Lecture Notes in Computer Science   10419

Commenced Publication in 1973
Founding and Former Series Editors:
Gerhard Goos, Juris Hartmanis, and Jan van Leeuwen

More information about this series at http://www.springer.com/series/7407

Alessandro Abate · Gilles Geeraerts (Eds.)

Formal Modeling and Analysis of Timed Systems

15th International Conference, FORMATS 2017
Berlin, Germany, September 5–7, 2017
Proceedings

 Springer

Editors
Alessandro Abate
Department of Computer Science
University of Oxford
Oxford
UK

Gilles Geeraerts
Dept. d'Informatique
Université Libre de Bruxelles
Brussels
Belgium

ISSN 0302-9743 ISSN 1611-3349 (electronic)
Lecture Notes in Computer Science
ISBN 978-3-319-65764-6 ISBN 978-3-319-65765-3 (eBook)
DOI 10.1007/978-3-319-65765-3

Library of Congress Control Number: 2017948642

LNCS Sublibrary: SL1 – Theoretical Computer Science and General Issues

Printed on acid-free paper

This Springer imprint is published by Springer Nature
The registered company is Springer International Publishing AG
The registered company address is: Gewerbestrasse 11, 6330 Cham, Switzerland

Preface

The 15th International Conference on Formal Modelling and Analysis of Timed Systems (FORMATS 2017) was held during September 5–7, 2017, in Berlin, Germany. FORMATS 2017 was part of QONFEST and was co-located with CONCUR 2017, QEST 2017, and EPEW 2017.

Control and analysis of the timing of computations are crucial to many domains of system engineering, be it, e.g., for ensuring timely response to stimuli originating in an uncooperative environment, or for synchronizing components in VLSI. Reflecting this broad scope, timing aspects of systems from a variety of domains have been treated independently by different communities in computer science and control. Researchers interested in semantics, verification, and performance analysis study models such as timed automata and timed Petri nets, the digital design community focuses on propagation and switching delays, while designers of embedded controllers have to take account of the time taken by controllers to compute their responses after sampling the environment, as well as of the dynamics of the controlled process during this span.

Timing-related questions in these separate disciplines have their particularities. However, there is a growing awareness that there are basic problems (of both scientific and engineering level) that are common to all of them. In particular, all these sub-disciplines treat systems whose behavior depends upon combinations of logical and temporal constraints; namely, constraints on the temporal distances between occurrences of successive events. Often, these constraints cannot be separated, as the intrinsic dynamics of processes couples them, necessitating models, methods, and tools facilitating their combined analysis. Reflecting this, FORMATS 2017 promoted submissions on hybrid discrete-continuous systems, and held a special session on this topic.

FORMATS 2017 was a three-day event, featuring three invited talks (two of which co-located with QEST 2017 and CONCUR 2017), and single-track regular podium sessions.

In all, 28 Program Committee members helped to provide at least three reviews of the 31 submitted contributions, 18 of which were accepted and presented during the single-track sessions and appear as full papers in these proceedings. We furthermore put in place a process of shepherding for a few of the 18 accepted submissions.

A highlight of FORMATS 2017 was the presence of the invited speaker Laurent Fribourg (CNRS and ENS, Université Paris-Saclay), who gave a talk titled "Euler's Method Applied to the Control of Switched Systems."

Furthermore, FORMATS 2017 sponsored two additional speakers: Morten Bisgaard, (GomSpace), co-sponsored with QEST 2017, and Hongseok Yang (Department of Computer Science, Oxford University) co-sponsored with CONCUR 2017 and QEST 2017.

Further details on FORMATS 2017 are featured at: http://formats17.ulb.be.

Finally, a few words of acknowledgment are due. Thanks to Katinka Wolter (FU Berlin), and to Uwe Nestmann (TU Berlin), for the supportive and can-do attitude as well as the local seamless organization of QONFEST. Thanks to Springer for publishing the FORMATS proceedings in its *Lecture Notes in Computer Science*. Thanks to Oded Maler and Martin Fränzle from the Steering Committee for support and direction, to Thao Dang for the help with publicity, to all the Program Committee members and additional reviewers for their work (105 reviews in total) in ensuring the quality of the contributions to FORMATS 2017, and to all the participants for contributing to this event. Finally, thanks to the EasyChair website for providing us with the necessary support in the selection process.

July 2017   Alessandro Abate
                                                             Gilles Geeraerts

Organization

Program Committee

Alessandro Abate	University of Oxford, UK
Erika Abraham	RWTH Aachen University, Germany
Étienne André	Université Paris 13, LIPN, CNRS, UMR 7030, France
Bernard Berthomieu	LAAS/CNRS, France
Sergiy Bogomolov	IST, Austria
Patricia Bouyer	LSV, CNRS and ENS Cachan, Université Paris Saclay, France
Thomas Brihaye	Université de Mons, Belgium
Alexandre David	Google Inc.
Uli Fahrenberg	École polytechnique, Palaiseau, France
Martin Fränzle	Carl von Ossietzky Universität Oldenburg, Germany
Gilles Geeraerts	Université libre de Bruxelles, Belgium
Jane Hillston	University of Edinburgh, UK
David N. Jansen	Institute of Software, Chinese Academy of Sciences, China
Jan Křetínský	Masaryk University, Czech Republic
Giuseppe Lipari	Université de Lille 1, France
Nicolas Markey	IRISA, CNRS, Inria and the University of Rennes 1, France
Dejan Nickovic	Austrian Institute of Technology AIT, Austria
Jens Oehlerking	Robert Bosch GmbH, Germany
Pavithra Prabhakar	Kansas State University, USA
Karin Quaas	Universität Leipzig, Germany
Jan Reineke	Saarland University, Germany
Olivier H. Roux	IRCCyN/Ecole Centrale de Nantes, France
Krishna S.	IIT Bombay, India
Sibylle Schupp	Institute for Software Systems, Hamburg University of Technology, Germany
Ana Sokolova	University of Salzburg, Austria
Oleg Sokolsky	University of Pennsylvania, USA
Jiří Srba	Aalborg University, Denmark
Nathalie Sznajder	LIP6, Université Pierre et Marie Curie, UMR CNRS 7606, France
Stavros Tripakis	University of California, Berkeley, USA
Majid Zamani	Technische Universität München, Germany

Additional Reviewers

Akshay, S.
Althoff, Matthias
Asarin, Eugene
Ashok, Pranav
Bollig, Benedikt
Chen, Xin
Colange, Maximilien
Dal Zilio, Silvano
Faucou, Sébastien
Ferrère, Thomas
Fippo Fitime, Louis
Fokkink, Wan
Fu, Hongfei
Garcia Soto, Miriam
Giacobbe, Mirco
Guha, Shibashis
Hahn, Ernst Moritz

Hladik, Pierre-Emmanuel
Ho, Hsi-Ming
Ivanov, Dmitry
Jaziri, Samy
Jezequel, Loïg
Krämer, Julia
Lal, Ratan
Le Botlan, Didier
Lehmann, Sascha
Lime, Didier
Meggendorfer, Tobias
Mikučionis, Marius
Monmege, Benjamin
Muniz, Marco
Norman, Gethin
Nyman, Ulrik
Parker, David

Phawade, Ramchandra
Rungger, Matthias
Sankur, Ocan
Schilling, Christian
Soudjani, Sadegh
Stierand, Ingo
Sun, Youcheng
Turrini, Andrea
Ulus, Dogan
Westphal, Bernd
Wimmer, Ralf
Wojtczak, Dominik
Zhang, Teng

Contents

Quantitative Logics and Monitoring

Reachability Analysis

Testing and Simulation

Invited Talk

Euler's Method Applied to the Control of Switched Systems

Laurent Fribourg[✉]

LSV, CNRS & ENS Paris-Saclay & INRIA, Cachan, France
fribourg@lsv.ens-cachan.fr

Abstract. Hybrid systems are a powerful formalism for modeling and reasoning about cyber-physical systems. They mix the continuous and discrete natures of the evolution of computerized systems. Switched systems are a special kind of hybrid systems, with restricted discrete behaviours: those systems only have finitely many different modes of (continuous) evolution, with isolated switches between modes. Such systems provide a good balance between expressiveness and controllability, and are thus in widespread use in large branches of industry such as power electronics and automotive control. The control law for a switched system defines the way of selecting the modes during the run of the system. Controllability is the problem of (automatically) synthesizing a control law in order to satisfy a desired property, such as safety (maintaining the variables within a given zone) or stabilisation (confinement of the variables in a close neighborhood around an objective point). In order to compute the control of a switched system, we need to compute the solutions of the differential equations governing the modes. Euler's method is the most basic technique for approximating such solutions. We present here an estimation of the Euler's method local error, using the notion of "one-sided Lispchitz constant" for modes. This yields a general control synthesis approach which can encompass several features such as bounded disturbance and compositionality.

1 Introduction

In this paper, we present some recent results obtained for the control synthesis of nonlinear switched systems using the one-sided Lipschitz conditions of their dynamics. The main idea is to use "one-sided Lipschitz conditions" on the system vector fields in order to generate a sequence of balls enclosing the sets of trajectories. The method can be easily extended to take into account uncertainty and compositional synthesis. These results mainly originate from collaboration with A. Le Coënt, F. De Vuyst, L. Chamoin, J. Alexandre dit Sandretto and A. Chapoutot (see [13,14]).

The plan of the paper is as follows: in Sect. 2, we present the notions of switched systems and (R, S)-stability; in Sect. 3, we introduce a new error analysis for Euler's method, and explain how to use it for ensuring (R, S)-stability in control synthesis of switched systems; we extend this control synthesis method

© Springer International Publishing AG 2017
A. Abate and G. Geeraerts (Eds.): FORMATS 2017, LNCS 10419, pp. 3–21, 2017.
DOI: 10.1007/978-3-319-65765-3_1

to uncertain switched systems, and to compositional synthesis (Sect. 4); we conclude in Sect. 5.

2   Switched Systems and (R, S)-Stability

2.1   Switched Systems

A hybrid system is a system where the state evolves continuously according to several possible *modes*, and where the change of modes (switching) is done instantaneously. We consider here the special case of hybrid systems called "sampled switched systems" where the change of modes occurs periodically with a period of τ seconds. We will suppose furthermore that the state keeps its value when the mode is changed (no jump). More formally, we denote the state of the system at time t by $x(t) \in \mathbb{R}^n$. The set of modes $U = \{1, \ldots, N\}$ is *finite*. With each mode $j \in U$ is associated a vector field f_j that governs the state $x(t)$; we have:

$$\dot{x}(t) = f_j(x(t))$$

We make the following hypothesis:

(H0)   For all $j \in U, f_j$ is a locally Lipschitz continuous map.

We will denote by $\phi_j(t; x^0)$ the solution at time t of the system

$$\begin{aligned}\dot{x}(t) &= f_j(x(t)), \\ x(0) &= x^0.\end{aligned} \tag{1}$$

The existence of ϕ_j is guaranteed by assumption (H0). Let us consider $S \subset \mathbb{R}^n$ be a compact and convex set, typically a "box" or "rectangular set", that is a cartesian product of n closed intervals. We know by (H0) that there exists a constant $L_j > 0$ such that:

$$\|f_j(y) - f_j(x)\| \le L_j \|y - x\| \forall x, y \in S. \tag{2}$$

We also define, for all $j \in U$:

$$C_j = \sup_{x \in S} L_j \|f_j(x)\|. \tag{3}$$

Example 1. One consider the example (adapted from [12]) of a two rooms apartment, with one heater per room. See Fig. 1. There is heat exchange between the two rooms and with the environment. The objective is to control the temperature of the two rooms. The continuous dynamics of the system is given by the equation:

$$\begin{pmatrix} \dot{T_1} \\ \dot{T_2} \end{pmatrix} = \begin{pmatrix} -\alpha_{21} - \alpha_{e1} - \alpha_f j_1 & \alpha_{21} \\ \alpha_{12} & -\alpha_{12} - \alpha_{e2} - \alpha_f j_2 \end{pmatrix} \begin{pmatrix} T_1 \\ T_2 \end{pmatrix} + \begin{pmatrix} \alpha_{e1} T_e + \alpha_f T_f j_1 \\ \alpha_{e2} T_e + \alpha_f T_f j_2 \end{pmatrix}.$$

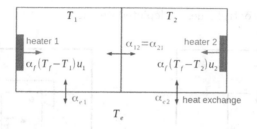

Fig. 1. 2-rooms example

Here the state of the system is (T_1, T_2) where T_1 and T_2 are the temperatures of the two rooms. The control mode of the system is of the form $j = (j_1, j_2)$ where variable j_1 (respectively j_2) can take the values 0 or 1 depending on whether the heater in room 1 (respectively room 2) is switched off or switched on (hence $U = U_1 \times U_2 = \{0,1\} \times \{0,1\}$). T_e corresponds to the temperature of the environment, and T_f to the temperature of the heaters. The values of the different parameters are the following: $\alpha_{12} = 5 \times 10^{-2}$, $\alpha_{21} = 5 \times 10^{-2}$, $\alpha_{e1} = 5 \times 10^{-3}$, $\alpha_{e2} = 5 \times 10^{-3}$, $\alpha_f = 8.3 \times 10^{-3}$, $T_e = 10$ and $T_f = 35$. We suppose that the heaters can be switched periodically at sampling instants $\tau, 2\tau, \ldots$ with $\tau = 5s$. The objective is to stabilize the state (T_1, T_2) of the system in the neighborhood of the region $R = [18, 22] \times [18, 22]$.

A *pattern* π is a finite sequence of modes; e.g., the expression $\left(\begin{pmatrix} 0 \\ 1 \end{pmatrix} \cdot \begin{pmatrix} 0 \\ 0 \end{pmatrix} \cdot \begin{pmatrix} 1 \\ 1 \end{pmatrix} \right)$ is a pattern in Example 1. The *(state-dependent) control synthesis problem* consists in finding at each sampling time $\tau, 2\tau, \ldots$, the appropriate *mode* $u \in U$ (in function of the current value of x) to be selected for satisfying some objective, for example a *safety* property. More generally, the control synthesis problem (with a "time-horizon" bounded by a positive integer K) consists first in selecting at time 0 a pattern π_1 of length, say $1 \leq k_1 \leq K$, according to the value of state $x(0)$; then after $k_1\tau$ seconds, selecting a new pattern π_2, according to the value of $x(k_1\tau)$, and so on repeatedly. This induces a control (or switching) rule σ which is a piecewise constant function of time, with discontinuities occurring at sampling times. By convention, the control law σ is right-continuous.

2.2 (R, S)-Stability

Among the classical objectives that one is generally aiming for, there are

- the *reachability* objective: given an initial region R_{init} and a target region R, find a pattern which drives $x(t)$ to R, for any initial state $x^0 = x(0) \in R_{init}$;
- the *stability* objective: for any initial point $x^0 = x(0) \in R$, find a pattern $\pi \in U^k$ (with $1 \leq k \leq K$) which makes the trajectory return in R (i.e.: $x(k\tau) \in R$) while always maintaining $x(t)$ in a *neighborhood* $S = R + \varepsilon$ of R, (i.e.: $x(t) \in S$ for $0 \leq t \leq k\tau$).

The effect of such control rules is depicted on Fig. 2.

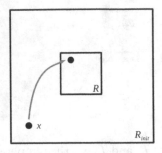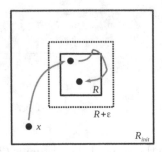

Fig. 2. Illustration of reachability (left) followed by stability (right)

For the sake of simplicity, we focus here on a property that we call "(R,S)-stability": given two rectangular sets (i.e., cartesian products of intervals) R and S with $R \subseteq S \subset \mathbb{R}^n$, called respectively "recurrence set" and "safety set", the (R,S)-*stability control problem* consists in finding a control σ ensuring, for all $x(0) \in R$.

1. *recurrence*: the state of the system $x(t)$ belongs to R for an infinite number of values of t;
2. *safety*: the state of the system $x(t)$ belongs to S for all $t \geq 0$.

The property of (R,S)-stability is illustrated in Fig. 3 in the case of Example 1, with $R = [18,22] \times [18,22]$.

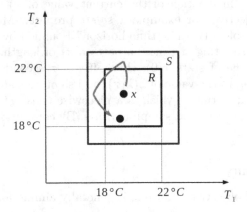

Fig. 3. (R,S)-stability

We now give the general scheme of control synthesis that has been proposed in MINIMATOR [10] for ensuring (R,S)-stability. This scheme consists in two steps:

1. *cover* R via a finite number m of subsets $B_1^0, B_2^0, ..., B_m^0$ of S (with $R \subset \bigcup_{i=1}^m B_i^0 \subseteq S$);
2. for each B_i^0 ($1 \le i \le m$), *find a pattern* π_i of length $k_i \le K$ such that, starting at $t = 0$ from any point of B_i^0, the trajectory $x(t)$ controlled by π_i satisfies:

$$x(t) \in S \quad \text{for all } t \in [0, k_i\tau] \quad \wedge \quad x(t) \in R \quad \text{for } t = k_i\tau.$$

Note that, when the system returns to R (after application of some pattern) at time, say $t = t_1$, the state $x(t_1)$ belongs to $B_{i_1}^0$ for some $1 \le i_1 \le m$; the pattern π_{i_1} is then applied, which makes the system return to R at time $t_2 = t_1 + k_{i_1}\tau$, and so on iteratively.

Remark 1. Let us give a rough estimation of the complexity of MINIMATOR scheme. Let N be the number of modes, n the state dimension, K the time-horizon (or maximum length of patterns), $m = 2^{nd}$ the number of modes (assuming a uniform covering obtained by bisection of depth d); the MINIMATOR scheme consists essentially in enumerating all the possible patterns of length $\le K$ until finding, for each B_i^0 ($1 \le i \le m$) a safe recurrent candidate; a simple calculation shows that there are $2^{nd}N^K$ candidate patterns; the complexity of the MINIMATOR scheme is thus *exponential* in n, d, K (note that the number of modes N may be itself exponential in the dimension n: for example, in a classical n-room heating example with one heater per room and two modes by heater, there are $N = 2^n$ modes).

Remark 2. Note that the set of trajectories starting at points of R form a (positive) *invariant set* included into S. There are classical methods for generating (maximal) invariant sets included into S [4,7]. Unfortunately, these general methods are based on a *backward* reachability constructs, which, as noticed by I.M. Mitchell [16], "are more likely to suffer from numerical stability issues, especially in systems with significant contraction – the very systems where forward simulation and reachability are most effective". The forward analysis used by the MINIMATOR scheme (application of patterns) avoids such a difficulty.

2.3   Guaranteed Integration

The MINIMATOR paradigm described in Sect. 2.2 relies implicitly on the existence of a process for overapproximating the set of trajectories originating from a subset B_i^0 during a multiple of sampling periods. Such a process is called "guaranteed integration" (or "set-integration"). As said in [18]:

"Methods of *guaranteed integration* are methods capable to compute bounds that are guaranteed to contain the solution of a given ODE at points t_j, $j = 1, 2, \ldots, m$ in the interval $(t_0, t_m]$ for some $t_m > t_0$. These methods are usually based on Taylor series or extension of Hermite-Obreschkoff schemes to interval methods. They usually consist of two phases. On an integration step from t_{j-1} to t_j, the first phase validates existence and uniqueness of the solution of (1) for all $[t_{j-1}, t_j]$ and computes a priori bounds for this solution for all $t \in [t_{j-1}, t_j]$, [19, 20]; and the second phase compute tight bounds for the solution of (1) at t_j. Note that a major problem in the second phase is the *wrapping effect* [16]. It occurs when a solution set that is not a box in $\mathbb{R}^n$, $n \geq 2$, is enclosed, or wrapped, by a box on each integration step. (...) As a result of such a wrapping, an overestimation is often introduced on each integration step. Those overestimations accumulate as the integration proceeds, and the computed bounds may soon become unacceptably large. Many methods have been proposed to reduce the wrapping effect in the context of interval methods."

In order to avoid such a wrapping effect, we proposed an alternate method which, instead of using interval arithmetic [17] and higher order Taylor series, has simply recourse to the basic (forward) Euler method [14]. This is made possible through a new error analysis of the Euler method via the notion of "one-sided Lipschitz constant".

3   Euler's Method and Error Estimation

3.1   One-Sided Lipschitz Constant

As remarked in [1]:

"The Lipschitz constant of [many] functions is usually region-based and often dramatically increases as the operating region is enlarged. On the other hand, even if the nonlinear system is Lipschitz in the region of interest, it is generally the case that the available observer design techniques can only stabilize the error dynamics for dynamical systems with small Lipschitz constants but fails to provide a solution when the Lipschitz constant becomes large. The problem becomes worse when dealing with stiff systems. Stiffness means that the ordinary differential equation (ODE) admits a smooth solution with moderate derivatives, together with nonsmooth ("transient") solutions rapidly converging towards the smooth ones (...) This problem has been recognized in the mathematical literature and specially in the field of numerical analysis for some time and a powerful tool has developed to overcome this problem. This tool is a generalization of the Lipschitz continuity to a less restrictive condition known as one-sided Lipschitz (OSL) continuity."

Unlike Lipschitz constants, OSL constants can be negative, which express a form of contractivity of the system dynamics. Even if the OSL constant is positive, it is in practice much lower than the Lipschitz constant [8]. The use of OSL thus allows us to obtain an upper bound for the error associated with Euler's method that is more precise than by using Lipschitz constants [14].

Let us denote by T a compact overapproximation of the image by ϕ_j of box S for $0 \leq t \leq \tau$ and $j \in U$, i.e. T is such that

$$T \supseteq \{\phi_j(t; x^0) \mid j \in U, 0 \leq t \leq \tau, x^0 \in S\}.$$

The existence of T is guaranteed by assumption $(H0)$. We now make the additional hypothesis that the vector fields f_j of the system are *one-sided Lipschitz* (OSL) [9]. Formally:

(H_U) For all $j \in U$, there exists a constant $\lambda_j \in \mathbb{R}$ such that

$$\langle f_j(y) - f_j(x), y - x \rangle \le \lambda_j \|y - x\|^2 \quad \forall x, y \in T,$$

where $\langle \cdot, \cdot \rangle$ denotes the scalar product of two vectors of $\mathbb{R}^n$.

Remark 3. Constants λ_j as well as L_j and C_j $(j \in U)$ can be computed using constrained optimization algorithms. See Sect. 3.5 for details.

3.2 Euler Approximate Solutions

Given an initial point $\tilde{x}^0 \in S$ and a mode $j \in U$, we define the following "linear approximate solution" $\tilde{\phi}_j(t; \tilde{x}^0)$ for $t \in [0, \tau]$ by:

$$\tilde{\phi}_j(t; \tilde{x}^0) = t f_j(\tilde{x}^0) + \tilde{x}^0. \tag{4}$$

Formula (4) is nothing else but the explicit forward Euler scheme with "time step" t. It is thus a consistent approximation of order 1 in t of the exact solution of (Sect. 2) under the hypothesis $\tilde{x}^0 = x^0$ (see Fig. 4). More generally, given an initial point $\tilde{x}^0 \in S$ and pattern π of U^k, we can define a "(piecewise linear) approximate solution" $\tilde{\phi}_\pi(t; \tilde{x}^0)$ of ϕ_π at time $t \in [0; k\tau]$ as follows:

- $\tilde{\phi}_\pi(t; \tilde{x}^0) = t f_j(\tilde{x}^0) + \tilde{x}^0$ if $\pi = j \in U$, $k = 1$ and $t \in [0, \tau]$, and
- $\tilde{\phi}_\pi(k\tau + t; \tilde{x}^0) = t f_j(\tilde{z}) + \tilde{z}$ with $\tilde{z} = \tilde{\phi}_{\pi'}((k-1)\tau; \tilde{x}^0)$, if $k \ge 2$, $t \in [0, \tau]$, $\pi = j \cdot \pi'$ for some $j \in U$ and $\pi' \in U^{k-1}$.

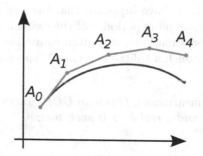

Fig. 4. Illustration of Euler's method (from Wikipedia)

We wish to synthesize a guaranteed control σ using approximate functions of the form $\tilde{\phi}_\pi$. We define the closed ball of center $x \in \mathbb{R}^n$ and radius $r > 0$, denoted $B(x, r)$, as the set $\{x' \in \mathbb{R}^n \mid \|x' - x\| \le r\}$. Given a positive real δ^0, we now define the expression $\delta_j(t)$ which, as we will see in Theorem 1, represents (an upper bound on) the error associated to $\tilde{\phi}_j(t; \tilde{x}^0)$ (i.e. $\|\tilde{\phi}_j(t; \tilde{x}^0) - \phi_j(t; x^0)\|$).

Definition 1. *Let δ^0 be a positive constant. Let us define, for all $0 \le t \le \tau$, $\delta_j(t)$ as follows:*

– *if $\lambda_j < 0$:*

$$\delta_j(t) = \left((\delta^0)^2 e^{\lambda_j t} + \frac{C_j^2}{\lambda_j^2} \left(t^2 + \frac{2t}{\lambda_j} + \frac{2}{\lambda_j^2} \left(1 - e^{\lambda_j t} \right) \right) \right)^{\frac{1}{2}}$$

– *if $\lambda_j = 0$:*

$$\delta_j(t) = \left((\delta^0)^2 e^t + C_j^2 (-t^2 - 2t + 2(e^t - 1)) \right)^{\frac{1}{2}}$$

– *if $\lambda_j > 0$:*

$$\delta_j(t) = \left((\delta^0)^2 e^{3\lambda_j t} + \frac{C_j^2}{3\lambda_j^2} \left(-t^2 - \frac{2t}{3\lambda_j} + \frac{2}{9\lambda_j^2} \left(e^{3\lambda_j t} - 1 \right) \right) \right)^{\frac{1}{2}}$$

Note that $\delta_j(t) = \delta^0$ for $t = 0$. The function $\delta_j(\cdot)$ depends implicitly on parameter: $\delta^0 \in \mathbb{R}_{>0}$. In Sect. 3.3, we will use the notation $\delta'_j(\cdot)$ where the value of $\delta'_j(t)$ for $t = 0$ is implicitly a parameter denoted by $(\delta')^0$.

Theorem 1. *Given an ODE system satisfying $(H0 - H_U)$, consider a point $\tilde{x}^0$ and a positive real δ^0. We have, for all $x^0 \in B(\tilde{x}^0, \delta^0)$, $t \in [0, \tau]$:*

$$\phi_j(t; x^0) \in B(\tilde{\phi}_j(t, \tilde{x}^0), \delta_j(t)).$$

The proof of this theorem is given in [14].

Remark 4. In Theorem 1, we have supposed that the step size h used in Euler's method was equal to the sampling period τ of the switching system. Actually, in order to have better approximations, it is often convenient to take a fraction of τ as for h (e.g., $h = \frac{\tau}{10}$). Such a splitting is called "sub-sampling" in numerical methods.

Corollary 1 *(one-step invariance). Given an ODE system satisfying $(H0-H_U)$, consider a point $\tilde{x}^0 \in S$ and a real $\delta^0 > 0$ such that:*

1. $B(\tilde{x}^0, \delta^0) \subseteq S$,
2. $B(\tilde{\phi}_j(\tau; \tilde{x}^0), \delta_j(\tau)) \subseteq S$, and
3. $\frac{d^2(\delta_j(t))}{dt^2} > 0$ *for all $t \in [0, \tau]$.*

Then we have, for all $x^0 \in B(\tilde{x}^0, \delta^0)$ and $t \in [0, \tau]$: $\phi_j(t; x^0) \in S$.

Corollary 1 is illustrated in Fig. 5. Note that condition 3 of Corollary 1 on the convexity of $\delta_j(\cdot)$ on $[0, \tau]$ can be established again using an optimization function.

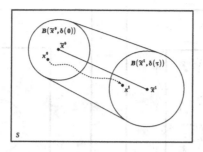

Fig. 5. Illustration of one-step invariance in S

3.3 Application to Control Synthesis for (R, S)-Stability

Consider a point $\tilde{x}^0 \in S$, a positive real δ^0 and a pattern π of length k. Let $\pi(k')$ denote the k'-th element (mode) of π for $1 \le k' \le k$. Let us abbreviate the k'-th approximate point $\tilde{\phi}_\pi(k'\tau; \tilde{x}^0)$ as $\tilde{x}_\pi^{k'}$ for $k' = 1, ..., k$, and let $\tilde{x}_\pi^{k'} = \tilde{x}^0$ for $k' = 0$. It is easy to show that $\tilde{x}_\pi^{k'}$ can be defined recursively for $k' = 1, ..., k$, by: $\tilde{x}_\pi^{k'} = \tilde{x}_\pi^{k'-1} + \tau f_j(\tilde{x}_\pi^{k'-1})$ with $j = \pi(k')$.

Let us now define the expression $\delta_\pi^{k'}$ as follows: for $k' = 0$: $\delta_\pi^{k'} = \delta^0$, and for $1 \le k' \le k$: $\delta_\pi^{k'} = \delta_j'(\tau)$ where $(\delta')^0$ denotes $\delta_\pi^{k'-1}$, and j denotes $\pi(k')$. Likewise, the expression $\delta_\pi(t)$ is defined, for $0 \le t \le k\tau$, by:

- for $t = 0$: $\delta_\pi(t) = \delta^0$,
- for $0 < t \le k\tau$: $\delta_\pi(t) = \delta_j'(t')$ with $(\delta')^0 = \delta_\pi^{\ell-1}$, $j = \pi(\ell)$, $t' = t - (\ell - 1)\tau$ and $\ell = \lceil \frac{t}{\tau} \rceil$.

Note that, for $0 \le k' \le k$, we have: $\delta_\pi(k'\tau) = \delta_\pi^{k'}$. Following the MINIMATOR paradigm (see Sect. 2.2), we are now ready to synthesize a control σ ensuring (R, S)-stability, using the approximate functions $\tilde{\phi}_\pi$.

Theorem 2. *Given a sampled switched system satisfying $(H0 - H_U)$, consider a point $\tilde{x}^0 \in S$, a positive real δ^0 and a pattern π of length k such that, for all $1 \le k' \le k$:*

1. $B(\tilde{x}_\pi^{k'}, \delta_\pi^{k'}) \subseteq S$ *and*
2. $\frac{d^2(\delta_j'(t))}{dt^2} > 0$ *for all $t \in [0, \tau]$, with $j = \pi(k')$ and $(\delta')^0 = \delta_\pi^{k'-1}$.*

Then we have, for all $x^0 \in B(\tilde{x}^0, \delta^0)$ and $t \in [0, k\tau]$: $\phi_\pi(t; x^0) \in S$.

Corollary 2. *Given a switched system satisfying $(H0 - H_U)$, consider a positive real δ^0 and a finite set of points $\tilde{x}_1, \ldots \tilde{x}_m$ of S such that all the balls $B(\tilde{x}_i, \delta^0)$ cover R and are included into S (i.e. $R \subseteq \bigcup_{i=1}^m D(\tilde{x}_i, \delta^0) \subseteq S$). Suppose furthermore that, for all $1 \le i \le m$, there exists a pattern π_i of length k_i such that:*

1. $B((\tilde{x}_i)_{\pi_i}^{k'}, \delta_{\pi_i}^{k'}) \subseteq S$, *for all $k' = 1, \ldots, k_i - 1$*
2. $B((\tilde{x}_i)_{\pi_i}^{k_i}, \delta_{\pi_i}^{k_i}) \subseteq R$.

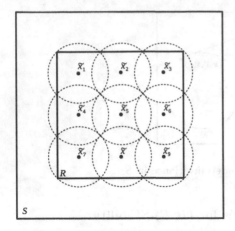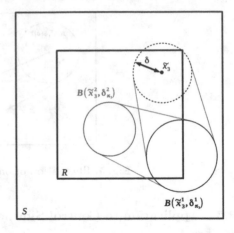

Fig. 6. Set of balls covering R (left) and safe recurrent pattern associated with one of these balls (right).

3. $\frac{d^2(\delta'_j(t))}{dt^2} > 0$ with $j = \pi_i(k')$ and $(\delta')^0 = \delta_{\pi_i}^{k'-1}$, for all $k' \in \{1, ..., k_i\}$ and $t \in [0, \tau]$.

These properties induce a control σ^1 which guarantees

- *(safety): if $x^0 \in R$, then $\phi_\sigma(t; x^0) \in S$ for all $t \geq 0$, and*
- *(recurrence): if $x^0 \in R$ then $\phi_\sigma(k\tau; x^0) \in R$ for some $k \in \{k_1, \ldots, k_m\}$.*

A covering of R with balls as stated in Corollary 2 is illustrated in Fig. 6 (left) with a pattern satisfying safety and recurrence in Fig. 6 (right). Corollary 2 thus leads to the following method (inspired by the MINIMATOR scheme described in Sect. 2.2), aiming for (R, S)-stability:

- we (pre-)compute λ_j, L_j, C_j for all $j \in U$;
- we find m points $\tilde{x}_1, \ldots, \tilde{x}_m$ of S and $\delta^0 > 0$ such that $\mathbb{R} \subseteq \bigcup_{i=1}^m B(\tilde{x}_i, \delta^0)) \subseteq S$;
- we find m patterns π_i ($i = 1, \ldots, m$) such that conditions 1-2-3 of Corollary 2 are satisfied.

3.4   Avoiding Wrapping Effect with Euler's Method

The problem of "wrapping effect" inherent to the method of interval analysis has been noticed from the outset: R. Moore [17] illustrates it on the simple rotation

$$\dot{x} = \begin{pmatrix} 0 & 1 \\ -1 & 0 \end{pmatrix} x; \quad x_0 \in A$$

---

[1] Given an initial point $x \in R$, the induced control σ corresponds to a sequence of patterns $\pi_{i_1}, \pi_{i_2}, \ldots$ defined as follows: Since $x \in R$, there exists a a point $\tilde{x}_{i_1}$ with $1 \leq i_1 \leq m$ such that $x \in B(\tilde{x}_{i_1}, \delta^0)$; then using pattern π_{i_1}, one has: $\phi_{\pi_{i_1}}(k_{i_1}\tau; x) \in R$. Let $x' = \phi_{\pi_{i_1}}(k_{i_1}\tau; x)$; there exists a point $\tilde{x}_{i_2}$ with $1 \leq i_2 \leq m$ such that $x' \in B(\tilde{x}_{i_2}, \delta^0)$, etc.

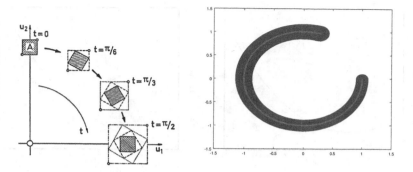

Fig. 7. left: guaranteed integration with interval method (from [17]); right: with Euler-based method.

for an initial set A which is rectangular. At each step, the rectangle is rotated and has to be wrapped by another one. At $t = 2\pi$, the blow up factor is by a factor $e^{2\pi} \approx 535$, as the step size tends to zero (Fig. 7: left). In contrast, the application of the Euler-based method starting from a ball of radius 0.1 with step size 0.005, does not blow up on this example (Fig. 7: right).

3.5 Numerical Results

Our Euler-based synthesis method has been implemented by Adrien Le Coënt in the interpreted language Octave, and the experiments performed on a 2.80 GHz Intel Core i7-4810MQ CPU with 8 GB of memory. The computation of constants L_j, C_j, λ_j $(j \in U)$ are realized with a constrained optimization algorithm. They are performed using the "sqp" function of Octave, applied on the following optimization problems:

- Constant L_j:

$$L_j = \max_{x,y \in S,\ x \neq y} \frac{\|f_j(y) - f_j(x)\|}{\|y - x\|}$$

- Constant C_j:

$$C_j = \max_{x \in S} L_j \|f_j(x)\|$$

- Constant λ_j:

$$\lambda_j = \max_{x,y \in T,\ x \neq y} \frac{\langle f_j(y) - f_j(x), y - x \rangle}{\|y - x\|^2}$$

The convexity test $\frac{d^2(\delta_j'(t))}{dt^2} > 0$ can be performed similarly. Note that in some cases, it is advantageous to use a time sub-sampling to compute the image of a ball. Indeed, because of the exponential growth of the radius $\delta_j(t)$ within time, computing a sequence of balls can lead to smaller ball images. It is particularly advantageous when a constant λ_j is negative. We illustrate this with the example of the DC-DC converter [6]. It has two switched modes, for which we have

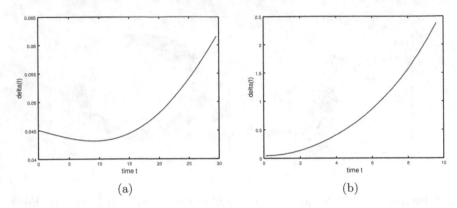

Fig. 8. Behavior of $\delta_j(t)$ for the DC-DC converter with $\delta_j(0) = 0.045$. (a) Evolution of $\delta_1(t)$ (with $\lambda_1 < 0$); (b) Evolution of $\delta_2(t)$ (with $\lambda_2 > 0$).

$\lambda_1 \approx -0.014$ and $\lambda_2 \approx 0.14$. In the case $\lambda_j < 0$, the associated formula $\delta_j(t)$ has the behavior of Fig. 8(a). In the case $\lambda_j > 0$, the associated formula $\delta_j(t)$ has the behavior of Fig. 8(b). In the case $\lambda_j < 0$, if the time sub-sampling is small enough, one can compute a sequence of balls with reducing radius, which makes the synthesis easier.

Example 2 (Four-room apartment). We describe a first application on a 4-room 16-switch building ventilation case study adapted from [15]. The model has been simplified in order to get constant parameters. The system is a four room apartment subject to heat transfer between the rooms, with the external environment, the underfloor, and human beings. The dynamics of the system is given by the following equation:

$$\frac{dT_i}{dt} = \sum_{j \in \mathcal{N}^* \setminus \{i\}} a_{ij}(T_j - T_i) + \delta_{s_i} b_i(T_{s_i}^4 - T_i^4) + c_i \max\left(0, \frac{V_i - V_i^*}{\bar{V}_i - V_i^*}\right)(T_u - T_i), \quad \text{for } i = 1, ..., 4.$$

The state of the system is given by the temperatures in the rooms T_i, for $i \in \mathcal{N} = \{1, \ldots, 4\}$. Room i is subject to heat exchange with different entities stated by the indices $\mathcal{N}^* = \{1, 2, 3, 4, u, o, c\}$. We have $T_0 = 30, T_c = 30, T_u = 17$, $\delta_{s_i} = 1$ for $i \in \mathcal{N}$. The (constant) parameters $T_{s_i}, V_i^*, \bar{V}_i, a_{ij}, b_i, c_i$ are given in [15]. The control input is V_i ($i \in \mathcal{N}$). In the experiment, V_1 and V_4 can take the values 0V or 3.5V, and V_2 and V_3 can take the values 0V or 3V. This leads to 16 switching modes corresponding to the different possible combinations of voltages V_i. The sampling period is $\tau = 30$ s. Compared simulations are given in Fig. 9. On this example, the Euler-based method works better than *DynIBEX* in terms of CPU time (see Table 1).

Table 1. Numerical results for the four-room example.

	Euler	DynIBEX
R	$[20, 22]^2 \times [22, 24]^2$	
S	$[19, 23]^2 \times [21, 25]^2$	
τ	30	
Time subsampling	No	
Complete control	Yes	Yes
$\max_{j=1,\dots,16} \lambda_j$ $\max_{j=1,\dots,16} C_j$	-6.30×10^{-3} 4.18×10^{-6}	
Number of balls/tiles	4096	252
Pattern length	1	1
CPU time	63 s	249 s

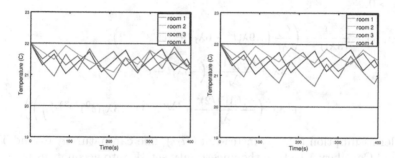

Fig. 9. Simulation of the four-room case study with Euler-based synthesis method (left) and with the synthesis method of [2] (right).

4   ODEs with Uncertainty

4.1   Bounded Uncertainty

Let us now consider the case where the mode j is governed by the *uncertain* ODE:

$$\dot{x}(t) = f_j(x(t), w(t)) \quad \text{with} \quad w(t) \in W$$

where W is a bounded set of diameter[2] denoted by $|W|$ (see, e.g., [3,5,11]).

Let us suppose that the uncertain ODE satisfies the assumption:

$(H_{U,W})$ For all $j \in U$, there exist $\lambda_j \in \mathbb{R}$ and $\gamma_j \in \mathbb{R}_{\geq 0}$ such that, for all $x, x' \in S$, and all $w, w' \in W$:

$$\langle f_j(x, w) - f_j(x', w'), x - x' \rangle \leq \lambda_j \|x - x'\|^2 + \gamma_j \|x - x'\|\|w - w'\|.$$

Definition 2. *Let δ^0 be a positive real, and W a rectangular set of diameter $|W|$. We define, for all $j \in U$ and $0 \leq t \leq \tau$, the expression $\delta_{j,W}(t)$ as follows:*

---

[2] The diameter of a set is the maximal distance of two elements.

– *if* $\lambda_j < 0$,

$$\delta_{j,W}(t) = \left(\frac{C_j^2}{-\lambda_j^4} \left(-\lambda_j^2 t^2 - 2\lambda_j t + 2e^{\lambda_j t} - 2 \right) \right.$$
$$+ \frac{1}{\lambda_j^2} \left(\frac{C_j \gamma_j |W|}{-\lambda_j} \left(-\lambda_j t + e^{\lambda_j t} - 1 \right) \right.$$
$$\left. \left. + \lambda_j \left(\frac{\gamma_j^2 (|W|/2)^2}{-\lambda_j} (e^{\lambda_j t} - 1) + \lambda_j (\delta^0)^2 e^{\lambda_j t} \right) \right) \right)^{1/2} \quad (5)$$

– *if* $\lambda_j = 0$,

$$\delta_{j,W}(t) = \left(C_j^2 \left(-t^2 - 2t + 2e^t - 2 \right) + \left(C_j \gamma_j |W| \left(-t + e^t - 1 \right) + \right. \right.$$
$$\left. \left. (\gamma_j^2 (|W|/2)^2 (e^t - 1) + (\delta^0)^2 e^t)) \right) \right)^{1/2} \quad (6)$$

– *if* $\lambda_j > 0$,

$$\delta_{j,W}(t) = \frac{1}{(3\lambda_j)^{3/2}} \left(\frac{C_j^2}{\lambda_j} \left(-9\lambda_j^2 t^2 - 6\lambda_j t + 2e^{3\lambda_j t} - 2 \right) \right.$$
$$+ 3\lambda_j \left(\frac{C_j \gamma_j |W|}{\lambda_j} \left(-3\lambda_j t + e^{3\lambda_j t} - 1 \right) \right.$$
$$\left. \left. + 3\lambda_j \left(\frac{\gamma_j^2 (|W|/2)^2}{\lambda_j} (e^{3\lambda_j t} - 1) + 3\lambda_j (\delta^0)^2 e^{3\lambda_j t} \right) \right) \right)^{1/2} \quad (7)$$

Under assumption $(H_{U,W})$ instead of (H_U), one can naturally extend Theorem 1 and Corollary 1 to take the uncertainty set W into account, using $\delta_{j,W}(\cdot)$ in place of $\delta_j(\cdot)$. These extended results are useful to control systems with uncertainty, for example when the coefficients in the vector field definitions are known with a limited precision. Such extended forms of Theorem 1 and Corollary 1 can also be applied to control *interconnected subsystems*, each component regarding the *input* from the other one as a form of bounded uncertainty (see Sect. 4.2).

4.2   Application to Distributed Control Synthesis

We now consider the distributed (or "compositional") approach which consists in splitting the original system into two sub-systems, in order to synthesize a controller σ_i ($i = 1, 2$) for each sub-system independently, then apply the control $\sigma = (\sigma_1 | \sigma_2)$ (by concurrent application of σ_1 and σ_2) to the global system. The interest of the approach is to break the exponential complexity of the original method w.r.t. the dimension of the system and the number of modes (see Sect. 2.2). We consider an ODE of the form $\dot{x} = f_j(x)$ with $x \in \mathbb{R}^n$, $j \in U$, which is of the form

$$\dot{x}_1 = f_{j_1}^1(x_1, x_2) \quad (8)$$
$$\dot{x}_2 = f_{j_2}^2(x_1, x_2) \quad (9)$$

where the state x is of the form (x_1, x_2) with $x_1 \in \mathbb{R}^{n_1}$, $x_2 \in \mathbb{R}^{n_2}$, $n_1 + n_2 = n$, the mode j is of the form (j_1, j_2), with $j_1 \in U_1$, $j_2 \in U_2$, $U = U_1 \times U_2$. Given an initial condition of the form $\begin{pmatrix} x_1^0 \\ x_2^0 \end{pmatrix}$, and a mode $j = (j_1, j_2) \in U = U_1 \times U_2$, the solution of the ODE is now denoted by $\phi_{(j_1,j_2)}(t; x^0)$, for all $t \in [0, \tau]$. The system (8, 9) can be seen as the *interconnection* of a 1st sub-system (8) where x_2 plays the role of an "input" given by (9), with a 2nd sub-system (9) where x_1 is an "input" given by (8).

Accordingly, the sets R, S and T are seen under their compositional form $R = R_1 \times R_2$, $S = S_1 \times S_2$, $T = T_1 \times T_2$. We will denote by x_1^m (resp. x_2^m) an arbitrary point of R_1 (resp. R_2), typically its central point. We denote by $L_{j_1}^1$ the Lipschitz constant for sub-system 1 under mode j_1:

$$\| f_{j_1}^1(x_1, x_2) - f_{j_1}^1(y_1, y_2) \| \leq L_{j_1}^1 \left\| \begin{pmatrix} x_1 \\ x_2 \end{pmatrix} - \begin{pmatrix} y_1 \\ y_2 \end{pmatrix} \right\|$$

We introduce also the constant:

$$C_{j_1}^1 = \sup_{x_1 \in S_1} L_{j_1}^1 \| f_{j_1}^1(x_1, x_2^m) \|$$

Similarly, we define the constants for sub-system 2:

$$\| f_{j_2}^2(x_1, x_2) - f_{j_2}^2(y_1, y_2) \| \leq L_{j_2}^2 \left\| \begin{pmatrix} x_1 \\ x_2 \end{pmatrix} - \begin{pmatrix} y_1 \\ y_2 \end{pmatrix} \right\|$$

and

$$C_{j_2}^2 = \sup_{x_2 \in S_2} L_{j_2}^2 \| f_{j_2}^2(x_1^m, x_2) \|$$

In the following, we assume that, for all $j_1 \in U_1$, there exist a real λ_{j_1} and a nonnegative real γ_{j_1} which make the 1st sub-system satisfy assumption (H_{U_1, W_2}) for some overapproximation W_2 of T_2. Symmetrically, we assume that, for all $j_2 \in U_2$, there exist a real λ_{j_2} and a non-negative real γ_{j_2} which make the 2nd sub-system satisfy (H_{U_2, W_1}) for some overapproximation W_1 of T_1.

Given two modes $j_1 \in U_1, j_2 \in U_2$, and two initial conditions $\tilde{x}_1^0, \tilde{x}_2^0$, we define the "decompositional" Euler approximate solutions $\tilde{\phi}_{j_1}^1$ and $\tilde{\phi}_{j_2}^2$, for $t \in [0, \tau]$, as follows:

$$\tilde{\phi}_{j_1}^1(t; \tilde{x}_1^0) = \tilde{x}_1^0 + t f_{j_1}^1(\tilde{x}_1^0, x_2^m) \tag{10}$$

$$\tilde{\phi}_{j_2}^2(t; \tilde{x}_2^0) = \tilde{x}_2^0 + t f_{j_2}^2(x_1^m, \tilde{x}_2^0) \tag{11}$$

We can now give the distributed version of Theorem 1.

Theorem 3. *Given a distributed sampled switched system satisfying, suppose that the 1st and 2nd sub-systems satisfy, for all $j_1 \in U_1$ and $j_2 \in U_2$, the assumptions (H_{U_1, W_2}) and (H_{U_2, W_1}) respectively. Consider a point $\tilde{x}_1^0$ and a positive real δ^0. We have, for all $x_1^0 \in B(\tilde{x}_1^0, \delta^0)$, $t \in [0, \tau]$, $j_1 \in U_1$:*

$$\phi_{(j_1,j_2)}(t; x^0)_{|1} \in B(\tilde{\phi}_{j_1}^1(t, \tilde{x}_1^0), \delta_{j_1, W_2}(t)) \quad \forall j_2 \in U_2, \forall x_2^0 \in S_2, x^0 = \begin{pmatrix} x_1^0 \\ x_2^0 \end{pmatrix}.$$

Table 2. Numerical results for centralized four-room example.

	Centralized
R	$[20, 22]^4$
S	$[19, 23]^4$
τ	30
Time subsampling	$\tau/20$
Complete control	Yes
Error parameters	$\max\limits_{j=1,\ldots,16} \lambda_j = -6.30 \times 10^{-3} \quad \max\limits_{j=1,\ldots,16} C_j = 4.18 \times 10^{-6}$
Number of balls/tiles	256
Pattern length	2
CPU time	48 s

Likewise, we have, for all $x_2^0 \in B(\tilde{x}_2^0, \delta^0)$, $t \in [0, \tau]$, $j_2 \in U_2$:

$$\phi_{(j_1,j_2)}(t; x^0)_{|2} \in B(\tilde{\phi}_{j_2}^2(t, \tilde{x}_2^0), \delta_{j_2, W_1}(t)) \quad \forall j_1 \in U_1, \forall x_1^0 \in S_1, x^0 = \begin{pmatrix} x_1^0 \\ x_2^0 \end{pmatrix}.$$

The proof of this theorem is in [13]. We can now state the distributed version of Corollary 2.

Corollary 3. *Given a positive real δ^0, consider two sets of points $\tilde{x}_1^1, \ldots, \tilde{x}_{m_1}^1$ and $\tilde{x}_1^2, \ldots, \tilde{x}_{m_2}^2$ such that all the balls $B(\tilde{x}_{i_1}^1, \delta^0)$ and $B(\tilde{x}_{i_2}^2, \delta^0)$, for $1 \leq i_1 \leq m_1$ and $1 \leq i_2 \leq m_2$, cover R_1 and R_2. Suppose that there exist patterns $\pi_{i_1}^1$ of length k_{i_1} for the 1st sub-system such that:*

1. $B((\tilde{x}_{i_1}^1)_{\pi_{i_1}^1}^{k'}, \delta_{\pi_{i_1}^1}^{k'}) \subseteq S_1$, for all $k' = 1, \ldots, k_{i_1} - 1$;

2. $B((\tilde{x}_{i_1}^1)_{\pi_{i_1}^1}^{k_{i_1}}, \delta_{\pi_{i_1}^1}^{k_{i_1}}) \subseteq R_1$;

3. $\frac{d^2(\delta'_{j_1}(t))}{dt^2} > 0$ *with* $j_1 = \pi_{i_1}^1(k')$ *and* $(\delta')^0 = \delta_{\pi_{i_1}^1}^{k'-1}$, *for all* $k' \in \{1, ..., k_{i_1}\}$ *and* $t \in [0, \tau]$.

and symmetrically for the 2nd sub-system. These properties induce a control σ_1 for the 1st sub-system, and σ_2 for the 2nd sub-system such that the composed control $\sigma = (\sigma_1|\sigma_2)$ ensures recurrence in R and safety in S, i.e.:

- *if $x^0 \in R$, then $\phi_\sigma(t; x^0) \in S$ for all $t \geq 0$;*
- *if $x^0 \in R$, then $\phi_\sigma(k_{i_1}\tau; x^0)_{|1} \in R_1$ for some $i_1 \in \{1, \ldots, m_1\}$, and symmetrically $\phi_\sigma(k_{i_2}\tau; x^0)_{|2} \in R_2$ for some $i_2 \in \{1, \ldots, m_2\}$.*

Example 3. We demonstrate the interest of the distributed approach by comparing it with respect to the (centralized) approach performed in Example 2. The main difficulty of this example is the large number of modes in the switching

Table 3. Numerical results for the distributed four-room example.

	Sub-system 1	Sub-system 2
R	$[20, 22]^2 \times [20, 22]^2$	
S	$[19, 23]^2 \times [19, 23]^2$	
τ	30	
Time subsampling	No	$\tau/10$
Complete control	Yes	Yes
Error parameters	$\displaystyle\max_{j_1=1,\dots,4} \lambda^1_{j_1} = -1.39 \times 10^{-3}$	$\displaystyle\max_{j_2=1,\dots,4} \lambda^2_{j_2} = -1.42 \times 10^{-3}$
	$\displaystyle\max_{j_1=1,\dots,4} \gamma^1_{j_1} = 1.79 \times 10^{-4}$	$\displaystyle\max_{j_2=1,\dots,4} \gamma^2_{j_2} = 2.47 \times 10^{-4}$
	$\displaystyle\max_{j_1=1,\dots,4} C^1_{j_1} = 4.15 \times 10^{-4}$	$\displaystyle\max_{j_2=1,\dots,4} C^2_{j_2} = 5.75 \times 10^{-4}$
Number of balls/tiles	16	16
Pattern length	2	2
CPU time	<1 s	<1 s

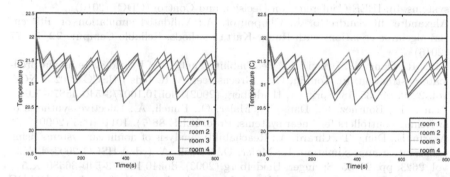

Fig. 10. Simulation of the centralized (left) and distributed (right) Euler-based controllers from the initial condition $(22, 22, 22, 22)$.

system, which induces a combinatorial issue. The centralized controller in Example 2 was obtained with 256 balls in 48 s, the distributed controller was obtained with $16 + 16$ balls in less than a second. In both cases, patterns of length 2 are used. A sub-sampling of $h = \tau/20$ is required to obtain a controller with the centralized approach (see Table 2). For the distributed approach, no sub-sampling is required for the first sub-system, while the second one requires a sub-sampling of $h = \tau/10$ (see Table 3). Simulations of the centralized and distributed controllers are given in Fig. 10, where the control objective is to stabilize the temperature in $[20, 22]^4$ while never going out of $[19, 23]^4$.

5   Final Remarks

We have presented a simple method of control synthesis for switched systems using a new scheme of guaranteed integration based on Euler's method. Preliminary experiments show that, on some examples, the method avoids the wrapping effect occurring with interval-based integration methods. On-going work is done for adapting this Euler-based method to the treatment of stochastic differential equations.

Acknowledgement. The results presented in this paper have been obtained through collaborations with Adrien Le Coënt, Florian De Vuyst, Ludovic Chamoin, Julien Alexandre dit Sandretto and Alexandre Chapoutot. I have also benefited from numerous insightful comments by Antoine Girard.

References

1. Abbaszadeh, M., Marquez, H.J.: Nonlinear observer design for one-sided lipschitz systems. In: IEEE Conference on Decision and Control (CDC) (2010)
2. Alexandre dit Sandretto, J., Chapoutot, A.: Validated simulation of differential algebraic equations with Runge-Kutta methods. Reliable Comput. **22**, 56–77 (2016)
3. Alur, R., Dang, T., Ivančić, F.: Reachability analysis of hybrid systems via predicate abstraction. In: Tomlin, C.J., Greenstreet, M.R. (eds.) HSCC 2002. LNCS, vol. 2289, pp. 35–48. Springer, Heidelberg (2002). doi:10.1007/3-540-45873-5_6
4. Asarin, E., Bournez, O., Dang, T., Maler, O., Pnueli, A.: Effective synthesis of switching controllers for linear systems. Proc. IEEE **88**(7), 1011–1025 (2000)
5. Asarin, E., Dang, T., Girard, A.: Reachability analysis of nonlinear systems using conservative approximation. In: Maler, O., Pnueli, A. (eds.) HSCC 2003. LNCS, vol. 2623, pp. 20–35. Springer, Heidelberg (2003). doi:10.1007/3-540-36580-X_5
6. Beccuti, A.G., Papafotiou, G., Morari, M.: Optimal control of the boost DC-DC converter. In: 44th IEEE Conference on Decision and Control (CDC) (2005)
7. Blanchini, F.: Set invariance in control: a survey. Automatica **35**(11), 1747–1768 (1999)
8. Dahlquist, G.: Error analysis for a class of methods for stiff non-linear initial value problems. In: Watson, G.A. (ed.) Numerical Analysis. LNM, vol. 506, pp. 60–72. Springer, Heidelberg (1976). doi:10.1007/BFb0080115
9. Donchev, T., Farkhi, E.: Stability and Euler approximation of one-sided lipschitz differential inclusions. SIAM J. Contr. Optim. **36**(2), 780–796 (1998)
10. Fribourg, L., Kühne, U., Soulat, R.: Finite controlled invariants for sampled switched systems. Formal Methods Syst. Des. **45**(3), 303–329 (2014)
11. Girard, A.: Reachability of uncertain linear systems using zonotopes. In: Morari, M., Thiele, L. (eds.) HSCC 2005. LNCS, vol. 3414, pp. 291–305. Springer, Heidelberg (2005). doi:10.1007/978-3-540-31954-2_19
12. Girard, A.: Low-complexity switching controllers for safety using symbolic models. In: Proceedings of 4th IFAC Conference on Analysis and Design of Hybrid Systems, pp. 82–87 (2012)
13. Le Coënt, A., Alexandre dit Sandretto, J., Chapoutot, A., Fribourg, L., De Vuyst, F., Chamoin, L.: Distributed control synthesis using Euler's method. In: International Workshop on Reachability Problems (2017)

14. Le Coënt, A., De Vuyst, F., Chamoin, L., Fribourg, L.: Control synthesis of nonlinear sampled switched systems using Euler's method. In: Proceedings 3rd International Workshop on Symbolic and Numerical Methods for Reachability Analysis, vol. 247 of Electronic Proceedings in Theoretical Computer Science, pp. 18–33. Open Publishing Association (2017)
15. Meyer, P.-J.: Invariance and symbolic control of cooperative systems for temperature regulation in intelligent buildings. Thesis, Université Grenoble Alpes (2015)
16. Mitchell, I.M.: Comparing forward and backward reachability as tools for safety analysis. In: Bemporad, A., Bicchi, A., Buttazzo, G. (eds.) HSCC 2007. LNCS, vol. 4416, pp. 428–443. Springer, Heidelberg (2007). doi:10.1007/978-3-540-71493-4_34
17. Moore, R.: Interval Analysis. Prentice Hall, Englewood Cliffs (1966)
18. Nedialkov N.S., Jackson K.R.: A new perspective on the wrapping effect in interval methods for initial value problems for ordinary differential equations. In: Kulisch U., Lohner R., Facius A. (eds) Perspectives on Enclosure Methods. Springer, Vienna (2001)

Timed Models

On the Determinization of Timed Systems

Patricia Bouyer[1]([⊠]), Samy Jaziri[1]([⊠]), and Nicolas Markey[2]([⊠])

[1] LSV – CNRS & ENS Paris-Saclay, Cachan, France
{bouyer,jaziri}@lsv.fr
[2] IRISA – CNRS & INRIA & Univ. Rennes 1, Rennes, France
nicolas.markey@irisa.fr

Abstract. We introduce a new formalism called *automata over a timed domain* which provides an adequate framework for the determinization of timed systems. In this formalism, determinization w.r.t. timed language is always possible at the cost of changing the timed domain. We give a condition for determinizability of automata over a timed domain without changing the timed domain, which allows us to recover several known determinizable classes of timed systems, such as strongly-non-zeno timed automata, integer-reset timed automata, perturbed timed automata, etc. Moreover in the case of timed automata this condition encompasses most determinizability conditions from the literature.

1 Introduction

Timed automata. Timed automata [AD94] extend finite-state automata with real-valued variables, called *clocks*, that can be used to constrain delays between transitions along executions of an automaton. This is performed by decorating transitions with *timing constraints* and *clock resets*: timing constraints compare some of the clocks to integer values; a transition is then available only at times when the timing constraint is satisfied; clock resets set some of the clocks back to value zero.

Figure 1 is a simple example representing the (simplified) behaviour of a computer mouse. Timed automata are very convenient to model real-time reactive systems: they enjoy polynomial-space analysis algorithms (with efficient implementations) for reachability (and many related verification problems), which is quite low in view of their expressiveness and handiness.

Determinization of timed automata. However, the situation is a bit less appealing in terms of the language-theoretic questions, where timed automata do not enjoy most of the nice properties of finite-state automata: they cannot be complemented nor determinized, and language inclusion and universality are undecidable [AD94]. As an example, the timed automaton of Fig. 2 does not admit a deterministic equivalent timed automaton: indeed, any deterministic[1] timed

---

This work was supported by ERC project EQualIS (308087).

[1] *Deterministic* for a timed automaton means that any two transitions out of the same state and carrying the same letter should have disjoint timing constraints.

© Springer International Publishing AG 2017
A. Abate and G. Geeraerts (Eds.): FORMATS 2017, LNCS 10419, pp. 25–41, 2017.
DOI: 10.1007/978-3-319-65765-3_2

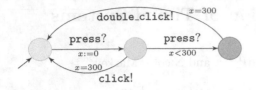

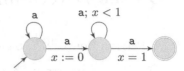

Fig. 1. Modelling a computer mouse

Fig. 2. A non-determinizable timed automaton

automaton accepting the same language would have to *guess* which occurrence of the letter a will have a matching a one time unit later. It can be proved that no finite timed automaton can achieve this. It has even been shown that determinizability of a timed automaton is undecidable [Tri06,Fin06].

Two research directions have emerged from this situation. First, several subclasses of timed automata have been shown to allow determinization:

- *Event-clock automata* [AFH94] are automata in which each letter σ of the alphabet is associated with two clocks x_σ and y_σ: the former clock keeps track of the time elapsed since the last occurrence of σ in the execution, while the latter stores the time until the next occurrence of σ (if any). The class of event-clock automata has been proven to be closed under determinization [AFH94]. This result heavily relies on the fact that event-clock automata are *input-determined* [DT04], i.e., the values of the clocks (hence also the satisfaction of the guards) all along any execution of the automaton only depend on the input word; they do not depend on the execution itself.
- The class of timed automata with 0 as the only constant has been proven determinizable in [OW04], by determinizing its region automaton (and augmenting the resulting DFA with one clock to detect time elapses);
- *Integer-reset timed automata* [VPKM08] are timed automata in which clock resets may only occur at integer times (by constraining resetting transitions with $x = c$ for some clock x and integer c). The class of integer-reset timed automata is closed under determinization [VPKM08], by determinizing an enriched version of the region automaton and augmenting it with one clock.
- A common phenomenon in timed automata is that of time convergence: for instance, Zeno runs are infinite executions of timed automata along which the sum of the delays remains bounded. *Strongly-non-Zeno timed automata* [AMPS98] are timed automata in which any two entries in the same location are at least one time unit apart. It is proved in [BBBB09] that the class of strongly-non-Zeno timed automata is determinizable.
- *Perturbed* timed automata [ALM05] are timed automata whose semantics is perturbed by clock drifts, making clocks have different rates in $[1 - \epsilon, 1 + \epsilon]$ for some $0 < \epsilon < 1$. It is proved in [ALM05] that the ϵ-*perturbed language* of a timed automaton can be captured as the (non-perturbed) language of a deterministic timed automaton. This result is different in nature from the previous one, as it is not a closure property.

A second direction has focused on developing incomplete or approximation techniques for determinization. Several approaches have been proposed:

- In [BBBB09], the input timed automaton is unfolded into a tree with unbound-edly many clocks; under some conditions, this tree may be refolded into a finite deterministic timed automaton. This technique can be used to (re)prove several of the results listed above (event-clock automata, integer-reset timed automata, strongly-non-Zeno timed automata).
- Approximating techniques have also been developed: in [KT09], an algorithm is developed to compute a deterministic timed automaton, using a limited number of clocks, that *over-approximates* the language of the original timed automaton, by trying to keep track (as much as possible) of the states the input automaton can be in at each step.
- Finally, a game-based approach has been developed in [BSJK15]: it turns an automaton $\mathcal{A}$ into a two-player turn-based game, where winning strategies of the first player (with safety objective) can be turned into deterministic timed automata accepting the same language as $\mathcal{A}$. If the strategy is not winning, the resulting automaton would only over-approximate the language of $\mathcal{A}$.

Our contributions. In this paper, we consider a novel approach, based on a very expressive formalism for representing timed automata (and much more). Our formalism is based on *timed domains*, which are a versatile tool for representing the dynamics of continuous variables. Timed domains are equipped with update functions, corresponding to (but extending) clock resets of timed automata. Then automata over timed domains are automata built on these formalisms.

We propose various notions of determinism, and we discuss determinization procedures for some of them. We also discuss finite representation of those deter-minized automata. This new approach to the determinization of automata over timed domains allows to recover several existing results.

Related works. Besides the works already listed above, our approach was inspired by the approach of [BL12], even if the latter is not directly linked to determiniza-tion. To tackle the problem of minimization, the authors introduce a super-class of timed automata called *constrained timed register automata*, which is decidable and closed under minimization.

An extended version of this work will be available under the same title as an arXiv paper.

2   Definitions

2.1   Timed Domains

Timed domains are our formalism for representing the evolution of continuous variables: a timed domain is made of *values* (e.g. vectors of nonnegative reals, which would correspond to clock valuations in timed automata) and a function encoding the evolution of those values when time elapses.

Definition 1. *A* timed domain *is a triple $\mathcal{D} = \langle \mathcal{V}, \hookrightarrow \rangle$ where $\mathcal{V}$ is a set of values, and $\hookrightarrow : \mathcal{V} \times \mathbb{R}_{\geq 0} \to \mathcal{V}$ is the* time transition function, *satisfying the condition $\hookrightarrow(v, d + d') = \hookrightarrow(\hookrightarrow(v, d), d')$ for all $v \in \mathcal{V}$ and all $d, d' \in \mathbb{R}_{\geq 0}$.*

In the sequel, we may write $v \xrightarrow{d} v'$ for $\hookrightarrow(v, d) = v'$.

Product and Subset Domains. Given two timed domains $\mathcal{D} = \langle \mathcal{V}, \hookrightarrow_{\mathcal{V}} \rangle$ and $\mathcal{D}' = \langle \mathcal{V}', \hookrightarrow_{\mathcal{V}'} \rangle$, we define their product $\mathcal{D} \times \mathcal{D}' = \langle \mathcal{V}_{\times}, \hookrightarrow_{\times} \rangle$ where $\mathcal{V}_{\times} = (\mathcal{V} \cup \{\bot\}) \times (\mathcal{V}' \cup \{\bot\})$ and $\hookrightarrow_{\times}((v, v'), d) = (\hookrightarrow_{\mathcal{V}}(v, d), \hookrightarrow_{\mathcal{V}'}(v', d))$ with $\hookrightarrow_{\mathcal{V}}(\bot, d) = \hookrightarrow_{\mathcal{V}'}(\bot, d) = \bot$. For $n \in \mathbb{N}_{>0}$, the timed domain $\mathcal{D}^n$ is defined inductively as $\mathcal{D}^1 = \mathcal{D}$ and $\mathcal{D}^{n+1} = \mathcal{D} \times \mathcal{D}^n$. Taking the product of timed domains can be viewed as considering multiple resources evolving synchronously. We add a special symbol $\bot$ to specify that a resource may be *inactive*; in that case, it does not evolve over time.

For a timed domain $\mathcal{D} = \langle \mathcal{V}, \hookrightarrow \rangle$, we also define its powerset $\mathcal{P}(\mathcal{D})$ as the timed domain $\langle \mathcal{V}_{\mathcal{P}}, \hookrightarrow_{\mathcal{P}} \rangle$ with $\mathcal{V}_{\mathcal{P}} = \mathcal{P}(\mathcal{V})$ and $\hookrightarrow_{\mathcal{P}}$ extends $\hookrightarrow$ to sets in the natural way.

Lemma 2. *Given timed domains $\mathcal{D}$ and $\mathcal{D}'$, and for any positive integer n, $\mathcal{D} \times \mathcal{D}'$, $\mathcal{D}^n$ and $\mathcal{P}(\mathcal{D})$ are timed domains.*

Example 1. Fix $M \in \mathbb{N}$. The M-bounded one-dimensional clock domain $\mathcal{D}_M = \langle \mathcal{C}_M, \hookrightarrow_{\mathcal{C}_M} \rangle$ is defined by $\mathcal{C}_M = [0; M] \cup \{+\infty\}$ equipped with the time transition function $\hookrightarrow_{\mathcal{C}_M}$ satisfying the requirements of the definition above, and such that $\hookrightarrow_{\mathcal{C}_M}(v, d) = v + d$ if $v + d \leq M$ and $\hookrightarrow(v, d) = \infty$ if $v + d > M$. The M-bounded n-dimensional clock domain is defined as the product $\mathcal{D}_M^n$, which we write $\mathcal{D}_{M^n} = \langle \mathcal{C}_{M^n}, \hookrightarrow_{\mathcal{C}_{M^n}} \rangle$. A value in the timed domain $\mathcal{D}_M^n$ corresponds to a clock valuation in timed automata [AD94]. Contrary to what is usually done, we explicitly replace every value larger than M with $+\infty$. As an example, $(0.3, 1.6, \bot) \in \mathcal{C}_2^3$ represents a clock valuation over three clocks, and $(0.3, 1.6, \bot) \xrightarrow{1.1}_{\mathcal{C}_2^3} (1.4, +\infty, \bot)$ represents a time-elapsing transition of 1.1 time units.

Example 2. Fix a continuous function $f \in \mathcal{C}^{\infty}(\mathbb{R}_{\geq 0}, \mathbb{R}^n \times \mathbb{R}^m)$ describing the evolution of two continuous variables x and y over time. We can define the timed domain $\mathcal{D}_f = \langle \mathbb{R}_{\geq 0} \times \mathbb{R}^n \times \mathbb{R}^m, \hookrightarrow_{\mathcal{D}_f} \rangle$ where $\hookrightarrow_{\mathcal{D}_f}$ satisfies the requirements of the definition above and such that $\hookrightarrow_{\mathcal{D}_f}((t, x, y), d) = (t + d, f(t + d))$. Such a timed domain would allow to define dynamical systems.

Many more examples of timed domains could be given, which would define rather complex systems evolving over time. For instance, we show in Sect. 4.3 how timed domains can be defined to represent *perturbed clocks*.

2.2 Updates

In this section, we introduce operations to be performed on values when taking transitions; it includes clock resets of timed automata, but is much more general. For $v \in \mathcal{V}$, we write $v^{\mathcal{V}}:\mathcal{V} \to \mathcal{V}$ for the constant function mapping all elements of $\mathcal{V}$ to v.

Definition 3. *Let $\mathcal{D} = \langle \mathcal{V}, \hookrightarrow \rangle$ be a timed domain, and Σ be a finite alphabet. An* update set *for $\mathcal{D}$ and Σ is a set $\Lambda \subseteq \Sigma \times \mathcal{V}^{\mathcal{V}}$.*

Given an update set Λ and a letter $\sigma \in \Sigma$, we write Λ_σ for the set $\{w \in \mathcal{V}^{\mathcal{V}} \mid (\sigma, w) \in \Lambda\}$. An element of Λ_σ is called a *σ-update*, or simply *update*.

Product Update Sets, Subset Update Sets. Take a timed domain $\mathcal{D}$ equipped with an update set Λ over Σ. We equip $\mathcal{D}^n$ with its canonical update set, denoted Λ^n, and defined as follows:

$$\Lambda^n = \Big\{ \big(\sigma, (w_i \circ \pi_{k_i}^n)_{1 \le i \le n}\big) \ \Big|$$

$$\sigma \in \Sigma \text{ and } \forall 1 \le i \le n. \ w_i \in \Lambda_\sigma \cup \{\perp^{\mathcal{V}}\} \text{ and } 1 \le k_i \le n \Big\}$$

where for $1 \le b \le a$, the function π_b^a is the projection $(d_j)_{1 \le j \le a} \mapsto d_b$. Notice that we add to Λ_σ a function $\perp^{\mathcal{V}}$ which allows to set a "resource" inactive.

Given an update set Λ over $\mathcal{D} = \langle \mathcal{V}, \hookrightarrow \rangle$ and Σ, and given $p \in \mathbb{N}_{>0}$, we define an update set $\mathcal{P}^p(\Lambda)$ over $\mathcal{P}(\mathcal{D})^p$ and Σ as follows. Fix $\sigma \in \Sigma$ and $\gamma = (\gamma_i)_{1 \le i \le p}$ with $\gamma_i \subseteq \mathcal{V} \times \Lambda_\sigma$ for all $1 \le i \le p$. Each relation γ_i defines the possible updates of Λ_σ we can apply to a value $v \in \mathcal{V}$. To each γ_i we can associate a function $o_{\sigma, \gamma_i}:\mathcal{V} \to \mathcal{P}(\mathcal{V})$ which aggregates all possible updated values of v following instructions in γ_i: $o_{\sigma, \gamma_i}(v) = \{w(v) \mid (v, w) \in \gamma_i\}$. We extend o_σ, γ_i on $\mathcal{P}(\mathcal{V})$ and obtain $O_{\sigma, \gamma_i}:\mathcal{P}(\mathcal{V}) \to \mathcal{P}(\mathcal{V})$ which aggregates this time the possible updated values of all values in V (following instructions in γ_i): $O_{\sigma, \gamma_i}(V) = \bigcup_{v \in V} o_{\sigma, \gamma_i}(v)$. Finally, $O_{\sigma, \gamma}:\mathcal{P}(\mathcal{V})^p \to \mathcal{P}(\mathcal{V})$ aggregates the possible updated values of $V_1, \ldots, V_p$, following respectively the instructions in $\gamma_1, \ldots, \gamma_p$: $O_{\sigma, \gamma}((V_i)_{1 \le i \le p}) = \bigcup_{1 \le i \le p} O_{\sigma, \gamma_i}(V_i)$. In one line:

$$O_{\sigma, \gamma}: \quad \mathcal{P}(\mathcal{V})^p \to \mathcal{P}(\mathcal{V})$$
$$(V_i)_{1 \le i \le p} \mapsto \bigcup_{1 \le i \le p} \{w(\nu) \mid (\nu, w) \in \gamma_i \text{ and } \nu \in V_i\}$$

Then $\mathcal{P}^p(\Lambda) =$ is the set

$$\Big\{ \big(\sigma, (O_{\sigma, \gamma^j})_{1 \le j \le p}\big) \ \Big| \ \sigma \in \Sigma \text{ and } \forall 1 \le j \le p, \ \gamma^j \subseteq \mathcal{P}(\mathcal{V} \times \Lambda_\sigma)^p \Big\}.$$

From the remarks above, the resulting sets are indeed update sets:

Lemma 4. *If Λ and Λ' are update sets for $\mathcal{D}$ and $\mathcal{D}'$ over Σ, and if $n \in \mathbb{N}_{>0}$, then $\Lambda \times \Lambda'$ and Λ^n are a update sets respectively for $\mathcal{D} \times \mathcal{D}'$ and $\mathcal{D}^n$ over Σ.*

Example 3. Given Σ a finite alphabet, the one-dimensional clock domain $\mathcal{D}_M$ defined in Example 1 can be equipped with the (canonical) update set $\Lambda_M = \Sigma \times \{\text{Id}, 0\}$, where $\text{Id}(v) = v$ (that is, it keeps the clock value unchanged), and $0 = 0^{C_M}$ (that is, it resets the clock to 0).

Then, $\mathcal{D}_M^n$ is equipped with operations of Λ_M^n (the product operations). Given an input vector $\mathbf{v} = (v_i)_{1 \le i \le n} \in \mathcal{C}_M^n$, an operation ω of Λ_M^n is characterized by $\iota : \{1, \dots, n\} \to \{1, \dots, n\} \cup \{0, \bot\}$ such that for every $\mathbf{v}' = (v_i')_{1 \le i \le n}$, $\mathbf{v}' = \omega(\mathbf{v})$ if, and only if:

$$v_i' = \begin{cases} 0 & \text{if } \iota(i) = 0 \\ \bot & \text{if } \iota(i) = \bot \\ v_j & \text{if } \iota(i) = j \end{cases}$$

Seeing $\mathbf{v}$ as a clock valuation, the i-th clock is reset in the first case, it is made inactive in the second case, and it takes the value of the j-th clock in the last case (note that if $j = i$, then the clock value is unchanged). We write ω_ι for the corresponding operation.

2.3   Automata over Timed Domains

Definition 5. *Fix a timed domain $\mathcal{D} = \langle \mathcal{V}, \hookrightarrow \rangle$ and an update set Λ for $\mathcal{D}$ over Σ. An automaton on $\mathcal{D}$ and Λ is a tuple $\mathcal{A} = \langle Q, q_{\mathit{init}}, \nu_{\mathit{init}}, T, F \rangle$ where Q is a finite set of states, $q_{\mathit{init}} \in Q$ is an initial state, ν_{init} is an initial value, $T \subseteq Q \times \mathcal{V} \times \Lambda \times Q$ is the transition function, and $F \subseteq Q$ is the set of final states.*

Given an automaton $\mathcal{A}$ over $\mathcal{D}$ and Λ, we write $S_{\mathcal{A}}$ for the set $Q \times \mathcal{V}$ of *configurations* of $\mathcal{A}$. An automaton $\mathcal{A}$ induces a (possibly infinite) state transition system $\mathcal{S} = \langle S_{\mathcal{A}}, \to_{\mathcal{A}} \rangle$ where $\to_{\mathcal{A}} = (\xrightarrow{d}_{\mathcal{A}})_{d \in \mathbb{R}_{\ge 0}} \uplus (\xrightarrow{\sigma, w}_{\mathcal{A}})_{(\sigma, w) \in \Lambda}$, defined as follows:

$$(q, \nu) \to d_{\mathcal{A}}(q', \nu') \quad \Leftrightarrow \quad q = q' \text{ and } \nu \xrightarrow{d} \nu'$$

$$(q, \nu) \xrightarrow{\sigma, w}_{\mathcal{A}} (q', \nu') \quad \Leftrightarrow \quad (q, \nu, (\sigma, w), q') \in T \text{ and } \nu' = w(\nu).$$

Given a timed domain $\mathcal{D}$ and its update set Λ, and given $n \in \mathbb{N}_{>0}$, we write $\mathbb{A}_n(\mathcal{D}, \Lambda)$ for the set of all automata on $\mathcal{D}^n$ and Λ^n. Notice that $\mathbb{A}_n(\mathcal{D}, \Lambda) = \mathbb{A}_1(\mathcal{D}^n, \Lambda^n)$. We let $\mathbb{A}(\mathcal{D}, \Lambda) = \bigcup_{n \in \mathbb{N}_{>0}} \mathbb{A}_n(\mathcal{D}, \Lambda)$. Similarly, for $n \in \mathbb{N}$, we let $\mathcal{P}\mathbb{A}_n(\mathcal{D}, \Lambda) = \bigcup_{p \in \mathbb{N}} \mathbb{A}(\mathcal{P}(\mathcal{D}^n)^p, \mathcal{P}^p(\Lambda^n))$, and $\mathcal{P}\mathbb{A}(\mathcal{D}, \Lambda) = \bigcup_{n \in \mathbb{N}} \mathcal{P}\mathbb{A}_n(\mathcal{D}, \Lambda)$.

Remark 1. This definition of an automaton is half-way between standard automata and transition systems: there is no symbolic guards and symbolic guarded transitions, but a "list" of transitions, specifying, for each state, and for each value in the timed domain, what the next state should be, and how the value should be updated. This general form of automaton will be useful to apply a determinization procedure.

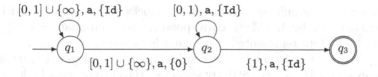

Fig. 3. A finitely-representable timed automaton $\mathcal{B}$

Example 4. An example of an automaton in $\mathbb{A}_1(\mathcal{D}_M, \Lambda_M)$ over $\Sigma = \{a\}$ is $\mathcal{A} = \langle \{q_1, q_2, q_3\}, q_1, 0, T, \{q_3\} \rangle$ where $T = \{(q_1, \nu, (a, 0^{\mathcal{C}_M}), q_2) \mid \nu \in \mathcal{C}_M\} \cup \{(q_2, \nu, (a, \mathrm{Id}), q_3) \mid \nu \in \mathcal{C}_M \cap \mathbb{Q}\}$. It generates (for instance) the sequences

$$(q_1, 0) \xrightarrow{d_1}_{\mathcal{A}} (q_1, d_1) \xrightarrow{a, 0^{\mathcal{C}_M}} (q_2, 0) \xrightarrow{d_2}_{\mathcal{A}} (q_2, d_2) \xrightarrow{a, \mathrm{Id}} (q_3, d_2)$$

requiring that d_2 is a rational number bounded by M.

2.4 Finite Representation of Automata over Timed Domains

With our definition, each transition $(q, \nu, (\sigma, w), q')$ is only available from configuration (q, ν). In general, the set of transitions is infinite. However, in order to get a finite representation, we may group transitions together.

Let $\mathcal{G} \subseteq \mathcal{P}(\mathcal{V})$; we call it a *set of guards*. A $\mathcal{G}$-*guarded update* for $\sigma \in \Sigma$ is a pair $(G, O) \in \mathcal{G} \times \mathcal{P}(\Lambda_\sigma)$. A set $\{(G_i, O_i) \mid i \in I\}$ (I being a finite or infinite subset of $\mathbb{N}$) of $\mathcal{G}$-guarded updates for σ is *(i)* sound from q to q' whenever for every $i \in I$, for every $\nu \in G_i$, for every $w \in O_i$, $(q, \nu, (\sigma, w), q') \in T$; and *(ii)* complete from q to q' whenever for every $(q, \nu, (\sigma, w), q') \in T$, there exists $i \in I$ such that $\nu \in G_i$ and $w \in O_i$.

An automaton $\mathcal{A} = \langle Q, q_{\mathsf{init}}, \nu_{\mathsf{init}}, T, F \rangle$ is *finitely representable* using $\mathcal{G}$ whenever for every q and q' in Q, for every $\sigma \in \Sigma$, there exists a finite set of $\mathcal{G}$-guarded updates for σ, which is sound and complete from q to q'. In that case, there is a natural way to graphically represent the automaton, by depicting a transition for every $\mathcal{G}$-guarded update involved in the representation. We illustrate those representations in the following example.

Example 5. We consider the automaton $\mathcal{B} \in \mathbb{A}(\mathcal{D}_1, \Lambda_1)$ (over the one-dimensional clock domain) represented on Fig. 3, which as we explain corresponds to the timed automaton of Fig. 2. The guarded transition $q_1 \xrightarrow{[0,1]\cup\{\infty\},\mathsf{a},\{0\}} q_2$ represents all the transitions $(q_1, \nu, (\mathsf{a}, 0), q_2)$ of $\mathcal{B}$, with $\nu \in [0, 1] \cup \{\infty\} = \mathcal{C}_1 \setminus \{\bot\}$. This automaton has a single clock variable, and the above transition resets the variable to 0, whatever its original value. The guarded transition $q_2 \xrightarrow{\{1\},\mathsf{a},\{\mathrm{Id}\}} q_3$ checks that the value of the variable is 1 prior to going to q_3. Later we may write $[0, \infty)$ for $[0, 1] \cup \{\infty\}$ when considering the one-dimensional clock domain $\mathcal{D}_1$.

Following this example, we remark that n-clocks timed automata with clock constraints bounded by M [AD94] correspond to those automata in $\mathbb{A}(\mathcal{C}_M^n, \Lambda_M^n)$, which can be finitely represented using guards of the form $(I_1, \ldots, I_n) \in \mathcal{I}_M^n$, where $\mathcal{I}_M$ is the set of intervals I whose bounds are nonnegative integral constants bounded by M, or $+\infty$. Strictly speaking, the current model allows transfers of clocks (using the updates $\omega_\iota \in \Lambda_M^n$ – see page 5), but we know that such updates can be expressed in timed automata [BDFP04]. In the following, we call *timed automata* those automata in the set:

$$\bigcup_{M \in \mathbb{N}} \bigcup_{n \in \mathbb{N}} \left\{ \mathcal{A} \in \mathbb{A}(\mathcal{C}_M^n, \Lambda_M^n) \;\middle|\; \begin{array}{l} \mathcal{A} \text{ can be finitely represented} \\ \text{using guards of the form } (I_1, \ldots, I_n) \in \mathcal{I}_M^n \end{array} \right\}$$

2.5   Commands

We now introduce the notion of *commands*, which we use to define different kinds of determinism.

Definition 6. *Let $\mathcal{D}$ be a timed domain and Λ be an update set. Let $\mathcal{A} \in \mathbb{A}(\mathcal{D}, \Lambda)$. Let Γ be a set (called* command alphabet*). Let $c \in \Gamma$. The c-command of $\mathcal{A}$ is a subset $\xrightarrow{c}_{\mathcal{A}} \subseteq S_{\mathcal{A}} \times S_{\mathcal{A}}$ s.t., writing $\xrightarrow{+}_{\mathcal{A}}$ for the transitive closure of $\to_{\mathcal{A}}$,*

$$(q, \nu) \xrightarrow{c}_{\mathcal{A}} (q', \nu') \implies (q, \nu) \xrightarrow{+}_{\mathcal{A}} (q', \nu')$$

A command for a class $\mathbf{C}$ of automata over a timed domain $\mathcal{D}$ is a set $\kappa = (\xrightarrow{c})_{c \in \Gamma}$ where $\xrightarrow{c}$ maps each automaton $\mathcal{A}$ of $\mathbf{C}$ to a command $\xrightarrow{c}_{\mathcal{A}}$ of $\mathcal{A}$.

Notice that some transitions from the automaton may be lost, and correspond to no command.

Fix a timed domain $\mathcal{D}$ and an update set Λ, a set $\mathbf{C}$ of automata over $\mathcal{D}$ and Λ, a command $\kappa = (\xrightarrow{c})_{c \in \Gamma}$ over $\mathbf{C}$. Let $\mathcal{A}$ be an automaton in $\mathbf{C}$. A κ-trace from a configuration (q, ν) is a finite sequence $\tau = (q_i, \nu_i)_{0 \le i \le n}$ where $(q_0, \nu_0) = (q, \nu)$, and for which there exists a word $C = (c_i)_{1 \le i \le n} \in \Gamma^n$ such that $(q_i, \nu_i) \xrightarrow{c_i} (q_{i+1}, \nu_{i+1})$ for all $1 \le i \le n$. Trace τ is then said to be *generated* by C. Notice that a single word $C \in \Gamma^n$ may generate several traces (even from a single configuration), and that several words may generate the same trace. For a word $C \in \Gamma^n$, we write $\mathcal{T}_{\mathcal{A}}^\kappa((q, \nu), C)$ for the set of traces from (q, ν) generated by C.

Definition 7. *An automaton $\mathcal{A} \in \mathbf{C}$ is said κ-deterministic if, for any $C \in \Gamma^*$, the cardinality of $\mathcal{T}_{\mathcal{A}}^\kappa((q_{init}, \nu_{init}), C)$ is at most 1.*

A word $C \in \Gamma^*$ reaches a configuration (q', ν') from (q, ν) w.r.t. κ if there exists a trace $\tau = (q_i, \nu_i)_{0 \le i \le n} \in \mathcal{T}_{\mathcal{A}}^\kappa(C)$ from (q, ν) with $(q_n, \nu_n) = (q', \nu')$. Then (q', ν') is said κ-reachable from (q, ν); we write $S_{\mathcal{A}}^\kappa(q, \nu)$ for the set of κ-reachable configurations from (q, ν). For all the notations introduced above, we may omit to mention (q, ν) when we mean (q_{init}, ν_{init}).

Finally, a word $C \in \Gamma^n$ is accepted by $\mathcal{A}$ from (q, ν) if there is a trace $\tau \in T_{\mathcal{A}}^{\kappa}((q, \nu), C)$ whose last configuration is in $F \times \mathcal{V}$. For a set of configurations $S \subseteq S_{\mathcal{A}}$, we write $\mathcal{L}_{\kappa}(\mathcal{A}, S)$ for the set of words accepted by $\mathcal{A}$ from some $(q, \nu) \in S$. Finally, $\mathcal{L}_{\kappa}(\mathcal{A})$ corresponds to $\mathcal{L}_{\kappa}(\mathcal{A}, \{q_{\mathrm{init}}, \nu_{\mathrm{init}}\})$.

Proposition 8. *An automaton $\mathcal{A} \in \mathbf{C}$ is κ-deterministic if, and only if, for any $c \in \Gamma$ and any κ-reachable configuration (q, ν) of $\mathcal{A}$, there is at most one configuration (q', ν') such that $(q, \nu) \xrightarrow{c}_{\mathcal{A}} (q', \nu')$.*

2.6   Different Notions of Determinism

We consider two different types of commands, leading to two notions of accepted language and two notions of determinism that we study in the sequel.

Full command. The *full command* corresponds to $\Gamma_{\mathrm{F}} = \mathbb{R}_{\geq 0} \uplus \Lambda$: in this setting, a word contains full information about the operations that have been performed on the values. More precisely, the *full command* of $\mathcal{A}$ over Γ_{F} is the relation $\twoheadrightarrow_{\mathcal{A}}^{\mathrm{F}}$ defined as

$$(q, \nu) \xrightarrow{d}{}_{\mathcal{A}}^{\mathrm{F}}(q, \nu') \Leftrightarrow \nu \xrightarrow{d} \nu' \qquad\qquad \forall d \in \mathbb{R}_{\geq 0}$$

$$(q, \nu) \xrightarrow{a,w}{}_{\mathcal{A}}^{\mathrm{F}}(q', \nu') \Leftrightarrow (q, \nu, (a, w), q') \in T \text{ and } \nu' = w(\nu) \quad \forall (a, w) \in \Lambda.$$

Then $\kappa_{\mathrm{F}} = (\xrightarrow{c}{}^{\mathrm{F}})_{c \in \Gamma_{\mathrm{F}}}$ is the *full command* over $\mathbb{A}(\mathcal{D}, \Lambda)$.

Being deterministic for the full command is not very demanding: it just amounts to satisfying that if $(q, \nu, (a, w), q_1) \in T$ and $(q, \nu, (a, w), q_2) \in T$, then $q_1 = q_2$. Thus the operator (of the commands) has access to all the variables of the system.

This is the kind of determinism that is used e.g. for event-clock timed automata [AFH94]—we discuss this further in Sect. 4.2.

Timed command. The *timed command* corresponds to $\Gamma_{\mathrm{T}} = \mathbb{R}_{\geq 0} \uplus \Sigma$: this gives rise to the classical setting of *timed words*, with $\twoheadrightarrow_{\mathcal{A}}^{\mathrm{T}}$ defined as

$$(q, \nu) \xrightarrow{d}{}_{\mathcal{A}}^{\mathrm{T}}(q, \nu') \Leftrightarrow \nu \xrightarrow{d} \nu' \qquad\qquad \forall d \in \mathbb{R}_{\geq 0}$$

$$(q, \nu) \xrightarrow{a}{}_{\mathcal{A}}^{\mathrm{T}}(q', \nu') \Leftrightarrow (q, \nu, (a, w), q') \in T \text{ and } \nu' = w(\nu) \quad \forall (a, w) \in \Lambda.$$

Then $\kappa_{\mathrm{T}} = (\xrightarrow{c}{}^{\mathrm{T}})_{c \in \Gamma_{\mathrm{T}}}$ is the *timed command* over $\mathbb{A}(\mathcal{D}, \Lambda)$.

This corresponds to the usual notion of determinism used for timed automata [AD94]. In a sense, the operator (of the commands) has access to the absolute time value (starting from value ν_0 at time 0) and to the action to be played.

Remark 2. We could define many other command sets, with the idea to finely describe which resources of the system the operator can access. Interesting command alphabets include partial observation (either of the variables or of the action alphabet of the system). For instance, following [DM02], consider a plant $\mathcal{P}$ given by a timed automaton with controllable (Σ_c) and uncontrollable (Σ_u) actions; an interesting command set would then be $\mathbb{R}_{\geq 0} \cup \Sigma_c$: the operator would then control delays and controllable actions, but could not control nor observe uncontrollable actions. Exploring such commands is part of our future work.

3   Determinization of ATD

3.1   Full-Command Determinization

In this section, we consider the full command κ_F, over the alphabet $\Gamma_F = \mathbb{R}_{\geq 0} \cup \Lambda$.

Theorem 9. *Let $\mathcal{D}$ be a timed domain and Λ be an update set. For any $\mathcal{A} \in \mathbb{A}_1(\mathcal{D}, \Lambda)$, there exists a κ_F-deterministic automaton $\mathcal{A}_{det} \in \mathbb{A}_1(\mathcal{D}, \Lambda)$ such that $\mathcal{L}_{\kappa_F}(\mathcal{A}) = \mathcal{L}_{\kappa_F}(\mathcal{A}_{det})$.*

Proof (Sketch). The proof follows the classical determinization procedure by powerset construction. We fix $\mathcal{A} = \langle Q, q_{\mathsf{init}}, \nu_{\mathsf{init}}, T, F \rangle \in \mathbb{A}_1(\mathcal{D}, \Lambda)$, and construct $\mathcal{A}_{\mathsf{det}} = \langle \mathcal{P}(Q), \{q_{\mathsf{init}}\}, \nu_{\mathsf{init}}, T_{\mathsf{det}}, F_{\mathsf{det}} \rangle$ with $F_{\mathsf{det}} = \{P \in \mathcal{P}(Q) \mid F \cap P \neq \emptyset\}$ and

$$(P, \nu, (a, w), P') \in T_{\mathsf{det}} \text{ iff } P' = \{q' \in Q' \mid \exists q \in P, (q, \nu, (a, w), q') \in T\}.$$

This automaton is in $\mathbb{A}_1(\mathcal{D}, \Lambda)$. κ_F-determinism is straightforward from the definition of T_{det} and κ_F. Finally, it is easily proven that $\mathcal{L}_{\kappa_F}(\mathcal{A}) = \mathcal{L}_{\kappa_F}(\mathcal{A}_{\mathsf{det}})$.   □

Finite representation. If $\mathcal{A}$ can be finitely represented using guards in some set $\mathcal{G}$, then the automaton $\mathcal{A}_{\mathsf{det}}$ constructed in the previous can be (straightforwardly) finitely represented using boolean combinations of guards in $\mathcal{G}$.

3.2   Timed-Command Determinization

We recall that $\Gamma_T = \mathbb{R}_{\geq 0} \uplus \Sigma$ is the timed-command alphabet. Determinizing with regards to that alphabet is the standard point-of-view used for timed systems.

3.2.1   General Determinization

We first formalize a kind of powerset construction for our general automata. Note the change in the timed domain of the determinized automaton.

Theorem 10. *Let $\mathcal{D}$ be a timed domain and Λ be an update set. For any $\mathcal{A} \in \mathbb{A}_1(\mathcal{D}, \Lambda)$, there exists a κ_T-deterministic automaton $\mathcal{A}_{det} \in \mathcal{P}\mathbb{A}_1(\mathcal{D}, \Lambda)$ such that $\mathcal{L}_{\kappa_T}(\mathcal{A}) = \mathcal{L}_{\kappa_T}(\mathcal{A}_{det})$.*

Proof. Write $\mathcal{D} = \langle \mathcal{V}, \hookrightarrow \rangle$ and $\mathcal{A} = \langle Q, q_{\text{init}}, \nu_{\text{init}}, T, F \rangle$, and let Σ be the alphabet used by Λ. Write $Q = \{q_1, \ldots, q_p\}$, and assume w.l.o.g. that $q_{\text{init}} = q_1$. For every $q \in Q$, define ind(q) the index of q, that is, i such that $q = q_i$.

We now construct a κ_T-deterministic automaton in $\mathbb{A}_1(\mathcal{P}(\mathcal{D})^p, \mathcal{P}^p(\Lambda)) \subseteq \mathcal{P}\mathbb{A}_1(\mathcal{D}, \Lambda)$ accepting the same κ_T-language as $\mathcal{A}$. For every $\mathbf{V} = (V_i)_{1 \leq i \leq p} \in \mathcal{P}(\mathcal{V})^p$, we define the set $Q_{\mathbf{V}} = \{q \in Q \mid V_{\text{ind}(q)} \neq \emptyset\}$. Intuitively, each set V_i represents the set of possible values at state q_i, hence $Q_{\mathbf{V}}$ represents the set of states the system can be in, when the possible values in each state is given by $\mathbf{V}$.

Fix $\sigma \in \Sigma$. For every $1 \leq i, j \leq p$, let $\gamma_\sigma^{i \to j}$ be the set $\{(\nu, w) \in \mathcal{V} \times \Lambda_\sigma \mid (q_i, \nu, (\sigma, w), q_j) \in T\}$ and $\gamma_\sigma^{\to j} = (\gamma_\sigma^{i \to j})_{1 \leq i \leq p}$. We define the following operation, which belongs to $\mathcal{P}^p(\Lambda)$ (see page 5):

$$O_{\sigma, \mathcal{A}} = (O_{\sigma, \gamma_\sigma^{\to 1}}, \ldots, O_{\sigma, \gamma_\sigma^{\to p}})$$

Somehow, $\gamma_\sigma^{i \to j}$ records how one can reach state q_j from state q_i with letter σ, i.e. the set of possible values, together with the set of updated values; and the operation $O_{\sigma, \gamma_\sigma^{\to j}}(\mathbf{V})$ aggregates all the possible ways to reach q_j, if we start from some (q_i, ν) with $\nu \in V_i$ (with $1 \leq i \leq p$).

Lemma 11. *Let* $\mathbf{V} = (V_i)_{1 \leq i \leq p} \in \mathcal{P}(\mathcal{V})^p$, *and* $\mathbf{V}' = (V_i')_{1 \leq i \leq p} = O_{\sigma, \mathcal{A}}(\mathbf{V})$. *Then, for every* $q' \in Q$, *for every* $\nu' \in \mathcal{V}$:

$$\nu' \in V_{\text{ind}(q')}' \iff \exists (q, \nu, (\sigma, w), q') \in T \ s.t. \ \nu \in V_{\text{ind}(q)} \ and \ \nu' = w(\nu)$$

We then let $\mathcal{A}_{\text{det}} = \langle \mathcal{P}(Q), \{q_{\text{init}}\}, (\{\nu_{\text{init}}\}, \emptyset, \ldots, \emptyset), T_{\text{det}}, F_{\text{det}} \rangle$ where:

- T_{det} is made of the transitions $(Q_{\mathbf{V}}, \mathbf{V}, (\sigma, O_{\sigma, \mathcal{A}}), Q')$ where:
  - $\mathbf{V} \in \mathcal{P}(\mathcal{V})^p$
  - $Q' = Q_{\mathbf{V}'}$ where $\mathbf{V}' = O_{\sigma, \mathcal{A}}(\mathbf{V})$
- $F_{\text{det}} = \{Q' \subseteq Q \mid Q' \cap F \neq \emptyset\}$.

Proposition 12. $\mathcal{A}_{det}$ *is* κ_T-*deterministic and* $\mathcal{L}_{\kappa_T}(\mathcal{A}) = \mathcal{L}_{\kappa_T}(\mathcal{A}_{det})$.

Proof (Sketch). The κ_T-determinism of $\mathcal{A}_{\text{det}}$ is obvious (by Proposition 8) since, for every $\sigma \in \Sigma$, there is a unique operation associated with σ, namely $O_{\sigma, \mathcal{A}}$. It remains to show the equality of the two languages. We first define a correspondence between vectors $\mathbf{V}$ and sets of configurations of $\mathcal{A}$ as follows:

$$\phi: \mathcal{P}(\mathcal{V})^p \to \mathcal{P}(S^{\mathcal{A}})$$
$$\mathbf{V} \mapsto \{(q, \nu) \mid q \in Q_{\mathbf{V}} \text{ and } \nu \in V_{\text{ind}(q)}\}$$

It is easy to see that this is a bijection. By induction, we can prove that for every $\mathbf{V} \in \mathcal{P}(\mathcal{V})^p$, $\mathcal{L}_{\kappa_T}(\mathcal{A}_{\text{det}}, (Q_{\mathbf{V}}, \mathbf{V})) = \mathcal{L}_{\kappa_T}(\mathcal{A}, \phi(\mathbf{V}))$.

Finite representation. We discuss now the finite representability of automaton $\mathcal{A}_{\mathsf{det}}$ constructed in the previous proof. We only consider the case of timed automata here, and have a more general discussion in the corresponding research report. The operations allowed in timed automata are ω_ι, where $\iota{:}\{1,\dots,n\} \to \{1,\dots,n\} \cup \{0,\bot\}$ (see page 5). We assume that in $\mathcal{A}$, there is a guard $G_{q,q',\sigma,\iota}$ defined with disjunctions and conjunctions (involving several clocks) of intervals constraints such that $(G_{q,q',\sigma,\iota},\omega_\iota)$ is a guarded update from q to q' for σ.

The transitions between two states Q_1 and Q_2 of $\mathcal{A}_{\mathsf{det}}$ labelled by σ can then be written as:

- a constraint requiring that $\forall q_j \in Q_2,\ \exists q_i \in Q_1,\ V_i \cap \left(\bigcup_{\iota(j)\neq\bot} G_{q_i,q_j,\sigma,\iota}\right) \neq \emptyset$;
- a constraint requiring that $\forall q_j \notin Q_2,\ \forall q_i \in Q_1,\ V_i \cap \left(\bigcup_{\iota(j)\neq\bot} G_{q_i,q_j,\sigma,\iota}\right) = \emptyset$;
- for each $q_i \in Q_1$, for each $q_j \in Q_2$, for every ι, there are rules $V_i \xmapsto{\ G_{q_i,q_j,\sigma,\iota,\omega_\iota}\ } V_j'$, representing a transfer of valuations from V_i (for those valuations of V_i which belong to $G_{q_i,q_j,\sigma,\iota}$) to V_j', after update ω_ι.

Example 6. Consider again the automaton $\mathcal{B}$ depicted on Fig. 3. The κ_{T}-deterministic automaton $\mathcal{B}_{\mathsf{det}}$ is depicted on Fig. 4, with the convention we have just discussed. Given that there are three states in $\mathcal{B}$ and one clock, the timed domain of $\mathcal{B}_{\mathsf{det}}$ is $\mathcal{P}(\mathcal{D}_1)^3$; hence there are three sets of clocks, one for each state of $\mathcal{B}$. We write V_1 (resp. V_2, V_3) for the set of clocks corresponding to q_1 (resp. q_2, q_3). As explained before, the guarded updates are represented explicitly as follows: we write $V_i \xmapsto{G,O} V_j$ for "for each element $\nu \in V_i \cap G$, for each $w \in O$, add $w(\nu)$ to V_j". So, for instance, the transition between $\{q_1,q_2\}$ and $\{q_1,q_2,q_3\}$ is

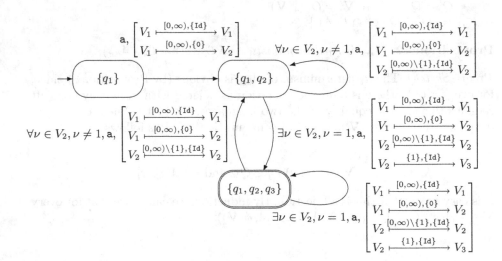

Fig. 4. Determinization of $\mathcal{B}$ of Fig. 3

guarded by the existence of some $\nu \in V_2$ such that $\nu = 1$, and if this holds, then we perform action a and take the transition while keeping all values in V_1, adding a 0 to V_2, keeping all values but value 1 in V_2, and initializing V_3 with 1.

We realize that, while this is not really a timed automaton (since it involves unboundedly many clocks), all these clocks can be partitioned, and can be manipulated using first-order quantifications.

3.2.2 Strong Determinization

We now focus on the case where the previously constructed deterministic automaton satisfies some nice boundedness property, which allows to *flatten* it (that is, if the original automaton is in $\mathbb{A}(\mathcal{D}^n, \Lambda^n)$, then so will be the determinized automaton).

We fix $\mathcal{A} = \langle Q, q_{\text{init}}, \nu_{\text{init}}, T, F \rangle \in \mathbb{A}_1(\mathcal{D}^n, \Lambda^n)$, and write $p = |Q|$. Borrowing notations from the proof of Theorem 10, every reachable state in $\mathcal{A}_{\text{det}}$ is characterized by some $\mathbf{V} \in \mathcal{P}(\mathcal{V}^n)^p$. Furthermore, for such a vector $\mathbf{V}$, we write V_i for its i-th component (for every $1 \le i \le p$), and we use this implicit convention for all the vectors we manipulate; we also extend operations componentwise.

We say that $\mathcal{A}_{\text{det}}$ is m-*weakly monotonic* whenever there exists $\mathbf{M} \in \mathbb{N}^p$, with $m = \sum_{i=1}^{p} M_i$, such that for every $\mathbf{V} \in \mathcal{P}(\mathcal{V}^n)^p$ in $\mathcal{A}_{\text{det}}$, there exists $\mathbf{V}' \in \mathcal{P}(\mathcal{V}^n)^p$ such that (i) $Q_{\mathbf{V}} = Q_{\mathbf{V}'}$, (ii) $\mathbf{V}' \subseteq \mathbf{V}$, (iii) $|\mathbf{V}'| \le \mathbf{M}$ (that is, $|V_i'| \le M_i$ for every $1 \le i \le p$) and (iv) $\mathcal{L}_{\kappa_T}(\mathcal{A}_{\text{det}}, \mathbf{V}') = \mathcal{L}_{\kappa_T}(\mathcal{A}_{\text{det}}, \mathbf{V})$. The intuition behind this condition is that $\mathbf{V}'$ selects a bounded number of values out of $\mathbf{V}$, which are enough to pursue the computation correctly (reading and accepting only relevant words). Condition (i) is for ensuring one should stay in the same discrete state of the automaton for pursuing the computation; Condition (ii) ensures that one can keep the same kinds of updates (we preserve the set of values on which we can apply the updates); Condition (iii) bounds the size of the sets of selected values; Finally, condition (iv) ensures the correctness of $\mathbf{V}'$ w.r.t. $\mathbf{V}$.

Theorem 13. *Let $\mathcal{D}$ be a timed domain and Λ be an action domain. Let $\mathcal{A} \in \mathbb{A}_n(\mathcal{D}, \Lambda) = \mathbb{A}_1(\mathcal{D}^n, \Lambda^n)$, and write $\mathcal{A}_{det}$ for the automaton constructed in the proof of Theorem 10. Assume furthermore that there exists $m \in \mathbb{N}$ such that $\mathcal{A}_{det}$ is m-weakly monotonic. Then, there exists a κ_T-deterministic automaton $\mathcal{A}_{sdet} \in \mathbb{A}_1(\mathcal{D}^{nm}, \Lambda^{nm})$ such that $\mathcal{L}_{\kappa_T}(\mathcal{A}) = \mathcal{L}_{\kappa_T}(\mathcal{A}_{sdet})$.*

The idea is to represent each vector $\mathbf{V}$ such that $|\mathbf{V}| \le \mathbf{M}$ by a single huge vector $\nu \in (\mathcal{V}^n)^m$ such that the first M_1 components of ν stores the elements of V_1, the next M_2 components stores the elements of V_2, etc. The element $\perp^n$ is used to fill the components of ν which are not used by some element of V_i (this can happen when the cardinal of V_i is (strictly) smaller than M_i). Through this correspondence, we transform the transitions of $\mathcal{A}_{\text{det}}$ into transitions over $(\mathcal{V}^n)^m$. In particular, to compute an update for some $\sigma \in \Sigma$ on ν, which corresponds to some $\mathbf{V}$, we apply $O_{\sigma, \mathcal{A}}$ on $\mathbf{V}$, reduce it using the condition given m-weak monotonicity, and reorder the resulting "small" vector of $\mathcal{P}(\mathcal{V}^n)^p$ into a vector $\nu' \in (\mathcal{V}^n)^m$.

Finite representation. It is not possible to obtain a finite representation for $\mathcal{A}_{\text{sdet}}$ in general, even if $\mathcal{A}_{\text{det}}$ can be finitely represented; indeed, the construction relies on a choice of $\mathbf{V}' \subseteq \mathbf{V}$, which is a priori arbitrary. This can however be used when all reachable $\mathbf{V}$ are such that $|\mathbf{V}| \leq \mathbf{M}$.

Actually, we can modify the m-weak monotonicity assumption of Theorem 13 into a more complex and abstract condition, so that the obtained deterministic automaton has a finite representation as soon as $\mathcal{A}_{\text{det}}$ has a finite representation.

4 Applications

4.1 Applications to Plain Timed Automata

We have already explained how Theorem 10 applies to timed automata, yielding deterministic automata $\mathcal{A}_{\text{det}}$ in $\mathbb{P}\mathbb{A}(\mathcal{D}_M, \Lambda_M)$. Theorem 13 can be used to get a deterministic automaton in $\mathbb{A}(\mathcal{D}_M, \Lambda_M)$: our notion of m-weak monotonicity in a sense corresponds to the clock-boundedness condition of [BBBB09].

Our approach is actually a bit stronger, as it can capture other classes of determinizable timed automata, such as the class of finally-imprecise timed automata: a location q is imprecise if any word accepted from some configuration (q, ν) is also accepted from any other configuration (q, ν') in the same region; a timed automaton is then said finally-imprecise if after a fixed number m of discrete steps, it only visits imprecise states. We can prove that finally-imprecise timed automata do have an equivalent deterministic timed automata. This class actually encompasses all timed automata with 0 as the only constant [OW04].

4.2 Applications to Event-Clock Automata

In order to capture event-clock automata [AFH94] in our formalism, we first define the *event-clock domain*. We fix a maximal constant M, and let $\mathcal{E}_M = ([0, M] \cup \{+\infty, \bot\})^2$: the first component corresponds to an event-recording clock, while the second is for event-predicting clocks. For $d \in \mathbb{R}_{\geq 0}$, we then set $(x, y) \xrightarrow{d}_{\mathcal{E}_M} (x', y')$ whenever $x \xrightarrow{d}_{\mathcal{C}_M} x'$, and $y' = y - d$ if $y - d \geq 0$, and $y' = +\infty$ otherwise (and $y' = \bot$ if, and only if, $y = \bot$). Thus the first component corresponds to the M-bounded one-dimensional clock domain defined at Example 1 (with an additional symbol $\bot$ when the clock is inactive). This defines the M-bounded one-letter event-clock domain $\mathcal{F}_M = \langle \mathcal{E}_M, \hookrightarrow_{\mathcal{E}_M} \rangle$. Given an alphabet $\Sigma = \{\sigma_i \mid 1 \leq i \leq n\} \uplus \{\text{init}\}$ (see below), the M-bounded Σ-event-clock domain, denoted $\mathcal{F}_M^\Sigma$, is the timed domain $\mathcal{F}_M^n$.

We now associate updates with this timed domain; for this we reuse the projections π_b^a we defined in Sect. 2.2: we define the action domain Θ_M on $\mathcal{E}_M$ as $\{(\sigma, (w \circ \pi_1^2, w' \circ \pi_2^2)) \mid \sigma \in \Sigma, w \in \{\text{Id}, 0, \bot\}, w' \in \{\text{Id}, \bot\} \cup \{d \mid d \in \mathbb{R}_{\geq 0}\}\}$. Again, we extend this action domain to $\mathcal{F}_M^\Sigma$, denoting the resulting action domain with Θ_M^Σ.

We now define M-bounded Σ-event-clock automata. For this, we set $\Sigma = \{\sigma_i \mid 1 \leq i \leq n\} \cup \{\text{init}\}$, where init is a special symbol used only for initializing the automaton. An automaton $\mathcal{A} = \langle Q, q_{\mathsf{init}}, \nu_{\mathsf{init}}, T, F \rangle$ is in the class $\mathsf{ECA}(\Sigma, M)$ of M-bounded Σ-event-clock automata if

- $\nu_{\mathsf{init}} = (\bot)_{1 \leq i \leq 2n}$, and $(q_{\mathsf{init}}, \nu_{\mathsf{init}})$ only initializes the computation, with transitions $(q_{\mathsf{init}}, \nu_{\mathsf{init}}, (\mathsf{init}, (\bot, d_i)_{1 \leq i \leq n}), q_1)$ for each $(d_i)_{1 \leq i \leq n} \in (\mathbb{R}_{\geq 0} \cup \{\bot\})^n$;
- for any transition $(q, \nu, (\sigma_i, w), q') \in T$ with $\sigma \neq \mathsf{init}$ and $q \neq q_{\mathsf{init}}$, variable y_i must have value 0 in ν, and operation w must set variable x_i to 0, variable y_i to some value in $[0, M] \cup \{\bot\}$, and leave the other variables unchanged.
- finally, for any transition $(q, \nu, (\sigma_i, w), q_f)$ with $q_f \in F$, we require that $y_j = \bot$ in ν for any $j \neq i$, and that $y_i = 0$.

An important feature of event-clock automata is that they are *input-determined*: in our setting, this can be expressed as an isomorphism between $\mathcal{L}_{\kappa_T}(\mathcal{A})$ and $\mathcal{L}_{\kappa_F}(\mathcal{A})$: intuitively, the operations performed on the clocks can be derived from observing the time of occurrence of the letters along words. Now, applying Theorem 9 to an event-clock automaton $\mathcal{A}$, we get a κ_F-deterministic automaton $\mathcal{A}_{\mathsf{det}}$ accepting the same κ_F-language as $\mathcal{A}$, hence also the same language (in the usual sense). Moreover, $\mathcal{A}_{\mathsf{det}}$ is easily proved to lie in $\mathsf{ECA}(\Sigma, M)$.

Remark 3. The automaton $\mathcal{A}_{\mathsf{det}}$ is *not* κ_T-deterministic, since from any configuration, there are several transitions, each having a different "guess" for updating the clock y_i associated with the letter carried by the transition. This is also the case of the determinization result of [AFH94].

If $\mathcal{A}$ only involves *event-recording* clocks, then so does $\mathcal{A}_{\mathsf{det}}$. Thus the resulting automaton does not have to guess values for clocks y_i, and it is κ_T-deterministic.

4.3   Application to Perturbed Timed Automata

The model of *perturbed timed automata* has been proposed in [ALM05], with the idea that adding perturbations to the system can indeed help having interesting properties like determinizability. The syntax of this model is a standard timed automaton, but its semantics is parametrized by some $\epsilon \in (0, 1)$: in this model, we consider that the slope of a clock can be perturbed by at most ϵ. It is shown in [ALM05] that single-clock perturbed timed automata can be determinized into standard timed automata. We can fit this model into our framework.

To track the possible slopes of a clock, we use two "variables", one which runs at speed $1 - \epsilon$, and the other at speed $1 + \epsilon$. If $M \in \mathbb{N}$, the M-bounded one-dimensional ϵ-perturbed clock domain is $\mathcal{D}_{M,\epsilon} = \langle \mathcal{C}_{M,\epsilon}, \hookrightarrow_{\mathcal{C}_{M,\epsilon}} \rangle$ with:

- $\mathcal{C}_{M,\epsilon} = ([0, M(1 + \epsilon)] \cup \{\infty\})^2$;
- $(x^-, x^+) \xrightarrow{d}_{\mathcal{C}_{M,\epsilon}} (x^- + d(1 - \epsilon), x^+ + d(1 + \epsilon))$ with conventions similar to the clock domain for manipulating ∞.

The two values x^- and x^+ represent respectively the lowest and greatest value that the perturbed clock x can take.

We equip this one-dimensional perturbed clock domain with a subset of the canonical action domain on two clocks, where updates on x^- and x^+ are forced to be the same. It is then easy to define a set of guards $\mathcal{I}_{M,\epsilon}$ such that any one-clock perturbed timed automata of [ALM05] can be represented by an automaton in $\mathbb{A}_1(\mathcal{D}_{M,\epsilon}, \Lambda_{M,\epsilon})$, which is finitely representable using guards in $\mathcal{I}_{M,\epsilon}$.

We can show that a proof very similar to that of Theorem 13 (or to its modified version) can be used to determinize the automaton. The result is not a timed automaton, but can be modified into a real timed automaton. This allows to recover the determinizability result of [ALM05].

5   Conclusions and Future Work

In this work, we have proposed a general model of automata based on a timed domain, and general notions of updates over that domain. We have discussed the notion of determinism for this model, by defining the notion of commands and discussing some possible sets of such commands. For two of these sets of commands (the full command, and the timed command), we have designed a generic procedure for determinizing the automata. While the full-command determinization stays within the class of automata we start with, the timed-command determinization involves a powerset construction, which increases the number of "variables" the automaton can manipulate. We have exhibited conditions under which this construction can be flattened into the original class of automata. We have applied our approach mostly to timed-automata-like classes of systems, and recovered many existing determinizability results. In particular, our approach gives a good understanding of event-clock timed automata [AFH94], gives a fresh view over the generic unfolding procedure for standard timed automaton of [BBBB09], and allows to recover the determinizability result for single-clock perturbed timed automata [ALM05].

As illustrated all along the paper, our framework encompasses timed automata and can represent various kinds of dynamical systems, but also timed systems with richer discrete structures. We can e.g. fit into our framework some families of pushdown timed automata, by encoding in the timed domain the "clock values" possibly stored in a stack. While it is not clear yet whether our approach can yield new results for those systems, we believe it is worth investigating.

Further, we believe that the notion of commands and the different kinds of determinism it generates are interesting. As illustrated in Example 2, we believe this approach could be worth investigating for monitoring or controller synthesis.

Finally, it is not completely clear to us how our approach for timed automata compares to the game approach of [BSJK15], so this would be worth investigating as well. Also, the fact that perturbations can be encoded in the timed domain (recall Sect. 4.3) might also have some interest for robustness issues.

References

[AD94] Alur, R., Dill, D.L.: A theory of timed automata. Theoret. Comput. Sci. **126**(2), 183–235 (1994)

[AFH94] Alur, R., Fix, L., Henzinger, T.A.: A determinizable class of timed automata. In: Dill, D.L. (ed.) CAV 1994. LNCS, vol. 818, pp. 1–13. Springer, Heidelberg (1994). doi:10.1007/3-540-58179-0_39

[ALM05] Alur, R., Torre, S., Madhusudan, P.: Perturbed timed automata. In: Morari, M., Thiele, L. (eds.) HSCC 2005. LNCS, vol. 3414, pp. 70–85. Springer, Heidelberg (2005). doi:10.1007/978-3-540-31954-2_5

[AMPS98] Asarin, E., Maler, O., Pnueli, A., Sifakis, J.: Controller synthesis for timed automata. In: SSC 1998, pp. 469–474. Elsevier (1998)

[BBBB09] Baier, C., Bertrand, N., Bouyer, P., Brihaye, T.: When are timed automata determinizable? In: Albers, S., Marchetti-Spaccamela, A., Matias, Y., Nikoletseas, S., Thomas, W. (eds.) ICALP 2009. LNCS, vol. 5556, pp. 43–54. Springer, Heidelberg (2009). doi:10.1007/978-3-642-02930-1_4

[BDFP04] Bouyer, P., Dufourd, C., Fleury, E., Petit, A.: Updatable timed automata. Theoret. Comput. Sci. **321**(2–3), 291–345 (2004)

[BL12] Bojańczyk, M., Lasota, S.: A machine-independent characterization of timed languages. In: Czumaj, A., Mehlhorn, K., Pitts, A., Wattenhofer, R. (eds.) ICALP 2012. LNCS, vol. 7392, pp. 92–103. Springer, Heidelberg (2012). doi:10.1007/978-3-642-31585-5_12

[BSJK15] Bertrand, N., Stainer, A., Jéron, T., Krichen, M.: A game approach to determinize timed automata. Formal Meth. Syst. Des. **46**(1), 42–80 (2015)

[DM02] D'souza, D., Madhusudan, P.: Timed control synthesis for external specifications. In: Alt, H., Ferreira, A. (eds.) STACS 2002. LNCS, vol. 2285, pp. 571–582. Springer, Heidelberg (2002). doi:10.1007/3-540-45841-7_47

[DT04] D'Souza, D., Tabareau, N.: On timed automata with input-determined guards. In: Lakhnech, Y., Yovine, S. (eds.) FORMATS/FTRTFT -2004. LNCS, vol. 3253, pp. 68–83. Springer, Heidelberg (2004). doi:10.1007/978-3-540-30206-3_7

[Fin06] Finkel, O.: Undecidable problems about timed automata. In: Asarin, E., Bouyer, P. (eds.) FORMATS 2006. LNCS, vol. 4202, pp. 187–199. Springer, Heidelberg (2006). doi:10.1007/11867340_14

[KT09] Krichen, M., Tripakis, S.: Conformance testing for real-time systems. Formal Meth. Syst. Des. **34**(3), 238–304 (2009)

[OW04] Ouaknine, J., Worrell, J.: On the language inclusion problem for timed automata: closing a decidability gap. In: LICS 2004, pp. 54–63. IEEE Computer Society Press (2004)

[Tri06] Tripakis, S.: Folk theorems on the determinization and minimization of timed automata. Inf. Process. Lett. **99**(6), 222–226 (2006)

[VPKM08] Suman, P.V., Pandya, P.K., Krishna, S.N., Manasa, L.: Timed automata with integer resets: language inclusion and expressiveness. In: Cassez, F., Jard, C. (eds.) FORMATS 2008. LNCS, vol. 5215, pp. 78–92. Springer, Heidelberg (2008). doi:10.1007/978-3-540-85778-5_7

On Global Scheduling Independency in Networks of Timed Automata

Sergio Feo-Arenis, Milan Vujinović, and Bernd Westphal(✉)

Albert-Ludwigs-Universität Freiburg, Freiburg, Germany
westphal@informatik.uni-freiburg.de

Abstract. Networks of timed automata are a widely used formalism to model timed systems. Models are often concise and convenient since timed automata abstract from many details of actual implementations. One such abstraction is that the semantics of networks of timed automata introduces an implicit global scheduler which blocks edges which are sending on a channel until a matching receiving edge is enabled. When models are used a priori, that is, to develop, e.g., a communication protocol which is supposed to have a (non-shared memory) distributed implementation, a corresponding global scheduler is not desired.

To facilitate distributed implementations of timed automata models, we introduce a new class of networks of timed automata whose behaviour does not depend on the blocking of sending edges. We show that the membership problem for this new class of networks of timed automata is decidable and evaluate our new decision procedure.

1 Introduction

Timed automata [2], in particular in the flavour of Uppaal [4], are widely used as a modelling formalism for timed systems. There are efforts on a-posteriori analysis of timed systems (like LUNAR as analysed in [14] or AODV in [5]), and a-priori verification, for example, for the self monitoring and notification protocols of a wireless fire alarm system (WFAS) [6]. In an a-posteriori analysis, the timed system to be analysed already exists, or has a clear specification or even an implementation, so certain aspects of the system can safely be abstracted for effective analyses without compromising implementability. In the a-priori setting, new communication protocols are developed using a model based approach. Formal models of design ideas for communication protocols are created and thoroughly analysed before the system as such is built, in particular before any implementation activities. In this a-priori setting, the final implementation of the communication protocol is desired to reflect the properties of the model.

In the case of the wireless fire alarm system (WFAS) mentioned above, a distributed implementation is necessary: the final system consists of individual components such as sensors, so-called repeaters, and a central unit, which exchange messages exclusively via wireless communication. The code for each component is supposed to implement the protocol aspects modelled by a corresponding component timed automaton in the model. In this motivating WFAS

A. Abate and G. Geeraerts (Eds.): FORMATS 2017, LNCS 10419, pp. 42–57, 2017.
DOI: 10.1007/978-3-319-65765-3_3

(a) Blocking send.

(b) Non-blocking send.

Fig. 1. Networks of timed automata (double outline indicates initial location).

example, the components only share a common, synchronised notion of time and can exchange information only via messages. We call exactly these kinds of non-shared memory systems *distributed*, in contrast to partially distributed programs consisting of multiple processes running, e.g., on the same host or on different cores of a multi-core CPU. Timed automata models of timed systems do not necessarily have a distributed implementation due to the fact that the formal semantics of timed automata introduces an implicit, global scheduler. This implicit global scheduler resolves non-determinism, and, more crucially, blocks sending edges if there is no matching receiving edge available. Conversely, transitions sending on broadcast channels are never blocked. Similarly, transitions from non-committed locations are blocked if at least one committed location is assumed in the current global configuration.

For example, in the network of timed automata shown in Fig. 1a, the timed automaton on the left is in principle ready to send in location ℓ_0 right from the initial configuration but the synchronisation is effectively blocked until the timed automaton on the right reaches location ℓ_3. By the semantics of timed automata, sending edges are only taken if a corresponding receiving edge is enabled. In order to determine a schedule, the implicit global scheduler needs information from the processes participating in (or affecting a) synchronisation, e.g., which location is assumed and which edges are enabled according to the guards which may depend on local and global variables. The information whether an edge of another component is enabled is in general not available in an architecture which only provides synchronised time and message exchange as the WFAS. Ensuring that all receiving edges are enabled at each point in time is often not a realistic option under energy considerations. For example, in the WFAS, being ready to receive consumes about as much energy as sending so the required battery lifetimes would not be realisable (cf. [6]). The amount of information exchanged using messages is similarly limited due to energy concerns, so extensive information exchange about enabled edges is not feasible either.

In the network of timed automata shown in Fig. 1b in contrast, the sending edge is never blocked by the absence of a corresponding receiving edge, since the timing constraints ensure that the receiver is enabled whenever the sending edge is enabled in the timed automaton on the left hand side. So there is strictly speaking no *need for the implicit* global scheduler in this case since the two timed automata in the network work according to a common time scheme. Thus, a distributed implementation exists.

In this work, we investigate a class of networks of timed automata where the behaviour *does not depend on a global scheduler*. More formally, a network of timed automata does not depend on a global scheduler if its behaviour under a new non-blocking semantics is equal to the behaviour in the classical semantics. In this regard, our work is similar to [15] who also study a different semantics, called ASAP. We show that the problem whether a given network of timed automata does not depend on a global scheduler is decidable. We give a decision procedure for this problem which reduces the problem to classical timed automata model-checking using an efficient syntactical transformation, thus a strictly easier procedure than required for ASAP.

We see our work as a contribution towards the automatic generation of distributed code for timed automata models of timed systems, which will be available for models which do not depend on a global scheduler. Automatic code generation promises to avoid human errors during manual implementations and to be cost and time efficient, so there is a need to automatically derive (at least parts of) an implementation from an existing Uppaal model. Generating code from Uppaal models has been approached before [1,3,7,8,13]. These works have in common that they also generate code for a scheduler (as an additional, explicit component) which corresponds to the implicit, global scheduler introduced by the timed automata semantics. So they are not immediately applicable if a distributed implementation is required.

This paper is structured as follows. We introduce necessary preliminaries in Chap. 2 and the concept of non-blocking semantics in Chap. 3. We present our decision procedure for global scheduling independency in Chap. 4, and finalise with an experimental evaluation (Chap. 5) and conclusions (Chap. 6).

2   Preliminaries

In this section, we recall the necessary preliminaries for self-containedness. The presentation of extended timed automata (as used by Uppaal) follows [12] with the addition of broadcast channels. Readers familiar with the theory of timed automata may still consider our definition of the operational semantics where we introduce some non-standard notations which will be used throughout the subsequent chapters.

An (extended) *timed automaton* $\mathcal{A} = (L, C, A, B, X, V, I, E, \ell_{ini})$ consists of a finite set L of *locations* with a subset $C \subseteq L$ of *committed locations*, a set A of *channels* with a subset $B \subseteq A$ of *broadcast channels*, disjoint sets X and V of *clocks* and *data variables*, a *location invariant* function I, a finite set of directed *edges* E, and an *initial location* $\ell_{ini} \in L$. The location invariant function I assigns to each location $\ell \in L$ an expression $I(\ell) \in \Phi(X, V)$, where $\Phi(X, V)$ denotes a set of boolean expressions over X and V. The boolean terms containing clocks in X are *clock constraints*, i.e., comparisons of a clock variable with an integer.

An element $(\ell, \alpha, \varphi, \vec{r}, \ell') \in E$ describes an edge from location ℓ to ℓ' with *action* $\alpha \in A_{!?} := \{a!, a? \mid a \in A\} \,\dot{\cup}\, \{\tau\}$, *guard* φ, and a finite sequence of *reset operations* $\vec{r} \in R(X, V)^*$, where $R(X, V)$ denotes a set of *reset operations* (updates of the valuations of clock and variables that occur during a transition, e.g., $x := 0$, where clock x is reset to the value 0) on X and V. We write $L(\mathcal{A})$ etc. to denote the set of locations L of timed automaton $\mathcal{A}$.

A *network* (of timed automata) is a finite set $\mathcal{N} = \{\mathcal{A}_1, \ldots, \mathcal{A}_n\}$ of *compatible* timed automata, i.e., if a channel α is a broadcast channel of some $\mathcal{A} \in \mathcal{N}$ then $\alpha \notin A(\mathcal{A}_i) \backslash B(\mathcal{A}_i)$ for all $i \in \{1, \ldots, n\}$, if $x \in X(\mathcal{A})$ then $x \notin V(\mathcal{A}_i)$ for all $i \in \{1, \ldots, n\}$, and if $v \in V(\mathcal{A})$ then $v \notin X(\mathcal{A}_i)$ for all $i \in \{1, \ldots, n\}$.

Let X be a set of clocks and V a disjoint set of variables. A *valuation* of X and V is a function $\nu : X \cup V \to \mathbb{R}_0^+ \cup \mathcal{D}$ such that $\nu(x) \in \mathbb{R}_0^+$ for all $x \in X$, and $\nu(v) \in \mathcal{D}$ for all $v \in V$, where $\mathcal{D} \supseteq \{0, 1, 2\}$ [1] is a non-empty, finite subset of the integers. Valuations are canonically lifted to integer and boolean expressions. We write $\nu \models \varphi$ if and only if boolean expression $\varphi \in \Phi(X, V)$ evaluates to *true* under ν, and $\nu \not\models \varphi$ otherwise. For a valuation ν and $t \in \mathbb{R}_0^+$, we use $\nu + t$ to denote the valuation with $(\nu + t)(x) = \nu(x) + t$ for all $x \in X$ and $(\nu + t)(v) = \nu(v)$ for all $v \in V$ (*time shift*). We use $\nu[r]$ to denote the valuation which is the effect of the reset operation $r \in R(X, V)$ on ν and set $\nu[r_1, \ldots, r_n] := ((\nu[r_1])[r_2] \ldots)[r_n]$.

The *operational semantics* of network $\mathcal{N} = \{\mathcal{A}_1, \ldots, \mathcal{A}_n\}$ is defined by the (labelled) transition system $(Conf(\mathcal{N}), \mathbb{R}_0^+ \cup \{\tau\}, \{\xrightarrow{\lambda} \mid \lambda \in \mathbb{R}_0^+ \cup 2^{A \cup B}\}, C_{ini})$ with $A = \bigcup_{i=1}^n A(\mathcal{A}_i)$ and $B = \bigcup_{i=1}^n B(\mathcal{A}_i)$. It consists of a set of *configurations*

$$Conf(\mathcal{N}) = \{\langle \vec{\ell}, \nu \rangle \mid \vec{\ell} \in L(\mathcal{A}_1) \times \cdots \times L(\mathcal{A}_n), \ \nu : X \cup V \to \mathbb{R}_0^+ \cup \mathcal{D}, \ \nu \models I(\vec{\ell})\}$$

where $X = \bigcup_{i=1}^n X(\mathcal{A}_i)$, $V = \bigcup_{i=1}^n V(\mathcal{A}_i)$, and $I(\ell_1, \ldots, \ell_n) = \bigwedge_{i=1}^n I(\mathcal{A}_i)(\ell_i)$, a set of *initial configurations* $C_{ini} = Conf(\mathcal{N}) \cap \{\langle (\ell_{ini}(\mathcal{A}_1), \ldots, \ell_{ini}(\mathcal{A}_n)), \nu_{ini} \rangle\}$ where $\nu_{ini} = \{x \mapsto 0, v \mapsto 0 \mid x \in X, v \in V\}$ (C_{ini} is empty if the conjunction of the invariants of the initial locations of the timed automaton in the network is not satisfied by ν_{ini}), and the transition relations defined below.

For convenience, we introduce a set of helper notations for the definition of the transition relations. Given a timed automaton $\mathcal{A}$ from $\mathcal{N}$, we use $E(\mathcal{A})|_\tau$ to denote the set $\{(\ell, \alpha, \varphi, \vec{r}, \ell') \in E(\mathcal{A}) \mid \alpha = \tau\}$ of non-sychronising edges, and similarly $E(\mathcal{A})|_{a!}$ and $E(\mathcal{A})|_{a?}$ for any channel $a \in A$. Let $e_0, e_1, \ldots, e_m$, $m \geq 0$, be edges of different automata $\mathcal{A}_{k_i}$ in $\mathcal{N}$, $i \in \{0, \ldots, m\}$, with guards φ_i, reset operations $\vec{r}_i$, and destination locations ℓ_i', $i \in \{0, \ldots, m\}$. Let $\langle \vec{\ell}, \nu \rangle \in Conf(\mathcal{N})$ be a configuration of network $\mathcal{N}$. We write $\langle \vec{\ell}, \nu \rangle[e_0; e_1, \ldots, e_m]$ to denote the effect of sending (or τ) edge e_0 with receiving edges $e_1, \ldots, e_m$ (in general, the order matters), i.e. $\langle \vec{\ell}', \nu' \rangle$ with $\vec{\ell}' = \vec{\ell}[\ell_0 := \ell_0'] \ldots [\ell_m := \ell_m']$ and $\nu' = \nu[\vec{r}_0] \ldots [\vec{r}_m]$. In case $m = 0$, we may just write $\langle \vec{\ell}, \nu \rangle[e_0]$. In our non-blocking semantics, we will extend this notation to a sequence of sending edges before the semicolon.

For $e_0 \in E(\mathcal{A}_{k_0})|_{a!}$ and $e_i \in E(\mathcal{A}_{k_i})|_{a?}$, $i \in \{1, \ldots, m\}$, (or $e_0 \in E(\mathcal{A})|_\tau$ for some $\mathcal{A} \in \mathcal{N}$ and $m = 0$) we say that $e_0, \ldots, e_m$ are *enabled* in $\langle \vec{\ell}, \nu \rangle$, denoted by $\langle \vec{\ell}, \nu \rangle \vdash e_0; e_1, \ldots, e_m$ (or $\langle \vec{\ell}, \nu \rangle \vdash e_0$), if and only if $\nu \vdash \bigwedge_{j=0}^m \psi_j$ and $\langle \vec{\ell}', \nu' \rangle = \langle \vec{\ell}, \nu \rangle[e_0; e_1, \ldots, e_m]$ is an element of $Conf(\mathcal{N})$ (that is, after applying

---

[1]   We need at least the values $0, 1, 2$ (and the standard interpretation of increment and decrement) in our transformation presented in Sect. 4.

the reset operations of the considered edges, the invariants of the destination locations are satisfied by ν').

Using our helper notations, the transition relations are defined as follows:

- (*delay transition*) $\langle \vec{\ell}, \nu \rangle \xrightarrow{t} \langle \vec{\ell}, \nu + t \rangle$, $t \in \mathbb{R}_0^+$, if and only if $\nu + t' \models I(\vec{\ell})$ holds for all $t' \in [0, t]$ and $\ell_i \notin C(\mathcal{A}_i)$ for all $i \in \{1, \dots, n\}$ (that is, there is no delay transition if at least one timed automaton is in a committed location).
- (*local action transition*) $\langle \vec{\ell}, \nu \rangle \xrightarrow{\tau} \langle \vec{\ell'}, \nu' \rangle$, if and only if for some $\mathcal{A} \in \mathcal{N}$, there is an edge $e \in E(\mathcal{A})|_\tau$ such that $\langle \vec{\ell}, \nu \rangle \vdash e$ and $\langle \vec{\ell'}, \nu' \rangle = \langle \vec{\ell}, \nu \rangle[e]$.
- (*rendezvous transition*) $\langle \vec{\ell}, \nu \rangle \xrightarrow{a} \langle \vec{\ell'}, \nu' \rangle$, if and only if there are edges $e_0 \in E(\mathcal{A}_{k_0})|_{a!}$ and $e_1 \in E(\mathcal{A}_{k_1})|_{a?}$ of two different automata $\mathcal{A}_{k_0}$ and $\mathcal{A}_{k_1}$ in $\mathcal{N}$ such that $a \in A(\mathcal{A}_{k_0}) \backslash B(\mathcal{A}_{k_0})$ (that is, a is not a broadcast channel), and $\langle \vec{\ell}, \nu \rangle \vdash e_0; e_1$ and $\langle \vec{\ell'}, \nu' \rangle = \langle \vec{\ell}, \nu \rangle[e_0; e_1]$.
- (*broadcast transition*) $\langle \vec{\ell}, \nu \rangle \xrightarrow{a} \langle \vec{\ell'}, \nu' \rangle$, if and only if there are edges $e_0 \in E(\mathcal{A}_{k_0})|_{a!}$ and $e_i \in E(\mathcal{A}_{k_i})|_{a?}$, $i \in \{1, \dots, m\}$, with $k_0, \dots, k_m$ pairwise different and m maximal, such that $a \in B(\mathcal{A}_i)$, and $\langle \vec{\ell}, \nu \rangle \vdash e_0; e_1, \dots, e_m$ and $\langle \vec{\ell'}, \nu' \rangle = \langle \vec{\ell}, \nu \rangle[e_0; e_1, \dots, e_m]$. [2]
- Local action, rendezvous and broadcast transitions are further constrained by the condition that if there is $i \in \{1, \dots, n\}$ such that $\ell_i \in C(\mathcal{A}_i)$, then for at least one of the participating edges, the source location is also committed.[3]

Note that the transition relations are well-defined because enabledness implies that the invariants of the destination locations are satisfied after applying the reset operations of the involved edges in the given order.

A *transition sequence* is any finite or infinite sequence of the form $\langle \vec{\ell_0}, \nu_0 \rangle \xrightarrow{\lambda_1} \langle \vec{\ell_1}, \nu_1 \rangle \xrightarrow{\lambda_2} \dots$ which is *initial*, i.e., $\langle \vec{\ell_0}, \nu_0 \rangle \in C_{ini}$, and *consecutive*, i.e., for all $i \in \mathbb{N}_0$, $\langle \vec{\ell_i}, \nu_i \rangle$ and $\langle \vec{\ell_{i+1}}, \nu_{i+1} \rangle$ are in transition relation $\xrightarrow{\lambda_{i+1}}$. A configuration $\langle \vec{\ell}, \nu \rangle$ is called *reachable* (in $\mathcal{T}(\mathcal{N})$) if and only if there is a finite transition sequence of length n such that $\langle \vec{\ell_n}, \nu_n \rangle = \langle \vec{\ell}, \nu \rangle$. A location ℓ is called *reachable* (in $\mathcal{T}(\mathcal{N})$) if and only if a configuration $\langle \vec{\ell}, \nu \rangle$ with $\ell_i = \ell$ is reachable. We write $\mathcal{T}(\mathcal{N})|_{reach}$ to denote the restriction of $\mathcal{T}(\mathcal{N})$ to reachable configurations.

The configuration reachability problem is decidable for appropriate choices of the expression language $\Phi(X, V)$ [2]; in the following, we only consider networks with decidable configuration reachability problem.

3   Non-blocking Operational Semantics

In the following, we introduce two new semantics for networks of timed automata. The *local enabledness semantics* considers a notion of *local enabledness* of edges

---

[2]   The Uppaal tool considers only one sequence of receiving edges induced by the so-called system declaration.

[3]   We consider committed locations (although any model with committed locations does depend on a global scheduler) since we will use committed locations in our source-to-source transformation based decision procedure in Sect. 4.

and we observe that the behaviour of networks of timed automata without global variables or committed locations in the local enabledness semantics is equal to the classical semantics, which we just recalled in Sect. 2. In the second, *non-blocking semantics*, sending edges are not blocked, i.e., sending edges can be taken without a corresponding receiving edge.

Definition 1 (Locally Enabled). *An edge* $e = (\ell, \alpha, \varphi, \vec{r}, \ell')$ *of some timed automaton* $\mathcal{A}_i$ *in network* $\mathcal{N} = \{\mathcal{A}_1, \ldots, \mathcal{A}_n\}$ *is called* locally enabled *in configuration* $\langle \vec{\ell}, \nu \rangle \in Conf(\mathcal{N})$, *denoted by* $\langle \vec{\ell}, \nu \rangle \vdash_{loc} e$, *if and only if* $\ell_i = \ell$, $\nu \models \varphi$, *and* $\nu[\vec{r}] \models I(\ell')$. $\Diamond$

In the following, we use $\mathcal{N}_{loc}$ to denote networks of timed automata with only local clocks and variables, and without committed locations, that is, in $\mathcal{N}_{loc} = \{\mathcal{A}_1, \ldots, \mathcal{A}_n\}$, the sets $X(\mathcal{A}_i)$, $i \in \{1, \ldots, n\}$ are pairwise disjoint, the sets $V(\mathcal{A}_i)$ are pairwise disjoint, and $C(\mathcal{A}_i) = \emptyset$ for all $i \in \{1, \ldots, n\}$. We call these networks *closed component networks*.

Definition 2 (Local Enabledness Semantics). *Let* $\mathcal{N}_{loc} = \{\mathcal{A}_1, \ldots, \mathcal{A}_n\}$ *be a closed component network. The* local-enabledness *operational semantics of network* $\mathcal{N}_{loc}$ *is defined by the transition system* $\mathcal{T}_{loc}(\mathcal{N}_{loc}) = (Conf(\mathcal{N}_{loc}), \mathbb{R}_0^+ \cup \{\tau\}, \{\xrightarrow{\lambda} | \lambda \in \mathbb{R}_0^+ \cup 2^{A \cup B}\}, C_{ini})$ *where*

- *configurations, initial configurations, and transition labels are as in* $\mathcal{T}(\mathcal{N}_{loc})$,
- *the transition relations are defined as follows:*
  - *delay: same as in* $\mathcal{T}(\mathcal{N}_{loc})$,
  - *local: use* $\langle \vec{\ell}, \nu \rangle \vdash_{loc} e$ *as enabledness condition instead of* $\langle \vec{\ell}, \nu \rangle \vdash e$,
  - *rendezvous: use* $\langle \vec{\ell}, \nu \rangle \vdash_{loc} e_0 \land \langle \vec{\ell}, \nu \rangle \vdash_{loc} e_1$ *as enabledness condition instead of* $\langle \vec{\ell}, \nu \rangle \vdash e_0; e_1$
  - *broadcast: use* $\langle \vec{\ell}, \nu \rangle \vdash_{loc} e_0 \land \langle \vec{\ell}, \nu \rangle \vdash_{loc} e_k$, $k \in \{1, \ldots, m\}$, m *maximal, as enabledness condition instead of* $\langle \vec{\ell}, \nu \rangle \vdash e_0; e_1, \ldots, e_m$. $\Diamond$

Lemma 1. *Let* $\mathcal{N}_{loc} = \{\mathcal{A}_1, \ldots, \mathcal{A}_n\}$ *be a closed component network. Then* $\mathcal{T}_{loc}(\mathcal{N}_{loc}) = \mathcal{T}(\mathcal{N}_{loc})$.

Proof. Let $j_0, j_1, \ldots, j_m \in \{1, \ldots, n\}$, $m \geq 0$ and m maximal, be pairwise different indices and let $e_0 = (\ell_{j_0}, a!, \varphi_{j_0}, \vec{r}_{j_0}, \ell'_{j_0}) \in E(\mathcal{A}_{j_0})$ and $e_k = (\ell_{j_k}, a?, \varphi_{j_k}, \vec{r}_{j_k}, \ell'_{j_k}) \in E(\mathcal{A}_{j_k})$, $k \in \{1, \ldots, m\}$ be edges of timed automata in $\mathcal{N}_{loc}$. Then:

$\langle \vec{\ell}, \nu \rangle \vdash e_0; e_1, \ldots, e_m$
$\iff \nu \models \bigwedge_{j=0}^{m} \varphi_j$ and $\langle \vec{\ell}', \nu' \rangle = \langle \vec{\ell}, \nu \rangle [e_0; e_1, \ldots, e_m]$ is an element of $Conf(\mathcal{N})$
$\iff \nu \models \bigwedge_{j=0}^{m} \varphi_j$, $\nu' = \nu[r_1] \ldots [r_n]$, and $\nu' \models \bigwedge_{j=0}^{m} I(\mathcal{A}_{k_j})(\ell'_j)$,
$\iff$ (reset operations in $\mathcal{N}_{loc}$ only affect local variables, hence their overall effect is independent from the order of application)
$\bigwedge_{j=0}^{m} \nu \vdash \psi_j$, and $\bigwedge_{j=0}^{m} \nu[r_j] \models I(\mathcal{A}_{k_j})(\ell'_j)$, $\iff \bigwedge_{j=0}^{m} \langle \vec{\ell}, \nu \rangle \vdash_{loc} e_j$.

Thus the enabledness conditions in the construction of $\mathcal{T}(\mathcal{N}_{loc})$ and $\mathcal{T}_{loc}(\mathcal{N}_{loc})$ are equivalent for $\mathcal{N}_{loc}$, thus $\mathcal{T}_{loc}(\mathcal{N}_{loc}) = \mathcal{T}(\mathcal{N}_{loc})$; since $\mathcal{N}_{loc}$ does not have any committed locations, the corresponding constraints in the definition of $\mathcal{T}(\mathcal{N}_{loc})$ are all trivially satisfied. $\square$

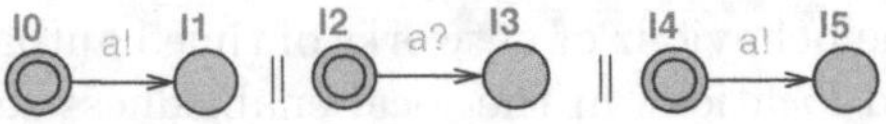

Fig. 2. Network of timed automata with multiple senders.

Definition 3. *Let $\mathcal{N}_{loc} = \{\mathcal{A}_1, \ldots, \mathcal{A}_n\}$ be a closed component network. The non-blocking operational semantics of $\mathcal{N}_{loc}$ is defined by the transition system $\mathcal{T}_{nb}(\mathcal{N}_{loc}) = (Conf(\mathcal{N}_{loc}), \mathbb{R}_0^+ \cup \{\tau\}, \{\xrightarrow{\lambda} \mid \lambda \in \mathbb{R}_0^+ \cup 2^{A \cup B}\}, C_{ini})$ where*

1. *configurations, initial configurations, and transition labels are as in $\mathcal{T}_{loc}(\mathcal{N}_{loc})$,*
2. *the transition relations are defined as follows:*
   (a) *delay and local transitions are as in $\mathcal{T}_{loc}(\mathcal{N}_{loc})$,*
   (b) *rendezvous: $\langle \vec{\ell}, \nu \rangle \xrightarrow{a_0, \ldots, a_{m+1}} \langle \vec{\ell'}, \nu' \rangle$, if and only if there are sending edges $e_i \in E(\mathcal{A}_{k_i})|_{a_i!}$, $i \in \{0, \ldots, m\}$, with $k_0, \ldots, k_m$ pairwise different and $m \geq 0$ maximal, $a_i \in A(\mathcal{A}_{k_i}) \backslash B(\mathcal{A}_{k_i})$, all locally enabled, i.e., $\langle \vec{\ell}, \nu \rangle \vdash_{loc} e_i$, $i \in \{0, \ldots, m\}$ and*
      i. *there is a receiving edge $e_{m+1} \in E(\mathcal{A}_{k_{m+1}})|_{a_{m+1}?}$ with $a_{m+1} = a_i$ for $i \in \{0, \ldots, m\}$ in an automaton $\mathcal{A}_{k_{m+1}}$ which is different from $k_0, \ldots, k_m$ such that e_{m+1} is locally enabled, i.e., $\langle \vec{\ell}, \nu \rangle \vdash_{loc} e_{m+1}$, and $\langle \vec{\ell'}, \nu' \rangle = \langle \vec{\ell}, \nu \rangle[e_0, \ldots, e_m; e_{m+1}]$, or*
      ii. *there is no locally enabled edge $e_{m+1} \in E(\mathcal{A}_{k_{m+1}})|_{a_{m+1}?}$ in any different automaton $\mathcal{A}_{k_{m+1}}$ in $\mathcal{N}$ with $a_{m+1} = a_i$, $i \in \{0, \ldots, m\}$, and $\langle \vec{\ell'}, \nu' \rangle = \langle \vec{\ell}, \nu \rangle[e_0, \ldots, e_m]$.*
      Here, $\langle \vec{\ell}, \nu \rangle[e_0, \ldots, e_m; e_{m+1}]$ denotes the effect of applying the reset vectors of edges e_i, $i \in \{0, \ldots, m\}$, on $\langle \vec{\ell}, \nu \rangle$ in any order, and then the reset vector of e_{m+1} (if given).
   (c) *broadcast: similar to rendezvous with*

   $$\langle \vec{\ell'}, \nu' \rangle = \langle \vec{\ell}, \nu \rangle[e_0, \ldots, e_m; e_{m+1}, \ldots, e_M]$$

   where $e_{m+1}, \ldots, e_M$ is a maximal set of edges receiving on a broadcast channel from $a_0, \ldots, a_m$ which belong to automata in the network which are not sending by edges $e_0, \ldots, e_m$. ◊

The transition system $\mathcal{T}_{nb}(\mathcal{N}_{loc})$ may have behaviour which is not present in $\mathcal{T}(\mathcal{N}_{loc})$, Additional behaviour may be caused by taking a sending edge (that is, an edge with a sending action $a!$) without an enabled corresponding receiver (that is, an edge with receiving action $a?$), or when more than one sending edge is locally enabled in a configuration. For example, in the classical (and the local enabledness) semantics the network of timed automata in Fig. 1a has only computation paths of the form

$$\langle (\ell_0, \ell_2), x = y = 0 \rangle \xrightarrow{t} \langle (\ell_0, \ell_2), x = y = t \rangle \xrightarrow{\tau} \langle (\ell_0, \ell_3), x = y = t \rangle$$
$$\xrightarrow{t'} \langle (\ell_0, \ell_3), x = y = t + t' \rangle \xrightarrow{a} \langle (\ell_2, \ell_4), x = y = t + t' \rangle, \quad t, t' \in \mathbb{R}_0^+.$$

In the non-blocking semantics, there are also computation paths of the form

$$\langle(\ell_0,\ell_2),x=y=0\rangle \xrightarrow{t} \langle(\ell_0,\ell_2),x=y=t\rangle \xrightarrow{a} \langle(\ell_1,\ell_2),x=y=t\rangle, \quad t\in\mathbb{R}_0^+,$$

since the edge sending on channel a can be taken before the receiving edge is enabled.

The transition system $\mathcal{T}(\mathcal{N}_{loc})$ may conversely have behaviour which is not present in $\mathcal{T}_{nb}(\mathcal{N}_{loc})$. For example, if more than one sending edge is locally enabled, then they are taken in a strict interleaving in $\mathcal{T}(\mathcal{N}_{loc})$; this interleaving will in general not be present in $\mathcal{T}_{nb}(\mathcal{N}_{loc})$. For example, in the classical (and local enabledness) semantics, the network shown in Fig. 2 has only computation paths of the two forms

$$\langle(\ell_0,\ell_2,\ell_4),x=y=0\rangle \xrightarrow{t} \langle(\ell_0,\ell_2,\ell_4),x=y=t\rangle \xrightarrow{a} \langle(\ell_1,\ell_3,\ell_4),x=y=t\rangle \text{ and}$$

$$\langle(\ell_0,\ell_2,\ell_4),x=y=0\rangle \xrightarrow{t} \langle(\ell_0,\ell_2,\ell_4),x=y=t\rangle \xrightarrow{a} \langle(\ell_0,\ell_3,\ell_5),x=y=t\rangle.$$

In the non-blocking semantics, there are only computation paths of the form

$$\langle(\ell_0,\ell_2,\ell_4),x=y=0\rangle \xrightarrow{t} \langle(\ell_0,\ell_2,\ell_4),x=y=t\rangle \xrightarrow{a} \langle(\ell_1,\ell_3,\ell_5),x=y=t\rangle.$$

Note that, in Definition 3, we consider all situations where multiple sending edges are enabled to be undesirable. Here, we consider channels to represent messages sent over a globally shared medium, so sending more than one message at a time could cause message collisions (and loss). It is possible to extend Definition 3 to consider multiple media. If, for example, message a is always sent on one medium and message b on a separate medium, then sending a and b at the same time could be allowed as long as each sending edge has an enabled receiving automaton (there is an interleaving in the classical semantics).

Our choice of taking a maximum number of enabled senders is arbitrary; for our purposes it would be sufficient to allow two sending edges to be taken in one transition. Our purpose is to make two conditions semantically visible which are undesirable for a distributed implementation of a model on a platform where global scheduling cannot be assumed:

- a sending edge is effectively blocked because the global scheduler waits for at least one corresponding receiving edge to be enabled,
- a sending edge is effectively blocked because the global scheduler chooses a different sending edge which is also enabled in the current configuration.

Lemma 2. *Let $\mathcal{N}_{loc}$ be a closed component network. Any rendezvous transition of edges e_0 and e_1 in $\mathcal{T}_{nb}(\mathcal{N}_{loc})$ is also present in $\mathcal{T}(\mathcal{N}_{loc})$, i.e.,*

$$\forall c\in Conf(\mathcal{N}_{loc}) \; \forall a\in A \bullet c \xrightarrow{a}_{nb} c[e_0;e_1] \implies c \xrightarrow{a} c[e_0;e_1],$$

where $\xrightarrow{a}_{nb}$ denotes the transition relation $\xrightarrow{a}$ of $\mathcal{T}_{nb}(\mathcal{N}_{loc})$; similar for broadcast.

The following lemma observes that the non-blocking semantics is in general different from changing all rendezvous channels to be broadcast channels. With broadcast channels, more than one receiving edge may synchronise. In the non-blocking semantics, at most one receiver participates in a transition.

Lemma 3. *Let* $\mathcal{N}_{loc} = \{\mathcal{A}_1, \ldots, \mathcal{A}_n\}$ *be a closed component network. Let each non-broadcast channel* $a \in A(\mathcal{N}_{loc})$ *have at most one automaton* $\mathcal{A}_{i_0} \in \mathcal{N}_{loc}$ *where action* $a!$ *occurs and at most one automaton* $\mathcal{A}_{i_1}$ *where action* $a?$ *occurs. Then*

$$\mathcal{T}(B_i := A(\mathcal{A}_i) \mid 1 \leq i \leq n_{loc}) = \mathcal{T}_{nb}(\mathcal{N}_{loc})[\xrightarrow{a_1,\ldots,a_m} := \emptyset \mid m > 1],$$

that is, the behaviour of the network obtained from $\mathcal{N}_{loc}$ *by turning all channels into broadcast channels is the same as* $\mathcal{T}_{nb}(\mathcal{N}_{loc})$ *up to those transitions in* $\mathcal{T}_{nb}(\mathcal{N}_{loc})$ *where multiple senders are enabled at the same time in different automata.* ◇

Our goal is to identify networks of timed automata where none of the two situations of a locally enabled sending edge without any locally enabled receiving edge, or multiple sending edges locally enabled in a configuration, ever occurs in any reachable configuration. These situations are undesired when modelling for a distributed implementation without global scheduling where senders "just proceed" according to their internal time schedule. In the first situation, messages get lost because no other component is listening; in the second situation, messages may get lost due to message collision on a shared medium. Those networks of timed automata are then not in principle un-implementable in a distributed way on a platform where a global scheduler cannot be assumed. We call networks of timed automata which *do not* reach any of the two situations discussed here to not depend on a global scheduler as follows.

Definition 4. *A closed component network* $\mathcal{N}_{loc}$ *is said* not to depend on a global scheduler *if and only if* $\mathcal{T}_{nb}(\mathcal{N}_{loc})|_{reach} = \mathcal{T}(\mathcal{N}_{loc})|_{reach}$. ◇

Intuitively, a network of timed automata does not depend on a global scheduler if the non-blocking semantics does not add or remove any behaviour from $\mathcal{T}(\mathcal{N}_{loc})$ on the reachable configurations. *Local*, discrete non-determinism does not necessarily affect the non-blocking semantics; a timed automaton in a network may have multiple sending or receiving edges locally enabled, and a distributed implementation can devise a *local* scheduler to resolve this non-determinism. If determinism is desired for an implementation, the network of timed automata model may be checked for being deterministic before beginning with the implementation.

The set of networks of timed automata which do not depend on a global scheduler is non-empty, and it is a strict subset of the set of all networks of timed automata. For example, the network shown in Fig. 1a does depend on a global scheduler while the network shown in Fig. 1b does not.

4   Deciding Independency from Global Scheduling

In the following, we establish a sufficient and necessary condition for independency from global scheduling, and we use this condition to devise a source-to-source transformation of networks of timed automata on which independency from global scheduling can be decided by a configuration reachability analysis.

We begin by stating the independency of closed component networks from a global scheduler.

Lemma 4. *Let $\mathcal{N}_{loc} = \{\mathcal{A}_1, \ldots, \mathcal{A}_n\}$ be a closed component network. $\mathcal{N}_{loc}$ does not depend on a global scheduler if and only if*

$$\forall c \in Conf(\mathcal{N}_{loc})|_{reach} \; \forall 1 \leq i \leq n \; \forall a \in A \; \forall e \in E(\mathcal{A}_i)|_{a!} \bullet c \vdash_{loc} e \qquad (1)$$
$$\implies (c \vdash e \wedge \forall 1 \leq j \leq n \; \forall b \in A \; \forall e' \in E(\mathcal{A}_j)|_{b!} \bullet c \vdash_{loc} e' \implies j = i).$$

Proof. Equation (1) states that $\mathcal{N}_{loc}$ depends on central control if and only if, for each sending edge which is locally enabled in some reachable configuration of $\mathcal{N}_{loc}$, there is exactly one receiving edge that is locally enabled (i.e., the edge is the only sending edge globally enabled).

We show the contra-position. If Eq. (1) does not hold for $\mathcal{N}_{loc}$, then there is a configuration c reachable such that c locally enables an edge e sending on channel a, but e is not (globally) enabled or there is another edge e' sending on channel b locally enabled.

If e is not enabled in c, Case 2(b)ii of Definition 3 applies. Then there is a transition $c \xrightarrow{a} c'$ in $\mathcal{T}_{nb}(\mathcal{N}_{loc})$ but not in $\mathcal{T}(\mathcal{N}_{loc})$, thus $\mathcal{N}_{loc}$ depends on a global scheduler. If at least two edges e_1 and e_2 (of different automata) sending on channels a_1 and a_2 are locally enabled in c, then there is a transition $c \xrightarrow{a_1, a_2, \ldots} c'$ in $\mathcal{T}_{nb}(\mathcal{N}_{loc})$ but not in $\mathcal{T}(\mathcal{N}_{loc})$, thus $\mathcal{N}_{loc}$ depends on a global scheduler. $\square$

Now, we define a source-to-source transformation useful for our analysis.

Definition 5. *Let $\mathcal{N}_{loc} = \{\mathcal{A}_1, \ldots, \mathcal{A}_n\}$ be a closed component network. The transformed network $\mathcal{N}'_{loc} = \{\mathcal{A}'_1, \ldots, \mathcal{A}'_n\}$ is obtained by transforming each timed automaton $\mathcal{A} = (L, C, A, B, X, V, I, E, \ell_{ini})$ in $\mathcal{N}_{loc}$ to the transformed automaton $\mathcal{A}' = (L', C', A', B', X', V', I', E', \ell'_{ini})$ as follows:*

- $B' = B$, $X' = X$, $\ell'_{ini} = \ell_{ini}$,
- $V' = V \cup \{enabled\}$, '*enabled*' *a fresh integer variable,*
- $L' = L \cup L_E$, $C' = L \cup L_E$, $L_E = \{\ell^e \mid e \in \bigcup_{a \in A} E|_{a!}\}$ *fresh locations,*
- $I' = I \cup \{\ell^e \mapsto I(\ell') \mid e = (\ell, \alpha, \varphi, \vec{r}, \ell') \in E, \ell^e \in L_E\}$,
- $A' = A \cup \{addEnabled\}$, '*addEnabled*' *a fresh channel,*
- $E' = \{(\ell, addEnabled!, \varphi, \vec{r}; enabled{+}{+}, \ell^e), (\ell^e, \tau, \varphi, \vec{r}; enabled{+}{+}, \ell^e),$
  $(\ell^e, addEnabled?, enabled \leq 1, \langle\rangle, \ell^e), (\ell^e, a!, enabled = 1, enabled{-}{-}, \ell')$
  $\mid e = (\ell, \alpha, \varphi, \vec{r}, \ell') \in E|_{a!}, a \in A\} \cup E \setminus \bigcup_{a \in A} \mathcal{A}|_{a!}.$ $\Diamond$

Figure 3b shows the transformed timed automaton for the left timed automaton in Fig. 3a. The idea is to split up each sending edge into two edges. The first edge from ℓ_0 to ℓ_e has the same guard and action as the original edge, but is a τ-transition. Thus this first edge can be taken whenever it is locally enabled. Location ℓ_e has an edge to ℓ_1 which comprises the send action. Since ℓ_e is committed (and since the original network is a closed component network), the absence of an enabled receiver results in a deadlock. In addition, the first edge increments the counter *enabled*. If another sending edge is enabled while in ℓ_e, this sending will have been split up similarly, so a synchronisation on channel *addEnabled* is possible, and enforced by the committed location. This synchronisation will increment the counter *enabled* to 2, so *enabled* reaches a value of 2 if and only if at least two sending edges are locally enabled in two different timed automata.

Theorem 1. *Let $\mathcal{N}_{loc}$ be a closed component network. Then the following statements are equivalent:*

1. *$\mathcal{N}_{loc}$ does not depend on a global scheduler.*
2. *Condition (1) of Lemma 4 holds for $\mathcal{N}_{loc}$.*
3. *$\mathcal{N}'_{loc} \models \mathsf{E}\Diamond\,(enabled \geq 1 \wedge deadlock)$.[4]*

Thus, checking whether a given network $\mathcal{N}_{loc}$ depends on global scheduling reduces to applying the transformation from Definition 5 and the reachability query given above. The approach based on a source-to-source transformation has the advantage that it is independent from tools for timed automata model-checking. The transformed network $\mathcal{N}'_{loc}$ is again a proper timed automaton, so any available checking tool can be applied and their full language features (from which in particular Uppaal may draw its popularity) are immediately supported,

The convenience of performing a syntactic transformation comes at a price. The number of configurations reachable in $\mathcal{N}'_{loc}$ is at least as large as for $\mathcal{N}_{loc}$ (cf. Lemma 5). The transformation introduces one new location per sending edge, so for each configuration $\langle \vec{\ell}, \nu \rangle$ which is reached by a synchronisation, i.e., there is some c_0 such that $c_0 \xrightarrow{a} \langle \vec{\ell}, \nu \rangle$, there is $\langle \vec{\ell'}, \nu' \rangle$ with $\nu'(enabled) = 1$ and the corresponding committed location in $\vec{\ell'}$ reachable in $\mathcal{N}_{loc}$. In networks which *do not* depend on a global scheduler, there is (by definition) at most one sending edge per configuration enabled, so $\mathcal{N}'_{loc}$ has at most twice as many reachable configurations as $\mathcal{N}_{loc}$. In networks which do depend on a global scheduler, a relevant measure is the amount of configurations which need to be explored in order to detect the dependency. As long as the configurations which do not satisfy the condition of Lemma 4 are explored, the overall number will again be at most twice as much as would be explored in $\mathcal{N}_{loc}$. For instance, the breadth- and depth-first explorations of Uppaal stop as soon as either a blocked sending or multiple enabled senders are detected, so at most two more configurations as in the original network will be explored. Overall, we expect that for most networks for which it is feasible to *verify* (in the sense of confirm) some invariant (which is usually part of model-based development of, e.g., new communication protocols), it will be feasible to detect whether the network depends on a global scheduler. Showing that a network *does* depend on a global scheduler will in average be much faster than verifying an invariant of the network. See Sect. 5 for a preliminary, quantitative evaluation of our approach.

In the following, we show the equivalence of statements (2) and (3) of Theorem 1 by using a *two-step* bisimulation relation. The two-step bisimulation

---

[4] We write $\mathcal{N}'_{loc} \models \mathsf{E}\Diamond\,(enabled \geq 1 \wedge deadlock)$ if and only if $\mathcal{T}(\mathcal{N}_{loc})$ has a reachable configuration c with $c \models (enabled \geq 1 \wedge deadlock)$; $c \models deadlock$ if and only if, for all configurations c', c'' and $t \in \mathbb{R}_0^+$, $c \xrightarrow{t} c' \xrightarrow{\lambda} c''$ implies $\lambda \in \mathbb{R}_0^+$.

relation focuses on reachability of configurations in the original and the transformed network. The transformed network $\mathcal{N}'_{loc}$ can simulate the behaviour of the original network $\mathcal{N}_{loc}$ if it just exits a committed location immediately without doing any synchronisation on *addEnabled* (which detects multiple enabled senders). $\mathcal{N}'_{loc}$ may reach a deadlock, but only in some *unrelated* intermediate configurations $\langle \vec{\ell}_c, \nu_c \rangle$, so the blocking of not globally enabled sends is preserved.

Definition 6. *A relation $\approx_{2stp} \subseteq Conf(\mathcal{N}_1) \times Conf(\mathcal{N}_2)$ is called two-step bisimulation relation on networks $\mathcal{N}_1$ and $\mathcal{N}_2$ iff the following conditions hold:*

1. *$C_{ini,1} \cup C_{ini,2} = \emptyset$, or $C_{ini,1} \neq \emptyset$, $C_{ini,2} \neq \emptyset$, and $C_{ini,1} \times C_{ini,2} \subseteq \approx_{2stp}$,*
2. *$\forall \langle \vec{\ell}_1, \nu_1 \rangle, \langle \vec{\ell}_2, \nu_2 \rangle \in \approx_{2stp} \forall \varphi \in \Phi(X,V) \bullet \nu_1 \models \varphi \iff \nu_2 \models \varphi$*
   where X and V are the common variables of $\mathcal{N}_1$ and $\mathcal{N}_2$,
3. *for all $\langle \vec{\ell}_1, \nu_1 \rangle, \langle \vec{\ell}_2, \nu_2 \rangle \in \approx_{2stp}$*

   (a) *if $\langle \vec{\ell}_1, \nu_1 \rangle \xrightarrow{\lambda} \langle \vec{\ell}_1', \nu_1' \rangle$ for some $\langle \vec{\ell}_1', \nu_1' \rangle \in Conf(\mathcal{N}_1)$, then there are $\langle \vec{\ell}_c, \nu_c \rangle, \langle \vec{\ell}_2', \nu_2' \rangle \in Conf(\mathcal{N}_2)$ such that $\langle \vec{\ell}_1', \nu_1' \rangle, \langle \vec{\ell}_2', \nu_2' \rangle \in \approx_{2stp}$ and*

   $$\langle \vec{\ell}_2, \nu_2 \rangle \xrightarrow{\lambda} \langle \vec{\ell}_2', \nu_2' \rangle \text{ or } \langle \vec{\ell}_2, \nu_2 \rangle \xrightarrow{\tau} \langle \vec{\ell}_c, \nu_c \rangle \xrightarrow{\lambda} \langle \vec{\ell}_2', \nu_2' \rangle,$$

   (b) *if $\langle \vec{\ell}_2, \nu_2 \rangle \xrightarrow{\lambda} \langle \vec{\ell}_2', \nu_2' \rangle$ or $\langle \vec{\ell}_2, \nu_2 \rangle \xrightarrow{\tau} \langle \vec{\ell}_c, \nu_c \rangle \xrightarrow{\lambda} \langle \vec{\ell}_2', \nu_2' \rangle$ for some $\langle \vec{\ell}_c, \nu_c \rangle$, $\langle \vec{\ell}_2', \nu_2' \rangle \in Conf(\mathcal{N}_2)$ then there is $\langle \vec{\ell}_1', \nu_1' \rangle \in Conf(\mathcal{N}_1)$ such that $\langle \vec{\ell}_1', \nu_1' \rangle, \langle \vec{\ell}_2', \nu_2' \rangle \in \approx_{2stp}$ and $\langle \vec{\ell}_1, \nu_1 \rangle \xrightarrow{\lambda} \langle \vec{\ell}_1', \nu_1' \rangle$.*

We write $\mathcal{N}_1 \approx_{2stp} \mathcal{N}_2$ if and only if there exists a two-step bisimulation relation on $Conf(\mathcal{N}_1)$ and $Conf(\mathcal{N}_2)$. ◇

Lemma 5. *Let $\mathcal{N}_{loc}$ be a closed component network. Then $\mathcal{N}_{loc} \approx_{2stp} \mathcal{N}'_{loc}$.*

Proof. Set $\approx_{2stp} = \{ \langle \vec{\ell}, \nu \rangle, \langle \vec{\ell}', \nu' \rangle \mid \vec{\ell} = \vec{\ell}', \nu' = \nu \cup \{enabled \mapsto 0\}\}$ and let $c_1 \approx_{2stp} c_2$.

- Let $c_1 \xrightarrow{\lambda} c_1'$ be a transition in $\mathcal{T}(\mathcal{N}_{loc})$. Any delay or local transition of $\mathcal{T}(\mathcal{N}_{loc})$ is also present in $\mathcal{T}(\mathcal{N}'_{loc})$ (since edges with action τ are not modified by the transformation), thus there is $c_2' \in Conf(\mathcal{N}_{loc})$ such that $c_1' \approx_{2stp} c_2'$ and $c_2 \xrightarrow{\lambda} c_2'$. If $\lambda = a \in A$, then let $e_0 = (\ell_0, a!, \varphi_0, \vec{r}_0, \ell_0')$ and $e_1 = (\ell_1, a?, \varphi_1, \vec{r}_1, \ell_1')$ be the edges in $\mathcal{N}_{loc}$ which justify the considered transition in $\mathcal{T}(\mathcal{N}_{loc})$. By construction, the edge $e_{0,1}$ from ℓ_0 to ℓ^{e_0} is enabled thus $c_1' \xrightarrow{\tau} c_1'[e_{0,1}] =: c_c$. In c_c, e_1 is enabled since only local variables are affected by the transition as well as the edge $e_{0,2}$ from ℓ^{e_0} to ℓ_0'. Thus $c_c \xrightarrow{a} c_1'[e_{0,1}][e_{0,2}; e_1] =: c_2'$. By construction of $\mathcal{N}'_{loc}$, $c_1' \approx_{2stp} c_2'$.

- Let $c_2 \xrightarrow{\lambda} c_2'$ be a transition in $\mathcal{T}(\mathcal{N}'_{loc})$. Any delay and local transition of $\mathcal{T}(\mathcal{N}'_{loc})$ is also present in $\mathcal{T}(\mathcal{N}_{loc})$ (since not modified by the transformation). All rendezvous and broadcast transitions in $\mathcal{N}'_{loc}$ involve originating at one of the fresh, committed locations where $\nu_2(enabled) \neq 0$ (by construction). Thus $\lambda \notin A$.

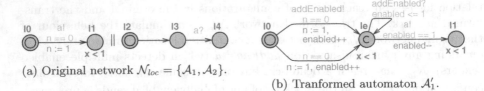

(a) Original network $\mathcal{N}_{loc} = \{\mathcal{A}_1, \mathcal{A}_2\}$.

(b) Tranformed automaton $\mathcal{A}_1'$.

Fig. 3. Network transformation example.

Let $c_2 \xrightarrow{\tau} c_c \xrightarrow{\lambda} c_2'$ be a transition in $\mathcal{T}(\mathcal{N}_{loc}')$. If the second transition is a delay or local transition, the previous case applies. Otherwise (in case of rendezvous; broadcast similar) there is an edge $e_0 = (\ell_0, a!, \varphi_0, \vec{r}_0, \ell_0') \in E(\mathcal{A}_{i_0})$ of some automaton $\mathcal{A}_{i_0} \in \mathcal{N}_{loc}'$ such that $\ell_{c,i_0} = \ell^{e_0}$ for some of the fresh locations in $\mathcal{N}_{loc}'$ and an edge e_1 receiving on a in an automaton $\mathcal{A}_{i_1} \in \mathcal{N}_{loc}$ with $i_1 \neq i_0$. Since enabledness of e_1 does not depend on the local transition (by construction of $\mathcal{N}_{loc}'$), e_1 is also (locally) enabled in c_2 and thus in c_1.

Thus $c_1 \xrightarrow{a} c_1[e_0; e_1] =: c_1'$ and $c_1' \approx_{2stp} c_2'$.   □

Lemma 6. *Configuration* $\langle \vec{\ell}, \nu \rangle \in Conf(\mathcal{N}_{loc})$ *is reachable in closed component network* $\mathcal{N}_{loc}$ *if and only if* $\langle \vec{\ell}, \nu \cup \{enabled \mapsto 0\} \rangle$ *is reachable in* $\mathcal{N}_{loc}'$.

Proof. Induction over the length of computation paths and Lemma 5.   □

Proof. (of Theorem 1). Statements (1) and (2) are equivalent by Lemma 4.

- Statement (2) implies (3): Let $\mathcal{N}_{loc} = \{\mathcal{A}_1, \ldots, \mathcal{A}_n\}$ depend on a global scheduler. By (2), it follows that there is a edge $e_0 = (\ell_0, \alpha_0, \varphi_0, \vec{r}_0, \ell_0')$ of automataon $\mathcal{A}_{i_0}$ sending on some channel $a_0 \in A(\mathcal{A}_{i_0})$ (in case of rendezvous; broadcast similar) and a configuration $c = \langle \vec{\ell}, \nu \rangle$ reachable in $\mathcal{N}_{loc}$ such that e_0 is locally but not globally enabled in c, or another edge e_1 of a different automaton $\mathcal{A}_{i_1}$, i.e., $i_0 \neq i_1$, is also locally enabled in c. By Lemma 6, the configuration $c' = \langle \vec{\ell}, \nu \cup \{enabled \mapsto 0\} \rangle$ is reachable in $\mathcal{N}_{loc}'$. Then the edge $(\ell_0, \tau, \varphi_0, \vec{r}_0; enabled++, \ell^{e_0})$, which has the same guard and reset operations as e and whose destination ℓ^{e_0} has the same location invariant as ℓ_0' added by the transformation (cf. Definition 5) is locally and (since $\mathcal{N}_{loc}$ only has local clocks and variables) also globally enabled. Thus $c'' = \langle \vec{\ell}[\ell_{i_0} := \ell^{e_0}], \nu[\vec{r}_0] \cup \{enabled \mapsto 1\} \rangle$ is reachable in $\mathcal{N}_{loc}$. If another edge $e_1 = (\ell_1, \alpha_1, \varphi_1, \vec{r}_1, \ell_1')$ of $\mathcal{A}_{i_1}$ is also locally enabled in c, then the pair of $(\ell_1, addEnabled!, \varphi_1, \vec{r}_1; enabled++, \ell^{e_1})$ in $\mathcal{A}_{i_1}$ and $(\ell^{e_0}, addEnabled?, enabled = 1, \langle \rangle, \ell^{e_0})$ in $\mathcal{A}_{i_0}$ are enabled in c'' (in the classical semantics) and thus $\langle \vec{\ell}[\ell_{i_0} := \ell^{e_0}][\ell_{i_1} := \ell^{e_1}], \nu[\vec{r}_0][\vec{r}_1] \cup \{enabled \mapsto 2\} \rangle$ is reachable in $\mathcal{N}_{loc}'$. Since the edges with source location ℓ^{e_0} have guards $enabled \leq 1$ and $enabled = 1$ respectively, none of them is enabled in c''. Thus (since c'' includes committed location ℓ^{eo} and $\mathcal{N}_{loc}$ does not have any committed locations), c'' is a deadlock configuration, hence $\mathcal{N}'_{loc} \models \mathsf{E}\Diamond\,(enabled \geq 1 \wedge deadlock)$.

Otherwise, e_0 is the only locally enabled sending edge and there is no locally enabled edge receiving on a_0. Again, by edge $(\ell_0, \tau, \varphi_0, \vec{r}_0; enabled{+}{+}, \ell^{eo})$, c' is reachable in $\mathcal{N}'_{loc}$. Since this edge only changes the local clocks and variables of $\mathcal{A}_0$, there is still no locally enabled edge receiving on a_0, so the edge from ℓ^{eo} to ℓ'_0 is not enabled. And since e_0 was the only locally enabled sending edge, the self-loop on ℓ^{eo} is also not enabled, c' is a deadlock configuration, hence $\mathcal{N}'_{loc} \models \mathsf{E}\Diamond\,(enabled \geq 1 \wedge deadlock)$.

– Statement (3) implies Statement (2): Let $\mathcal{N}'_{loc} \models \mathsf{E}\Diamond\,(enabled \geq 1 \wedge deadlock)$. Then there is a configuration $c' = \langle \vec{\ell}', \nu' \rangle \in Conf(\mathcal{N}'_{loc})$ reachable in $\mathcal{T}(\mathcal{N}'_{loc})$ such that $\nu'(enabled) \geq 1$ and c' is a deadlock. Since $\nu'(enabled) > 0$ for fresh variable $enabled$, and since $enabled$ is only incremented on edges added by the transformation (cf. Definition 5), there is an edge $e_0 = (\ell_0, a!, \varphi_0, \vec{r}_0, \ell'_0)$ with $a \in A$ of an automaton $\mathcal{A}_{i_0} \in \mathcal{N}_{loc}$ such that $\ell'_0 = \ell^{eo}$. Since ℓ^{eo} is not initial, there is a configuration $c'' = \langle \vec{\ell}'', \nu'' \rangle$ in $\mathcal{T}(\mathcal{N}'_{loc})$ such that $\nu''(enabled) = 0$ and either (a) $c'' \xrightarrow{\tau} c'$ or (b) $c'' \xrightarrow{\tau} c''' \xrightarrow{addEnabled} c'$, since there are only two edges reaching ℓ^{eo}, one incrementing $enabled$ and the self-loop on ℓ^{eo}, which has guard $enabled = 1$, so the self-loop on ℓ^{eo} can be taken at most once. As $\nu''(enabled) = 0$, there is a configuration $c \in Conf(\mathcal{N}_{loc})$ with $c \approx_{2stp} c''$ reachable in $\mathcal{T}(\mathcal{N}_{loc})$ by Lemma 6. In case (a), in particular the edge with source ℓ^{eo} is not enabled in c', thus there is no edge receiving on a enabled in c' and, since all variables are local, also not in c. Thus Statement (2) holds. In case (b), the first transition is similar to the one just discussed, and in addition the self-loop on ℓ^{eo} is taken. By construction of $\mathcal{N}'_{loc}$, there is another sending edge e_1 of an automaton $\mathcal{A}_{i_1} \in \mathcal{N}_{loc}$ with $i_1 \neq i_0$ enabled in c. Thus Statement (2) holds. $\square$

5   Evaluation

We have implemented Definition 5 in our tool Saset [11] and applied it to a selection of Uppaal models: The simple desktop lamp from [4] does not depend on a global scheduler since there is always a receiving edge enabled; the generalised train/gate controller from [12] does not depend on a global scheduler since the protocol design ensures that the receiving edges in the gate controller are enabled when the train sends; the simplified self-monitoring protocol of the wireless fire alarm system (WFAS) as presented in [9,10] does not depend on a global scheduler since the master (which is running on wall power) is always ready to receive messages and sends acknowledgements to the monitored sensors only at expected times according to the protocol. In [6], the fully detailed self-monitoring is presented. It does depend on a global scheduler in its original form, which is surprising since the WFAS *has* a distributed implementation. The reason is an artificial *monitor* (or observer, or test automaton) which has been added to the model to observe violations of the desired deadlines. If this monitor

Table 1. Evaluation results.

$|\mathcal{N}|$	L	E	states	Memory/MB	time/s	depends	model
2	4	5	3	4.78	< 0.01		Fig. 1 in [4]
	5	8	6	4.80	< 0.01	no	
2	7	9	5	4.81	< 0.01		Example 4.18 in [12]
	9	15	8	4.83	< 0.01	no	
11	73	92	2,088	5.78	0.09		Sect. 1.3 in [10]; [9]
	93	152	2,108	5.93	0.08	no	
23	190	274	6,292,287	987.94	3840.29		[6] with monitor
	273	523	4	5.87	0.03	yes	
22	187	271	4,194,721	715.89	2428.94		[6] without monitor
	249	457	4,194,844	715.06	2345.94	no	

is disabled in the model, we can show that the protocol as such does not depend on a global scheduler.

Table 1 presents the evaluation results. Columns $|\mathcal{N}|$, L, and E give the number of automata (not templates), and the overall number of locations and edges in the network. Column 'states' gives the number of states explored as reported by verifyta(1), version 4.1.19. Memory (as reported by verifyta(1)) and time ('usr' as reported by time(1)) are averages over 3 runs (AMD Opteron 6174, 2.2 GHz, 64 GB, Debian 3.16.39-1). For each model, the first row reports on checking deadlock freedom on the original model, the second row on checking dependency on a global scheduler on the transformed model. Transformation takes about 30 ms on the large models.

6 Conclusion

We have identified a new class of networks of timed automata defined by the property of independency from a global scheduler. We have shown that it is practically feasible to prove independency from a global scheduler for the large industrial case-study of a wireless fire alarm system.

We plan to exploit independency from a global scheduler to extend the existing work on code generation from timed automata models (like [1]) by the generation of a distributed implementation on a platform where we can only assume a common notion of time and message exchange, but no global variables or global scheduling. Independency from a global scheduler is a *necessary* criterion for the existence of a distributed implementation, but not *sufficient*. Real-world platforms (of course) do not guarantee an exactly equal common notion of time in a distributed system and neither do they provide synchronisation in zero-time. We will opt for a notion of correct implementation whose behaviour is sufficiently similar to the model behaviour. By our results, the necessary criterion of independency from a global scheduler is decidable.

References

1. Abdellatif, T., Combaz, J., Sifakis, J.: Model-based implementation of real-time applications. In: EMSOFT, pp. 229–238. ACM (2010)
2. Alur, R., Dill, D.: A theory of timed automata. TCS **126**(2), 183–235 (1994)
3. Amnell, T., Fersman, E., Pettersson, P., Sun, H., Wang, Y.: Code synthesis for timed automata. Nordic J. Comput. (NJC) **9**, 1–32 (2002). http://www2.imm.dtu.dk/pubdb/p.php?1957
4. Behrmann, G., David, A., Larsen, K.G.: A tutorial on UPPAAL. In: Bernardo, M., Corradini, F. (eds.) SFM-RT 2004. LNCS, vol. 3185, pp. 200–236. Springer, Heidelberg (2004). doi:10.1007/978-3-540-30080-9_7
5. Fehnker, A., Glabbeek, R., Höfner, P., McIver, A., Portmann, M., Tan, W.L.: Automated analysis of AODV using UPPAAL. In: Flanagan, C., König, B. (eds.) TACAS 2012. LNCS, vol. 7214, pp. 173–187. Springer, Heidelberg (2012). doi:10.1007/978-3-642-28756-5_13
6. Feo-Arenis, S., Westphal, B., Dietsch, D., Muñiz, M., Andisha, A.S., Podelski, A.: Ready for testing: ensuring conformance to industrial standards t formal verification. Formal Asp. Comput. **28**(3), 499–527 (2016)
7. Hendriks, M.: Translating Uppaal to not quite C (2001). http://repository.ubn.ru.nl/bitstream/handle/2066/19058/19058.pdf?sequence=1
8. Kristensen, J., Mejlholm, A., Pedersen, S.: Automatic translation from Uppaal to C (2005). http://mejlholm.org/uni/pdfs/dat4.pdf
9. Muñiz, M., Westphal, B., Podelski, A.: Timed automata with disjoint activity. In: Jurdziński, M., Ničković, D. (eds.) FORMATS 2012. LNCS, vol. 7595, pp. 188–203. Springer, Heidelberg (2012). doi:10.1007/978-3-642-33365-1_14
10. Muñiz, M.: Model checking for time division multiple access systems. Ph.D. thesis, Albert-Ludwigs-Universität Freiburg, December 2014
11. Muñiz, M., Westphal, B., Podelski, A.: Detecting Quasi-equal clocks in timed automata. In: Braberman, V., Fribourg, L. (eds.) FORMATS 2013. LNCS, vol. 8053, pp. 198–212. Springer, Heidelberg (2013). doi:10.1007/978-3-642-40229-6_14
12. Olderog, E.R., Dierks, H.: Real-Time Systems - Formal Specification and Automatic Verification. Cambridge University Press, Cambridge (2008)
13. Senthooran, I., Watanabe, T.: On generating soft real-time programs for non-real-time environments. In: Nishizaki, S., Numao, M., Caro, J., Suarez, M.T. (eds.) Theory and Practice of Computation, pp. 1–12. Springer, Tokyo (2013)
14. Wibling, O., Parrow, J., Pears, A.: Ad hoc routing protocol verification through broadcast abstraction. In: Wang, F. (ed.) FORTE 2005. LNCS, vol. 3731, pp. 128–142. Springer, Heidelberg (2005). doi:10.1007/11562436_11
15. Wulf, M.D., Doyen, L., Raskin, J.F.: Almost ASAP semantics: from timed models to timed implementations. Formal Asp. Comput. **17**, 319–341 (2005)

Optimal Reachability in Cost Time Petri Nets

Hanifa Boucheneb[1], Didier Lime[2], Baptiste Parquier[2], Olivier H. Roux[2],
and Charlotte Seidner[3]([✉])

[1] École Polytechnique de Montréal, Québec, Canada
[2] École Centrale de Nantes, LS2N UMR CNRS 6004, Nantes, France
[3] Université de Nantes, LS2N UMR CNRS 6004, Nantes, France
`charlotte.seidner@univ-nantes.fr`

Abstract. In order to model resource-consumption or allocation problems in concurrent real-time systems, we propose an extension of time Petri nets (TPN) with a linear cost function and investigate the minimum/infimum cost reachability problem. We build on the good properties of the state class symbolic abstraction, which is coarse and requires no approximation (or k-extrapolation) to ensure finiteness, and extend this abstraction to symbolically compute the cost of a given sequence of transitions. We show how this can be done, both by using general convex polyhedra, but also using the more efficient Difference Bound Matrix (DBM) data structure. Both techniques can then be used to obtain a symbolic algorithm for minimum cost reachability in bounded time Petri nets with possibly negative costs (provided there are no negative cost cycles). We prove that this algorithm terminates in both cases by proving that it explores only a finite number of extended state classes for bounded TPN, without having to resort to a bounded clock hypothesis, or to an extra approximation/extrapolation operator. All this is implemented in our tool Romeo and we illustrate the usefulness of these results in a case study.

1 Introduction

Time Petri nets (TPN for short) have been introduced by Merlin in 1974 to extend the modelling and analysis powers of Petri nets to time dependent systems. They allow to specify different kinds of time constraints by means of intervals associated with transitions. Furthermore, they offer effective reachability analysis methods that take into account the time constraints of systems. These methods are generally based on the state space abstraction where all the firing sequences and reachable markings are represented. Even if the reachability problem is not decidable for TPN, there are some subclasses of TPN, such as bounded TPN, for which the reachability problem is decidable. Using reachability analysis methods, tools such as Tina and Romeo provide an interesting platform to verify various qualitative and quantitative properties of TPN.

Cost time Petri nets (cTPN for short) extend TPN with costs associated with transitions and markings. The cost of a transition represents its firing cost while the cost of a marking is the price per time unit for staying in the marking. As

© Springer International Publishing AG 2017
A. Abate and G. Geeraerts (Eds.): FORMATS 2017, LNCS 10419, pp. 58–73, 2017.
DOI: 10.1007/978-3-319-65765-3_4

a run in the TPN is a succession of discrete transitions interspersed with time elapsing (delay transitions), the cost of the run is the accumulation of the costs of its discrete and delay transitions. Several runs may lead with different costs to a goal marking. These costs represent in general resource-consumptions such as memory and power consumptions. In such cases, it would be interesting to be able to determine the runs that yield the optimal cost. This problem, called the optimal-cost reachability, can be stated formally as follows in the context of cTPN: Given a goal marking m, what is the optimal (minimal/infimum) cost to reach m in the cTPN?

This paper deals with the optimal-cost problem for cTPN. It proposes a forward exploration of cost state classes that provides the optimal cost to reach a given goal marking for all bounded cTPN with no negative-cost cycles.

1.1 Related Works

In the literature, the optimal-cost problem has been addressed for Priced Timed automata (PTA) in [2–4,9,12] and Priced Timed Petri nets (PTPN) in [1]. A PTA is a timed automaton where locations have *rate costs* and edges have *costs*. The rate cost of a location gives the cost per time unit for staying in the location, whereas the cost of a transition indicates its firing cost. A PTPN is a timed arc Petri net where each place has a rate cost, each transition has a firing cost and the firing semantics of its transitions is weak. It is well known that many verification problems such as reachability and coverability are undecidable under the strong semantics but decidable under the weak semantics. However, timed models based on strong semantics are more appropriate to specify urgency than those based on weak semantics. Moreover, they do not need to manage dead tokens or transitions.

For PTA with non negative integer costs, two different solutions based on priced regions and priced zones have been proposed, in [2,12], respectively for the optimal-cost problem. The solution proposed in [2] has allowed the authors to prove decidability of the optimal-cost problem. However, from a practical point of view, region graphs are less useful than zone graphs. In [3,4,9,12], the computation of the optimal-cost to reach a goal location is based on a forward exploration of priced zones, where an extra variable COST gives the currently best known cost of reaching the goal location. A priced zone extends a zone with a linear cost function specifying the optimal cost to reach every state of that zone [3,4,9,12]. The optimal cost of a priced zone is obtained by minimising its cost function under the constraints of the zone. The priced zones of the discrete and continuous successors are computed by considering some zone facets[1]. The exploration is performed congruently with a "bigger and cheaper" inclusion relation over priced zones. The inclusion relation used in [4,12] and implemented in the UPPAAL-CORA tool ensures termination of the exploration for all *bounded*

---

[1] A zone facet is obtained by adding a constraint of the form $x = c$ (or $x - y = c$), where c is a constant and $x \prec c$ (or $x - y \prec c$) is an atomic constraint of the zone.

PTA (meaning all clocks are bounded). However, the termination is not guaranteed for PTA with unbounded clocks. Furthermore, if negative costs are allowed, the exploration does not necessarily provide the optimal-cost to reach the goal location. Indeed, if a path leading to the goal location goes through a priced zone belonging to some cycle with negative cost, the optimal cost to reach the goal location may be $-\infty$. In [9], the authors have improved the approach, developed in [3,4,12], by refining and combining the inclusion relation over priced zones with an over-approximation relation over clock valuations, by ignoring clock values that exceed some bound when priced zones are compared together. This improvement ensures termination of the forward exploration algorithm even when clocks are not bounded and costs are negative, provided that the PTA is free of negative cost cycles.

For PTPN, the optimal-cost reachability problem is also decidable, but only if all costs are non negative integers. The computation of the optimal-cost for reaching a goal marking is based on similar techniques to those of PTA [1].

1.2   Our Contribution

While weighted, priced, or cost timed automata have been well-studied in the literature, very few comparable results exist for time Petri nets. Yet, beyond subjective preferences for one or another formalism, time Petri nets exhibit some interesting properties. In particular, while the symbolic techniques defined for timed automata can be adapted to TPN, the symbolic abstraction of choice remains the so-called state classes. They are naturally very coarse and have the great advantage of not requiring any further approximation (as in k-extrapolation, LU-extrapolation, etc.), or any boundedness hypothesis on the clock variables, to ensure their finite number. This has proven quite problematic and the restriction that clocks should be bounded to ensure termination has has been lifted only recently in [9], 15 years after the the initial approach of [12].

We therefore investigate here how this specific abstraction can be adapted to symbolically compute optimal costs. As we expected, the state class abstraction, even extended with costs, does not require any approximation. While the results we obtain are similar, in terms of what we can do in the end, to the results obtained for timed automata, the underlying techniques are quite specific. For instance, an important result is that we can partition the domains (encoded as Difference Bound Matrices or DBMs) to ensure that the constraints on the cost remain simple as in [12] but the notion of facet used in that paper does not apply to our model.

Outline. The paper is structured as follows. Section 2 presents the TPN formalism, its extension with costs (cTPN) and their semantics. Section 3 extends the state class method to cTPN. In Sect. 4, we present the symbolic algorithm used to compute the optimal cost. In Sect. 5, by describing how cost state classes can be partitioned, we both improve the algorithm efficiency and provide a key result for the termination proof of the symbolic algorithm, given in Sect. 6. In Sect. 7, we present our implementation in the Romeo tool and a case study to illustrate how cTPN can be useful for the design of real-time systems. Finally, Sect. 8 concludes this paper.

2 Cost Time Petri Nets

2.1 Preliminaries

We denote the set of natural numbers by $\mathbb{N}$, the set of integers by $\mathbb{Z}$, the set of rational numbers by $\mathbb{Q}$, the set of real numbers by $\mathbb{R}$ and the set of non-negative real numbers by $\mathbb{R}_{\geq 0}$.

For $I \in \mathcal{I}_{\mathbb{Q}_{\geq 0}}$, $\underline{I}$ denotes its left end-point and $\overline{I}$ denotes its right end-point if I is bounded and ∞ otherwise. Moreover, for any $\theta \in \mathbb{R}_{\geq 0}$, we let $I \dot{-} \theta$ be the interval defined by $\{x - \theta \mid x \in I \wedge x - \theta \geq 0\}$.

Let F and F' be two systems of linear inequalities over a set of variables X; $F \equiv F'$ denotes that both systems have the same set of solutions over X. Furthermore, $F_{|Y}$ (with $Y \subseteq X$) denotes the projection of F over Y obtained for instance by a Fourier–Motzkin elimination of all variables that are in X but not in Y.

2.2 Time Petri Nets

Definition 1 (Time Petri Net (TPN)). *A* Time Petri Net *is a sextuple* $\mathcal{N} = (P, T, {}^{\bullet}., .^{\bullet}, m_0, I_s)$ *where:*

- *P is a finite non-empty set of places,*
- *T is a finite set of transitions such that $T \cap P = \emptyset$,*
- *${}^{\bullet}. : T \to \mathbb{N}^P$ is the backward incidence mapping,*
- *$.^{\bullet} : T \to \mathbb{N}^P$ is the forward incidence mapping,*
- *$m_0 : P \to \mathbb{N}$ is the initial marking,*
- *$I_s : T \to \mathcal{I}_{\mathbb{Q}_{\geq 0}}$ is a function assigning a firing interval to each transition.*

The distribution of tokens over the places of $\mathcal{N}$ is called a marking which is a mapping from P to $\mathbb{N}$. For a marking $m \in \mathbb{N}^P$, $m(p)$ denotes the number of tokens in place p. A Petri net $\mathcal{N}$ is said to be k-bounded or simply bounded if the number of tokens in each place does not exceed a finite number k for any marking reachable from m_0.

A transition $t \in T$ is said to be *enabled* by a given marking $m \in \mathbb{N}^P$ if m supplies t with at least as many tokens as required by the backward incidence mapping ${}^{\bullet}$. We define $En(m)$ as the set of transitions that are enabled by the marking m:

$$En(m) = \{t \in T \mid m \geq {}^{\bullet}(t)\}$$

A transition $t' \in T$ is said to be *newly enabled* by the firing of a transition t from a given marking $m \in \mathbb{N}^P$ if it is enabled by $m - {}^{\bullet}t + t^{\bullet}$ but not by $m - {}^{\bullet}t$. The set of transitions that are newly enabled by the firing of t from the marking m is:

$$NewlyEn(m, t) = \{t' \in En(m - {}^{\bullet}t + t^{\bullet}) \mid t' \notin En(m - {}^{\bullet}t) \text{ or } t = t'\}$$

Definition 2 (State). *A state of the net $\mathcal{N}$ is described by an ordered pair (m, I) in $\mathbb{N}^P \times \mathcal{I}_{\mathbb{Q}_{\geq 0}}^T$, where m is a marking of $\mathcal{N}$ and I is a function called the interval function. $I : T \to \mathcal{I}_{\mathbb{Q}_{\geq 0}}$ associates a temporal interval with every transition enabled by m.*

Definition 3 (Semantics of a TPN). *The semantics of a TPN is defined by a timed transition system $(Q, q_0, \to)$ where:*

- $Q \subseteq \mathbb{N}^P \times \mathcal{I}_{\mathbb{Q}_{\geq 0}}^T$
- $q_0 = (m_0, I_0)$ *s.t.* $\forall t \in En(m_0)$ $I_0(t) = I_s(t)$
- $\to$ *consists of two types of transitions:*
  - *discrete transitions:* $(m, I) \xrightarrow{t} (m', I')$ *iff*
    * $m \geq {}^\bullet t$, $m' = m - {}^\bullet t + t^\bullet$ *and* $\underline{I(t) = 0}$,
    * $\forall t' \in En(m')$
      · $I'(t') = I_s(t')$ *if* $t' \in NewlyEn(m, t)$,
      · $I'(t') = I(t')$ *otherwise*
  - *time transitions:* $(m, I) \xrightarrow{\theta \in \mathbb{Q}_{\geq 0}} (m, I \dot{-} \theta)$ *iff* $\forall t \in En(m)$, $\overline{(I \dot{-} \theta)(t)} \geq 0$.

A run of a time Petri Net $\mathcal{N}$ is a (finite or infinite) path starting in state q_0 and whose steps follow the semantics described above. The set of runs of a TPN $\mathcal{N}$ is denoted by $\mathsf{Runs}(\mathcal{N})$. A run is therefore a succession of time and discrete transitions; let us for instance consider the elapsing of a duration θ followed by the firing of a transition t: $(m, I) \xrightarrow{\theta} (m, I \dot{-} \theta) \xrightarrow{t} (m', I')$. In the following, such a succession is denoted by $(m, I) \xrightarrow{t@\theta} (m', I')$.

Furthermore, $sequence(\rho)$ denotes the projection of the run ρ over T. The sequence σ corresponding to the run $\rho = q_0 \xrightarrow{t_0@\theta_0} q_1 \xrightarrow{t_1@\theta_1} q_2 \xrightarrow{t_2@\theta_2} q_3$ is therefore $\sigma = sequence(\rho) = t_0 t_1 t_2$.

Definition 4 (Discrete state graph of a TPN). *The discrete state graph (DSG) of a TPN is the structure $DSG = (S, s_0, \hookrightarrow)$ where $S \in \mathbb{N}^P \times \mathcal{I}_{\mathbb{Q}_{\geq 0}}^T$, $s_0 = (m_0, I_s)$ and $s \xrightarrow{t} s'$ iff $\exists \theta \in \mathbb{Q}_{\geq 0} \mid s \xrightarrow{t@\theta} s'$*

Any state of the DSG is a state of the semantics of the TPN and any state of the semantics which is not in the DSG is reachable from some state of the DSG by a continuous transition. The DSG is a dense graph and a state may have infinite number of successors by $\xrightarrow{t}$. Finitely representing state spaces involves grouping some sets of states.

State Classes. For an arbitrary sequence of transitions $\sigma = t_1 \ldots t_n \in T^*$, let C_σ be the set of all states that can be reached by the sequence σ from s_0: $C_\sigma = \{s \in S | s_0 \xrightarrow{t_1} s_1 \cdots \xrightarrow{t_n} s\}$. All the states of C_σ share the same marking and can therefore be written as a pair (m, D) where m is the common marking and D is the union of all points belonging to the set of firing intervals. D is called the *firing domain*.

$\cong$ denotes the relation satisfied by two such sets of states when they have both the same marking and the same firing domain.

Definition 5. *Let $C_\sigma = (m, D)$ and $C'_{\sigma'} = (m', D')$ be two sets of states; $C_\sigma \cong C_{\sigma'}$ iff $m = m'$ and $D \equiv D'$.*

If $C_\sigma \cong C_{\sigma'}$, any firing schedule firable from some state in C_σ is firable from state in $C_{\sigma'}$ and conversely. The state classes as defined in [5,6] are the equivalence classes of the $\cong$ relation defined on the set of classes C_σ.

Definition 6. *The state class graph (SCG) of [5,6] is defined by the set of state classes equipped with a transition relation: $C_\sigma \xrightarrow{t} X$ iff $C_{\sigma.t} \cong X$.*

Hence the SCG computes the smallest set C of state classes w.r.t. $\cong$. The SCG is finite iff the net is bounded. Moreover, the SCG is a complete and sound state space abstraction of the TPN.

Given a state class $C = (m, D)$, a point $x = (\theta_1, \theta_2, ..., \theta_n) \in D$ is composed of the values of variables $\theta_1, \theta_2, ..., \theta_n$ that refers to the firing instants in C of transitions $t_1, t_2...t_n$ that are enabled by m. The firing domain may be described by linear inequations of the form $\theta_j - \theta_i \le c$ or $\theta_i \le c$ where $c \in \mathbb{Q}$; therefore, they can be encoded as a Difference Bound Matrix (DBM) [6,10].

Let $\Theta = \{\theta_1...\theta_n\}$ and $\mathcal{C}$ a set of constraints over Θ. Let θ_0 a reference variable whose value is always 0 and $\Theta_0 = \Theta \cup \{\theta_0\}$. A DBM M representing $\mathcal{C}$ is a matrix of size $|\Theta_0| \times |\Theta_0|$ such that $M_{ij} = inf\{c|(\theta_j - \theta_i \le c) \in \mathcal{C}\}$ where $inf(\emptyset) = +\infty$. A DBM has a unique canonical form which gives the tightest bounds on all differences between variables.

2.3   Cost Time Petri Nets

Definition 7 (Cost Time Petri Net (cTPN)). *A Cost Time Petri Net is a tuple $\mathcal{N}_c = (P, T, {}^\bullet., .{}^\bullet, m_0, I_s, \omega, cr)$ where:*

- $\mathcal{N} = (P, T, {}^\bullet., .{}^\bullet, m_0, I_s)$ *is a TPN,*
- $\omega : T \to \mathbb{Z}$ *is the discrete cost function,*
- $cr : \mathbb{N}^P \to \mathbb{Z}$ *is the cost rate function; as a matter of fact, cr is a linear function over markings.*

Definition 8 (Semantics of a cTPN). *The semantics of a cTPN $\mathcal{N}_c = (P, T, {}^\bullet., .{}^\bullet, m_0, I_s, \omega, cr)$ is the semantics of the TPN $\mathcal{N} = (P, T, {}^\bullet., .{}^\bullet, m_0, I_s)$.*

The cost state of a cTPN is $(m, I, c) \in \mathbb{N}^P \times \mathcal{I}_{\mathbb{Q}_{\ge 0}}^T \times \mathbb{R}$, where (m, I) is a TPN state and c is the accumulation, from the initial state, of the costs of the discrete and timed transitions of a run that leads to (m, I). More specifically:

- the cost of a discrete transition $(m, I, c) \xrightarrow{t} (m', I', c')$ is $c' - c = \omega(t)$;
- the cost of a timed transition $(m, I, c) \xrightarrow{d} (m, I', c')$ is $c' - c = d * cr(m)$.

Definition 9 (Cost of a run (Ω_r)). *The cost of a run $\rho = (m_0, I_0, c_0) \xrightarrow{t_0 @ \theta_0}$ $(m_1, I_1, c_1) \xrightarrow{t_1 @ \theta_1} (m_2, I_2, c_2) \cdots \xrightarrow{t_{n-1} @ \theta_{n-1}} (m_n, I_n, c_n)$ is*

$$\Omega_r(\rho) = \sum_{i=0}^{n-1} \theta_i * cr(m_i) + \omega(t_i)$$

Definition 10 (Optimal cost of a sequence). *The optimal cost $\Omega(\sigma)$ of the sequence of transitions σ is $\Omega(\sigma) = \Omega_r(\rho)$ such that $sequence(\rho) = \sigma$ and $\nexists \rho' \in \mathsf{Runs}(\mathcal{N}) \mid \Omega_r(\rho') < \Omega_r(\rho)$.*

Since C_σ is the set of all states that can be reached by the sequence σ, we also denote $\Omega(C_\sigma) = \Omega(\sigma)$.

3   Cost State Classes

We now extend the notion of state class to additionally include an information on the cost of the corresponding runs. We call *cost state classes* these extended state classes.

Recall that the firing domain D of a classic state class $C_\sigma = (m, D)$ of [5,6] is a convex polyhedron constraining the firing times of the transitions enabled by m. Note that these firing times are relative to the absolute firing date of the last transition of σ (or 0 for the initial class). For an enabled transition t_i, θ_i denotes the corresponding variable in D.

Cost state classes $L_\sigma = (m, F)$ extend the firing domain with an additional cost variable c, initially null, and evolving as described in the semantics above, and using the following observation: since firing dates are relative to the last fired transition, the time spent in a class before firing some transition t_i is exactly θ_i.

Computing the successive cost state classes then naturally extends the classic computation of [5,6] as follows:

- the initial cost state class is: $L_\varepsilon = (m_0, \{\theta_i \in I_s(t_i) | t_i \in En(m_0)\} \wedge \{c = 0\})$
- a transition t_f is firable from class $L_\sigma = (m, F)$ iff:
  - t_f is enabled by m;
  - $F \wedge \bigwedge_{i \neq f} \theta_f \leq \theta_i \neq \emptyset$.
- the successor $L_{\sigma.t_f}$ of cost state class L_σ by a transition t_f firable from L_σ is given by Algorithm 1.

Algorithm 1. Successor $L' = (m', F')$ of $L = (m, F)$ by firing t_f: $L' = Next(L, t_f)$

1: $m' \leftarrow m' = m - {}^\bullet t_f + t_f^\bullet$
2: $F' \leftarrow F \wedge \bigwedge_{i \neq f} \theta_f \leq \theta_i$
3: for all $i \neq f$, add variable θ_i' to F', constrained by $\theta_i = \theta_i' + \theta_f$ to F'
4: add variable c' to F', constrained by $c' = c + \theta_f * cr(m) + \omega(t_f)$
5: eliminate (by projection) variables c, θ_i for all i, and θ_j' for all t_j disabled by firing t_f, from F'
6: for all $t_j \in NewlyEn(m, t_f)$, add variable θ_j', constrained by $\theta_j' \in I_s(t_j)$

Remark that the only change to the classic successor computation in Algorithm 1 is the addition of line 4 (and of course the elimination of c in line 5).

By iteratively computing the extended state classes, we obtain a possibly infinite graph with edges labeled by fired transitions and nodes by classes. The quotient of the graph by the equivalence relation $\equiv$ defined by $(m, F) \equiv (m', F')$ iff $m = m'$ and $F = F'$ (in the sense that the polyhedra contain the same points), provides a finite graph for regular state classes, when the net is bounded. This is however not necessarily the case with cost state classes since the cost variable c may increase or decrease unboundedly, and its relation to the other variables may be arbitrarily complex (though still linear).

Lemma 1 $(L_{\sigma|\theta} \cong C_\sigma)$. *Let σ a firable sequence from the initial state, $L_{\sigma|\theta} \cong C_\sigma$.*

A corollary of lemma 1 is that $Next(L_{\sigma|\theta}, t) \cong Next(L_\sigma, t)_{|\theta}$.

Lemma 2 (Optimal cost of L_σ). $\Omega(\sigma) = inf(L_{\sigma|c})$.

We will now denote $\Omega(L_\sigma) = \Omega(C_\sigma) = \Omega(\sigma)$.

4   Symbolic Algorithm

Now that we have a symbolic abstraction, we can reuse the symbolic algorithm from [12,15], originally designed for priced zones. The only property we need to ensure correctness and soundness is that we can extract the minimum cost for a given sequence of transitions. We have seen how to do that for cost state classes in the previous section.

So, given a target set of markings Goal, if Algorithm 2 terminates, it will provide the optimal cost to reach Goal.

Algorithm 2. Symbolic algorithm for optimal cost

1: COST ← ∞
2: PASSED ← ∅
3: WAITING ← $\{(m_0, F_0)\}$
4: **while** WAITING $\neq \emptyset$ **do**
5:    select $L_\sigma = (m, F)$ from WAITING
6:    **if** $m \in$ Goal and $\Omega(L_\sigma) <$ COST **then**
7:       COST ← $\Omega(L_\sigma)$
8:    **end if**
9:    **if** for all $L' \in$ PASSED, $L_\sigma \not\preceq L'$ **then**
10:       add L_σ to PASSED
11:       for all $t \in \mathcal{F}irable(L_\sigma)$, add $L_{\sigma.t}$ to WAITING
12:    **end if**
13: **end while**
14: **return** COST

The algorithm consists in a classic exploration of the symbolic state-space, updating the optimal cost whenever we visit a marking in Goal. It uses a passed list to store already visited symbolic states but since the cost is not bounded a priori there is no reason the same states will eventually repeat.

To overcome this difficulty the algorithm uses a dedicated comparison operator $\preccurlyeq$ between symbolic states that is easily adapted to cost state classes as follows.

For any cost state class $L = (m, F)$ and any point $\theta \in F_{|\theta}$, the optimal cost of θ in F is defined by $\Omega_F(\theta) = \min_{(\theta,c) \in F} c$.

In the sequel, given a point $\theta = (\theta_1, \ldots, \theta_n) \in F_{|\theta}$, we often write (θ, c) instead of $(\theta_1, \ldots, \theta_n, c)$ for the corresponding point in F with cost value c.

Definition 11. *Let $L = (m, F)$ and $L' = (m', F')$ two cost state classes. We say that L is subsumed by L', which we denote by $L \preccurlyeq L'$ iff $m = m'$ and for all $F_{|\theta} \subseteq F'_{|\theta}$, and for all $\theta \in F_{|\theta}, \Omega_{F'}(\theta) \leq \Omega_F(\theta)$.*

Relation $\preccurlyeq$ can be checked for cost state classes in the same way proposed for priced zones in [15]: consider $(m, F) \preccurlyeq (m', F')$, then $m = m'$ and $F \subset F'$ are easy to check as polyhedral operations. To check the last condition, if c is the cost variable in F and c' the cost variable in F', we need only minimize $c - c'$ on F and check that it is non negative. This minimisation can again be done using classic polyhedral operations, such as the simplex method.

We can however also reduce $\preccurlyeq$ checking to standard inclusion on polyhedra.

Given a cost state class $L_\sigma = (m, F)$, we denote by $\uparrow F$ the convex polyhedron obtained from F by removing all upper bound constraints on cost variable c (or equivalently, by adding an extremal ray in the direction of c). By extension, we note $\uparrow L_\sigma = (m, \uparrow F)$.

It is easy to see that for all points $(\theta_1, \ldots, \theta_n, c')$ in $\uparrow F$ there exists a point $(\theta_1, \ldots, \theta_n, c)$, with $c \leq c'$ in F and therefore $\Omega(\uparrow L_\sigma) = \Omega(L_\sigma)$. This also implies that for any transition t firable from L_σ, the successor of $\uparrow L_\sigma$ by t (obtained with Algorithm 1) is equal to $\uparrow L_{\sigma.t}$. Furthermore, we have the following lemma.

Lemma 3. *Let L and L' be two cost state classes. We have $L \preccurlyeq L'$ iff $\uparrow L \subseteq \uparrow L'$.*

Now, to prove that the algorithm indeed always terminates, we first have to show that relaxed cost state classes can always be partitioned in a finite number of cost state classes with only one lower bound constraint on the cost variable.

Definition 12. *A simple cost state class is a cost state class such that its domain contains only one constraint over the cost variable and this constraint is a lower bound constraint.*

This will also give us a usually more efficient way to symbolically compute the optimal cost, using the efficient DBM datastructure and, in particular, minimisation of a linear expression over a DBM, instead of the simplex or polyhedral inclusion, using the results of [15]. Suppose we have two simple cost state classes L and L': their firing domains F and F' can be decomposed as DBMs D and D', each with an additional constraint on the cost variable, $c \geq \ell(\theta)$ and $c' \geq \ell'(\theta)$. Then instead of minimizing $c - c'$ over F, we only need to minimize $\ell(\theta) - \ell'(\theta)$ over D, which is usually much easier [15].

5 Computing the Simple Cost State Classes

We now show how we can partition relaxed cost state classes into *simple* cost state classes. Note that the initial cost state class, once relaxed with $\uparrow$, is indeed a simple cost state class. We then focus on computing the successors of simple cost state classes.

Let us consider a simple cost state class $L = (m, F)$ where F is a combination of a classic firing domain D, written as a DBM, and of a linear inequality over variables θ_i constraining the cost c. To ease further reading, we also define sets $\mathcal{E}$ as $En(m)$ and $\mathcal{E}_f$ as $En(m)\backslash\{t_f\}$. The firing domain F is thus defined:

$$F : \begin{cases} D : \begin{cases} \forall t_i \in \mathcal{E} & \alpha_i \leq \theta_i \leq \beta_i \\ \forall t_i, t_j \in \mathcal{E} & \theta_i - \theta_j \leq \gamma_{ij} \end{cases} \\ c \geq \sum_{t_i \in \mathcal{E}} a_i \theta_i + b \end{cases}$$

Let us compute its successor $L' = (m', F')$ by firing transition t_f following Algorithm 1 and show that L' can be written as a finite union of simple cost state classes.

Applying line 2 simply means that we modify D by adding the constraint $\theta_f \leq \theta_i$ for all t_i in $\mathcal{E}_f$. Following line 3, we then replace θ_i by $\theta_i' + \theta_f$; after simplification, we obtain the following domain:

$$F_3 : \begin{cases} D_3 : \begin{cases} \alpha_f \leq \theta_f \leq \beta_f & (5.1) \\ \forall t_i \in \mathcal{E}_f & \begin{cases} \alpha_i - \theta_i' \leq \theta_f \leq \beta_i - \theta_i' & (5.2) \\ \max(0, -\gamma_{fi}) \leq \theta_i' \leq \gamma_{if} \end{cases} \\ \forall t_i, t_j \in \mathcal{E}_f & \theta_i' - \theta_j' \leq \gamma_{ij} \end{cases} \\ c \geq \sum_{t_i \in \mathcal{E}_f} a_i \theta_i' + \left(\sum_{t_i \in \mathcal{E}} a_i \right) \theta_f + b \end{cases}$$

We then compute the constraint on the new cost c', according to line 4 of the algorithm: $c' \geq \sum_{t_i \in \mathcal{E}_f} a_i \theta_i' + C * \theta_f + B$ (5.3) where $C = cr(m) + \sum_{t_i \in \mathcal{E}} a_i$ and $B = b + \omega(t_f)$.

Before proceeding to line 5 of the algorithm, in which we need to eliminate θ_f (amongst other variables) from the system, let us notice that only inequalities (5.1), (5.2) and (5.3) involve θ_f. To eliminate θ_f by projection, we use Fourier–Motzkin elimination (FME): we keep all the inequalities in F_4 that don't involve θ_f and we add all the inequalities stating that any lower bound of θ_f should be lower than any of its upper bounds. We obtain the following system:

$$F_5 : \begin{cases} D_5 : \begin{cases} \forall t_i \in \mathcal{E}_f & \max(0, -\gamma_{fi}, \alpha_i - \beta_f \leq \theta_i' \leq \min(\gamma_{if}, \beta_i - \alpha_f) \\ \forall t_i, t_j \in \mathcal{E}_f & \theta_i' - \theta_j' \leq \min(\gamma_{ij}, \beta_i - \alpha j) \end{cases} \\ c' \geq \begin{cases} \max\left(\alpha_f, \max_{t_i \in \mathcal{E}_f}(\alpha_i - \theta_i') \right) * C + \sum_{t_i \in \mathcal{E}_f} a_i \theta_i' + B & \text{if } C \geq 0 \\ \min\left(\beta_f, \min_{t_i \in \mathcal{E}_f}(\beta_i - \theta_i') \right) * C + \sum_{t_i \in \mathcal{E}_f} a_i \theta_i' + B & \text{otherwise} \end{cases} \end{cases}$$

Again, D_5 is a DBM; following Lemma 1, it is indeed equal to the DBM obtained by a computation of the next state without considering the cost. On a side note, exact expressions for the bounds of the canonical form of this DBM can be found in [7,8]. We now consider that D_5 is defined by:

$$D_5 : \begin{cases} \forall t_i \in \mathcal{E}_f & \alpha_i' \le \theta_i' \le \beta_i' \\ \forall t_i, t_j \in \mathcal{E}_f & \theta_i' - \theta_j' \le \gamma_{ij}' \end{cases}$$

In our aim to obtain an union of simple cost state classes, we shall now consider the constraints on the new cost c'. Let us suppose that $C \ge 0$; the constraint over c' can be split in two cases: either α_f is the largest coefficient, or one transition $t_I \in \mathcal{E}_f$ yields largest coefficient. Supposing that α_f is indeed the largest coefficient, we know that $\alpha_i - \theta_i' \le \alpha_f$ for all t_i in $\mathcal{E}_f$ and that $c' \ge \alpha_f * C + \sum_{t_i \in \mathcal{E}_f} a_i \theta_i' + B$. By combining these constraints with F_5, we obtain the following simple cost state class:

$$F_5' : \begin{cases} D_5' : \begin{cases} \forall t_i \in \mathcal{E}_f & \max(\alpha_i', \alpha_i - \alpha_f) \le \theta_i' \le \beta_i' \\ \forall t_i, t_j \in \mathcal{E}_f & \theta_i' - \theta_j' \le \gamma_{ij}' \end{cases} \\ c' \ge \alpha_f * C + \sum_{t_i \in \mathcal{E}_f} a_i \theta_i' + B \end{cases}$$

All other cases (e.g. one of the $\alpha_I - \theta_I'$ is the greatest coefficient, and also the cases when $C < 0$) also lead to adding constraints preserving the DBM form, and we can thus show that F_5 can indeed be split as a finite union of simple cost state classes of the following form:

$$F_5' : \begin{cases} D_5' : \begin{cases} \forall t_i \in \mathcal{E}_f & \alpha_i'' \le \theta_i' \le \beta_i'' \\ \forall t_i, t_j \in \mathcal{E}_f & \theta_i' - \theta_j' \le \gamma_{ij}'' \end{cases} \\ c' \ge \sum_{t_i \in \mathcal{E}_f} a_i' \theta_i' + B' \end{cases}$$

In order to complete line 5 of the algorithm, we need to eliminate in all domains F_5' all variables refering to transitions that have been disabled by the firing of t_f. Let t_k be such a transition; to eliminate θ_k' from F_5', we apply the FME method again. Note that, to eliminate θ_k' in D_5', provided D_5' is in canonical form, we simply erase any inequality involving this variable, which gives us DBM D_5''; we therefore focus on inequalities over the cost c' and obtain the following domain:

$$F_5' : \begin{cases} D_5'' \\ c' \ge \begin{cases} \max\left(\alpha_k'', \displaystyle\max_{t_i \in \mathcal{E}_f \setminus \{t_k\}} (\theta_i' - \gamma_{ik}'')\right) * a_k' + \displaystyle\sum_{t_i \in \mathcal{E}_f \setminus \{t_k\}} a_i' \theta_i' + B' & \text{if } a_k' \ge 0 \\ \min\left(\beta_f'', \displaystyle\min_{t_i \in \mathcal{E}_f \setminus \{t_k\}} (\theta_i' + \gamma_{ki}'')\right) * a_k' + \displaystyle\sum_{t_i \in \mathcal{E}_f} a_i' \theta_i' + B' & \text{otherwise} \end{cases} \end{cases}$$

Again, we can split the constraint on c' to obtain a finite union of simple cost state classes and iterate the process for all the transitions that have been disabled by the firing of t_f.

Finally, we add the constraints given by line 6 to finish the computation of F'. In the end, we indeed obtain the successor of our initial simple cost state class as a finite union of simple cost state classes.

Each of the elements of this finite union can then be considered as a stand-alone successor of that state class in Algorithm 2 much like in [12,15].

6   Termination of the Algorithm

To prove the termination, we consider $\succcurlyeq$ the symmetric relation to $\preccurlyeq$, such that $x \succcurlyeq y$ iff $y \preccurlyeq x$, and prove that it is a well quasi-order (wqo), i.e., that for every infinite sequence of cost state classes, there are at least L and L' in the sequence, with L strictly preceding L' such that $L \succcurlyeq L'$. This implies that the exploration of children in Algorithm 2 will always eventually stop.

The idea is to first prove that $\succcurlyeq$ is a wqo on *simple* cost state classes, and then to lift this result to a certain quasi-order derived from $\succcurlyeq$ and defined on *sets* of simple cost state classes. To ensure the lifted order is indeed a wqo, $\succcurlyeq$ has to have a stronger property: indeed, we need to prove that it is a *better* quasi-order (bqo). The definition of bqo's is a bit involved and we actually do not need to use it explicitly so we refer the interested reader to [14] for instance.

Proposition 1. *Let $\mathcal{N}$ be a bounded TPN such that the cost of all runs is uniformly lower-bounded by some constant M, then relation $\succcurlyeq$ is a better quasi-order on the simple cost state classes of $\mathcal{N}$.*

The wqo on cost state classes and the termination of Algorithm 2 are rather direct consequences of Proposition 1.

Corollary 1. *Let $\mathcal{N}$ be a bounded TPN such that the cost of all runs is uniformly lower-bounded by some constant M, then relation $\succcurlyeq$ is a well quasi-order on the cost state classes of $\mathcal{N}$.*

Corollary 2. *When $\mathcal{N}$ is bounded and the cost of all runs is uniformly lower-bounded by some constant M, Algorithm 2 terminates.*

7   Practical Results

We have implemented the above algorithms in Romeo[2], a tool for the verification of (parametric) time Petri nets [13]. In this section, we illustrate the above approaches with a practical example. It uses negative costs, the point here being to show how to obtain a scheduler using prediction about environmental features.

---

[2] http://romeo.rts-software.org.

7.1 EPOC (Energy Proportional and Opportunistic Computing systems)

The EPOC project [11] focusses on energy-aware task execution in the context of a mono-site and small data center which is connected to the regular electric grid and to local renewable energy sources (such as windmills or solar cells).

Given a reliable prediction model, it is possible to design a scheduling that aims at optimizing resource utilization and energy usage. A power-driven approach allows shifting or scheduling the postponable workloads to the time period when the electricity is available (from the renewable energy sources) or at the best price.

Description. We consider here a small system with four tasks: Task1 can be scheduled at any time with non-renewable energy whereas the other tasks must be computed using renewable energy. To run the four tasks, there are two processors: Task2, Task3 and Task4 can run on both, but Task1 must run on the first processor. Furthermore, the second processor, which can only use renewable energy, is twice as slow as the first processor.

The energy source is assumed to rely on solar cells and wind turbines; as illustrated by Fig. 2, the weather pattern used in the case study is the following:

- 10 a.m.–11:20 a.m.: windy, with a mix of sunny and cloudy;
- 11:20 a.m.–11:30 a.m.: calm and cloudy;
- 11:30 a.m.–11:40 a.m.: calm and weakly sunny;
- 11:40 a.m.–12 p.m. (noon): calm and sunny.

If a task is executed after the deadline, the cost rate is 100. Using non-renewable energy for Task1 has a cost rate of 40. If tasks 2, 3 and 4 are executed during a sunny period, the cost rate is -20; during a period of weak sun, it is -10; and during a windy period, it is -10. Evidently, costs add up: e.g. when the weather is sunny and windy, the cost rate is $-20 - 10 = -30$.

The TPN model is presented in Fig. 1. Proc1 and Proc2 stand for the processors (1 and 2).

The associated cost function is: $40 * R1\_1 + (DL) * (R1\_1 + R2\_1 + R2\_2 + R3\_1 + R3\_2 + R4\_1 + R4\_2) * 100 - (1 * Windy + 2 * (Sun1 + Sun2 + Sun3 + Sun4) + 1 * WeakSun) * (R2\_1 + R2\_2 + R3\_1 + R3\_2 + R4\_1 + R4\_2) * 10$.

Objective. We want to reach a marking corresponding to the situation where all tasks have been executed, which corresponds to all places in the upper net being empty except Proc1 and Proc2, which contains exactly one token.

Results. The minimal cost to reach a state such that all the tasks are executed is -1560 and from the associated trace, given by Romeo, we can derive the Gantt chart in Fig. 2. As for Fig. 3, it shows the evolution of the cost rate during the scenario proposed in the Gantt chart Fig. 2.

Table 1 summarizes the performances of Romeo to reach the minimal cost using cost state classes (and polyhedral operations) or simple cost state classes

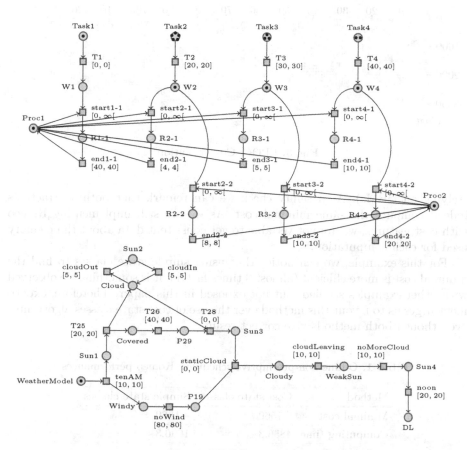

Fig. 1. EPOC example

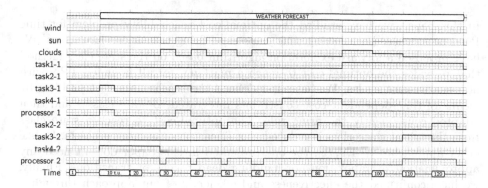

Fig. 2. EPOC: Gantt chart

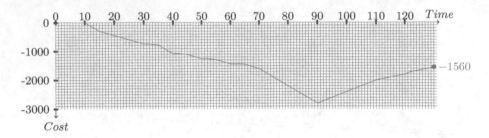

Fig. 3. EPOC: Cost evolution

(relying on DBMs). As a sanity check we can remark that both abstractions indeed compute the same minimal cost. As we are still implementing Romeo with cost features, we are not yet able to get consistent data about the memory used for each computation.

For this example, we can notice that using simple state classes to find the minimal cost is more efficient (almost 3 times faster): it is something we observed with other examples studied, but not exposed in this paper. Therefore, experiment urges us to favour this method over the use of cost state classes algorithms, even though both methods give correct results.

Table 1. Offline non-preemptive scheduler: Romeo performances

Method	Cost state classes	Simple state classes
Minimal cost	−1560	−1560
Computing time	4856.3 s	1696.3 s

8   Conclusion

In this paper, we have studied the optimal-cost reachability problem for time Petri nets, where both letting time elapse and firing transitions have costs. We have proposed a forward exploration algorithm based on the state class method that provides the optimal-cost to reach a marking, for all bounded TPN with no negative-cost cycles. We have first defined the reachability cost problem by means of time-dependent cost constraints integrated to state classes and then adapted consequently the firing rule. The optimal-cost to reach a state class from the initial state class is reduced to a linear programming problem. Unlike other approaches [1–4,9,12], the one presented in this paper doesn't need any approximation/extrapolation nor handling dead tokens or transitions. Finally, we have confirmed the effectiveness and efficiency of our approach through a case study.

References

1. Abdulla, P.A., Mayr, R.: Priced timed petri nets. Logical Methods Comput. Sci. **9**(4) (2013)
2. Alur, R., La Torre, S., Pappas, G.J.: Optimal paths in weighted timed automata. Theoret. Comput. Sci. **318**(3), 297–322 (2004)
3. Behrmann, G., Fehnker, A., Hune, T., Larsen, K., Pettersson, P., Romijn, J., Vaandrager, F.: Minimum-cost reachability for priced time automata. In: Benedetto, M.D., Sangiovanni-Vincentelli, A. (eds.) HSCC 2001. LNCS, vol. 2034, pp. 147–161. Springer, Heidelberg (2001). doi:10.1007/3-540-45351-2_15
4. Behrmann, G., Larsen, K.G., Rasmussen, J.I.: Optimal scheduling using priced timed automata. SIGMETRICS Perform. Eval. Rev. **32**(4), 34–40 (2005)
5. Berthomieu, B., Diaz, M.: Modeling and verification of time dependent systems using time petri nets. IEEE Trans. Software Eng. **17**(3), 259–273 (1991)
6. Berthomieu, B., Menasche, M.: An enumerative approach for analyzing time petri nets. In: IFIP Congress, pp. 41–46 (1983)
7. Boucheneb, H., Mullins, J.: Analyse des réseaux temporels: calcul des classes en $O(n^2)$ et des temps de chemin en $O(m \times n)$. TSI. Technique et science informatiques **22**(4), 435–459 (2003)
8. Bourdil, P.A., Berthomieu, B., Dal Zilio, S., Vernadat, F.: Symmetry reduction for time petri net state classes. Sci. Comput. Program. **132**, 209–225 (2016)
9. Bouyer, P., Colange, M., Markey, N.: Symbolic optimal reachability in weighted timed automata. In: Chaudhuri, S., Farzan, A. (eds.) CAV 2016. LNCS, vol. 9779, pp. 513–530. Springer, Cham (2016). doi:10.1007/978-3-319-41528-4_28
10. Dill, D.L.: Timing assumptions and verification of finite-state concurrent systems. In: Sifakis, J. (ed.) CAV 1989. LNCS, vol. 407, pp. 197–212. Springer, Heidelberg (1990). doi:10.1007/3-540-52148-8_17
11. EPOC. Energy proportional and opportunistic computing systems. http://www.epoc.cominlabs.ueb.eu/fr
12. Larsen, K., Behrmann, G., Brinksma, E., Fehnker, A., Hune, T., Pettersson, P., Romijn, J.: As cheap as possible: effcient cost-optimal reachability for priced timed automata. In: Berry, G., Comon, H., Finkel, A. (eds.) CAV 2001. LNCS, vol. 2102, pp. 493–505. Springer, Heidelberg (2001). doi:10.1007/3-540-44585-4_47
13. Lime, D., Roux, O.H., Seidner, C., Traonouez, L.-M.: Romeo: a parametric model-checker for petri nets with stopwatches. In: Kowalewski, S., Philippou, A. (eds.) TACAS 2009. LNCS, vol. 5505, pp. 54–57. Springer, Heidelberg (2009). doi:10.1007/978-3-642-00768-2_6
14. Marcone, A.: Fine analysis of the quasi-orderings on the power set. Order **18**(4), 339–347 (2001)
15. Rasmussen, J.I., Larsen, K.G., Subramani, K.: On using priced timed automata to achieve optimal scheduling. Formal Methods Syst. Des. **29**(1), 97–114 (2006)

Hybrid Systems

Optimal Control for Multi-mode Systems with Discrete Costs

Mahmoud A.A. Mousa[✉], Sven Schewe, and Dominik Wojtczak

University of Liverpool, Liverpool, UK
mahmoud.mousa@liverpool.ac.uk

Abstract. This paper studies optimal time-bounded control in multi-mode systems with discrete costs. Multi-mode systems are an important subclass of linear hybrid systems, in which there are no guards on transitions and all invariants are global. Each state has a continuous cost attached to it, which is linear in the sojourn time, while a discrete cost is attached to each transition taken. We show that an optimal control for this model can be computed in NExpTime and approximated in PSpace. We also show that the one-dimensional case is simpler: although the problem is NP-complete (and in LogSpace for an infinite time horizon), we develop an FPTAS for finding an approximate solution.

1 Introduction

Multi-mode systems [8] are an important subclass of linear hybrid systems [4], which consist of multiple continuous variables and global invariants for the values that each variable is allowed to take during a run of the system. However, unlike for the full linear hybrid systems model, multi-mode systems have no guards on transitions and no local invariants. In this paper, we study multi-mode systems with discrete costs, which extend linear hybrid systems by adding both continuous and discrete costs to states. Every time a transition is taken (i.e. when the current state changes), the discrete cost assigned to the target state is incurred. The continuous cost is the sum of the products of the sojourn time in each state and the cost assigned to this state. Our aim is to minimise the total cost over a finite-time horizon or a long-time average cost over an infinite time horizon. We exemplify this by applying this model to the optimal control of heating, ventilation, and air-conditioning (HVAC) systems. HVAC systems account for about 50% of the total energy cost in buildings [27], so a lot of energy can be saved by optimising their control. Many simulation programs have been developed to analyse the influence of control on the performance of HVAC system components such as TRNSYS [3], EnergyPlus [1], and the Matlab's IBPT [2]. Our approach has the advantage over the existing control theory techniques that it provides approximation guarantees. Although the actual dynamics of a HVAC system is governed by linear differential equations, one can argue [22,24,25] that constant rate dynamic, as in our model, can approximate well such a behaviour.

The simplest subclass of our model is multi-mode systems with a single dimension. It naturally occurs when controlling the temperature in a single room

© Springer International Publishing AG 2017
A. Abate and G. Geeraerts (Eds.): FORMATS 2017, LNCS 10419, pp. 77–96, 2017.
DOI: 10.1007/978-3-319-65765-3_5

or building to stay in a pleasant range. For this, the system can be in different modes, e.g. the air-conditioning can be switched on or off, or one can choose to switch on an electrical radiator or a gas burner. Each such a configuration can be modelled as mode of our multi-mode system. Modes have start-up cost (gas burners, e.g. may suffer some wear and tear when switched on) as well as continuous costs.

When keeping an office building in a pleasant temperature range during opening hours, we face a control problem for multi-mode systems with a finite time horizon. We show that finding an optimal schedule in such a case is NP-complete and significantly more challenging than for the infinite time horizon (LogSPACE). However, we devise an FPTAS for the finite time horizon problem.

Heating multiple rooms simultaneously can be naturally modelled by multi-mode systems (with multiple dimensions). In such a scenario, we might have different pleasant temperature ranges in different rooms and the temperatures of the individual rooms may influence each other. Naturally, controlling a multi-dimensional multi-mode systems is more complex than controlling a one-dimensional multi-mode system. We develop a nondeterministic exponential time algorithm for the construction of optimal control, whose complexity is only driven by potentially required high precision in exponentially many mode switches. Allowing for an ε-deviation from the ranges of pleasant temperatures reduces the complexity to PSPACE.

Related Work. Our model can be viewed as a weighted extension of the linear hybrid automata model [5,17], but with global constraints only. Even basic questions for the general linear hybrid automata model are undecidable already for three variables and not known to be decidable for two variables [9]. Most of the research for this model has focused on qualitative objectives such as reachability. Various subclasses of hybrid systems with a decidable reachability problem were considered, see e.g. [9] for an overview. In particular, reachability in linear hybrid systems, where the derivative of each variable in each state is constant, can be shown to be decidable for one continuous variable by using the techniques from [19]. In [6], it has been shown that reachability is decidable for timed automata, which are a particular subclass of hybrid automata where the slope of all variables is equal to 1.

In [22] we only studied the one-dimensional case of our model with the simplifying assumption that there is exactly one mode that can bring the temperature down and it is cost-free. In this paper, we drop this assumption and generalise the model to multiple dimensions. In the one-dimensional setting, we manage to prove similar nice algorithmic properties as in [22], i.e. the existence of finitely many patterns for optimal schedules, polynomial constant-factor approximation algorithm and an FPTAS. However, as opposed to the existence of a unique pattern for an optimal schedule in [22], we show that there can be 44 different patterns when the simplifying assumption is dropped. To show this, we need to devise five safety-preserving and cost-non-increasing operations on schedules, while in [22] it sufficed for each mode to just lump together all timed actions that use this mode. Also, our constant-factor approximation algorithm requires a careful analysis of the interplay between different sections of the normal form for schedules, which results in an $\mathcal{O}(n^7)$ algorithm, while in [22] it sufficed to use one mode all the time and the algorithm ran in linear time.

Multi-mode systems were studied in [8], but with no discrete costs and with infinite time horizons only. They were later extended in [7] to a setting where the rate of change of each variable in a mode belonging to an interval instead of being constant. [28] studied a hybrid automaton model where the dynamics are governed by linear differential equations, but again without switching costs and only with an infinite time horizon. Both of these papers show that, for any number of variables, a schedule with the optimal long-time average cost can be computed in polynomial time. In [24,25], the same models without switching costs have been studied over the infinite time horizon, with the objective of minimising the peak cost, rather than the long-time average cost. In [11], long-time average and total cost games have been shown to be decidable for hybrid automata with strong resets, in which all variables are reset to 0 after each discrete transition. The long-time average and total cost optimisation for the weighted timed automata model have been shown to be PSPACE-complete (see e.g. [10] for an overview).

There are many practical approaches to the reduction of energy consumption and peak demand in buildings. One particularly popular one is model predictive control (MPC) [12]. In [26], stochastic MPC was used to minimise the energy consumption in a building. In [21], On-Off optimal control was considered for air conditioning and refrigeration. The drawback of using MPC is its high computational complexity and the fact that it cannot provide any worst-case guarantees. UPPAAL Stratego [15] supports the analysis of the expected cost in linear hybrid systems, but uses a stochastic semantics of these models [14,16]. I.e. a control strategy induces a stochastic model where the time delay in each state is uniformly or exponentially distributed. This is different to the standard nondeterministic interpretation of the model, which we use in this paper. In [20], an on-line controller synthesis combined with machine learning and compositional synthesis techniques was applied for optimal control of a floor heating system.

Structure of the Paper. The paper is organised as follows. We introduce all necessary notation and formally define the model in Sect. 2. In Sect. 3, we study the computational complexity of limit-safe and ϵ-safe control in multiple dimensions. In Sect. 4, we show that in one dimension every schedule can be transformed without increasing its cost into a schedule following one of 44 different patterns. In Sect. 5, we show that the cost optimisation decision problem in one-dimension with infinite and finite horizon is LOGSPACE and NP-complete, respectively. In Sect. 6, still for the one-dimension case, we first show a constant factor approximation algorithm and, building on it, develop an FPTAS by a reduction to the 0-1 knapsack problem. Due to the space constraints, some of the proofs and algorithms are only available in the extended version of this paper [23].

2   Preliminaries

Let $\mathbb{0}_N$ and $\mathbb{1}_N$ be N-dimensional vectors with all entries equal to 0 and 1, respectively. By $\mathbb{R}_{\geq 0}$ and $\mathbb{Q}_{\geq 0}$ we denote the sets of all non-negative real and rational numbers, respectively. We assume that $0 \cdot \infty = \infty \cdot 0 = 0$. For a vector v, let $\|v\|$ be its ∞-norm (i.e. the maximum coordinate in v). We write $v_1 \leq v_2$ if every coordinate vector of vector v_1 is smaller than or equal to the corresponding coordinate in vector v_2, and $v_1 < v_2$ if, additionally, $v_1 \neq v_2$ holds.

2.1   Formal Definition of Multi-mode Systems

Motivated by our application of keeping temperature in multiple rooms within comfortable range, we restrict ourselves to safe sets being hyperrectangles, which can be specified by giving its two extreme corner points. A *multi-mode system with discrete costs*, $\mathcal{A}$, henceforth referred to simply as *multi-mode system*, is formally defined as a tuple $\mathcal{A} = (M, N, A, \pi_c, \pi_d, V_{\min}, V_{\max}, V_0)$ where:

- M is a finite set of modes;
- $N \geq 1$ is the number of continuous variables in the system;
- $A : M \to \mathbb{Q}^N$ is the slope of all the variables in a given mode;
- $\pi_c : M \to \mathbb{Q}_{\geq 0}$ is the cost per time unit spent in a given mode;
- $\pi_d : M \to \mathbb{Q}_{\geq 0}$ is the cost of switching to a given mode;
- $V_{\min}, V_{\max} \in \mathbb{Q}^N$: $V_{\min} < V_{\max}$, define the safe set, S, as follows $\{x \in \mathbb{R}^N : V_{\min} \leq x \leq V_{\max}\}$;
- $V_0 \in \mathbb{Q}^N$, such that $V_0 \in S$, defines the initial value of all the variables.

2.2   Schedules, Their Cost and Safety

A *timed action* is a pair $(m, t) \in M \times \mathbb{R}_{\geq 0}$ of a mode m and time delay $t > 0$. A *schedule* σ (of length k) with time horizon $t_{\max}$ is a finite sequence of timed actions $\sigma = \langle (m_1, t_1), (m_2, t_2), \ldots, (m_k, t_k) \rangle$, such that $\sum_{i=1}^{k} t_i = t_{\max}$. A *schedule* σ with infinite time horizon is either an infinite sequence of timed actions $\sigma = \langle (m_1, t_1), (m_2, t_2), \ldots, (m_k, t_k), \ldots \rangle$, such that $\sum_{i=1}^{\infty} t_i = \infty$ or a finite sequence of timed actions $\sigma = \langle (m_1, t_1), (m_2, t_2), \ldots, (m_k, t_k) \rangle$, such that $t_k = \infty$. The *run* of a finite schedule $\sigma = \langle (m_1, t_1), (m_2, t_2), \ldots, (m_k, t_k) \rangle$ is a sequence of *states* $\mathrm{run}(\sigma) = \langle V_0, V_1, \ldots, V_k \rangle$ such that, for all $0 \leq i \leq k - 1$, we have that $V_{i+1} = V_i + t_i A(m_i)$.

A schedule and its run are called *safe* if $V_{\min} \leq V_i \leq V_{\max}$ holds for all $1 \leq i \leq k$. A schedule and its run are called *ϵ-safe* if $V_{\min} - \epsilon \cdot \mathbb{1}_N < V_i < V_{\max} + \epsilon \cdot \mathbb{1}_N$ holds for all $1 \leq i \leq k$. The run of an infinite schedule and its safety and ϵ-safety are defined accordingly.

The *total cost* of a schedule $\sigma = \langle (m_1, t_1), (m_2, t_2), \ldots, (m_k, t_k) \rangle$ with a finite time horizon is defined as $\pi(\sigma) = \sum_{i=1}^{k} \pi_d(m_i) + \pi_c(m_i) t_i$. The *limit-average cost* for a finite schedule $\sigma = \langle (m_1, t_1), (m_2, t_2), \ldots, (m_k, t_k) \rangle$ with an infinite time horizon is defined as $\pi_{avg}(\sigma) = \pi_c(m_k)$ and for an infinite schedule $\sigma = \langle (m_1, t_1), (m_2, t_2), \ldots \rangle$ it is defined as

$$\pi_{avg}(\sigma) = \limsup_{k \to \infty} \left(\sum_{i=1}^{k} \pi_d(m_i) + \pi_c(m_i) t_i \right) \Big/ \sum_{i=1}^{k} t_i$$

A safe finite schedule σ is ϵ-*optimal* if, for all safe finite schedules σ', we have that $\pi(\sigma') \geq \pi(\sigma) - \epsilon$. A safe finite schedule is *optimal* if it is 0-optimal. A safe infinite schedule σ is *optimal* if, for all safe infinite schedules σ', we have that $\pi_{avg}(\sigma') \geq \pi_{avg}(\sigma)$.

The following example shows that there may not be an optimal schedule for a multi-mode system with a finite time horizon.

Example 1. Consider a multi-mode system with three modes: M_1, M_2, M_3. The slope vectors in these modes are $A(M_1) = (1, 1)$, $A(M_2) = (1, -1)$ and $A(M_3) = (-1, 1)$, respectively. The continuous cost of using M_1 is $\pi_c(M_1) = 1$ and all the other costs are 0. Let $V_0 = V_{\min} = \mathbb{0}_2$ and $V_{\max} = \mathbb{1}_2$. Notice that we can only use M_2 or M_3 once we get out of the initial corner V_0. This can only be done using M_1. Now let the time horizon be $t_{\max}$. Note that the following schedule $\sigma_\epsilon = (M_1, \epsilon), ((M_2, t), (M_3, t))^l$, where $t' = t_{\max} - \epsilon$, $l = \lceil t'/\epsilon \rceil$, and $t = t'/2l$, has time horizon $t_{\max}$ and total cost $\epsilon > 0$. As ϵ can be made arbitrarily small but has to be > 0, σ_ϵ is an ϵ-optimal schedule for all $\epsilon > 0$, but no optimal schedule exists.

Note that in Example 1, for any $\epsilon > 0$, there exists an optimal ϵ-safe schedule σ with total cost 0: $\sigma_0 = \langle ((M_2, t), (M_3, t))^l \rangle$ where l is defined as in Example 1. Our aim is to find an "abstract schedule" that, for any given $\epsilon > 0$, can be used to construct in polynomial time an ϵ-safe ϵ-optimal schedule.

Let $M^* = \{ m \in M \mid \pi_d(m) = 0 \}$ be the subset of modes without discrete costs. Note that, as shown in [8], the cost and safety of a schedule with M^* modes only, depends only on the total amount of time spent in each of the M^* modes. We therefore lump together any sequence of timed actions that only use M^* modes and define an *abstract timed action (over M^*)* as a function $\mathbf{t} : M^* \to \mathbb{R}_{\geq 0}$. A finite *abstract schedule* with time horizon $t_{\max}$ (of length k) is a finite sequence $\tau = \langle \mathbf{t}_1, (m_1, t_1), \mathbf{t}_2, (m_2, t_2), \ldots, (m_{k-1}, t_{k-1}), \mathbf{t}_k \rangle$ such that $\forall_i \, m_i \in M \backslash M^*$ and $\sum_{i \leq k, m \in M^*} \mathbf{t}_i(m) + \sum_{i < k} t_i = t_{\max}$. The run of the abstract schedule τ is a sequence $\langle V_0, V_1, \ldots, V_{2k+1} \rangle$ such that, for all $i \leq k$, we have $V_{2i} = V_{2i-1} + A(m_i) t_i$ and $V_{2i+1} = V_{2i} + \sum_{m \in M^*} A(m) \mathbf{t}_i(m)$. We say that an abstract schedule is *limit-safe* if its run is safe. The total cost of an abstract schedule τ is defined as

$$\sum_{i \leq k, m \in M^*} \pi_c(m, \mathbf{t}_i(m)) + \sum_{i < k} \left(\pi_d(m_i) + \pi_c(m_i) t_i \right).$$

Note that any safe schedule can be turned into a limit-safe abstract schedule with the same cost by simply replacing any maximal subsequence of consecutive timed actions that only use M^* modes by a single abstract timed action. A limit-safe abstract schedule σ is optimal if the total cost of all other limit-safe abstract schedules is higher than $\pi(\sigma)$. The following statement justifies the name "limit-safe".

Proposition 1. *Given a limit-safe abstract schedule τ and $\epsilon > 0$, we can construct in polynomial time an ϵ-safe schedule σ such that $\pi(\tau) = \pi(\sigma)$.*

Proof. Let $M^* = \{m_1, m_2, \ldots, m_j\}$. To obtain σ from τ, we replace each abstract timed action $\{(m, t_m) \mid m \in M^*\}$ by a sequence $((m_1, t_{m_1}/l), \ldots, (m_j, t_{m_j}/l))^l$ for a sufficiently large $l \in \mathbb{N}$.

Sufficiently large means that, for $t^* = \sum_{m \in M^*} t_m, l > t^* \cdot \max_{m \in M^*} \|A(m)\|/\epsilon$. This choice guarantees that $\sum_{m \in M^*} \|A(m)\| \cdot t_m/l < \varepsilon$. Thus, when the abstract action $\{(m, t_m) \mid m \in M^*\}$ joins two states V_{2i}, V_{2i+1} along the run $\langle V_0, V_1, \ldots, \ldots, V_{2k+1}\rangle$ of τ, we know that this concrete schedule will cover the l-th part of V_{2i}, V_{2i+1} after every sequence $(m_1, t_{m_1}/l), (m_2, t_{m_2}/l), \ldots, (m_j, t_{m_j}/l)$. As the safe set is convex, the start and end points of this sequence are safe points. Also, $\sum_{m \in M^*} \|A(m)\| \cdot t_m/l < \varepsilon$ implies that the points in the middle are ϵ-safe. $\square$

Example 1 continues. *An example limit-safe abstract schedule of length 1 is $\tau = \{(m_1, t_{max}/2), (m_2, t_{max}/2)\}$. Based on τ we can construct an ϵ-safe schedule $\langle((m_1, t_{max}/2l), (m_2, t_{max}/2l))^l\rangle$ where l is any integer greater than t_{max}/ϵ.*

2.3   Structure of Optimal Schedules

We show here that it later suffices to consider only schedules with a particular structure.

Definition 1. *We call a finite schedule σ angular if there are no two consecutive timed actions $(m_i, t_i), (m_{i+1}, t_{i+1})$ in σ such that $A(m_i) = A(m_{i+1})$.*

We show that while looking for an $(\epsilon$-)safe $(\epsilon$-)optimal finite schedule, we can restrict our attention to angular schedules only.

Proposition 2. *For every finite $(\epsilon$-)safe schedule with time horizon t_{max} there exists an angular safe schedule with the same or lower cost.*

Henceforth, we assume that all finite schedules are angular. Let $M^0 = \{m \mid A(m) = 0\}$, which we will also refer to as *zero-modes*.

Proposition 3. *For every finite safe schedule with time horizon t_{max} there exists a safe schedule with the same or lower cost, in which at most one zero-mode is used at the very beginning.*

Henceforth, we assume that all finite schedules use at most one zero-mode timed action and only at the very beginning.

2.4   Approximation Algorithms

We study approximation algorithms for the total cost minimisation problem in multi-mode systems. We say that an algorithm is a *constant factor approximation algorithm* with a *relative performance* ρ iff, for all inputs x, the cost of the solution that it computes, $f(x)$, satisfies $OPT(x) \leq f(x) \leq (1 + \rho) \cdot OPT(x)$, where $OPT(x)$ is the optimal cost for the input x. We are particularly interested in polynomial-time approximation algorithms. A polynomial-time approximation scheme (PTAS) is an algorithm that, for every $\rho > 0$, runs in polynomial-time and has relative performance ρ. Note that the running time of a PTAS may depend in an arbitrary way on ρ. Therefore, we typically strive to find a fully polynomial-time approximation scheme (FPTAS), which is an algorithm that runs in polynomial-time in the size of the input and $1/\rho$.

The 0-1 Knapsack problem is a well-known NP-complete optimisations problem, which possess multiple FPTASes (see e.g. [18]). In this problem we are given a knapsack with a fixed volume and a list of items, each with an integer volume and value. The aim is to pick a subset of these items that together do not exceed the volume of the knapsack and have the maximum total value.

3   Complexity of Limit-Safe and ϵ-safe Finite Control

As our one-dimensional model strictly generalises the simple linear hybrid automata considered in [22], we immediately obtain the following result.

Theorem 1 (follows from [22], Theorem 3).   *Given (one-dimensional) multi-mode system $\mathcal{A}$, constants t_{max} and C (both in binary), checking whether there exists a safe schedule in $\mathcal{A}$ with time horizon t_{max} and total cost at most C is NP-hard.*

In the rest of this section we fix a (multi-dimensional) multi-mode system $\mathcal{A}$ and time horizon t_{max}.

Theorem 2. *If a limit-safe abstract schedule exists in $\mathcal{A}$, then there exists one of exponential length and it can be constructed in polynomial time.*

Proof (sketch). Before we formally prove this theorem, we need to introduce first a bit of terminology. We call a mode m *safe for time* $t > 0$ at $V \in S := \{x \in \mathbb{R}^N : V_{min} \leq x \leq V_{max}\}$ if $V + A(m)t \in S$. Also, m is *safe* at V if there exists $t > 0$ such that m is safe for time t at V. We say that a *coordinate of a state*, $V \in S$, *is at the border* if that coordinate in V is equal to the corresponding coordinate in V_{min} or V_{max}.

Our algorithm first removes from M all modes that will never be safe to use in a limit-safe schedule (and it can be found in the extended version of this paper [23]). This is an adaptation of [8, Theorem 7] where an algorithm was given for finding safe modes that can ever be used in a schedule with no time horizon. The main difference here is that the modes in M^* can always be used in a limit-safe abstract schedule even if they are not safe to use. We find here a sequence of sets of modes $M^* = M_0 \subset M_1 \subset M_2 \subset \ldots$ such M_{i+1} is the set of modes that are safe at a state reachable from V_0 via a limit-safe abstract schedule that only uses modes from M_i. Note that at some step $k \leq |M|$ this sequence will stabilise, i.e. $M_k = M_{k+1}$. Similarly as in the proof of [8, Theorem 7], we can show that no mode from $M \setminus M_k$ can ever be used by a limit-safe abstract schedule. As a result, we can remove all these modes from M.

Next, we remove all modes that cannot be part of a limit-safe abstract schedule with time horizon $t_{\max}$. For this, for each m, we formulate a very similar linear programme (LP) as above (again, more details in [23]), where we ask for the time delay of m to be positive and the total time delay of all the modes to be $t_{\max}$. By a simple adaptation of the proof of [8, Theorem 4], if this LP is not satisfiable then m can be removed from $\mathcal{A}$.

Next, we look for the easiest possible target state V_{end} that can potentially be reached using a limit-safe abstract schedule from V_0 with time horizon $t_{\max}$. For this, V_{end} has to have the least number of coordinates at the border of the safe set. Note that this is well-defined, because if V and V' are two points reachable from V_0 via a limit-safe abstract schedules τ and τ' with time horizon $t_{\max}$, respectively, then $\tau/2$ (i.e. divide all abstract and timed actions delays in τ by 2) followed by $\tau'/2$, is also a limit-safe abstract schedule with time horizon $t_{\max}$, which reaches $(V + V')/2$. However, $(V + V')/2$ has a coordinate at the border iff both V and V' have it as well. This shows that there is a state with a minimum number of coordinates at the border.

To find the coordinates that need to be at the border we will use the following LP. We have a variable x_i for each dimension $i \leq N$ and a constraint that requires x_i to be less or equal to the i-th coordinate of $V_{\max} - V_{\mathrm{end}}$ **and** $V_{\mathrm{end}} - V_{\min}$. We also add that $\sum_{m \in M} t_m = t_{\max}$ and $V_{\mathrm{end}} = V_0 + \sum_{m \in M} t_m \cdot A(m)$, with the objective *Maximise* $\sum_i x_i$. If the value of the objective is > 0, we will get to know a new coordinate that does not have to be at the border. We then remove it from the LP and run it again. Once the objective is 0, then all the remaining coordinates, I, have to be at the border and the solution to this LP tells us, at which border the solution has to be located (it cannot possibly be at the border of both $V_{\min}$ and $V_{\max}$ as then we could reach the middle).

Next, in order to bound the length of a limit-safe abstract schedule by an exponential in the size of the input, we not only need a state with the minimum number of coordinates at the border, but also sufficiently far way from the border. Otherwise, we may need super-exponentially many timed actions to reach it. In order to find such a point, we replace all x_i-s in the previously defined LP by a single variable x which is smaller or equal to all the coordinates of $V_{\max} - V_{\mathrm{end}}$ and $V_{\mathrm{end}} - V_{\min}$ from I. We then set the objective to *Maximise* x, which will give us a suitable easy target state V_{end}.

Now, consider $\mathcal{A}'$, which is the same as $\mathcal{A}$ but with all slopes negated (i.e. $A'(m) = -A(m)$ for all $m \in M$). We claim that V_{end} is reachable from V_0 using a limit-safe abstract schedule τ iff $(V_0 + V_{\mathrm{end}})/2$ is reachable from V_0 in $\mathcal{A}$ with time horizon $t_{\max}/2$ and $(V_0 + V_{\mathrm{end}})/2$ is reachable from V_{end} in $\mathcal{A}'$ with time horizon $t_{max}/2$; this again follows by considering $\tau/2$. Note that a coordinate of $(V_0 + V_{end})/2$ is at the border iff it is at the border in both V_0 and V_{end}.

This way we reduced our problem to just checking whether a limit-safe abstract schedule exists from one point to another more permissive point (i.e. where the set of safe modes is at least as big) within a given time horizon. The algorithm that solves this problem is provided in the extended version. It again reuses the same constructions as above, e.g. constructs exactly the same sequence of sets of modes $M^* = M_0 \subset M_1 \subset \ldots \subset M_k$, and its correctness follows by a similar reasoning as above. We now need to invoke this algorithm twice: to check that $(V_0 + V_{end})/2$ is reachable from V_0 with time horizon $t_{max}/2$ and that $(V_0 + V_{end})/2$ is reachable from V_{end} with time horizon $t_{max}/2$ in $\mathcal{A}'$. If at least one of these calls return NO, then no limit-safe abstract schedule from V_0 to V_{end} can exist. Otherwise, let σ and σ' be the schedules returned by these two calls, respectively. Then the concatenation of σ with the reverse of σ' is a limit-safe abstract schedule that reaches V_{end} from V_0 with time horizon t_{max}. $\square$

Theorem 3. *Finding an optimal limit-safe abstract schedule in $\mathcal{A}$ can be done in nondeterministic exponential time.*

Proof. The limit-safe abstract schedule constructed in Theorem 2 has an exponential length. To establish a nondeterministic exponential upper bound, we can guess the modes (and the order in which they occur). With them, we can produce an exponentially sized linear program, which encodes that the run of the abstract schedule is safe and minimises the total cost incurred. $\square$

Theorem 3 and Proposition 1 immediately give us the following.

Corollary 1. *If a limit-safe abstract schedule exists in $\mathcal{A}$, then for any $\epsilon > 0$ an ϵ-safe schedule with the same cost can be found in nondeterministic exponential time.*

Moreover, from Theorem 2 and the fact that in the case of multi-mode systems with no discrete costs all abstract schedules have length 1, we get the following.

Corollary 2. *Finding an optimal limit-safe abstract schedule for multi-mode systems with no discrete costs can be done in polynomial time.*

We can reduce the computational complexity in the general model if we are willing to sacrifice optimality for ϵ-optimality.

Theorem 4. *If a limit-safe abstract schedule exists, then finding an ϵ-safe ϵ-optimal strategy can be done in deterministic polynomial space.*

Proof. When reconsidering the linear programme from the end of the proof of Theorem 3, we can guess the intermediate states in polynomial space (and thus guess and output the schedule) as long as all states along the run (including the time passed so far) are representable in polynomial space.

Otherwise we use the opportunity to deviate by up to ϵ from the safe set by increasing or decreasing the duration of each timed action up to some $\delta > 0$, in order to keep the intermediate values representable in space polynomial in $|\mathcal{A}|$ and ϵ. However, we apply these changes in a way that the overall time remains t_{max}. Clearly this is possible, because within $\delta/2$ of the actual time point of each state along the run, there is a value whose number of digits in the standard decimal notation is at most equal to the sum of the number of digits in $\delta/2$ and t_{max}. Picking any such point for every interval would induce a schedule with the required property and they can be simply guessed one by one.

The final imprecision introduced by this operation is at most $b \cdot \delta \cdot \max_{m \in M} |A(m)|$, where b is a bound on the number of timed actions in a limit-safe schedule, which is exponential in $|\mathcal{A}|$. If we choose $\delta = \epsilon/(b \cdot \max_{m \in M} |A(m)|)$, then we will get the required precision.

Although our algorithm is nondeterministic, due to Savitch's theorem, it can be implemented in deterministic polynomial space.   □

4   Structure of Finite Control in One-Dimension

We show in this section that any finite safe schedule in one-dimension can be transformed without increasing its cost into a safe schedule, which follows one of finitely many regular patterns. The crucial component of this normal form will be a "leap" that we define below. We first introduce some notation. Let $M^+ = \{m \mid A(m) > 0\}$ and $M^- = \{m \mid A(m) < 0\}$. Recall that $M^0 = \{m \mid A(m) = 0\}$. We will call a mode, m, an *up mode, down mode, or zero-mode* if $m \in M^+$, $m \in M^-$, or $m \in M^0$, respectively. Similarly, the *trend* of a timed action (m, t) is *up, down, flat* if m is an up, down, zero-mode, respectively. For any subsequence of timed actions $\sigma' = \langle (m_i, t_i), \ldots, (m_j, t_j) \rangle$ in a schedule σ, whose run is $run(\sigma) = \langle V_0, V_1, \ldots, V_k \rangle$, we say that σ' *starts at state* v and *ends at state* v' iff $v = V_{i-1}$ and $v' = V_j$. We use the same terminology for a single timed action (in this case this subsequence has length 1).

Definition 2. *A* partial leap *is a pair of consecutive timed actions* $(m_i, t_i), (m_{i+1}, t_{i+1})$ *in a safe schedule such that* $m_i \in M^+$, $m_{i+1} \in M^-$, *and* $A(m_i)t_i + A(m_{i+1})t_{i+1} = 0$, *i.e. the state of a multi-mode system does not change after any partial leap. A partial leap is* complete *if* $A(m_i)t_i = V_{max} - V_{min}$. *We will simply refer to complete leaps as* leaps.

There are $|M^+ \times M^-|$ *types of leap. A leap is of type* $(m, m') \in M^+ \times M^-$ *iff* $m_i = m$ *and* $m_{i+1} = m'$. *Let* Δt_m *and* $\Delta \pi_m$ *denote the time and cost it takes for an up mode* m *to get from* V_{min} *to* V_{max} *or a down mode* m *to get from* V_{max} *to* V_{min}. *Note that* $\Delta t_m = |(V_{max} - V_{min})/A(m)|$ *and* $\Delta \pi_m = \pi_d(m) + \pi_c(m) \cdot \Delta t_m$. *By* $\Delta t_{m,m'}$ *and* $\Delta \pi_{m,m'}$ *we denote the time duration and the cost of a leap of type* $(m, m') \in M^+ \times M^-$, *respectively. Note that* $\Delta t_{m,m'} = \Delta t_m + \Delta t_{m'}$ *and* $\Delta \pi_{m,m'} = \Delta \pi_m + \Delta \pi_{m'}$.

Any safe schedule σ can be decomposed into three sections that we will call its *head, leaps, and tail*. The *head section* ends after the first timed action that ends at $V_{\min}$. The *leaps section* contains only leaps of possibly different types following the head section. Finally, the *tail section* starts after the last leap in the leaps section has finished. Note that any of these sections can be empty and the tail section can in principle contain further leaps. We show here that, for any safe schedule of length at least three, there exists another safe one with the same or a smaller cost, whose head and tail sections follow one of the 10 patterns presented in Figs. 3 and 4, respectively, where *partial up/down* means that the next state is not at the border. For each of these patterns, there exists an example which shows that an optimal safe schedule may need to use such a pattern and hence it is necessary to consider it. In order to prove this, we first need to define several cost-nonincreasing and safety-preserving operations that can be applied to safe schedules. These will later be applied in Theorem 5 to transform any safe schedule into one of the just mentioned regular patterns. These operations are easy to explain via a picture, but cumbersome to define formally. Therefore, the formal definitions can be found in the extended version of this paper [23] and we present here only the intuition behind them.

Let σ be any safe finite schedule. Following Propositions 2 and 3, we can assume that σ is angular and only contains at most one timed action with a zero-mode, and if it contains one, this action occurs at the very beginning. Unless explicitly stated, the operations below are defined for timed actions with up or down trend only.

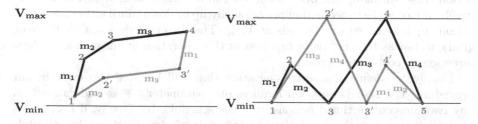

Fig. 1. On the left, the rearrange operation applied to three timed actions 1-2-3 with modes m_1, m_2, m_3 results in $1'-2'-3'$ with modes m_2, m_3, m_1. On the right, the shift operation is being applied to a partial leap 1-2-3 which will be moved after the (complete) leap 3-4-5.

The first operation that we need is the *rearrange* operation, which simply changes the order of any subsequence of timed actions with the same trend. The next one is the *shift* operation. It cuts any subsequence of timed actions that start and end at the same state, V, and pastes this subsequence after any timed action that ends at V. The effect of these two operations can be seen in Fig. 1.

Next is the *shift-down* operation. We can see an example of applying this operation in Fig. 2. Intuitively, it can rearrange any subsequence of timed actions that start and end at the same state and move them after any timed action that ends at $V_{\min}$. The most complicated operation we define is the *wedge* operation.

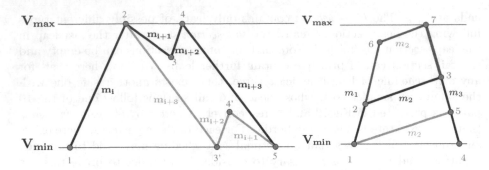

Fig. 2. On the left, an example of applying the shift-down operation to timed actions m_{i+1}, m_{i+2}. These actions are rearranged to move after point 5, which becomes point 3' (i.e. following timed action m_{i+3}). On the right, an example of applying the wedge operation to three timed actions m_1, m_2, m_3. This operation is a (parallel) translation of the action m_2, which changes the time duration of each of theses actions. After this operation either the m_2 line touches $V_{\min}$, which would remove m_1 from the schedule, or the m_2 line touches $V_{\max}$, which would change a state along the run of the schedule to be at the border.

It acts on three consecutive timed actions in a safe schedule and simultaneously shrinks the middle action while extending the other two, or stretches the middle action while shrinking the other two. We can see its behaviour in Fig. 2. Intuitively, it moves the timed action m_2 parallelly up or down, until either the timed action m_1 is removed or m_2 ends at $V_{\max}$. The direction depends on the cost gradient, but as the cost delta function of this operation is linear, one of these directions is cost-nonincreasing.

Finally, we define the *resize* operation that will be used the most in our procedure. The resize operation requires one parameter $t \in \mathbb{R}$ and can act on any two consecutive timed actions in a safe schedule. Intuitively, if $t < 0$, this operation decreases the total time of this pair of timed actions by $|t|$ while changing only the middle state between these two timed actions along the run of the schedule. If $t > 0$, this operation increases the duration of this pair of timed actions by t while again changing only the state between them along the run. If $t > 0$ then we will also refer to this operation as the *stretch* operation and if $t < 0$ as the *shrink* operation with parameter $-t > 0$. If the stretch and shrink operations are simultaneously applied with the same parameter t to two non-overlapping pairs of timed actions, the result is a safe schedule with the same time horizon as before, but with a possibly different total cost. We will call a *flexi* any subsequence of length 2 in a safe schedule such that both shrink and stretch operations can be applied to it for some $t > 0$ without compromising its safety. A simultaneous application of these two operations to flexis is demonstrated in Figs. 5 and 6.

Consider two non-overlapping flexis at positions i and j in a safe schedule σ. Let $\sigma' = \mathrm{resize}(\sigma, i, t)$ be the resulting schedule of applying the resize operation with parameter t to the i-th and $i + 1$-th timed actions in σ and resize-domain(σ, i) be the maximal closed interval from which t can be picked to ensure that σ' is safe. Similarly, let $\sigma'' = \text{resize}(\sigma, j, -t)$ and $\sigma''' = \text{resize}(\text{resize}(\sigma, i, t), j, -t)$. Note that σ''' has the same time horizon as σ and it is safe as long as $t \in \text{resize-domain}(\sigma, i) \cap \text{resize-domain}(\sigma, j)$ and let us denote this closed interval by I. Furthermore, $\pi(\sigma''') - \pi(\sigma) = \pi(\sigma') - \pi(\sigma) + \pi(\sigma'') - \pi(\sigma)$ because the two flexis did not overlap. As it is shown in the extended version, both $\pi(\sigma') - \pi(\sigma)$ and $\pi(\sigma'') - \pi(\sigma)$ are linear functions in t in the interior of I. As a result, $\pi(\sigma''') - \pi(\sigma)$ is also a linear function in t and so its minimum value is achieved at one of the endpoints of I. Also, at such an endpoint, one of the time actions in these two flexis will disappear and as a result the total cost would be reduced even further. It follows, that there is an endpoint of I such that selecting it as t will not increase the cost of the schedule, but it will remove a flexi from σ. As the zero-mode timed action and the last timed action in a schedule can have flexible time delay, we can also define the resize operation for them in a similar way. As a result, we can apply the resize operation with parameter t to any of these (including a flexi) and with parameter $-t$ to the other. Reasoning as above, there is a value for t such that the cost of the resulting schedule does not increase, the schedule remains safe, and at least one of the timed actions is removed from σ or one more state along the run of σ becomes $V_{\min}$ or $V_{\max}$.

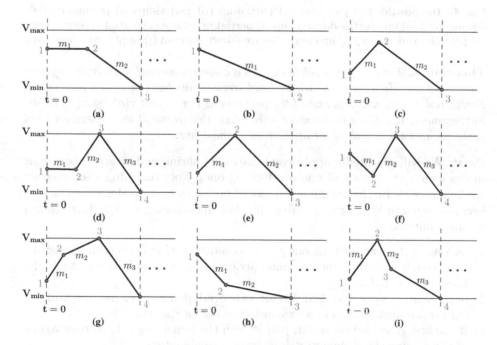

Fig. 3. Ten possible head patterns: (a) flat+down (b) down (c) partial-up+down (d) flat+up+down (e) up+down (f) partial-down+up+down (g) partial-up+up+down (h) partial-down+down (i) up+partial-down+down and (j) empty (not depicted).

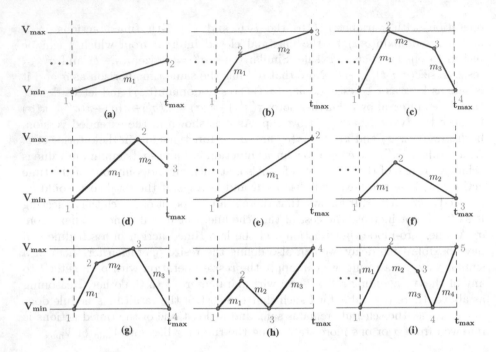

Fig. 4. Ten possible tail patterns: (a) partial-up (b) partial-up+up (c) up+partial-down+down (d) up+partial-down (e) up (f) partial-up+down (g) partial-up+up+down (h) partial-up+down+up (i) up+partial-down+down+up and (j) empty (not depicted).

Theorem 5. *For every safe schedule σ in a one-dimensional multi-mode system there exists a safe schedule σ' whose head section matches one of the patterns in Fig. 3, tail section matches one of the patterns in Fig. 4, and $\pi(\sigma') \leq \pi(\sigma)$ holds. Furthermore, it suffices to consider only 44 combinations of these head and tail patterns, and the length of all of them is at most five.*

Proof. We will repeatedly apply combination of shrink and stretch operations to flexis until we remove all non-overlapping ones. Note that after each such an application either a timed action is removed or one more state along the run of σ becomes equal to $V_{\max}$ or $V_{\min}$. We claim that the following steps will transform σ into a suitable σ':

1. as long as there are at least one pair of non-overlapping flexis then shrink one and stretch the other until a timed action is removed or a new state at the border is created;
2. once there is only one flexi left or two overlapping ones, use the shift or shift-down operation to move them to the end of the schedule;
3. if the first timed action is flat, pair it with the remaining flexi to remove one of them using the shrink-stretch operation combination;
4. if the last state of $run(\sigma)$ is not at the border and a flexi or flat timed action remains after the previous step, they should be paired with each other for the shrink-stretch operation combination;

5. if two overlapping flexis exist, use the wedge operation to resolve them;
6. finally, if the tail section still does not follow any of the patterns, apply the shift-down operation to the (unique) segment that starts and ends at $V_{\max}$.

A graphical representation of this procedure when applied to an example schedule is provided in the extended version. It is easy to see that the first step of this procedure will stop eventually because σ has a finite number of timed actions and states along its run. The rest of the steps of this procedure just try to reduce the number of possibilities for the head and tail sections. Note that, apart from the initial state, there can be only one state, along the run of the resulting σ', which is not at the border. This is because otherwise a shrink-stretch or wedge operation could still be applied. Drawing all possible patterns with one point not at the border and eliminating the ones that are inter-reducible using one of these operations, results in Fig. 3 for the head section and Fig. 4 for the tail section.

If we try to combine all these head and tail pattern together then this would result in $10 \cdot 10 = 100$ possible combinations. However, as just mentioned, there can be only one point not at the border or a zero-mode timed action in a schedule so these combinations of head and tail patterns can be reduced further. In particular, any head pattern can be combined with tail patterns (e) and (j), but only (b), (e), (j) head patterns can be combined with the remaining tail ones. Therefore, there are $10 \cdot 2 + 3 \cdot 8 = 44$ combined patterns and it is easy to check that none of them has length larger than five (this is important for the computational complexity stated in Theorem 8).   □

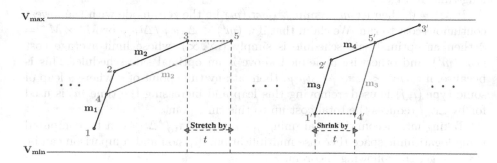

Fig. 5. Shrink and stretch operations being applied to two up-up flexis. The 1-2-3 one is stretched by t, which results in 1-4-5, and $1'$-$2'$-$3'$ is shrunk by t, which results in $4'$-$5'$-$3'$. Note that 3 and 5 (also, $1'$ and $4'$) are the same states but shifted in time. In fact, all states along the run of the schedule stay the same apart from 2 and $2'$, and as a result the schedule stays safe.

5   Complexity of Optimal Control in One-Dimension

We start with considering the easy case of infinite time horizons, before turning to the interesting case of finite time horizons.

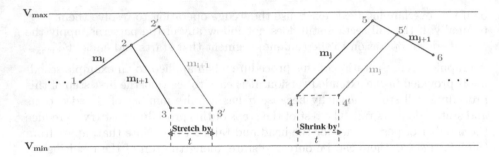

Fig. 6. Shrink and stretch operations being applied to two up-down flexis.

5.1 Infinite Time Horizon

First let us consider the case $M^0 = \emptyset$. If also $M^+ \times M^- = \emptyset$ then there are no safe schedules with infinite horizon at all. Otherwise, let $(i', j') = \operatorname{argmin}_{(i,j) \in M^+ \times M^-} \Delta\pi_{i,j}/\Delta t_{i,j}$. Let us pick any mode $m^- \in M^-$ and denote $t^- := (V_{\min} - V_0)/A(m^-)$. Consider the infinite schedule σ, which starts with the timed action (m^-, t^-) followed by infinitely many complete leaps of type (i', j'). Obviously, at all times $t = t^- + k \cdot \Delta t_{i',j'}$ where $k \in \mathbb{N}$, σ is more expensive by at most $\pi_d(m^-) + \pi_c(m^-)t^-$ from the cheapest schedule with time horizon t. Consequently, as $k \to \infty$, this shows that the limit superior of the average cost cannot be smaller than $\Delta\pi_{i',j'}/\Delta t_{i',j'}$. At the same time, σ realises this long-time average.

If $M^0 \neq \emptyset$, then let $m' = \min_{m \in M^0} \pi_c(m)$ be the zero-mode with the lowest continuous cost to run. We claim that if $\pi_c(m') < \Delta\pi_{i',j'}/\Delta t_{i',j'}$ or $M^+ \times M^- = \emptyset$ then an optimal safe schedule is simply (m', ∞), whose limit-average cost is $\pi_c(m')$, and otherwise σ defined above is an optimal safe schedule. This is because, if $\pi_c(m') < \Delta\pi_{i',j'}/\Delta t_{i',j'}$, then, at any time point of σ where a leap of some type (i, j) is used, removing this leap and increasing the time m' is used for by $\Delta t_{i,j}$ reduces the total cost up to this time point.

Taking into account that $\operatorname{argmin}_{(i,j) \in M^+ \times M^-} \Delta\pi_{i,j}/\Delta t_{i,j}$ can be computed using logarithmic space (because multiplication, division and comparison can be [13]) we get the following theorem.

Theorem 6. *An optimal safe infinite schedule for one-dimensional multi-mode systems can be computed in deterministic* LOGSPACE.

5.2 Finite Time Horizon

Due to Theorem 1, we already know that the decision problem for optimal schedules in one-dimensional multi-mode systems is at least NP-hard. Here, we show that the problem is NP-complete by showing that an optimal schedule exists and that each section of an optimal schedule can be guessed.

Note that the existence of an optimal schedule for the one-dimensional case sets it apart from the general case. In Example 1, we have shown that optimal schedules are not even guaranteed to exist for two-dimensional multi-mode systems.

Theorem 7. *For any one-dimensional multi-mode systems $\mathcal{A}$ and $t_{max} \geq 0$, there exists an optimal schedule with time horizon t_{max}, and checking for the existence of an optimal schedule with cost $\leq C$ is NP-complete. (When t_{max} and C are given in binary.)*

Proof. First, we can simply iterate over all schedules of length one and directly calculate their costs. Next, we can iterate over pairs of modes, m_1 and m_2, and for each of them solve a linear program (LP) which will give us the cheapest schedule of length two using these two modes. This LP finds the cheapest partition of $t_{\max}$ between the two modes and has the following form: Minimise $\pi_c(m_1)t_1 + \pi_c(m_2)(t_{\max} - t_1) + \pi_d(m_1) + \pi_d(m_2)$

$$\text{Subject to: } 0 \leq t_1 \leq t_{\max}, \quad V_{\min} \leq V_0 + A(m_1)t_1 \leq V_{\max} \text{ and}$$
$$V_{\min} \leq V_0 + A(m_1)t_1 + A(m_2)(t_{\max} - t_1) \leq V_{\max}.$$

This can be done in $\mathcal{O}(|\mathcal{A}|^2)$ time.

Now, for schedules of length at least three, we showed in Sect. 4 that any such a schedule can be transformed without increasing its cost into one that can be split into three sections: the head section, the leaps section, and the tail section (some of which may be empty). Due to Theorem 5, there are 44 combined patterns for the tail and head sections. Note that, when considering only the cost of the whole schedule, it suffices for us to know the number of leaps of each type in the leaps section and not their precise order. Notice that a schedule with time horizon $t_{\max}$ can contain at most $\lfloor t_{\max}/\Delta\pi_{i,j}\rfloor$ leaps of type (i,j). The size of this number is polynomial in the size of the input $\mathcal{A}$. There are $\mathcal{O}(|M|^2)$ types of leaps so the number of leaps of each type and the combined pattern of the schedule can be guessed non-deterministically with polynomially many bits. This guess uniquely determines the cost of the schedule. This is because, after the total time of the leaps section is deducted from $t_{\max}$, we get the exact time the head and tail section have to last for. Each combined pattern has at most one of the following: a flexi, a zero-mode, or the last state not at the border. The time remaining will determinate exactly (if at all possible) the value of this single flexible point along this schedule. Now, computing the cost of the resulting schedule and checking whether it is lower than C can be done in polynomial time. This shows that the problem is in NP. It also shows that optimal schedules exist, because there are only finitely many options to choose from. □

6   Approximate Optimal Control in One-Dimension

We first show an approximation algorithm with a 3-relative performance for the cost minimisation problem in one-dimensional multi-mode systems, which runs in $\mathcal{O}(|\mathcal{A}|^7)$ time. Our algorithm tries all possible patterns for an optimal schedule and for the leaps section always picks leaps of the same type. It then adds, if necessary or for cost efficiency, a partial leap to the leaps section and minimises the total cost of the just constructed schedule by optimising the time duration of this partial leap. This constant approximation algorithm is crucial for showing the existence of an FPTAS for the same problem in the next subsection.

Theorem 8. *Computing a safe schedule with total cost at most three times larger than the optimal one for one-dimensional multi-mode system $\mathcal{A}$ can be done in $\mathcal{O}(|\mathcal{A}|^7)$ time.*

We now show that the cost minimisation problem for one dimensional multi-mode systems is in FPTAS by a polynomial time reduction to the 0-1 Knapsack problem, for which many FPTAS algorithms are available (see e.g. [18]). This is similar to the FPTAS construction in [22], but differs in how the modes with fractional duration are handled. First we iterate over all possible schedules of length at most two and find the cheapest one in polynomial time. Next, thanks to Theorem 5, all optimal schedules longer than two can be transformed into one of 44 different patterns. Each of these patterns results in a slightly different FPTAS formulation. An FPTAS for the general model consists of all of these individual FPTASes executed one after another. The details of the proof are provided in the extended version.

Theorem 9. *Solving the optimal control problem for multi-mode systems with relative performance ρ takes $\mathcal{O}(\text{poly}(1/\rho)\text{poly}(\text{size of the instance}))$ time and is therefore in FPTAS.*

Acknowledgement. This work was supported by EPSRC EP/M027287/1 grant "Energy Efficient Control".

References

1. EnergyPlus: Building energy simulation program. https://energyplus.net/
2. IBPT: International building physics toolbox in simulink. http://www.ibpt.org/
3. TRaNsient SYstems simulation program. http://sel.me.wisc.edu/trnsys/
4. Alur, R., Courcoubetis, C., Halbwachs, N., Henzinger, T.A., Ho, P.-H., Nicollin, X., Olivero, A., Sifakis, J., Yovine, S.: The algorithmic analysis of hybrid systems. Theor. Comput. Sci. **138**(1), 3–34 (1995)
5. Alur, R., Courcoubetis, C., Henzinger, T.A., Ho, P.-H.: Hybrid automata: An algorithmic approach to the specification and verification of hybrid systems. In: Grossman, R.L., Nerode, A., Ravn, A.P., Rischel, H. (eds.) HS 1991-1992. LNCS, vol. 736, pp. 209–229. Springer, Heidelberg (1993). doi:10.1007/3-540-57318-6_30
6. Alur, R., Dill, D.L.: A theory of timed automata. Theor. Comput. Sci. **126**(2), 183–235 (1994)
7. Alur, R., Forejt, V., Moarref, S., Trivedi, A.: Safe schedulability of bounded-rate multi-mode systems. In: HSCC, pp. 243–252. ACM (2013)
8. Alur, R., Trivedi, A., Wojtczak, D.: Optimal scheduling for constant-rate multi-mode systems. computation and control. In: Proceedings of Hybrid Systems (2012)

9. Asarin, E., Mysore, V.P., Pnueli, A., Schneider, G.: Low dimensional hybrid systems – decidable, undecidable, don't know. Inf. Comput. **211**, 138–159 (2012)
10. Bouyer, P.: Weighted timed automata: model-checking and games. Electron. Notes Theor. Comput. Sci. **158**, 3–17 (2006)
11. Bouyer, P., Brihaye, T., Jurdziński, M., Lazić, R., Rutkowski, M.: Average-price and reachability-price games on hybrid automata with strong resets. In: Cassez, F., Jard, C. (eds.) FORMATS 2008. LNCS, vol. 5215, pp. 63–77. Springer, Heidelberg (2008). doi:10.1007/978-3-540-85778-5_6
12. Camacho, E.F., Alba, C.B.: Model Predictive Control. Springer, London (2013). doi:10.1007/978-0-85729-398-5
13. Chiu, A., Davida, G.I., Litow, B.E.: Division in logspace-uniform NC^1. ITA **35**(3), 259–275 (2001)
14. David, A., Du, D., Guldstrand Larsen, K., Legay, A., Mikučionis, M.: Optimizing control strategy using statistical model checking. In: Brat, G., Rungta, N., Venet, A. (eds.) NFM 2013. LNCS, vol. 7871, pp. 352–367. Springer, Heidelberg (2013). doi:10.1007/978-3-642-38088-4_24
15. David, A., Jensen, P.G., Larsen, K.G., Mikučionis, M., Taankvist, J.H.: UPPAAL STRATEGO . In: Baier, C., Tinelli, C. (eds.) TACAS 2015. LNCS, vol. 9035, pp. 206–211. Springer, Heidelberg (2015). doi:10.1007/978-3-662-46681-0_16
16. David, A., Larsen, K.G., Legay, A., Mikučionis, M., Wang, Z.: Time for statistical model checking of real-time systems. In: Gopalakrishnan, G., Qadeer, S. (eds.) CAV 2011. LNCS, vol. 6806, pp. 349–355. Springer, Heidelberg (2011). doi:10. 1007/978-3-642-22110-1_27
17. Henzinger, T.A.: The theory of hybrid automata. In: Proceedings of the 11th IEEE LICS 1996 Symposium, Washington, DC (1996)
18. Kellerer, H., Pferschy, U., Pisinger, D.: Knapsack Problems. Springer, Heidelberg (2004). doi:10.1007/978-3-540-24777-7
19. Laroussinie, F., Markey, N., Schnoebelen, P.: Model checking timed automata with one or two clocks. In: Gardner, P., Yoshida, N. (eds.) CONCUR 2004. LNCS, vol. 3170, pp. 387–401. Springer, Heidelberg (2004). doi:10.1007/978-3-540-28644-8_25
20. Larsen, K.G., Mikučionis, M., Muñiz, M., Srba, J., Taankvist, J.H.: Online and compositional learning of controllers with application to floor heating. In: Chechik, M., Raskin, J.-F. (eds.) TACAS 2016. LNCS, vol. 9636, pp. 244–259. Springer, Heidelberg (2016). doi:10.1007/978-3-662-49674-9_14
21. Li, B., Alleyne, A.G.: Optimal on-off control of an air conditioning and refrigeration system. In: American Control Conference (ACC), pp. 5892–5897. IEEE (2010)
22. Mousa, M.A.A., Schewe, S., Wojtczak, D.: Optimal control for simple linear hybrid systems. In: 23rd International Symposium on Temporal Representation and Reasoning (TIME), pp. 12–20. IEEE (2016)
23. Mousa, M.A.A., Schewe, S., Wojtczak, D.: Optimal control for multi-mode systems with discrete costs. CoRR, 1706.09886 (2017). http://arxiv.org/abs/1706.09886
24. Nghiem, T.X., Behl, M., Mangharam, R., Pappas, G.J.: Green scheduling of control systems for peak demand reduction. In: 2011 50th IEEE Conference on Decision and Control and European Control Conference (CDC-ECC), pp. 5131–5136. IEEE (2011)
25. Nghiem, T.X., Pappas, G.J., Mangharam, R.: Event-based green scheduling of radiant systems in buildings. In: American Control Conference (ACC), pp. 455–460. IEEE (2013)

26. Oldewurtel, F., Ulbig, A., Parisio, A., Andersson, G., Morari, M.: Reducing peak electricity demand in building climate control using real-time pricing and model predictive control. In: 2010 49th IEEE Conference on Decision and Control (CDC), pp. 1927–1932. IEEE (2010)
27. Pérez-Lombard, L., Ortiz, J., Pout, C.: A review on buildings energy consumption information. Energy Build. **40**(3), 394–398 (2008)
28. Wojtczak, D.: Optimal control for linear-rate multi-mode systems. In: Braberman, V., Fribourg, L. (eds.) FORMATS 2013. LNCS, vol. 8053, pp. 258–273. Springer, Heidelberg (2013). doi:10.1007/978-3-642-40229-6_18

Augmented Complex Zonotopes for Computing Invariants of Affine Hybrid Systems

Arvind Adimoolam$^{(\boxtimes)}$ and Thao Dang

Verimag, Grenoble, France
{santosh.adimoolam,thao.dang}@univ-grenoble-alpes.fr

Abstract. Zonotopes are a useful set representation for bounded time reach set computation of affine hybrid systems because of their closure under Minkowski sum and matrix multiplication operations. For unbounded time reach set approximation of arbitrarily switched affine hybrid systems, template complex zonotopes and a corresponding invariant computation procedure were introduced, which utilized the possibly complex eigenstructure of the affine maps. But a major hurdle in extending the technique for computing invariants of more general affine hybrid systems, where switching is state dependent and controlled by linear constraints, is that the class of template complex zonotopes is not closed under intersection with linear constraints. In this paper, we use a more expressive set representation called augmented complex zonotopes, for which we propose an algebraic over-approximation of the intersection with linear constraints. This over-approximation is then used to derive a set of second order conic constraints for computing an augmented complex zonotopic positive invariant for discrete time affine hybrid systems with additive disturbance input and linear safety constraints. We demonstrate the efficiency of this approach by experimenting on some benchmark examples.

1 Introduction

In the design of embedded and cyber-physical systems, one of the most important requirements is safety, which can be roughly stated as that the system will never enter a bad state. Safety verification for such systems are known to be computationally challenging due to the complexity resulting from the interactions among heterogenous components, having mixed (continuous and discrete) dynamics. In this paper, we focus on the problem of finding invariants for hybrid systems, which are widely recognized as appropriate for modelling embedded and cyber-physical systems. An invariant is a property that is satisfied in every state that the system can reach. Therefore a common approach for proving a safety property is to find an invariant that implies the safety property. Invariant computation has been studied extensively in the context of verification of transition systems and program analysis (see for example [8,10,11,16,34] and

This research work is partially supported by ANR project MALTHY.

A. Abate and G. Geeraerts (Eds.): FORMATS 2017, LNCS 10419, pp. 97–115, 2017.
DOI: 10.1007/978-3-319-65765-3_6

the developed techniques have been extended to continuous and hybrid systems [9,12,26,30,31,33]. Barrier certificates [23] are closely related to invariants in the sense that they describe a boundary that the system starting from a given initial set will never cross to enter a region containing bad states. Another common approach to safety verification is to compute or over-approximate the reachable set of the system, and these reachability computation techniques have been developed for continuous and hybrid systems. Many such techniques are based on iterative approximation of the reachable state on a step-by-step basis, which can be thought of as a set-based extension of numerical integration. A major drawback of this approach, inherent to undecidability of general hybrid systems with non-trivial dynamics, is that such an iterative procedure may not terminate and thus can only be used for bounded-time safety verification (except when the over-approximation error accumulation is not too bad that the safety can be decided). In contrast, invariants and barrier certificates are based on conditions that are satisfied at all times. Although solving these conditions often involves fixed point computation, by exploiting the structure of the dynamics (such as eigenstructures of linear systems), one can derive meaningful conditions which can significantly reduce the number of iterations until convergence.

Zonotopes have the advantage that they accurately capture matrix multiplication and linear transformation operations, but they are used mainly for bounded time reachability computation. For approximating unbounded time reachable sets of arbitrarily switched affine hybrid systems based on positive invariants, template complex zonotopes were introduced in [1], which have the following useful property. Any template complex zonotope generated by the eigenvectors of a Schur stable linear transformation is positively invariant with respect to the transformation. Therefore, template complex zonotopes can exploit the possibly complex eigenstructure of the system dynamics for computing invariants, while real zonotopes can not. However, a formidable hurdle using them for invariant computation of more general affine hybrid systems, where switching is state-dependent and controlled by linear constraints, is that we have to handle the intersection of template complex zonotopes with the guard sets that trigger switching. In this regard, template complex zonotopes share the drawback of usual zonotopes that these classes of sets are not closed under intersection with linear constraints. In this paper, we address this problem as follows. We use a slightly more general set representation, called *augmented complex zonotope*, based on which we propose an algebraic overapproximation of the intersection with a class of linear constraints, called sub-parallelotopic. Henceforth, we derive a numerically efficiently solvable sufficient condition for computing an augmented complex zonotopic invariant satisfying linear safety constraints, for a discrete-time affine hybrid system with subparallelotopic switching constraints and bounded additive disturbance input. The sufficient condition is expressed as a set of second order conic constraints. We also note that the class of subparallelotopic constraints that we consider are quite general and can be used in the specification of many practical affine hybrid systems. We corroborate our approach by presenting the experimental results for three benchmark examples from the literature.

Related work. For hybrid systems verification, convex polyhedra [11,18], and their special classes such as octagons [22] and zonotopes [15,20] and tropical polyhedra [5] are the most commonly used set representations. During reachability analysis, which requires operations under which a set representation is not closed (such as the union or join operations for convex polyhedra and additionally intersection for zonotopes), the complexity of generated sets increases rapidly in order to guarantee a desired error bound. One way to control this complexity increase is to fix the face normal vectors or generators, which leads to template convex polyhedra [12,29]. Although our template complex zonotopes proposed in [1] do not belong to the class of convex polyhedra, they follow the same spirit of controlling the complexity using templates. Set representations defined by non-linear constraints include ellipsoids [19], polynomial inequalities [7] and equalities [25], quadratic templates and piecewise quadratic templates [3,27,28], which are used for computing non-linear invariants. A major problem of template based approaches finding good templates. In this regard, using template complex zonotopes and the augmented version introduced in this paper, we can exploit eigen-structures of linear dynamics which reflect the contraction or expansion of a set by the dynamics, and define good templates for efficient convergence to an invariant (see Proposition 4.3 of [2]).

The extension to complex zonotope [2] is very similar in spirit to quadratic zonotopes [4] and more generally polynomial zonotopes [6]. Nevertheless, while a polynomial zonotope is a set-valued polynomial function of *intervals*, a complex zonotope is a set-valued function of unit *circles* in the complex plane. Our idea in this paper of coupling additional linear constraints with complex zonotopes is inspired by the work on constrained zonotopes proposed in [14,32] for computing intersection with linear constraints. But while [14,32] compute the intersection or its overapproximation, algorithmically, we instead derive a simple algebraic expression to overapproximate the intersection. This algebraic expression is latter used to obtain second order conic (convex) constraints, for invariant computation in a single step of convex optimization.

Organization. The rest of the paper is organized as follows. Firstly, we explain some of the mathematical notation used in this paper. Then in Sect. 2, we describe the model of a discrete-time affine hybrid system, controlled by sub-parallelotopic switching conditions and having a bounded additive disturbance input. In Sect. 3, we present the set representation of augmented complex zonotopes and discuss some important operations and relations, in particular intersection with sub-parallelotopic constraints, projection in any direction, linear transformation, Minkowski sum and inclusion checking. In Sect. 4, we derive a set of second order conic constraints to compute an augmented complex zonotopic invariant, satisfying linear safety constraints and containing an initial set. Furthermore, we explain how to choose the template. In Sect. 5, we report some experimental results. The conclusion and future work are given in Sect. 6.

Notation. Some notations for which we consider explanation may be required is described below. We denote $\overline{\mathbb{R}} = \mathbb{R} \bigcup \{-\infty, \infty\}$. If S is a set of complex numbers, then $\mathrm{Re}(S)$ and $\mathrm{Im}(S)$ represent the real and imaginary projections of S, respectively. If z is a complex number, then $|z|$ denotes the absolute value of z. On the other hand, if X is a complex matrix (or vector), then $|X|$ denotes the matrix (or vector) containing the absolute values of the elements of X. The diagonal square matrix containing the entries of a complex vector z along the diagonal is denoted by $\mathcal{D}(z)$. The conjugate transpose of a matrix $V \in \mathbb{M}_{m \times n}(\mathbb{C})$ is denoted $V^* = (\mathrm{Re}(V) - i \, \mathrm{Im}(V))^T$. If VV^* is invertible, then $V^\dagger = V^* (VV^*)^{-1}$, which is the pseudo-inverse of V. Given two vectors $l, u \in \mathbb{R}^k$ and any relation $\bowtie$ between numbers in $\overline{\mathbb{R}}$, we say $l \bowtie u$ if $l_i \bowtie u_i$, $\forall i \in \{1, ..., k\}$. The meet of the two vectors l and u is denoted $l \bigwedge u$, defined as $(l \bigwedge u)_i = \min (l_i, u_i) \; \forall i \in \{1, ..., k\}$. The join is denoted $l \bigvee u$, defined as $(l \bigvee u)_i = \max (l_i, u_i) \; \forall i \in \{1, ..., k\}$.

2   Hybrid Systems and Positive Invariants

In a discrete-time affine hybrid system, there is a finite set of discrete variables, called locations, and a finite set of continuous variables, whose valuation is in the real Euclidean space of dimension $n \in \mathbb{Z}_{>0}$. For each location, a set of linear constraints called staying conditions constrain the continuous state of the system in the location. Also, there is an affine transition map with a (possibly) additive uncertain but bounded disturbance input set, which specifies the evolution of the continuous variables in the location. A set of labeled directed edges specify the discrete transitions, which result in a possible change of locations along with an affine reset of continuous variables, where the reset has a bounded additive uncertainty. Also, each edge transition can have a set of preconditions, called a guard, given by linear constraints.

In this paper, we consider a specific class of linear constraints called sub-parallelotopic, for defining guards and staying conditions, such that their intersection with the reachable set represented by augmented complex zonotopes (introduced later) can be effectively computed. The sets corresponding to sub-parallelotopic constraints can be seen as a generalization of parallelotopes to possibly unbounded sets.

Definition 1 (Sub-parallelotope).   *Let $K \in \mathbb{M}_{k \times n}(\mathbb{R})$ such that $k \leq n$ and (KK^T) is non-singular. We call such a matrix K as a sub-parallelotopic template. Let $\widehat{u}, \widehat{l} \in \overline{\mathbb{R}}^k$ such that $\widehat{l} \leq \widehat{u}$. Then a sub-parallelotopic set is* $\mathcal{P}\left(K, \widehat{l}, \widehat{u}\right) = \left\{ x \in \mathbb{R}^n : \widehat{l} \leq Kx \leq \widehat{u} \right\}$.

For example, the set of linear constraints $-1 \leq x + y - z \leq 1 \; \wedge \; x - y + z \leq 3$ is equivalent to a sub-parallelotope

$$\mathcal{P}\left(\begin{bmatrix} 1 & 1 & -1 \\ 1 & -1 & 1 \end{bmatrix}, \begin{bmatrix} -1 \\ -\infty \end{bmatrix}, \begin{bmatrix} 1 \\ 3 \end{bmatrix} \right),$$

because the rows of the sub-parallelotopic template are linearly independent. On the other hand, the set of constraints $-1 \leq x + y - z \leq 1 \ \wedge \ x + y + z \leq 2 \ \wedge \ -1 \leq x + y$ do not constitute a sub-parallelotope, because the three row vectors $[1\ 1\ -1]$, $[1\ 1\ 1]$, and $[1\ 1\ 0]$ together are linearly dependent. Sub-parallelotopic constraints are algebraically related to a generator representation. We can express $\mathcal{P}\left(K_{k \times n}, \widehat{l}, \widehat{u}\right) = \{c + K^{\dagger}\zeta : c \in \mathbb{R}^n, \zeta \in \mathbb{R}^k, Kc = 0,$ $\widehat{l} \leq \zeta \leq \widehat{u}\}$. Here, the columns vectors in the pseudo-inverse $K^{\dagger}$ can be considered as generators. Therefore, it is possible to express the intersection of sub-parallelotope with a suitably aligned zonotope as a simple algebraic expression, as we will see latter.

System model. We consider discrete-time affine hybrid systems defined by a tuple $\mathbb{H} = (Q, \mathcal{K}, \gamma, \mathcal{A}, U, E)$. Here, Q is a finite set of locations. For each location $q \in Q$, a sub-parallelotopic template $\mathcal{K}_q \in \mathrm{M}_{k_q \times n}(\mathbb{R})$, i.e., $\mathcal{K}_q (\mathcal{K}_q)^T$ is non-singular, and k_q is the number of rows of the template, is used for defining the staying conditions and the guards on edges emanating from the location. A pair of upper and lower bounds $\gamma_q = (\gamma_q^-, \gamma_q^+) \in \mathbb{R}^{k_q} \times \mathbb{R}^{k_q} : \ \gamma_q^- \leq \gamma_q^+$ together with the sub-parallelotopic template define the sub-parallelotopic staying set, given as $\mathcal{P}(\mathcal{K}_q, \gamma_q^-, \gamma_q^+)$. A matrix A_q and a bounded set $U_q \subseteq \mathbb{R}^n$ correspond to the affine transformation in the location. The set of edges is E, where $\sigma \in E$ is a tuple $\sigma = (\sigma_1, \sigma_2, \sigma^-, \sigma^+, \Theta_\sigma, \Omega_\sigma)$. The pre and post locations of the edge are $\sigma_1 \in Q$ and $\sigma_2 \in Q$, respectively. The pair of upper and lower bounds $(\sigma^-, \sigma^+) \in \mathbb{R}^{k_{\sigma_1}} \times \mathbb{R}^{k_{\sigma_1}} : \ \sigma^- \leq \sigma^+$, gives the sub-parallelotopic guard set $\mathcal{P}(\mathcal{K}_{\sigma_1}, \sigma^-, \sigma^+)$, which is a precondition on the edge transition. The matrix Θ_σ and a bounded set $\Omega_\sigma \subseteq \mathbb{R}^n$ correspond to the affine transition map along the edge.

Dynamics. The state of the hybrid system is a pair (x, q), where $x \in \mathbb{R}^n$ is called the continuous state and $q \in Q$ is called the discrete state. The evolution of the state of the system in time is called a *trajectory* of the system. The trajectory is a function $(\mathbf{x}, \mathbf{q}) : \mathbb{Z}_{\geq 0} \to \mathbb{R}^n \times Q$, such that for all $t \in \mathbb{Z}_{\geq 0}$, one of the following is true.

1. Continuous transition.

$\exists u \in U_{\mathbf{q}(t)}$ such that all of the following are collectively true.

$$\mathbf{x}(t + 1) = \mathcal{A}_{\mathbf{q}(t)}\mathbf{x}(t) + u, \quad \mathbf{q}(t + 1) = \mathbf{q}(t) \text{ and} \tag{1}$$

$$\mathbf{x}(t), \ \mathbf{x}(t + 1) \in \mathcal{P}\left(\mathcal{K}_{\mathbf{q}(t)}, \gamma_{\mathbf{q}(t)}^-, \gamma_{\mathbf{q}(t)}^+\right).$$

2. Discrete transition.

$\exists \sigma \in E$ and $u \in \Omega_\sigma$ such that all of the following are collectively true.

$$\mathbf{q}(t) = \sigma_1, \quad \mathbf{x}(t) \in \mathcal{P}\left(\mathcal{K}_{\sigma_1}, \sigma^- \bigvee \gamma_{\sigma_1}^-, \sigma^+ \bigwedge \gamma_{\sigma_1}^+\right)$$

$$\mathbf{x}(t + 1) = \Theta_{\mathbf{q}(t)}\mathbf{x}(t) + u, \quad \mathbf{q}(t + 1) = \sigma_2 \tag{2}$$

$$\mathbf{x}(t + 1) \in \mathcal{P}\left(\mathcal{K}_{\sigma_2}, \gamma_{\sigma_2}^-, \gamma_{\sigma_2}^+\right).$$

Given a set of continuous states $S \in \mathbb{R}^n$ in a location, for computing the set of reachable continuous states in the next step of continuous or discrete transition, we define the following functions, respectively.

$$R_q (S) = \left\{ \begin{array}{l} (\mathcal{A}_q (S \bigcap \mathcal{P} (\mathcal{K}_q, \gamma_q^-, \gamma_q^+)) \oplus U_q) \\ \bigcap \mathcal{P} (\mathcal{K}_q, \gamma_q^-, \gamma_q^+) \end{array} \right. .$$

$$R_\sigma (S) = \left\{ \begin{array}{l} (\Theta_\sigma (S \bigcap \mathcal{P} (\mathcal{K}_{\sigma_1}, \sigma^- \bigvee \gamma_{\sigma_1}^-, \sigma^+ \bigwedge \gamma_{\sigma_1}^+)) \oplus \Omega_\sigma) \\ \bigcap \mathcal{P} (\mathcal{K}_{\sigma_2}, \gamma_{\sigma_2}^-, \gamma_{\sigma_2}^+) \end{array} \right. .$$

We shall identify a set of states by a mapping of the kind $\Gamma : Q \to 2^{\mathbb{R}^n}$, called a *state set*, which corresponds to the set of states $\{(x, q) : x \in \Gamma (q)\}$. For notational convenience, we shall denote Γ_q as the set of continuous states of Γ in a location q. A *positive invariant* is a set of states of the system such that all trajectories beginning at any state in the positive invariant remain within the positive invariant. Equivalently, a state set is a positive invariant if the reachable set in one time step by both the intralocation and interlocation dynamics is contained within the original state set.

Definition 2. *A state set Γ is a positive invariant if $\forall q \in Q$, $R_q (\Gamma_q) \subseteq \Gamma_q$ and $\forall \sigma \in E$, $R_\sigma (\Gamma_{\sigma_1}) \subseteq \Gamma_{\sigma_2}$.*

3   Augmented Complex Zonotopes

Before introducing augmented complex zonotope, we briefly review the related set representations used in this paper. First, polytopes can be defined in terms of halfspace representation. Let $T \in \mathbb{M}_{n \times k}(\mathbb{R})$ and $d \in \mathbb{R}^k$. Then a (possibly unbounded) *polytope*, denoted by $\mathcal{J}(T, d)$, is defined as $\mathcal{J}(T, d) = \left\{ x \in \overline{\mathbb{R}}^k : Tx \leq d \right\}$. Usual zonotopes form a subclass of polytopes, which are geometrically Minkowski sums of line segments. They are represented as a linear combination of real vectors, called *generators*, whose combining coefficients are bounded in real-valued intervals. Let $W \in \mathbb{M}_{n \times k}(\mathbb{R})$ and $l, u \in \mathbb{R}^m : l \leq u$. Then a *real zonotope* is $\mathcal{Z}(W, l, u) = \left\{ W\zeta : \zeta \in \mathbb{R}^k, \zeta_i \in [l_i, u_i] \forall i \in \{1, ..., k\} \right\}$. For simple examples of zonotopes like boxes and octagons, efficient interconversion between the zonotopic representation and the halfspace polytopic representation is possible. However, in general, zonotopes do not admit efficient halfspace representations as polytopes. The reason is that a zonotope with m generators in an n-dimensional space has $\binom{m}{n-1}$ faces (bounding hyperplanes), if all combinations of any n generators are linearly independent. That is, the halfspace representation of a zonotope can be exponentially large, compared to the above generator representation.

Zonotopes are closed under linear transformations and Minkowski sums, which can be computed efficiently. Hence, zonotopes are considered efficient for reachability analysis of continuous linear systems. Nevertheless, a major drawback of zonotopes is that their intersection with sets defined by linear constraints need not be zonotopes. Also, there is no unique smallest zonotope that overapproximates such intersections. However, we observe that when the linear constraints constitute a sub-parallelotope with a template aligned with that of the zonotope, their intersection can be exactly computed. This is also the reason we considered the case of staying conditions and guards specified as sub-parallelotopes in this work. As a simple example, the intersection of $\mathcal{Z} \left(\begin{bmatrix} 1 & 0 \\ 0 & 1 \end{bmatrix}, \begin{bmatrix} -1 \\ -1 \end{bmatrix}, \begin{bmatrix} 2 \\ 2 \end{bmatrix} \right)$ with $x_1 \leq 1 \wedge x_2 \geq 0.5$ gives $\mathcal{Z} \left(\begin{bmatrix} 1 & 0 \\ 0 & 1 \end{bmatrix}, \begin{bmatrix} -1 \\ 0.5 \end{bmatrix}, \begin{bmatrix} 1 \\ 2 \end{bmatrix} \right)$. The general case is described in the following lemma.

Lemma 1. *Let* $K \in \mathbb{M}_{k \times n}(\mathbb{R})$ *such that* $k \leq n$ *and* $\left(KK^T \right)$ *is non-singular. Then*

$$\mathcal{Z} \left(K^\dagger, l, u \right) \bigcap \mathcal{P} \left(K, \widehat{l}, \widehat{u} \right) = \mathcal{Z} \left(K^\dagger, l \bigvee \widehat{l}, u \bigwedge \widehat{u} \right)$$

A template complex zonotope introduced in [1] has complex valued vectors as generators, whose combining coefficients are complex and bounded in their absolute values. It has the useful property that when multiplied by a Schur stable matrix whose (possibly complex) eigenvectors are its generators, the transformed complex zonotope is contained inside the original complex zonotope. A formal statement of a similar property is given in Proposition 4.3 of [2]. Because of this property, template complex zonotopes can utilize the possibly complex eigenstructure while computing invariants.

Definition 3 (Template complex zonotope). *Let* $V \in \mathbb{M}_{n \times m}(\mathbb{C})$ *(template) and* $s \in \mathbb{R}_{\geq 0}^m$ *(scaling factors) and* $c \in \mathbb{R}^n$ *(center). Then the following is a template complex zonotope:* $\mathcal{C} \left(V, c, s \right) = \{ c + V\epsilon : \epsilon \in \mathbb{C}^m, \ |\epsilon_i| \leq s_i \ \forall i \in \{1, ..., m\} \}$.

We note that unlike real zonotopes, template complex zonotopes can have non-polyhedral real projections because they describe Minkowski sums of ellipsoids and line segments. We now introduce an *augmented complex zonotope*, which is a Minkowski sum of a template complex zonotope and a real zonotope. In terms of expressivity, an augmented complex zonotope is slightly more general than template complex zonotopes. But geometrically, the sets that can be described as real projections of augmented complex zonotopes can also be described as real projections of template complex zonotopes. However, with augmented complex zonotopes, the intersection with subparallelotopic constraints can be succinctly specified, as we will see latter. Consequently, this representation is more convenient to derive conditions for computing invariants for the affine hybrid system.

Definition 4 (Augmented complex zonotope). *Let* $V \in \mathbb{M}_{n \times m}(\mathbb{C})$ *called primary template,* $W \in \mathbb{M}_{n \times k}(\mathbb{R})$ *called secondary template,* $c \in \mathbb{R}^n$ *called primary offset,* $s \subset \mathbb{R}^m$ *called scaling factors,* $u, l \subset \mathbb{R}^k$ *called lower and upper interval bounds, respectively, such that* $l \leq u$. *The following is an augmented complex zonotope*

$$\mathcal{G} \left(V, c, s, W, l, u \right) = \mathcal{C} \left(V, c, s \right) \oplus \mathcal{Z} \left(W, l, u \right).$$

We first discuss the intersection operation of an augmented complex zonotope with sub-parallelotopic constraints, before discussing other operations. Note that due to the space limit, we do not include all the proofs but only those of the key results.

For deriving a formula for the intersection, we first prove some results on intersection among convex sets. Let us define the support of a vector v in a set $S \subset \mathbb{R}^n$ relative to a point $w \in \mathbb{R}^n$ as $\rho(v, w, S) = \max_{x \in S} v^T (x - w)$. The following lemma states a relationship between the support of vectors and inclusion between sets.

Lemma 2. *Let $S_1, S_2 \subseteq \mathbb{R}^n$ be two closed convex sets such that $S_1 \bigcap S_2 \neq \emptyset$. Let $w \in S_1 \bigcap S_2$. Then $S_1 \subseteq S_2$ iff $\forall v \in \mathbb{R}^n : \rho(v, w, S_1) \leq \rho(v, w, S_2)$.*

Let us say that two convex and closed sets S_1 and S_2 have non-empty intersection and w is a common point, i.e., inside the sets. According to the above lemma, saying that S_1 is contained inside S_2, is equivalent to saying that the maximum possible displacement in S_1 from w along the direction of any vector v is less than the maximum possible displacement in S_2 from w along the direction of the vector v.

Recall that an augmented complex zonotope is a Minkowski sum of a complex zonotope and a real zonotope, i.e., $\mathcal{C}(V, c, s) \oplus \mathcal{Z}(W, l, u)$. From Lemma 1, we see that the intersection of a sub-parallelotope $\mathcal{P}\left(K, \widehat{l}, \widehat{u}\right)$ with a zonotope $\mathcal{Z}(W, l, u)$ can be computed when $W = K^{\dagger}$. Motivated by this, we want to find a condition under which we can overapproximate the intersection $(\mathcal{C}(V, c, s) \oplus \mathcal{Z}(W, l, u)) \bigcap \mathcal{P}\left(K, \widehat{l}, \widehat{u}\right)$ by $\mathcal{C}(V, c, s) \oplus \left(\mathcal{Z}(W, l, u) \bigcap \mathcal{P}\left(K, \widehat{l}, \widehat{u}\right)\right)$, that is computing first the intersection (which can be done efficiently) and then the Minkowski sum. Indeed we can find the required condition for a more general case of any three closed convex sets S_1, S_2, S_3 (that is, find a condition under which $(S_1 \oplus S_2) \bigcap S_3$ can be overapproximated by $S_1 \oplus (S_2 \bigcap S_3)$) and apply this result to augmented complex zonotopes. We state this condition as follows.

Lemma 3. *Let $S_1 \subseteq \mathbb{C}^n$ and $S_2, S_3 \in \mathbb{R}^n$ be closed convex sets such that $S_2 \bigcap S_3 \neq \emptyset$ and $0 \in S_1$. Then $(S_1 \oplus S_2) \bigcap S_3 \subseteq S_1 \oplus (S_2 \cap S_3)$.*

Proof. Firstly, the imaginary parts of both sides of above inequality are equal to $\mathrm{Im}(S_1)$ because $\mathrm{Im}(S_2) = \mathrm{Im}(S_3) = 0$. So, we show the inclusion of real parts. Let $w \in S_2 \bigcap S_3$. Then, since $0 \in S_1$, so $w = w + 0 \in S_1 \oplus S_2 \implies w \in (\mathrm{Re}(S_1) \oplus S_2) \bigcap S_3$. So, based on Lemma 2, it sufficient to prove that for all $v \in \mathbb{R}^n$,

$$\rho\left(v, w, (\mathrm{Re}(S_1) \oplus S_2) \bigcap S_3\right) \leq \rho(v, w, \mathrm{Re}(S_1) \oplus (S_2 \cap S_3)).$$

Let us define $a = \rho(v, 0, \mathrm{Re}(S_1))$, $b = \rho(v, w, S_2)$ and $c = \rho(v, w, S_3)$. Since, $0 \in \mathrm{Re}(S_1)$, so $a = \max_{x \in \mathrm{Re}(S_1)} v^T x \geq v^T 0 = 0$, i.e., $a \geq 0$. Furthermore, $\rho(v, w, (\mathrm{Re}(S_1) \oplus S_2) \bigcap S_3) = \min(\rho(v, w, \mathrm{Re}(S_1) \oplus S_2), \rho(v, w, S_3))$. As $w = w + 0$, so the above equals $\min(\rho(v, 0, \mathrm{Re}(S_1)) + \rho(v, w, S_2), \rho(v, w, S_3)) =$

$\min(a+b,c)$. By a similar calculation, we can show $\rho\left(v, w, \text{Re}\left(S_1\right) \oplus \left(S_2 \cap S_3\right)\right) = a + \min(b,c)$. So, we need to prove that $\min(a+b,c) \leq a + \min(b,c)$. Since $a \geq 0$, so $\min(a + b, c) \leq \min(a + b, a + c) = a + \min(b, c)$. $\qquad\square$

Now we introduce the following *affine* functions which are used latter to express the overapproximation of the intersection between an augmented complex zonotope and a sub-parallelotope. A binary function $\widehat{\Lambda} : \mathbb{R}^k \times \overline{\mathbb{R}}^k$, called *min-approximation* function, is defined as follows: for $u \in \mathbb{R}^k$ and $\widehat{u} \in \overline{\mathbb{R}}^k$,

$$\left(\widehat{\Lambda}\left(u, \widehat{u}\right)\right)_i = \begin{cases} \widehat{u}_i & \text{if } \widehat{u}_i < \infty \\ u_i & \text{if } \widehat{u}_i = \infty \end{cases}$$. Similarly, another binary function $\overline{\Lambda} : \mathbb{R}^k \times \overline{\mathbb{R}}^k$,

called *max-approximation* function, is defined as follows: for $l \in \mathbb{R}^k$ and $\widehat{l} \in \overline{\mathbb{R}}^k$,

$$\left(\overline{\Lambda}\left(l, \widehat{l}\right)\right)_i = \begin{cases} \widehat{l}_i & \text{if } \widehat{l}_i > \infty \\ l_i & \text{if } \widehat{l}_i = -\infty \end{cases}$$. It is easy to see that the min-approximation

and max-approximation functions are affine, because for any one coordinate, a respective function is either a constant function or equal to the first argument, i.e., identity function. The following theorem states that an overapproximation of the intersection of an augmented complex zonotope with a sub-parallelotope can be expressed using these affine approximation functions.

Theorem 1. *Given a sub-parallelotope* $\mathcal{P}\left(\mathcal{K}, \widehat{l}, \widehat{u}\right)$ *and an augmented complex zonotope* $\mathcal{G}\left(V, c, s, \mathcal{K}^\dagger, l, u\right)$ *such that* VV^* *is non-singular,* $|V^\dagger c| \leq s$, $l \leq \overline{\Lambda}\left(l, \widehat{l}\right) \leq \widehat{\Lambda}(u, \widehat{u}) \leq u$, *then* $\mathcal{G}\left(V, c, s, \mathcal{K}^\dagger, l, u\right) \cap \mathcal{P}\left(\mathcal{K}, \widehat{l}, \widehat{u}\right) \subseteq \mathcal{G}\left(V, c, s, \mathcal{K}^\dagger, \overline{\Lambda}\left(l, \widehat{l}\right), \widehat{\Lambda}(u, \widehat{u})\right)$.

Proof Sketch. Consider $S_1 = \mathcal{C}\left(V, c, s\right)$, $S_2 = \mathcal{Z}\left(\mathcal{K}^\dagger, l, u\right)$ and $S_3 = \mathcal{P}\left(\mathcal{K}, \widehat{l}, \widehat{u}\right)$. First, we check that $0 \in S_1$ and $S_2 \cap S_3 \neq \emptyset$, and then we subsitute S_1, S_2 and S_3 in Lemma 3. To compute the intersection between S_2 and S_3, we use Lemma 1. $\qquad\square$

Similar to usual zonotopes, augmented complex zonotopes are closed under Minkowski sums and linear transformations, and their computations are also similar. The computation of some important operations are summarized as follows.

1. $A\mathcal{G}\left(V, c, s, W, l, u\right) = \mathcal{G}\left(AV, Ac, s, AW, l, u\right)$.
2. Given $\mathcal{G}_1 = \mathcal{G}\left(V, c, s, W, l, u\right)$ and $\mathcal{G}_2 = \mathcal{G}\left(V', c', s', W', l', u'\right)$, we have $\mathcal{G}_1 \oplus \mathcal{G}_2 = \mathcal{G}\left(\left[V \; V'\right], c + c', \begin{bmatrix} s \\ s' \end{bmatrix}, \left[W \; W'\right], \begin{bmatrix} l \\ l' \end{bmatrix}, \begin{bmatrix} u \\ u' \end{bmatrix}\right)$.
3. The limits of the projection of an augmented complex zonotope along any direction can be computed as follows. For $v \in \mathbb{R}^n$,

$$\max_{x \in \mathcal{G}(V,c,s,W,l,u)} v^T x = v^T \left(c + W \frac{l+u}{2}\right) + \left|v^T [V \; W]\right| \left(\begin{bmatrix} s \\ \frac{u-l}{2} \end{bmatrix}\right) \qquad (3)$$

To derive (3), we multiply the linear constraints with the center of the augmented complex zonotope and add an error term proportional to a set of scaling factors.

The center is $\left(c + W\frac{l+u}{2}\right)$, while the scaling factors are $\left[\begin{array}{c} s \\ \frac{u-l}{2} \end{array}\right]$. Based on (3), we derive the following Lemma relating the real projection of an augmented complex zonotope and a template complex zonotope.

Lemma 4. $\mathrm{Re}\left(\mathcal{G}\left(V, c, s, W, l, u\right)\right) = \mathrm{Re}\left(\mathcal{C}\left([V\ W], c + W\left(\frac{u+l}{2}\right), \left[\begin{array}{c} s \\ \frac{u-l}{2} \end{array}\right]\right)\right).$

Because of the above relationship, checking the inclusion between the real projections of two augmented complex zonotopes amounts to checking the inclusion between real projections of two template complex zonotopes. Therefore, we first review an inclusion relation between template complex zonotopes, which was earlier stated in [1].

Unlike usual zonotopes, template complex zonotopes can have non-polyhedral real projections. Checking the exact inclusion between two template complex zonotopes, in general, amounts to solving a non-convex optimization problem, which could be computationally intractable. Instead, a convex condition was proposed in [1], which is sufficient to guarantee the inclusion between template complex zonotopes. Here, we present this condition as a relation between template complex zonotopes.

Definition 5. *We define a relation "$\sqsubseteq$" between template complex zonotopes as* $\mathcal{C}\left(V'_{n\times m'}, c', s'\right) \sqsubseteq \mathcal{C}\left(V_{n\times m}, c, s\right)$ *if all of the below statements are collectively true.*

$$\exists X \in \mathbb{M}_{m\times m'}(\mathbb{C})\ and\ y \in \mathbb{C}^m\ s.t.$$

$$VX = V'\mathcal{D}\left(s'\right), \quad Vy = c' - c, \quad and \quad \max_{i=1}^{m}\left(|y_i| + \sum_{j=1}^{m'}|X_{ij}| - s_i\right) \leq 0 \tag{4}$$

Lemma 5 (Inclusion: template complex zonotopes). *The inclusion* $\mathcal{C}\left(V', c', s'\right) \subseteq \mathcal{C}\left(V, c, s\right)$ *holds if the relation* $\mathcal{C}\left(V', c', s'\right) \sqsubseteq \mathcal{C}\left(V, c, s\right)$ *is true.*

Proof idea. We relate the combining coefficients of the two template complex zonotopes by a linear transformation, with appropriate bounds on the transformation matrix such that the inclusion holds.   □

We extend the above inclusion relation to augmented complex zonotopes, based on Lemma 4 as follows.

Definition 6. *We say that* $\mathcal{G}\left(V', c', s', W', l', u'\right) \sqsubseteq \mathcal{G}\left(V, c, s, W, l, u\right)$ *if*

$$\mathcal{C}\left([V'\ W'], c' + W'\left(\frac{u'+l'}{2}\right), \left[\begin{array}{c} s' \\ \frac{u-l}{2} \end{array}\right]\right) \sqsubseteq \mathcal{C}\left([V\ W], c + W\left(\frac{u+l}{2}\right), \left[\begin{array}{c} s \\ \frac{u-l}{2} \end{array}\right]\right).$$

Lemma 6 (Inclusion between augmented complex zonotopes). *The real inclusion* $\mathrm{Re}\left(\mathcal{G}\left(V', c', s', W', l', u'\right)\right) \subseteq \mathrm{Re}\left(\mathcal{G}\left(V, c, s, W_{n\times k}, l, u\right)\right)$ *holds if the relation* $\mathcal{G}\left(V', c', s', W', l', u'\right) \sqsubseteq \mathcal{G}\left(V, c, s, W, l, u\right)$ *is true.*

For fixed V and V', we observe that (4) is equivalent to a set of convex constraints called second order conic constraints. Recall that a constraint of the form $\|Ax\|_2 + v^T x + w \leq 0$ on an n-dimensional variable x, given $A \in \mathbb{M}_{n \times k}(\mathbb{R})$, $v \in \mathbb{R}^n$ and $w \in \mathbb{R}$, is a second order conic constraint (SOCC). We also note that linear inequalities and equalities can be expressed in the form of SOCC described above. There are many convex optimization tools that can efficiently solve SOCC up to a high numerical precision. Our aforementioned observation about (4) is extended to augmented complex zonotopes and formalized as below.

Proposition 1. *For constant V, V', W, W', the relation $\mathcal{G}\left(V', c', s', W', l', u'\right) \sqsubseteq \mathcal{G}\left(V, c, s, W, l, u\right)$ is equivalent to a set of second order conic constraints on the variables $c, c', s, s', l, l', u, u'$ and some additional variables.*

4 Computation of Positive Invariants

In this section, we first derive a sufficient condition for positive invariance of an augmented complex zonotope. Also, we state conditions for containment of an initial set and satisfaction of polytopic safety constraints. Latter, we explain how to compute the augmented complex zontope based on these conditions.

Earlier, we had computed the linear transformations and Minkowki sums of augmented complex zonotope and possible overapproximations of their intersection with subparalleotopic constraints. Accordingly, we can compute the overapproximation of the reachable set of an augmented complex zonotope as another augmented complex zonotope. Then, we utilize the relation given in Definition 6 to deduce a sufficient condition for positive invariance, as follows. We consider a state set Γ given as, for a location $q \in Q$, $\Gamma_q = \mathrm{Re}\left(\mathcal{G}\left(V_q, c_q, s_q, \mathcal{K}_q^\dagger, l_q, u_q\right)\right)$ such that $V_q V_q^*$ is invertible. Let us consider that the additive input for an intralocation transition in any location $q \in Q$ is overapproximated as $U_q \subseteq \mathcal{G}\left(V_q^{in}, c_q^{in}, s_q^{in}, W_q^{in}, l_q^{in}, u_q^{in}\right)$. Similarly, for an edge $\sigma \in E$, let the additive input set be overapproximated as $\Omega_\sigma \subseteq \mathcal{G}\left(V_\sigma^{in}, c_\sigma^{in}, s_\sigma^{in}, W_\sigma^{in}, l_\sigma^{in}, u_\sigma^{in}\right)$. Furthermore, for any $q \in Q$, the safe set in the location is $\mathcal{S}_q = \mathcal{J}\left(T_q, d_q\right)$ and the initial set is $\mathcal{I}_q = \mathrm{Re}\left(\mathcal{G}\left(V_q^I, c_q^I, s_q^I, W_q^I, l_q^I, u_q^I\right)\right)$.

Lemma 7 (Positive invariance). *For all locations $q \in Q$ and all edges $\sigma \in E$, the inclusions $R_q\left(\Gamma_q\right) \subseteq \Gamma_q$ and $R_\sigma\left(\Gamma_{\sigma_1}\right) \subseteq \Gamma_{\sigma_2}$ holds if $\forall q \in Q$ and $\forall \sigma \in E$, all of the below statements are collectively true.*

/* intersection with staying conditions and one continuous transition */

$$|V_q^\dagger c_q| \leq s_q, \quad l_q \leq \overline{\Lambda}\left(l_q, \gamma_q^-\right) \leq \widehat{\Lambda}\left(u_q, \gamma_q^+\right) \leq u_q \tag{5}$$

there exist real vectors $c_q', s_q', l_q', u_q', l_q'', u_q''$ such that

$$c_q' = A_q c_q + c_q^{in}, \quad s_q' = \begin{bmatrix} s_q \\ s_q^{in} \end{bmatrix}, \quad l_q' = \begin{bmatrix} \overline{\Lambda}\left(l_q, \gamma_q^-\right) \\ l_q^{in} \end{bmatrix}, \quad u' = \begin{bmatrix} \widehat{\Lambda}\left(u_q, \gamma_q^+\right) \\ u_q^{in} \end{bmatrix} \tag{6}$$

/* inclusion condition */

$$\mathcal{G}\left(\left[A_q V_q \ \ V_q^{in}\right], c_q', s_q', \left[A_q \mathcal{K}_q^\dagger \ \ W_q^{in}\right], l_q', u_q'\right) \sqsubseteq \mathcal{G}\left(V_q, c_q, s_q, \mathcal{K}_q^\dagger, l_q'', u_q''\right)$$
$$l_q'' \leq \overline{\Lambda}\left(l_q'', \gamma_q^-\right) \leq \widehat{\Lambda}\left(u_q'', \gamma_q^+\right) \leq u_q'', \quad \overline{\Lambda}\left(l_q'', \gamma_q^-\right) \geq l_q \ \text{and} \ \widehat{\Lambda}\left(u_q'', \gamma_q^+\right) \leq u_q. \tag{7}$$

/* intersection with staying and guard condition of current location and one discrete transition*/

there exist real vectors $c_{\sigma_2}', s_{\sigma_2}', l_{\sigma_2}', u_{\sigma_2}', l_{\sigma_2}'', u_{\sigma_2}''$ such that

$$c_\sigma' = \Theta_\sigma c_{\sigma_1} + c_\sigma^{in}, \quad s_\sigma' = \begin{bmatrix} s_{\sigma_1} \\ s_\sigma^{in} \end{bmatrix}, \quad l_{\sigma_1} \leq \overline{\Lambda}\left(l_{\sigma_1}, \gamma_{\sigma_1}^-\right) \leq \widehat{\Lambda}\left(u_{\sigma_1}, \gamma_{\sigma_1}^+\right) \leq u_{\sigma_1} \tag{8}$$

$$l_\sigma' = \begin{bmatrix} \overline{\Lambda}\left(l_{\sigma_1}, \gamma_{\sigma_1}^- \bigvee \sigma^-\right) \\ l_\sigma^{in} \end{bmatrix}, \quad u_\sigma' = \begin{bmatrix} \widehat{\Lambda}\left(u_{\sigma_1}, \gamma_{\sigma_1}^+ \bigwedge \sigma^+\right) \\ u_\sigma^{in} \end{bmatrix} \tag{9}$$

/* intersection with staying condition of target location and inclusion condition */

$$\mathcal{G}\left(\left[\Theta_\sigma V_{\sigma_1} \ \ V_\sigma^{in}\right], c_\sigma', s_\sigma', \left[\Theta_\sigma \mathcal{K}_{\sigma_1}^\dagger \ \ W_\sigma^{in}\right], l_\sigma', u_\sigma'\right) \sqsubseteq \mathcal{G}\left(V_{\sigma_2}, c_{\sigma_2}, s_{\sigma_2}, \mathcal{K}_{\sigma_2}^\dagger, l_\sigma'', u_\sigma''\right)$$
$$l_\sigma'' \leq \overline{\Lambda}\left(l_\sigma'', \gamma_{\sigma_2}^-\right) \leq \widehat{\Lambda}\left(u_\sigma'', \gamma_{\sigma_2}^+\right) \leq u_\sigma''$$
$$\overline{\Lambda}\left(l_\sigma'', \gamma_{\sigma_2}^-\right) \geq l_{\sigma_2} \ \text{and} \ \widehat{\Lambda}\left(u_\sigma'', \gamma_{\sigma_2}^+\right) \leq u_{\sigma_2}. \tag{10}$$

Next, for the augmented complex zonotopic state set to contain the initial set, we state the following sufficient condition based on the inclusion relation between augmented complex zonotopes from Lemma 6. For a location $q \in Q, \mathcal{I}_q \subseteq \Gamma_q$ if,

$$\mathcal{G}\left(V_q^I, c_q^I, s_q^I, W_q^I, l_q^I, u_q^I\right) \sqsubseteq \mathcal{G}\left(V_q, c_q, s_q, \mathcal{K}_q^\dagger, l_q, u_q\right). \tag{11}$$

For satisfaction of polytopic safety constraints, i.e., for a location $q \in Q, \Gamma_q \subseteq \mathcal{S}_q$, the following is a necessary and sufficient condition, which is a reformulation of (3).

$$T_q\left(c_q + \mathcal{K}_q^\dagger\left(\frac{u_q + l_q}{2}\right)\right) + |T\left[V_q, \ \mathcal{K}_q^\dagger\right]| \begin{bmatrix} s \\ \frac{u_q - l_q}{2} \end{bmatrix} \leq d_q. \tag{12}$$

By simply collecting all the results of this section for computing a safe positive invariant, we state the following theorem.

Theorem 2. *If $\forall q \in Q$ and $\forall \sigma \in E$, all of the Eqs. (5–12) are collectively true, then the state set Γ is a positive invariant, satisfies the given safety constraints and contains the given initial set.*

Solving the conditions. First we note that the secondary template in a location is predefined as the pseudoinverse of the subparallelotopic template in the location, in accordance with the above results in this section. Then, we observe that for a fixed primary template in each location, the set of Eqs. (5–12) are equivalent to second order conic constraints on the primary offset, upper and lower interval bounds in each location and some additional variables. This can be inferred from the Proposition 1 and the fact that the min-approximation and max approximation functions are affine. So, we first fix the primary template in each location and solve the aforementioned constraints as a convex program. The choice of the primary template is explained below.

Choosing the primary template. Ensuring that the primary template has full rank, so that its pseudo-inverse as defined exists, we may collect all or some of the following vectors in the primary template. (1) Eigenvectors of the transformation matrices and their products, for the different transition maps. This is motivated by the observation that complex zonotopes generated by eigenvectors of a Schur stable matrix contract when multiplied by the matrix (see Proposition 4.3 of [2]). (2) The primary and secondary templates of the zonotopes which overapproximate the additive disturbance input sets and their products with the linear matrices of the transition maps. This is because the input set and its transformations are added in continuous step computation. (3) Orthogonal projections of the above vectors on the null space of the subparallelotopic template. This is because the proposed intersection in Theorem 1 is exact when the primary template belongs to the null space of the subparallelotopic template. (4) Adding any set of arbitrary vectors will increase the chance of computing a desired invariant, but at a computational expense. This is because the scaling factors will be adjusted accordingly by the optimizer.

5 Experiments

We performed experiments on 3 benchmark examples from the literature and compared the results with that obtained by the tool SpaceEx [13] which performs verification by step-by-step reachability computation. On one example, we compared the computational time with the reported results of the MPT tool [24]. For convex optimization, we used CVX (version 2.1) with MOSEK solver (version 7.1) and Matlab (version: 8.5/R2015a) on a computer with 1.4 GHz Intel Core i5 processor and 4 GB 1600 MHz DDR3. The precision of the solver is set to the default precision of CVX.

Robot with a Saturated Controller. Our first example is a benchmark model of a self-balancing two wheeled robot called NXTway-GS1 by Yorihisa Yamamoto, presented in the ARCH workshop [17]. We consider the sampled data (discrete time) networked control system model presented in the paper. In our experiment, we decoupled some unbounded directions of the dynamics of the system from bounded directions by making an appropriate linear transformation of the coordinates. The transformation is such that the coordinates corresponding to the body pitch angle and controller inputs are among the bounded directions. We do not explain the transformation here because it is beyond the scope of this paper.

The state space of the saturated system can be divided into 9 different regions such that the system exhibits different affine dynamics in different regions. Therefore, the saturated sampled data system can be seen as a discrete time affine

Table 1. Unsaturated robot model: results

Method		$|\psi| \leq$	Comp. time (s)
SpaceEx	Octagon template	UB	NT
	400 support vectors	UB	NT
Suggested in [17]		1.39	n/a
ACZ invariant		1.29	4

UB: >1000, NT: Not terminating in more than 180s, n/a: Not applicable/not available, ACZ: Augmented complex zonotope.

Table 2. Saturated robot model: results

Method		$|\psi| \leq$	Comp. time (s)
SpaceEx	Octagon template	UB	NT
	400 support vectors	UB	NT
Suggested in [17]		$1.571 - \epsilon :$ $\epsilon > 0$	n/a
ACZ invariant		1.13	45

UB: >1000, NT: Not terminating in more than 180s, n/a: Not applicable/not available, ACZ: Augmented complex zonotope.

Table 3. Small invariant computation: Perturbed double integrator

Method		$|x_1| \leq$	$|x_2| \leq$	Comp. time (s)
SpaceEx	Octagon template	0.38	0.43	1.7
	100 support vectors	0.38	0.43	23.6
ACZ invariant		0.38	0.36	5.1

Table 4. Large invariant computation: Perturbed double integrator

Method	Comp. time (s)
MPT tool [24]	107
ACZ	12

hybrid system. On the other hand, the unsaturated system has just one affine dynamics and is not a hybrid system. We model the saturated system using one location and nine self edges, corresponding to the nine different affine dynamics in different regions, which are specified by the guards on the edges. The unsaturated system is modelled with one location and no edges such that the only dynamics is the continuous affine dynamics in the location. The same discrete time models are specified in SpaceEx for comparison of performance.

Size of unsaturated model: 10 dimensional, 1 location, 0 edges.

Size of saturated model: 10 dimensional, 1 location and 9 edges.

The safety requirement is that the *body pitch angle* of the robot, which in our model is denoted by x_1, should be bounded within some value. In the benchmark, it was suggested that $x_1 \in \left[-\frac{\pi}{2} + \epsilon, \frac{\pi}{2} - \epsilon\right] : \epsilon > 0$ for the saturated system, while $x_1 \in \left[\frac{-\pi}{2.26}, \frac{\pi}{2.26}\right]$ for the unsaturated system. The initial set is the origin.

Experiment settings. The primary template for the hybrid system is chosen as the collection of the (complex) eigenvectors of linear matrices of all affine maps for the edge transitions, the orthonormal vectors to the guarding hyperplane normals and the projections of the eigenvectors on the subspace spanned by the orthonormal vectors. For the linear system, it consists of the eigenvectors of the linear map, the input set template and its multiplication by the linear matrix (related to affine map) and square of the linear matrix. Concerning the experiment using SpaceEx, we tested with the octagon template and a template with 400 uniformly sampled support vectors. For the hybrid system, we com-

Table 5. Networked vehicle platoon: results and matrices

Method		Slow switching				Fast switching			
		$-x_1 \leq$	$-x_4 \leq$	$-x_7 \leq$	Comp.time (s)	$-x_1 \leq$	$-x_4 \leq$	$-x_7 \leq$	Comp. time (s)
SpaceEx	Octagon template	28	27	10	NT	UB	UB	UB	NT
	100 support vectors	28	25	13	1.3	UB	UB	UB	NT
Real zonotope [21]		25	25	10	n/a	n/a	n/a	n/a	n/a
ACZ invariant		28	26	12	12	46	54	57	12.6

UB: >1000, NT: Not terminating in more than 180s, n/a: Not applicable/not available, ACZ: Augmented complex zonotope.

puted a single augmented complex zonotopic invariant satisfying both the upper and lower safety bounds. But for the linear system, we computed two different invariants, each of which satisfies the upper and lower bounds, respectively.

Results. For both the hybrid and the linear systems, we could verify smaller magnitudes for the bounds on the pitch angle than what is proposed in the benchmark [17]. But the SpaceEx tool could not find a finite bound for either of the above systems. The results are reported in the Tables 1 and 2.

Perturbed Double Integrator. Our second example is a perturbed double integrator system given in [24]. The closed loop system with a feedback control is piecewise affine, having four different affine dynamics in four different regions of space, as $\mathbf{x}(t+1) = M_i\mathbf{x}(t) + w$, $i \in \{1, 2, 3, 4\}$. The additive disturbance input w is bounded as $\|w\|_\infty \leq 0.2$.

We perform two different experiments on this system. In the first experiment, we try to verify the smallest possible magnitude of bounds on the two coordinates, denoted x_1 and x_2. We compare these bounds with that found by the SpaceEx tool. In the second experiment, we try to quickly compute a large invariant for the system under the safety constraints given in [24]. We draw comparison in terms of the computation time with the reported result for the MPT tool [24].

In our formalism, we model the system with 4 locations and 12 edges connecting all the locations. Appropriate staying conditions are specified in each location, reflecting the division of the state space into different regions where the dynamics is affine. The initial set is the origin. The same model is specified in SpaceEx.

Size of model: 2 dimensions, 4 locations and 12 edges.

Experiment settings. For the primary template, we collected the (complex) eigenvectors of all linear matrices of the affine maps and their binary products. For the SpaceEx tool, we experimented with two different templates, the octagon template and a template with 100 uniformly sampled support vectors.

Results. In the first experiment, we verified smaller bounds for x_2 than that of SpaceEx, while the bounds verified for x_1 were equal for both methods. In our second experiment on this example, the computation time for finding a large invariant by our method is significantly smaller than that of the reported result for the MPT tool. The results are summarized in the Tables 3 and 4.

Networked Platoon of Vehicles. Our third example is a model of a networked cooperative platoon of vehicles, which is presented as a benchmark in the ARCH workshop [21]. The platoon consists of three vehicles M_1, M_2 and M_3 along with a leader board ahead. In the benchmark proposal, the continuous time dynamics of the vehicles is described as a hybrid system with two possible dynamics, related to the presence and absence of communication between the vehicles, respectively. Furthermore, there are time constraints on when the switching can happen. The state of the system is a 9 dimensional vector x. Any upper bounds on $-x_1$, $-x_4$, and $-x_7$ provide lower limits on the reference distances of M_1, M_2 and M_3 to their successor vehicles, beyond which the platoon is will not collide. Therefore, the verification challenge is to find the smallest possible upper bounds on $-x_1$, $-x_4$, and $-x_7$. The benchmark then provides the experimental results for the case when the minimum dwell time is 20 s, i.e., $C = \{c > 20\}$ (also specified in the distributed SpaceEx implementation[1]). In our experiment, apart from the case of the minimum dwell time of 20s (slow switching), we also study a case of fast switching, where the possible switching times C is the set of all non-negative integers. We could specify discrete time models that overapproximate the reachable sets of both these above models.

Size of slow switching model: 9 dimensions, 2 locations and 4 edges.

Size of fast switching (integer times) model: 9 dimensions, 2 locations, 2 edges.

Experiment settings. We chose the primary template as the collection of the (complex) eigenvectors of linear matrices of the affine maps in the two locations and their binary products, the axis aligned box template and the templates used for overapproximating the input sets. For the SpaceEx tool, we experimented with two templates, octagon and hundred uniformly sampled support vectors.

Results. For the large minimum dwell time of 20 s, the discrete time SpaceEx implementation and also a method based on using real zonotopes [21] could verify slightly smaller bounds compared to our approach. But for the small minimum dwell time (1 s) model, SpaceEx could not even find a finite set of bounds, whereas our approach could verify a finite set of bounds. The reason is that the system is more stable under slow switching as compared to fast switching. These results are reported in the Table 5.

6   Conclusion

We introduced augmented complex zonotopes as a more general set representation than template complex zonotopes, based on which we derived efficiently

---

[1] http://cps-vo.org/node/15096.

solvable conditions for computing invariants, subject to linear safety constraints, for discrete time affine hybrid systems with linear guards and additive disturbance input. Like template complex zonotopes, augmented complex zonotopes have the advantage that we can meaningfully choose the templates for efficient fixpoint computation, based on the eigenstructure and other relevant aspects of the dynamics. But additionally, we overcame a drawback of template complex zonotopes in that we derived a simple algebraic expression for reasonable overapproximation of the intersection with a class of linear constraints. We use this algebraic expression to obtain of a set of second order conic constraints that can be efficiently solved to compute an invariant. In contrast to the step-by-step reachability computation approaches that iteratively accumulate overapproximation error, we instead compute an invariant in a single convex optimization step such that the optimizer inherently minimizes the overapproximation error. We demonstrated the efficiency of our approach on some benchmark examples.

As future work, we can investigate ways to minimize the overapproximation error in the intersection operation, such that the overapproximation can still be algebraically computed. In particular, the relation between the choice of the template and the over-approximation error in the intersection has to be analyzed. Also, we would like to extend this computational framework to continuous time hybrid systems.

References

1. Adimoolam, A., Dang, T.: Template complex zonotopes for stability and invariant computation. In: American Control Conference (ACC). IEEE (2017)
2. Adimoolam, A.S., Dang, T.: Using complex zonotopes for stability verification. In: American Control Conference (ACC), pp. 4269–4274. IEEE (2016)
3. Adjé, A.: Coupling policy iterations with piecewise quadratic lyapunov functions. In: Proceedings of the 20th International Conference on Hybrid Systems: Computation and Control (HSCC 2017), Pittsburgh, 18–20 April 2017, pp. 143–152 (2017)
4. Adjé, A., Garoche, P., Werey, A.: Quadratic zonotopes - an extension of zonotopes to quadratic arithmetics. In: Proceedings of the 13th Asian Symposium on Programming Languages and Systems (APLAS 2015), pp. 127–145 (2015)
5. Allamigeon, X., Gaubert, S., Goubault, É.: Inferring min and max invariants using max-plus polyhedra. In: Alpuente, M., Vidal, G. (eds.) SAS 2008. LNCS, vol. 5079, pp. 189–204. Springer, Heidelberg (2008). doi:10.1007/978-3-540-69166-2_13
6. Althoff, M.: Reachability analysis of nonlinear systems using conservative polynomialization and non-convex sets. In: Proceedings of the 16th International Conference on Hybrid Systems: Computation and Control (HSCC 2013), pp. 173–182 (2013)
7. Dagnaia, R., Rodríguez-Carbonell, E., Zaffanella, E.: Generation of basic semialgebraic invariants using convex polyhedra. In: Hankin, C., Siveroni, I. (eds.) SAS 2005. LNCS, vol. 3672, pp. 19–34. Springer, Heidelberg (2005). doi:10.1007/11547662_4
8. Bensalem, S., Lakhnech, Y.: Automatic generation of invariants. Form. Methods Syst. Des. 15(1), 75–92 (1999)

9. Bouissou, O., Goubault, E., Putot, S., Tekkal, K., Vedrine, F.: HybridFluctuat: a static analyzer of numerical programs within a continuous environment. In: Bouajjani, A., Maler, O. (eds.) CAV 2009. LNCS, vol. 5643, pp. 620–626. Springer, Heidelberg (2009). doi:10.1007/978-3-642-02658-4_46

10. Colón, M.A., Sankaranarayanan, S., Sipma, H.B.: Linear invariant generation using non-linear constraint solving. In: Hunt, W.A., Somenzi, F. (eds.) CAV 2003. LNCS, vol. 2725, pp. 420–432. Springer, Heidelberg (2003). doi:10.1007/978-3-540-45069-6_39

11. Cousot, P., Halbwachs, N.: Automatic discovery of linear restraints among variables of a program. In: Conference Record of the Fifth Annual ACM SIGPLAN-SIGACT Symposium on Principles of Programming Languages, Tucson, pp. 84–97 (1978)

12. Dang, T., Gawlitza, T.M.: Template-based unbounded time verification of affine hybrid automata. In: Yang, H. (ed.) APLAS 2011. LNCS, vol. 7078, pp. 34–49. Springer, Heidelberg (2011). doi:10.1007/978-3-642-25318-8_6

13. Frehse, G., et al.: SpaceEx: scalable verification of hybrid systems. In: Gopalakrishnan, G., Qadeer, S. (eds.) CAV 2011. LNCS, vol. 6806, pp. 379–395. Springer, Heidelberg (2011). doi:10.1007/978-3-642-22110-1_30

14. Ghorbal, K., Goubault, E., Putot, S.: The zonotope abstract domain Taylor1+. In: Bouajjani, A., Maler, O. (eds.) CAV 2009. LNCS, vol. 5643, pp. 627–633. Springer, Heidelberg (2009). doi:10.1007/978-3-642-02658-4_47

15. Girard, A.: Reachability of uncertain linear systems using zonotopes. In: Morari, M., Thiele, L. (eds.) HSCC 2005. LNCS, vol. 3414, pp. 291–305. Springer, Heidelberg (2005). doi:10.1007/978-3-540-31954-2_19

16. Goubault, E.: Static analysis by abstract interpretation of numerical programs and systems, and FLUCTUAT. In: Logozzo, F., Fähndrich, M. (eds.) SAS 2013. LNCS, vol. 7935, pp. 1–3. Springer, Heidelberg (2013). doi:10.1007/978-3-642-38856-9_1

17. Heinz, T., Oehlerking, J., Woehrle, M.: Benchmark: reachability on a model with holes. In: ARCH@ CPSWeek, pp. 31–36 (2014)

18. Jeannet, B., Miné, A.: APRON: a library of numerical abstract domains for static analysis. In: Bouajjani, A., Maler, O. (eds.) CAV 2009. LNCS, vol. 5643, pp. 661–667. Springer, Heidelberg (2009). doi:10.1007/978-3-642-02658-4_52

19. Kurzhanski, A., Varaiya, P.: Ellipsoidal techniques for reachability analysis: internal approximation. Syst. Control Lett. 41(3), 201–211 (2000)

20. Maïga, M., Combastel, C., Ramdani, N., Travé-Massuyès, L.: Nonlinear hybrid reachability using set integration and zonotopic enclosures. In: European Control Conference (ECC 2014), Strasbourg, 24–27 June 2014, pp. 234–239 (2014)

21. Makhlouf, I.B., Kowalewski, S.: Networked cooperative platoon of vehicles for testing methods and verification tools. In: ARCH@ CPSWeek, pp. 37–42 (2014)

22. Miné, A.: The octagon abstract domain. High. Order Symb. Comput. 19(1), 31–100 (2006)

23. Prajna, S., Jadbabaie, A.: Safety verification of hybrid systems using barrier certificates. In: Alur, R., Pappas, G.J. (eds.) HSCC 2004. LNCS, vol. 2993, pp. 477–492. Springer, Heidelberg (2004). doi:10.1007/978-3-540-24743-2_32

24. Rakovic, S., Grieder, P., Kvasnica, M., Mayne, D., Morari, M.: Computation of invariant sets for piecewise affine discrete time systems subject to bounded disturbances. In: 43rd IEEE Conference on Decision and Control (CDC 2004), vol. 2, pp. 1418–1423. IEEE (2004)

25. Rodríguez-Carbonell, E., Kapur, D.: Automatic generation of polynomial invariants of bounded degree using abstract interpretation. Sci. Comput. Program. 64(1), 54–75 (2007)

26. Rodríguez-Carbonell, E., Tiwari, A.: Generating polynomial invariants for hybrid systems. In: Morari, M., Thiele, L. (eds.) HSCC 2005. LNCS, vol. 3414, pp. 590–605. Springer, Heidelberg (2005). doi:10.1007/978-3-540-31954-2_38

27. Roux, P., Garoche, P.-L.: Computing quadratic invariants with min- and max-policy iterations: a practical comparison. In: Jones, C., Pihlajasaari, P., Sun, J. (eds.) FM 2014. LNCS, vol. 8442, pp. 563–578. Springer, Cham (2014). doi:10.1007/978-3-319-06410-9_38

28. Roux, P., Jobredeaux, R., Garoche, P., Feron, E.: A generic ellipsoid abstract domain for linear time invariant systems. In: Hybrid Systems: Computation and Control (part of CPS Week 2012) (HSCC 2012), Beijing, 17–19 April 2012, pp. 105–114 (2012)

29. Sankaranarayanan, S., Dang, T., Ivančić, F.: Symbolic model checking of hybrid systems using template polyhedra. In: Ramakrishnan, C.R., Rehof, J. (eds.) TACAS 2008. LNCS, vol. 4963, pp. 188–202. Springer, Heidelberg (2008). doi:10.1007/978-3-540-78800-3_14

30. Sankaranarayanan, S., Sipma, H.B., Manna, Z.: Constructing invariants for hybrid systems. In: Alur, R., Pappas, G.J. (eds.) HSCC 2004. LNCS, vol. 2993, pp. 539–554. Springer, Heidelberg (2004). doi:10.1007/978-3-540-24743-2_36

31. Sassi, M.A.B., Girard, A., Sankaranarayanan, S.: Iterative computation of polyhedral invariants sets for polynomial dynamical systems. In: 53rd IEEE Conference on Decision and Control (CDC 2014), Los Angeles, 15–17 December 2014, pp. 6348–6353 (2014)

32. Scott, J.K., Raimondo, D.M., Marseglia, G.R., Braatz, R.D.: Constrained zonotopes: a new tool for set-based estimation and fault detection. Automatica **69**, 126–136 (2016)

33. Sogokon, A., Ghorbal, K., Jackson, P.B., Platzer, A.: A method for invariant generation for polynomial continuous systems. In: Jobstmann, B., Leino, K.R.M. (eds.) VMCAI 2016. LNCS, vol. 9583, pp. 268–288. Springer, Heidelberg (2016). doi:10.1007/978-3-662-49122-5_13

34. Tiwari, A., Rueß, H., Saïdi, H., Shankar, N.: A technique for invariant generation. In: Margaria, T., Yi, W. (eds.) TACAS 2001. LNCS, vol. 2031, pp. 113–127. Springer, Heidelberg (2001). doi:10.1007/3-540-45319-9_9

Conic Abstractions for Hybrid Systems

Sergiy Bogomolov[1,2], Mirco Giacobbe[2(✉)], Thomas A. Henzinger[2], and Hui Kong[2(✉)]

[1] Australian National University, Canberra, Australia
[2] IST Austria, Klosterneuburg, Austria
{mgiacobbe,hui.kong}@ist.ac.at

Abstract. Despite researchers' efforts in the last couple of decades, reachability analysis is still a challenging problem even for linear hybrid systems. Among the existing approaches, the most practical ones are mainly based on bounded-time reachable set over-approximations. For the purpose of unbounded-time analysis, one important strategy is to abstract the original system and find an invariant for the abstraction. In this paper, we propose an approach to constructing a new kind of abstraction called conic abstraction for affine hybrid systems, and to computing reachable sets based on this abstraction. The essential feature of a conic abstraction is that it partitions the state space of a system into a set of convex polyhedral cones which is derived from a uniform conic partition of the derivative space. Such a set of polyhedral cones is able to cut all trajectories of the system into almost straight segments so that every segment of a reach pipe in a polyhedral cone tends to be straight as well, and hence can be over-approximated tightly by polyhedra using similar techniques as *HyTech* or *PHAVer*. In particular, for diagonalizable affine systems, our approach can guarantee to find an invariant for unbounded reachable sets, which is beyond the capability of bounded-time reachability analysis tools. We implemented the approach in a tool and experiments on benchmarks show that our approach is more powerful than *SpaceEx* and *PHAVer* in dealing with diagonalizable systems.

Keywords: Affine system · Hybrid system · Reachability analysis · Conic abstraction · Discrete abstraction

1 Introduction

Hybrid systems [1,2] are systems that admit interacting discrete and continuous dynamics. Reachability analysis of hybrid systems has been a major research issue over the past couple of decades [3–8]. An important part of the effort has been devoted to hybrid systems where the continuous dynamics is described by linear or affine differential equations or inclusions. For the purpose of efficient computation, a number of representations of convex set have been proposed, including polyhedrons [9,10], ellipsoids [11,12], hyperrectangles [13], zonotopes [14,15], and support functions [16]. A common feature of these approaches is

© Springer International Publishing AG 2017
A. Abate and G. Geeraerts (Eds.): FORMATS 2017, LNCS 10419, pp. 116–132, 2017.
DOI: 10.1007/978-3-319-65765-3_7

that all of them apply only to reachability analysis with bounded continuous time although sometimes a fixed point could be found.

For the purpose of unbounded-time analysis, a very useful strategy is to use lightweight runtime technique for continuous online verification [17,18], and another important strategy is to abstract the original system and find an invariant for the abstraction [19]. However, obtaining a high-quality abstraction automatically for the original system is challenging by itself and this is why *PHAVer* chooses to leave this important work to users, who have some domain expertise available for this purpose [20]. Roughly speaking, the ultimate goal of abstraction is to use a partition of the state space which is as coarse as possible, to derive an over-approximation of the original system which is as accurate as possible and allows a computation of the reachable state set which is as efficient as possible. Depending on the set representation that is used, the schemes that have been proposed for state space partition vary significantly [5,21–28]. When polyhedra are used for the set representation of states, a guiding principle for state space partitioning is that the partition should result in a set of regions that are as "straight" as possible. By "straight region", we mean that the maximal angle between the derivative vectors in that region (which we define as the *twisting* of the region) is small, so that every trajectory tends to be straight in the region. The benefit of straight regions is that they can be over-approximated accurately by polyhedra. However, for a given system, obtaining the least number of straight regions under a given threshold of twisting is by no means trivial.

With this principle in mind, we propose a new abstraction called *conic abstraction* for affine hybrid systems and we compute reachable state sets based on the abstraction. Given an n-D linear system defined by $\dot{x} = Ax$, assume that A is an invertible matrix (note that any affine system $\dot{x} = Ax + b$ can be transformed into a linear system under this assumption). The basic idea behind conic abstraction is as follows. First, the derivative space of the system is partitioned uniformly into a set D of convex polyhedral cones. Then, D is mapped back from the derivative space to the state space to obtain a conic partition C of state space, i.e., $\forall C_i \in C : \exists D_i \in D : C_i = \{A^{-1}y \mid y \in D_i\}$. Finally, every state region C_i is treated as a discrete location ("mode") and the discrete transitions between these modes are decided on-the-fly according to whether there exists a trajectory between them. By doing so, we can easily obtain the differential inclusion D_i for each polyhedral cone C_i. Therefore, for any subset I_i of C_i, the reachable set of I_i in C_i can be overapproximated by $(I_i \oplus D_i) \cap C_i$, where $\oplus$ denotes the Minkowski sum. More importantly, since the twisting of C_i is determined by the maximal angle of D_i, the partition can be refined easily to any desired precision, by shrinking the maximal angle of the conic partition of the derivative space. Note that an important feature of C_i is that it is an unbounded set, however, with a bounded twisting, which means that each C_i captures infinitely long trajectories only if they are straight enough. *Diagonalizable* affine systems, for which the matrix A is diagonalizable, form such a class of systems, because for diagonalizable systems all trajectories eventually evolve into approximately straight lines.

Using properties of diagonalizable affine systems, we develop an algorithm that constructs a conic abstraction as a directed acyclic graph (DAG) for which an invariant (i.e., an over-approximation of the reachable state set) exists and the computation of the invariant is guaranteed to terminate. The algorithm is implemented in a tool and experiments on randomly generated examples as well as published benchmarks show that our approach is more powerful than *PHAVer* in finding unbounded invariants. Note that computing an unbounded invariant for diagonalizable affine systems lies beyond the capability of tools for time-bounded reachability analysis, such as *SpaceEx* [29].

The main contributions of this paper are as follows. First, we propose conic abstractions and a method for constructing them for affine hybrid systems. The core idea lies in deriving a state space partition from a uniform partition of the derivative space. Second, we develop an algorithm for building conic abstractions as DAGs for diagonalizable affine systems and for computing invariants on these abstractions. Finally, we implement and evaluate our approach in a tool.

The paper is organized as follows. Section 2 is devoted to preliminary definitions. In Sect. 3, we introduce conic abstractions for affine systems. In Sect. 4, we show how to construct conic abstractions as DAGs for diagonalizable systems. Section 5 describes how we compute invariants for continuous systems and affine hybrid systems. In Sect. 6, we present our experimental results. Finally, we conclude with Sect. 7.

2 Preliminaries

In this section, we recall some concepts used throughout the paper. We first clarify some notation conventions. We use bold uppercase letters such as A to denote matrices and bold lowercase letters such as b to denote vectors and $diag(\lambda_1, \cdots, \lambda_n)$ to denote a diagonal matrix with $\lambda_1, \cdots, \lambda_n$ as its diagonal elements. We call a dynamical system defined as $\dot{x} = Ax + b$ an affine system and we use a superscript T for the transpose of a matrix.

Definition 1 (Affine System). *An n-dimensional affine system consists of a matrix $A \in \mathbb{R}^{n \times n}$ and a vector $b \in \mathbb{R}^n$, which define the vector flow $\dot{x} = Ax + b$, and an initial region $X_0 \subseteq \mathbb{R}^n$ defined by a polyhedron.*

Whenever the initial set is immaterial, we refer to an affine system just as to $\dot{x} = Ax + b$. We next introduce the concept of Lie derivative.

Definition 2 (Lie derivative). *For a given polynomial $p \in \mathbb{K}[x]$ and a continuous system $\dot{x} = f$, the **Lie derivative** of $p \in \mathbb{K}[x]$ along f is defined as $\mathcal{L}_f p \stackrel{def}{=} \langle \nabla p, f^T \rangle$.*

For an affine system $\dot{x} = Ax + b$, we can simply write the Lie derivative as $\mathcal{L}_A \langle a, x \rangle = \langle aA, x^T \rangle + \langle a, b^T \rangle$. We call a polyhedral cone C an intersection of linear inequalities of the form $\langle a, x \rangle \leq 0$, and we denote its boundary as ∂C. For $X, Y \subseteq \mathbb{R}^n$, $X \oplus Y$ denotes their Minkowski sum $\{x + y : x \in X \text{ and } y \in Y\}$, and for $A \in \mathbb{R}^{n \times n}$ and $X \subseteq \mathbb{R}^n$, AX denotes the linear transformation $\{Ax : x \in X\}$.

3   Conic Abstractions of Affine Systems

Discrete abstraction is a basic strategy for verifying continuous and hybrid systems. There are many abstraction approaches proposed for this purpose. Rectangular abstraction [5,19,30] and nonlinear abstraction [22–24,26] are widely used. However, even for linear systems, the existing abstraction approaches are still inefficient. In this section, focusing on linear systems, we propose a new abstraction approach called *conic abstraction*. However, since every affine system can be transformed into an equivalent linear system $\dot{x} = Ax$, as we discuss in Sec. 4, our discussion applies to affine systems too.

The idea is that we partition the state space of a linear system into a set of convex polyhedral cones. We call this set a *conic partition*.

Definition 3 (Conic Partition). *A conic partition is a set of polyhedral cones Δ such that $\cup_{C_i \in \Delta} C_i = \mathbb{R}^n$ and every two cones $C_1, C_2 \in \Delta$ have disjoint interiors, i.e., $(C_1 \backslash \partial C_1) \cap (C_2 \backslash \partial C_2) = \emptyset$.*

We call an element of the partition $C \in \Delta$ a region. Then we construct a graph whose vertices correspond to partition regions and edges indicate possible flow between them. We call such a graph a *conic abstraction*.

Definition 4 (Conic Abstraction). *The conic abstraction of the linear system $\dot{x} = Ax$ derived from the conic partition Δ consists of the finite directed graph (L, E) as follows. Every vertex $l_C \in L$ corresponds to one and only one cone $C \in \Delta$. There exists an edge $(l_{C_1}, l_{C_2}) \in E$ if and only if there exists a plane $F_1 = \{x \mid \langle a, x^T \rangle = 0\}$ such that (1) $\partial C_1 \cap \partial C_2 \subseteq F_1$, (2) $C_1 \subseteq \{x \mid \langle a, x^T \rangle \leq 0\}$, (3) the Lie derivative of $\langle a, x^T \rangle$ is non-negative at some common point, i.e., $\mathcal{L}_A \langle a, x^T \rangle \geq 0$ for some $x \in \partial C_1 \cap \partial C_2$.*

We elaborate on how to construct a conic abstraction for diagonalizable systems in Sect. 4. A conic abstraction can be seen as a Linear Hybrid Automaton (LHA, [1]), whose locations l_C are such that its invariant is given by C, its flow is given by a differential inclusion defined as $\dot{x} \in AC$, and whose switch guards consist of the common facet of the respective adjacent cones.

Example 1 (running example). Consider the linear system described by $\dot{x} = -2x - 2y, \dot{y} = -5x + y$. A conic partition of the state space, the corresponding differential inclusion and the conic abstraction of the system is shown in Fig. 1a, b and c, respectively. As you can see, both the invariant and the differential inclusion of each location are polyhedral cones.   □

Similarly as for the symbolic reachability analysis of LHA [2], the set of states that are reachable from an initial set $X \subseteq \mathbb{R}^n$ through the continuous flow at location $l_C \in L$ corresponding to $C \in \Delta$ is given by

$$(X \oplus AC) \cap C. \tag{1}$$

A conic abstraction represents an overapproximation of the system, whose tightness depends on the maximum angle between any two points in the cone

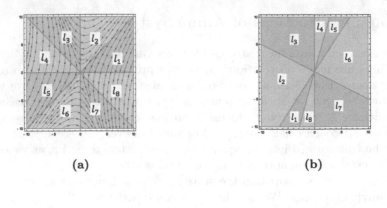

(a)   (b)

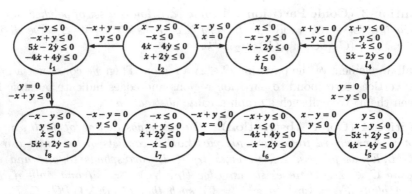

(c)

Fig. 1. Example 1. (a) Conic partition of state space. (b) Conic differential inclusion. (c) Conic abstraction of the system.

AC in derivative space. Roughly speaking, the more acute the cone AC in derivative space, the more accurate the overapproximation. Figure 2a shows a comparison between conic partitions with different accuracies (depicted in two different shades) for the same initial region. We encapsulate the accuracy given by a partition with the notion of twisting.

Definition 5 (Twisting of a state region). *Let $\dot{x} = Ax$ be a linear system and $P \subseteq \mathbb{R}^n$ be a (not necessarily conic) region of the state space. Then P is said to have a twisting of θ (or to be θ twisted) if it satisfies that*

$$\sup_{x_1, x_2 \in P} \arccos\left(\frac{\langle \dot{x}_1, \dot{x}_2 \rangle}{\|\dot{x}_1\|\|\dot{x}_2\|}\right) = \theta. \tag{2}$$

Intuitively, a cone with smaller twisting allows only trajectory segments that are almost straight, inducing a more accurate overapproximation. In the context of conic abstraction, properly inducing smaller and smaller twistings induce refinements of the abstraction, providing a better overapproximation.

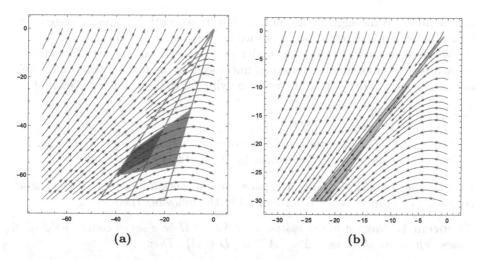

Fig. 2. (a) Overapproximation inside different cones. The smaller the cone, the more precise the overapproximation. (b) A cone capable of offering accurate overapproximation for unbounded reach pipe.

Definition 6 (Conic abstraction refinement). *Given two conic abstractions* (L_1, E_1) *and* (L_2, E_2) *for a linear system* $\dot{x} = Ax$, (L_2, E_2) *refines* (L_1, E_1) *if* $|L_2| > |L_1|$ *and for all* $l_1 \in L_1$ *with cone* C_1 *there does always exist* $l_2^1, \ldots, l_2^m \in L_2$ *with cones* $C_2^1, \ldots, C_2^m$ *such that* $C_1 = C_2^1 \cup \cdots \cup C_2^m$.

It is subject of Sect. 4 how to generate abstraction refinements by tuning the value of twisting.

The property we desire is that the twisting of every state partition is bounded by a small angle θ. A common strategy to achieve this goal is to split the state space into small rectangles iteratively until the twisting of each rectangle falls below θ [19,30,31]. However, such strategy is inefficient, as the twisting may not change uniformly in a rectangular partition. On the contrary, a conic partition naturally enjoys bounded twisting using unbounded regions. This allows a conic partition to accurately overapproximate both bounded and unbounded reach pipes, if in the latter case the trajectories are straight enough. Figure 2b shows such an example, where the tiny cone overapproximates all trajectories entering it, as they tend to be parallel to its left boundary.

3.1 Conic Abstractions Derived from Derivative Space Partitions

In existing work on discrete abstraction of continuous systems, to obtain a high-quality state space partition, the focus is mostly placed on state space. However, what really matters here is the derivative space. Therefore, our state space partition should be derived from a derivative space partition. Given a continuous system $\dot{x} = f(x)$, every convex cone D in the derivative space with a maximal angle θ corresponds to a set C of states which has a twisting of θ. Moreover, C

can be obtained through simple substitution. However, for nonlinear systems, C is nonlinear and is hard to handle, so we leave it for future work.

We assume that the systems under consideration are linear. To derive a conic abstraction for an n-dimensional linear system, we first partition the whole derivative space into a set Ω of convex polyhedral cones which satisfies that

1. $\bigcup_{D_i \in \Omega} D_i = \mathbb{R}^n$;
2. $\forall D_i, D_j \in \Omega : (D_i \backslash \partial D_i) \bigcap (D_i \backslash \partial D_j) = \emptyset$;
3. $\forall D_i \in \Omega : \sphericalangle D_i \leq \theta$, where $\sphericalangle D_i$ denotes the maximal angle of D_i (i.e. the maximal angle between the vectors in D_i) and θ is a given bound.

By mapping Ω back to the state space, we can obtain another set Δ of state regions. The property of Δ is formalized in the following theorem.

Theorem 1. *Given a linear system $\dot{x} = Ax$ let Ω be a set of convex polyhedral cones defined as above and $\Delta = \{A^{-1}D \mid D \in \Omega\}$. Then,*

1. *every $C_i \in \Delta$ is a convex polyhedral cone and the twisting of C_i is θ-bounded;*
2. $\bigcup_{C_i \in \Delta} C_i = \mathbb{R}^n$;
3. $\forall C_i, C_j \in \Delta : (C_i \backslash \partial C_i) \bigcap (C_i \backslash \partial C_j) = \emptyset$;

Remark 1. According to Theorem 1, we know that, given any linear system $\mathcal{H}$ with an invertible matrix A and a θ-bounded conic partition Ω of the derivative space, a conic partition Δ for the state space with θ-bounded twisting can be obtained by a linear transformation. Note that the twisting of C_i is θ-bounded does not mean that C_i is θ-bounded. Conversely, the maximal angle of each cone C_i varies significantly depending on how straight the trajectories are in that cone. Roughly speaking, the straighter the trajectories are, the larger the maximal angle of C_i is, provided that the twisting is the same. □

Now, let us get back to the issue of generating a conic partition of the derivative space. Our approach borrows the idea of slicing watermelons. Concretely, given an n-dimensional derivative space, we first choose a group of seed planes passing through the origin and then generate a cluster of planes by rotating each seed plane counterclockwise around an independent axis by a fixed angle θ_1, step by step until no further θ_1 rotation is possible. Finally, the whole vector space can be sliced into a set of convex polyhedral cones by the generated planes and each of them is θ_2-bounded for some θ_2. By mapping these cones into the state space, we can achieve a conic partition of θ_2-bounded twisting for the state space. The following example shows how a conic state space partition derived from a uniform derivative space partition looks like.

Example 2 (running example). Consider the following linear system $\mathcal{H}$ described by $\dot{x} = -2x - 2y, \dot{y} = -5x + y$. As shown in Fig. 3a, the derivative space is first uniformly partitioned into 18 cones. Then, these cones are mapped into the state space. As can be seen in Fig. 3b, in every cone, the straighter the trajectories are, the larger the maximal angle of the cone is. □

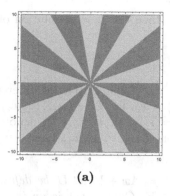

(a)

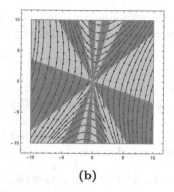

(b)

Fig. 3. Example 2 (a) Uniformly conic partition of the the derivative space. (b) Conic partition of state space derived from the derivative space partition.

The reachable set computation of a conic abstraction is a basic operation of linear hybrid automata. As usual, due to the undecidable nature of the issue, the reachable set computation of a conic abstraction cannot guarantee to terminate for a general linear system. However, for the conic abstraction of a specific class of systems, the reachable set computation can be guaranteed to terminate, which is shown in the next section.

4   Diagonalizable Systems

In this section, we focus on a class of affine systems for which the matrix used to describe the system dynamics is diagonalizable in $\mathbb{R}$, called diagonalizable systems. The reason why diagonalizable systems are interesting is that, given a conic abstraction, the reachable set computation is guaranteed to terminate. Formally, a diagonalizable system is defined as follows.

Definition 7 (Diagonalizable system). *An affine system $\dot{x} = Ax+b$ is diagonalizable if there exist a real matrix Q such that $Q^{-1}AQ = diag(\lambda_1, \cdots, \lambda_n)$, where $\lambda_i \in \mathbb{R}, \lambda_i \neq 0, i = 1, \cdots, n$.*

In the following, we introduce how to derive a conic abstraction for a diagonalizable system and how to overapproximate their reachable sets by the conic abstraction. We also extend the theory to hybrid affine systems.

4.1   Properties of Diagonalizable Systems

The most important feature of diagonalizable system is that all of their eigenvalues are real numbers. Given a diagonalizable affine system $\dot{x} = Ax+b$ with initial region X_0, by doing a translation on the coordinate system with $y = x + A^{-1}b$, we can always transform the system into a linear system $\dot{y} = Ay$ with initial region $Y_0 = X_0 \oplus \{A^{-1}b\}$. Let $\lambda_1, \ldots, \lambda_n$ be the eigenvalues of A and $u_1, \ldots, u_j$

be the corresponding eigenvectors respectively, then the general solution of the linear system can be written as (refer to [32])

$$x(t) = c_1 e^{\lambda_1 t} u_1 + \cdots + c_n e^{\lambda_n t} u_n \tag{3}$$

where $c_1, \ldots, c_n$ depends on the initial value x_0 of the system of differential equations and can be obtained by solving $x(0) = x_0$. Let $U = (u_1, \ldots, u_n)$ and $c = (c_1, \ldots, c_n)$, $Cone(c, U) = \{x \in \mathbb{R}^n \mid x = \sum_{i=1}^n t_i c_i u_i, t_i \geq 0\}$ denote the convex polyhedral cone generated by the vectors $c_1 u_1, \ldots, c_n u_n$. Then, we have the following theorem.

Theorem 2. *Given a diagonalizable system $\dot{x} = Ax + b$, let U be defined as above and $\Xi = \{-1, 1\}^n$. Then, for every $\xi \in \Xi$, $Cone(\xi, U)$ is an invariant and the twisting of $Cone(\xi, U)$ is bounded by radian π.*

Remark 2. According to Theorem 2, the state space of a diagonalizable system can always be partitioned into a set of invariant cones and the twisting of every invariant cone is bounded by radian π. Therefore, given a diagonalizable system, to overapproximate the reachable set, we do not have to construct a conic abstraction for the whole state space. Instead, we only need to figure out which invariant cones the initial set spans and then construct a conic abstraction for each of them respectively. As mentioned previously, we would start from partitioning the derivative space. Based on the property of diagonalizable system, we develop a partitioning scheme which can construct a conic abstraction as a directed acyclic graph.

4.2   Diagonalization and Conic Partition

The first step of constructing a conic partition consists of diagonalizing the original system. Given a diagonalizable system $\dot{y} = Ay$ with initial region Y_0, a diagonalization of it is a linear system $\dot{z} = A_\lambda z$ with initial region Z_0 where $A_\lambda = Q^{-1}AQ$ is a diagonal matrix and $Z_0 = Q^{-1}Y_0$ for some Q. In theory, the diagonalized system is equivalent to the original system in terms of safety verification. However, by doing diagonalization, we manage to transform every invariant cone and its derivative cone into an independent orthant respectively. Since an orthant as a cone has some good properties such as having a fixed maximal angle of $\frac{\pi}{2}$ and all the generating vectors of the invariant cones are orthogonal to each other, we propose a special conic partition scheme, called *radial partition*, which can result in a directed acyclic graph for the conic abstraction.

Given a diagonalized n-dimensional system $\dot{z} = A_\lambda z$ and an orthant $O = \{z \in \mathbb{R}^n \mid Bz \leq 0\}$ in derivative space, where $B = diag(b_{11}, \ldots, b_{nn})$ with $b_{ii} = 1$ or -1. Let B_i, B_j be the i'th and j'th row vectors of B respectively, where $i \neq j$. The basic idea of *radial partition* is as follows. For every pair of (B_i, B_j), we generate a sequence of vectors $S_{ij} : v_{ij1}, \ldots, v_{ij(K_{ij}+1)}$ by rotating the vector $v_{ij1} = B_j$ from B_i to B_j step by step with an rotating amplitude $\frac{\pi}{2K_{ij}}$. Then, S_{ij} is used as the sequence of normal vectors of partitioning planes. Thus, each pair of adjacent vectors v_{ijk}, v_{ijk+1} forms a slice

---

Algorithm 1. Reach pipe overapproximation of affine systems

---

input : System $\dot{x} = Ax + b$ and initial set X_0;
local : Heap of partition regions H; /*stores unique elements only*/
output: Map from partition region to polyhedron R; /*by default maps to $\emptyset$*/

1   $A_\lambda \leftarrow Q^{-1}AQ$; /*diagonalize*/
2   $Z_0 \leftarrow Q^{-1}(X_0 \oplus \{A^{-1}b\})$; /*transform into linear system and diagonalize*/
3   **foreach** C *partition region in state space such that* $Z_0 \cap C \neq \emptyset$ **do**
4   insert into $\mathrm{R}(C)$ the template polyhedron of $[(Z_0 \cap C) \oplus A_\lambda C] \cap C$;
5   push C into H;
6   **end**
7   **while** H *is not empty* **do**
8      $C \leftarrow$ pop the top of H;
9   **foreach** D *successor partition region of* C *such that* $R(C) \cap D \neq \emptyset$ **do**
10   join $\mathrm{R}(D)$ with the template polyhedron of $[(R(C) \cap D) \oplus A_\lambda D] \cap D$;
11   push D into H;
12   **end**
13 **end**

$\{z \in \mathbb{R}^n \mid \langle v_{ijk}, z^T \rangle \leq 0, \langle -v_{ijk+1}, z^T \rangle \leq 0\}$ of the orthant O and O will be partitioned into K_{ij} slices by all the planes formed by S_{ij}. Hence, we can get $\frac{n(n-1)}{2}$ ordered sequences of planes at most totally. These planes intersecting each other yield a conic partition D for the orthant O. However, we do not really need so many sequences of partitioning planes. Actually, $n-1$ sequences of planes suffices to construct a partition with an arbitrarily small maximal angle.

For the conic abstraction derived from radial partition, we have the following theorem.

Theorem 3. *Every conic abstraction derived from a radial partition of the derivative space is a directed acyclic graph.*

Remark 3. By Theorem 3, the reachable set exploration of the conic abstraction derived from a radial partition is guaranteed to terminate. Moreover, as indicated in the proof, the direction of the discrete transition between locations can be easily determined by the sign of the Lie derivatives of the partitioning planes at the beginning [33]. $\qquad\square$

5   Time-Unbounded Reachability Analysis

In this section, we present how to compute the overapproximation of reach pipe of a given affine system based on the conic abstraction.

We first diagonalize the system (as in Sect. 4.2) and we identify the regions that hit the initial region. Then we iteratively explore the adjacent regions, while computing and storing the reach pipe. In particular, we build the control graph of the conic abstraction incrementally and only for those locations that are indeed reachable. We outline our procedure in Algorithm 1.

- The first two lines aim to translate the equilibrium point to the origin and further diagonalize the system. The initial set X_0 undergoes a similar transformation.
- In line 3–6, we split the initial set into multiple regions. For each split, we compute the overapproximation of the reach pipe inside the respective region, as defined in Eq. 1. We store the result in R and we push the region to H for further exploration.
- In line 7–13, we compute the overapproximation of following reach pipes inside the adjacent regions. The result is joined to what previously computed in the same region. The join consists of taking a convex hull between template polyhedra. Each such successor region is pushed to H.

We optimize the exploration order so to explore the successors of a specific region at most once, namely we want the heap H to never pop a region twice at line 8. To this aim, we instruct H to maintain a topological order between regions given by the graph of the conic abstraction (see Definition 4). Such order always exists, as a radial partition always induces an acyclic one (see Theorem 3). Similarly, on the enumeration of line 9, each region D must satisfy the same order w.r.t. C. Concretely, the order between regions is the closure of the order given by the Lie derivative of their common facets (as in Definition 4).

We produce a map from partition regions to template polyhedra, where each template polyhedron overapproximates the reach pipe at the respective region. Precisely, the template polyhedron of a convex set $X \subseteq \mathbb{R}^n$ w.r.t. the finite set of directions $D \subseteq \mathbb{R}^n$, which we call the template, is the tightest polyhedron enclosing X whose facets are normal to all and only the directions in D. We efficiently compute the template polyhedra at lines 4 and 10 using linear programming [34] and the convex hull at line 10 by simply taking for each direction the facet that is the loosest between the two. The choice of template is critical for the quality of the abstraction and the efficiency of the procedure. In each region we use the octagonal template, augmented with the normals of the facets of both the derivative and the state space cones.

In the following, we exemplify the result of the procedure on our running example under different granularities of the partition.

Example 3 (running example). Consider the system in Example 1, let the initial set be $X_0 = \{(x, y) \in \mathbb{R}^2 \mid -30 \leq x \leq -28, -45 \leq y \leq -43\}$ and the invariant be $\mathbb{R}^2$. We diagonalize and transform the system dynamics into $\dot{x} = -4x, \dot{y} = 3y$ with initial state $Z_0 = \{(x, y) \in \mathbb{R}^2 \mid -x + \frac{2}{5}y \leq 30, x - \frac{2}{5}y \leq -28, -x - y \leq 45, x + y \leq -43\}$. By partitioning the orthant into 5, 20 and 60 cones respectively, we got 3 overapproximations of different accuracies for the unbounded reachable set, which is shown in Fig. 4. As can be seen, the precision of the overapproximation increases rapidly with the number of cones. □

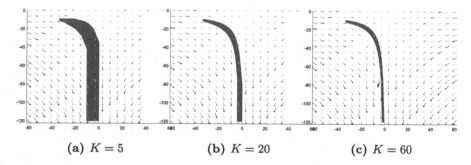

(a) $K = 5$ **(b)** $K = 20$ **(c)** $K = 60$

Fig. 4. Unbounded invariants obtained for Example 3 under different numbers of slices of partition.

5.1   Mode Switching

The theory presented in the previous sections can be easily extended to deal with hybrid systems. Given a hybrid system, the conic abstraction of each discrete location can be done as presented. However, due to the transformation of the system dynamics in each location, the same transformation also needs to be applied to the guards and reset operations of the discrete transitions between locations.

Concretely, let $\dot{y} = A_i y + b_i$ and $\dot{y} = A_j y + b_j$ be the dynamics of two discrete locations l_i, l_j of a hybrid system, $G_{ij} = \{ y \in \mathbb{R}^n \mid J_{ij} y \leq h_{ij} \}$ be the guard of the transition (l_i, l_j) and $T_{ij} : y' \mapsto M_{ij} y + e_{ij}$ be the reset operation. Suppose the diagonalization of A_i, A_j are $A_{\lambda_i} = Q_i^{-1} A_i Q_i$, $A_{\lambda_j} = Q_j^{-1} A_j Q_j$, respectively. Let x be the variable name after transformation, then we have $l_i : y = Q_i x + A_i^{-1} b_i$ and $l_j : y = Q_j x + A_j^{-1} b_j$. Thus, the guard and the reset operation are transformed into the following.

$$G_{ij}^* = \{ x \in \mathbb{R}^n \mid J_{ij} Q_i x \leq h_{ij} - J_{ij} A_i^{-1} b_i \} \tag{4}$$

$$T_{ij}^* : x \mapsto Q_j^{-1} (M_{ij} Q_i x + M_{ij} A_i^{-1} b_i + e_{ij} - A_j^{-1} b_j) \tag{5}$$

Location invariants I_j are transformed as well using the formula $I_j' = \{ x \in \mathbb{R}^n \mid x = Q^{-1}(y + A^{-1} b), y \in I_j \}$. By applying the above transformations to the whole hybrid system and then performing the conic abstraction, we obtain an LHA, whose reachability analysis can be done as usual. However, unlike for pure continuous systems, termination is not guaranteed.

6   Experiments

We have implemented the procedure presented above in C++ using the GLPK library for linear programming [35], and we have performed two experiments. In the first, we have performed a scalability test using purely continuous systems given by random matrices of increasing size and for increasing precision of the

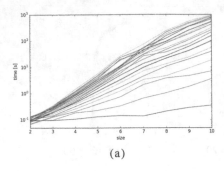
(a)

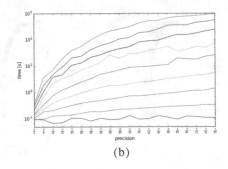
(b)

Fig. 5. Scalability of our method in computing the abstraction of purely continuous systems. The abscissa of (a) refer to the number of variables and each curve refers to a precision (maximum angle), while the abscissa of (b) refers to precisions and each curve refers to a system size (# variables). Both ordinates show the average runtime for 50 randomly generated systems for each system size and precision.

analysis. In the second, we have considered the room heating benchmark and compared against *SpaceEx* under scenarios `supp` and `stc` and *PHAVer* [16,20,36].

We generated random diagonal matrices with non-zero distinct integer values between -10 and 10 on the diagonal. Then we measured the runtime of our procedure for the maximum angles of $\frac{\pi}{2k}$ for increasing k (two by two) and the initial state being a unit box centered in $(50, \dots, 50)$. Figure 5a shows that the runtime increases exponentially with the number of variables, while the more the precision increases the less (for fixed system size) the difference in runtime is affected. The latter is also confirmed by Fig. 5b, which shows that the runtime increases polynomially with the increase in precision and that the number of variables affects the degree of the polynomial as, in fact, the number of partitions is worst case k^n.

The room heating benchmark describes a protocol for heating a number of rooms with a limited number of shared heaters [37]. We consider houses with 2 to 6 ordered rooms, each room is only adjacent to the previous and the following room, and all but one room have a heater. The temperature of room i is governed by a linear ODE of the form

$$\dot{x}_i = ch + b_i(u - x_i) + \sum_{j \neq i} a_{ij}(x_j - x_i) \tag{6}$$

where c is the heater efficiency, h indicates whether the heater is present, b_i is the room dispersion, u is external temperature, and a_{ij} is the heat exchange between rooms ($a_{ij} = 0$ for non-adjacent rooms). The switching logic moves a heater from a room to an adjacent room if the temperature difference exceeds a threshold and the latter is colder. In addition, we augmented every mode with a dummy self switch, so to force *SpaceEx* to perform time-unbounded reachability.

We have verified the room heating benchmark using *SpaceEx* with both scenarios `supp` and `stc` and in both cases it either crashes or timeouts. Conversely, using *PHAVer* the procedure terminated, but for small models only. Similarly to

Table 1. Runtimes for the abstraction of the room heating benchmark with 2 to 6 rooms. *SpaceEx* has been run with scenarios `supp` and `stc`, template `oct`, and time horizon of 1. *PHAVer* has been run on explicit conic partitions for the given precisions whose generation time is excluded here. We used a 2.6 GHz CPU with 4 Gb RAM. The key err indicates error, oot out of time (24 h), and - experiment not executed, i.e., the explicit partitioning run out of 24 h time.

| | Time part. | | Conic part. | | | | | | | |
| | *SpaceEx* | | *PHAVer* | | | | Our method | | | |
	supp	**stc**	$\pi/4$	$\pi/20$	$\pi/40$	$\pi/80$	$\pi/4$	$\pi/20$	$\pi/40$	$\pi/80$
heat-2	err	oot	0.17	2.20	9.86	50.86	0.24	0.25	0.31	0.41
heat-3	err	oot	oot	oot	oot	–	147	2.41	5.18	12.32
heat-4	err	oot	oot	–	–	–	14155	278	190	1217
heat-5	err	oot	oot	–	–	–	oot	oot	27467	56671
heat-6	err	oot	–	–	–	–	oot	oot	oot	oot

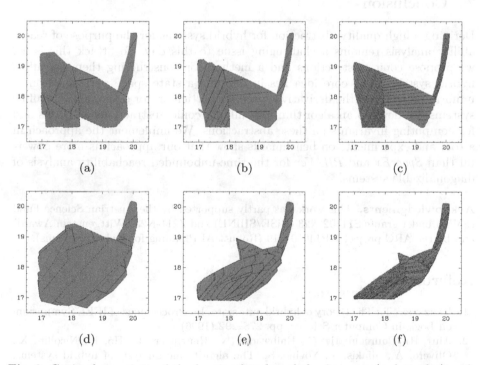

(a)   (b)   (c)

(d)   (e)   (f)

Fig. 6. Conic abstractions of the heating benchmark for 2 rooms (a, b, and c) and 2-dimensional projection for 3 rooms (d, e, and f) for resp. precisions $\pi/20$ (a and d), $\pi/80$ (b and e), and $\pi/400$ (c and f).

our method, *PHAVer* abstracts affine systems into LHA, but it requires the user to provide an explicit partition of the state space (rather than the derivative space). We have generated equivalent conic abstractions in the form of explicit LHA and verified them with *PHAVer*. Note that if such LHA is not provided, *PHAVer* computes trivial abstractions by using the whole mode invariants as partitions. *PHAVer* uses quantifier elimination for forward reachability, while we compute template polyhedra.

The time results are shown in Table 1. First, PHAver always times out for systems with more than 2 variables and even for 2-dimensional it scales poorly in precision compared to our method. Second, beyond three dimensional systems our method is even faster than generating the explicit LHA. The scalability in dimensionality indicated the advantage of using template polyhedra rather than quantifier elimination while the scalability in precision demonstrates the advantage of using our incremental construction of the conic partition. Figure 6 depicts the abstractions for the 2 and 3 rooms systems and for precisions $\pi/20$, $\pi/80$, and additionally $\pi/400$, computed using our method. Predictably, one can see how the quality of the abstraction increases as the precision increases.

7   Conclusion

Deriving a high-quality abstraction for hybrid systems for the purpose of reachability analysis remains a challenging issue to this day. To attack this issue, we propose conic abstractions and a method for constructing them for affine hybrid systems. The core idea lies in deriving a state space partition from a uniform partition of the derivative space. In particular, for diagonalizable affine systems, we develop an algorithm for building conic abstractions as DAGs and for computing invariants on these abstractions. We implement the approach in a tool and experiments on benchmarks show that our approach is more powerful than *SpaceEx* and *PHAVer* for the time-unbounded reachability analysis of diagonalizable systems.

Acknowledgments. This work was partly supported by the Austrian Science Fund (FWF) under grants S11402-N23 (RiSE/SHiNE) and Z211-N23 (Wittgenstein Award) and by the ARC project DP140104219 (Robust AI Planning for Hybrid Systems).

References

1. Henzinger, T.: The theory of hybrid automata. In: Proceedings of IEEE Symposium on Logic in Computer Science, pp. 278–292 (1996)
2. Alur, R., Courcoubetis, C., Halbwachs, N., Henzinger, T., Ho, P., Nicollin, X., Olivero, A., Sifakis, J., Yovine, S.: The algorithmic analysis of hybrid systems. Theor. Comput. Sci. **138**(1), 3–34 (1995)
3. Chen, X., Ábrahám, E., Sankaranarayanan, S.: Flow*: an analyzer for non-linear hybrid systems. In: Sharygina, N., Veith, H. (eds.) CAV 2013. LNCS, vol. 8044, pp. 258–263. Springer, Heidelberg (2013). doi:10.1007/978-3-642-39799-8_18

4. Dang, T., Maler, O.: Reachability analysis via face lifting. In: Henzinger, T.A., Sastry, S. (eds.) HSCC 1998. LNCS, vol. 1386, pp. 96–109. Springer, Heidelberg (1998). doi:10.1007/3-540-64358-3_34

5. Kloetzer, M., Belta, C.: Reachability analysis of multi-affine systems. In: Hespanha, J.P., Tiwari, A. (eds.) HSCC 2006. LNCS, vol. 3927, pp. 348–362. Springer, Heidelberg (2006). doi:10.1007/11730637_27

6. Prabhakar, P., Viswanathan, M.: A dynamic algorithm for approximate flow computations. In: HSCC, pp. 133–142 (2011)

7. Lal, R., Prabhakar, P.: Bounded error flowpipe computation of parameterized linear systems. In: 2015 International Conference on Embedded Software (EMSOFT 2015), Amsterdam, Netherlands, 4–9 October 2015, pp. 237–246 (2015)

8. Kong, H., Bogomolov, S., Schilling, C., Jiang, Y., Henzinger, T.A.: Safety verification of nonlinear hybrid systems based on invariant clusters. In: HSCC, ser. (HSCC 2017), pp. 163–172. ACM, New York (2017)

9. Chutinan, A., Krogh, B.H.: Verification of polyhedral-invariant hybrid automata using polygonal flow pipe approximations. In: Vaandrager, F.W., Schuppen, J.H. (eds.) HSCC 1999. LNCS, vol. 1569, pp. 76–90. Springer, Heidelberg (1999). doi:10.1007/3-540-48983-5_10

10. Asarin, E., Bournez, O., Dang, T., Maler, O.: Approximate reachability analysis of piecewise-linear dynamical systems. In: Lynch, N., Krogh, B.H. (eds.) HSCC 2000. LNCS, vol. 1790, pp. 20–31. Springer, Heidelberg (2000). doi:10.1007/3-540-46430-1_6

11. Kurzhanski, A., Varaiya, P.: Ellipsoidal techniques for reachability analysis: internal approximation. Syst. Contr. Lett. **41**(3), 201–211 (2000)

12. Botchkarev, O., Tripakis, S.: Verification of hybrid systems with linear differential inclusions using ellipsoidal approximations. In: Lynch, N., Krogh, B.H. (eds.) HSCC 2000. LNCS, vol. 1790, pp. 73–88. Springer, Heidelberg (2000). doi:10.1007/3-540-46430-1_10

13. Stursberg, O., Krogh, B.H.: Efficient representation and computation of reachable sets for hybrid systems. In: Maler, O., Pnueli, A. (eds.) HSCC 2003. LNCS, vol. 2623, pp. 482–497. Springer, Heidelberg (2003). doi:10.1007/3-540-36580-X_35

14. Girard, A.: Reachability of uncertain linear systems using zonotopes. In: Morari, M., Thiele, L. (eds.) HSCC 2005. LNCS, vol. 3414, pp. 291–305. Springer, Heidelberg (2005). doi:10.1007/978-3-540-31954-2_19

15. Girard, A., Guernic, C., Maler, O.: Efficient computation of reachable sets of linear time-invariant systems with inputs. In: Hespanha, J.P., Tiwari, A. (eds.) HSCC 2006. LNCS, vol. 3927, pp. 257–271. Springer, Heidelberg (2006). doi:10.1007/11730637_21

16. Guernic, C., Girard, A.: Reachability analysis of hybrid systems using support functions. In: Bouajjani, A., Maler, O. (eds.) CAV 2009. LNCS, vol. 5643, pp. 540–554. Springer, Heidelberg (2009). doi:10.1007/978-3-642-02658-4_40

17. Jiang, Y., Song, H., Wang, R., Gu, M., Sun, J., Sha, L.: Data-centered runtime verification of wireless medical cyber-physical system. IEEE Trans. Ind. Inform. **PP**(99), 1 (2016)

18. Jiang, Y., Zhang, H., Li, Z., Deng, Y., Song, X., Gu, M., Sun, J.: Design and optimization of multiclocked embedded systems using formal techniques. IEEE Trans. Ind. Electron. **62**(2), 1270–1278 (2015)

19. Henzinger, T.A., Ho, P.-H., Wong-Toi, H.: HyTech: a model checker for hybrid systems. In: Grumberg, O. (ed.) CAV 1997. LNCS, vol. 1254, pp. 460–463. Springer, Heidelberg (1997). doi:10.1007/3-540-63166-6_48

20. Frehse, G.: Phaver: algorithmic verification of hybrid systems past hytech. Int. J. Softw. Tools Technol. Transfer **10**(3), 263–279 (2008)
21. Batt, G., Belta, C., Weiss, R.: Temporal logic analysis of gene networks under parameter uncertainty. Trans. Autom. Contr. **53**(Special Issue), 215–229 (2008)
22. Alur, R., Dang, T., Ivančić, F.: Progress on reachability analysis of hybrid systems using predicate abstraction. In: Maler, O., Pnueli, A. (eds.) HSCC 2003. LNCS, vol. 2623, pp. 4–19. Springer, Heidelberg (2003). doi:10.1007/3-540-36580-X_4
23. Tiwari, A., Khanna, G.: Series of abstractions for hybrid automata. In: Tomlin, C.J., Greenstreet, M.R. (eds.) HSCC 2002. LNCS, vol. 2289, pp. 465–478. Springer, Heidelberg (2002). doi:10.1007/3-540-45873-5_36
24. Tiwari, A.: Abstractions for hybrid systems. Formal Methods Syst. Des. **32**(1), 57–83 (2008)
25. Roohi, N., Prabhakar, P., Viswanathan, M.: Hybridization based CEGAR for hybrid automata with affine dynamics. In: Chechik, M., Raskin, J.-F. (eds.) TACAS 2016. LNCS, vol. 9636, pp. 752–769. Springer, Heidelberg (2016). doi:10.1007/978-3-662-49674-9_48
26. Sogokon, A., Ghorbal, K., Jackson, P.B., Platzer, A.: A method for invariant generation for polynomial continuous systems. In: Jobstmann, B., Leino, K.R.M. (eds.) VMCAI 2016. LNCS, vol. 9583, pp. 268–288. Springer, Heidelberg (2016). doi:10.1007/978-3-662-49122-5_13
27. Asarin, E., Dang, T., Girard, A.: Hybridization methods for the analysis of nonlinear systems. Acta Informatica **43**(7), 451–476 (2007)
28. Henzinger, T., Wong-Toi, H.: Linear phase-portrait approximations for nonlinear hybrid systems. Hybrid Syst. **III**, 377–388 (1996)
29. Frehse, G., Guernic, C., Donzé, A., Cotton, S., Ray, R., Lebeltel, O., Ripado, R., Girard, A., Dang, T., Maler, O.: SpaceEx: scalable verification of hybrid systems. In: Gopalakrishnan, G., Qadeer, S. (eds.) CAV 2011. LNCS, vol. 6806, pp. 379–395. Springer, Heidelberg (2011). doi:10.1007/978-3-642-22110-1_30
30. Frehse, G.: PHAVer: algorithmic verification of hybrid systems past HyTech. In: Morari, M., Thiele, L. (eds.) HSCC 2005. LNCS, vol. 3414, pp. 258–273. Springer, Heidelberg (2005). doi:10.1007/978-3-540-31954-2_17
31. Doyen, L., Henzinger, T.A., Raskin, J.-F.: Automatic rectangular refinement of affine hybrid systems. In: Pettersson, P., Yi, W. (eds.) FORMATS 2005. LNCS, vol. 3829, pp. 144–161. Springer, Heidelberg (2005). doi:10.1007/11603009_13
32. Hirsch, M.W., Smale, S., Devaney, R.L.: Differential Equations, Dynamical Systems, and an Introduction to Chaos. Academic press, Amsterdam (2012)
33. Kong, H., Bartocci, E., Bogomolov, S., Grosu, R., Henzinger, T.A., Jiang, Y., Schilling, C.: Discrete abstraction of multiaffine systems. In: Cinquemani, E., Donzé, A. (eds.) HSB 2016. LNCS, vol. 9957, pp. 128–144. Springer, Cham (2016). doi:10.1007/978-3-319-47151-8_9
34. Sankaranarayanan, S., Sipma, H.B., Manna, Z.: Scalable analysis of linear systems using mathematical programming. In: Cousot, R. (ed.) VMCAI 2005. LNCS, vol. 3385, pp. 25–41. Springer, Heidelberg (2005). doi:10.1007/978-3-540-30579-8_2
35. GLPK (GNU linear programming kit). www.gnu.org/software/glpk
36. Frehse, G., Kateja, R., Le Guernic, C.: Flowpipe approximation and clustering in space-time. In: Proceedings of the 16th International Conference on Hybrid Systems: Computation and Control, pp. 203–212. ACM (2013)
37. Fehnker, A., Ivančić, F.: Benchmarks for hybrid systems verification. In: Alur, R., Pappas, G.J. (eds.) HSCC 2004. LNCS, vol. 2993, pp. 326–341. Springer, Heidelberg (2004). doi:10.1007/978-3-540-24743-2_22

Time-Triggered Conversion of Guards
for Reachability Analysis of Hybrid Automata

Stanley Bak[1($\boxtimes$)], Sergiy Bogomolov[2], and Matthias Althoff[3]

[1] Air Force Research Laboratory, Dayton, OH, USA
stanleybak@gmail.com
[2] Australian National University, Canberra, Australia
sergiy.bogomolov@anu.edu.au
[3] Technische Universität München, Munich, Germany
althoff@in.tum.de

Abstract. A promising technique for the formal verification of embedded and cyber-physical systems is flow-pipe construction, which creates a sequence of regions covering all reachable states over time. Flow-pipe construction methods can check whether specifications are met for all states, rather than just testing using a finite and incomplete set of simulation traces. A fundamental challenge when using flow-pipe construction on high-dimensional systems is the cost of geometric operations, such as intersection and convex hull. We address this challenge by showing that it is often possible to remove the need to perform high-dimensional geometric operations by combining two model transformations, direct time-triggered conversion and dynamics scaling. Further, we prove the overapproximation error in the conversion can be made arbitrarily small. Finally, we show that our transformation-based approach enables the analysis of a drivetrain system with up to 51 dimensions.

1 Introduction

Hybrid automata [6] are often used to model embedded and cyber-physical systems with a combination of discrete and continuous dynamics. Due to their expressiveness, however, hybrid automata can be difficult to verify. The flow-pipe construction technique [39] performs analysis with *regions* of states; it starts with a given initial set of states and propagates the set forward in time, constructing a sequence of regions that overapproximate the reachable set of states up to a time bound. To check which states can take a discrete transition, a geometric intersection is performed between the continuous reachable region and a transition's guard set. Afterwards, the intersected states are combined together in an aggregation step, often done by taking their convex hull or performing a template polytope overapproximation. Without guards, methods exist which can scale to analyze purely continuous systems with thousands of state variables [10], but

DISTRIBUTION A. Approved for public release; Distribution unlimited. (Approval AFRL PA #88ABW-2017-1923, 25 APR 2017).

A. Abate and G. Geeraerts (Eds.): FORMATS 2017, LNCS 10419, pp. 133–150, 2017.
DOI: 10.1007/978-3-319-65765-3_8

no such scalability results exist for systems with guards, due to the complexity of high-dimensional intersection and aggregation. For this reason, we propose a new method to try to remove the need for these costly geometric operations.

In particular, we leverage time-triggered transitions [2,8]. In a system with time-triggered transitions, the discrete mode change occurs after a certain amount of time has elapsed. In contrast, space-triggered transitions have mode changes based on the system's continuous state, and may arise from models of switched systems, or continuous systems with gain-scheduled controllers. Propagating sets of states through time-triggered transitions is practically free; it does not require performing high-dimensional intersection or convex hull.

In this paper, we present a transformation that can, under certain assumptions, convert a space-triggered transition to a series of time-triggered transitions. The main assumption for this conversion is that all executions of the hybrid automaton must pass through the guard completely (partial intersections with the guard are not considered here), and resets along transitions are not allowed. The main contributions of this paper are as follows:

- We present a new transformation process to convert a space-triggered transition to a series of time-triggered transitions;
- We prove that, in theory, the overapproximation error due to the proposed transformation can be reduced to an arbitrarily small constant;
- We demonstrate that, in practice, the approach works well on a numerical example of a high-dimensional drivetrain system.

This paper first introduces key definitions (Sect. 2), provides descriptions of the proposed transformations and accuracy proof (Sect. 3), and then evaluates the approach on a numerical example (Sect. 4). Related approaches are then discussed (Sect. 5), followed by a conclusion (Sect. 6).

2   Preliminaries

In order to define and justify the soundness of the model transformation steps used in our approach, we need to first precisely define the syntax and semantics of hybrid automata and some related concepts.

Definition 1 (Hybrid Automaton). *A* **hybrid automaton** $\mathcal{H}$ *is a tuple* $\mathcal{H} \triangleq (Modes, Var, Init, Flow, Trans, Inv)$, *where: (a) Modes is a finite set of discrete elements, each of which we call a mode; (b) $Var = (x_1, \ldots, x_n)$ is a list of real-valued variables. (c) $Init(m) \subseteq \mathbb{R}^n$ is a bounded set of initial values for Var for each mode $m \in Modes$; (d) For each $m \in Modes$, the flow relation $Flow(m)$ has the form of $\dot{x} \in f_m(x)$, where $x \in \mathbb{R}^n$ and $f_m : \mathbb{R}^n \to 2^{\mathbb{R}^n}$. (e) Trans is a set of discrete transitions, each of which is a 4-tuple (m, G, υ, m'), where m and m' are the source and the target modes, $G \subseteq \mathbb{R}^n$ is the guard, and $\upsilon : \mathbb{R}^n \to \mathbb{R}^n$ is the update or reset of the transition; (f) $Inv(m) \subseteq \mathbb{R}^n$ is an invariant for each mode $m \in Modes$.*

When a hybrid automaton has n real-valued variables, we say that $\mathcal{H}$ is n-dimensional, and has states with continuous part in $\mathbb{R}^n$. Note that f_m is a set-valued function, i.e., differential inclusions, $\dot{x} \in f_m(x)$, are allowed [46]. When the flows are deterministic, we may simply write them as a differential equation $\dot{x} = f_m(x)$. Now, we introduce a notion of distance which is useful to quantify properties of hybrid automata as well as errors.

Definition 2 (Distance). *Let $\|\cdot\|$ be the L^2 norm of a point in $\mathbb{R}^n$ and $d(\mathbf{x}, \mathbf{x}') = \|\mathbf{x} - \mathbf{x}'\|$ be the **distance** between two points in $\mathbb{R}^n$. We will write $d_S(\mathbf{x})$ to mean the lower bound on the distance between the point $\mathbf{x}$ and a set S, $d_S(\mathbf{x}) = \inf\{d(\mathbf{x}, \mathbf{x}') \mid \mathbf{x}' \in S\}$.*

Although the flows can be non-deterministic, they must obey a Lipschitz continuity property: in each mode m, there exists a constant L_m such that, for any two points $\mathbf{x_1}, \mathbf{x_2} \in \mathbb{R}^n$, for any $\mathbf{y_1} \in f_m(\mathbf{x_1})$, there exists a $\mathbf{y_2} \in f_m(\mathbf{x_2})$ with $d(\mathbf{y_1}, \mathbf{y_2}) \leq L_m \cdot d(\mathbf{x_1}, \mathbf{x_2})$. To define the formal semantics of hybrid automata, we introduce the notion of a state.

Definition 3 (State). *A **state** $s \in States$ of an n-dimensional hybrid automaton is a pair $(m, \mathbf{x})$, with mode $m \in Modes$ and continuous part $\mathbf{x} \in \mathbb{R}^n$.*

The semantics of hybrid automata is defined in terms of executions where an execution is a sequence of states. A state can change either due to a continuous flow or discrete transition, which requires the definition of successors.

Definition 4 (Continuous Successor). *A state $(m', \mathbf{x}')$ is a **continuous successor** of another state $(m, \mathbf{x})$ if $m' = m$ and there exists a positive time t and a differentiable function $g : [0, t] \to \mathbb{R}^n$ such that the following holds: (1) $g(0) = \mathbf{x}$, (2) $g(t) = \mathbf{x}'$ and (3) for all $\delta \in (0, t)$: $g(\delta) \in Inv(m)$ and $(g(\delta), \dot{g}(\delta)) \in Flow(m)$.*

We refer to the time t as a dwell time spent in the mode m.

Definition 5 (Discrete Successor). *A state $(m, \mathbf{x}')$ is a **discrete successor** of another state $(m, \mathbf{x})$ if there exists a transition $(m, G, \upsilon, m') \in Trans$ such that $\mathbf{x} \in G$ and $\upsilon(\mathbf{x}) = \mathbf{x}'$.*

Based on these definitions, we can define an execution of a hybrid automaton:

Definition 6 (Execution). *An **execution** $\xi = s_0 s_1 \ldots$ of a hybrid automaton $\mathcal{H}$ is a (finite or infinite) sequence which starts at an initial state s_0 of $\mathcal{H}$, i.e. for $s_0 = (m, \mathbf{x})$ it holds that $\mathbf{x} \in Init(m)$. Each of s_{i+1} is either a continuous or discrete successor of s_i. For finite executions, we call the last state in the sequence the end state, and can refer to the duration of the execution as the sum of the dwelling times over all continuous successors in the execution. Given two executions of a hybrid automaton ξ and ξ', where ξ is finite, we say ξ is a prefix of ξ' if the sequence ξ' begins with ξ.*

The consideration of all possible executions defines the reachable states:

Definition 7 (Reachable States).   *A state s is a **reachable state** of a hybrid automaton $\mathcal{H}$ if s is the end state of some execution of $\mathcal{H}$. In this paper, we primarily compare the continuous parts of reachable states. The set of all points which are the continuous part of some reachable state of $\mathcal{H}$ is written as $\mathsf{Reach}(\mathcal{H})$. The set of time-bounded continuous reachable states, which corresponds to the continuous parts of end states of all executions with durations no longer than T, is written as $\mathsf{Reach}_{\leq T}(\mathcal{H})$.*

To analyze our time-triggered transformation, we introduce overapproximating hybrid automata as well as a definition of error in the overapproximation. Note that, when considering continuous overapproximations (and later their errors), if $\mathcal{H}'$ has more variables than $\mathcal{H}$, the variables exclusive to $\mathcal{H}'$ are projected away before doing the comparison. That is, the projection of $\mathsf{Reach}(\mathcal{H}')$ onto Var, $\mathsf{Reach}(\mathcal{H}') \downarrow_{Var}$, is used instead of $\mathsf{Reach}(\mathcal{H}')$, where Var are the variables of the original automaton $\mathcal{H}$.

Definition 8 (Continuous Overapproximation).   *A hybrid automaton $\mathcal{H}'$ is a **continuous overapproximation** of another hybrid automaton $\mathcal{H}$ if the inclusion $\mathsf{Reach}(\mathcal{H}') \supseteq \mathsf{Reach}(\mathcal{H})$ holds. A time-bounded version can also be defined. We say that $\mathcal{H}'$ with time bound T' is a time-bounded continuous overapproximation of automaton $\mathcal{H}$ with time bound T if $\mathsf{Reach}_{\leq T}(\mathcal{H}) \subseteq \mathsf{Reach}_{\leq T'}(\mathcal{H}')$.*

Definition 9 (Time-Bounded Continuous Overapproximation Error). *Let $\mathcal{H}$ be a hybrid automaton with a time bound T, and $\mathcal{H}'$ with time bound T' be a time-bounded continuous overapproximation of $\mathcal{H}$. Then, the **time − bounded continuous overapproximation error** is $\sup_{\mathbf{x}' \in \mathsf{Reach}_{\leq T'}(\mathcal{H}')} d_{\mathsf{Reach}_{\leq T}(\mathcal{H})}(\mathbf{x}')$.*

This measurement of error is equal to the asymmetric Hausdorff distance from $\mathsf{Reach}_{\leq T'}(\mathcal{H}')$ to $\mathsf{Reach}_{\leq T}(\mathcal{H}')$. Further, such a measurement is relevant for model transformations, such as the ones proposed in this paper. Rather than computing the reachable set of states of an automaton $\mathcal{H}$ with time bound T, we can instead compute reachable sets on a modified automaton $\mathcal{H}'$ with a different time bound T'. The time-bounded continuous overapproximation error can be used to measure the amount of error, in space, that an ideal reachability computation would have due to the use of $\mathcal{H}'$ instead of the original $\mathcal{H}$.

3   Transformations

In this section, we describe a way to convert certain space-triggered transitions into time-triggered ones. This is beneficial for reachability analysis algorithms, since time-triggered transitions can be handled efficiently. In order to do this, we first describe a direct time-triggered conversion transformation in Sect. 3.1, followed by a dynamics scaling transformation in Sect. 3.2. We combine the two transformations to construct the final automaton in Sect. 3.3, which we prove is an overapproximation with an error that can be made arbitrarily small in Theorem 1. We make four assumptions about the original automaton.

Assumption 1. *We present the conversion assuming that the original automaton $\mathcal{H}$ consists of two modes m_1 and m_2 with deterministic dynamics connected by a single transition (see top of Fig. 1), and all the initial states are in m_1.*

It is often possible to apply the transformation to a more general hybrid automaton, by adapting the proposed process and considering a single transition at a time for the finite time-bound, as will be shown later in our evaluation in Sect. 4. In this conversion, there are two cases to consider: (1) The reachable set hits one guard set at a time. (2) Several guard sets are hit at once. Again, by removing the parts of the reachable set that are already hit by other guards, one can extract cases with a single guard intersection, as studied in this work (also see Sect. 5.5 of [2]). The only difference is that now a tree of possible next discrete states is spanned instead of consecutive next discrete states as in case 1). Notice that due to the finite time bound, and under a non-Zeno assumption, it is possible to unroll any loops in the automaton.

Assumption 2. *The single transition of $\mathcal{H}$ is space-triggered with a single linear condition, $G = \{\mathbf{x} \mid a \cdot \mathbf{x} = b\}$. Since the transition is space-triggered, there is no reset and the invariant of m_1 is $a \cdot \mathbf{x} \leq b$ (one side of the guard).*

The approach may be generalizable to more complex guards, but it would require a more complicated dynamics scaling process.

Assumption 3. *At some time t_{max}, all executions have taken the transition.*

Not all transitions satisfy Assumption 3, and it is one of the main restrictions of the approach.

Assumption 4. *For any amount of time t_γ, there exists a distance γ from the guard G, such that any execution that gets within distance γ of the guard must take the transition before t_γ time.*

Assumption 4 ensures that there are no executions that can touch the guard set and then back away without crossing the guard. One way to ensure this is by examining the Lie derivative of the guard level-set function, $B(\mathbf{x}) = a \cdot \mathbf{x} - b$ with respect to the mode's flow vector field. Due to the continuity of the flows, the condition is satisfied if there is some constant $\epsilon > 0$, such that at every point $\mathbf{x}$ where a transition might occur, $\frac{\partial B}{\partial \mathbf{x}} f_{m_1}(\mathbf{x}) \geq \epsilon$.

3.1   Direct Time-Triggered Conversion Transformation

First, we aim to replace the space-triggered transition of $\mathcal{H}$ with two time-triggered transitions. This is done by constructing a new automaton $\mathcal{H}_{tt}$, which is a continuous overapproximation of $\mathcal{H}$. We proceed with the following steps to transform the original hybrid automaton $\mathcal{H}$ to $\mathcal{H}_{tt}$:

1. We remove the space-triggered transition between m_1 and m_2.

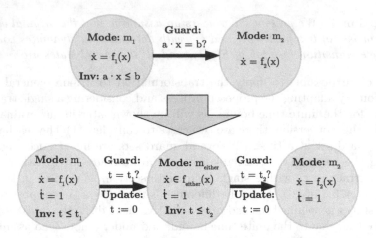

Fig. 1. The direct time-triggered conversion transformation, described in Sect. 3.1, converts the original automaton $\mathcal{H}$ (top), to an overapproximating automaton that only has time-triggered transitions, $\mathcal{H}_{tt}$ (bottom), using the parameters t_1 and t_2.

2. We add a new intermediate mode m_{either} and transitions such that the hybrid automaton switches from m_1 to m_{either} and then to m_2.
3. We add a new time variable, t, to the automaton with derivative $\dot{t} = 1$ in each mode. This will be used to force certain dwell times (exact times spent in each mode) as part of the new time-triggered transitions.
4. We equip the newly-introduced transitions with *time-triggered* guards. In other words, the guards are of the form $t = t_1$ and $t = t_2$, with invariants of the modes set to when t is less than t_1 or t_2, and resets $t := 0$ upon entering each mode. The first dwell time t_1 is selected to be the minimum duration when, in the original automaton, every finite execution with duration up to t_1 has an end state still in mode m_1. Similarly, t_2 is selected to be the smallest time such that the sum $t_1 + t_2$ is a time after which every finite execution with duration greater than or equal to $t_1 + t_2$ has an end state with mode m_2. Time t_2 exists because by Assumption 3, all executions eventually take the transition.
5. We assign the continuous dynamics in the mode m_{either} so that it *overapproximates* the dynamics in m_1 and m_2. This means that for any state $\mathbf{x}$, the flow in m_{either} contains the flows in m_1 and m_2, $f_1(\mathbf{x}) \cup f_2(\mathbf{x}) \subseteq f_{either}(\mathbf{x})$. In this way, we express the fact that executions of $\mathcal{H}$ with durations in the range $[t_1, t_1 + t_2]$ end in states that can be in either mode.

The conversion of $\mathcal{H}$ to $\mathcal{H}_{tt}$ is illustrated in Fig. 1. Notice that, in practice, the times t_1 and t_2 would be available during flow-pipe construction since a tool must check at each step if a guard can be reached. This transformation results in a time-bounded overapproximation, which we prove next.

Lemma 1. *For any time bound T, the constructed $\mathcal{H}_{tt}$ is a time-bounded continuous overapproximation of the original automaton $\mathcal{H}$ with the same time bound.*

Proof. Consider any execution ξ of $\mathcal{H}$ which ends at a state s with continuous part $\mathbf{x}$. If the mode of s is m_1, then ξ is also directly an execution of $\mathcal{H}_{tt}$, and so an execution exists that ends with a state with continuous part equal to $\mathbf{x}$. In the other case, if the mode of s is m_2, then let t_{trans} be the maximum duration of any prefix of ξ ending in a state with mode m_1 (t_{trans} is the time of the transition). By the construction of $\mathcal{H}_{tt}$, $t_{trans} \geq t_1$.

The duration of ξ is either (1) less than or (2) greater than or equal to $t_1 + t_2$. In the first case, there is an execution of $\mathcal{H}_{tt}$ which first spends t_1 time in m_1, then spends $t_{trans} - t_1$ using the dynamics of m_1 in mode m_{either} (because m_{either}'s dynamics are a differential inclusion containing the dynamics of m_1), and finally spends the remaining time using the dynamics of m_2 in mode m_{either} (again, because, m_{either}'s dynamics contain m_2's dynamics). This execution ends in a state with continuous part equal to $\mathbf{x}$. In the second case, the execution would spend $t_2 - (t_{trans} - t_1)$ in mode m_{either} using the dynamics of m_2, and then use the remaining time in mode m_2 to also end at a state with continuous part $\mathbf{x}$. In all cases, we have constructed an execution of $\mathcal{H}_{tt}$ of equal duration with an end state with continuous part equal to $\mathbf{x}$, and this holds for any execution ξ of $\mathcal{H}$, and so $\mathsf{Reach}_{\leq T}(\mathcal{H}) \subseteq \mathsf{Reach}_{\leq T}(\mathcal{H}_{tt})$. $\square$

The time-bounded continuous overapproximation error of $\mathcal{H}_{tt}$ crucially depends on the dwell time t_2 spent in the intermediate mode m_{either}. This follows from the fact that the dynamics in m_{either} is nondeterministic, subsuming both the dynamics of m_1 and m_2. This can be reduced by choosing the dynamics f_{either} to be as small as possible while still containing both f_1 and f_2. In general, however, the error cannot be eliminated without a further transformation.

3.2 Dynamics Scaling Transformation

Next, we introduce a dynamics scaling transformation that is later used to substantially reduce the overapproximation error in $\mathcal{H}_{tt}$. We first describe this transformation in isolation since it is quite general and we can show that it theoretically does not modify the continuously reachable states (Lemma 2).

Let $\mathcal{H}_{single}$ be a hybrid automaton with a single mode m with continuous dynamics $\dot{\mathbf{x}} = f(\mathbf{x})$. We proceed with the following steps to transform to construct a new automaton $\mathcal{H}_{scaling}$ from a copy of $\mathcal{H}_{single}$:

1. We create two additional copies of m: $m_{scaling}$ and m'.
2. We add a new time variable t in the automaton to measure the dwell time (unless such a variable already exists), with $\dot{t} = 1$ in all three modes.
3. We equip the automaton with time-triggered transitions with dwell times t_{begin} (from m to $m_{scaling}$) and $t_{scaling}$ (from $m_{scaling}$ to m'), where $t_{begin} > 0$ and $t_{scaling} > 0$ are parameters of the transformation.
4. We change the flow of $m_{scaling}$ to $\dot{\mathbf{x}} = g(\mathbf{x}) \cdot f(\mathbf{x})$ where $f(\mathbf{x})$ is the original dynamics in m, and $g(\mathbf{x})$, a user-defined function, is a scalar function that outputs a nonnegative number for every reachable state $\mathbf{x}$.

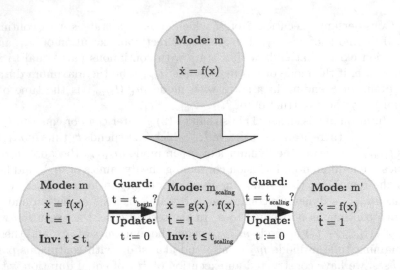

Fig. 2. The dynamics scaling transformation, described in Sect. 3.1, converts a single-mode automaton $\mathcal{H}_{single}$ (top), to an automaton with an identical continuous reachable set $\mathcal{H}_{scaling}$ (bottom).

The dynamics scaling transformation is shown in Fig. 2. It does not change the time-bounded continuous reachable set of states, which is proved next.

Lemma 2. *For any times T and $t_{scaling}$, the reachable set of the constructed $\mathcal{H}_{scaling}$ with time bound $T' = T + t_{scaling}$ is a zero-error time-bounded continuous overapproximation of the reachable set of $\mathcal{H}_{single}$ with time bound T.*

Proof. First, we show that $\mathcal{H}_{scaling}$ is a time-bounded continuous overapproximation, and then we analyze its error.

Consider any execution of $\mathcal{H}$ ending with a continuous state $\mathbf{x} \in \mathsf{Reach}_{\leq T}(\mathcal{H})$. The dynamics of each mode in $\mathcal{H}_{scaling}$ are identical to the original $\mathcal{H}_{single}$, except in $m_{scaling}$, where they get multiplied by a non-negative value at each point in space. This has the effect of scaling the vector field, without changing any of the directions. In the worst-case, the scaling factor in $m_{scaling}$, g can be zero, which effectively pauses the executions for at most $t_{scaling}$ time. Since the time bound of $\mathcal{H}_{scaling}$ is $T' = T + t_{scaling}$, we can ensure that $\mathbf{x} \in \mathsf{Reach}_{\leq T'}(\mathcal{H}_{scaling}) \downarrow Var$, and so $\mathcal{H}_{scaling}$ is a time-bounded continuous overapproximation. Notice that if ever $g(x) > 1$, more states may be reached by $\mathcal{H}_{scaling}$ than $\mathcal{H}$ for the same time-bound. However, any execution of $\mathcal{H}$ up to time T is still contained in (the larger) $\mathsf{Reach}_{\leq T'}(\mathcal{H}_{scaling})$.

In terms of error, consider any point in $\mathbf{x}' \in \mathsf{Reach}_{\leq T'}(\mathcal{H}_{scaling})$. Since the direction of the vector field in each of the modes of $\mathcal{H}_{scaling}$ is unchanged from $\mathcal{H}$, the point $\mathbf{x}'$ will eventually be the continuous part of a reachable state of $\mathcal{H}$. Thus, $d_{\mathsf{Reach}(\mathcal{H})}(\mathbf{x}') = 0$, and so the overapproximation error is zero. $\square$

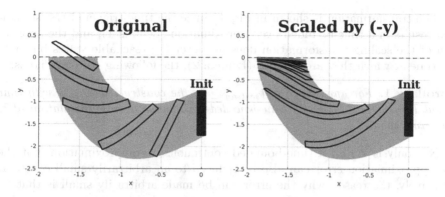

Fig. 3. For the Van der Pol dynamics, the currently-tracked set of states becomes flattened against the x axis when using a scaling function $g(\mathbf{x}) = -y$. The time-invariant set of reachable states below the x axis (grey states) is unchanged.

Dynamics scaling can alter the set of states reachable with executions of a fixed duration, without altering the final (time-invariant) continuous reachable set. This is practically useful, because reachability algorithms usually perform their computations using sets which correspond to continuous trajectories of a fixed duration, which is sometimes called the *currently-tracked set of states* [8].

To reduce the error in the time-triggered conversion, we use dynamics scaling to flatten the currently-tracked set of states against a guard boundary. An illustration of this for the Van der Pol system, with dynamics $\dot{x} = y$ and $\dot{y} = (1 - x^2) \cdot y - x$, is shown in Fig. 3. Here, when the dynamics is scaled based on the distance from the $y = 0$ guard, the currently-tracked set of states becomes flattened as it approaches the x axis.

3.3   Combined Scaled Time-Triggered Transformation

We now combine the transformations from Sects. 3.1 and 3.2 into a single transformation, which can theoretically be done with arbitrary accuracy. The steps to produce the final automaton $\mathcal{H}_{final}$ starting from $\mathcal{H}$ are as follows:

1. We first apply the time-triggered transformation on $\mathcal{H}$ to produce $\mathcal{H}_{tt}$.
2. Next, we apply a version of the dynamics scaling transformation to mode m_1 of $\mathcal{H}_{tt}$. For the time t_{begin} of the transformation we use t_1. Time $t_{scaling}$ is a parameter of the transformation. For the scaling function $g(\mathbf{x})$, we use the minimum distance from the point to the guard set, $d_G(\mathbf{x})$. Since the guard set is defined with a single linear condition, $G = \{x \mid a \cdot \mathbf{x} = b\}$, we use the dynamics scaling function $g(\mathbf{x}) = \hat{a} \cdot \mathbf{x} + b$, where $\hat{a} = \frac{a}{\|a\|}$ is the normal vector associated with a and $\cdot$ is the standard dot product. This function is nonnegative for any $\mathbf{x}$ in m_1, meeting the required condition for g in step 4 of the dynamics scaling transformation.
3. We directly transition from $m_{scaling}$ to m_{either}, deleting m_1' and its associated transitions.

The transformation is shown in Fig. 4. Since the time-triggered transformation results in a time-bounded overapproximation (Lemma 1), and the application of the scaling transformation does not alter the reachable states but only the time at which they are reached (Lemma 2), the following corollary holds:

Corollary 1. *For any choice of $t_{scaling} \geq 0$, the constructed $\mathcal{H}_{final}$ with time bound $T' = T + t_{scaling}$ is a time-bounded continuous overapproximation of $\mathcal{H}$ with time bound T.*

Not only is $\mathcal{H}_{final}$ a time-bounded continuous overapproximation, but the overapproximiation error can also be reduced to an arbitrarily small constant. Intuitively, the reason why the error can be made arbitrarily small is that by increasing $t_{scaling}$, the set of states upon entering m_{either} becomes more and more flattened against the original guard's boundary. Since all states are then about to cross the guard, the time needed in m_{either} becomes arbitrarily small, reducing the only source of overapproximation error in the time-triggered conversion. Then, by the Lipschitz continuity of the dynamics, in finite time, the total divergence can also be made arbitrarily small as shown next.

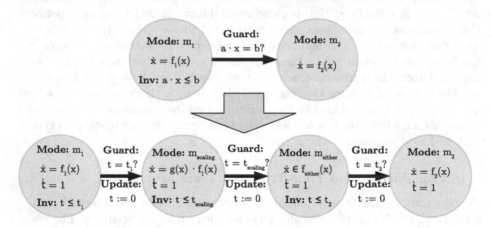

Fig. 4. The original automaton $\mathcal{H}$ (top) is transformed using both time-triggered conversion and dynamics scaling to produce the final automaton $\mathcal{H}_{final}$ (bottom). Theorem 1 proves that the error due to this transformation can be reduced to an arbitrarily small constant by increasing $t_{scaling}$.

Theorem 1. *For any time T and any desired error $\delta > 0$, there exists a $t_{scaling}$ such that the time-bounded continuous overapproximation error between $\mathcal{H}$ with time bound T and $\mathcal{H}_{final}$ with time bound $T' = T + t_{scaling}$ is less than δ.*

Proof. First, by Corollary 1, we know that $\mathcal{H}_{final}$ is a time-bounded overapproximation. Second, to show the error can be reduced to less than any $\delta > 0$, we will find a $t_{scaling}$ such that, given any point $\mathbf{x}' \in \text{Reach}_{\leq T'}(\mathcal{H}_{final})$, there exists a point $\mathbf{x} \in \text{Reach}_{\leq T}(\mathcal{H})$ such that $d(\mathbf{x}, \mathbf{x}') < \delta$.

Consider any $\delta > 0$. Let s' be the final state of an execution ξ' of $\mathcal{H}_{final}$ that has continuous part $\mathbf{x}'$, such that $s' = (m', \mathbf{x}')$. We proceed by showing there exists a $t_{scaling}$ for each of the four possible cases of m'.

Case $m' = m_1$: ξ' is directly an execution of $\mathcal{H}$ for any value of $t_{scaling}$, so s' is reachable in $\mathcal{H}$. Thus, $\mathbf{x} = \mathbf{x}'$ with $d(\mathbf{x}, \mathbf{x}') = 0 < \delta$.

Case $m' = m_{scaling}$: since the execution ξ' only reaches m_1 and $m_{scaling}$, we can apply the same reasoning as in Lemma 2, and for any value of $t_{scaling}$, find an execution of $\mathcal{H}$ that ends with continuous part $\mathbf{x} = \mathbf{x}'$. Again, $d(\mathbf{x}, \mathbf{x}') = 0 < \delta$.

Case $m' = m_{either}$: the execution ξ' will contain a prefix execution ξ'_{prefix} of maximum duration that ends in mode $m_{scaling}$. Let $\mathbf{x}'_{prefix}$ be the continuous part of the end state of ξ'_{prefix}, and let t_{either} be the time ξ' spends in m_{either} (the duration of ξ' minus the duration of ξ'_{prefix}). Notice that by the same argument as in the second case, $\mathbf{x}'_{prefix}$ is the continuous part of some reachable state of $\mathcal{H}$. Let L_{either} be the Lipschitz constant of the flows in m_{either}. Using the definition of Lipschitz constants, the distance between $\mathbf{x}'_{prefix}$ and $\mathbf{x}'$ will be bounded by $\|\mathbf{x}'_{prefix}\|(e^{L_{either} \cdot t_{either}} - 1)$. Thus, if we can show that t_{either} can be made arbitrarily small, we can also make the distance between $\mathbf{x}'_{prefix}$ and $\mathbf{x}'$ less than δ. Notice that t_{either} is upper bounded by t_2, which is the maximum amount of time it takes for all executions reach the single guard G of the original automaton. Further, by Assumption 4 of the original automaton, for any amount of time t, there exists a distance γ from the guard G, such that any execution that gets within distance γ of G must take G's transition before t_γ time. We instantiate this assumption taking t_γ to be small enough such that $\|\mathbf{x}'_{prefix}\|(e^{L_{either} \cdot t_\gamma} - 1) < \delta$. Next, we assign a value of $t_{scaling}$ that ensures all continuous parts of executions are within γ distance of the guard set G upon entering m_{either}. By Assumption 3, all executions of $\mathcal{H}$ eventually take the transition. Let t_{max} be the maximum duration needed to take the transition using the original dynamics of m_1. Since the scaling function g was taken to be the distance from the guard set G (step 2 of the construction of $\mathcal{H}_{final}$), if we take $t_{scaling} \geq \frac{t_{max} - t_1}{\gamma}$, we can ensure that all executions, upon transitioning to m_{either}, are within γ distance of G (because if the dynamics of $m_{scaling}$ were used from the start, all executions would get within γ distance of G in at most $\frac{t_{max}}{\gamma}$ time). In this case, we have $t_{either} \leq t_2 \leq t_\gamma$, which ensures that $\|\mathbf{x}'_{prefix}\|(e^{L_{either} \cdot t_{either}} - 1) \leq \|\mathbf{x}'_{prefix}\|(e^{L_{either} \cdot t_\gamma} - 1) < \delta$. Taking $\mathbf{x} = \mathbf{x}'_{prefix}$, this ensures the desired $d(\mathbf{x}, \mathbf{x}') < \delta$.

Case $m' = m_2$: Any execution of $\mathcal{H}'$ will have an intermediate continuous state at the moment it takes the transition to m_2 which we call $\mathbf{x}'_i$. By the same reasoning as in the above case, when $t_{scaling}$ is large enough, we can guarantee there is an execution of $\mathcal{H}$ that ends at a state that has just transitioned to m_2 with continuous part $\mathbf{x}_i$, with $\|\mathbf{x}_i - \mathbf{x}'_i\|$ less than any positive constant. If L_{m_2} is a Lipschitz constant of m_2, then the divergence in trajectories between two points $\mathbf{x_i}$ and $\mathbf{x'_i}$ under m_2's dynamics is bounded by $\|\mathbf{x_i} - \mathbf{x'_i}\|e^{L_{m_2} \cdot t}$, for any time t. Pick $t_{scaling}$ such that $\|\mathbf{x_i} - \mathbf{x'_i}\|e^{L_{m_2} \cdot T} < \delta$. Now, since t_{m_2}, the amount of time spent in mode m_2, is less than the time bound T, we have $\|\mathbf{x_i} - \mathbf{x'_i}\|e^{L_{m_2} \cdot t_{m_2}} < \|\mathbf{x_i} - \mathbf{x'_i}\|e^{L_{m_2} \cdot T} < \delta$. Thus, we can take $\mathbf{x}$ as the end point of the execution that goes through $\mathbf{x_i}$, and then uses the flow in m_2. This guarantees $d(\mathbf{x}, \mathbf{x'}) < \delta$.

In all cases, there exists a $t_{scaling}$ so that the error can be reduced to less than δ. □

Constructing $t_{scaling}$: One way to construct the final value of $t_{scaling}$ is: Following the reasoning in the m_2 case, we must ensure $\|\mathbf{x_i} - \mathbf{x'_i}\|e^{L_{m_2} \cdot T} < \delta$. This can be done by ensuring the error after m_{either} (which bounds $\|\mathbf{x_i} - \mathbf{x'_i}\|$) is less than $\delta/(e^{L_{m_2} \cdot T})$. By the reasoning in the m_{either} case, this occurs when $\|\mathbf{x'_{prefix}}\|(e^{L_{either} \cdot t_{either}} - 1) < \delta/(e^{L_{m_2} \cdot T})$, where $\|\mathbf{x'_{prefix}}\|$ is the norm of the continuous part of the state upon entering m_{either}, which is less than $\|Init(m_1)\|e^{L_{m_1} t_1}$. Substituting and solving for t_{either}, we get the condition $t_{either} < (\ln(\delta/(e^{L_{m_2} \cdot T})/\|Init(m_1)\|e^{L_{m_1} t_1}) + 1)/L_{either}$. Using Assumption 4, we get the γ corresponding to the t_{either} condition, and then need to find $t_{scaling}$ to ensure all executions are within γ distance of the guard upon switching to m_{either}. This can be ensured by taking the maximum time an execution can remain in the first mode t_{max}, multiplied by the maximum slowdown due to scaling γ, resulting in the value of $t_{scaling}$ that ensures the desired error, $t_{scaling} > t_{max}\gamma$. Notice that although theoretically the error can be made arbitrarily small by choosing a large enough $t_{scaling}$, flow-pipe construction methods often have overapproximation error, which may prevent this in practice.

Also notice that the proposed transformations do not depend on Assumption 4, but only the proof that we can make the error small uses it. By using a different scaling function g, we may be able to remove it.

4   Evaluation

We evaluate the proposed approach using a drivetrain system model [38]. The complete system dynamics, controller, and initial set description are available in another work [2], and here we only provide a brief description.

The model is a parameterized vehicle drivetrain, where one can add any number θ of rotating masses, corresponding to gears and other parts of the drivetrain such as transmission shafts. Given θ rotating masses, the model contains $n = 7 + 2\theta$ dimensions. The hybrid behavior of the drivetrain originates from backlash [42], which is caused by a physical gap between two components that are normally touching, such as gears. When the rotating components switch direction, for a short time they temporarily disconnect, and the system is said to be in the *dead zone*. All flows are linear ODEs.

We analyze an extreme maneuver from an assumed maximum negative acceleration that lasts for 0.2 [s], followed by a maximum positive acceleration that lasts for 1.8 [s]. The initial states of the model are taken to be a zonotope with a single generator (a line segment in the n-dimensional space). We can make the reachability problem easier by considering scaling down the initial states by some percentage. The model has the following specification: after the change of direction of acceleration, the drivetrain completely passes the dead zone before being able to transmit torque again. Due to oscillations in the torque transmission, the drivetrain should not re-enter the dead zone of the backlash. The system has three modes with two transitions between them, and so as mentioned after Assumption 1, we needed to apply the proposed transformation twice.

Table 1. Computational times in seconds ($n = 2\theta + 7$).

Dimensions	11	21	31	41	51
SpaceEx (smaller init)	541	1669	T/O	T/O	T/O
CORA Total	75	264	475	654	1073
CORA 1st guard					
Scaling Mode	36.95	132.00	281.44	377.25	620.54
Either Mode	0.06	0.11	0.37	1.49	2.96
CORA 2nd guard					
Scaling Mode	28.87	122.17	182.22	259.96	427.98
Either Mode	0.05	0.12	0.19	0.72	1.68

The implementation was done in CORA [1], a MATLAB-based tool, on an i7 Processor and 6 GB memory. We computed reachable sets with a varying number of rotating masses, where the total number of dimensions $n \in \{11, 21, 31, 41, 51\}$ (plots are shown in Fig. 5). Using the transformation approach from this paper, we could successfully analyze the model using initial states up to 40% of the desired size, while provably meeting the specification. The overall computational time, as well as the individual intersection times with the two guard sets are listed in Table 1. The total CPU time for the largest system with 51 dimensions is about 18 min. The table also shows that the runtime is dominated by computation in the scaling modes. This demonstrates a trade-off of our approach: Although we can eliminate geometric intersections, the dynamics in the scaling mode becomes more complicated. Further, the error can be reduced by spending more time in the scaling mode, at the cost of additional computation time.

We also analyzed the same system using SpaceEx [27], the state-of-the art reachability tool for linear systems which performs geometric operations for guard intersection and successor aggregation. Note that SpaceEx is a more general-purpose tool, while the approach here requires that all executions eventually reach the guard set. For SpaceEx, we used the space-time clustering analysis scenario [29], and, for each of the models, we tried to maximize the size of the initial set while ensuring the specification was not violated and the analysis time was less than 20 min. For the $n = 11$ model, using a `flowpipe-tolerance` parameter of 0.0005, in 541 seconds we could successfully analyze the system with up to 1.1% of the desired initial set size (1.2% violated the error specification). For the $n = 21$ model, using a `flowpipe-tolerance` value of 0.01, in 1669 s we could successfully analyze the system with up to 0.2% of the desired initial set size (0.3% exceeded the time bound). We did not find parameters which succeeded for the other models within the 20 min timeout. This demonstrates that this model is particularly hard for techniques which do geometric intersection and aggregation as part of reachability analysis. A plot of the reachable states using SpaceEx and our technique with CORA is shown in Fig. 5.

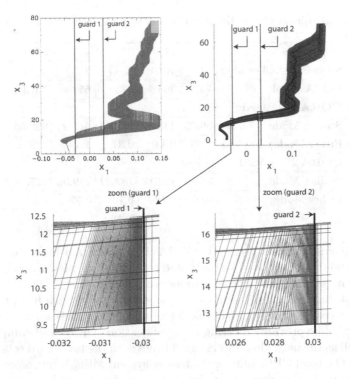

Fig. 5. Reachable set using SpaceEx with $n = 11$ (top left), and using our transformation approach with $n = 31$ (others).

5   Related Work

Hybrid automata [6] can be analyzed by a number of methods [45]. These range from SMT [19,25,36], deduction [43], level sets [41], and simulation [24] based to flow-pipe construction based methods. In this paper, we compute time-bounded reachability [18] using flow-pipe construction. These methods work by propagating regions of states, which can be represented using constraint polyhedra [26], support functions [32], orthogonal polyhedra [23], zonotopes [5], Taylor models [21,44] or ellipsoids [17,37]. These representations have been implemented in powerful analysis tools for hybrid automata including HyTech [34], Ariadne [13], Flow* [20], PHAVer [26], SpaceEx [27], CORA [1], and Hylaa [11].

Research on intersection in flowpipe construction involves techniques which avoid the intersection operation by employing a nonlinear mapping onto the guard [2]. Continuization methods [3,4,12] eliminate intersections using abstractions that get rid of fast-switching dynamics or eliminate guard intersections between similar continuous dynamics, as performed for m_{either} in this work. Frehse et al. [30] cast the intersection operator as a convex minimization problem. Other research examines the problem of efficiently computing geometric intersections for particular choices of data structures [31,33,35,40].

Our approach was presented using model transformations [9]. Model transformations can be used to derive abstractions [14–16,28]. Bak et al. [8] use model transformations to encode a hybridization process, i.e. reduction of the analysis of non-linear hybrid automata to linear ones, also using time-triggered transitions. The pseudo-invariants model transformation [7] can be used to reduce wrapping-effect error, which may also be possible with the dynamics scaling approach described in this work, without requiring geometric intersections.

In terms of applicability, benchmarks for various classes of hybrid systems have been proposed [22]. Of these proposed hybrid benchmarks, the main limit to applicability is the presence of resets along transitions. Some models, such as the filtered oscillator or glycemic control system, only use identity resets and do not have synchronization points, and so may be applicable for our method.

6 Conclusion

In this paper, we have presented a new way to handle certain types of discrete transitions when performing hybrid systems reachability analysis. We do this by creating an overapproximation abstraction of the original hybrid automaton that uses only time-triggered transitions. Given a space-triggered transition, our technique works in two steps: (1) we first add an intermediate mode which accounts for a "grey" zone when executions can be in either mode; (2) we scale the continuous dynamics in the first mode to decrease the time interval executions must spend in previously-mentioned "grey" zone. By applying these transformations, we remove the need to perform high-dimensional set intersection and set aggregation, which can be both time-consuming and error-prone.

The trade-off with this approach is that the system dynamics become more complicated when the dynamics are scaled. A system with linear ODEs, for example, becomes a quadratic system when scaling is being performed. The proposed method can also work for systems that originally have nonlinear dynamics, and so it is a promising approach to address part of the grand challenge of verifying high-dimensional nonlinear hybrid systems.

Acknowledgment. This work was partly supported by the ARC project DP140104219 (Robust AI Planning for Hybrid Systems), the German Research Foundation (DFG) grant number AL 1185/5-1, and the Air Force Office of Scientific Research (AFOSR).

References

1. Althoff, M.: An introduction to CORA 2015. In: Proceeding of the Workshop on Applied Verification for Continuous and Hybrid Systems, pp. 120–151 (2015)
2. Althoff, M., Krogh, B.H.: Avoiding geometric intersection operations in reachability analysis of hybrid systems. In: Hybrid Systems: Computation and Control, HSCC 2012, Beijing, China, 17–19 April 2012, pp. 45–54 (2012)
3. Althoff, M., Le Guernic, C., Krogh, B.H.: Reachable set computation for uncertain time-varying linear systems. In: Hybrid Systems: Computation and Control, pp. 93–102 (2011)
4. Althoff, M., Rajhans, A., Krogh, B.H., Yaldiz, S., Li, X., Pileggi, L.: Formal verification of phase-locked loops using reachability analysis and continuization. In: Proceeding of the International Conference on Computer Aided Design, pp. 659–666 (2011)
5. Althoff, M., Stursberg, O., Buss, M.: Computing reachable sets of hybrid systems using a combination of zonotopes and polytopes. Nonlinear Anal. Hybrid Syst. 4(2), 233–249 (2010)
6. Alur, R., Courcoubetis, C., Halbwachs, N., Henzinger, T.A., Ho, P.-H., Nicollin, X., Olivero, A., Sifakis, J., Yovine, S.: The algorithmic analysis of hybrid systems. Theoret. Comput. Sci. 138(1), 3–34 (1995)
7. Bak, S.: Reducing the wrapping effect in flowpipe construction using pseudo-invariants. In: 4th ACM SIGBED International Workshop on Design, Modeling, and Evaluation of Cyber-Physical Systems (CyPhy 2014), pp. 40–43 (2014)
8. Bak, S., Bogomolov, S., Henzinger, T.A., Johnson, T.T., Prakash, P.: Scalable static hybridization methods for analysis of nonlinear systems. In: Proceedings of the 19th International Conference on Hybrid Systems: Computation and Control, HSCC 2016, pp. 155–164. ACM, New York (2016)
9. Bak, S., Bogomolov, S., Johnson, T.T.: HYST: a source transformation and translation tool for hybrid automaton models. In: 18th International Conference on Hybrid Systems: Computation and Control (HSCC 2015), pp. 128–133. ACM (2015)
10. Bak, S., Duggirala, P.S.: Direct verification of linear systems with over 10000 dimensions. In: 4th International Workshop on Applied Verification for Continuous and Hybrid Systems (2017)
11. Bak, S., Duggirala, P.S.: Hylaa: A tool for computing simulation-equivalent reachability for linear systems. In: Proceedings of the 20th International Conference on Hybrid Systems: Computation and Control, pp. 173–178. ACM (2017)
12. Bak, S., Johnson, T.T.: Periodically-scheduled controller analysis using hybrid systems reachability and continuization. In: 36th IEEE Real-Time Systems Symposium (RTSS), San Antonio, Texas. IEEE Computer Society, December 2015
13. Benvenuti, L., Bresolin, D., Collins, P., Ferrari, A., Geretti, L., Villa, T.: Assume-guarantee verification of nonlinear hybrid systems with ARIADNE. Int. J. Robust Nonlinear Control 24, 699–724 (2014)
14. Bogomolov, S., Frehse, G., Greitschus, M., Grosu, R., Pasareanu, C., Podelski, A., Strump, T.: Assume-guarantee abstraction refinement meets hybrid systems. In: Yahav, E. (ed.) HVC 2014. LNCS, vol. 8855, pp. 116–131. Springer, Cham (2014). doi:10.1007/978-3-319-13338-6_10
15. Bogomolov, S., Frehse, G., Grosu, R., Ladan, H., Podelski, A., Wehrle, M.: A box-based distance between regions for guiding the reachability analysis of SpaceEx. In: Madhusudan, P., Seshia, S.A. (eds.) CAV 2012. LNCS, vol. 7358, pp. 479–494. Springer, Heidelberg (2012). doi:10.1007/978-3-642-31424-7_35

16. Bogomolov, S., Mitrohin, C., Podelski, A.: Composing reachability analyses of hybrid systems for safety and stability. In: Proceeding of the 8th International Symposium on Automated Technology for Verification and Analysis, pp. 67–81 (2010)

17. Botchkarev, O., Tripakis, S.: Verification of hybrid systems with linear differential inclusions using ellipsoidal approximations. In: Lynch, N., Krogh, B.H. (eds.) HSCC 2000. LNCS, vol. 1790, pp. 73–88. Springer, Heidelberg (2000). doi:10.1007/3-540-46430-1_10

18. Brihaye, T., Doyen, L., Geeraerts, G., Ouaknine, J., Raskin, J.-F., Worrell, J.: Time-bounded reachability for monotonic hybrid automata: complexity and fixed points. In: Hung, D., Ogawa, M. (eds.) ATVA 2013. LNCS, vol. 8172, pp. 55–70. Springer, Cham (2013). doi:10.1007/978-3-319-02444-8_6

19. Bu, L., Li, Y., Wang, L., Chen, X., Li, X.: Bach 2: bounded reachability checker for compositional linear hybrid systems. In: Proceeding of Design, Automation & Test in Europe, pp. 1512–1517 (2010)

20. Chen, X., Ábrahám, E., Sankaranarayanan, S.: Flow*: an analyzer for non-linear hybrid systems. In: Sharygina, N., Veith, H. (eds.) CAV 2013. LNCS, vol. 8044, pp. 258–263. Springer, Heidelberg (2013). doi:10.1007/978-3-642-39799-8_18

21. Chen, X., Sankaranarayanan, S., Ábrahám, E.: Taylor model flowpipe construction for non-linear hybrid systems. In: Proceeding of the 33rd IEEE Real-Time Systems Symposium (2012)

22. Chen, X., Schupp, S., Makhlouf, I.B., Ábrahám, E., Frehse, G., Kowalewski, S.: A benchmark suite for hybrid systems reachability analysis. In: Havelund, K., Holzmann, G., Joshi, R. (eds.) NFM 2015. LNCS, vol. 9058, pp. 408–414. Springer, Cham (2015). doi:10.1007/978-3-319-17524-9_29

23. Dang, T.: Vérification et synthèse des systèmes hybrides. PhD thesis, Institut National Polytechnique de Grenoble (2000)

24. Donzé, A., Maler, O.: Systematic simulation using sensitivity analysis. In: Bemporad, A., Bicchi, A., Buttazzo, G. (eds.) HSCC 2007. LNCS, vol. 4416, pp. 174–189. Springer, Heidelberg (2007). doi:10.1007/978-3-540-71493-4_16

25. Fränzle, M., Herde, C.: HySAT: an efficient proof engine for bounded model checking of hybrid systems. Formal Methods Syst. Des. 30(3), 179–198 (2007)

26. Frehse, G.: PHAVer: algorithmic verification of hybrid systems past HyTech. In: Morari, M., Thiele, L. (eds.) HSCC 2005. LNCS, vol. 3414, pp. 258–273. Springer, Heidelberg (2005). doi:10.1007/978-3-540-31954-2_17

27. Frehse, G., Guernic, C., Donzé, A., Cotton, S., Ray, R., Lebeltel, O., Ripado, R., Girard, A., Dang, T., Maler, O.: SpaceEx: scalable verification of hybrid systems. In: Gopalakrishnan, G., Qadeer, S. (eds.) CAV 2011. LNCS, vol. 6806, pp. 379–395. Springer, Heidelberg (2011). doi:10.1007/978-3-642-22110-1_30

28. Frehse, G., Jha, S.K., Krogh, B.H.: A counterexample-guided approach to parameter synthesis for linear hybrid automata. In: Egerstedt, M., Mishra, B. (eds.) HSCC 2008. LNCS, vol. 4981, pp. 187–200. Springer, Heidelberg (2008). doi:10.1007/978-3-540-78929-1_14

29. Frehse, G., Kateja, R., Le Guernic, C.: Flowpipe approximation and clustering in space-time. In: Proceedings of the 16th International Conference on Hybrid Systems: Computation and Control, pp. 203–212. ACM (2013)

30. Frehse, G., Ray, R.: Flowpipe-guard intersection for reachability computations with support functions. In: Proceeding of Analysis and Design of Hybrid Systems, pp. 94–101 (2012)

31. Ghorbal, K., Goubault, E., Putot, S.: A logical product approach to zonotope intersection. In: Proceeding of the 27th International Conference on Computer Aided Verification, pp. 212–226 (2010)

32. Girard, A., Le Guernic, C.: Efficient reachability analysis for linear systems using support functions. In: Proceeding of the 17th IFAC World Congress, pp. 8966–8971 (2008)

33. Girard, A., Guernic, C.: Zonotope/Hyperplane intersection for hybrid systems reachability analysis. In: Egerstedt, M., Mishra, B. (eds.) HSCC 2008. LNCS, vol. 4981, pp. 215–228. Springer, Heidelberg (2008). doi:10.1007/978-3-540-78929-1_16

34. Henzinger, T.A., Ho, P.-H., Wong-Toi, H.: HYTECH: the next generation. In: Proceeding. of the 16th IEEE Real-Time Systems Symposium, pp. 56–65 (1995)

35. Immler, F.: A verified algorithm for geometric zonotope/hyperplane intersection. In: Proceeding of the Conference on Certified Programs and Proofs, pp. 129–136 (2015)

36. Kong, S., Gao, S., Chen, W., Clarke, E.: dReach: δ-reachability analysis for hybrid systems. In: Proceeding of Tools and Algorithms for the Construction and Analysis of Systems, pp. 200–205 (2015)

37. Kurzhanski, A., Varaiya, P.: Ellipsoidal techniques for hybrid dynamics: the reachability problem. In: Dayawansa, W.P., Lindquist, A., Zhou, Y. (eds.) New Directions and Applications in Control Theory, vol. 321, pp. 193–205. Springer, Heidelberg (2005). doi:10.1007/10984413_12

38. Lagerberg, A.: A benchmark on hybrid control of an automotive powertrain with backlash. Technical report R005/2007, Signals and Systems, Chalmers University of Technology (2007)

39. Le Guernic, C., Girard, A.: Reachability analysis of linear systems using support functions. Nonlinear Anal. Hybrid Syst. **4**(2), 250–262 (2010)

40. Maïga, M., Ramdani, N., Travé-Massuyès, L., Combastel, C.: A CSP versus a zonotope-based method for solving guard set intersection in nonlinear hybrid reachability. Math. Comput. Sci. **8**, 407–423 (2014)

41. Mitchell, I.M., Susuki, Y.: Level set methods for computing reachable sets of hybrid systems with differential algebraic equation dynamics. In: Egerstedt, M., Mishra, B. (eds.) HSCC 2008. LNCS, vol. 4981, pp. 630–633. Springer, Heidelberg (2008). doi:10.1007/978-3-540-78929-1_51

42. Nordin, M., Gutman, P.-O.: Controlling mechanical systems with backlash - a survey. Automatica **38**, 1633–1649 (2002)

43. Platzer, A.: Logical Analysis of Hybrid Systems: Proving Theorems for Complex Dynamics. Springer, Heidelberg (2010). doi:10.1007/978-3-642-14509-4

44. Ramdani, N., Nedialkov, N.S.: Computing reachable sets for uncertain nonlinear hybrid systems using interval constraint-propagation techniques. Nonlinear Anal. Hybrid Syst. **5**(2), 149–162 (2010)

45. Schupp, S., Ábrahám, E., Chen, X., Ben Makhlouf, I., Frehse, G., Sankaranarayanan, S., Kowalewski, S.: Current challenges in the verification of hybrid systems. In: Proceeding of the Fifth Workshop on Design, Modeling and Evaluation of Cyber Physical Systems, pp. 8–24 (2015)

46. Smirnov, G.V.: Introduction to the Theory of Differential Inclusions. American Mathematical Society (2002)

Probabilistic Models

Symbolic Dependency Graphs for PCTL$\gtrless$ Model-Checking

Anders Mariegaard[(✉)] and Kim Guldstrand Larsen

Department of Computer Science, Aalborg University,
Selma Lagerlöfs Vej 300, 9220 Aalborg, Denmark
{am,kgl}@cs.aau.dk

Abstract. We consider the problem of model-checking a subset of probabilistic CTL, interpreted over (discrete-time) Markov reward models,
allowing the specification of lower bounds on the probability of the set of
paths satisfying a cost-bounded path formula. We first consider a reduction to fixed-point computations on a graph structure that encodes a
division of the problem into smaller sub-problems by explicit unfolding
of the given formula into sub-formulae. Although correct, the size of the
graph constructed is highly dependent on the size of the cost bound. To
this end, we provide a symbolic extension, effectively ensuring independence between the size of the graph and the cost-bound.

Keywords: Model-checking · Probabilistic CTL · Dependency graphs

1 Introduction

Addressing non-functional properties of embedded and distributed systems has
been studied intensely in recent years. This has called for extensions of traditional
modeling formalisms and specification languages to directly incorporate information such as resource consumption, timing constraints and probabilistic behavior. For real-time systems, various extensions of the popular Timed Automata
[1] formalism have been studied and successfully implemented in model-checking
tools such as UPPAAL[17] and PRISM [16]. These extensions include variations
and combinations of Priced Timed Automata [4], where costs are associated to
both locations and transitions, and Probabilistic Timed Automata [19] where
edges have associated probability distributions. Various extensions of Markov
chains such as Markov Reward Models [12] assigning cost expressions to states
and transitions, have been studied and successfully incorporated in tools such as
MRMC [14], PRISM and recently STORM [10]. The underlying semantics of
all these models can be given in terms of traditional transition systems where the
transition relation is endowed with costs and probabilities. To reason about the
costs and probabilities of the underlying (discrete) quantitative models, probabilistic CTL (PCTL) [11] extends the classical logic CTL [7] with probabilistic
quantification over path formulae. Various extensions of PCTL have been developed, notably PRCTL [2] for specification of constraints over reward measures.

© Springer International Publishing AG 2017
A. Abate and G. Geeraerts (Eds.): FORMATS 2017, LNCS 10419, pp. 153–169, 2017.
DOI: 10.1007/978-3-319-65765-3_9

Devising efficient techniques for verifying such specifications for complex models is non-trivial as any naïve exploration of the entire state space is many times not possible due to time and memory constraints, even when the state space is finite.

Our contribution. We consider model-checking a subset of PCTL. Our formalism allows for specification of non-trivial properties such as "the probability to reach a goal state through only approved states (indicated by labels), using no more than X amounts of some resource, is strictly greater than 90%". Thus, we consider a cost-bounded logic. This is natural for verification of embedded systems as resources such as time and energy are often sparse and one often wants to ensure that the probability of reaching a goal configuration without running out of resources, is above a certain threshold. We show that the problem can be reduced to fixed-point computations on a probabilistic extension of *dependency graphs* first introduced by Liu and Smolka [18]. They provide linear-time algorithms for computing least fixed-point for a Boolean domain, lending itself to e.g. CTL model checking. They offer both a global and local approach, where the global approach computes the fixed-point value for each node while the local approach in many cases will only explore parts of the entire graph. Our contribution is a lifting of the approach from the Boolean domain to a domain of probabilities for model-checking a subset of PCTL. The first approach is a new type of *probabilistic* dependency graph, constructed by a simple unfolding of the formula. Although correct, this approach is highly dependent on the size of the concrete cost bounds. To this end we provide a *symbolic* extension of probabilistic dependency graphs that effectively ensures independence between the size of the graph and the cost-bound. Although this paper does not describe a concrete implementation, the framework is constructed in such a way that it lends itself to an adaptation of the local algorithm by Liu and Smolka [18].

Related work. The framework of dependency graphs and the local algorithm of Liu and Smolka [18] has recently been extended in various ways. For the Boolean domain, a distributed implementation of the local algorithm has been developed [9] and very recently extended to express negation [8] with promising experimental results. Several extension to different domains have also been proposed. In [5] an extension to time bounds is presented to efficiently analyse Timed Games [5] and in [6,13] the approach was lifted to a (parametric) weighted domain for model-checking a (parametric) weighted variant of CTL. This paper further extends the theory behind this framework by a novel extension to the probabilistic domain. In [2] the notion of a *Path Graph* is used to solve similar model-checking problems. These graphs also express an unfolding of the model, but instead of nodes encoding probabilities for a certain state and formula, as is the case in this paper, the nodes represent possible rewards for path fragments and the associated probabilities. It will be interesting in the future to compare a distributed implementation of our approach to the Path Graph approach.

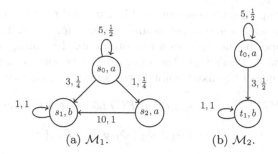

Fig. 1. Two MRMs, $\mathcal{M}_1$ and $\mathcal{M}_2$.

2   Models and Properties

This section introduces the modeling formalism and specification language. Our models will be instances of Markov Reward Models (MRMs) [12]. As we are interested in upper bounds on the non-probabilistic quantities we will from now on refer to them as *costs* instead of rewards, hence the inclusion of a transition cost function.

Definition 1 (Markov Reward Model). *A Markov Reward Model (MRM) is a structure $\mathcal{M} = (S, P, c, \mathcal{L})$ where S is a finite set of states, $P \colon S \times S \to [0,1]$ is the transition probability function such that for all $s \in S$, $\sum_{s' \in S} P(s, s') = 1$, $c \colon S \times S \to \mathbb{N}^+$ is the transition cost function and $\mathcal{L} \colon S \to 2^{AP}$ is the labeling function, assigning to each state a set of atomic propositions from a set AP.*

For two states s, s' with s being the current state, $P(s, s')$ is the probability that the next state will be s' and $c(s, s')$ represents the cost of exercising the transition. As our approach requires all paths to diverge w.r.t cost, we simply impose all weights to be strictly positive. Our approach also works for the case where all loops are required to have at least one transition with a strictly positive cost[1]. We denote such a transition from s to s' with probability p and cost w by $s \xrightarrow{w,p} s'$[2]. Thus, any MRM, defines a transition system for which we want to model-check properties. A *path* from a state s_0 is an infinite sequence of states $\pi = s_0, s_1, s_2, s_3, s_4, \ldots$ with $P(s_i, s_{i+1}) > 0$ for any $i \in \mathbb{N}$. We denote by $\pi[j]$ the j'th state of π, s_j.

Example 1. Consider the MRMs in Fig. 1. Each circle represents a state and the set of atomic propositions of that state. Set notation is omitted as each state has exactly one atomic proposition.

---

[1] Note that using costs from $\mathbb{Q}^+$ does not change the expressivity of the formalism; as any model is finite, one can always multiply all costs by the least common denominator to obtain a model with costs in $\mathbb{N}^+$.

[2] Any such transition could be replaced by a number of unit length transitions with probability 1, transforming the MRM into a (much larger) Markov chain.

As specification language, we consider PCTL restricted to strict lower bounds on the probabilistic modality and upper bounds on path formulae. The combination of a lower and upper bound induces a monotonic fixed point operator while the strict lower bound is needed for the operator to be chain-continuous, which implies the existence of the fixed point in the symbolic case (see Lemma 2).

Definition 2 (PCTL$_{\leq}^{\geq}$). *The syntax of PCTL$_{\leq}^{\geq}$ state formulae is as follows:*

$$\Phi ::= a \mid \neg a \mid \Phi_1 \wedge \Phi_2 \mid \Phi_1 \vee \Phi_2 \mid \mathcal{P}_{>\lambda}(\varphi)$$

where $a \in AP$ and $\lambda \in [0,1)$. The path formulae *are then constructed according to the following grammar, with $k \in \mathbb{N}$:*

$$\varphi ::= X_{\leq k}\Phi \mid \Phi_1 U_{\leq k}\Phi_2.$$

Informally, a state s satisfies $\mathcal{P}_{>\lambda}(\Phi_1 U_{\leq k}\Phi_2)$ if the probability of the set of paths from s satisfying $\Phi_1 U_{\leq k}\Phi_2$ is greater than λ. A path satisfies $\Phi_1 U_{\leq k}\Phi_2$ if, from the beginning of the path, all states satisfy Φ_1 until a state satisfying Φ_2 is reached while the sum of the costs between the start of the path and the state satisfying Φ_2 is less than or equal to k.

The probability associated with a given path-formula is well defined based on the σ-algebra generated from the standard cylinder-set construction (see [3, Chap. 10]) assigning probabilities to sets of infinite paths sharing a finite prefix. This construction ensures that the following PCTL$_{\leq}^{\geq}$ semantics is well defined. $\mathbb{P}$ will be used to denote the (unique) probability measure.

For a state formula Φ and an MRM $\mathcal{M}$ with state s, we denote by $\mathcal{M}, s \models \Phi$ the satisfiability of Φ in s. Similarly $\mathcal{M}, \pi \models \varphi$ denotes the satisfaction of path formula φ by the path π of $\mathcal{M}$.

Definition 3 (PCTL$_{\leq}^{\geq}$ Semantics). *For MRM $\mathcal{M} = (S, P, c, \mathcal{L})$ with state s, the* satisfiability relation $\models$ *is defined inductively on PCTL$_{\leq}^{\geq}$ formulae:*

$$
\begin{aligned}
\mathcal{M}, s &\models a && \text{iff} && a \in \mathcal{L}(s) \\
\mathcal{M}, s &\models \neg a && \text{iff} && a \notin \mathcal{L}(s) \\
\mathcal{M}, s &\models \Phi_1 \wedge \Phi_2 && \text{iff} && \mathcal{M}, s \models \Phi_1 \text{ and } \mathcal{M}, s \models \Phi_2 \\
\mathcal{M}, s &\models \Phi_1 \vee \Phi_2 && \text{iff} && \mathcal{M}, s \models \Phi_1 \text{ or } \mathcal{M}, s \models \Phi_2 \\
\mathcal{M}, s &\models \mathcal{P}_{>\lambda}(\varphi) && \text{iff} && \mathbb{P}(\pi \mid \pi[0] = s, \mathcal{M}, \pi \models \varphi) > \lambda \\
\mathcal{M}, \pi &\models X_{\leq k}\Phi && \text{iff} && \mathcal{M}, \pi[1] \models \Phi \text{ and } c(\pi[0], \pi[1]) \leq k \\
\mathcal{M}, \pi &\models \Phi_1 U_{\leq k}\Phi_2 && \text{iff} && \text{there exists a } j \text{ such that } \mathcal{M}, \pi[j] \models \Phi_2,
\end{aligned}
$$

$$\mathcal{M}, \pi[i] \models \Phi_1 \text{ for all } i < j \text{ and}$$

$$\sum_{l=0}^{j-1} c(\pi[l], \pi[l+1]) \leq k.$$

The satisfiability of a formula of the form $\mathcal{P}_{>\lambda}(\varphi)$ for a state s can be model-checked by deciding satisfiability of certain sub-formulae in the successor states of s.

Proposition 1. *If* $\mathcal{M}, s \models \mathbb{P}_{>\lambda}(\Phi_1 U_{\leq k}\Phi_2)$ *then at least one of the two following properties must hold:*

1. *there exists transitions* $s \xrightarrow{w_i, p_i} s_i$ *with* $w_i \leq k$ *such that*
   $\mathcal{M}, s_i \models \mathbb{P}_{>\lambda_i}(\Phi_1 U_{\leq k-w_i}\Phi_2)$ *with* $\sum p_i \cdot \lambda_i > \lambda$.
2. $\mathcal{M}, s \models \Phi_2$.

Proposition 1 suggests a procedure for generation of *dependencies* for PCTL$_{\leq}^{\geq}$ model checking as a disjunction between the dependencies represented by property (1) and the dependency of property (2). In Sect. 3 we will explicitly encode these dependencies as a probabilistic *dependency graph*. This involves a recursive application of property (1) At some point, a cost bound of less than or equal to 0 is reached. At this point, the generation of dependencies stops, as we do not allow 0-weights in a MRM.

Finally, the probability measure associated with path formulae is monotonically increasing w.r.t cost bounds.

Proposition 2. *For any MRM* $\mathcal{M}$ *and state* s,

$$\mathcal{M}, s \models \mathbb{P}_{>\lambda}(\Phi_1 U_{\leq k}\Phi_2) \implies \mathcal{M}, s \models \mathbb{P}_{>\lambda'}(\Phi_1 U_{\leq k'}\Phi_2)$$

whenever $\lambda' \leq \lambda$ *and* $k' \geq k$.

Example 2. Consider the formula $\Phi = \mathcal{P}_{>\frac{1}{2}}(\varphi)$ with $\varphi = a\, U_{\leq k}\, b$, $k \in \mathbb{N}$ and the MRM $\mathcal{M}_1$ in Fig. 1a. For $k = 10$, $\mathbb{P}(\pi \mid \pi[0] = s_0, \mathcal{M}_1, \pi \models \varphi) = P(s_0, s_1) + P(s_0, s_0) \cdot P(s_0, s_1) = \frac{1}{4} + \frac{1}{8} = \frac{3}{8} < \frac{1}{2}$ If instead $k = 11$ the direct path through s_2 affects the total probability i.e. $\mathbb{P}(\pi \mid \pi[0] = s_0, \mathcal{M}_1, \pi \models \varphi) = \frac{3}{8} + P(s_0, s_2) \cdot P(s_2, s_1) = \frac{5}{8} > \frac{1}{2}$. Thus, $\mathcal{M}_1, s_0 \models \mathcal{P}_{>\frac{1}{2}}(a\, U_{\leq 11}\, b)$. By Proposition 2 we conclude $\mathcal{M}_1, s_0 \models \mathcal{P}_{>\frac{1}{2}}(a\, U_{\leq k} b)$ for any $k \geq 11$. Similarly for $\mathcal{M}_2$ of Fig. 1b we conclude $\mathcal{M}_2, t_0 \models \mathcal{P}_{>\frac{5}{8}}(a\, U_{\leq k}\, b)$ for any $k \geq 8$.

3   Probabilistic Dependency Graphs

This section introduces *probabilistic dependency graphs* to explicitly represent the dependencies implied by Proposition 1. We show that PCTL$_{\leq}^{\geq}$ model checking can be solved by computing the *least* fixed-point on a complete lattice of probability *assignments* to nodes of the graph. These assignments will be concrete probabilities.

Consider the model-checking problem $\mathcal{M}, t_0 \models \mathcal{P}_{>\frac{1}{3}}(a\, U_{\leq 8}\, b)$ for t_0 of Fig. 1b. To encode this problem, a node representing the entire problem is constructed. This can be seen in Fig. 2. Now, the probability mass for the set of paths that satisfy the path formula $a\, U_{\leq 8}\, b$ must be strictly greater than $\frac{1}{3}$. This dependency is encoded by a special *cover edge* (dashed edge), labeled by the probability, to a successor node encoding the sub-problem. The semantics is that the *assignment* (probability) of the successor node must be strictly greater than $\frac{1}{3}$ for the node to have value 1. At this point we can directly apply Proposition 1 to construct new nodes. If $\mathcal{M}, t_0 \models b$, then the problem is trivial and must have associated probability 1, hence the labeling of max on the outgoing edge, indicating that a maximum will be computed. If $\mathcal{M}, t_0 \not\models b$, then $\mathcal{M}, t_0 \models a$ must be the case (value 1) and at the same time we have to apply Proposition 1 (1) to reason about successors of t_0 in the MRM, hence the minimum. A *hyper edge* is created, labeled by the transition probabilities out of t_0 with target nodes encoding the sub-problems by Proposition 1 (1). The rest of the graph can be generated in a similar manner, but one can also apply a *local* approach in lieu of Liu and Smolka [18]. If we choose to locally expand the tree at node $\langle t_1, a\, U_{\leq 5}\, b \rangle$ and first construct the node $\langle t_1, b \rangle$ it is trivial that the value of $\langle t_1, a\, U_{\leq 5}\, b \rangle$ should be 1 as $\langle t_1, b \rangle$ would have value 1. The value for the node $\langle \Sigma \rangle$ would then be $p \cdot \frac{1}{2} + \frac{1}{2} \cdot 1$ which, no matter the value for p, is strictly greater than $\frac{1}{3}$. Hence the root gets the value 1 and we can stop, even though p is completely unknown.

Our aim is in the future to use this approach to implement an extension of the local fixed-point algorithm by Liu and Smolka [18].

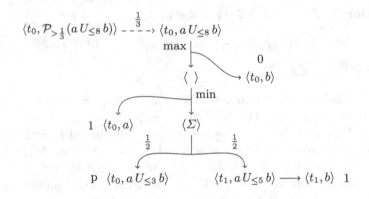

Fig. 2. On-the-fly unfolding of dependencies.

Definition 4 (Probabilistic dependency graph). *A probabilistic dependency graph (PDG) is a structure* $G = (N, C, E_\Sigma, E_{\min}, E_{\max})$ *where*

- *N is a finite set of* nodes.
- *$C \subseteq N \times [0,1] \times N$ is a finite set of* cover edges.
- *$E_\Sigma \subseteq N \times 2^{[0,1] \times N}$ is a finite set of (probabilistic weighted)* sum-edges *where*
  - *for any $E \in E_\Sigma$ with $E = (n, T)$, $\sum_{(w_i, p_i, n_i) \in T} p_i = 1$.*
- *$E_{\min}, E_{\max} \subseteq N \times 2^N$ are finite sets of* minimum/maximum-edges.

All nodes are restricted to have at most one outgoing edge.

PDGs for PCTL$^{\geq}_{\leq}$ model checking will mostly have nodes of the types $\langle s, \Phi \rangle$ or $\langle s, \varphi \rangle$ where Φ is a state-formula and φ is a path-formula. Figure 3 shows the concrete construction rules. Given an MRM state and a PCTL$^{\geq}_{\leq}$ formula, one can apply the rules in a recursive manner to obtain a PDG. The rules for $\neg a$ are omitted as they are simply the inverse of the rules for a. Maximum/minimum edges are labeled with max/min, cover edges are represented by dashed lines and sum edges by solid lines. Note that any PDG will be finite and without cycles as MRMs are finite and 0-costs are not allowed. Cover edges abstract away the probability bound before unfolding the until formula by the until rule (Fig. 3h) according to Proposition 1. The semantic value of a node $\langle s, \varphi \rangle$ is a value in the interval $[0, 1]$ corresponding to the probability of the set of paths out of s that satisfy φ. Nodes $\langle s, \Phi \rangle$ will be assigned either 1 or 0, depending on whether Φ is satisfied in s or not.

Example 3. Consider MRM $\mathcal{M}_2$ in Fig. 1b with formula $\Phi = \mathcal{P}_{> \frac{5}{8}}(a \, U_{\leq 8} \, b)$. After applying the construction rules we get the PDG in Fig. 3. As the entire PDG is quite large, a few nodes have been omitted, indicated by dots. These nodes all represent the unfolding of $a \, U_{\leq k} \, b$ in state t_1 for various k. The size of the PDG is therefore highly dependent on the cost bound.

The formal semantics of a node is given by an *assignment*.

Definition 5 (Assignments). *Given a PDG $G = (N, C, E_\Sigma, E_{\min}, E_{\max})$, an assignment, $A \colon N \to [0, 1]$ on G is a mapping from each node to a probability.*

An assignment represents the probability associated with the satisfiability of a PCTL$^{\geq}_{\leq}$ formula in an MRM state. We denote by $\mathcal{A}^G$, the set of all assignments for a PDG G and order assignments by the partial order $\sqsubseteq$: for two assignments $A_1, A_2, A_1 \sqsubseteq A_2$ iff $\forall n \in N . A_1(n) \leq A_2(n)$. $(\mathcal{A}^G, \sqsubseteq)$ then constitutes a complete lattice as the meet and join of any (possibly infinite) subset $D = \{A_1, A_2, \ldots\}$ is given by the well defined supremum and infimum defined on elements of the unit interval $[0, 1]$. The join is given by $\bigvee D = A_\vee$ where $\forall n \in N . A_\vee(n) = \sup_{A_i \in D} A_i(n)$. The meet can be defined similarly, using infimum.

As we are interested in the least fixed point of $(\mathcal{A}^G, \sqsubseteq)$, we define a monotone function that iteratively refines assignments. In the following we let $\max \emptyset = 1$.

Definition 6 (Iterator). *For a PDG $G = (N, C, E_\Sigma, E_{\min}, E_{\max})$, $F \colon \mathcal{A}^G \to \mathcal{A}^G$ is a function that, given an assignment A on G, produces a new updated assignment, $F(A)$, defined for any node $n \in N$:*

$$F(A)(n) = \begin{cases} \begin{cases} 1 & \text{if } A(n') > \lambda \\ 0 & \text{otherwise} \end{cases} & \text{if } (n, \lambda, n') \in C \\ \sum_{(p_i, n_i) \in T} (A(n_i) \cdot p_i) & \text{if } (n, T) \in E_\Sigma \\ \max_{n' \in T} \{A(n')\} & \text{if } (n, T) \in E_{\max} \\ \min_{n' \in T} \{A(n')\} & \text{if } (n, T) \in E_{\min} \\ 0 & \text{otherwise} \end{cases}$$

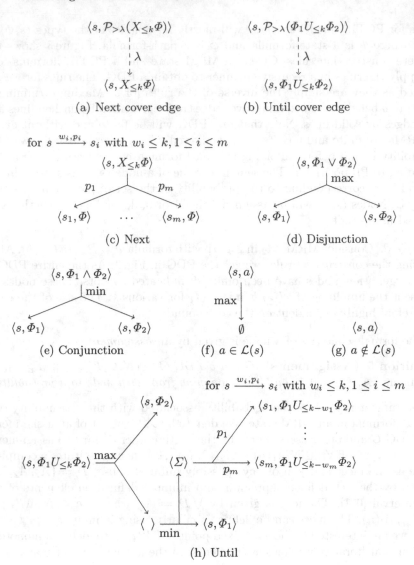

Fig. 3. PDG construction rules

For a formula $\varphi = \Phi_1 U_{\leq k}\Phi_2$ and a state s, a cover edge is created to abstract away the cost bound. The target node of this edge will compute the probability for the set of paths from s that satisfy φ which is compared to λ in the cover edge case of F. By Proposition 1, this probability can be split into a weighted sum of probabilities for similar formula in successor states. This is implemented in the sum-edge case of F. To argue that F is well defined we note that assignments are closed under maximum and minimum. Furthermore, for the case $(n, T) \in E_\Sigma$ we have, by definition of E_Σ, that $\sum_{(p_i, n_i) \in T} p_i = 1$ for any $(n, T) \in E_\Sigma$. Thus,

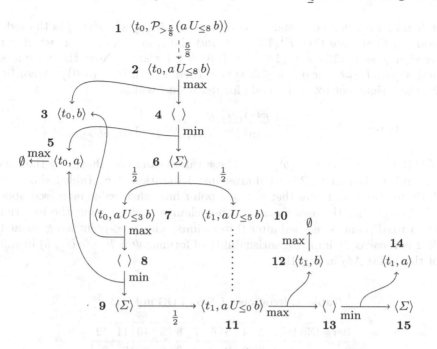

Fig. 4. PDG constructed from $\mathcal{M}_2$ (Fig. 1) and $\Phi = \mathcal{P}_{>\frac{5}{8}}(a\,U_{\leq 8}\,b)$

each term of the sum can be at most p_i implying that the sum is within $[0,1]$. We now argue for the existence of a least fixed point of F. To this end we show that F is monotone on the complete lattice of assignments.

Lemma 1 (Monotonicity). *F is monotone on the complete lattice $(\mathcal{A}^G, \sqsubseteq)$.*

Let $F^i(A)$ denote i repeated applications of F on assignment A i.e. $F^i(A) = F(F^{i-1}(A))$ for $i > 0$ and $F^0(A) = A$. As F is monotone on the complete lattice $(\mathcal{A}^G, \sqsubseteq)$, Tarski's fixed point theorem [21] guarantees the existence of a least (pre-) fixed point assignment $A_{\min}$. As the PDG is finite and has no cycles, the least fixed point is computable by a repeated application of the monotone function F on the bottom element of the complete lattice of assignments. The following theorem states the correctness of our approach.

Theorem 1 (Correctness). *Given a state s of an MRM $\mathcal{M}$, a PCTL$^{\geq}_{\leq}$ state-formula Φ and the generated PDG $\mathcal{G}$ with root node $\langle s, \Phi \rangle$,*

- *$\mathcal{M}, s \models \Phi \iff A_{\min}(\langle s, \Phi \rangle) = 1$*
- *For any node $n = \langle s', \varphi' \rangle$ where φ' is a path-formula,*

$$A_{\min}(n) = \mathbb{P}(\pi \mid \pi[0] = s', \mathcal{M}, s' \models \varphi').$$

Example 4. We now apply F on the PDG in Fig. 4. Our starting assumption is that the assignment to all nodes is 0. The node indices in bold will be used as shorthand for a given node and $F^i(\mathbf{j})$ denotes $F^i(\mathbf{0})(n)$ whenever $\mathbf{j}$ is the index of node n. First note that $F^1(\mathbf{12}) = 1$ and therefore $F^2(\mathbf{11}) = 1$, which will never change as $F^i(\mathbf{13}) = F^i(\mathbf{14}) = F^i(\mathbf{15}) = 0$ for any i. Now, there are a set of nodes $\langle s_1, a\, U_{\leq k}\, b \rangle$ for $0 \leq k \leq 5$, two of them shown ($k \in \{5, 0\}$). According to F, the assignment to such a node for iteration i will be

$$F^i(\langle t_1, aU_{\leq k}b \rangle) = \max \left\{ \begin{array}{l} F^{i-1}(\langle t_1, b \rangle), \\ \min\{F^{i-1}(\langle t_1, a \rangle), F^{i-1}(\langle t_1\, aU_{\leq k-1}\, b \rangle\} \end{array} \right\}.$$

As $F^1(\mathbf{12}) = 1$, $F^2(\langle t_1, aU_{\leq k}b \rangle) = 1$. These values can never change by the maximum and the fact that $\mathbf{12}$ is fixed after just 1 iteration of F. Table 1 shows the first 10 iterations for nodes that at some point have their value increased above 0. '−' denotes that the assignment did not change from previous the iteration; hence a fixed point is reached after 9 iterations. The fixed-point assignment to node $\mathbf{1}$ is 1, correctly implying satisfiability of formula $\Phi = \mathcal{P}_{> \frac{5}{8}}(a\, U_{\leq 8}\, b)$ in state t_0 of the MRM $\mathcal{M}_2$ in Fig. 1b.

Table 1. Iterations of F on PDG in Fig. 3

Iter#/Node	1	2	4	5	6	7	8	9	10	11	12
0	0	0	0	0	0	0	0	0	0	0	0
1	-	-	-	1	-	-	-	-	-	-	1
2	-	-	-	-	-	-	-	-	1	1	-
3	-	-	-	-	$\frac{1}{2}$	-	-	$\frac{1}{2}$	-	-	-
4	-	-	$\frac{1}{2}$	-	-	-	$\frac{1}{2}$	-	-	-	-
5	-	$\frac{1}{2}$	-	-	-	$\frac{1}{2}$	-	-	-	-	-
6	-	-	-	-	$\frac{3}{4}$	-	-	-	-	-	-
7	-	-	$\frac{3}{4}$	-	-	-	-	-	-	-	-
8	-	$\frac{3}{4}$	-	-	-	-	-	-	-	-	-
9	1	-	-	-	-	-	-	-	-	-	-
10	-	-	-	-	-	-	-	-	-	-	-

4   Probabilistic Symbolic Dependency Graphs

As witnessed by the previous section, a simple unfolding of the dependencies arising from a probabilistic formula can be used for PCTL$_{\leq}^{\geq}$ model-checking. Although correct, the approach implies that larger cost bounds on path formula results in larger PDGs as illustrated in Example 4. In this section we introduce a symbolic version of PDGs that abstracts away the cost bound, effectively collapsing many concrete nodes into *symbolic* nodes of the form $\langle s, \Phi_1 U_{\leq ?}\Phi_2 \rangle$. This reduces the size of the graph significantly but may introduce cycles.

Definition 7 (Probabilistic symbolic dependency graph). *A probabilistic symbolic dependency graph (PSDG) is a structure* $G = (N, C, E_\Sigma, E_{\min}, E_{\max})$ *where*

- $N, E_{\min}, E_{\max}$ *are defined as for PDGs.*
- $E_\Sigma \subseteq N \times 2^{\mathbb{N}^+ \times [0,1] \times N}$ *is a finite set of sum-edges.*
- $C \subseteq N \times \mathbb{N}^+ \times [0,1] \times N$ *is a finite set of cover edges.*

All nodes are restricted to have at most one outgoing edge.

The new construction rules for cover edges and symbolic nodes are shown in Fig. 5. From the rules, we see that symbolic nodes imply independence between the size of the PSDG and the cost-bound.

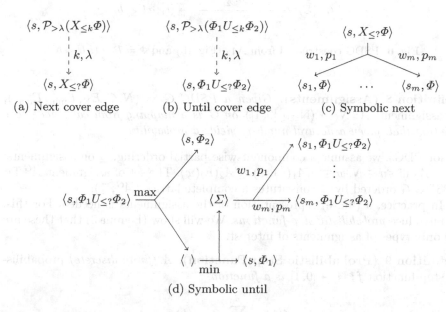

(a) Next cover edge   (b) Until cover edge   (c) Symbolic next

(d) Symbolic until

Fig. 5. PSDG construction rules for state s where $s \xrightarrow{w_i, p_i} s_i$ for all i with $1 \leq i \leq m$.

Example 5. Consider again the MRM $\mathcal{M}_2$ in Fig. 1. Figure 6 shows the constructed PSDG for $\mathcal{M}_2, t_0 \models \mathcal{P}_{>\frac{5}{8}}(a\, U_{\leq 8}\, b)$ which is much smaller than the corresponding PDG in Fig. 3.

As for PDGs, the semantics of each node is given by an *assignment*. Now that the upper bound on path formulae is abstracted away, each node represents a function from strictly positive naturals to concrete probabilities. Thus, an assignment to a node $\langle s, \Phi_1 U_{\leq ?}\Phi_2 \rangle$ is a function f from cost bounds to probabilities such that $f(k)$ is the probability of the set of paths from s that satisfy $\Phi_1 U_{\leq k}\Phi_2$.

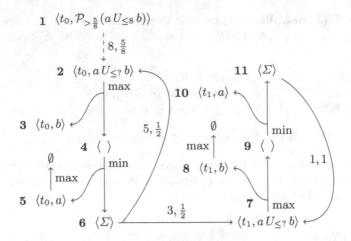

Fig. 6. PSDG constructed from $\mathcal{M}_2$ (Fig. 1b) and $\Phi = \mathcal{P}_{>\frac{5}{8}}(a\,U_{\leq 8}\,b)$

Definition 8 (Assignments). *Given a PSDG* $G = (N, C, E_\Sigma, E_{\min}, E_{\max})$, *an* assignment, $A: N \to (\mathbb{N} \to [0,1])$ *on* G *is a mapping from each node to a function that, given a natural number, yields a probability.*

As for PDGs, we assume a component-wise partial ordering, $\sqsubseteq$ on assignments; $A_1 \sqsubseteq A_2$ iff $\forall n \in N, w \in \mathbb{N}.A_1(n)(w) \leq A_2(n)(w)$. The set of assignment $\mathcal{A}^G$ for a PSDG G ordered by $\sqsubseteq$ constitutes a complete lattice $(\mathcal{A}^G, \sqsubseteq)$.

In practice, a (finite) representation of the assignments is needed. For this, we introduce *probabilistic step-functions*. We will show (Lemma 3) that these are the only types of assignments of interest.

Definition 9 (Probabilistic Step Function). *A (finite discrete) probabilistic step-function* $f: \mathbb{N} \to [0,1]$ *is a function*

$$f(k) = \sum_{i=0}^{n} p_i \chi_{B_i}(k)$$

where $n \in \mathbb{N}$ *is the number of* steps, $p_i \in [0,1]$ *denotes the probability associated with step* i, B_i *is the interval of step* i *and* χ_{B_i} *is the* indicator *function for the interval* B_i. *The intervals partition* $\mathbb{N}$ *and all intervals* B_i *are on the form* $[l, u)$ *with* $l < u$, $l \in \mathbb{N}$, $u \in \mathbb{N} \cup \{\infty\}$.

Note that our definition of (probabilistic) step-function requires a finite number of steps, implying that any step-function is bounded. We will represent a step-function f as a set $\mathbf{C}_f = \{(k_i, p_i - p_{i-1}) \mid k_i = \mathtt{low}(B_i), 0 < i \leq n\}$ where $\mathtt{low}(B_i)$ is the lower end of the interval B_i. Thus, for each step, $\mathbf{C}_f$ includes a pair describing the position and size of the step. As we will show, all assignments of interest are probabilistic step-functions (cf. Lemma 3) i.e. any assignment A of interest is *weight-monotonic*; for any node n, $A(n)(w) \geq A(n)(w')$ whenever

$w \geq w'$, capturing that the probability measure associated with properties increases with an increased cost bound (see Proposition 1). An assignment will be referred to as a step-function assignment if it assigns a probabilistic step-function to each node in the PSDG.

Example 6. Consider again the MRM $\mathcal{M}_2$ in Fig. 1b and the path formula $a\,U_{\leq k}\,b$. For $k \leq 13$, the step-function depicted in Fig. 7 correctly computes the probability of the set of paths outgoing of t_0 that satisfy $a\,U_{\leq k}\,b$. This function is represented by the set $\{(3, \frac{1}{2}), (8, \frac{1}{4}), (13, \frac{1}{8})\}$.

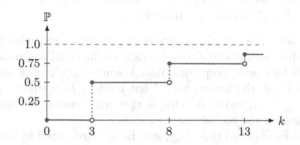

Fig. 7. Step-function for probability of set of paths outgoing of t_0 (MRM $\mathcal{M}_2$, Fig. 1b) satisfying $a\,U_{\leq k}\,b$ for $k \leq 13$.

We now define the fixed-point iterator for a PSDG $G = (N, C, E_\Sigma, E_{\min}, E_{\max})$, to iteratively refine assignments. In the following we let $\boldsymbol{x}$ be an assignment such that for any node $n \in N$ and natural number w, $\boldsymbol{x}(n)(w) = x$.

Definition 10 (Iterator). *For a PSDG $G = (N, C, E_\Sigma, E_{\min}, E_{\max})$, $F: \mathcal{A}^G \to \mathcal{A}^G$ is a function that, given an assignment A on G, produces a new updated assignment, $F(A)$. For any node $n \in N$ and weight $w \in \mathbb{N}$:*

$$
F(A)(n)(w) = \begin{cases} \begin{cases} 1 \text{ if } A(n')(k) > \lambda \\ 0 \text{ otherwise} \end{cases} & \text{if } (n, k, \lambda, n') \in C \\ \sum_{\substack{(w_i, p_i, n_i) \in T \\ w_i \leq w}} (A(n_i)(w - w_i) \cdot p_i) & \text{if } (n, T) \in E_\Sigma \\ \max_{n' \in T}\{A(n')(w)\} & \text{if } (n, T) \in E_{\max} \\ \min_{n' \in T}\{A(n')(w)\} & \text{if } (n, T) \in E_{\min} \\ 0 & \text{otherwise} \end{cases}
$$

Monotonicity of F is straightforward. Thus, by Tarski's fixed point theorem [21], a least fixed point, $A_{\min}$, exists.

As the complete lattice $(\mathcal{A}^G, \sqsubseteq)$ of assignments is of arbitrary size, in addition to the possibility of cycles in the PSDG, applying only the fixed-point theorem by Tarski does not imply a way of constructing $A_{\min}$. To this end, we prove that F is chain (Scott [20])-continuous and apply the Kleene fixed point theorem [15] to show that $A_{\min} = \sup_{n \in \mathbb{N}} F^n(\mathbf{0})$. A function $f : U \to U$ on a partially ordered set U with order $\sqsubseteq$ is *chain-continuous* iff, for any subset $D \subseteq U$ totally ordered by $\sqsubseteq$ (*a chain*), $f(\sup D) = \sup_{u_i \in D} f(u_i)$. By the Kleene fixed point theorem [15], we have that if f is chain-continuous on a complete lattice $(U, \sqsubseteq)$ with bottom element $\bot$, then $lfp(f) = \sup_n f^n(\bot)$ where $lfp(f)$ denotes the least fixed-point of f. As F is monotone on $(\mathcal{A}^G, \sqsubseteq)$ the least fixed-point $A_{\min}$ exists and a repeated application of F on the bottom element $\mathbf{0}$ produces the chain $F^0(\mathbf{0}) \sqsubseteq F^1(\mathbf{0}) \dots$. Thus, if F is chain-continuous, $A_{\min} = \sup_n F^n(\mathbf{0})$. Chain-continuity of F thus implies an iterative procedure to approximate the least fixed-point $A_{\min}$. The following lemma shows that F is chain-continuous.

Lemma 2 (*F* chain-continuity). *The iterator F defined for a PSDG $G = (N, C, E_\Sigma, E_{\min}, E_{\max})$ is chain-continuous.*

Note that, if instead $\geq \lambda$ was the cover-condition for a cover edge $(n, k, \lambda, n') \in C$, there would be cases where F computes a chain D' of assignments A_i converging to λ. In this case, $(\sup D)(n') = \lambda$ while $A_i(n') < \lambda$ for all i. Thus $F(\sup D')(n) = 1$ and the lemma would not hold as $F(A_i)(n) = 0$ for any A_i, implying $\sup_{A_i \in D'} F(A_i)(n) = 0$. This is the exact reason for our choice of a strict lower bound on the probabilistic modality.

We have now established that $A_{\min}$ can be approximated by repeated application of F on $\mathbf{0}$. We now argue that all assignments of interest are step-function assignments.

Lemma 3. *For a PSDG $G = (N, C, E_\Sigma, E_{\min}, E_{\max})$, node $n \in N$ and assignment $A \in \mathcal{A}^G$, if A is a step-function assignment then $F(A)$ is a step-function assignment.*

The following lemma states that for any i, the $i'th$ repeated application of F on the top (bottom) element gives an over(under)-approximation of the least fixed-point. This follows directly from the definition of the least fixed-point.

Lemma 4. *For an arbitrary PSDG $\mathcal{G}$, node n, iteration m and weight w,*

$$A_{\min}(n)(w) \in [F^m(\mathbf{0})(n)(w), F^m(\mathbf{1})(n)(w)].$$

Similarly, the approximations provide upper and lower bounds on the probability associated with the set of paths satisfying a given path formula.

Lemma 5. *For any symbolic node $n = \langle s, \Phi_1 U_{\leq ?} \Phi_2 \rangle$, iteration m and weight w, $\mathbb{P}(\pi \mid \pi[0] = s, \mathcal{M}, s \models \Phi_1 U_{\leq w} \Phi_2) \in [F^m(\mathbf{0})(n)(w), F^m(\mathbf{1})(n)(w)].$*

Finally, the next theorem states that we only need a finite number of iterations to guarantee these approximations to be equal to the least fixed-point, up to a given cost. Combining this result with Lemma 5 implies correctness of our approach; for any given concrete cost bound, we can compute the exact probability of the set of paths outgoing from a state that satisfy the formula, in a finite number of steps.

Theorem 2. *For an arbitrary PSDG $\mathcal{G}$, node n and weight w, there exists an iteration i such that for any $w' \leq w$, $F^i(\mathbf{0})(n)(w') = F^i(\mathbf{1})(n)(w').$*

Example 7. We now apply the iterator F to the PSDG in Fig. 6 to correctly verify $\mathcal{M}_2, t_0 \models \mathcal{P}_{>\frac{5}{8}}(a\, U_{\leq 8}\, b)$. We will use $\mathbf{C}_x = \{(0, x)\}$ to represent the constant step-function with value x. Table 2 shows the first 9 iterations of F for the nodes that change value, starting from $\mathbf{C}_0$. After 9 iterations, node $\mathbf{1}$ is assigned $\mathbf{C}_1$ as $\mathbf{2}$ was assigned $\{(3, \frac{1}{2}), (8, \frac{1}{4})\}$ in iteration 8. This represents the fact that $t_0 \xrightarrow{3, \frac{1}{2}} t_1$ adds $\frac{1}{2}$ to the probability if the cost bound is equal to or greater than 3 and $t_0 \xrightarrow{5, \frac{1}{2}} t_0 \xrightarrow{3, \frac{1}{2}} t_1$ adds $\frac{1}{2} \cdot \frac{1}{2} = \frac{1}{4}$ if the bound is 8 or greater. Thus, for a bound of exactly 8 the two steps are added and we get the probability $\frac{6}{8} > \frac{5}{8}$. Note that the fixed-point is not reached as there is a cycle between nodes $\mathbf{2, 4, 6}$. Hence the set $\{(3, \frac{1}{2}), (8, \frac{1}{4}), (13, \frac{1}{8})\}$ will be propagated to $\mathbf{2}$, but this will not change the assignment to $\mathbf{1}$. Thus, at iteration 9 we can stop.

Table 2. Iterations of F on PDG in Fig. 6

Iter#/Node	1	2	4	5	6	7	8
0	$\mathbf{C}_0$	$\mathbf{C}_0$	$\mathbf{C}_0$	$\mathbf{C}_0$	$\mathbf{C}_0$	$\mathbf{C}_0$	$\mathbf{C}_0$
1	-	-	-	$\mathbf{C}_1$	-	-	$\mathbf{C}_1$
2	-	-	-	-	-	$\mathbf{C}_1$	-
3	-	-	-	-	$\{(3, \frac{1}{2})\}$	-	-
4	-	-	$\{3, \frac{1}{2})\}$	-	-	-	-
5	-	$\{(3, \frac{1}{2})\}$	-	-	-	-	-
6	-	-	-	-	$\{(3, \frac{1}{2}), (8, \frac{1}{4})\}$	-	-
7	-	-	$\{(3, \frac{1}{2}), (8, \frac{1}{4})\}$	-	-	-	-
8	-	$\{(3, \frac{1}{2}), (8, \frac{1}{4})\}$	-	-	-	-	-
9	$\mathbf{C}_1$	-	-	-	$\{(3, \frac{1}{2}), (8, \frac{1}{4}), (13, \frac{1}{8})\}$	-	-

5   Conclusion

We presented an approach for model-checking PCTL$_\leq^\geq$, a subset of PCTL restricted to strict lower bounds on the probabilistic modalities and lower bounds on the path formulae, against weighted probabilistic transition systems by reduction to fixed-point computations on new probabilistic versions of dependency graphs. First, we presented a simple encoding by unfolding of the path formula, leading to graphs highly dependent on the size of the cost-bound. To this end, a symbolic approach was developed to ensure independence between the size of the graph and the cost-bound, by collapsing many concrete nodes into one symbolic node. For the symbolic approach, all assignments are step-functions that, given a cost bound return a probability that corresponds to the probability mass of the set of paths that satisfy the path formula with the specified cost-bound.

Future work includes efficient data-structures for step-functions and operations on step-function in order to develop an efficient implementation based on the polynomial time on-the-fly algorithm presented in [13]. Another direction could be to lift the approach to parametric model-checking of probabilistic weighted systems.

References

1. Alur, R., Dill, D.L.: A theory of timed automata. Theor. Comput. Sci. **126**(2), 183–235 (1994). http://dx.doi.org/10.1016/0304-3975(94)90010-8
2. Andova, S., Hermanns, H., Katoen, J.-P.: Discrete-time rewards model-checked. In: Larsen, K.G., Niebert, P. (eds.) FORMATS 2003. LNCS, vol. 2791, pp. 88–104. Springer, Heidelberg (2004). doi:10.1007/978-3-540-40903-8_8
3. Baier, C., Katoen, J.: Principles of Model Checking. MIT Press, Cambridge (2008)
4. Behrmann, G., Fehnker, A., Hune, T., Larsen, K., Pettersson, P., Romijn, J., Vaandrager, F.: Minimum-cost reachability for priced time automata. In: Benedetto, M.D., Sangiovanni-Vincentelli, A. (eds.) HSCC 2001. LNCS, vol. 2034, pp. 147–161. Springer, Heidelberg (2001). doi:10.1007/3-540-45351-2_15
5. Cassez, F., David, A., Fleury, E., Larsen, K.G., Lime, D.: Efficient on-the-fly algorithms for the analysis of timed games. In: Abadi, M., Alfaro, L. (eds.) CONCUR 2005. LNCS, vol. 3653, pp. 66–80. Springer, Heidelberg (2005). doi:10.1007/11539452_9
6. Christoffersen, P., Hansen, M., Mariegaard, A., Ringsmose, J.T., Larsen, K.G., Mardare, R.: Parametric verification of weighted systems. In: 2nd International Workshop on Synthesis of Complex Parameters, SynCoP 11, 2015, London, UK, pp. 77–90 (2015). http://dx.doi.org/10.4230/OASIcs.SynCoP.2015.77
7. Clarke, E.M., Emerson, E.A., Sistla, A.P.: Automatic verification of finite-state concurrent systems using temporal logic specifications. ACM Trans. Program. Lang. Syst. **8**(2), 244–263 (1986). http://doi.acm.org/10.1145/5397.5399
8. Dalsgaard, A.E., et al.: Extended dependency graphs and efficient distributed fixed-point computation. In: van der Aalst, W., Best, E. (eds.) PETRI NETS 2017. LNCS, vol. 10258, pp. 139–158. Springer, Cham (2017). doi:10.1007/978-3-319-57861-3_10
9. Dalsgaard, A.E., Enevoldsen, S., Larsen, K.G., Srba, J.: Distributed computation of fixed points on dependency graphs. In: Fränzle, M., Kapur, D., Zhan, N. (eds.) SETTA 2016. LNCS, vol. 9984, pp. 197–212. Springer, Cham (2016). doi:10.1007/978-3-319-47677-3_13
10. Dehnert, C., Junges, S., Katoen, J., Volk, M.: A storm is coming: a modern probabilistic model checker. CoRR abs/1702.04311 (2017). http://arxiv.org/abs/1702.04311
11. Hansson, H., Jonsson, B.: A logic for reasoning about time and reliability. Formal Asp. Comput. **6**(5), 512–535 (1994). http://dx.doi.org/10.1007/BF01211866
12. Howard, R.A.: Dynamic Probabilistic Systems, vol. 2. Wiley, New York (1971)
13. Jensen, J.F., Larsen, K.G., Srba, J., Oestergaard, L.K.: Efficient model-checking of weighted CTL with upper-bound constraints. STTT **18**(4), 409–426 (2016). http://dx.doi.org/10.1007/s10009-014-0359-5
14. Katoen, J., Khattri, M., Zapreev, I.S.: A Markov reward model checker. In: Second International Conference on the Quantitative Evaluaiton of Systems (QEST 2005), Torino, Italy, 19–22 September 2005, pp. 243–244 (2005). http://dx.doi.org/10.1109/QEST.2005.2
15. Kleene, S.C.: Introduction to metamathematics. Van Nostrand, Princeton (1952)

16. Kwiatkowska, M., Norman, G., Parker, D.: PRISM 4.0: verification of probabilistic real-time systems. In: Gopalakrishnan, G., Qadeer, S. (eds.) CAV 2011. LNCS, vol. 6806, pp. 585–591. Springer, Heidelberg (2011). doi:10.1007/978-3-642-22110-1_47

17. Larsen, K.G., Pettersson, P., Yi, W.: UPPAAL in a nutshell. STTT 1(1–2), 134–152 (1997). http://dx.doi.org/10.1007/s100090050010

18. Liu, X., Smolka, S.A.: Simple linear-time algorithms for minimal fixed points. In: Larsen, K.G., Skyum, S., Winskel, G. (eds.) ICALP 1998. LNCS, vol. 1443, pp. 53–66. Springer, Heidelberg (1998). doi:10.1007/BFb0055040

19. Norman, G., Parker, D., Sproston, J.: Model checking for probabilistic timed automata. Formal Methods Syst. Des. 43(2), 164–190 (2013). http://dx.doi.org/10.1007/s10703-012-0177-x

20. Scott, D.: Continuous lattices. In: Lawvere, F.W. (ed.) Toposes, Algebraic Geometry and Logic. LNM, vol. 274, pp. 97–136. Springer, Heidelberg (1972). doi:10.1007/BFb0073967

21. Tarski, A., et al.: A lattice-theoretical fixpoint theorem and its applications. Pacific J. Math. 5(2), 285–309 (1955)

Distribution-Based Bisimulation
for Labelled Markov Processes

Pengfei Yang[1,2], David N. Jansen[1], and Lijun Zhang[1,2(✉)]

[1] State Key Laboratory of Computer Science,
Institute of Software, CAS, Beijing, China
{yangpf,dnjansen,zhanglj}@ios.ac.cn
[2] University of Chinese Academy of Sciences, Beijing, China

Abstract. In this paper we propose a (sub)distribution-based bisimulation for labelled Markov processes and compare it with earlier definitions of state and event bisimulation, which both only compare states. In contrast to those state-based bisimulations, our distribution bisimulation is weaker, but corresponds more closely to linear properties. We construct a logic and a metric to describe our distribution bisimulation and discuss linearity, continuity and compositional properties.

1 Introduction

1.1 Labelled Markov Processes

Markov processes are one of the most popular types of stochastic processes in the fields of mathematics, physics, biology, economics, and computer science. Markov processes have a common property, called *Markov property:* Given exact information on the present, the future is independent of the past. There are many examples of Markov processes, like Brownian motion, spread of infectious diseases, option pricing, and quantitative information flow. In some of these, the state space is continuous, so it is worth studying such Markov processes.

Labelled Markov processes (LMPs) were first studied in [4,14]. Contrary to common Markov processes, they contain action labels on the transitions: There is a set of actions, and for each action there is exactly one subprobabilistic transition function to describe the transition with this action. That is to say, labelled Markov processes are transition systems with action labels and (sub)probabilistic transitions. They are input-enabled if all transitions are fully probabilistic. We adapt the following example from [2] to show what is an LMP.

Example 1.1. There are n rooms in a building, and each room has a heater that is either **On** or **Off**. The state space is the state of the heaters and the temperatures of every room, i.e. $S = \{\mathbf{On}, \mathbf{Off}\}^n \times \mathbb{R}^n$. On every transition we can change the states of heaters, so the set of actions $\mathcal{A} = 2^{\{1,2,\dots,n\}}$. The temperature of the i-th room at time k is denoted by x_i^k, and these x_i are determined by the following stochastic difference equation:

$$x_i^{k+1} = x_i^k + b_i(x_0 - x_i^k) + \sum_{j \neq i} a_{ij}(x_j^k - x_i^k) + c_i \mathbb{I}_{\{q_i^k = \mathbf{On}\}} + w_i^k.$$

© Springer International Publishing AG 2017
A. Abate and G. Geeraerts (Eds.): FORMATS 2017, LNCS 10419, pp. 170–186, 2017.
DOI: 10.1007/978-3-319-65765-3_10

Here x_0 is the outside temperature, b_i is the rate of heat transfer between the i-th room and the outside environment, a_{ij} is the rate of heat transfer from the j-th room to the i-th room. $q_i(k) = \textbf{On}$ means from time k to $k+1$ the heater of the i-th room is $\textbf{On}$, c_i describes the temperature influence of this heater, and $w_i(k)$ are independent normally distributed random variables which represent errors. Now the state space is no longer discrete, but hybrid, and we have a discrete-time evolution. At every step we choose an action from the set $\mathcal{A}$, and the probabilistic transition is determined by a system of difference equations.

1.2 Motivation and Related Work

A bisimulation is a relation that describes which states of an automaton or process exhibit equivalent behaviour. It can help us simplify the models and grasp the core properties of systems. Bisimulation relations were first studied in [24,25] for discrete probabilistic systems. On the downside, bisimulations for probabilistic systems are known to lack *robustness:* a small perturbation of the probabilities may change bisimilar states to become different. As a result, metrics for probabilistic systems have been proposed, such that a smaller distance between two states implies their behaviours are more similar. A distance of zero agrees with the standard (precise) bisimulation. We refer to [26, Chap. 8] for a detailed discussion. In [3,5,7,28], decision algorithms and optimisations for bisimulation metrics have been investigated. Bisimulation distance between probabilistic processes composed by standard process is characterised in [21]. In [1], approximating bisimulation based on relations, metrics, and approximating functions for LMPs were discussed systematically.

Bisimulations for Markov processes with continuous state spaces (especially analytic spaces) were studied in [4,13,14]. These papers also introduced the name "labelled Markov processes". They defined bisimulation for LMPs in a coalgebraic way and constructed a simple logic to characterise this bisimulation. This work led to a lot of further research on bisimulations for LMPs [26].

Metrics, approximations and other topics based on bisimulation for labelled Markov processes were studied in [8–10,15,16]. In [6], a bisimulation relation was defined in a categoric way for abstract Markov processes, and that paper also discussed logical characterisation and approximation based on their definition of bisimulation. [11] discussed state and event bisimulation for non-deterministic LMPs and gave a logic characterisation of event bisimulation.

The work mentioned above all focuses on bisimulations between states. That is to say, their bisimulations are binary relations on the state space. Inspired by [17], research on bisimulations based on *distributions* (or *subdistributions*) for probabilistic systems with discrete state spaces bloomed up [19,22,23].

Distribution-based bisimulations are usually coarser than state-based bisimulations, i.e. they declare more states in probabilistic systems equivalent. We are not aware of any research on distribution-based bisimulation for LMPs or other probabilistic systems with continuous state spaces or time evolution, which motivates us to carry on with such research. There are many methods and results which are inspired by the discrete situation, but also some new problems, observations and differences have appeared.

Different from state-based bisimulation, distribution-based bisimulation has a tight connection with linear-time properties. In [19], an equivalence metric is put forward to measure the distance between two systems. Basically the metric characterising bisimulation is equal to this equivalence metric, so their distribution-based bisimulation corresponds to trace distribution equivalence. In our setting, similar results hold, which indicates that our distribution-based bisimulation characterises equivalence of linear properties. When discussing distribution bisimulation, we can construct a logical characterization even for state spaces that are not analytic. Also, some proofs which are trivial for discrete models need a second thought.

Summarising, the main contributions of our paper are:

- First, we propose a distribution-based bisimulation for LMPs (Sect. 2). We show that our definition conservatively extends standard state-based and event-based bisimulations in the literature.
- Second, We provide a logical characterisation result for our bisimulation based on extensions of the Hennessy–Milner logic (Sect. 3).
- Also, we define a (pseudo)metric between distributions of LMPs with discounting factor $0 < c \leq 1$ (Sect. 4). A distance of 0 is equivalent to our notion of bisimilarity. Further, we investigate the notion of equivalence metric, characterising trace equivalence distance, and show that our metric matches the trace equivalence distance in a natural manner. We study some useful properties and then investigate the compositional properties.

2   Subdistribution Bisimulation

We assume that the readers have basic knowledge of measure theory, like measurable spaces, (sub)probability measures, Borel σ-algebras, and integration of measurable functions. We refer to [18] for details.

2.1   Bisimulations for Labelled Markov Processes

First we introduce the definition of labelled Markov processes (LMPs) formally [4,26]. We equip an LMP with an initial distribution.

Definition 2.1. *A labelled Markov process (LMP) is a tuple $(S, \Sigma, (\tau_a)_{a \in \mathcal{A}}, \pi)$, where*

- *(S, Σ) is a measurable space;*
- *$\tau_a : S \times \Sigma \to [0, 1]$ is a subprobability transition function indexed with an element a in the set $\mathcal{A}$ of actions, where we assume that $\mathcal{A}$ is countable;*
- *$\pi \in Dist(S)$ is the initial distribution.*

Here $(\tau_a)_{a \in \mathcal{A}}$ induces a relation $\to$ on $S \times \mathcal{A} \times subDist(S)$: $(s, a, \mu) \in \to$, also denoted by $s \xrightarrow{a} \mu$, if $\tau_a(s, \cdot) = \mu(\cdot)$. For $\mu, \mu' \in subDist(S)$, we write $\mu \xrightarrow{a} \mu'$, if

$$\mu'(\cdot) = \int \tau_a(s, \cdot) \mu(\mathrm{d}s).$$

Moreover, the relation $\to$ can be expanded to $subDist(S) \times \mathcal{A}^* \times subDist(S)$ by:

- *$\mu \xrightarrow{\varepsilon} \mu$, where ε is the empty word;*
- *For $w \in \mathcal{A}^*$ and $a \in \mathcal{A}$, write $\mu \xrightarrow{wa} \mu'$ if there exists μ'' s.t. $\mu \xrightarrow{w} \mu'' \xrightarrow{a} \mu'$.*

Now we will define subdistribution bisimulation, state bisimulation and event bisimulation for LMPs so that we can compare these bisimulations. Subdistribution bisimulation extends the discrete version in [19].

Definition 2.2. *Let $(S, \Sigma, (\tau_a)_{a \in \mathcal{A}}, \pi)$ be an LMP. We say a symmetric relation $R \subseteq subDist(S) \times subDist(S)$ is a (subdistribution) bisimulation relation, if $\mu \, R \, \nu$ implies:*

- *$\mu(S) = \nu(S)$;*
- *For any $a \in \mathcal{A}$ and $\mu \xrightarrow{a} \mu'$, there exists $\nu \xrightarrow{a} \nu'$, s.t. $\mu' \, R \, \nu'$.*

We say $\mu, \nu \in subDist(S)$ are bisimilar, denoted by $\mu \sim_d \nu$, if there exists a bisimulation relation R, s.t. $\mu \, R \, \nu$.

Remark. The wording of Definition 2.2 is classical and can be used for non-deterministic LMPs [11] as well. Since our LMPs do not contain non-determinism, the second condition holds if and only if for any $a \in \mathcal{A}$, $\mu \xrightarrow{a} \mu'$ and $\nu \xrightarrow{a} \nu'$ implies $\mu' \, R \, \nu'$.

Like other bisimilarity relations, the relation $\sim_d$ is an equivalence relation, and the proof is classical.

Proposition 2.3. *The relation $\sim_d$ is an equivalence relation.*

The following example from [19] shows an LMP with a finite state space, which is classical in discussing bisimulation based on distributions.

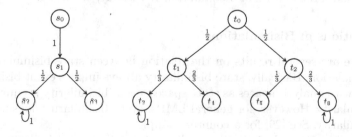

Fig. 1. An example of subdistribution bisimulation: $\delta_{s_0} \sim_d \delta_{t_0}$.

Example 2.4. Figure 1 shows an LMP with a single action in its action set $\mathcal{A} = \{a\}$. In this LMP, we have $\delta_{s_0} \sim_d \delta_{t_0}$. Let the relation R be $\{(\delta_{s_0}, \delta_{t_0}), (\delta_{s_1}, \frac{1}{2}\delta_{t_1} + \frac{1}{2}\delta_{t_2}), (\frac{1}{2}\delta_{s_2} + \frac{1}{2}\delta_{s_3}, \frac{1}{6}\delta_{t_3} + \frac{1}{3}\delta_{t_4} + \frac{1}{6}\delta_{t_5} + \frac{1}{3}\delta_{t_6}), (\frac{1}{2}\delta_{s_2}, \frac{1}{6}\delta_{t_3} + \frac{1}{3}\delta_{t_6})\}$. Then it is easy to check that its symmetric and reflexive closure $\bar{R}$ is a subdistribution bisimulation relation. Therefore, we have $\delta_{s_0} \sim_d \delta_{t_0}$.

Then we recall state bisimulation according to [8]. Given a binary relation $R \subseteq S \times S$, we say $A \subseteq S$ is R-closed, if $R(A) := \{t \in S | \exists s \in A, \ s \, R \, t\} \subseteq A$.

Definition 2.5. *Let $(S, \Sigma, (\tau_a)_{a \in \mathcal{A}}, \pi)$ be an LMP. We say an equivalence relation $R \subseteq S \times S$ is a state bisimulation relation, if $s \, R \, t$ implies that for any $a \in \mathcal{A}$ and R-closed set $A \in \Sigma$,*

$$\tau_a(s, A) = \tau_a(t, A). \tag{1}$$

We say $s, t \in S$ are state-bisimilar, denoted by $s \sim_s t$, if there exists a state bisimulation relation R, s.t. $s \, R \, t$.

In Definition 2.5, we check (1) only for measurable R-closed sets. We do not require all R-equivalence classes to be measurable, just as the following example shows.

Example 2.6. ([8]). Let $(\mathbb{R}, \mathcal{B}(\mathbb{R}), (\tau_a)_{a \in \{*\}}, \pi)$ be an LMP. The transitions are defined by $\tau_*(s, \{s\}) = 1$ for all $s \in \mathbb{R}$. Let $A \subseteq \mathbb{R}$ be a set which is not Lebesgue-measurable. Then the relation $R := (A \times A) \cup (A^c \times A^c)$ is a state bisimulation relation with non-measurable equivalence classes.

In the example, intuitively we dislike such a bisimulation relation, since the separation is too fine. To avoid this problem, [8] defined event bisimulation by:

Definition 2.7. *Let $(S, \Sigma, (\tau_a)_{a \in \mathcal{A}}, \pi)$ be an LMP. We say a sub-σ-algebra $\Lambda \subseteq \Sigma$ is an event bisimulation, if $(S, \Lambda, (\tau_a)_{a \in \mathcal{A}}, \pi)$ is still an LMP. We define the the Λ-indistinguishable relation $\mathcal{R}(\Lambda)$ to contain all pairs of states $x, y \in S$ for which there is no set $A \in \Lambda$ that distinguishes x from y (i.e. $\{x, y\} \cap A$ contains exactly one element). If Λ is an event bisimulation, we sometimes also call $\mathcal{R}(\Lambda)$ an event bisimulation relation. We say $s, t \in S$ are event-bisimilar, denoted by $s \sim_e t$, if there exists an event bisimulation relation R, s.t. $s \, R \, t$.*

2.2 Relations of Bisimulations

In [8], there are several results on the relation between state bisimulation and event bisimulation. Basically, state bisimilarity always implies event bisimilarity. For LMPs with analytic spaces as state spaces, event bisimilarity is equivalent to state bisimilarity. However, for general LMPs, event bisimilarity does not imply state bisimilarity. See [29] for a counterexample.

We show that state bisimilarity implies subdistribution bisimilarity.

Theorem 2.8. *Given an LMP with measurable single-point sets. $s \sim_s t$ implies $\delta_s \sim_d \delta_t$, but $\delta_s \sim_d \delta_t$ does not imply $s \sim_s t$.*

Consequently, we can extend state bisimilarity $\sim_s$ to $subDist(S) \times subDist(S)$: We write $\mu \sim_s \nu$ if there is a state bisimulation R, s.t. for any R-closed set $A \in \Sigma$, $\mu(A) = \nu(A)$. While $\mu \sim_s \nu$ now implies $\mu \sim_d \nu$, they are not equivalent.

In [1], instead of R-closed sets, only equivalence classes are checked in Eq. (1) of Definition 2.5. However, these two definitions differ, and using equivalence class has counterintuitive consequences. In particular, Theorem 2.8 does not hold any more. The following example shows this fact.

Example 2.9. Let $\mathcal{M} = ([0,], \mathcal{B}([0,1]), (\tau_a)_{a \in \mathcal{A}}, \pi)$ be an LMP, where $\mathcal{A} = \{a\}$ and τ_a is defined as follows:

$$\tau_a(0, A) = \frac{1}{2} m(A); \quad \tau_a(1, A) = \frac{1}{2} \int_A \left(x + \frac{1}{2}\right) dx;$$

$$\tau_a(s, \{0\}) = \tau_a(s, \{1\}) = \frac{s}{2}, \quad \tau_a(s, (0, 1)) = 0, \quad 0 < s < 1.$$

Here m is the Lebesgue measure on $(\mathbb{R}, \mathcal{B}(\mathbb{R}))$. Let $R \subseteq [0,1] \times [0,1]$ be the smallest equivalence relation that satisfies $0\ R\ 1$. Then, the set of equivalence classes contains all singletons $\{x\}$, for $0 < x < 1$, and $\{0, 1\}$. It is easy to check that R is not a state bisimulation, since for the R-closed set $I = (0, 1/2)$, $\tau_a(0, I) \neq \tau_a(1, I)$. However, if we replace "R-closed set" with "equivalence class" in Definition 2.5, then R is a state bisimulation.

Now we show that $\delta_0 \sim_d \delta_1$ does not hold. Otherwise, there exists a bisimulation relation R', s.t. $\delta_0\ R'\ \delta_1$. Now $\delta_0 \xrightarrow{a} \mu_0$ and $\delta_1 \xrightarrow{a} \mu_1$, where μ_0 has density $p_0(x) = 1/2$ and μ_1 has density $p_1(x) = 1/2(x + 1/2)$, both on $[0, 1]$. Then we consider the next step $\mu_0 \xrightarrow{a} \mu_0'$ and $\mu_1 \xrightarrow{a} \mu_1'$. Here we have $\mu_0'(\{0\}) = \mu_0'(\{1\}) = \int_{(0,1)} \frac{s}{2} \mu_0(ds) = \int_{(0,1)} \frac{1}{2} \cdot \frac{s}{2} ds = \frac{1}{8}$ and $\mu_1'(\{0\}) = \mu_1'(\{1\}) = \int_{(0,1)} \frac{s}{2} \mu_1(ds) = \int_{(0,1)} \frac{1}{2}\left(s + \frac{1}{2}\right) \cdot \frac{s}{2} ds = \frac{7}{48}$. Because R' is a bisimulation relation, $\mu_0'\ R'\ \mu_1'$, but $\mu_0'(S) \neq \mu_1'(S)$. Contradiction!

Intuitively, the states 0 and 1 should not be bisimilar, since transitions from 0 and 1 induce different distributions on $(0, 1)$, where no states appear to be bisimilar. Therefore, we prefer Definition 2.5.

In this example, if we replace $\tau_a(1, \cdot)$ with any non-uniform subdistribution that has measure 1/2 on $[0, 1]$ and mean 1/2, then we have $\delta_0 \sim_d \delta_1$. However, $0 \sim_s 1$ still does not hold. This is a counterexample with a continuous state space showing that subdistribution bisimulation does not imply state bisimulation.

The proof that event bisimulation implies subdistribution bisimulation is more intricate; we postpone it to the end of the next section.

3   Logical Characterisation

Inspired by [4,8,13,14,19], we construct a logic to characterise subdistribution bisimulation in this section. Also, we compare our logical characterisation with that for state bisimulation [4,13,14] and event bisimulation [8].

3.1   Logical Characterisation for Subdistribution Bisimulation

Definition 3.1. *We assume a fixed set $\mathcal{A}$ of actions and define a logic given by*

$$\mathcal{L}_0 ::= \mathbb{T} \mid \varphi_1 \wedge \varphi_2 \mid \langle a \rangle_q \varphi \mid \langle \varepsilon \rangle_q,$$

where $a \in \mathcal{A}$ and $q \in \mathbb{Q} \cap [0,1]$, and the formula $\langle \varepsilon \rangle_q$ does not appear in the scope of any diamond operator $\langle a \rangle_q$. Given an LMP $\mathcal{M} = (S, \Sigma, (\tau_a)_{a \in \mathcal{A}}, \pi)$, the semantics are defined inductively as follows:

- $\mathcal{M}, \mu \models \mathbb{T}$,
- $\mathcal{M}, \mu \models \varphi_1 \wedge \varphi_2$ *iff* $\mathcal{M}, \mu \models \varphi_1$ *and* $\mathcal{M}, \mu \models \varphi_2$,
- $\mathcal{M}, \mu \models \langle a \rangle_q \varphi$ *iff* $\mu'(S) \geq q$ *and* $\mu' \models \varphi$, *where* $\mu \xrightarrow{a} \mu'$,
- $\mathcal{M}, \mu \models \langle \varepsilon \rangle_q$ *iff* $\mu(S) \geq q$.

We write $\mathcal{M} \models \varphi$, if $\mathcal{M}, \pi \models \varphi$. If there is no misunderstanding, we simply write $\mu \models \varphi$ instead of $\mathcal{M}, \mu \models \varphi$.

Our formulae $\langle a \rangle_q \varphi$ look similar to the logic defined in [4], but their semantics are quite different. We only care about whether the subdistribution of the next step satisfies φ and not about the states any more. In addition, we have added $\langle \varepsilon \rangle_q$ to measure how "large" the subdistribution is, since subdistribution bisimulation requires that two subdistributions have the same measure on S. If we only consider bisimulation between full distributions, then $\langle \varepsilon \rangle_q$ can be omitted. Also, we request that $\langle \varepsilon \rangle_q$ does not appear in the scope of any diamond operator $\langle a \rangle_q$ because $\langle a \rangle_0 (\langle \varepsilon \rangle_q \wedge \varphi)$ is semantically equivalent to $\langle a \rangle_q \varphi$.

Now we show that the logic $\mathcal{L}_0$ characterises subdistribution bisimulation.

Theorem 3.2. *$\mu \sim_{\mathrm{d}} \nu$ if and only if μ and ν satisfy the same formulae in $\mathcal{L}_0$, i.e. $\mathcal{L}_0$ characterises subdistribution bisimulation.*

Next we define four extensions of $\mathcal{L}_0$, which are inspired by [4,13,14].

$$\mathcal{L}_{\mathrm{Can}} := \mathcal{L}_0 \mid \mathrm{Can}(a), \qquad\qquad \mathcal{L}_{\neg} := \mathcal{L}_0 \mid \neg \varphi,$$

$$\mathcal{L}_{\Delta} := \mathcal{L}_0 \mid \Delta_a, \qquad\qquad \mathcal{L}_{\wedge} := \mathcal{L}_{\neg} \mid \bigwedge_{i \in \mathbb{N}} \varphi_i,$$

where $a \in \mathcal{A}$. Given an LMP $\mathcal{M} = (S, \Sigma, (\tau_a)_{a \in \mathcal{A}}, \pi)$, the semantics are defined inductively as follows:

- $\mu \models \mathrm{Can}(a)$ iff $\mu'(S) > 0$, where $\mu \xrightarrow{a} \mu'$;
- $\mu \models \Delta_a$ iff $\mu'(S) = 0$, where $\mu \xrightarrow{a} \mu'$;
- $\mu \models \neg \varphi$ iff $\mu \not\models \varphi$;
- $\mu \models \bigwedge_{i \in \mathbb{N}} \varphi_i$ iff for all $i \in \mathbb{N}$, $\mu \models \varphi_i$.

These four extended logics all characterise subdistribution bisimulation.

Proposition 3.3. *$\mathcal{L}_{\mathrm{Can}}$, $\mathcal{L}_{\Delta}$, $\mathcal{L}_{\neg}$ and $\mathcal{L}_{\wedge}$ all characterise subdistribution bisimulation.*

In previous research of state bisimulation [4,14], only $\mathcal{L}_\wedge$ characterises equivalence classes. Here we have the following similar result.

Proposition 3.4. $\mathcal{L}_\wedge$ *characterises bisimilarity equivalence classes, i.e. for any LMP and any equivalence class $C \subseteq subDist(S)$, there exists a formula $\varphi \in \mathcal{L}_\wedge$, s.t. for any $\mu \in subDist(S)$, $\mu \in C$ if and only if $\mu \models \varphi$.*

Proof. Let $C \subseteq subDist(S)$ be a bisimilarity equivalence class. Let $F(C)$ be the set of $\mathcal{L}_0$ formulae which are satisfied by the subdistributions in C. It is easy to see that $F(C)$ is countable. Let $\varphi = \bigwedge_{\psi \in F(C)} \psi \in \mathcal{L}_\wedge$. Then for any $\mu \in subDist(S)$, $\mu \in C$ if and only if for any $\psi \in F(C)$, $\mu \models \psi$, i.e. $\mu \models \varphi$.

However, the other logics cannot characterise equivalence classes.

Example 3.5. Let $\mathcal{M}_0$ be an LMP with one action a and only one state s_0 going to itself through the action a with probability 1. Let $\mathcal{M}_n$ be an LMP with one action a and n states which can do the action $n - 1$ times and finally goes to a dead state. Consider the union LMP $\mathcal{M} = \bigcup_{n=0}^{\infty} \mathcal{M}_n$, then the equivalence class of δ_{s_0} cannot be characterised by any finite formula.

While for state bisimulation, $\mathcal{L}_\neg$ characterises equivalence classes of any finite LMP, its subdistribution bisimilarity equivalence classes still cannot be characterised by $\mathcal{L}_0$, $\mathcal{L}_{Can}$, $\mathcal{L}_\Delta$ or $\mathcal{L}_\neg$, as shown by the next example.

Example 3.6. Let $\mathcal{M}$ be an LMP with one action a and two states: s going to itself with probability 1, and t going to itself with probability 0.5. We can see that the two states (or rather δ_s and δ_t) are not bisimilar. Then the equivalence class $\{\sqrt{2}/2\, \delta_s\}$ cannot be characterised by any finite formula because an irrational number must be characterised by an infinite sequence of rational numbers. Moreover, even $\mathcal{L}_0$ ($\mathcal{L}_{Can}$, $\mathcal{L}_\Delta$ or $\mathcal{L}_\neg$) cannot characterise equivalence classes of distributions. Consider the equivalence class $\{\sqrt{2}/2\, \delta_s + (1 - \sqrt{2}/2)\, \delta_t\}$: it is still impossible to characterise an irrational number.

3.2 Comparison of Logical Characterisations

In this part we recall the logical characterisation for state-based bisimulation and compare it with ours, to understand the difference between them deeper. Also, we will show that event bisimilarity implies subdistribution bisimilarity. First let's recall the logic that characterises state-based bisimulation [4,14].

Definition 3.7. *We assume a fixed set $\mathcal{A}$ of actions and define a logic given by*

$$\mathcal{L} ::= \mathbb{T} \mid \phi_1 \wedge \phi_2 \mid \langle a \rangle_q^{sl} \phi,$$

where $a \in \mathcal{A}$ and $q \in \mathbb{Q}$. Given an LMP $\mathcal{M} = (S, \Sigma, (\tau_a)_{a \in \mathcal{A}}, \pi)$, the semantics are defined inductively as follows:

– $\mathcal{M}, s \models \mathbb{T}$,

- $M, s \models \phi_1 \wedge \phi_2$ iff $M, s \models \phi_1$ and $M, s \models \phi_2$,
- $M, s \models \langle a \rangle_q^{\mathrm{st}} \phi$ iff there exists $A \in \Sigma$, s.t. $\mu(A) \geq q$, and $t \models \phi$ for all $t \in A$.

If there is no misunderstanding, we simply write $s \models \phi$ instead of $M, s \models \phi$.

The formula $\langle a \rangle_q^{\mathrm{st}} \phi$ looks similar to $\langle a \rangle_q \varphi$ in $\mathcal{L}_0$. However, their semantics differ. For $\langle a \rangle_q^{\mathrm{st}} \phi$, satisfiability requests a measurable set which is large enough and only contains states satisfying ϕ, but for $\langle a \rangle_q \varphi$, we only request that after an action a, the resulting subdistribution should be large enough and satisfy φ.

From [4,14], we know that the logic $\mathcal{L}$ can characterise state bisimulation for LMPs with analytic state spaces. In [8], it is proven that $\mathcal{L}$ characterises event bisimulation for arbitrary LMPs. We summarise their results as follows:

Proposition 3.8.

(1) For an LMP with an analytic state space, $s \sim_s t$ if and only if s and t satisfy the same formulae in $\mathcal{L}$.
(2) For any LMP, $s \sim_e t$ if and only if s and t satisfy the same formulae in $\mathcal{L}$.

Now we consider whether event bisimilarity implies subdistribution bisimilarity. We only need to show that, if s and t satisfy the same formulae in $\mathcal{L}$, then δ_s and δ_t (provided that every single-point set is measurable) satisfy the same formulae in $\mathcal{L}_0$. We note that δ_s and δ_t satisfy the same formulae of the form $\langle \varepsilon \rangle_q$, so we do not consider such formulae any more. Then the syntaxes of the two logics $\mathcal{L}$ and $\mathcal{L}_0$ become very similar. We inductively define a mapping $f : \mathcal{L} \rightarrow \mathcal{L}_0$ by:

- $f(\mathbb{T}) = \mathbb{T}$,
- $f(\phi_1 \wedge \phi_2) = f(\phi_1) \wedge f(\phi_2)$,
- $f(\langle a \rangle_q^{\mathrm{st}} \phi) = \langle a \rangle_q f(\phi)$.

Basically we just replace every $\langle a \rangle_q^{\mathrm{st}}$ in $\mathcal{L}$ formulae with $\langle a \rangle_q$. Obviously this f is surjective. First we have the following observation:

Proposition 3.9.

(1) In $\mathcal{L}_0$, we have $\langle a \rangle_q (\varphi_1 \wedge \varphi_2) \equiv (\langle a \rangle_q \varphi_1) \wedge (\langle a \rangle_q \varphi_2)$, where $\equiv$ means semantic equivalence.
(2) In $\mathcal{L}$, $s \models \langle a \rangle_q^{\mathrm{st}} (\phi_1 \wedge \phi_2)$ implies $s \models \langle a \rangle_q^{\mathrm{st}} \phi_1$ and $s \models \langle a \rangle_q^{\mathrm{st}} \phi_2$.

The proposition is easy to prove from the semantics of $\mathcal{L}_0$ and $\mathcal{L}$. From this observation, first we can turn every formula in $\mathcal{L}_0$ to a conjunctive normal form (CNF) $\bigwedge_{i=1}^{m} \varphi_i$, where every φ_i has the form $\langle a_1 \rangle_{q_1} \cdots \langle a_{n_i} \rangle_{q_{n_i}} \mathbb{T}$. First we deal with formulae like ϕ_i. We have the following proposition:

Proposition 3.10. *Given an LMP with measurable single-point sets. We have that $s \models \langle a_1 \rangle_{q_1}^{\mathrm{st}} \cdots \langle a_n \rangle_{q_n}^{\mathrm{st}} \mathbb{T}$ is equivalent to $\delta_s \models \langle a_1 \rangle_{q_1} \cdots \langle a_n \rangle_{q_n} \mathbb{T}$.*

For a general formula in $\mathcal{L}_0$, we compare its f^{-1}-image with the f^{-1}-image of its CNF. The latter implies the former, as transforming a formula in $\mathcal{L}$ to CNF may lead to a weaker formula. Therefore we get the following result:

Proposition 3.11. *Given an LMP with measurable single-point sets. If s and t satisfy the same formulae in $\mathcal{L}$, then δ_s and δ_t satisfy the same formulae in $\mathcal{L}_0$.*

Then from Proposition 3.8, we immediately get the following result:

Theorem 3.12. *Given an LMP with measurable single-point sets. $s \sim_e t$ implies $\delta_s \sim_d \delta_t$, but the other direction does not hold.*

4   Metrics

In this section we will introduce a pseudometric and an approximating subdistribution bisimulation.

Given a nonempty set X, we say a function $d : X \times X \to [0, \infty)$ is a pseudometric on X, if for all $x, y, z \in X$, we have $d(x, x) = 0$, symmetry $d(x, y) = d(y, x)$, and the triangle inequality $d(x, y) + d(y, z) \geq d(x, z)$. If in addition $d(x, y) = 0$ implies $x = y$, then d is a metric.

4.1   Metrics and Approximating Bisimulation

First we give the definition of the pseudometric d^c, which is inspired by [16].

Definition 4.1. *Let $(S, \Sigma, (\tau_a)_{a \in \mathcal{A}}, \pi)$ be an LMP. We define $d^c : subDist(S) \times subDist(S) \to [0, 1]$ as follows:*

$$d^c(\mu, \nu) := \sup_{w \in \mathcal{A}^*, \mu \xrightarrow{w} \mu', \nu \xrightarrow{w} \nu'} c^{|w|} |\mu'(S) - \nu'(S)|,$$

where $c \in (0, 1]$ is a constant called the discounting factor, and $|w|$ is the length of the word w.

It is obvious that d^c is indeed a pseudometric. Although d^c is not a proper metric since different subdistributions may have distance 0, we follow earlier literature and call this d^c a metric.

Then, the (pseudo)metric d^c characterises subdistribution bisimulation.

Theorem 4.2. *(1) $\mu \sim \nu$ implies that for any $c \in (0, 1]$, $d^c(\mu, \nu) = 0$;*
(2) $\mu \sim \nu$ if there exists $c \in (0, 1]$, s.t. $d^c(\mu, \nu) = 0$.

With a metric d^c characterising subdistribution bisimulation, we can define approximating bisimilarity through this metric.

Definition 4.3. *Let $(S, \Sigma, (\tau_a)_{a \in \mathcal{A}}, \pi)$ be an LMP. Given $\epsilon \geq 0$ and $c \in (0, 1]$, we say $\mu, \nu \in subDist(S)$ are ϵ-bisimilar with the discounting factor c, denoted by $\mu \sim_\epsilon^c \nu$, if $d^c(\mu, \nu) \leq \epsilon$.*

It is easy to prove the following properties of approximating bisimilarity.

Proposition 4.4.

(1) For any $c \in (0,1]$, $\sim_d = \sim_0^c$;
(2) For any $c \in (0,1]$ and $0 \leq \epsilon \leq \epsilon'$, $\sim_\epsilon^c \subseteq \sim_{\epsilon'}^c$;
(3) For any $c \in (0,1]$, $\sim_d = \bigcap_{\epsilon>0} \sim_\epsilon^c$;
(4) For any $\epsilon \geq 0$ and $0 < c \leq c' \leq 1$, $\sim_\epsilon^c \subseteq \sim_\epsilon^{c'}$;
(5) If $\mu_1 \sim_\epsilon^c \mu_2$ and $\mu_2 \sim_{\epsilon'}^c \mu_3$, then $\mu_1 \sim_{\epsilon+\epsilon'}^c \mu_3$.

Different from other papers [1,19], we directly define our approximating bisimilarity based on the metric, not on an approximating bisimulation relation. In fact, we could also do the latter, and the two definitions are equivalent:

Definition 4.5. *Given a discounting factor $c \in (0,1]$, we say a collection of symmetric relations $\{R_\epsilon^c\}_{\epsilon>0}$ on $subDist(S)$ is an approximating bisimulation relation with the discounting factor c, if $\mu\ R_\epsilon^c\ \nu$ implies:*

- $|\mu(S) - \nu(S)| \leq \epsilon$;
- *For any $a \in \mathcal{A}$ and $\mu \xrightarrow{a} \mu'$, there exists $\nu \xrightarrow{a} \nu'$, s.t. $\mu'\ R_{\epsilon/c}^c\ \nu'$.*

We write $\mu \approx_{\epsilon'}^c \nu$, if there exists an approximating bisimulation relation $\{R_\epsilon^c\}_{\epsilon>0}$, s.t. $\mu\ R_{\epsilon'}^c\ \nu$.

Then we have the following property:

Proposition 4.6. $\sim_{\epsilon'}^c = \approx_{\epsilon'}^c$ for any $c \in (0,1]$ and $\epsilon' > 0$.

4.2   Equivalence Metric for LMP

In [19], distribution-based bisimulation for probabilistic automata [27] is constructed, and an equivalence metric to describe linear-time properties is defined. Basically, their equivalence metric is the supremum of the distribution difference on finite words. In probabilistic automata, every state is labelled with a set of atomic propositions. Not so in LMPs; however, we can label every state in an LMP with the same label $\top$, with the intuitive meaning: the process has not stopped or blocked; then, distribution on traces are just the same as distributions on paths. Then we can define trace equivalence for two subdistributions in an LMP as follows: Given an LMP $\mathcal{M} = (S, \Sigma, (\tau_a)_{a\in\mathcal{A}}, \pi)$, we say $\pi_1, \pi_2 \in subDist(S)$ are trace equivalent, if for any $w \in \mathcal{A}^*$, $\pi_1(w) = \pi_2(w)$, where $\pi(w) = \mu(S)$, provided $\pi \xrightarrow{w} \mu$. Also we can define equivalence metric for LMPs as follows:

Definition 4.7 (Equivalence Metric). *Let $\mathcal{M}_i = (S_i, \Sigma_i, (\tau_a^i)_{a\in\mathcal{A}}, \pi_i)$ for $i = 1, 2$ be two LMPs. We say $\mathcal{M}_1$ and $\mathcal{M}_2$ are ϵ-equivalent, denoted by $\mathcal{M}_1 \sim_\epsilon \mathcal{M}_2$, if for any word $w \in \mathcal{A}^*$, $|\pi_1(w) - \pi_2(w)| \leq \epsilon$. The equivalence metric between $\mathcal{M}_1$ and $\mathcal{M}_2$ is defined by $D(\mathcal{M}_1, \mathcal{M}_2) = \inf\{\epsilon \geq 0 : \mathcal{M}_1 \sim_\epsilon \mathcal{M}_2\}$.*

From the definition, it is obvious that this metric D is equivalent to our metric d^1. From Proposition 4.6, it also corresponds to our approximating bisimulation relation $\sim_\epsilon^1$. Therefore, we claim that our approximating bisimulation describes the distance between two LMPs with respect to linear properties. Also, subdistribution bisimilarity is equivalent to trace equivalence.

In some papers [16,19], metrics are defined through a logic. Here in a similar way we can define a metric d_l^c based on a logic. Furthermore, we will show that this metric is equivalent to d^c.

Definition 4.8. *Let $c \in (0,1]$ be a discounting factor. Let $\mathcal{M} = (S, \Sigma, (\tau_a)_{a\in\mathcal{A}}, \pi)$ be an LMP. We define a logic given by*

$$\mathcal{L}_\mathcal{M}^c ::= \mathbf{1} \mid \varphi \oplus p \mid \neg\varphi \mid \bigwedge_{i\in I} \varphi_i \mid \langle a \rangle^c \varphi,$$

where $p \in [0,1]$, $a \in \mathcal{A}$ and I is an index set. The semantics of the formula φ in $\mathcal{L}_\mathcal{M}^c$ is a function on $subDist(S)$, defined inductively as follows:

$$\mathbf{1}(\mu) := \mu(S)$$
$$(\varphi \oplus p)(\mu) := \min\{\varphi(\mu) + p, 1\}$$
$$\neg\varphi(\mu) := 1 - \varphi(\mu)$$
$$(\bigwedge_{i\in I} \varphi_i)(\mu) := \inf\{\varphi_i(\mu) : i \in I\}$$
$$\langle a \rangle^c \varphi(\mu) := c \cdot \varphi(\mu'), \text{ where } \mu \xrightarrow{a} \mu'.$$

Definition 4.9. *Let $\mathcal{M} = (S, \Sigma, (\tau_a)_{a\in\mathcal{A}}, \pi)$ be an LMP. For $\mu, \nu \in subDist(S)$, we define $d_l^c : subDist(S) \times subDist(S) \to [0,1]$ as follows:*

$$d_l^c(\mu, \nu) := \sup_{\varphi\in\mathcal{L}_\mathcal{M}^c} |\varphi(\mu) - \varphi(\nu)|.$$

Obviously d_l^c is indeed a pseudometric. The next theorem shows that d_l^c defined through logic is equivalent to d^c.

Proposition 4.10. *Let $\mathcal{M} = (S, \Sigma, (\tau_a)_{a\in\mathcal{A}}, \pi)$ be an LMP. Then for any $\mu, \nu \in subDist(S)$ and $c \in (0,1]$, $d^c(\mu, \nu) = d_l^c(\mu, \nu)$.*

4.3   Linearity and Continuity of Subdistribution Bisimulation

Theorem 4.2 is powerful, because with it we can prove some properties of the relation $\sim_d$ more easily. In this part, we illustrate how to exploit them to prove the linearity and continuity of our subdistribution bisimulation. In [12,19], similar results have been proven for discrete models. However, for LMPs with arbitrary state spaces, the proofs are quite different. Here approximation with simple functions and the monotone convergence theorem are applied multiple times, which indicates the intuition that it is a good way to use finite models to approximate an LMP in many problems.

Given a sequence of subdistributions $\{\mu_n\}$ on $(X, \mathcal{F})$, we say $\{\mu_n\}$ converges to μ, denoted by $\mu_n \to \mu$, or $\lim_{n\to\infty} \mu_n = \mu$, if for any $A \in \mathcal{F}$, $\mu_n(A) \to \mu(A)$ as $n \to \infty$. Now we give the definitions of linearity, σ-linearity and continuity of a relation on $subDist(S)$.

Definition 4.11. *We say a relation $R \subseteq subDist(S) \times subDist(S)$ is linear, if for any $\mu_i \, R \, \nu_i$, $i = 1, 2, \ldots, n$, and $\{a_i\}_{i=1}^n$ s.t. $\sum_{i=1}^n a_i\mu_i$ as well as $\sum_{i=1}^n a_i\nu_i$ are subdistributions, where $a_i \geq 0$, we have $\sum_{i=1}^n a_i\mu_i \, R \, \sum_{i=1}^n a_i\nu_i$.*

We say a relation $R \subseteq subDist(S) \times subDist(S)$ is σ-linear, if for any $\mu_i \, R \, \nu_i$, $i = 1, 2, \ldots$, and $\{a_i\}_{i=1}^\infty$ s.t. $\sum_{i=1}^\infty a_i\mu_i$ as well as $\sum_{i=1}^\infty a_i\nu_i$ are subdistributions, where $a_i \geq 0$, we have $\sum_{i=1}^\infty a_i\mu_i \, R \, \sum_{i=1}^\infty a_i\nu_i$.

We say a relation $R \subseteq subDist(S) \times subDist(S)$ is continuous, if for any $\mu_i \, R \, \nu_i$, $i = 1, 2, \ldots$, with $\mu_i \to \mu$ and $\nu_i \to \nu$ as $n \to \infty$, we have $\mu \, R \, \nu$.

We first discuss linearity and σ-linearity. We need a lemma showing that the relation $\xrightarrow{w} \subseteq subDist(S) \times subDist(S)$ is linear and σ-linear on the space of Borel-measurable functions.

Lemma 4.12. *For any $w \in \mathcal{A}^*$, the relation $\xrightarrow{w}$ is linear and σ-linear.*

Then we have the following linear and σ-linear properties.

Proposition 4.13. *The relation $\sim_d$ is linear and σ-linear.*

Proof. We assume $\mu_i \sim_d \nu_i$, and we have $d^c(\mu_i, \nu_i) = 0$, i.e. for any $w \in \mathcal{A}^*$, $\mu_i'(S) = \nu_i'(S)$, where $\mu_i \xrightarrow{w} \mu_i'$ and $\nu_i \xrightarrow{w} \nu_i'$. Then from the linearity of $\xrightarrow{w}$, we have $\sum_{i=1}^n a_i\mu_i \xrightarrow{w} \sum_{i=1}^n a_i\mu_i'$ and $\sum_{i=1}^n a_i\nu_i \xrightarrow{w} \sum_{i=1}^n a_i\nu_i'$, and naturally

$$\sum_{i=1}^n a_i\mu_i'(S) = \sum_{i=1}^n a_i\nu_i'(S),$$

which indicates $d^c(\sum_{i=1}^n a_i\mu_i, \sum_{i=1}^n a_i\nu_i) = 0$ since w is arbitrary.

By taking the limit $n \to \infty$ in the proof above, we can see that the relation $\sim_d$ also is σ-linear.

Now we discuss continuity. Similarly we only need to prove that the relation $\xrightarrow{w}$ is continuous.

Lemma 4.14. *The relation $\xrightarrow{w}$ is continuous.*

Actually from the proof of Lemma 4.14, we can get a stronger result: If $\mu_i \xrightarrow{w} \nu_i$ and $\lim_{i\to\infty} \mu_i = \mu$, then there exists a subdistribution ν, s.t. $\lim_{i\to\infty} \nu_i = \nu$. Then it is natural that the relation $\sim_d$ is continuous.

Proposition 4.15. *The relation $\sim_d$ is continuous.*

Proof. We assume $\mu_i \sim_d \nu_i$, $\mu_i \to \mu$ and $\nu_i \to \nu$. We need to prove $\mu \sim_d \nu$. From Theorem 4.2 we have $d^c(\mu_i, \nu_i) = 0$, i.e. for any $w \in \mathcal{A}^*$, $\mu_i'(S) = \nu_i'(S)$, where $\mu_i \xrightarrow{w} \mu_i'$ and $\nu_i \xrightarrow{w} \nu_i'$. Because $\mu_i \to \mu$ and $\nu_i \to \nu$, there exist μ' and ν', s.t. $\lim_{i\to\infty} \mu_i' = \mu'$ and $\lim_{i\to\infty} \nu_i' = \nu'$, and we have $\mu \xrightarrow{w} \mu'$ and $\nu \xrightarrow{w} \nu'$. Then $\mu'(S) = \lim_{i\to\infty} \mu_i'(S) = \lim_{i\to\infty} \mu_i'(S) = \nu'(S)$, which indicates $d^c(\mu, \nu) = 0$ since w was arbitrary.

What's more, if the LMP has a Borel measurable space as its state space, and all its subprobability transition functions $\tau_a(\cdot, A)$ are continuous almost everywhere, then the subdistribution bisimilarity relation $\sim_d$ is continuous w.r.t. weak convergence. (See [18] for the definition of weak convergence and other details.) The following example illustrates this fact.

Example 4.16. Let $\mathcal{M} = (S, \Sigma, (\tau_a)_{a\in\mathcal{A}}, \pi)$ be an LMP, where $S = [0, 1]$, $\Sigma = \mathcal{B}([0, 1])$, and $\mathcal{A} = \mathbb{N}$. We use E_0 to denote the set $[0, 1] \setminus (\frac{1}{3}, \frac{2}{3})$, and E_n to denote the set obtained by removing the middle third of each interval that remains in E_{n-1}. The limit set $C = \lim_{n\to\infty} E_n$ is called the Cantor set. (See [18] for more details.) We define the transitions as follows:

$$\tau_i(x, A) = \begin{cases} \frac{1}{2}(\frac{3}{2})^{i+1} m(A \cap E_i^c), & \text{if } x \in E_i, \\ \delta_x(A), & \text{otherwise,} \end{cases}$$

where m is the Lebesgue measure on $([0, 1], \mathcal{B}([0, 1]))$. First, it is easy to see that this $\mathcal{M}$ is indeed an LMP. We use $U(E)$ to denote the uniform distribution over $E \in \mathcal{B}([0, 1])$ with $m(E) > 0$. We can see that $U([0, 3^{-n-1}])$ and $U(E_n)$ are subdistribution bisimilar because these two distributions have the same subdistribution after any a_i-transition. We have that $U([0, 3^{-n-1}])$ converges weakly to the Dirac distribution δ_0 as $n \to \infty$. Also, the sequence of distributions $U(E_n)$ converges because the distribution function F_n of the distribution $U(E_n)$ converges uniformly to some F as $n \to \infty$, and obviously F is also a distribution function. We call the distribution with the distribution function F the uniform distribution on the Cantor set, denoted by $U(C)$, and obviously $U(E_n)$ converges to $U(C)$ as $n \to \infty$. Therefore, we have $\delta_0 \sim_d U(C)$.

4.4   Compositionality

Compositionality is a great help in simplifying model checking: When a large system is composed from several small systems, we would like to work on these small systems to see whether their composition satisfy some property. In this part we discuss the compositionality of our subdistribution bisimilarity. This part also relies on Theorem 4.2 heavily. We will see that two large systems are subdistribution bisimilar if their composition components are subdistribution bisimilar, respectively, in our LMP setting. We assume that all the LMPs in this part have the same action set $\mathcal{A}$. First we introduce the definition of the composition for two LMPs:

Definition 4.17. *Let* $\mathcal{M}_i = (S_i, \Sigma_i, (\tau_a^i)_{a \in \mathcal{A}}, \pi_i)$, $i = 1, 2$ *be two LMPs. Their composition* $\mathcal{M}_1 \parallel \mathcal{M}_2 = (S, \Sigma, (\tau_a)_{a \in \mathcal{A}}, \pi)$ *is defined as follows:*

- $(S, \Sigma) = (S_1 \times S_2, \sigma(\Sigma_1 \times \Sigma_2))$;
- $\tau_a((s_1, s_2), \cdot) = \tau_a^1(s_1, \cdot) \times \tau_a^2(s_2, \cdot)$ *for* $(s_1, s_2) \in S$;
- $\pi = \pi_1 \times \pi_2$.

Then we show that composition preserves bisimilarity:

Theorem 4.18. $\mathcal{M}_1 \sim_d \mathcal{M}_1'$ *and* $\mathcal{M}_2 \sim_d \mathcal{M}_2'$ *imply* $\mathcal{M}_1 \parallel \mathcal{M}_2 \sim_d \mathcal{M}_1' \parallel \mathcal{M}_2'$.

From Theorem 4.18, we can immediately know that for any LMP $\mathcal{M}$, $\mathcal{M}_1 \sim_d$ $\mathcal{M}_1'$ implies $\mathcal{M}_1 \parallel \mathcal{M} \sim_d \mathcal{M}_1' \parallel \mathcal{M}$. Actually Theorem 4.18 is a special case of the following theorem, by taking $\epsilon_1 = \epsilon_2 = 0$:

Theorem 4.19. *Given the discounting factor* $c \in (0, 1]$ *and approximation* $\epsilon_1, \epsilon_2 \in [0, 1]$, $\mathcal{M}_1 \sim_{\epsilon_1}^c \mathcal{M}_1'$ *and* $\mathcal{M}_2 \sim_{\epsilon_2}^c \mathcal{M}_2'$ *imply* $\mathcal{M}_1 \parallel \mathcal{M}_2 \sim_{\epsilon_1 + \epsilon_2 - \epsilon_1 \epsilon_2}^c$ $\mathcal{M}_1' \parallel \mathcal{M}_2'$.

Theorem 4.19 bounds the distance between the composed LMPs. This bound $\epsilon_1 + \epsilon_2 - \epsilon_1 \epsilon_2$ can be approximated by $\epsilon_1 + \epsilon_2$, which is a linear function of ϵ_1 and ϵ_2. Also we can see that composition with bisimilar LMPs does not make the distance of two LMPs larger, so bisimulation is compositional in this sense. Observe the bound in Theorem 4.19 is tight.

5   Conclusion

In this paper we propose to define subdistribution bisimulation for LMPs based on distributions rather than states, and we described its basic properties. We compare it with earlier bisimulations to show that it is a weaker relation. Following a common way to study a bisimulation, we construct a logic and a metric both characterising our subdistribution bisimulation.

There are several interesting directions for future work. First, we plan to investigate an approximation scheme for our subdistribution bisimulation. Another direction is to deal with systems that are more complex than LMPs. For example, we can add non-deterministic choice for the same action, as the model in [11]. In addition, we can add the internal action τ to the set of actions and investigate weak bisimulation for LMPs/ Further, we can investigate the metric definition for continuous-time models [20].

Last but not least, using coalgebras is a popular way to describe bisimulation and simulation relations for probabilistic systems (e.g. [30,31]), and we expect that our distribution-based bisimulation for LMPs and other more complex models will have a pretty coalgebraic description.

Acknowledgement. This work has been supported by the National Natural Science Foundation of China (Grants 61532019, 61472473), the CAS/SAFEA International Partnership Program for Creative Research Teams, the Sino-German CDZ project CAP (GZ 1023).

References

1. Abate, A.: Approximation metrics based on probabilistic bisimulations for general state-space Markov processes: a survey. Electr. Notes Theor. Comput. Sci. **297**, 3–25 (2013)
2. Abate, A., Katoen, J.-P., Lygeros, J., Prandini, M.: Approximate model checking of stochastic hybrid systems. Eur. J. Control **16**(6), 624–641 (2010)
3. Bacci, G., Bacci, G., Larsen, K.G., Mardare, R.: On-the-fly exact computation of bisimilarity distances. In: Piterman, N., Smolka, S.A. (eds.) TACAS 2013. LNCS, vol. 7795, pp. 1–15. Springer, Heidelberg (2013). doi:10.1007/978-3-642-36742-7_1
4. Blute, R., Desharnais, J., Edalat, A., Panangaden, P.: Bisimulation for labelled Markov processes. In: IEEE Symposium on Logic in Computer Science (LICS), pp. 149–158. IEEE Computer Society (1997)
5. van Breugel, F., Sharma, B., Worrell, J.: Approximating a behavioural pseudometric without discount for probabilistic systems. Logical Methods Comput. Sci. **4**(2), 123–137 (2008)
6. Chaput, P., Danos, V., Panangaden, P., Plotkin, G.D.: Approximating Markov processes by averaging. J. ACM **61**(1), 5:1–5:45 (2014)
7. Daca, P., Henzinger, T.A., Křetínský, J., Petrov, T.: Linear distances between Markov chains. In: Concurrency Theory (CONCUR). Leibniz International Proceedings in Informatics (LIPIcs), vol. 59, pp. 20:1–20:15. Schloss Dagstuhl-Leibniz-Zentrum fuer Informatik (2016)
8. Danos, V., Desharnais, J., Laviolette, F., Panangaden, P.: Bisimulation and cocongruence for probabilistic systems. Inf. Comput. **204**(4), 503–523 (2006)
9. Danos, V., Desharnais, J., Panangaden, P.: Conditional expectation and the approximation of labelled markov processes. In: Amadio, R., Lugiez, D. (eds.) CONCUR 2003. LNCS, vol. 2761, pp. 477–491. Springer, Heidelberg (2003). doi:10.1007/978-3-540-45187-7_31
10. Danos, V., Desharnais, J., Panangaden, P.: Labelled Markov processes: stronger and faster approximations. Electr. Notes Theor. Comput. Sci. **87**, 157–203 (2004)
11. D'Argenio, P.R., Terraf, P.S., Wolovick, N.: Bisimulations for non-deterministic labelled Markov processes. Math. Struct. Comput. Sci. **22**(1), 43–68 (2012)
12. Deng, Y.: Semantics of Probabilistic Processes. Springer, Heidelberg (2014)
13. Desharnais, J., Edalat, A., Panangaden, P.: A logical characterization of bisimulation for labeled Markov processes. In: IEEE Symposium on Logic in Computer Science (LICS), pp. 478–487. IEEE Computer Society (1998)
14. Desharnais, J., Edalat, A., Panangaden, P.: Bisimulation for labelled Markov processes. Inf. Comput. **179**(2), 163–193 (2002)
15. Desharnais, J., Gupta, V., Jagadeesan, R., Panangaden, P.: Approximating labelled Markov processes. Inf. Comput. **184**(1), 160–200 (2003)
16. Desharnais, J., Gupta, V., Jagadeesan, R., Panangaden, P.: Metrics for labelled Markov processes. Theor. Comput. Sci. **318**(3), 323–354 (2004)
17. Doyen, L., Henzinger, T.A., Raskin, J.F.: Equivalence of labeled Markov chains. Int. J. Found. Comput. Sci. **19**(3), 549–563 (2008)
18. Durrett, R.: Probability: Theory and Examples, 3rd edn. Duxbury Press, Belmont (2004)
19. Feng, Y., Zhang, L.: When equivalence and bisimulation join forces in probabilistic automata. In: Jones, C., Pihlajasaari, P., Sun, J. (eds.) FM 2014. LNCS, vol. 8442, pp. 247–262. Springer, Cham (2014). doi:10.1007/978-3-319-06410-9_18

20. Ferns, N., Panangaden, P., Precup, D.: Bisimulation metrics for continuous Markov decision processes. SIAM J. Comput. **40**(6), 1662–1714 (2011)
21. Gebler, D., Larsen, K.G., Tini, S.: Compositional metric reasoning with probabilistic process calculi. In: Pitts, A. (ed.) FoSSaCS 2015. LNCS, vol. 9034, pp. 230–245. Springer, Heidelberg (2015). doi:10.1007/978-3-662-46678-0_15
22. Hennessy, M.: Exploring probabilistic bisimulations, part I. Formal Asp. Comput. **24**(4–6), 749–768 (2012)
23. Hermanns, H., Krčál, J., Křetínský, J.: Probabilistic bisimulation: naturally on distributions. In: Baldan, P., Gorla, D. (eds.) CONCUR 2014. LNCS, vol. 8704, pp. 249–265. Springer, Heidelberg (2014). doi:10.1007/978-3-662-44584-6_18
24. Kemeny, J.G., Snell, J.L.: Finite Markov chains. Springer, Heidelberg (1960)
25. Larsen, K.G., Skou, A.: Bisimulation through probablistic testing. Inf. Comput. **94**(1), 1–28 (1991)
26. Panangaden, P.: Labelled Markov Processes. Imperial College Press, London (2009)
27. Segala, R., Lynch, N.A.: Probabilistic simulations for probabilistic processes. Nord. J. Comput. **2**(2), 250–273 (1995)
28. Tang, Q., van Breugel, F.: Computing probabilistic bisimilarity distances via policy iteration. In: Concurrency Theory (CONCUR). LIPIcs, vol. 59, p. 22:1–22:15. Schloss Dagstuhl - Leibniz-Zentrum fuer Informatik (2016)
29. Terraf, P.S.: Unprovability of the logical characterization of bisimulation. CoRR abs/1005.5142 (2010)
30. Urabe, N., Hasuo, I.: Generic forward and backward simulations III: quantitative simulations by Matrices. In: Baldan, P., Gorla, D. (eds.) CONCUR 2014. LNCS, vol. 8704, pp. 451–466. Springer, Heidelberg (2014). doi:10.1007/978-3-662-44584-6_31
31. Vink, E.P., Rutten, J.J.M.M.: Bisimulation for probabilistic transition systems: a coalgebraic approach. In: Degano, P., Gorrieri, R., Marchetti-Spaccamela, A. (eds.) ICALP 1997. LNCS, vol. 1256, pp. 460–470. Springer, Heidelberg (1997). doi:10.1007/3-540-63165-8_202

Quantitative Logics and Monitoring

On the Quantitative Semantics of Regular Expressions over Real-Valued Signals

Alexey Bakhirkin[1,2]([✉]), Thomas Ferrère[3], Oded Maler[1,2], and Dogan Ulus[1,2]

[1] Université Grenoble-Alpes, VERIMAG, 38000 Grenoble, France
alexey.bakhirkin@univ-grenoble-alpes.fr
[2] CNRS, VERIMAG, 38000 Grenoble, France
[3] IST Austria, Am Campus 1, 3400 Klosterneuburg, Austria

Abstract. Signal regular expressions can specify sequential properties of real-valued signals based on threshold conditions, regular operations, and duration constraints. In this paper we endow them with a quantitative semantics which indicates how robustly a signal matches or does not match a given expression. First, we show that this semantics is a safe approximation of a distance between the signal and the language defined by the expression. Then, we consider the robust matching problem, that is, computing the quantitative semantics of every segment of a given signal relative to an expression. We present an algorithm that solves this problem for piecewise-constant and piecewise-linear signals and show that for such signals the robustness map is a piecewise-linear function. The availability of an indicator describing how robustly a signal segment matches some regular pattern provides a general framework for quantitative monitoring of cyber-physical systems.

1 Introduction

Regular expressions (RE) are among the cornerstones of computer science, being one of several formalism that can express sets of sequences (languages) acceptable by finite-state automata. In addition to their application in domains such as lexical analysis and pattern matching, regular expression are used in verification as a specification formalism to express correct or erroneous behaviors of reactive systems. In this context they are used along with another popular specification formalism, linear-time temporal logic (LTL) [27] that can express (star-free) regular languages in a different and complementary style. For both formalisms, the commonly-used semantics consists of discrete-time sequences often defined over finite small alphabets without a rich structure.

Over the years several extensions related to these two aspects, namely, discrete time and discrete non-numerical values, have been pursued in various contexts. To model real-time systems, finite automata have been augmented with

This research was supported in part by the European Research Council under the European Union's Seventh Framework Programme (FP/2007-2013)/ERC Grant Agreement nr. 306595 "STATOR", and by the Austrian Science Fund (FWF) under grants S11402-N23 (RiSE/SHiNE) and Z211-N23 (Wittgenstein Award).

A. Abate and G. Geeraerts (Eds.): FORMATS 2017, LNCS 10419, pp. 189–206, 2017.
DOI: 10.1007/978-3-319-65765-3_11

continuously-evolving clocks resulting in timed automata [2] that can generate
and accept sets of timed behaviors consisting of Boolean signals or time-event
sequences, where events and state transitions are embedded in the dense real-
time axis, not forced to occur at pre-specified sampling points or clock ticks.
On the specification side, temporal logics have been extended with real-time
constructs resulting in logics such as metric temporal logic (MTL) [22] and its
decidable fragment MITL [3]. These logics can express quantitative timing properties such as bounds on the temporal distance between two events. Likewise,
timed regular expressions have been defined and one of their variants has been
proved to be expressively equivalent to timed automata [5,6].

In terms of alphabets, recent years saw a growing interest in large or infinite
alphabets taken from richer domains such as $\mathbb{N}$ or $\mathbb{R}$, admitting order and arithmetic operations. Such languages are accepted by symbolic automata [33] whose
transitions are labeled by predicates such as inequalities. Various questions, such
as minimization [10], closure under various operations and learnability [25] have
been studied in this context. Temporal logics over sequences of numbers [28]
and first-order temporal logics in general [9], as well as regular expressions over
quantitative domains [4] have also been defined and investigated.

The starting point of this work is *signal temporal logic* (STL) [23,24], which
combines the dense time of MTL with predicates over real-valued variables. As
such it can be used to express properties of continuous and mixed signals resulting from the simulation (or measurement) of continuous and hybrid systems such
as analog circuits or cyber-physical control systems. Given a simulation trace w
and an STL formula φ, simple and efficient algorithms [23], linear in the length
of the trace, can check whether w satisfies φ and liberate users from the tedious
and error-prone task of evaluating such traces manually. These algorithms have
been implemented in tools such as AMT [26] and Breach [14] and have been
applied to case-studies in domains ranging from control systems and robotics,
via electronic circuits to systems biology.

Satisfaction (or membership) is traditionally a yes/no matter and it cannot
distinguish between robust and non-robust satisfaction, a meaningful issue in
numerical domains. To take a simple example, the requirement that some variable x is always positive is equally satisfied by safe behaviors being all the time
far above zero and more dangerous and edgy ones that approach zero but do not
cross it. To capture this distinction, quantitative semantics have been proposed
for various temporal logics [15,17,28] including STL along with efficient algorithms to compute it [16]. In a nutshell, with every STL formula φ and signal
w, a real-valued robustness measure $\rho = \rho(\varphi, w)$ is associated, admitting the
following two important properties:

1. The robustness ρ is positive if w satisfies φ, negative if w violates φ;
2. The φ-satisfaction of a signal w', whose maximal pointwise distance from w
   is smaller than ρ, is equal to that of w.

The inductive definition of the quantitative semantics of STL is isomorphic to the
standard definition of the qualitative semantics. The semantics of atomic predicates such as $x \geq 0$ at a point t is defined as $x[t]$. Boolean operations ($\wedge, \vee, \neg$)

are interpreted in the algebra $(\min, \max, -)$, and temporal operators are interpreted as min or max over time windows according to the disjunctive/conjunctive nature of the operator.

In this paper we define and compute such a quantitative semantics for *signal regular expressions* (SRE), which are timed regular expressions that use numerical predicates as atoms. Our semantics satisfies the same two important properties stated above. For regular expressions, due to the special nature of concatenation which requires to check all possible factorizations of a sequence or signal, it is natural to solve the more general pattern matching problem: given an expression φ and a signal w, find the set of all segments $w[t, t')$ that satisfy (match) φ. The set of all segments of a signal w is captured by the triangle $T_w = \{(t, t') \in \mathbb{T}^2 \mid 0 \le t \le t' \le |w|\}$. The segments that satisfy φ define a subset of T_w that we call the *match set* of φ in w and denote by $\mathcal{M}(\varphi, w)$. In [32] it was proven that for every Boolean signal of bounded variability, the match set is a finite union of zones that can be computed by induction on the structure of the expression. The analogous problem for the quantitative semantics is to compute the robust satisfaction degree ρ of φ w.r.t. w for every segment $(t, t') \in T_w$. This is the problem we solve in this paper.

2   Signal Regular Expressions

In this section, we introduce signal regular expressions (SRE), recall their qualitative semantics and introduce a quantitative semantics. Signal regular expressions are an adaptation of the timed regular expressions (TRE) of [5,6] designed to deal with real-valued, rather than Boolean signals. They are built from atomic constraints (e.g., $x \ge 2$ specifies a signal segment where x is above 2), standard regular operations, and *duration constraints*. For an expression φ and an interval I, the duration constraint $\langle \varphi \rangle_I$ specifies that the duration of the signal segment that matches φ should be within I.

Signals. A *signal* is a function $w : \mathbb{T} \to \mathbb{R}^n$ where $\mathbb{T} = [s, s')$ is a bounded interval of $\mathbb{R}_{\ge 0}$, called the *temporal domain*. We usually take $s = 0$. The length of signal w is given by $|w| = s' - s$. By $w[t] \in \mathbb{R}^n$, we denote the value of w at time $t \in \mathbb{T}$. By $w[t, t')$, we denote the signal that has the temporal domain $[t, t') \subseteq [s, s')$ and agrees with w on $[t, t')$. We call such a signal a *factor* of w. Signal values are accessed by variables from the set $\mathbb{X} = \{x_1, \ldots x_n\}$. For a variable $x \in \mathbb{X}$ we denote by $w_x : \mathbb{T} \to \mathbb{R}$ the projection of w on x. We say that w_x is a *component* of w.

Definition 1 (Syntax of SRE). *SREs are formed according to the grammar:*

$$\varphi ::= \varnothing \mid \epsilon \mid x \ge c \mid x \le c \mid \varphi \vee \varphi \mid \varphi \wedge \varphi \mid \varphi \cdot \varphi \mid \varphi^* \mid \langle \varphi \rangle_I$$

where $x \in \mathbb{X}$, $c \in \mathbb{R}$, and I is an interval of $\mathbb{R}$ with integer bounds.

As standard, we write iterated concatenation of an expression φ using power notation: $\varphi^0 = \epsilon$, and $\varphi^k = \varphi^{k-1} \cdot \varphi$ for an integer $k > 0$.

The *qualitative semantics* of expression φ w.r.t. a signal w is given by the function μ that returns a Boolean value (in $\{0,1\}$), indicating whether w *matches* φ.

Definition 2 (Qualitative Semantics of SRE). *The semantics $\mu(\varphi, w)$ of expression φ w.r.t a signal w is defined inductively as follows:*

$$\mu(\varnothing, w) = 1 \quad \Leftrightarrow \quad \bot$$
$$\mu(\epsilon, w) = 1 \quad \Leftrightarrow \quad |w| = 0$$
$$\mu(x \geq c, w) = 1 \quad \Leftrightarrow \quad |w| > 0 \text{ and } \forall t \in [0, |w|), w_x[t] \geq c$$
$$\mu(x \leq c, w) = 1 \quad \Leftrightarrow \quad |w| > 0 \text{ and } \forall t \in [0, |w|), w_x[t] \leq c$$
$$\mu(\varphi \vee \psi, w) = 1 \quad \Leftrightarrow \quad \mu(\varphi, w) = 1 \text{ or } \mu(\psi, w) = 1$$
$$\mu(\varphi \wedge \psi, w) = 1 \quad \Leftrightarrow \quad \mu(\varphi, w) = 1 \text{ and } \mu(\psi, w) = 1$$
$$\mu(\varphi \cdot \psi, w) = 1 \quad \Leftrightarrow \quad \exists uv = w, \mu(\varphi, u) = 1 \text{ and } \mu(\psi, v) = 1$$
$$\mu(\varphi^*, w) = 1 \quad \Leftrightarrow \quad \exists k \geq 0, \mu(\varphi^k, w) = 1$$
$$\mu(\langle\varphi\rangle_I, w) = 1 \quad \Leftrightarrow \quad \mu(\varphi, w) = 1 \text{ and } |w| \in I$$

where uv denotes the concatenation of signals u and v.

The set of signals that matches an expression φ is called the *language* of φ; $\mathcal{L}(\varphi) = \{w \mid \mu(\varphi, w) = 1\}$.

We introduce a *quantitative* semantics of an expression φ w.r.t. a signal w, given by the function ρ that returns a real value (in $\mathbb{R} \cup \pm\infty$) and indicates how robustly w matches φ. We call it the *robustness* of φ w.r.t. w (or the robustness of w w.r.t. φ).

Definition 3 (Quantitative Semantics of SRE). *The robustness $\rho(\varphi, w)$ of an expression φ w.r.t. a signal w is defined inductively as follows:*

$$\rho(\varnothing, w) = -\infty$$
$$\rho(\epsilon, w) = \begin{cases} +\infty, & \text{if } |w| = 0 \\ -\infty, & \text{otherwise} \end{cases}$$
$$\rho(x \geq c, w) = \begin{cases} \inf_{t \in [0, |w|)} w_x[t] - c & \text{if } |w| > 0 \\ -\infty & \text{otherwise} \end{cases}$$
$$\rho(x \leq c, w) = \begin{cases} \inf_{t \in [0, |w|)} c - w_x[t] & \text{if } |w| > 0 \\ -\infty & \text{otherwise} \end{cases}$$
$$\rho(\varphi \vee \psi, w) = \max\{\rho(\varphi, w), \rho(\psi, w)\}$$
$$\rho(\varphi \wedge \psi, w) = \min\{\rho(\varphi, w), \rho(\psi, w)\}$$
$$\rho(\varphi \cdot \psi, w) = \sup_{uv=w} \min\{\rho(\varphi, u), \rho(\psi, v)\}$$
$$\rho(\varphi^*, w) = \sup_{k \geq 0} \rho(\varphi^k, w)$$
$$\rho(\langle\varphi\rangle_I, w) = \begin{cases} \rho(\varphi, w), & \text{if } |w| \in I \\ -\infty, & \text{otherwise} \end{cases}$$

where $\sup \emptyset = \inf \mathbb{R} = -\infty$ and $\inf \emptyset = \sup \mathbb{R} = +\infty$.

In what follows, we can assume without loss of generality that atomic expressions are of the form $x \geq 0$. Given a constraint $x \geq c$ (resp. $x \leq c$), we can replace it by the constraint $y \geq 0$, where y is a fresh variable, and the projection of w on y is defined as $w_y[t] = w_x[t] - c$ (resp. $c - w_x[t]$). This replacement preserves the quantitative and qualitative semantics, as well as the assumptions that we make later (e.g., the signal being piecewise-constant or continuous piecewise-linear, etc.).

3   Properties of the Quantitative Semantics

In this section, we present two important properties of our semantics. First, we relate the qualitative and quantitative semantics based on a notion of a *distance*. Second, we show that the quantitative semantics of a Kleene star expression φ^* can be computed as a finite iteration of φ.

3.1   Robustness Estimate

We now introduce a metric on the signal space and then derive two notions of distance between signals and expressions.

Definition 4 (Signal Distance). *The (uniform norm) distance between signals v and w, denoted $\mathrm{d}(v, w)$, is defined by $\mathrm{d}(v, w) = \sup_{t \in \mathbb{T}} \max_{x \in \mathbb{X}} |v_x[t] - w_x[t]|$ if v and w have the same temporal domain $\mathbb{T}$, otherwise $\mathrm{d}(v, w) = +\infty$.*

Definition 5 (Expression Distance). *The distance from signal w to expression φ, denoted $\underline{\mathrm{d}}(\varphi, w)$, is defined by $\underline{\mathrm{d}}(\varphi, w) = \inf_{v \in \mathcal{L}(\varphi)} \mathrm{d}(v, w)$. The co-distance from signal w to expression φ, denoted $\overline{\mathrm{d}}(\varphi, w)$, is defined by $\overline{\mathrm{d}}(\varphi, w) = \inf_{v \notin \mathcal{L}(\varphi)} \mathrm{d}(v, w)$.*

Such (Hausdorff) distances indicate by how much w needs to be changed to satisfy or violate φ, respectively. The quantitative semantics of SRE has the following characteristics: on a given signal its sign indicates membership in the language of the expression, and its magnitude estimates the distance to language boundary.

Theorem 1 (Soundness). *Let φ be an expression, and w a signal. If $\rho(\varphi, w) > 0$ then $w \in \mathcal{L}(\varphi)$. Symmetrically if $\rho(\varphi, w) < 0$ then $w \notin \mathcal{L}(\varphi)$.*

Theorem 2 (Correctness). *Let φ be an expression, and v, w two signals. If $w \in \mathcal{L}(\varphi)$ and $\mathrm{d}(v, w) < \rho(\varphi, w)$ then $v \in \mathcal{L}(\varphi)$. Symmetrically if $w \notin \mathcal{L}(\varphi)$ and $\mathrm{d}(v, w) < -\rho(\varphi, w)$ then $v \notin \mathcal{L}(\varphi)$.*

These two characteristics are in fact direct corollaries of the following statement:

Lemma 1 (Distance Bounds). *Let φ be an expression and w a signal. Then, we have $-\underline{\mathrm{d}}(\varphi, w) \leq \rho(\varphi, w) \leq \overline{\mathrm{d}}(\varphi, w)$.*

Due to space constraints, we cannot give the full proof here. It proceeds by straightforward induction on the expression structure, using lattice properties of min, max, inf and sup.

Theorems 1 and 2 derive from Lemma 1 as follows. Assume $\rho(\varphi, w) > 0$. We have $\overline{d}(\varphi, w) > 0$ and thus $w \in \mathcal{L}(\varphi)$ by definition of $\overline{d}(\varphi, w)$; the statement of Theorem 1 is proved. If $d(v, w) < \rho(\varphi, w)$, then $\overline{d}(\varphi, v) \geq \overline{d}(\varphi, w) - d(v, w) > 0$ and again $v \in \mathcal{L}(\varphi)$; the statement of Theorem 2 is proved. Symmetrical reasoning applies to the case $\rho(\varphi, w) < 0$; when $\rho(\varphi, w) = 0$ both statements hold vacuously true.

3.2 Star Boundedness

We now prove that for every signal w (from a broad class of *well-behaved* signals) there exists some index m such that $\rho(\varphi^*, w) = \rho(\bigvee_{n=0}^{m} \varphi^n, w)$. Intuitively, this is because for practical signals, there is a limit to how many non-redundant factors it can be partitioned into. In particular, if a factor v is *sufficiently short*, $\rho(\varphi^2, v) \leq \rho(\varphi, v)$, and v does not need to be partitioned further during the computation of $\rho(\varphi^*, w)$. A similar result was obtained in [32] for the qualitative semantics of SRE, but for the quantitative case the proof is much more complicated since we do not assume the signals to be piecewise-constant.

Let us formalize what is a *sufficiently short* signal. For a pair of signals f and g over temporal domain $\mathbb{T}$, we write $f \leq g$ when $f[t] \leq g[t]$ for every $t \in \mathbb{T}$. A real signal f is *increasing* (*decreasing*) if $f[t] \leq f[t']$ (respectively $f[t] \geq f[t']$) for all $t < t' \in \mathbb{T}$. A signal that is increasing or decreasing is called *monotone*.

Definition 6 (Unitary Signal). *A signal w is unitary when $|w| < 1$, for every $x \in X$, w_x is monotone, and for every $x, y \in \mathbb{X}$, $w_x \leq w_y$ or $w_y \leq w_x$.*

Intuitively, a unitary signal is sufficiently short and need not be partitioned further during the computation of $\rho(\varphi^*, w)$. More formally, we have the following.

Lemma 2 (Square). *For a unitary signal u and an expression φ, $\rho(\varphi^2, u) \leq \rho(\varphi, u)$.*

Let us delay the proof of Lemma 2, and instead state and prove (using Lemma 2) an important result of this section.

Definition 7 (Well-behaved signal). *A signal w is* well-behaved *if there exists $k \in \mathbb{N}$ such that w can be factored into $w = u_1 u_2 \ldots u_k$ where every u_i for $i \in \{1, \ldots, k\}$ is unitary. The smallest such k is denoted $\kappa(w)$.*

Theorem 3 (Star is Bounded). *For a well-behaved signal w with $\kappa(w) = k$ we have $\rho(\varphi^*, w) = \rho(\bigvee_{n=0}^{2k+1} \varphi^n, w)$.*

Proof. Assume, in search of a contradiction, that $\rho(\varphi^{n+1}, w) > \rho(\varphi^n, w)$ for some $n > 2k + 1$. This means that there exists a decomposition $w = u_1 u_2 \ldots u_{n+1}$ such that for every $1 \leq i \leq n+1$, $\rho(\varphi, u_i) > \rho(\varphi^n, w)$. However $\kappa(w) = k$, so by pigeon hole principle there exists j such that the factor $u' = u_j u_{j+1}$ is unitary. From Lemma 2, $\rho(\varphi, u') \geq \rho(\varphi^2, u') \geq \min\{\rho(\varphi, u_j), \rho(\varphi, u_{j+1})\}$ and thus $\rho(\varphi, u') > \rho(\varphi^n, w)$. We obtain the decomposition $w = u_1 \ldots u_{j-1} u' u_{j+2} \ldots u_{n+1}$ with n factors, s.t. robustness of φ on every factor is greater than $\rho(\varphi^n, w)$, which contradicts the definition of $\rho(\varphi^n, w)$. Thus, it has to be that $\rho(\varphi^{n+1}, w) \leq \rho(\varphi^n, w)$ for every $n > 2k + 1$. According to the semantics of Kleene star, $\rho(\varphi^*, w) = \sup_{n \geq 0} \rho(\varphi^n, w) = \max_{n=0}^{2k+1} \rho(\varphi^n, w) = \rho(\bigvee_{n=0}^{2k+1} \varphi^n, w)$. □

Due to space constraints, we cannot give the proof of Lemma 2 in full, but we guide the reader through its most important steps. Let us write $\varphi \approx_w \psi$ when $\rho(\varphi, v) = \rho(\psi, v)$ for every factor v of w; and $\varphi \preccurlyeq_w \psi$ when $\rho(\varphi, v) \leq \rho(\psi, v)$ for every factor v of w. It turns out, given a unitary signal w, we can always rewrite an expression φ into another expression γ, s.t. $\gamma \approx_w \varphi$ and for which we can prove $\gamma^2 \preccurlyeq_w \gamma$. Let us give an example of such a rewriting.

Example 1. Consider the unitary signal w defined on $[s_1, s_2)$ in Fig. 1 and the expression $\varphi = \langle x \geq 0 \cdot z \geq 0 \rangle_{(0,2)} \vee y \geq 0$. Let v be an arbitrary factor $w[r_1, r_2)$. Observe that $\rho(x \geq 0 \cdot z \geq 0, v) = \sup_{r' \in (r_1, r_2)} \min\{\inf_{[r_1, r')} w_x, \inf_{[r', r_2)} w_z\} = \inf_{[r_1, r')} w_x$ (since w_x is increasing and everywhere below w_z). That is $x \geq 0 \cdot z \geq 0 \approx_w x \geq 0$. Then, notice that the duration constraint has no influence on signals of length less than one. Finally, since w_y is pointwise below w_x, $x \geq 0 \vee y \geq 0 \approx_w x \geq 0$. Thus, $\varphi = \langle x \geq 0 \cdot z \geq 0 \rangle_{(0,2)} \vee y \geq 0 \approx_w x \geq 0$.

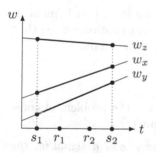

Fig. 1. A unitary signal w defined on $[s_1, s_2)$.

Example 2. Consider the same unitary signal, the expression $\varphi = x \geq 0 \cdot z \geq 0 \cdot y \geq 0$ and let v be an arbitrary factor $w[r_1, r_2)$. Observe that $\rho(\varphi, v) = \sup_{r', r'' \in (r_1, r_2)} \min\{\inf_{[r_1, r')} w_x, \inf_{[r', r'')} w_z, \inf_{[r'', r_2)} w_y\}$. To maximize the minimum, we want to move the time point r'' infinitely close to r_2 and obtain $\rho(\varphi, v) = \min\{\inf_v w_x, \sup_v w_y\}$ (since w_z is everywhere above w_x and w_y, the corresponding term is discarded). Similarly, we can show that $\rho(x \geq 0 \cdot y \geq 0, v) = \min\{\inf_v w_x, \sup_v w_y\}$ and thus $\varphi \approx_w x \geq 0 \cdot y \geq 0$.

In general, the robustness of an expression over a unitary signal *and over its every factor* is given by some min-max expression. We prefer to state this in a more algebraic way and say that for a given unitary signal, every expression can be rewritten to an equivalent *quadratic expression*.

Definition 8 (Monomial, Polynomial) *A monomial expression (of degree n) is of the form $\epsilon \cdot \alpha_1 \cdot \alpha_2 \cdots \alpha_n$, where every α_i is and atomic expression. A polynomial expression (of degree n) is of the form $\varnothing \vee \bigvee_{j=1}^m \beta_j$ where each β_j is a monomial expression (of degree at most n). A polynomial expression of degree at most 2 is called quadratic.*

Quadratic expressions are sufficient to represent the robustness of an arbitrary expressions over unitary signals. They are also necessary, as illustrated in Example 2, in the sense that atomic expressions cannot replace arbitrary expressions.

Proposition 1 (Quadratic Expressions). *For every expression φ and unitary signal u, there exists a quadratic expression γ such that $\varphi \approx_u \gamma$.*

The proof proceeds by structural induction, rewriting the expressions using Kleene algebra and lattice equivalences. Lemmas 3 and 4 state the key property of polynomial expressions relative to unitary signals. By proving them, we prove Lemma 2.

Lemma 3 (Product of Monomials). *Let u be a unitary signal. For every pair of monomials β_1, β_2 there exists a monomial β_3 of degree at most 2 such that the following is true: $\beta_1 \cdot \beta_2 \approx_u \beta_3 \preccurlyeq_u \beta_1 \vee \beta_2$*

Proof idea. To find β_3, we want to find an atomic expression $y \geq 0$ appearing in $\beta_1 \cdot \beta_2$ such that y is minimal. Then if y is increasing, all factors in $\beta_1 \cdot \beta_2$ at the right of $y \geq 0$ can be ignored, and only the leftmost factor $x \geq 0$ is needed. We let $\beta_3 = x \geq 0 \cdot y \geq 0$, and check that monotonicity and ordering entail the equation of Lemma 3; the case where y is decreasing is symmetrical.   □

Lemma 4 (Squaring Polynomials). *For every unitary signal u and polynomial expression γ we have $\gamma^2 \preccurlyeq_u \gamma$.*

Proof idea. For every pair of monomials β_1, β_2 appearing in γ, (via Lemma 3) we have $\beta_1 \cdot \beta_2 \preccurlyeq_u \beta_1 \vee \beta_2$. Distributing unions over concatenation we see that every monomial in γ^2 is dominated according to $\preccurlyeq_u$ by a monomial in γ.   □

4   The Robust Matching Problem

Given an expression φ and a signal w, *robust matching* is the problem of computing the quantitative semantics of φ for every segment $w[t, t')$ of w.

Definition 9 (Robustness Map). *For an expression φ and a signal w, the robustness map is the function $(t, t') \mapsto \rho(\varphi, w[t, t'))$ that maps every t, t' (s.t. $0 \leq t \leq t' \leq |w|$) to the robustness of φ w.r.t w on $[t, t')$.*

It is convenient to represent the robustness map indirectly, using the following notion of *robustness support*.

Definition 10 (Robustness Support). *For a signal w and an expression φ, the robustness support is the set $\mathcal{R}(\varphi, w) = \{(t, t', r) \mid r < \rho(\varphi, w[t, t'))\}$*

The robustness map can be extracted from the robustness support by taking its pointwise supremum: $\rho(\varphi, w[t, t')) = \sup\{r \mid (t, t', r) \in \mathcal{R}(\varphi, w)\}$.

In what follows, we consider two classes of signals, continuous piecewise-linear and piecewise-constant. We show that for these signals, the robustness support can be represented as a finite union of polyhedra or *zones* respectively. As a result, the robustness map for these signals is respectively piecewise-linear or piecewise-constant.

Definition 11 (Zone). *A zone is a polyhedron formed by intersection of constraints of the form $x \bowtie c$ or $x - y \bowtie c$ where x and y are variables, c is a constant, and $\bowtie \in \{<, \leq, =, \geq, >\}$.*

Zones are often used in verification of timed systems. They admit efficient representation and computation via difference bound matrices [13].

Connection to Qualitative Matching. The *match set* $\mathcal{M}(\varphi, w)$ of an expression φ w.r.t. a signal w is the set of pairs (t, t') such that the factor $w[t, t']$ matches φ. That, is, $(t, t') \in \mathcal{M}(\varphi, w)$ iff $w[t, t'] \in \mathcal{L}(\varphi)$. For a signal of bounded variability (i.e., when the truth value of every atomic proposition has finitely many switching points), this set was shown [32] to be computable and representable by a finite union of zones.

4.1 Finite Representation of Signals

Signals are typically represented by finitely many sampling points and interpolated between them. When computing robustness, we are interested in simple interpolation schemes that produce piecewise-constant or *continuous* piecewise-linear signals (our theoretical results are applicable to a larger class of signals). Formally, we can define

Definition 12 (Piecewise-Constant Signal). *A signal $w : \mathbb{T} \to \mathbb{R}^n$ is piecewise-constant if there exists a partition of $\mathbb{T}$ into a finite ordered sequence of left-closed right-open intervals $(J_1, \ldots, J_n)$, s.t. for every $i = 1 \ldots n$, the value of w on J_i is constant.*

Definition 13 (Piecewise-Linear Signal). *A signal $w : \mathbb{T} \to \mathbb{R}^n$ is piecewise-linear if there exists a partition of $\mathbb{T}$ into a finite sequence of left-closed right-open intervals $(J_i)_{1 \leq i \leq n}$, and there exist sequences of vectors $(a_i)_{1 \leq i \leq n}$ and $(b_i)_{1 \leq i \leq n}$ such that $w[t] = a_i t + b_i$ for every $t \in J_i$, for every $1 \leq i \leq n$.*

For both classes of signals, we call the endpoints of the intervals, $\inf J_i$ and $\sup J_i$, the *switching points*. When computing the robustness, we are only interested in piecewise-linear signals that are also continuous, i.e., where $a_k(\sup J_k) + b_k = a_{k+1}(\sup J_{k+1}) + b_{k+1}$ for every two adjacent segments J_k, J_{k+1}.

The notion of a piecewise-constant or a piecewise-linear function can be extended to higher dimensions. In particular, for $\mathbb{T}^2 \to \mathbb{R}$, we can define:

Definition 14 (Piecewise-Constant and Piecewise-Linear Functions).
We say that a function $f : \mathbb{T}^2 \to \mathbb{R}$ is piecewise-constant if there exists a finite set of convex polyhedra $\{P_i\}_{1 \leq i \leq n}$ over t, t', s.t. $dom(f) = \bigcup_{i=1}^{n} P_i$, and on every P_i, f is constant. If on every P_i, f is linear in t, t', we say that f is piecewise-linear.

Theorem 4 (Piecewise-Linear Decomposition). *For an expression φ and piecewise-constant signal w, the robustness map $(t, t') \mapsto \rho(\varphi, w[t, t'])$ is piecewise-constant. For a continuous piecewise-linear signal w, the robustness map is piecewise-linear.*

Section 5 gives a constructive proof of this.

As a final remark, we note that if we sample and interpolate an analog signal, for which we know the bound on its derivative, we can infer the bound on the pointwise distance between this analog signal and its piecewise representation. This number will also be the bound on the difference between the robustness of the original signal and the robustness of its piecewise representation.

5   Algorithms

In this section we present robust matching algorithms for piecewise-constant and continuous piecewise-linear signals. More specifically, our algorithms compute a polyhedral representation of the robustness support. For a signal w and an expression φ, by induction on the structure of φ, we compute a set $\mathcal{S}_\varphi$ of convex polyhedra (over t, t', and r), whose union is $\mathcal{R}(\varphi, w)$. In particular, for a piecewise-constant signal, $\mathcal{S}_\varphi$ is a set of zones. We use the robustness support as an implicit representation of the robustness map: given a pair (t, t'), we take the maximum value of r over all (t, t', r) in the polyhedra in $\mathcal{S}_\varphi$. First, we show how to compute $\mathcal{S}_\varphi$ for the atomic propositions ($x \geq c$, $x \leq c$). Then, for the other operations, the robustness support is characterized by induction on the structure of the expression using basic operations on sets of convex polyhedra.

Atomic Propositions. Recall that we only need an algorithm to compute the robustness support for the basic atomic proposition $x \geq 0$. For a proposition such

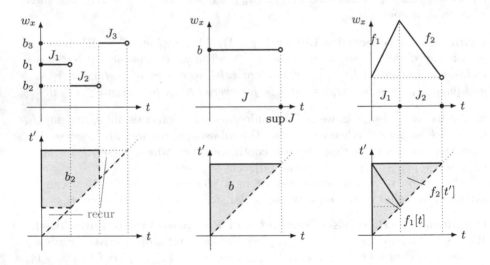

Fig. 2. A piecewise-constant signal component and a step of the algorithm for the expression $x \geq 0$

Fig. 3. A constant segment and its robustness for $x \geq 0$.

Fig. 4. A signal component consisting of two segments and its robustness for $x \geq 0$.

as $x \geq c$, we introduce an auxiliary signal component y defined as $w_y[t] = w_x[t] - c$ and then compute the support for $y \geq 0$. For the expression $x \geq 0$, robustness support can be characterized as follows

$$\mathcal{R}(x \geq 0, w) = \{(t, t', r) \mid r < \rho(x \geq 0, w, [t, t'])\} = \{(t, t', r) \mid r < \inf_{t'' \in (t,t')} w_x[t'']\}$$

That is, $\mathcal{S}_{x \geq 0}$ should be a set of polyhedra, where for every t and t', the value of r is bounded from above by the infimum of w_x on the interval (t, t'). For both piecewise-constant and continuous piecewise-linear signals we can compute it by induction on the *signal* structure, although in slightly different ways.

Piecewise-Constant Signals. Assume we are given a signal w and a finite sequence of intervals $(J_1, \ldots, J_n)$, s.t., on every J_i the signal is constant. Also assume that on an interval J_k, w_x reaches its global minimum b_k. Then, we immediately know that for every interval (t, t') that intersects with J_k, the robustness value is given by b_k. Based on this observation, we build the following recursive algorithm.

1. Given a sequence $(J_1, \ldots, J_n)$, find an interval J_k, where component w_x achieves its minimum value b_k.
2. Add to $\mathcal{S}_{x \geq 0}$ the zone ($\inf J_1 \leq t < \sup J_k \wedge \inf J_k < t' \leq \sup J_n \wedge t < t' \wedge r < b_k$). It corresponds to the shaded area in Fig. 2.
3. If $k > 1$, apply the procedure recursively to the sequence $(J_1, \ldots, J_{k-1})$.
4. If $k < n$, apply the procedure recursively to the sequence $(J_{k+1}, \ldots, J_n)$.

In Fig. 2, we give an example of one step of this procedure.

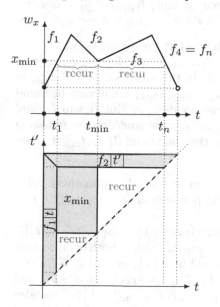

The procedure produces one *zone* for every constant segment of the signal (every recursive call produces one zone and removes one segment from consideration). Also, every constraint on r is of the form $r < c$. This is important for Theorem 4.

Continuous   Piecewise-Linear Signals. To simplify the presentation, we make two assumptions. First, we define the value of the signal at the right endpoint: $w[\sup \mathbb{T}] = \lim_{t \to \sup \mathbb{T}} w[t]$. Second, we assume that w_x reaches the minimum on both endpoints: $w_x[0] = w_x[\sup \mathbb{T}] = \min w_x$ (recursively, this will be preserved). We can always extend a signal to ensure this property, which saves us from extra case analysis. To get the idea of the algorithm, consider Fig. 5, which shows the general form of a signal with $n \geq 3$ segments. Let $x_{\min}$ be the

Fig. 5. A signal component with more than two segments and a step of the algorithm for the expression $x \geq 0$.

minimal value of the signal on segments 2 to $n - 1$, that is, excluding the first and the last segments, and let t_{min} be the corresponding time point. This information is sufficient for computing the robustness value for certain segments.

(1) In all segments that contain t_{min} and where the values in the first and last segments is above x_{min}, the robustness value is the constant x_{min}. This holds in the rectangle defined by $t \in [t_1, t_{min}]$ and $t' \in [t_{min}, t_n]$ where t_1 and t_n satisfy $f_1[t_1] = f_n[t_n] = x_{min}$.

(2) When $t \leq t_1$ and $t' \leq t_n$, the robustness value is given by $f_1[t]$ and likewise when $t > t_1$ and $t' > t_n$, the value is given by $f_n[t']$.

(3) When $t \leq t_1$ and $t' > t_n$ the value is given by either $f_1[t]$ or $f_n[t']$ depending on a linear inequality based on their respective slopes.

(4) Other segments not covered by the above and where the minimal value is larger than x_{min}, are subject to two recursive calls over the intervals $[t_1, t_{min}]$ and $[t_{min}, t_n]$.

More formally, Let w be a signal, x be a variable, and J be a time interval. We consider three cases, displayed in Figs. 3, 4, and 5.

Case 1: When w_x has one segment, because of our assumption, it is constant: $w_x[t] = b$, for $t \in J$, as shown in Fig. 3. Then for $t < t' \in J$, the robustness value is b. That is, we add to $\mathcal{S}_{x \geq 0}$ the zone $(t, t' \in J, t < t' \wedge r < b)$.

Case 2: When w_x consists of two segments, it always has a wedge-like shape as in Fig. 4. In this case we again can immediately produce the result. More formally, let J be split into J_1, J_2, s.t. $w_x[t] = a_1 t + b_1 = f_1[t]$ when $t \in J_1$, $a_2 t + b_2 = f_2[t]$ when $t \in J_2$, and (since w_x is continuous) $f_1[\sup J_1] = f_2[\inf J_2]$. Then, for $t < t' \in J_1 \cup J_2$, robustness is given by $\min\{f_1[t], f_2[t']\}$. Thus, we add to $\mathcal{S}_{x \geq 0}$ the polyhedron $(t, t' \in J_1 \cup J_2, t < t' \wedge r < a_1 t + b_1 \wedge r < a_2 t' + b_2)$.

Case 3: Now assume that w_x consists of three or more segments, i.e., J can be split into a sequence of adjacent intervals $J_1, \ldots, J_n$, s.t., for $t \in J_i$, $w_x[t] = f_i[t] = a_i t + b_i$. We show an example in Fig. 5. In this case, let us find $x'_{min} = \min_{t \in J_2 \ldots J_{n-1}} w_x[t]$ and some t_{min}, s.t. $w_x[t_{min}] = x'_{min}$ (t_{min} can always be found at a switching point). Then we find the time points $t_1 \in [\inf J_1, \sup J_1]$ and $t_n \in [\inf J_n, \sup J_n]$, s.t. $f_1[t_1] = f_n[t_n] = x'_{min}$. Now we consider the following sub-cases, based on where t and t' lie w.r.t the time points $\inf J_1, t_1, t_{min}, t_n$, and $\sup J_n$.

1. When $t \in [t_1, t_{min}]$ and $t' \in [t_{min}, t_n]$, we know that the robustness value should be x'_{min}. Thus, we add to $\mathcal{S}_{x \geq 0}$ the polyhedron $(t \in [t_1, t_{min}] \wedge t' \in [t_{min}, t_n] \wedge r < x'_{min} \wedge t < t')$;
2. When $t \leq t_1$ and $t' \geq t_n$, the robustness value is given by $\min\{w_x[t_1], w_x[t_n]\}$. More formally, when $t_1 > \inf J_1$ and $t_n < \sup J_n$ (either both will be true or, if $x'_{min} = w_x[\inf J_1] = w_x[\sup J_n]$, both will be false), we add to $\mathcal{S}_{x \geq 0}$ two polyhedra: $(t \in [\inf J_1, t_1] \wedge t < t' \wedge a_1 t + b_1 \leq a_2 t' + b_2 \wedge r \leq a_1 t + b_1)$ and $(t' \in [t_n, \sup J_n] \wedge t < t' \wedge a_2 t' + b_2 \leq a_1 t + b_1 \wedge r \leq a_n t' + b_n)$. This also accounts for the cases where $t \leq t_1$, but $t' < t_n$ (robustness is $w_x[t]$) and where $t > t_1$ and $t' \geq t_n$ (robustness is $w_x[t']$).

3. If $t_{min} > t_1$, we apply the procedure recursively to the interval $J = [t_1, t_{min}]$ (there may be a degenerate case where $t_{min} = t_1 = \sup J_1$);
4. If $t_{min} < t_n$, we apply the procedure recursively to the interval $J = [t_{min}, t_n]$ (there may be a degenerate case where $t_{min} = t_n = \inf J_n$).

One can show that this procedure produces a number of polyhedra linear in the number of segments of the signal. The total number of recursive calls of the second and third kind is bounded by the number of switching points, since every call consumes the interior point of a wedge or a point of local minimum and this point cannot appear in either role in the other recursive calls. Additionally, we make a number of recursive calls of the first kind bounded by the number of segments. Also, observe that in the resulting polyhedra, r is always unbounded from below.

Other Expressions. Robustness support can be characterized by induction on the expression structure using basic set operations. The rules below can be derived from this inductive characterization.

Empty word. For the expression ϵ, one can show that $\mathcal{R}(\epsilon, w) = \{(t, t', r) \mid t = t'\}$, which is represented using the singleton *zone*: $\mathcal{S}_\epsilon = \{(t = t')\}$.

Falsehood. In this case, robustness support is empty, thus $\mathcal{S}_\emptyset = \emptyset$.

Disjunction. For the disjunction $\varphi \vee \psi$, we have $\mathcal{R}(\varphi \vee \psi, w) = \mathcal{R}(\varphi, w) \cup \mathcal{R}(\psi, w)$, thus we take the union of the sets of polyhedra, $\mathcal{S}_{\varphi \vee \psi} = \mathcal{S}_\varphi \cup \mathcal{S}_\psi$.

Conjunction. For the conjunction $\varphi \wedge \psi$, $\mathcal{R}(\varphi \wedge \psi, w) = \mathcal{R}(\varphi, w) \cap \mathcal{R}(\psi, w)$, thus we take the pairwise intersection: $\mathcal{S}_{\varphi \wedge \psi} = \bigcup_{\substack{P_\varphi \in \mathcal{S}_\varphi \\ P_\psi \in \mathcal{S}_\psi}} \{P_\varphi \cap P_\psi\}$

Concatenation. Notice that we identify polyhedra (or zones) with conjunctions of constraints. Thus, for two polyhedra P and Q, the formula $P \wedge Q$ denotes the polyhedron that is the intersection of P and Q. For a polyhedron P with 4 dimensions t, t', t'' and r, the formula $\exists t''. P[t, t', t'', r]$ denotes the polyhedron that is the projection of P on t, t', r. For concatenation, one can show that $\mathcal{R}(\varphi \cdot \psi, w) = \{(t, t', r) \mid \exists t''. (t, t'', r) \in \mathcal{R}(\varphi, w) \wedge (t'', t', r) \in \mathcal{R}(\psi, w)\}$. Thus, $\mathcal{S}_{\varphi \cdot \psi}$ is the set of polyhedra $\{\exists t''. P_\varphi[t, t'', r] \wedge P_\psi[t'', t', r] \mid P_\varphi \in \mathcal{S}_\varphi, P_\psi \in \mathcal{S}_\psi\}$.

Kleene star. From Theorem 3 it follows that for every signal w and expression φ, there exists $k \geq 0$, s.t. (i) $\mathcal{R}(\varphi^k, w) \supseteq \mathcal{R}(\varphi^{k+1}, w)$; and (ii) $\mathcal{R}(\varphi^*, w) = \bigcup_{i=0}^k \mathcal{R}(\varphi^i, w)$. By definition of the Kleene star, $\mathcal{R}(\varphi^*, w) = \bigcup_{k \geq 0} \mathcal{R}(\varphi^k, w)$, hence $\mathcal{S}_{\varphi^*} = \bigcup_{i=0}^k \mathcal{S}_{\varphi^i}$ where k is the smallest index, s.t. $\mathcal{R}(\varphi^k, w) \supseteq \mathcal{R}(\varphi^{k+1}, w)$. A sufficient stopping condition thus is to check whether the set of polyhedra $\mathcal{S}_{\varphi^k}$ *geometrically covers* the set of polyhedra $\mathcal{S}_{\varphi^{k+1}}$ (it can be implemented, e.g., by checking intersection with the complement). In [32], it was shown that for the pattern matching problem, a sufficient stopping condition can be formulated using pairwise inclusion rather than geometric coverage. Whether this is also true in the case of *robust* pattern matching relative to arbitrary polyhedra, is yet to be shown.

Duration Restriction. For the duration restriction $\langle \varphi \rangle_I$, one can show $\mathcal{R}(\langle \varphi \rangle_I, w) = \mathcal{R}(\varphi, w) \cap \{(t, t', r) \mid t' - t \in I\}$. Thus, we restrict every element of $\mathcal{S}_\varphi$ as follows: $\mathcal{S}_{\langle \varphi \rangle_I} = \{P \wedge (t' - t \in I) \mid P \in \mathcal{S}_\varphi\}$.

Proof (of Theorem 4). We can now prove Theorem 4. For a piecewise-constant signal w and an expression φ, $\mathcal{S}_\varphi$ is a set of *zones* over t, t', r, s.t. every constraint on r is of the form $r < c$. This holds for the base cases and is preserved by intersection and projection operations performed for the inductive cases. When a zone Z, bounds r from above by c (possibly ∞), the pointwise supremum function $(t, t') \mapsto \sup\{r \mid (t, t', r) \in Z\}$ is piecewise-constant. The robustness map $(t, t') \mapsto \rho(\varphi, w, [t, t'])$ is a pointwise maximum of finitely many piecewise-constant functions, and is piecewise-constant. Similarly, for a continuous piecewise-linear signal, $\mathcal{S}_\varphi$ is a set of polyhedra, where r is unbounded from below. For every such polyhedron P, the function $(t, t') \mapsto \sup\{r \mid (t, t', r) \in P\}$ is piecewise-linear. The robustness map is a pointwise maximum of finitely many piecewise-linear functions and is piecewise-linear. $\square$

Possible Optimizations. A practical issue of computing robustness support in this bottom-up way is that we have to compute and store the robustness value for every segment of the signal and every sub-expression, regardless of how small this value is and whether it will be used when matching the higher-level expressions. One workaround is to approximate robustness by replacing the values that are below some threshold with $-\infty$ (discarding the corresponding polyhedra). Another optimization is to rewrite the original expression and propagate time restriction operations to the sub-expressions. This will allow to earlier discard the polyhedra that would anyway be discarded by the time restriction later in the computation.

6   Experiments

In this section, we evaluate our matching algorithms on a problem of finding ringing patterns in a signal. Ringing is a damped oscillation of an output of a system as a response to a sudden change in the input. In Fig. 6 (left), we give an example of a ringing behavior of a linear system with respect to a square wave input. We define ringing using the following expression:

$$\langle x \leq 0.2 \rangle_{\leq 0.05} \cdot \langle 0.1 \leq x \leq 0.9 \rangle_{\leq 0.05} \cdot \langle 0.7 \leq x \leq 1.3 \rangle_{[0.3,\ 1]} \cdot \langle 0.9 \leq x \leq 1.1 \rangle_{[3,\ 6]}$$

This is a concatenation of constraints that describe (from left to right) low value, rising edge, ringing, and stable high value periods, using thresholds on the value and duration. We discretize the input signal and feed it to our matching tool Montre [31], which was extended to support robust matching of piecewise-constant signals. In Fig. 6 (right), we show the robustness map produced by Montre, where darker colors correspond to time segments with higher robustness values. In particular, thin dark bands correspond to the segments that start on the rising edge of the signal and end at high signal value. These segments also

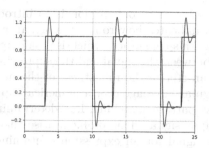 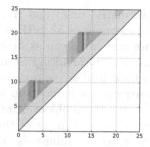

Fig. 6. A ringing signal w (left) and its robustness map (right).

satisfy the expression qualitatively. The surrounding lighter areas correspond to the segments that do not satisfy the expression qualitatively, but are close to satisfaction. These are the segments that start before the rising edge of the signal, or during or after the second ringing oscillation.

To evaluate the practical complexity of robust matching, we generate longer input signals, consisting of multiple square waves with ringing. In Table 1, we give execution times and numbers of output zones for different lengths of the input (measured in the number of discrete samples). We observe that for this example the runtime of the algorithm is linear in the length of the input, which is expected when the duration constraints in the expression are much shorter than the input itself. Additionally (not shown in Table 1) we measured the overhead of performing matching on piecewise-linear interpolation of a signal compared to piecewise-constant, which is due to using polyhedra instead of zones. To represent and manipulate polyhedra, we use Parma Polyhedra Library (PPL) [7]. Our experiments with PPL suggest that individual operations on polyhedra (corresponding to SRE operators) are 30 to 40 times slower than those on zones. The implementation of zones is optimized for the particular form of constraints, while for polyhedra, PPL implements the double-description method [8], where a polyhedron is represented by a system of constraints and a system of generators.

Table 1. Experimental results

Input length	10 K	20 K	40 K
Execution Time (sec)	3.88	7.80	15.5
Number of output zones	156 K	315 K	631 K

7 Conclusion

This work can be seen as part of the trend of extending formal language theory and its related formalisms towards the quantitative; somewhat in the spirit of

[29,30] (for metric time) and [18,19]. Our first contribution is to introduce a quantitative semantics for SRE which indicates how robustly a signal matches or does not match a given expression. This semantics, which is a safe approximation of the uniform norm distance between the signal and the expression, can also be applied in discrete time to characterize the robustness of the membership of a sequence of numbers in a regular language over a numerical alphabet. We then define the problem of robust pattern matching, i.e., determining the robustness of every segment of the input signal. This problem arises naturally when computing the robustness of a signal for an expression containing concatenation. Moreover, this additional information can be very useful in novel applications of such specification formalisms, for example [1,11,21]. Unlike classical verification, where we want to verify properties of the whole behavior, in monitoring of real systems or in data mining, we would like to detect the occurrence of patterns at various parts of the signal. We developed algorithms to solve this robust matching problem for two classes of signals: piecewise-constant and continuous piecewise-linear, which are both common in digital signal processing based on sampled signals. We observe that robust pattern matching can be seen as constructing a 3-dimensional surface, and show that this surface is piecewise-linear for piecewise-linear signals. Practically, we represent the volume under this surface as a set of zones or convex polyhedra.

Future Work. We consider the following directions for future work. First, we observe that our definition of robustness represents purely *spatial* distance and thus does not address *time* robustness (see discussion in [15]). This issue is best demonstrated with the duration operator. Consider an expression $\langle \varphi \rangle_{[2,3]}$ and a signal that matches φ but with duration $2 - \delta$, for a small δ. With our current semantics, its robustness is $-\infty$, regardless of how small δ is. An alternative more continuous semantics of the time restriction operator will bring our semantics closer to other (non-pointwise) metrics that allow stretching and shrinking of behaviors [12,20].

Also, as mentioned in the end of Sect. 5, unlike the very efficient qualitative matching [32], our quantitative matching algorithm is costly. One reason is the use of arbitrary convex polyhedra for piecewise-linear signals. Another is the fact that we need to cover the whole triangle $0 \leq t \leq t' \leq |w|$ by polyhedra or zones, while for the qualitative semantics, the match set is very sparse. In addition to the ad-hoc optimizations mentioned in the end of Sect. 5, we foresee two more rigorous ways to address this problem. First, we can use an approximate semantics that quantizes the robustness values into a finite set of ranges. Second, if we are only interested in the robustness with respect to the whole signal, we may be able to replace the current bottom-up algorithm by a more sophisticated top-down scheme that will compute robustness only with respect to a subset of the sub-expressions and time segments.

References

1. Abbas, H., Rodionova, A., Bartocci, E., Smolka, S.A., Grosu, R.: Regular expressions for irregular rhythms. arXiv preprint arXiv:1612.07770 (2016)
2. Alur, R., Dill, D.L.: A theory of timed automata. Theoret. Comput. Sci. **126**(2), 183–235 (1994)
3. Alur, R., Feder, T., Henzinger, T.A.: The benefits of relaxing punctuality. J. ACM **43**(1), 116–146 (1996)
4. Alur, R., Fisman, D., Raghothaman, M.: Regular programming for quantitative properties of data streams. In: Thiemann, P. (ed.) ESOP 2016. LNCS, vol. 9632, pp. 15–40. Springer, Heidelberg (2016). doi:10.1007/978-3-662-49498-1_2
5. Asarin, E., Caspi, P., Maler, O.: Timed regular expressions. J. ACM **49**(2), 172–206 (2002)
6. Asarin, E., Caspi, P., Maler, O.: A Kleene theorem for timed automata. In: Logic in Computer Science (LICS), pp. 160–171 (1997)
7. Bagnara, R., Hill, P.M., Zaffanella, E.: The Parma Polyhedra Library: Toward a complete set of numerical abstractions for the analysis and verification of hardware and software systems. Sci. Comput. Program. **72**(1–2), 3–21 (2008)
8. Bagnara, R., Hill, P.M., Zaffanella, E.: Not necessarily closed convex polyhedra and the double description method. Formal Asp. Comput. **17**(2), 222–257 (2005)
9. Basin, D., Klaedtke, F., Müller, S., Zălinescu, E.: Monitoring metric first-order temporal properties. J. ACM (JACM) **62**(2), 15 (2015)
10. D'Antoni, L., Veanes, M.: Minimization of symbolic automata. In: POPL, pp. 541–554. ACM (2014)
11. Deshmukh, J.V., Jin, X., Seshia, S., et al.: Learning auditable features from signals using unsupervised temporal projection (2017)
12. Deshmukh, J.V., Majumdar, R., Prabhu, V.S.: Quantifying conformance using the skorokhod metric. In: Kroening, D., Păsăreanu, C.S. (eds.) CAV 2015. LNCS, vol. 9207, pp. 234–250. Springer, Cham (2015). doi:10.1007/978-3-319-21668-3_14
13. Dill, D.L.: Timing assumptions and verification of finite-state concurrent systems. In: Sifakis, J. (ed.) CAV 1989. LNCS, vol. 407, pp. 197–212. Springer, Heidelberg (1990). doi:10.1007/3-540-52148-8_17
14. Donzé, A.: Breach, a toolbox for verification and parameter synthesis of hybrid systems. In: Touili, T., Cook, B., Jackson, P. (eds.) CAV 2010. LNCS, vol. 6174, pp. 167–170. Springer, Heidelberg (2010). doi:10.1007/978-3-642-14295-6_17
15. Donzé, A., Maler, O.: Robust satisfaction of temporal logic over real-valued signals. In: Chatterjee, K., Henzinger, T.A. (eds.) FORMATS 2010. LNCS, vol. 6246, pp. 92–106. Springer, Heidelberg (2010). doi:10.1007/978-3-642-15297-9_9
16. Donzé, A., Ferrère, T., Maler, O.: Efficient robust monitoring for STL. In: Sharygina, N., Veith, H. (eds.) CAV 2013. LNCS, vol. 8044, pp. 264–279. Springer, Heidelberg (2013). doi:10.1007/978-3-642-39799-8_19
17. Fainekos, G.E., Pappas, G.J.: Robustness of temporal logic specifications. In: Havelund, K., Núñez, M., Roşu, G., Wolff, B. (eds.) FATES/RV -2006. LNCS, vol. 4262, pp. 178–192. Springer, Heidelberg (2006). doi:10.1007/11940197_12
18. Henzinger, T.A.: Quantitative reactive modeling and verification. Comput. Sci. Res. Dev. **28**(4), 331–344 (2013)
19. Henzinger, T.A., Otop, J.: From model checking to model measuring. In: D'Argenio, P.R., Melgratti, H. (eds.) CONCUR 2013. LNCS, vol. 8052, pp. 273–287. Springer, Heidelberg (2013). doi:10.1007/978-3-642-40184-8_20

20. Jakšić, S., Bartocci, E., Grosu, R., Ničković, D.: Quantitative monitoring of STL with edit distance. In: Falcone, Y., Sánchez, C. (eds.) RV 2016. LNCS, vol. 10012, pp. 201–218. Springer, Cham (2016). doi:10.1007/978-3-319-46982-9_13

21. Jin, X., Donzé, A., Deshmukh, J.V., Seshia, S.A.: Mining requirements from closed-loop control models. IEEE Trans. Comput. Aided Des. Integr. Circuits Syst. **34**(11), 1704–1717 (2015)

22. Koymans, R.: Specifying real-time properties with metric temporal logic. Real-Time Syst. **2**(4), 255–299 (1990)

23. Maler, O., Nickovic, D.: Monitoring temporal properties of continuous signals. In: Lakhnech, Y., Yovine, S. (eds.) FORMATS/FTRTFT -2004. LNCS, vol. 3253, pp. 152–166. Springer, Heidelberg (2004). doi:10.1007/978-3-540-30206-3_12

24. Maler, O., Nickovic, D., Pnueli, A.: Checking temporal properties of discrete, timed and continuous behaviors. In: Avron, A., Dershowitz, N., Rabinovich, A. (eds.) Pillars of Computer Science. LNCS, vol. 4800, pp. 475–505. Springer, Heidelberg (2008). doi:10.1007/978-3-540-78127-1_26

25. Mens, I.E., Maler, O.: Learning regular languages over large ordered alphabets. Log. Methods Comput. Sci. (LMCS) **11**(3)

26. Nickovic, D., Maler, O.: AMT: A property-based monitoring tool for analog systems. In: FORMATS, pp. 304–319 (2007)

27. Pnueli, A.: The temporal logic of programs. In: Proceedings of the 18th Annual Symposium on Foundations of Computer Science (FOCS), pp. 46–57 (1977)

28. Rizk, A., Batt, G., Fages, F., Soliman, S.: On a continuous degree of satisfaction of temporal logic formulae with applications to systems biology. In: Heiner, M., Uhrmacher, A.M. (eds.) CMSB 2008. LNCS (LNAI), vol. 5307, pp. 251–268. Springer, Heidelberg (2008). doi:10.1007/978-3-540-88562-7_19

29. Trakhtenbrot, B.A.: Origins and metamorphoses of the trinity: Logic, nets, automata. In: LICS, pp. 506–507 (1995)

30. Trakhtenbrot, B.A.: Understanding basic automata theory in the continuous time setting. Fundam. Inform. **62**(1), 69–121 (2004)

31. Ulus, D.: Montre: A tool for monitoring timed regular expressions. CoRR abs/1605.05963 (2016)

32. Ulus, D., Ferrère, T., Asarin, E., Maler, O.: Timed pattern matching. In: Legay, A., Bozga, M. (eds.) FORMATS 2014. LNCS, vol. 8711, pp. 222–236. Springer, Cham (2014). doi:10.1007/978-3-319-10512-3_16

33. Veanes, M., Hooimeijer, P., Livshits, B., Molnar, D., Björner, N.: Symbolic finite state transducers: algorithms and applications. In: POPL, pp. 137–150. ACM (2012)

Combining the Temporal and Epistemic Dimensions for MTL Monitoring

Eugene Asarin[1], Oded Maler[2], Dejan Nickovic[3], and Dogan Ulus[2(✉)]

[1] IRIF, Paris Diderot University, Paris, France
[2] Verimag, CNRS/University of Grenoble-Alpes, Grenoble, France
doganulus@gmail.com
[3] Austrian Institute of Technology, Vienna, Austria

Abstract. We define a new notion of satisfaction of a temporal logic formula φ by a behavior w. This notion, denoted by $(w, t, t') \models \varphi$, is characterized by two time parameters: the position t from which satisfaction is considered, and the end of the (finite) behavior t' which indicates how much do we *know* about the behavior. We define this notion in dense time where φ is a formula in the future fragment of metric temporal logic (MTL) and w is a Boolean signal of bounded variability. We show that the set of all pairs (t, t') such that $(w, t, t') \models \varphi$ can be expressed as a finite union of two-dimensional zones and give an effective procedure to compute it.

1 Introduction and Motivation

Within the traditional use of temporal logic (TL) in verification, formulas are interpreted over non-terminating[1] behaviors, viewed mathematically as ω-words. These are sequences which are infinite in one dimension with a time domain order-isomorphic to $\mathbb{N}$ (to $\mathbb{R}_+$ or $\mathbb{Q}_+$, if we consider dense time). In this setting, the availability of a generative model of the system dynamics is assumed in a form of a transition system (automaton) where all those behaviors are represented by infinite runs that go through cycles. Likewise, the TL specification can also be translated to an ω-automaton and the verification problem reduces to a test of inclusion between two ω-regular languages [31]. This problem can be solved by reasoning about cycles in finite-state automata.

Historical Remark: This was not always the point of view in the early works of logicians on tense logic, before the importation of TL to verification by Pnueli [24,25]. Kamp [13] who added the *until* and *since* operators to the original tense logic of Prior [26], and showed expressive equivalence to the first-order theory of sequences, considered arbitrary time structures satisfying order axioms, that could be infinite in both directions. Regular languages over bi-infinite words, indexed by $\mathbb{Z}$ rather than $\mathbb{N}$, were considered by Nivat and Perrin in [23]. The

---

[1] In the context of reactive systems, finite behaviors are sometimes even considered anomalous, representing deadlocks.

© Springer International Publishing AG 2017
A. Abate and G. Geeraerts (Eds.): FORMATS 2017, LNCS 10419, pp. 207–223, 2017.
DOI: 10.1007/978-3-319-65765-3_12

current ω-view has been nailed down in the *anchored* interpretation of Manna and Pnueli [21] which associated an initial state with every computation and, moreover, considered satisfaction from this initial state as having a special status compared to satisfaction from an arbitrary point in time. Readers interested in more historical and technical details are advised to consult [30] and the references therein.   □

There are several contemporary motivations to consider finite, time bounded behaviors as the semantic model for TL. In many (if not most) real-life situations, especially in the hybrid cyber-physical world, exhaustive verification is impossible and one resorts to simulation-based (runtime, dynamic, lightweight) verification, where behaviors are generated individually. Each of these behaviors is checked for property satisfaction, or using a language-theoretic terminology, the inclusion test of model checking is replaced by numerous membership tests. We use the term *monitoring* for this activity. An important advantage of monitoring is that it can be applied to systems models not admitting a clean description (programs, simulators, black boxes) and hence not amenable to formal reasoning. For a behavior to be observed and checked by a mortal agent (or analyzed by a terminating program), it should be finite and the semantics of the specifications should be adapted to yield answers based on such finite behaviors.

This problem had to be (and has been) addressed by anyone developing such monitoring tools [1]. One way to tackle this issue is to provide finitary interpretation of TL. The truncated semantics for future TL is rigorously studied in [9], where weak, strong and neutral interpretation of the temporal specifications are proposed. This work is further developed in [8], providing the topological characterization of the weakness and strength of temporal formulas. In [6], the authors study LTL interpreted over finite behaviors and show the limited expressiveness of the logic in the finitary setting. They propose linear dynamic logic over finite traces (LDL_f) that significantly increases the expressiveness of the logic without additional computational cost. Another way to address the interpretation of TL over finite behaviors is to employ a 3-valued semantics ranging over $\{0, 1, \perp\}$ where $\perp$ is viewed as *unknown* to model the fact that the finite behavior does not contain sufficient information needed to determine the satisfaction or a violation of a temporal formula at a given instant in time [2,3,27]. We finally mention [20], which discusses various options of handling temporal logic over finite behaviors.

Another motivation comes from the application of specification formalisms outside the traditional design-time verification framework. After all, monitoring can be applied to data measured from real physical systems, not only to models [16]. In monitoring real systems during their execution we would like to detect some alarming patterns of behavior as they occur, so as to do something about them. In not so safety-critical situations, we would like to analyze a given behavior and distinguish, say, periods in which some bounded-response property has been satisfied from periods when it was not. All these application domains call for an approach where finite segments of a behavior, not necessarily starting at time zero, and certainly not ending at the "end", are the major objects of study. In this setting, monitoring has often to be performed *online*, with the values of the monitored behavior being disclosed progressively as time goes by.

The major contribution of this work is in defining a two-dimensional notion of satisfiability, denoted by $(w, t, t') \models \varphi$, where t indicates, as usual, the position from which satisfaction is considered, and t' indicates the endpoint of the signal, the limit of our current knowledge about it. This work is partially inspired by [28] where the relation $(w, t, t') \models \varphi$ means that the segment $w[t, t')$ of a Boolean signal w matches a timed regular expression. In that paper, the match set $\mathcal{M}(\varphi, w) = \{(t, t') : (w, t, t') \models \varphi\}$ was shown to be computable and to consist of a finite union of zones. While we borrow some of the two-dimensional techniques from [28], it turns out that for TL, which is less symmetric than regular expressions with respect to the direction of time, these notions are trickier and require a distinction between the temporal and epistemic components. Note that unlike other works that combine knowledge and time [10,12,29], where knowledge is relative to different agents in a distributed system who may observe different variables and events at different times, our notion is centralized and is focused on the knowledge associated with the unfolding of time.

The rest of the paper is organized as follows. In Sect. 2 we present the algorithm for MTL monitoring of Boolean signals as developed in [17,22]. It is based on two major operation, interval back-shifting to treat the *timed eventually* operator and another operation on intervals to handle the *untimed until*. In Sect. 3 we define the two-dimensional satisfaction relation for future MTL and its associated match-set computation problem. We show that the latter can be solved by extending the above two interval-based operations to deal with zones. In Sect. 4 we illustrate how our implementation of the algorithm works on MTL formulas of a practical interest. Section 5 is devoted to conclusions and suggestions for future work. Needless to say, the results and insights obtained for dense time and MTL hold, as a degenerate case, for the discrete time setting of LTL and sequences.

2 Preliminaries

A Boolean signal w is a function from an interval $dom(w) = [0, \ell)$ to $\mathbb{B}^n$. The signal is infinite when $\ell = \infty$, and finite, otherwise. We restrict ourselves to signals that satisfy the sanity condition of *bounded variability*, which for finite signals means that $dom(w)$ can be partitioned into finitely many intervals, and w is constant in each interval. Such an interval is said to be *maximal* if it is not strictly contained in another interval where the signal is constant.

The syntax of the future fragment of metric temporal logic (MTL) as defined in [15] is given by

$$\varphi := p \mid \neg\varphi \mid \varphi_1 \vee \varphi_2 \mid \varphi_1 \mathcal{U}_I \varphi_2$$

where $p \in \{p_1, \ldots, p_n\}$ is a propositional variable and I is any non-empty interval of the form $[a, b]$, $[a, b)$, $(a, b]$ or (a, b) with a and b being integers. To avoid tedious case analysis and focus on the new features introduced by the two-dimensional notion of satisfaction, we treat only the case $I = [a, b]$. It has been shown in [19] that with this restriction, if w decomposes into unions of maximal intervals which are left-closed right-open, all the other signals generated during the monitoring procedure admit such a decomposition without singular points, a fact that will simplify the presentation. For the same reason, we do not explore all variants of the timed *until* operator and focus on the non-strict version, whose semantics is given using the standard satisfaction relation $(w, t) \models \varphi$ indicating that w satisfies φ *from* position t:

$$(w, t) \models \varphi_1 \mathcal{U}_{[a,b]} \varphi_2 \text{ iff } \exists r \in [t+a, t+b](w, r) \models \varphi_2 \wedge \forall r' \in [t, r] \ (w, r') \models \varphi_1$$

The timed *eventually* operator $F_{[a,b]}$ is a degenerate case where φ_1 is replaced by *true*, $F_{[a,b]}\varphi = \top \mathcal{U}_{[a,b]}\varphi$. It only requires that t will occur sometime in $[t+a, t+b]$. Its dual, the timed *always*, which require φ to hold throughout the interval, is defined as $G_{[a,b]}\varphi = \neg(F_{[a,b]}\neg\varphi)$.

It has been shown in [7, 22] that the timed until operator can be rewritten as a combination of $F_{[a,b]}$ and the *untimed* until $\mathcal{U}$ which does not put any restriction on the future time point r:

$$\varphi_1 \mathcal{U}_{[a,b]} \varphi_2 = G_{[0,a]}\varphi_1 \mathcal{U}\varphi_2 \wedge F_{[a,b]}\varphi_2$$

Hence from now on we consider the syntax

$$\varphi := p \mid \neg\varphi \mid \varphi_1 \vee \varphi_2 \mid F_{[a,b]} \mid \varphi_1 \mathcal{U}\varphi_2$$

The monitoring procedure of [17, 22] is based on reformulating the time-dependent satisfaction relation in terms of *satisfaction signals*. A satisfaction signal for a formula φ relative to signal w is a one-dimensional Boolean signal[2] $\varphi(.)$ such that

$$\varphi(t) = \begin{cases} 1 \text{ if } (w, t) \models \varphi \\ 0 \text{ if } (w, t) \not\models \varphi \end{cases}$$

The standard semantics of MTL can be reformulated in terms of such signals. We use w_p to denote the projection of w on variable p.

Definition 1 (MTL Semantics with Satisfaction Signals). *The semantics of MTL formulas with respect to a Boolean signal w is defined inductively:*

$$p(t) = w_p(t)$$
$$(\neg\varphi)(t) = \neg(\varphi(t))$$
$$(\varphi \vee \psi)(t) = \varphi(t) \vee \psi(t)$$
$$(F_{[a,b]}\varphi)(t) = \bigvee_{r \in [t+a, t+b]} \varphi(r)$$
$$(\varphi_1 \mathcal{U}\varphi_2)(t) = \bigvee_{r \geq t} (\varphi_2(r) \wedge \bigwedge_{r' \in [t,r]} \varphi_1(r'))$$

---

[2] By a slight abuse of notation we use the same symbol for a formula and its satisfaction signal.

We say that w satisfies φ from t if $\varphi(t) = 1$. We use $M(\varphi, w)$, or simply $M(\varphi)$ when w is clear from the context, to denote the time points from which φ is satisfied. For every φ, $M(\varphi)$ admits a *canonical representation* as a minimal set $\mathcal{I}$ of maximal intervals. The above semantics can be viewed as specifying recursive calls that descend the parse tree of φ down to the atomic propositions whose satisfaction signals are just the appropriate projections of w. Then, while climbing up, it combines the lower-level satisfaction signals until it gets to the top formula. The crucial procedures are those that compute the satisfaction signals of $F_{[a,b]}\varphi$ and $\varphi_1 \mathcal{U} \varphi_2$ from those of their sub-formulas.

Let $\varphi' = F_{[a,b]}\varphi$. The back-shifting method of [17,22] for computing φ' from φ is based on the following simple concepts that generalize time shifts to the non-deterministic setting (more on these operations and their relation to determinism can be found in [18]).

Definition 2 (Forward and Backward Cones, Back-Shift). *Let t be a time point and let $I = [c, d]$ be an interval.*

1. *The $[a,b]$-forward cone of t is the interval $[t + a, t + b]$;*
2. *The $[a,b]$-back cone of t is the interval $[t - b, t - a]$;*
3. *The $[a,b]$-back shift of interval I is $I' = \sigma_{[a,b]}(I) = [c - b, d - a]$.*

The forward cone consists of all time points r such that $\varphi(r)$ may influence $\varphi'(t)$. The back cone specifies the points r such that $\varphi'(r)$ can be influenced by $\varphi(t)$, those that t is in their forward cone. The back-shift of I is the union of the back cones of its elements, the set of all time points t such that $\varphi'(t)$ is influenced by $\varphi(r), r \in I$. The following observation underlies the monitoring procedure of [17,22].

Observation 1 (Back Shifting). *The back-shift of interval I consists of all points whose forward cone intersects I: $\sigma_{[a,b]}(I) = \{t : [t + a, t + b] \cap I \neq \emptyset\}$.*

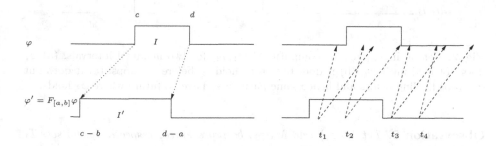

Fig. 1. A finite satisfaction signal φ which is true at interval $I = [c, d]$ (left): Back shifting $I' = \sigma_{[a,b]}(I)$; (right): the forward cones of points $t_1, t_2 \in I'$ do indeed intersect I hence $\varphi' = F_{[a,b]}\varphi$ holds there. On the other hand, $\varphi = 0$ throughout all the forward cone of t_3 and hence $\varphi'(t_3) = 0$. The forward cone of t_4 does not intersect I either but part of it goes outside $dom(\varphi)$. We use in this paper a semantics where $\varphi'(t_4) = 0$.

The satisfaction signal of $\varphi' = F_{[a,b]}\varphi$ is thus computed by back-shifting all maximal intervals in $M(\varphi)$ and their union characterizes φ', see Fig. 1. This procedure is obviously correct for points t such that $[t + a, t + b] \subseteq dom(\varphi)$. For other points like t_4 in the figure, the question is how to evaluate the disjunction (existential quantification) over the values of φ in that cone. A common approach, the one used implicitly in [22], is to consider $\varphi'(t) = 0$ if $\varphi(r) = 0$ for all $r \in [t + a, t + b] \cap dom(\varphi)$. We will use this semantics but our results can be easily adapted to an alternative 3-valued semantics where $\varphi(t) = \bot$ (unknown) if some possible completion of the signal lead to satisfaction and some others, to violation.

To illustrate the computation of $\varphi = \varphi_1 \mathcal{U} \varphi_2$ observe first that $(\varphi_1 \mathcal{U} \varphi_2)$ holds at t when φ_1 holds continuously between t and some future point r where φ_2 holds. This motivates the following operation between intervals $I_1 = [c, d)$ and $I_2 = [c', d')$:

$$\Omega(I_1, I_2) = \begin{cases} \emptyset & \text{if } d \le c' \\ [c, d) & \text{if } c' < d \wedge d \le d' \\ [c, d') & \text{if } c' < d \wedge d' < d \end{cases}$$

The three cases are illustrated Fig. 2. The following observation justifies the computation of the set $M(\varphi)$ of positive intervals in the satisfaction signal of φ, by applying this operation to all pairs of maximal intervals in $M(\varphi_1)$ and $M(\varphi_2)$.

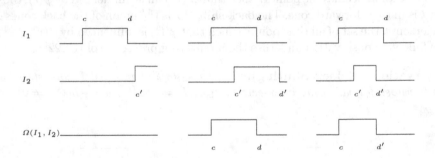

Fig. 2. Computing $\varphi_1 \mathcal{U} \varphi_2$ by computing $\Omega(I_1, I_2)$ for two maximal intervals. (a) φ_1 does not hold until φ_2; (b) it does but stops holding before φ_2 stops; (c) it does but φ_2 stops holding before and hence some parts of I_1 have no future where φ_2 holds.

Observation 2. *Let $M(\varphi_1)$ and $M(\varphi_2)$ be represented, respectively, by sets $\mathcal{I}_1$ and $\mathcal{I}_2$ of maximal intervals. Then*

$$M(\varphi) = \bigcup_{I_1 \in \mathcal{I}_1} \bigcup_{I_2 \in \mathcal{I}_2} \Omega(I_1, I_2).$$

The fact that $\mathcal{I}_1$ consists of maximal intervals is crucial here. If an interval $[c, d)$ satisfying $d' < d$ is split into non-maximal intervals $[c, e)$ and $[e, d)$ with $e < c'$, the points in $[c, e)$ will be wrongly considered as not satisfying $\varphi_1 \mathcal{U} \varphi_2$.

3 Satisfaction in Two Dimensions

The essence of our definition is to consider the end of the signal as an additional parameter t'. We would like to know what can be said about satisfaction at t after observing a prefix $w[0, t')$. Although this characterization of the pair (t, t') is different here from the matching property used for regular expressions in [28], we will use a similar terminology, partly because we have not yet found a simple name for this relation.

Let w be a Boolean signal defined over a bounded time domain $dom(w) = [0, \ell)$. Any sub-interval $[t, t')$ of $dom(w)$ defines a sub-segment of w that we denote by $w' = w[t, t')$. The set of all non-empty sub-segments of w can be represented by the triangle $T_w = \{(t, t') : 0 \le t < t' < \ell\}$ (Fig. 3-(a)).

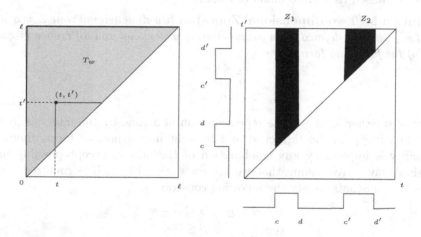

Fig. 3. (a) The triangle T_w associated with a signal defined over $[0, \ell)$. The length of the horizontal or vertical line from a point (t, t') to the diagonal is $t' - t$, the length of the segment $[t, t')$ that it represents; (b) A proposition which is true at the intervals $[c, d]$ and $[c', d']$. Its match set is $Z_1 \cup Z_2$.

Definition 3 (Matching and Match Sets). *A segment (t, t') of signal w matches an MTL formula φ, denoted as $(w, t, t') \models \varphi$, if $(w[0, t'), t) \models \varphi$. The match-set of φ in w is the set of all matching segments:*

$$\mathcal{M}(\varphi, w) = \{(t, t') : (w, t, t') \models \varphi\}.$$

The relation between matching in one and two dimensions can be expressed as

$$\mathcal{M}(\varphi, w) = \bigcup_{t' \in [0, \ell)} M(\varphi, w[0, t')) \times \{t'\} \tag{1}$$

We will use notation $\mathcal{M}(\varphi)$ when w is clear from the context. To compute $\mathcal{M}(\varphi)$ we first define the two-dimensional analog of satisfaction signal, the satisfaction map, where $\varphi(t, t')$ indicates the satisfaction status of φ by $w[t, t')$.

Definition 4 (MTL Matching Semantics with Satisfaction Maps). *The matching semantics of MTL formulas with respect to a Boolean signal w is defined inductively as follows:*

$$p(t, t') = w_p(t) \wedge t < t' < \ell$$
$$(\neg\varphi)(t, t') = \neg(\varphi(t, t'))$$
$$(\varphi \vee \psi)(t, t') = \varphi(t, t') \vee \psi(t, t')$$
$$(F_{[a,b]}\varphi)(t, t') = \bigvee_{r \in [t+a, t+b]} \varphi(r, t')$$
$$(\varphi_1 \mathcal{U} \varphi_2)(t, t') = \bigvee_{r \geq t} (\varphi_2(r, t') \wedge \bigwedge_{r' \in [t,r]} \varphi_1(r', t'))$$

In the sequel we will show that for a bounded-variability signal w, $\mathcal{M}(\varphi, w)$ can be expressed as a finite union of zones.

Definition 5 (Two-dimensional Zones). *A two-dimensional zone Z is a subset of $\mathbb{R}_+^2$ which is defined via a conjunction of orthogonal and difference inequalities of the following form*

$$\underline{\alpha} \prec t \prec \overline{\alpha}$$
$$\underline{\beta} \prec t' \prec \overline{\beta} \qquad\qquad (2)$$
$$\underline{\gamma} \prec t' - t \prec \overline{\gamma}$$

where $\prec$ is either $<$ or $\leq$. The representation of a zone by the intervals $[\underline{\alpha}, \overline{\alpha}]$, $[\underline{\beta}, \overline{\beta}]$ and $[\underline{\gamma}, \overline{\gamma}]$ can be tightened and brought into a normal form where no inequality is implied by any combination of the others, except possibly in a marginal way.[3] We assume that we always work with such normalized zones where the constants satisfy the following constraints.

$$\underline{\beta} - \overline{\gamma} \leq \underline{\alpha} \leq \overline{\alpha} \leq \overline{\beta} - \underline{\gamma}$$
$$\underline{\alpha} + \underline{\gamma} \leq \underline{\beta} \leq \overline{\beta} \leq \overline{\alpha} + \overline{\gamma}$$
$$\underline{\beta} - \overline{\alpha} \leq \underline{\gamma} \leq \overline{\gamma} \leq \overline{\beta} - \underline{\alpha}$$

As convex sets, zones are not closed under union and complementation and these operations yield the class of sets that we will call timed polyhedra. Non-convex timed polyhedra can be expressed as a finite union of zones but this representation is not unique, and there is no canonical minimal representation as in the case of intervals. Moreover, the choice of the zones in the representation may affect the correctness of the procedure we propose in the sequel for the until operator. For this reason we define explicitly the notion of a representation of a timed polyhedron.

Definition 6 (Timed Polyhedra, Representation). *A timed polyhedron $\mathbf{Z}$ is a set expressible as a Boolean combination of orthogonal and difference constraints as in (2). A set of zones $\mathcal{Z} = \{Z_1, \ldots, Z_k\}$ is a representation of $\mathbf{Z}$ if*

$$\mathbf{Z} = \bigcup_i Z_i$$

---

[3] It means that if a constraint $f(t, t') \leq c$ is implied by other constraints, the constraint $f(t, t') \leq c - \varepsilon$ is not implied by them for any $\varepsilon > 0$.

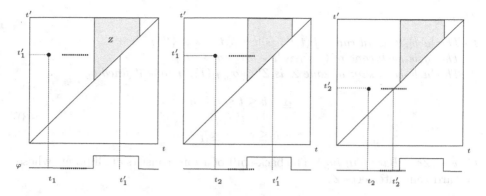

Fig. 4. The effect of t and t' on satisfaction of $\varphi' = F_{[a,b]}\varphi$ with respect to a given satisfaction signal φ whose match-set is the zone Z. The thick dashed lines indicate the forward cones of the respective values of t. (a) segment (t_1, t_1') does not satisfy φ' because the forward cone of t_1 does not intersect Z; (b) segment (t_2, t_1') which starts later does satisfy φ' because the forward cone of (t_2, t_1') intersects Z. In other words $[t_2 + a, t_2 + b]$ intersects φ^1 before t_1'; (c) segment (t_2, t_2') which ends earlier than (t_2, t_1') does not satisfy φ' because it ends before φ becomes true.

To characterize match sets we will first show that those of propositions are timed polyhedra and that the latter are closed under the operations in Definition 4. This is trivial for disjunction and negation and we focus on $F_{[a,b]}$ and U for which we provide constructive proofs.

When a proposition p holds throughout an interval $I = [c, d]$, $\mathcal{M}(p)$ contains segments of w whose starting point t is in I. The role of t' is just to ensure, in addition, that $[t, t')$ is a well-defined segment, a sub-interval of $dom(w)$. This can be written explicitly as $(c \leq t \leq d) \wedge (t < t' < \ell)$, or using a zone-like notation, $(c \leq t \leq d) \wedge (0 < t' - t) \wedge (0 \leq t' < \ell)$. This will hold for any p-interval and consequently $\mathcal{M}(p)$ is a timed polyhedron (see Fig. 3-(b)). The concepts of cones and back-shifting can be adapted to points and zones in $\mathbb{R}_+^2$. Recall that the satisfaction of $F_{[a,b]}\varphi$ at t is a function of the satisfaction of φ throughout $[t + a, t + b]$. The role of t' is to determine whether parts of the forward cone go outside $dom(\varphi)$ and should not be considered. Figure 4 illustrates the effect of t and t' on satisfaction.

Definition 7 (Cones and Back-Shifting in the Plane). *Let (t, t') be a point in $\mathbb{R}_+^2$ and let Z be a zone represented by the following (normalized) inequalities:*

$$\underline{\alpha} \leq t \leq \overline{\alpha}$$
$$\underline{\beta} \leq t' \leq \overline{\beta}$$
$$\underline{\gamma} \leq t' - t \leq \overline{\gamma}$$

Then

1. *The* $[a, b]$-*forward cone of* (t, t') *is* $[t + a, t + b] \times \{t'\}$;
2. *The* $[a, b]$-*back cone of* (t, t') *is* $[t - b, t - a] \times \{t'\}$;
3. *The* $[a, b]$-*back shift of zone* Z *is* $Z' = \sigma_{[a,b]}(I)$, *a zone defined by*

$$\begin{aligned} \underline{\alpha} - b \leq t \leq \overline{\alpha} - a \\ \underline{\beta} \leq t' \leq \overline{\beta} \\ \underline{\gamma} + a \leq t' - t \leq \overline{\gamma} + b \end{aligned} \tag{3}$$

Claim (Zone Back Shifting). The back-shift of a zone consists of all points whose forward cone intersects Z:

$$\sigma_{[a,b]}(Z) = \{(t, t') : [t + a, t + b] \times \{t'\} \cap Z \neq \emptyset\}$$

Proof. Given that Z is normalized, (3) is what you get by applying quantifier elimination to the following formula

$$\exists r \begin{pmatrix} a \leq r \leq b \\ \underline{\alpha} \leq t + r \leq \overline{\alpha} \\ \underline{\beta} \leq t' \leq \overline{\beta} \\ \underline{\gamma} \leq t' - (t + r) \leq \overline{\gamma} \end{pmatrix}$$

□

Figure 5 illustrates zone back-shifting. Perhaps the simplest way to view it is to back-shift the vertices of Z along the horizontal t dimension. The left vertices are shifted by b and the right ones by a.

What remains to be shown is that if both $\mathcal{M}(\varphi_1)$ and $\mathcal{M}(\varphi_2)$ are timed polyhedra, so is $\mathcal{M}(\varphi_1 \mathcal{U} \varphi_2)$. Recalling the relation between one-dimensional matching by intervals and two-dimensional matching as expressed in (1), we will associate with every $\mathbf{Z} \subseteq T_w$ and every t', a one-dimensional object, the t'-slice (projection) of $\mathbf{Z}$, defined as $I_{\mathbf{Z},t'} = \{t : (t, t') \in \mathbf{Z}\}$. For a convex zone Z, $I_{Z,t'}$ is a single interval and for this reason we first prove our result for the case where both match-sets are single zones.

Claim. Let $\mathcal{M}(\varphi_1) = Z_1$ and $\mathcal{M}(\varphi_2) = Z_2$ be zones, then $\mathcal{M}(\varphi_1 \mathcal{U} \varphi_2)$ is also a zone.

Proof. Following the semantics of until we have

$$\begin{aligned} (t, t') \in \mathcal{M}(\varphi_1 \mathcal{U} \varphi_2) \text{ iff } \quad & \exists r \in [t, t'] \ (r, t') \in Z_2 \\ & \text{and } \forall r' \in [t, r] \ (r', t') \in Z_1 \end{aligned}$$

which translates to

$$\exists r \in [t, t'] \left\{ \left\{ \begin{matrix} \underline{\alpha_2} \prec & r & \prec \overline{\alpha_2} \\ \underline{\beta_2} \prec & t' & \prec \overline{\beta_2} \\ \underline{\gamma_2} \prec t' - r & \prec \overline{\gamma_2} \end{matrix} \right\} \text{ and } \forall r' \in [t, r] \left\{ \begin{matrix} \underline{\alpha_1} \prec & r' & \prec \overline{\alpha_1} \\ \underline{\beta_1} \prec & t' & \prec \overline{\beta_1} \\ \underline{\gamma_1} \prec t' - r' & \prec \overline{\gamma_1} \end{matrix} \right\} \right\}$$

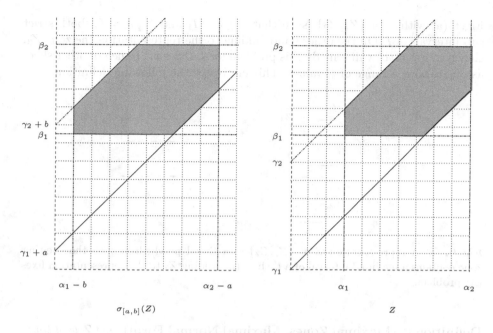

Fig. 5. An illustration of zone back-shifting.

First we eliminate the universal quantification by taking the dual and applying the Fourier-Motzkin procedure and then eliminate the existential quantifier to finally obtain

$$\mathcal{M}(\varphi_1 \mathcal{U} \varphi_2) = \left\{ \begin{array}{c} \underline{\alpha_1} \prec t \prec \min\{\overline{\alpha}_1, \overline{\alpha}_2\} \\[1ex] \max\left\{ \begin{array}{c} \underline{\beta}_1, \underline{\beta}_2, \\ \underline{\alpha}_2 + \underline{\gamma}_1 \end{array} \right\} \prec t' \prec \min\left\{ \begin{array}{c} \overline{\beta}_1, \overline{\beta}_2, \\ \overline{\alpha}_1 + \overline{\gamma}_2, \end{array} \right\} \\[2ex] \max\{\underline{\gamma}_1, \underline{\gamma}_2\} \prec t' - t \prec \overline{\gamma}_1 \end{array} \right\} \quad (4)$$

□

Let us denote this operation on zones as $\mathbf{\Omega}(Z_1, Z_2)$. It can be viewed as performing in a symbolic manner an uncountable number of interval-based until computations:

$$\mathbf{\Omega}(Z_1, Z_2) = \bigcup_{t' \in [0,\ell)} \Omega(I_{Z_1,t'}, I_{Z_2,t'}) \times \{t'\}.$$

Consider now the more general case where $\mathcal{M}(\varphi_1)$ is a non-convex timed polyhedron $\mathbf{Z}$, represented as a set of zones $\mathcal{Z}$. Trying to apply the procedure to every pair of zones in the respective representations, we may face the following problem. There might be a maximal interval I in $I_{\mathbf{Z},t'}$ which is not fully included in a single zone in $\mathcal{Z}$ but is spread over two or more zones. This is illustrated in

Fig. 6-(a) with $\mathcal{Z} = \{Z_1, Z_2\}$, such that $I_{Z_1, t'} = I_1$ and $I_{Z_2, t'} = I_2$, both strict sub-intervals of I. On the other hand, adding to the representation the zone Z_3, shown in Fig. 6-(b) will remedy this problem for I and for a bunch of other slices associate with a range of t' values. This motivates the following definition.

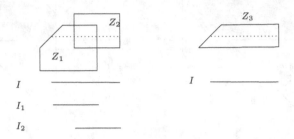

Fig. 6. (a) A representation $\mathcal{Z} = \{Z_1, Z_2\}$ of a timed polyhedron such that neither zone contains a maximal interval of a t'-slice. (b) Adding Z_3 to the representation fixes the problem.

Definition 8 (Maximal Zones, Maximal Normal Form). *Let $\mathbf{Z}$ be a timed polyhedron. A zone $Z \subseteq \mathbf{Z}$ is maximal in $\mathbf{Z}$ if there is no other zone Z' such that $Z \subset Z' \subseteq \mathbf{Z}$. A representation $\mathcal{Z}$ of $\mathbf{Z}$ is maximal if contains all maximal zones. A representation is reduced maximal if it consists of the set of all maximal zones.*

The notion of maximal representation is an adaptation of the concept of a *syllogistic form* of a Boolean function, a DNF representation that contains all maximal cubes. The reduced maximal representation corresponds to what is known as Blake normal form. Both were introduced in [4] and the reader can find more about it in [5]. In a maximal representation $\mathcal{Z}$ of $\mathbf{Z}$, every zone included in $\mathbf{Z}$ is included in some $Z \in \mathcal{Z}$, a fact which implies the following claim.

Claim (Pairwise Operation on Maximal Representation). Let $\mathcal{M}(\varphi_1) = \mathbf{Z}_1$ and $\mathcal{M}(\varphi_2) = \mathbf{Z}_2$ be timed polyhedra, represented by $\mathcal{Z}_1$ and $\mathcal{Z}_2$, respectively, with $\mathcal{Z}_1$ being maximal. Then $\mathcal{M}(\varphi_1 \mathcal{U} \varphi_2)$ is also a timed polyhedron computed as

$$\bigcup_{Z_1 \in \mathcal{Z}_1} \bigcup_{Z_2 \in \mathcal{Z}_2} \Omega(Z_1, Z_2).$$

Proof. The inclusion

$$\mathcal{M}(\varphi_1 \mathcal{U} \varphi_2) \supseteq \bigcup_{Z_1, Z_2} \Omega(Z_1, Z_2)$$

is trivial. Let us prove the opposite ($\subseteq$) inclusion. Consider any $(t, t') \in \mathcal{M}(\varphi_1 \mathcal{U} \varphi_2)$. By definition of the until satisfaction map, there exists $r \geq t$, such that

$$(r, t') \in \mathbf{Z}_2 \wedge \bigwedge_{r' \in [t, r]} ((r', t') \in \mathbf{Z}_1)$$

Applying the representation of $\mathbf{Z}_2$, we deduce from the first conjunct that $(r, t') \in Z_2$ for some zone $Z_2 \in \mathcal{Z}_2$. We rewrite the second conjunct as $I \subseteq \mathbf{Z}_1$, where I is the interval with extremities (t, t') and (r, t'). Using maximality of $\mathcal{Z}_1$, we deduce that $I \subseteq Z_1$ for some $Z_1 \in \mathcal{Z}_1$ or, in pointwise notation,

$$\bigwedge_{r' \in [t,r]} ((r', t') \in Z_1).$$

Gathering everything, we get that for some $r \geq t, Z_1 \in \mathcal{Z}_1, Z_2 \in \mathcal{Z}_2$, it holds that

$$(r, t') \in Z_2 \wedge \bigwedge_{r' \in [t,r]} ((r', t') \in Z_1),$$

in other words $(t, t') \in \mathbf{\Omega}(Z_1, Z_2)$. $\qquad\qquad\qquad\qquad\qquad\qquad\qquad$ $\square$

This concludes the proof of our main result.

Theorem 1 (Match Sets for MTL). *For any MTL formula φ and a bounded variability Boolean signal w, $\mathcal{M}(\varphi, w)$ is a timed polyhedron represented as a finite union of zones.*

We sketch below how one can transform a representation of a timed polyhedron into a maximal one. We apply the multiplication (intersection) technique [4,5] to complement a timed polyhedron $\mathbf{Z}$ represented by a set of zones. In essence it applies De Moragn rule to obtain a CNF representation of $\overline{\mathbf{Z}}$, and then opens the parentheses to collect the terms (zones). The representation of $\overline{\mathbf{Z}}$ thus obtained is maximal by a direct extension of the results proved by Blake [5]. Applying this operation twice we obtain a maximal representation of $\mathbf{Z}$.

While a maximal representation is sufficient for proving the results, in our implementation we keep the representation reduced by making incremental inclusion tests and other optimization such as plane sweep techniques that may avoid intersections between zones that are far apart.

4   Case Study

In this section, we illustrate the computation of match sets on an example of a bounded recurrence property, taken from the catalog of commonly-used real-time properties [14]:

$$\varphi_1 := (q \wedge \neg r \wedge Fr) \rightarrow (F_{[0,c]}(p \vee r) \, \mathcal{U} \, r)$$

Property φ_1 requires proposition p to hold at least every c time units between q and r. Such properties are commonly used to express periodic tasks to be performed between two events. Figure 7-(top left) depicts some input signals for propositions p, q, and r. The satisfaction maps for some sub-formulas are shown in Fig. 7-(left) followed by the satisfaction map for the top-level formula φ_1 in Fig. 7-(right). This figure illustrates the evolution of the formulas satisfaction with time and knowledge. Recall that a t'-section of the map gives us the satisfaction signal for the formula φ by $w[0, t']$. We depict t'-sections for time points t_1, t_2 and t_3 in Fig. 7-(bottom-right). We can observe that φ_1 is satisfied at all times $t \in [0, t_1)$ based on the knowledge available at t_1. However, it turns out to be violated at some times $t \in [0, t_1)$ when additional knowledge about the input signals is provided at times t_2 and t_3.

Our techniques also open the way for using MTL for specifying local timed properties (patterns) that only hold at some segments of the signal. We illustrate this using three examples. First, consider a formula $\varphi_2 = q \wedge \varphi_1$ and its satisfaction map which filters away segments that satisfy φ_1 trivially due to $\neg q$. Second, we consider an MTL formula $\varphi_3 = GF_{[0,c]}(p \vee r)$ which describes time periods where p or r holds periodically at least every c time units. Third, in

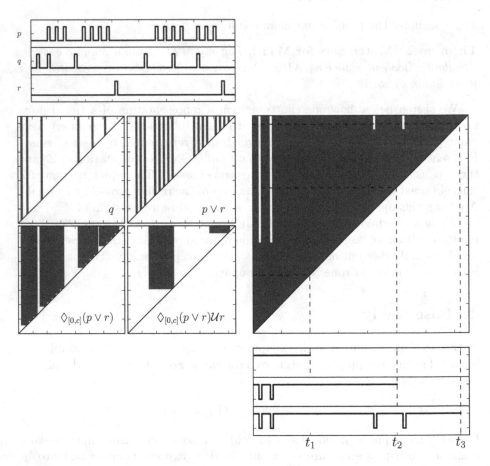

Fig. 7. Input signals p, q, and r, respectively (top left). Satisfaction maps for some subformulas (left). The satisfaction map for φ (right). Cross-sections of the satisfaction map for φ that corresponds to satisfaction signals at t_1, t_2, and t_3 (bottom right).

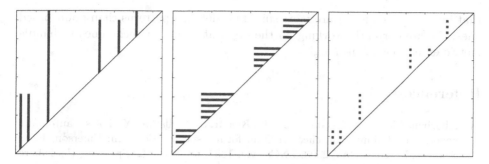

Fig. 8. Satisfaction maps for the formula $q \wedge \varphi_1$ (left), the formula $GF_{[0,c]}(p \vee r)$ (middle), and the formula $q \wedge GF_{[0,c]}(p \vee r)$ (right).

order to express a pattern describing time periods where p or r holds at least every c time units and starting with q, the formula φ_3 is intersected with q such that $\varphi_4 = q \wedge GF_{[0,c]}(p \vee r)$. Figure 8 depicts the satisfaction maps for φ_2, φ_3, and φ_4 using the same signals appearing in Fig. 7.

5   Conclusions and Future Work

The major contribution of this work is in exporting and adapting the two-dimensional segment matching technology from timed regular expressions [28] to MTL. On the way to prove the main result, namely that the match sets for MTL are unions of zones, we had to cope with the alternating nature of the until operator, using the maximal representation for timed polyhedra. This concept, adapted from the syllogistic representation of Boolean functions, may have some other applications in the analysis of timed systems. Our matching algorithm has been implemented and demonstrated on some non-trivial examples.

Regular expressions and temporal logic are inherently different due to various reasons, including the different nature of the major sequential operator (concatenation compared to *until*) and the positional and directed satisfaction relation of TL. Consequently, the MTL interpretation of the satisfaction map consists of separate positional and epistemological components. One way to go further in this direction is to consider a 3-dimensional satisfaction map defined on tuples (s, t, t') where $[t, t')$ stands for what is known about the signal and s is the position from which satisfaction is considered, not necessarily included in $[t, t')$. It looks a priori as if such an approach could handle full MTL with both future and past operators.

As mentioned, our technique can be adapted to a 3-values semantics with $\bot$ standing for unknown. To this end, the representation of the satisfaction map should be augmented with a second timed polyhedron $\mathcal{M}_\bot$, which should be shifted and manipulated in coordination with $\mathcal{M}$ and its complement.

Finally, the satisfaction of formulas in *interval temporal logics*, such as those studied in [11,32], is associated naturally with intervals. It might be the case that interval-based logics are more suited for defining patterns than point-based ones. We are currently working on the application of our techniques to handle metric extensions of such logics.

References

1. Abarbanel, Y., Beer, I., Gluhovsky, L., Keidar, S., Wolfsthal, Y.: FoCs – automatic generation of simulation checkers from formal specifications. In: Emerson, E.A., Sistla, A.P. (eds.) CAV 2000. LNCS, vol. 1855, pp. 538–542. Springer, Heidelberg (2000). doi:10.1007/10722167_40
2. Basin, D.A., Klaedtke, F., Zalinescu, E.: Failure-aware runtime verification of distributed systems. In: FSTTCS, pp. 590–603 (2015)
3. Bauer, A., Leucker, M., Schallhart, C.: Monitoring of real-time properties. In: Arun-Kumar, S., Garg, N. (eds.) FSTTCS 2006. LNCS, vol. 4337, pp. 260–272. Springer, Heidelberg (2006). doi:10.1007/11944836_25
4. Blake, A.: Canonical expressions in Boolean algebra. Ph.D. thesis (1938)
5. Brown, F.M.: Boolean Reasoning: The Logic of Boolean Equations. Springer, New York (2012). doi:10.1007/978-1-4757-2078-5
6. De Giacomo, G., Vardi, M.Y.: Linear temporal logic and linear dynamic logic on finite traces. In: IJCAI, pp. 854–860 (2013)
7. D'Souza, D., Tabareau, N.: On timed automata with input-determined guards. In: Lakhnech, Y., Yovine, S. (eds.) FORMATS/FTRTFT -2004. LNCS, vol. 3253, pp. 68–83. Springer, Heidelberg (2004). doi:10.1007/978-3-540-30206-3_7
8. Eisner, C., Fisman, D., Havlicek, J.: A topological characterization of weakness. In: PODC, pp. 1–8 (2005)
9. Eisner, C., Fisman, D., Havlicek, J., Lustig, Y., McIsaac, A., Campenhout, D.: Reasoning with temporal logic on truncated paths. In: Hunt, W.A., Somenzi, F. (eds.) CAV 2003. LNCS, vol. 2725, pp. 27–39. Springer, Heidelberg (2003). doi:10.1007/978-3-540-45069-6_3
10. Guelev, D.P., Dima, C., Enea, C.: An alternating-time temporal logic with knowledge, perfect recall and past: axiomatisation and model-checking. J. Appl. Non Class. Log. 21(1), 93–131 (2011)
11. Halpern, J.Y., Shoham, Y.: A propositional modal logic of time intervals. J. ACM (JACM) 38(4), 935–962 (1991)
12. Halpern, J.Y., Vardi, M.Y.: The complexity of reasoning about knowledge and time. I. lower bounds. J. Comput. Syst. Sci. 38(1), 195–237 (1989)
13. Kamp, H.: Tense logic and the theory of order. Ph.D. thesis, UCLA (1968)
14. Konrad, S., Cheng, B.H.C.: Real-time specification patterns. In: ICSE, pp. 372–381 (2005)
15. Koymans, R.: Specifying real-time properties with metric temporal logic. Real Time Syst. 2(4), 255–299 (1990)
16. Maler, O.: Some thoughts on runtime verification. In: Falcone, Y., Sánchez, C. (eds.) RV 2016. LNCS, vol. 10012, pp. 3–14. Springer, Cham (2016). doi:10.1007/978-3-319-46982-9_1
17. Maler, O., Nickovic, D.: Monitoring temporal properties of continuous signals. In: Lakhnech, Y., Yovine, S. (eds.) FORMATS/FTRTFT -2004. LNCS, vol. 3253, pp. 152–166. Springer, Heidelberg (2004). doi:10.1007/978-3-540-30206-3_12

18. Maler, O., Nickovic, D., Pnueli, A.: Real time temporal logic: past, present, future. In: Pettersson, P., Yi, W. (eds.) FORMATS 2005. LNCS, vol. 3829, pp. 2–16. Springer, Heidelberg (2005). doi:10.1007/11603009_2

19. Maler, O., Nickovic, D., Pnueli, A.: From MITL to timed automata. In: Asarin, E., Bouyer, P. (eds.) FORMATS 2006. LNCS, vol. 4202, pp. 274–289. Springer, Heidelberg (2006). doi:10.1007/11867340_20

20. Maler, O., Nickovic, D., Pnueli, A.: Checking temporal properties of discrete, timed and continuous behaviors. In: Avron, A., Dershowitz, N., Rabinovich, A. (eds.) Pillars of Computer Science. LNCS, vol. 4800, pp. 475–505. Springer, Heidelberg (2008). doi:10.1007/978-3-540-78127-1_26

21. Manna, Z., Pnueli, A.: The anchored version of the temporal framework. In: Bakker, J.W., Roever, W.-P., Rozenberg, G. (eds.) REX 1988. LNCS, vol. 354, pp. 201–284. Springer, Heidelberg (1989). doi:10.1007/BFb0013024

22. Nickovic, D.: Checking timed and hybrid properties: theory and applications. Ph.D. thesis, Université Joseph Fourier, Grenoble, France (2008)

23. Nivat, M., Perrin, D.: Ensembles reconnaissables de mots bi-infinis. In: STOC, pp. 47–59. ACM (1982)

24. Pnueli, A.: The temporal logic of programs. In: FOCS, pp. 46–57 (1977)

25. Pnueli, A.: The temporal semantics of concurrent programs. Theor. Comput. Sci. 13, 45–60 (1981)

26. Prior, A.N.: Past, present and future, vol. 154 (1967)

27. Reinbacher, T., Rozier, K.Y., Schumann, J.: Temporal-logic based runtime observer pairs for system health management of real-time systems. In: Ábrahám, E., Havelund, K. (eds.) TACAS 2014. LNCS, vol. 8413, pp. 357–372. Springer, Heidelberg (2014). doi:10.1007/978-3-642-54862-8_24

28. Ulus, D., Ferrère, T., Asarin, E., Maler, O.: Timed pattern matching. In: Legay, A., Bozga, M. (eds.) FORMATS 2014. LNCS, vol. 8711, pp. 222–236. Springer, Cham (2014). doi:10.1007/978-3-319-10512-3_16

29. Van Benthem, J., Pacuit, E.: The tree of knowledge in action: towards a common perspective (2006)

30. Vardi, M.Y.: From church and prior to PSL. In: Grumberg, O., Veith, H. (eds.) 25 Years of Model Checking. LNCS, vol. 5000, pp. 150–171. Springer, Heidelberg (2008). doi:10.1007/978-3-540-69850-0_10

31. Vardi, M.Y., Wolper, P.: An automata-theoretic approach to automatic program verification. In: LICS (1986)

32. Venema, Y.: A modal logic for chopping intervals. J. Log. Comput. 1(4), 453–476 (1991)

Efficient Online Timed Pattern Matching by Automata-Based Skipping

Masaki Waga[1][✉], Ichiro Hasuo[2], and Kohei Suenaga[3]

[1] University of Tokyo, Tokyo, Japan
mwaga@is.s.u-tokyo.ac.jp
[2] National Institute of Informatics, Tokyo, Japan
[3] Kyoto University and JST PRESTO, Kyoto, Japan

Abstract. The *timed pattern matching* problem is an actively studied topic because of its relevance in *monitoring* of real-time systems. There one is given a log w and a specification $\mathcal{A}$ (given by a *timed word* and a *timed automaton* in this paper), and one wishes to return the set of intervals for which the log w, when restricted to the interval, satisfies the specification $\mathcal{A}$. In our previous work we presented an efficient timed pattern matching algorithm: it adopts a skipping mechanism inspired by the classic Boyer–Moore (BM) string matching algorithm. In this work we tackle the problem of *online* timed pattern matching, towards embedded applications where it is vital to process a vast amount of incoming data in a timely manner. Specifically, we start with the Franek-Jennings-Smyth (FJS) string matching algorithm—a recent variant of the BM algorithm—and extend it to timed pattern matching. Our experiments indicate the efficiency of our FJS-type algorithm in online and offline timed pattern matching.

1 Introduction

Monitoring of real-time properties is an actively studied topic with numerous applications such as automotive systems [19], medical systems [8], data classification [6], web service [26], and quantitative performance measuring [12]. Given a specification $\mathcal{A}$ and a log w of activities, monitoring would ask questions like: *if w has a segment that matches $\mathcal{A}$; all the segments of w that match $\mathcal{A}$;* and so on.

For a monitoring algorithm *efficiency* is a critical matter. Since we often need to monitor a large number of logs, each of which tends to be very long, one monitoring task can take hours. Therefore even *constant* speed up can make significant practical differences. Another important issue is an algorithm's performance in *online usage scenarios*. Monitoring algorithms are often deployed in *embedded* applications [18], and this incurs the following online requirements:

- *Real-time properties*, such as: on prefixes of the log w, we want to know their monitoring result soon, possibly before the whole log w arrives.

© Springer International Publishing AG 2017
A. Abate and G. Geeraerts (Eds.): FORMATS 2017, LNCS 10419, pp. 224–243, 2017.
DOI: 10.1007/978-3-319-65765-3_13

- *Memory consumption*, such as: early prefixes of w should not affect the monitoring task of later segments of w, so that we can throw the prefixes away and free memory (that tends to be quite limited in embedded applications).
- *Speed* of the algorithm. In an online setting this means: if the log w arrives at a speed faster than the algorithm processes it, then the data that waits to be processed will fill up the memory.

Constant improvement in aspects like speed and memory consumption will be appreciated in online settings, too: if an algorithm is twice as fast, then this means the same monitoring task can be conducted with cheaper hardware that is twice slower.

The goal of the current paper is thus monitoring algorithms that perform well both in offline and online settings. We take a framework where *timed words*—they are essentially sequences of time-stamped events—stand for logs, and *timed automata* express a specification. Both constructs are well-known in the community of real-time systems. The problem we solve is that of *timed pattern matching*: see Sect. 2.1 for its definition; Fig. 1 for an example; and Table 1 for comparison with other matching problems.

Fig. 1. An example of timed pattern matching. For the pattern timed automaton $\mathcal{A}$ and the target timed word w, as shown, the output is the set of matching intervals $\{(t, t') \mid w|_{(t,t')} \in L(\mathcal{A})\} = \{(t, t') \mid t \in [3.7, 3.9), t' \in (6.0, \infty)\}$. Here $\$$ is a special terminal character.

Towards the goal our strategy is to exploit the idea of *skip values* in efficient string matching algorithms (such as Boyer–Moore (BM) [7]), together with their *automata-based extension* for pattern matching by Watson and Watson [35], to skip unnecessary matching trials. In our previous work [32] we took the strategy and introduced a timed pattern matching algorithm with BM-type skipping.

Table 1. Matching problems

	Log, target	Specification, pattern	Output
String matching	a word $w \in \Sigma^*$	a word $pat \in \Sigma^*$	$\{(i, j) \in (\mathbb{Z}_{>0})^2 \mid w(i, j) = pat\}$
Pattern matching	a word $w \in \Sigma^*$	an NFA $\mathcal{A}$	$\{(i, j) \subset (\mathbb{Z}_{>0})^2 \mid w(i, j) \in L(\mathcal{A})\}$
Timed pattern matching	a timed word $w \in (\Sigma \times \mathbb{R}_{>0})^*$	a timed automaton $\mathcal{A}$	$\{(t, t') \in (\mathbb{R}_{>0})^2 \mid w|_{(t,t')} \in L(\mathcal{A})\}$

The current work improves on this previous BM algorithm: it is based on the more recent *Franek–Jennings–Smyth (FJS) algorithm* [13] for string matching (instead of BM); and our new algorithm is faster than our previous BM-type one. Moreover, in online usage, our FJS-type algorithm better addresses the online requirements that we listed in the above. This is in contrast with our previous BM-type algorithm that works necessarily in an offline manner (it must wait for the whole log w before it starts).

Contributions. Our main contribution is an efficient algorithm for timed pattern matching that employs (an automata-theoretic extension of) skip values from the Franek–Jennings–Smyth (FJS) algorithm for string matching [13]. By experiments we show that the algorithm generally outperforms a brute-force one and our previous BM algorithm [32]: it is twice as fast for some realistic automotive examples. Through our theoretical analysis as well as experiments on memory consumption, we claim that our algorithm is suited for online usage scenarios, too. We also compare its performance with a recent tool *Montre* for timed pattern matching [29], and observe that ours is faster, at least in terms of the implementations currently available.

In its course we have obtained an FJS-type algorithm for *untimed* pattern matching, which is one of the main contributions too. The algorithm is explained rather in detail, so that it paves the way to our FJS-type *timed* pattern matching that is more complex.

A central theme of the paper is benefits of the formalism of *automata*, a mathematical tool whose use is nowadays widespread in fields like temporal logic, model checking, and so on. We follow Watson & Watson's idea of extending skipping from string matching to pattern matching [35], where the key is overapproximation of words and languages by states of automata. Our main contribution on the conceptual side is that the same idea applies to *timed* automata as well, where we rely on *zone*-based abstraction (see e.g. [4,5,14]) for computing reachability.

Related Works. Several algorithms have been proposed for online monitoring of real-time temporal logic specifications. An online monitoring algorithm for ptMTL (a past time fragment of MTL) is in [27] and an algorithm for MTL[U,S] (a variant of MTL with both forward and backward temporal modalities) is in [15]. In addition, a case study on an autonomous research vehicle monitoring [19] shows such procedures can be performed in an actual vehicle—this is where our motivation comes from, too.

We have chosen timed automata as a specification formalism. This is because of their expressivity as well as various techniques that operate on them. Some other formalisms can be translated to timed automata, and via translation, our algorithm offers to these formalisms an online monitoring algorithm. In [3], a variant of *timed regular expressions (TREs)* are proved to have the same expressive power as timed automata. For MTL and MITL, transformations into automata are introduced for many different settings; see e.g. [2,10,20,22,24].

The work with closest interests to ours is by Ulus, Ferrère, Asarin, Maler and their colleagues [29–31]. In their series of work, logs are presented by *signals*, i.e. values that vary over time. Their logs are thus *state-based* rather than *event-based* like timed words. Their specification formalism is timed regular expressions (TREs). An offline monitoring algorithm is presented in [30] and an online one is in [31]. These algorithms are implemented in the tool *Montre* [29], with which we conduct performance comparison. The difference between different specification formalisms (TREs, timed automata, temporal logics, etc.) are subtle, but for many realistic examples the difference does not matter. In the current paper we exploit various operations on automata, most notably zone-based abstraction.

Notations Let Σ be an alphabet and $w = a_1 a_2 \ldots a_n \in \Sigma^*$ be a string over Σ, where $a_i \in \Sigma$ for each $i \in [1, n]$. We let $w(i)$ denote the i-th character a_i of w. Furthermore, for $i, j \in [1, n]$, when $i \leq j$ we let $w(i, j)$ denote the substring $a_i a_{i+1} \ldots a_j$, otherwise we let $w(i, j)$ denote the empty string ε. The length n of the string w is denoted by $|w|$.

Organization of the Paper. In Sect. 2 are preliminaries on: our formulation of the problem of timed pattern matching; and the FJS algorithm for string matching. The FJS-type skipping is extended to (untimed) pattern matching in Sect. 3, where we describe the algorithm in detail. This paves the way to our FJS-type timed pattern matching algorithm in Sect. 4. In Sect. 4 we also sketch zone-based abstraction of timed automata, a key technical ingredient in the algorithm. In Sect. 5 we present our experiment results. They indicate our algorithm's performance advantage in both offline and online usage scenarios.

2   Preliminaries

2.1   Timed Pattern Matching

Here we formulate our problem. Our target strings are *timed words* [1], that are time-stamped words over an alphabet Σ. Our patterns are given by *timed automata* [1].

Definition 2.1 (timed word, timed word segment). For an alphabet Σ, a *timed word* is a sequence w of pairs $(a_i, \tau_i) \in (\Sigma \times \mathbb{R}_{>0})$ satisfying $\tau_i < \tau_{i+1}$ for any $i \in [1, |w| - 1]$. Let $w = (\overline{a}, \overline{\tau})$ be a timed word. We denote the subsequence $(a_i, \tau_i), (a_{i+1}, \tau_{i+1}), \cdots, (a_j, \tau_j)$ by $w(i, j)$. For $t \in \mathbb{R}_{\geq 0}$, the t-*shift* of w is $(\overline{a}, \overline{\tau}) + t = (\overline{a}, \overline{\tau} + t)$ where $\overline{\tau} + t = \tau_1 + t, \tau_2 + t, \cdots, \tau_{|\tau|} + t$. For timed words $w = (\overline{a}, \overline{\tau})$ and $w' = (\overline{a'}, \overline{\tau'})$, their *absorbing concatenation* is $w \circ w' = (\overline{a} \circ \overline{a'}, \overline{\tau} \circ \overline{\tau'})$ where $\overline{a} \circ \overline{a'}$ and $\overline{\tau} \circ \overline{\tau'}$ are usual concatenations, and their *non-absorbing concatenation* is $w \cdot w' = w \circ (w' + \tau_{|w|})$. We note that the absorbing concatenation $w \circ w'$ is defined only when $\tau_{|w|} < \tau'_1$.

For a timed word $w = (\overline{a}, \overline{\tau})$ on Σ and $t, t' \in \mathbb{R}_{>0}$ satisfying $t < t'$, a *timed word segment* $w|_{(t,t')}$ is defined by the timed word $(w(i, j) - t) \circ (\$, t')$ on the augmented alphabet $\Sigma \sqcup \{\$\}$, where i, j are chosen so that $\tau_{i-1} \leq t < \tau_i$ and $\tau_j < t' \leq \tau_{j+1}$. Here the fresh symbol $\$$ is called the *terminal character*.

Definition 2.2 (timed automaton). Let C be a finite set of *clock variables*, and $\Phi(C)$ denote the set of conjunctions of inequalities $x \bowtie c$ where $x \in C$, $c \in \mathbb{Z}_{\geq 0}$, and $\bowtie \in \{>, \geq, <, \leq\}$. A *timed automaton* $\mathcal{A} = (\Sigma, S, S_0, C, E, F)$ is a tuple where: Σ is an alphabet; S is a finite set of states; $S_0 \subseteq S$ is a set of initial states; $E \subseteq S \times S \times \Sigma \times \mathcal{P}(C) \times \Phi(C)$ is a set of transitions; and $F \subseteq S$ is a set of accepting states. The components of a transition $(s, s', a, \lambda, \delta) \in E$ represent: the source, target, action, reset variables and guard of the transition, respectively.

We define a *clock valuation* ν as a function $\nu : C \to \mathbb{R}_{\geq 0}$. We define the *t-shift* $\nu + t$ of a clock valuation ν, where $t \in \mathbb{R}_{\geq 0}$, by $(\nu + t)(x) = \nu(x) + t$ for any $x \in C$. For a timed automaton $\mathcal{A} = (\Sigma, S, S_0, E, C, F)$ and a timed word $w = (\overline{a}, \overline{\tau})$, a *run* of $\mathcal{A}$ over w is a sequence r of pairs $(s_i, \nu_i) \in S \times (\mathbb{R}_{\geq 0})^C$ satisfying the following: (initiation) $s_0 \in S_0$ and $\nu_0(x) = 0$ for any $x \in C$; and (consecution) for any $i \in [1, |w|]$, there exists a transition $(s_{i-1}, s_i, a_i, \lambda, \delta) \in E$ such that $\nu_{i-1} + \tau_i - \tau_{i-1} \models \delta$ and $\nu_i(x) = 0$ (for $x \in \lambda$) and $\nu_i(x) = \nu_{i-1}(x) + \tau_i - \tau_{i-1}$ (for $x \notin \lambda$). A run only satisfying the consecution condition is a *path*. A run $r = (\overline{s}, \overline{\nu})$ is *accepting* if the last element $s_{|s|-1}$ of s belongs to F. The *language* $L(\mathcal{A})$ is defined to be the set $\{w \mid$ there is an accepting run of $\mathcal{A}$ over $w\}$ of timed words.

Definition 2.3 (timed pattern matching). Let $\mathcal{A}$ be a timed automaton, and w be a timed word, over a common alphabet Σ. The *timed pattern matching* problem requires all the intervals (t, t') for which the segment $w|_{(t,t')}$ is accepted by $\mathcal{A}$. That is, it requires the *match set* $\mathcal{M}(w, \mathcal{A}) = \{(t, t') \mid w|_{(t,t')} \in L(\mathcal{A})\}$.

The match set $\mathcal{M}(w, \mathcal{A})$ is in general uncountable; however it allows finitary representation, as a finite union of special polyhedra called *zones*. See [32].

2.2 String Matching and the FJS Algorithm

String matching is a fundamental problem in computer science. Given a *pattern string pat* and a *target string* w, it requires the set $\{(i, j) \in (\mathbb{Z}_{>0})^2 \mid w(i, j) = pat\}$ of all the occurrences of *pat* in w. A brute-force algorithm, by trying to match $|pat|$ characters for all the possible $|w| - |pat|$ positions of the pattern string, solves the string matching problem in $O(|pat||w|)$. Efficient algorithms for this classic problem have been sought for a long time, with significant progress made as recently as in the last decade [11]. Among them the *Knuth–Morris–Pratt (KMP) algorithm* [21] and the *Boyer–Moore (BM) algorithm* [7] are well-known, where unnecessary matching trials are *skipped* utilizing *skip value functions*. Empirical studies have shown speed advantage of BM—and its variants like *Quick Search* [28]—over KMP, while theoretically KMP exhibits better worst-case complexity $O(|pat| + |w|)$. By combining KMP and Quick Search, the *Franek–Jennings–Smyth (FJS) algorithm* [13], proposed in 2007, achieves both linear worst-case complexity and good practical performance.

The current paper's goal is to introduce FJS-like optimization to timed pattern matching. We therefore take the FJS algorithm as an example and

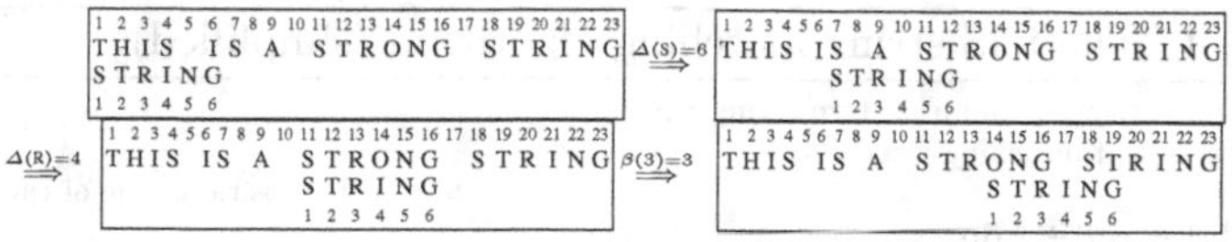

Fig. 2. The Franek–Jennings–Smyth (FJS) algorithm for string matching: an example

demonstrate how skip values are utilized in the string matching algorithms we have mentioned.[1]

The FJS algorithm combines two skip value functions: $\Delta \colon \Sigma \to [1, |pat| + 1]$ and $\beta \colon [0, |pat|] \to [1, |pat|]$; the former Δ comes from Quick Search and the latter β comes from KMP (the choice of symbols follows [13]). See Fig. 2 where the pattern string $pat = $ STRING is shifted by 6, 4 and 3 (instead of one-by-one).

In the first shift we use the Quick Search skip value $\Delta(S) = 6$: we try matching the tail of pat; it fails ($pat(6) \neq w(6)$); then we find that the next character $w(7) = S$ of the target only occurs in the first position of the pattern. Formally we define Δ by

$$\Delta(a) = \min(\{i \in [1, |pat|] \mid a = pat(|pat| - i + 1)\} \cup \{|pat| + 1\}) \quad \text{for } a \in \Sigma. \quad (1)$$

In the example of Fig. 2 we have $\Delta(I) = 3$ and $\Delta(Q) = 7$.

Now we are in the second configuration of Fig. 2 and we try matching the tail $pat(6) = G$ with $w(12)$. It fails and we invoke the Quick Search skip value function Δ; this results in a shift by $\Delta(R) = 4$ positions.

For the shift from the third configuration to the fourth in Fig. 2 we employ the KMP skip value function β. It is defined as follows. Observe first that, in the third configuration of Fig. 2, matching trials from the head succeed for three positions and then fail ($w(11, 13) = pat(1, 3), w(14) \neq pat(4)$). From this information alone we can see that, for a potential string match, the pattern string must be shifted at least by $\beta(3) = 3$. See Fig. 3 where shifting the pattern string pat by one or two positions necessarily leads to a mismatch with $pat(1, 3)$. It is important here that we know $pat(1, 3)$ coincides with $w(11, 13)$ from the previous successful matching trials. Formally:

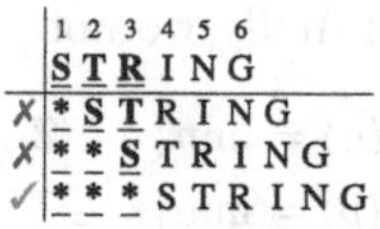

Fig. 3. $\beta(3) = 3$, where the argument 3 is the length of the successful partial match.

$$\beta(p) = \min\{n \in [1, pat] \mid pat(1, p - n) = pat(1 + n, p)\} \quad \text{for } p \in [0, |pat|]. \quad (2)$$

In the FJS algorithm we combine the two skip value function Δ and β. Specifically: let us be in a configuration where $pat(1)$ is in the position of $w(1 + n)$. We

---

[1] The FJS-typo algorithm we present here is a simplified version of the original FJS algorithm. Our simplification is equipped with all the features that we will exploit later for pattern matching and timed pattern matching; the original algorithm further omits some other trivially unnecessary matching trials. We note that, because of the difference (that is conceptually inessential), our simplified algorithm (for string matching) no longer enjoys linear worst-case complexity.

Algorithm 1. The FJS string matching algorithm (simplified)

Require: A target string w and a pattern string pat.
Ensure: Z is the set of matching intervals.
```
1:  n ← 1;                                              ▷ n is the position in w of the head of pat
2:  while n ≤ |w| − |pat| + 1 do
3:      while w(n + |pat| − 1) ≠ pat(|pat|) do          ▷ Try matching the tail of pat
4:      │   n ← n + Δ(w(n + |pat|))                      ▷ Quick Search-type skipping
5:      │   if n > |w| − m + 1 then return
6:      if pat = w(n, n + |pat| − 1) then                ▷ We try matching from left to right
7:      │   p ← |pat| + 1;    Z ← Z ∪ {[n, n + |pat| − 1]}
8:      else
9:      │   p ← min{p′ | pat(p′) ≠ w(n + p′ − 1)}        ▷ Matching trials fail at position p for the first time
10: │   n ← n + β(p)                                     ▷ KMP-type skipping
```

---

first try matching the pattern's tail $pat(|pat|)$ with its counterpart $w(|pat| + n)$; if it fails we invoke the Quick Search skipping Δ; otherwise we turn to the pattern's head $pat(1)$ try matching from left to right. After its success or failure we invoke the KMP skipping β. Note that preference is given to the Quick Search skipping. See Algorithm 1.

It is important that the skip value functions $\Delta\colon \Sigma \to [1, |pat| + 1]$ and $\beta\colon [0, |pat|] \to [1, |pat|]$ rely only on the pattern string pat. Therefore it is possible to pre-compute the function values in advance (i.e. before a target string w arrives); moreover since $|pat|$ is usually not large those values can be stored effectively in look-up tables. Skipping by these skip values does not improve the worst-case complexity, but practically it brings pleasing constant speed up, as demonstrated in Fig. 2.

Finally we note the following alternative presentation of Δ and β.

$$\begin{aligned}\Delta(a) &= \min\{n \in \mathbb{Z}_{>0} \mid \Sigma^n pat \cap \Sigma^{|pat|} a\Sigma^* \neq \emptyset\} && \text{for each } a \in \Sigma, \\ \beta(p) &= \min\{n \in \mathbb{Z}_{>0} \mid \Sigma^n pat(1, p) \cap pat(1, p)\Sigma^* \neq \emptyset\} && \text{for each } p \in [0, |pat|].\end{aligned} \tag{3}$$

3 An FJS-Type Algorithm for Pattern Matching

In this section we present our first main contribution, namely an adaptation of the FJS algorithm (Sect. 2.2) from string matching to *pattern matching*.

Definition 3.1 (pattern matching). Let $\mathcal{A}$ be a nondeterministic finite automaton over an alphabet Σ (a *pattern* NFA), and $w \in \Sigma^*$ be a *target* string. The *pattern matching* problem requires all the intervals (i, j) for which the substring $w(i, j)$ is accepted by $\mathcal{A}$. That is, it requires the set $\{(i, j) \mid 1 \leq i \leq j \leq |w| \text{ and } w(i, j) \in L(\mathcal{A})\}$.

For an example see Fig. 4, where the automaton $\mathcal{A}$ satisfies $L(\mathcal{A}) = L(\{ab, cd\}cc^*d)$.

A brute-force algorithm solves pattern matching in $O(|S||w|^2)$, where S is the state space of the pattern $\mathcal{A}$ (the factor $|S|$ is there due to nondeterminism). Some optimizations are known, among which is the adaptation of the Boyer–Moore algorithm by Watson & Watson [35]. In their algorithm they adapt the BM-type

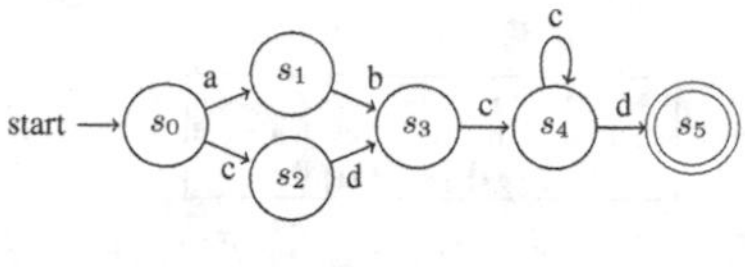

Fig. 4. Pattern matching. For the pattern NFA $\mathcal{A}$ on the left, for which it is easy to see that $L(\mathcal{A}) = L(\{ab, cd\}cc^*d)$, the output is $\{(9, 12)\}$ as shown on the right.

$$L(\mathcal{A}) = \left\{ \begin{array}{ll} abcd, & cdcd, \\ abccd, & cdccd, \\ abcccd, & cdcccd, \\ & \vdots \end{array} \right\} \quad \rightsquigarrow \quad L'' = L' \cdot \Sigma^* = \left\{ \begin{array}{l} abcd, cdcd, \\ abcc, cdcc \end{array} \right\} \Sigma^*$$

Fig. 5. Overapproximation of the language $L(\mathcal{A})$

skip values to pattern matching: the core idea in doing so is to *overapproximate* languages and substrings, so that the skip value function can be organized as a finite table and hence can be computed in advance. Our adaptation of the FJS algorithm employs similar overapproximation.

In the original FJS algorithm (for string matching) one uses skip value functions

$$\Delta \colon \Sigma \to [1, |pat| + 1] \quad \text{and} \quad \beta \colon [0, |pat|] \to [1, |pat|]. \tag{4}$$

One may wonder what we can use in place of $|pat|$, now that the pattern $\mathcal{A}$ can accept infinitely many words that are unboundedly long.

It turns out that our adaptations have the types

$$\Delta \colon \Sigma \to [1, m + 1] \quad \text{and} \quad \beta \colon S \to [1, m], \tag{5}$$

where m is the length of the shortest words accepted by $\mathcal{A}$ and S is the state space of $\mathcal{A}$. Intuitively, the original Δ does a comparison of the pattern pat with a character $a \in \Sigma$ and the original β does a comparison of pat with the substring $w(i,j)$ of the target string we actually read in the last matching trial. Thus the adaptation can be done by a finite presentation of the overapproximation of $L(\mathcal{A})$ and $w(i,j)$.

More specifically, for the approximation of $L(\mathcal{A})$: (1) we focus on the length m of the shortest accepted strings (four in the example of Fig. 4); (2) we collect all the prefixes of length m that appear in $L(\mathcal{A})$ (abcd, cdcd, abcc, cdcc in the same example); and (3) we let an overapproximation L'' consist of any word that starts with those prefixes. See Fig. 5 for illustration; precise definitions are as follows.

$$m = \min\{|w| \mid w \in L(\mathcal{A})\} \quad L' = \{w' \in \Sigma^m \mid \exists w'' \in \Sigma^*. \, w'w'' \in L(\mathcal{A})\} \quad L'' = L' \cdot \Sigma^*$$

Here $L' \subseteq \Sigma^m$ is necessarily a finite set; thus $L'' = L' \cdot \Sigma^*$ is an overapproximation of $L(\mathcal{A})$ with a finite representation L'.

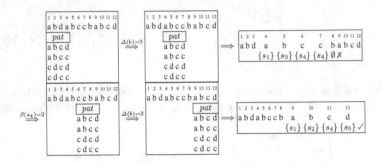

Fig. 6. Our FJS-type algorithm for pattern matching, for the example in Fig. 4

Algorithm 2. The FJS algorithm for pattern matching, for a target w and a pattern $\mathcal{A}$

Ensure: Z is the set of matching intervals.

1:    $n \leftarrow 1$;   ▷ n is the position in w of the head of pat

2:    **while** $n \leq |w| - m + 1$ **do**

3:        **while** $\forall w' \in L'. \, w(n + m - 1) \neq w'(m)$ **do**   ▷ Try matching the tail of L'

4:           $n \leftarrow n + \Delta(w(n + m))$ ▷ Quick Search-type skipping

5:           **if** $n > |w| - m + 1$ **then return**

6:        $Z \leftarrow Z \cup \{(n, n') \mid w(n, n') \in L(\mathcal{A})\}$ ▷ We try matching by feeding $w(n, |w|)$ to $\mathcal{A}$

7:        $n' \leftarrow \max\{n' \in [1, |w|] \mid \exists s_0 \in S_0, s \in S. \, s_0 \xrightarrow{w(n,n')} s\}$ ▷ n' is the position of the last successful match

8:        $S' \leftarrow \{s \in S \mid \exists s_0 \in S_0. \, s_0 \xrightarrow{w(n,n')} s\}$ ▷ Matching trials stack at the states S'

9:        $n \leftarrow n + \max_{s \in S'} \beta(s)$ ▷ KMP-type skipping

---

For the overapproximation of the substring $w(i, j)$ that we actually read at the last matching trial, we exploit the set $\mathcal{S}(w(i, j)) = \{s \in S \mid s_0 \xrightarrow{w(i,j)} s \text{ in } \mathcal{A}\}$ of states of $\mathcal{A}$. We have $w(i, j) \in \{w' \mid \forall s \in \mathcal{S}(w(i, j)), \exists s_0 \in S_0. \, s_0 \xrightarrow{w'} s \text{ in } \mathcal{A}\}$, when $\mathcal{S}(w(i, j)) \neq \emptyset$. Using the overapproximation same as the one for L', we obtain an overapproximation of such $w(i, j)$ represented by at most $2^{|S|}$ sets.

Let us demonstrate our two skip value functions Δ and β using the example in Fig. 4; the execution trace of our algorithm is in Fig. 6. In the first configuration we try to match the tail of all the possible length-4 prefixes of $L(\mathcal{A})$ with $w(4) = $ a, which fails. Then we invoke the Quick Search-type skipping $\Delta(w(5)) = \Delta(b)$; since b occurs no later than in the second position in $L' = \{abcd, abcc, cdcd, cdcc\}$, we can skip by three positions and reach the second configuration.

We again try matching from the tail; this time we succeed since $w(7) = $ c appears as a tail in L'. We subsequently move to the phase where we match from left to right, much like in the original FJS algorithm (Sect. 2.2). Concretely this means we feed the automaton $\mathcal{A}$ (see Fig. 6) the remaining segment $w(4)w(5)\ldots$ from left to right; we obtain $\{s_1\}\{s_3\}\{s_4\}\{s_4\}\emptyset$ as the sequence of reachable sets. Since no accepting states occur therein and we have reached the emptyset, we conclude that the matching trial starting at the position $w(4)$ is unsuccessful.

Now we invoke the KMP-type skipping β. In the original FJS algorithm we used the data of successful partial matching ($w(4,7) = $ abcc in the current case) for computing β; this is not possible, however, since it is infeasible to prepare skip values for all possible $w(i,j)$. Instead we use the data $\mathcal{S}(w(4,7)) = \{s_4\}$ and the set $L'_{s_4} = \{$abc, cdc$\}$ as an overapproximation of the partial match $w(4,7) = $ abcc. The intuition of the set L'_{s_4} is that: for a word w' to drive $\mathcal{A}$ from an initial state to s_4, w' must have either abc or cdc as its prefix. In Fig. 7 is how we compute the skip value $\beta(s_4)$, using the approximant L'_{s_4} of the partial match and the approximant L' of the pattern. Note also that it follows the same pattern as Fig. 3.

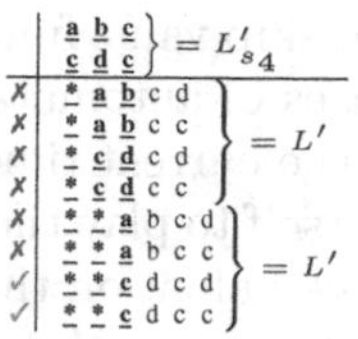

Fig. 7. $\beta(s_4)$

We are now in the fourth configuration in Fig. 6. The matching trial at the position 9 fails and we invoke the Quick Search-type skipping, much like before. In the fifth configuration, the matching trial at the position 12 succeeds, which makes us try matching from the left, feeding $\mathcal{A}$ with $w(9,12)$. We reach s_5 and thus succeed.

Overall our FJS-type algorithm for pattern matching is as in Algorithm 2. The skip value functions therein are defined as follows. They are similar to the ones in (3). Since L' and L'_s are all finite, computing Δ and β is straightforward.

Definition 3.2 (Skip values in our FJS-type pattern matching algorithm). Let $\mathcal{A} = (\Sigma, S, S_0, E, F)$ be a pattern NFA, $a \in \Sigma$ be a character, s be a state of $\mathcal{A}$, and $\mathcal{A}_s = (\Sigma, S, S_0, E, \{s\})$ be the automaton where s is the only accepting state. Let $m_s = \min\{|w| \mid w \in L(\mathcal{A}_s)\}$ (the length of a shortest word that leads to s) and $m = \min_{s \in F} m_s$ (the length of a shortest accepted word). The skip value functions $\Delta : \Sigma \to [1, m+1]$ and $\beta : S \to [1, m]$ are defined as follows.

$$L' = \{w(1,m) \mid w \in L(\mathcal{A})\} \qquad L'_s = \{w(1, \min\{m_s, m\}) \mid w \in L(\mathcal{A}_s)\}$$
$$\Delta(a) = \min\{n \in \mathbb{Z}_{>0} \mid \Sigma^n L' \cap \Sigma^m a \Sigma^* \neq \emptyset\}$$
$$\beta(s) = \min\{n \in \mathbb{Z}_{>0} \mid \Sigma^n L' \cap L'_s \Sigma^* \neq \emptyset\}$$

4 An FJS-Type Algorithm for Timed Pattern Matching

Here we present our second main contribution: an FJS-type algorithm for timed pattern matching. It is superior to our previous Boyer–Moore-type algorithm [32], in its performance both in offline and online scenarios. We fix a target timed word $w = (\bar{a}, \bar{\tau})$ and a pattern timed automaton $\mathcal{A} = (\Sigma \sqcup \{\$\}, S, S_0, C, E, F)$. We further assume the following that means $\mathcal{A}$ is a suitable pattern for timed pattern matching.

Assumption 4.1. $\mathcal{A}$ satisfies the following: any transition to an accepting state is labelled with the terminal character $\$$; no other transition is labelled with $\$$; and there is no transition from an accepting state.

The basic idea of our FJS-type algorithm here is the same as in Sect. 3: we use two skip value functions Δ and β; and and for their finitary representation we let states of automata overapproximate various infinitary data, as we explain later. In the current timed setting, however, we cannot use a pattern timed automaton $\mathcal{A}$ itself to play the same role—in a run of $\mathcal{A}$ a state is always accompanied with a clock valuation that takes continuous values. We overcome this difficulty relying on the *zone abstraction* of timed automata, a construction that turns a timed automaton into an NFA maintaining reachability (see e.g. [14]).[2]

Definition 4.2 (zone). Let $\mathcal{A}$ be a timed automaton over the set C of clock variables, and M be the maximum constant occurring in the guards of $\mathcal{A}$. A *zone* is a $|C|$-dimensional polyhedron specified with a conjunction of the constraints of the form $\nu(x_j) - \nu(x_i) \prec c$, $\nu(x_i) \prec c$ or $-\nu(x_i) \prec c$, where $\prec \in \{<, \leq\}$ and $c \in [-M, M]$.

A *zone automaton* $\mathcal{Z}$ for a timed automaton $\mathcal{A}$ is an NFA whose states are pairs (s, α) of a state s of $\mathcal{A}$ and a zone α; it is meant to be a finite abstraction of the timed automaton $\mathcal{A}$ via which we study properties of $\mathcal{A}$. There are many different known constructions of zone automata (see e.g. [4,14]): they come with different efficiency (i.e. the size of the resulting NFA), and with different preservation properties (bisimilarity to $\mathcal{A}$, similarity, etc.). For our current purpose it does not matter which precise construction we use; we chose a common construction SG^a from [14], mainly for its ease of implementation.

A *path* of a zone automaton $\mathcal{Z}$ is much like a run, but it is allowed to start at a possibly non-initial state. A path $r = (\overline{s}, \overline{\nu})$ of a timed automaton $\mathcal{A}$ is called an *instance* of a path $\overline{r} = (\overline{s}, \overline{\alpha})$ of a zone automaton $\mathcal{Z}$ for $\mathcal{A}$ if, for any $n \in [0, |s|-1]$, we have $\overline{\nu}_n \in \overline{\alpha}_n$. Conversely, such $\overline{r}$ is called an *abstraction* of r. In this paper we rely on the following preservation property of the specific construction $\mathcal{Z} = SG^a(\mathcal{A})$ of zone automata: every run in $SG^a(\mathcal{A})$ is an abstraction of some run of $\mathcal{A}$; conversely every run of $\mathcal{A}$ is an instance of some run in $SG^a(\mathcal{A})$. See [14] for details.

Our algorithm is in Algorithm 3. The constructs therein are defined as follows.

Definition 4.3 (FJS-type skip values for timed pattern matching). Let $\overline{r}$ be a path of the zone automaton $SG^a(\mathcal{A})$. The set $\mathcal{W}(\overline{r})$ of timed words represented by $\overline{r}$ is:

$$\mathcal{W}(\overline{r}) = \{w \in (\Sigma \times \mathbb{R}_{>0})^* \mid \text{there is a path } r \text{ of } \mathcal{A} \text{ over } w \text{ that is an instance of } \overline{r}\}.$$

For a set K of paths of $SG^a(\mathcal{A})$, the definition naturally extends by $\mathcal{W}(K) = \bigcup_{\overline{r} \in K} \mathcal{W}(\overline{r})$. Let $\mathcal{A}_s = (\Sigma, S, S_0, E, C, \{s\})$ be the modification of $\mathcal{A}$ in which s is the only accepting state. Let $m_s = \min\{|w| \mid w \in L(\mathcal{A}_s)\}$ and $m = \min_{s \in F} m_s$. Following the discussion in Sect. 3, we define the overapproximations L'' of $L(\mathcal{A})$

---

[2] In our previous work [32] we used *regions* [1] in place of zones. Though equivalent in terms of finiteness, zones give more efficient abstraction than regions.

Algorithm 3. Our FJS-type algorithm for timed pattern matching, for a target w and a pattern $\mathcal{A}$

Ensure: Z is the match set $\mathcal{M}(w, \mathcal{A})$ in Def. 2.3.
1:   $n \leftarrow 1$;   ▷ n is the position in w of the beginning of the current matching trial
2:   $\nu_0 \leftarrow$ (the clock valuation that returns 0 for any clock variable)
3: **while** $n \leq |w| - m + 2$ **do**
4:    | **while** $\forall \bar{\tau} \in L'.\bar{a}_{n+m-2} \neq a'$ (where a' is such that $\bar{\tau}_{m-2} \xrightarrow{a'} \bar{\tau}_{m-1}$) **do** ▷ Try matching the tail of L'
5:    | | $n \leftarrow n + \Delta(\bar{a}_{n+m-1})$ ▷ Quick Search-type skipping
6:    | **if** $n > |w| - m + 2$ **then return**
7:    | $Z \leftarrow Z \cup \{(t, t') \in [\tau_{n-1}, \tau_t) \times (\tau_{n-1}, \infty) \mid w|_{(t,t')} \in L(\mathcal{A})\}$ ▷ Try matching from left to right
8:    | $n' \leftarrow \max\{n' \in [1, |w|] \mid \exists s_0 \in S_0, s \in S, \nu \in (\mathbb{R}_{\geq 0})^C. (s_0, \nu_0) \xrightarrow{w(n,n')} (s, \nu)\}$
9:    | $S' \leftarrow \{s \in S \mid \exists s_0 \in S_0, \nu \in (\mathbb{R}_{\geq 0})^C. (s_0, \nu_0) \xrightarrow{w(n,n')} (s, \nu)\}$ ▷ Matching trials stack at the states S'
10:    | $n \leftarrow n + \max_{s \in S'} \beta(s)$ ▷ KMP-type skipping

---

and L'_s. as follows. Note that L' and L'_s are in fact sets of runs of $SG^a(\mathcal{A})$; L'' is a set of timed words.

$$L' = \{\bar{\tau}(0, m-1) \mid \bar{\tau} \text{ is a run of } SG^a(\mathcal{A}), \text{and } \mathcal{W}(\bar{\tau}) \cap L(\mathcal{A}) \neq \emptyset\}$$
$$L'' = \mathcal{W}(L') \cdot (\Sigma \times \mathbb{R}_{>0})^*$$
$$L'_s = \{\bar{\tau}(0, \min\{m_s, m-1\}) \mid \bar{\tau} \text{ is a run of } SG^a(\mathcal{A}), \text{and } \mathcal{W}(\bar{\tau}) \cap L(\mathcal{A}_s) \neq \emptyset\}$$

These are used in the following definition of skip values. Here $a \in \Sigma$ and $s \in S$.

$$\Delta(a) = \min\{n \in \mathbb{Z}_{>0} \mid$$
$$\exists t \in \mathbb{R}_{>0}. (\Sigma \times \mathbb{R}_{>0})^n \cdot \mathcal{W}(L') \cap (\Sigma \times \mathbb{R}_{>0})^{m-1} \cdot (a, t) \cdot (\Sigma \times \mathbb{R}_{>0})^* \neq \emptyset\} \quad (6)$$
$$\beta(s) = \min\{n \in \mathbb{Z}_{>0} \mid (\Sigma \times \mathbb{R}_{>0})^n \cdot \mathcal{W}(L') \cap \mathcal{W}(L'_s) \cdot (\Sigma \times \mathbb{R}_{>0})^* \neq \emptyset\}$$

Note the similarity between the last definition and (3).

Explanation is in order how some operations in Algorithm 3 (and in Definition 4.3) can be implemented. First note that $\mathcal{W}(\bar{\tau})$ is an infinite set. The set L' is finite and computable nevertheless: due to the preservation property of the zone automaton $SG^a(\mathcal{A})$, the condition $\mathcal{W}(\bar{\tau}) \cap L(\mathcal{A}) \neq \emptyset$ simply means $\bar{\tau}$ is accepting. The same goes for L'_s. For Δ, we realize that the second argument $(\Sigma \times \mathbb{R}_{>0})^{m-1} \cdot (a, t) \cdot (\Sigma \times \mathbb{R}_{>0})^*$ of the intersection does not pose any timing constraint. Therefore the timed nonemptiness problem reduces to an untimed one that is readily solved. Solving the timed nonemptiness problem for β in (6) is nontrivial. Here we use emptiness check in $SG^a(\mathcal{A} \times \mathcal{A})$—the zone automaton of the product of $\mathcal{A}$ with itself, changing its initial state suitably in order to address shift of words—to check whether the intersection of the two relevant languages is empty. Finally, the left-to-right matching on Line 7 is done by accumulating constraints on t in the course of necessary transitions. Further details are in Appendices A–B of [34].

A correctness proof (i.e. our skipping does not affect the output) is in Appendix C of [34].

One important idea in our algorithm is that we use timing constraints—in addition to character constraints like in Figs. 3 and 7—in calculating skip values.

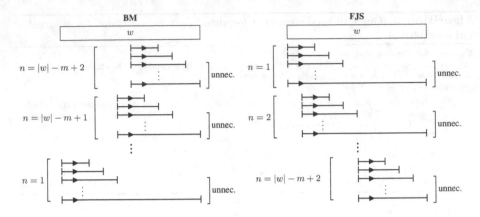

Fig. 8. How matching trials proceed: our previous BM-type algorithm (on the left) and our current FJS-type algorithm (on the right).

By this we achieve greater skip values, while keeping the computational overhead minimal by the use of the zone automaton $SG^a(\mathcal{A} \times \mathcal{A})$.

The way our algorithm (Algorithm 3) operates is very similar to the one in Sect. 3 for (untimed) pattern matching, as we already described earlier. There the zone automaton $SG^a(\mathcal{A})$ plays important roles in the calculation of skip values. For the record we include in Appendix B of [34] the illustration of our algorithm using the example in Fig. 1.

Online Properties. We claim that the current FJS-type algorithm is much better suited to online usage scenarios than our previous BM-type one [32]. See Fig. 8. In our FJS-type algorithm we can sometimes increment n before reading the whole target timed word w ("unnec." for "unnecessary" in Fig. 8); this is the case when we observe that no further transition is possible in the pattern automaton $\mathcal{A}$. (Additionally, thanks to the skip values Δ and β, sometimes we can increment n by more than one). For real-world examples we can assume that matches tend to be much shorter than the whole log w; this means the "unnec." parts are often big.

In the BM-type algorithm, in contrast, matching trials start almost at the tail of w,[3] and we have to wait until the arrival of the whole target word. This contrast is witnessed in our experimental results, specifically on those for memory usage.

5   Experiments

We implemented our FJS-type algorithm for timed pattern matching—its online and offline variations difference between which will be elaborated later.

---

[3] To be precise we can start without the last $m - 1$ characters, where m is the length of a shortest word accepted by $\mathcal{A}$. Usually m is by magnitude smaller than $|w|$.

We compared its performance with that of: brute-force algorithms (online and offline); the BM-type algorithm [32]; and the tool *Montre* [29] for timed pattern matching.

The BM- and FJS-type algorithms employ zone-based abstraction; it is implemented using *difference bound matrices*, following [9]. Zone construction and calculation of skip values are done in

	brute-force	BM	FJS	Montre
offline	from [32]	from [32]	new	from [29]
online	from [32]	—	new	from [29]

the preprocessing stage, where the most expensive is the emptiness checking for $\beta(s)$ (see (6)). We optimized this part, memorizing parts of zone automata and reusing them in computing $\beta(s)$ for different s. As a result the preprocessing stage takes a fraction of a second for each of our benchmark problems. See Appendix E of [34] for details.

For brute-force and FJS, the algorithms are the same in their online and offline implementations. In the online implementations, a target timed word is read lazily and a memory cell is deallocated as soon as we realize it is no longer needed. In the offline implementations, the whole target timed word is read and stored in memory in the beginning, and the memory cells are not deallocated until the end. The tool Montre employs different algorithms in its online and offline usage modes. See [29] for details.

In our current implementations, we hardcode a pattern timed automaton in the code. Developing a parser for user-defined timed automata should not be hard.

The benchmark problems we used are in Figs. 9, 10, 11, 12, 13 and 14 (the pattern automata $\mathcal{A}$ and the set W of target words). They are from automotive scenarios except for the first two.

5.1 Comparison with the Brute Force and BM-Type Algorithms

We implemented the brute-force, BM, FJS algorithms in C++ [33] and we compiled them by clang-800.0.42.1. All the experiments are done on MacBook Pro Early 2013 with 2.6 GHz Intel Core i5 processor and 8 GB 1600MHz DDR3 RAM.

Speed (i.e. Permissible Density in Online Usage). In Figs. 15, 16, 17, 18, 19 and 20 are the comparison of the offline implementations of the brute-force, BM and FJS algorithms, respectively (average of five runs). Preprocessing time is excluded (it is anyway negligible, see Appendix E of [34]). We also exclude time of loading the input timed word in memory; this is because in many deployment scenarios like embedded ones, I/O is pipelined by, for example, DMA.

The pattern automata for the benchmarks TORQUE, SETTING, and GEAR look similar to each other. However their input timed words—generated by a suitable Simulink model for each benchmark—exhibit different characteristics, such as how often the characters in the pattern automaton occur in the input timed words. Accordingly the performance of the timed pattern matching algorithms varies, as we see in Figs. 17, 18 and 19.

We observe that our FJS algorithm generally outperforms the BM and brute-force ones. For SETTLING and ACCEL the performance gap is roughly twice, and it possibly makes a big practical difference e.g. when a data set is huge and the monitoring task takes hours. For LARGE CONSTRAINTS it seems to depend on specific words which algorithm performs better. The advantage in performance is as we expected, given that the FJS algorithm combines the KMP-type skipping (that works well roughly when the BM-type one does) and the Quick Search-type skipping (that complements KMP). After all, it is encouraging to observe that our FJS algorithm performs better in the automotive examples, where our motivation is drawn.

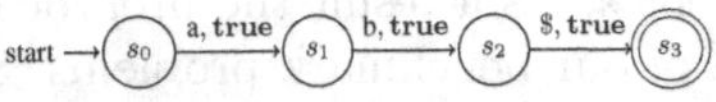

Fig. 9. SIMPLE from [32]. The set W consists of alternations of a and b whose length is from 20 to 1,024,000. Timing is random.

$$\langle \left(\left(\langle p \cdot \neg p \rangle_{(0,10]} \right)^* \wedge \left(\langle q \cdot \neg q \rangle_{(0,10]} \right)^* \right) \cdot \$ \rangle_{(0,80]}$$

Fig. 10. LARGE CONSTRAINTS from [32]. The pattern $\mathcal{A}$ is a translation of the above timed regular expression (5 states and 9 transitions). The set W consists of superpositions of the alternations $p, \neg p, p, \neg p, \ldots$ and $q, \neg q, q, \neg q, \ldots$ whose timing follows a certain exponential distribution. The length of words in W is from 1,934 to 31,935. The pattern $\mathcal{A}$ is in Fig. 24 of [34]

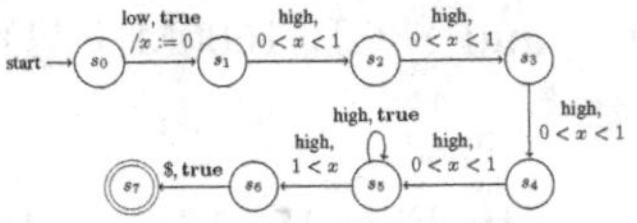

Fig. 11. TORQUE, an automotive example from [32]. It monitors for five or more consecutive occurrences of high in one second. The target words in W (length 242,808–4,873,207) are generated by the model `sldemo_enginewc.slx` in the Simulink Demo palette [23] with random input.

Fig. 12. SETTLING. The set W (length 472–47,200,000) is generated by the Simulink powertrain model in [17]. The pattern (Requirement (32) in [17]) is for an event in which the system remains unsettled for 100 s after moving to the normal mode.

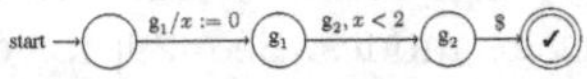

Fig. 13. GEAR. The set W (length 307–1,011,427) is generated by the automatic transmission system model in [16]. The pattern, from ϕ_5^{AT} in [16], is for an event in which gear shift occurs too quickly (from the 1st to 2nd).

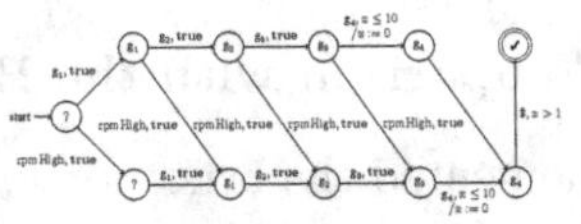

Fig. 14. ACCEL. The set W (length 25,002–17,280,002) is generated by the same automatic transmission system model as in GEAR. The pattern is from ϕ_8^{AT} in [16]: although the gear shifts from 1st to 4th and RPM is high enough somewhere in its course, the vehicle velocity is not high enough (i.e. the character veloHigh is absent).

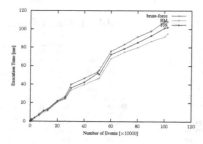

Fig. 15. SIMPLE: exec. time

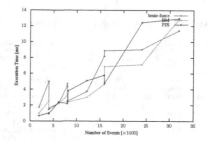

Fig. 16. LARGE CONSTRAINTS: exec. time

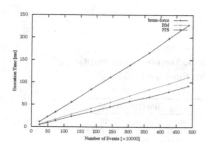

Fig. 17. TORQUE: exec. time

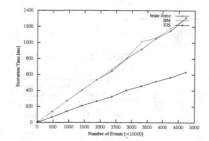

Fig. 18. SETTLING: exec. time

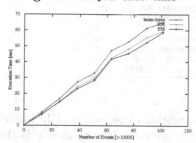

Fig. 19. GEAR: exec. time

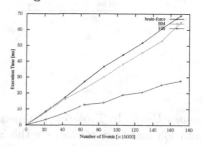

Fig. 20. ACCEL: exec. time

In every benchmark except for LARGE CONSTRAINT, the execution time grows roughly linearly on the length of the input word. This is a pleasant property for monitoring algorithms for which an input word can be very long.

These results for *offline* implementations also support our claim of FJS's superiority in *online* usage scenarios. In online usage we must process an input word faster than the speed with which the word arrives; otherwise the word eventually floods memory. Thus running twice as fast means that our algorithm can handle twice as dense input—or that we can use cheaper hardware to conduct the same monitoring task. Note that the difference between our online and offline implementations is only in the memory management and I/O. Thus their speed should be similar.

Table 2. SIMPLE (sec.)

$|w|$	FJS (online)	Montre (offline)	Montre (online)
32,000	0.01	0.05	3.00
64,000	0.02	0.10	6.06
100,000	0.03	0.16	9.41
128,000	0.04	0.20	12.54
200,000	0.07	0.31	18.89
256,000	0.09	0.40	23.76
300,000	0.10	0.48	28.19
400,000	0.14	0.63	38.24
500,000	0.18	0.78	46.33
512,000	0.18	0.81	48.77
600,000	0.21	0.96	56.76
700,000	0.25	1.13	66.53
800,000	0.28	1.28	74.91
900,000	0.32	1.43	84.58
1,000,000	0.36	1.60	93.52
1,024,000	0.37	1.62	95.62

Table 3. SETTLING (sec.)

$|w|$	FJS (online)	Montre (offline)	Montre (online)
300	0.00	0.01	0.01
30,000	0.01	0.01	0.01
300,000	0.11	0.01	0.01
3,000,000	1.11	3.85	299.85
6,000,000	2.23	7.74	600.66
9,000,000	3.34	11.66	893.88
12,000,000	4.46	15.65	1,188.02
15,000,000	5.58	19.75	1,475.89
18,000,000	6.72	24.48	1,788.18
21,000,000	9.27	27.80	Timeout
24,000,000	8.96	31.78	Timeout
27,000,000	10.09	37.10	Timeout
30,000,000	11.21	41.10	Timeout

Table 4. GEAR (sec.)

$|w|$	FJS (online)	Montre (offline)	Montre (online)
1,000	0.00	0.01	0.04
86,400	0.04	0.15	11.63
172,800	0.08	0.29	23.48
259,200	0.13	0.42	37.51
345,600	0.17	0.54	47.20
432,000	0.21	0.67	57.99
518,400	0.25	0.85	69.76
604,800	0.30	0.96	87.59
691,200	0.34	1.09	90.36

Table 5. ACCEL (sec.)

$|w|$	FJS (online)	Montre (offline)	Montre (online)
1,000	0.00	0.01	69.05
86,400	0.06	0.63	Timeout
172,800	0.13	1.25	Timeout
259,200	0.20	1.88	Timeout
345,600	0.26	2.50	Timeout
432,000	0.33	3.12	Timeout
518,400	0.40	3.75	Timeout
604,800	0.46	4.38	Timeout
691,200	0.53	4.99	Timeout

Table 6. Memory consumption of FJS (online) and BM

$|w|$	BM (MB)	FJS (MB)
300	1.16	1.16
30,000	2.61	1.16
300,000	15.55	1.16
3,000,000	145.21	1.16
6,000,000	289.25	1.16
9,000,000	433.31	1.16
12,000,000	577.32	1.19
15,000,000	721.37	1.18
18,000,000	865.42	1.19
21,000,000	1,009.46	1.16
24,000,000	1,153.50	1.16
27,000,000	1,297.57	1.16
30,000,000	1,441.61	1.16

Memory Usage. In Table 6 is the memory consumption of our *online* FJS implementation and that of BM, for the SETTLING benchmark (the tendency is the same for the other benchmarks). The absolute values are not very important because they include our program and dynamically linked libraries; what matters is the tendency that memory consumption is almost constant for online FJS while it increases for BM. Constant memory consumption is an important property for monitoring algorithms, especially in online usage. The results here also concurs with our theoretical observation at the end of Sect. 4 (see Fig. 8).

5.2   Comparison with Montre

Here we compare with Montre, a recent tool for (both online and offline) timed pattern matching [29]. Montre's online and offline algorithms differ from each other; both of them are quite different from our FJS algorithm, too. Montre's emphasis is on the algebraic structure of timed regular expressions and compositional reasoning thereby, while our algorithm features automata-theoretic views on the problem.

Since we had difficulty running Montre in the same environment as in Sect. 5.1, we instead used GCC 4.9.3 as a compiler, and conducted experiments on an Amazon EC2 c4.xlarge instance (April 2017, 4 vCPUs and 7.5 GB RAM) that runs Ubuntu 14.04 LTS (64 bit). The timeout is set to thirty minutes.

In Tables 2, 3, 4 and 5 are the results. Here we use the benchmarks SIMPLE, SETTLING, GEAR, and ACCEL, for which the translation between timed words (our input) and signals (Montre's input) makes sense. Our (online) FJS implementation is about 3 to 8 times faster than offline Montre and about 250 times faster than online Montre. The big performance advantage over *online* Montre can be attributed to various reasons, including: (1) online Montre needs to frequently compute derivatives of TREs; (2) online Montre is comparable to our brute-force algorithm in that there is no skipping involved; and (3) Montre is implemented in a functional language (Pure [25]) that is in general slower. The reason for the advantage over *offline* Montre is yet to be seen: given that the algorithms are very different, the advantage may well be solely attributed to implementation details. We claim however that good online performance of our FJS algorithm is a big advantage for monitoring applications.

6   Conclusions and Future Work

We continued [32] and presented an algorithm for timed pattern matching. Based on the FJS algorithm [13] it exhibits better online properties, as witnessed in our experiments. As future work we wish to implement an interface of our experimental implementation and distribute as a tool. We also wish to try the algorithm in actual embedded hardware, like [18].

Acknowledgments. Thanks are due to Sean Sedwards, Eugenia Sironi and the anonymous referees for useful discussions and comments. The authors are supported by JSPS Grant-in-Aid 15KT0012. M.W. and I.H. are supported by JST ERATO HASUO Metamathematics for Systems Design Project (No. JPMJER1603), and JSPS Grant-in-Aid No. 15K11984. K.S. is supported by JST PRESTO (No. JPMJPR15E5) and JSPS Grant-in-Aid No. 70633692.

References

1. Alur, R., Dill, D.L.: A theory of timed automata. Theor. Comput. Sci. **126**(2), 183–235 (1994)
2. Alur, R., Henzinger, T.A.: Back to the future: towards a theory of timed regular languages. In: 33rd Annual Symposium on Foundations of Computer Science, Pittsburgh, Pennsylvania, USA, 24–27 October 1992, pp. 177–186, IEEE Computer Society (1992)
3. Asarin, E., Caspi, P., Maler, O.: Timed regular expressions. J. ACM **49**(2), 172–206 (2002)
4. Behrmann, G., Bouyer, P., Fleury, E., Larsen, K.G.: Static guard analysis in timed automata verification. In: Garavel, H., Hatcliff, J. (eds.) TACAS 2003. LNCS, vol. 2619, pp. 254–270. Springer, Heidelberg (2003). doi:10.1007/3-540-36577-X_18

5. Behrmann, G., Bouyer, P., Larsen, K.G., Pelánek, R.: Lower and upper bounds in zone-based abstractions of timed automata. STTT 8(3), 204–215 (2006)
6. Bombara, G., Vasile, C.I., Penedo, F., Yasuoka, H., Belta, C.: A decision tree approach to data classification using signal temporal logic. In: Abate, A., Fainekos, G.E. (eds.) HSCC 2016, Vienna, Austria, April 12–14, 2016, pp. 1–10. ACM (2016)
7. Boyer, R.S., Moore, J.S.: A fast string searching algorithm. Commun. ACM 20(10), 762–772 (1977)
8. Chen, S., Sokolsky, O., Weimer, J., Lee, I.: Data-driven adaptive safety monitoring using virtual subjects in medical cyber-physical systems: a glucose control case study. JCSE 10(3), 75–84 (2016)
9. Dill, D.L.: Timing assumptions and verification of finite-state concurrent systems. In: Sifakis, J. (ed.) CAV 1989. LNCS, vol. 407, pp. 197–212. Springer, Heidelberg (1990). doi:10.1007/3-540-52148-8_17
10. DSouza, D., Matteplackel, R.: A clock-optimal hierarchical monitoring automaton construction for mitl. Technical report (2013)
11. Faro, S., Lecroq, T.: The exact online string matching problem: a review of the most recent results. ACM Comput. Surv. 45(2), 13:1–13:42 (2013)
12. Ferrère, T., Maler, O., Ničković, D., Ulus, D.: Measuring with timed patterns. In: Kroening, D., Păsăreanu, C.S. (eds.) CAV 2015. LNCS, vol. 9207, pp. 322–337. Springer, Cham (2015). doi:10.1007/978-3-319-21668-3_19
13. Franek, F., Jennings, C.G., Smyth, W.F.: A simple fast hybrid pattern-matching algorithm. J. Discrete Algorithms 5(4), 682–695 (2007)
14. Herbreteau, F., Srivathsan, B., Walukiewicz, I.: Efficient emptiness check for timed büchi automata. In: Touili, T., Cook, B., Jackson, P. (eds.) CAV 2010. LNCS, vol. 6174, pp. 148–161. Springer, Heidelberg (2010). doi:10.1007/978-3-642-14295-6_15
15. Ho, H.-M., Ouaknine, J., Worrell, J.: Online monitoring of metric temporal logic. In: Bonakdarpour, B., Smolka, S.A. (eds.) RV 2014. LNCS, vol. 8734, pp. 178–192. Springer, Cham (2014). doi:10.1007/978-3-319-11164-3_15
16. Hoxha, B., Abbas, H., Fainekos, G.E.: Benchmarks for temporal logic requirements for automotive systems. In: Frehse, G., Althoff, M. (eds.) 1st and 2nd International Workshop on Applied veRification for Continuous and Hybrid Systems, ARCH@CPSWeek 2014, Berlin, Germany, April 14, 2014 / ARCH@CPSWeek 2015, EPiC Series in Computing,Seattle, WA, USA, April 13, 2015, vol. 34, pp. 25–30. EasyChair (2014)
17. Jin, X., Deshmukh, J.V., Kapinski, J., Ueda, K., Butts, K.R.: Powertrain control verification benchmark. In: Fränzle M., Lygeros, J. (eds.) HSCC 2014, Berlin, Germany, April 15–17, 2014, pp. 253–262. ACM (2014)
18. Kane A.: Runtime monitoring for safety-critical embedded systems. Ph.D. thesis, Carnegie Mellon University, USA (2015)
19. Kane, A., Chowdhury, O., Datta, A., Koopman, P.: A case study on runtime monitoring of an autonomous research vehicle (ARV) system. In: Bartocci, E., Majumdar, R. (eds.) RV 2015. LNCS, vol. 9333, pp. 102–117. Springer, Cham (2015). doi:10.1007/978-3-319-23820-3_7
20. Kini, D.R., Krishna, S.N., Pandya, P.K.: On construction of safety signal automata for $MITL[\mathcal{U}, \mathcal{S}]$ using temporal projections. In: Fahrenberg, U., Tripakis, S. (eds.) FORMATS 2011. LNCS, vol. 6919, pp. 225–239. Springer, Heidelberg (2011). doi:10.1007/978-3-642-24310-3_16
21. Knuth, D.E., Morris Jr., J.H., Pratt, V.R.: Fast pattern matching in strings. SIAM J. Comput. 6(2), 323–350 (1977)

22. Maler, O., Nickovic, D., Pnueli, A.: From MITL to timed automata. In: Asarin, E., Bouyer, P. (eds.) FORMATS 2006. LNCS, vol. 4202, pp. 274–289. Springer, Heidelberg (2006). doi:10.1007/11867340_20
23. The MathWorks Inc, Natick, MA, USA. Simulink User's Guide (2015)
24. Ničković, D., Piterman, N.: From MTL to deterministic timed automata. In: Chatterjee, K., Henzinger, T.A. (eds.) FORMATS 2010. LNCS, vol. 6246, pp. 152–167. Springer, Heidelberg (2010). doi:10.1007/978-3-642-15297-9_13
25. Pure Programming Language. https://purelang.bitbucket.io
26. Raimondi, F., Skene, J., Emmerich, W.: Efficient online monitoring of web-service slas. In: Harrold, M.J., Murphy, G.C. (eds.) Proceedings of the 16th ACM SIGSOFT International Symposium on Foundations of Software Engineering, 2008, Atlanta, Georgia, USA, November 9–14, 2008, pp. 170–180. ACM (2008)
27. Reinbacher, T., Függer, M., Brauer, J.: Runtime verification of embedded real-time systems. Formal Meth. Syst. Des. 44(3), 203–239 (2014)
28. Sunday, D.: A very fast substring search algorithm. Commun. ACM 33(8), 132–142 (1990)
29. Ulus, D.: Montre: a tool for monitoring timed regular expressions. CoRR, abs/1605.05963 (2016)
30. Ulus, D., Ferrère, T., Asarin, E., Maler, O.: Timed pattern matching. In: Legay, A., Bozga, M. (eds.) FORMATS 2014. LNCS, vol. 8711, pp. 222–236. Springer, Cham (2014). doi:10.1007/978-3-319-10512-3_16
31. Ulus, D., Ferrère, T., Asarin, E., Maler, O.: Online timed pattern matching using derivatives. In: Chechik, M., Raskin, J.-F. (eds.) TACAS 2016. LNCS, vol. 9636, pp. 736–751. Springer, Heidelberg (2016). doi:10.1007/978-3-662-49674-9_47
32. Waga, M., Akazaki, T., Hasuo, I.: A boyer-moore type algorithm for timed pattern matching. In: Fränzle, M., Markey, N. (eds.) FORMATS 2016. LNCS, vol. 9884, pp. 121–139. Springer, Cham (2016). doi:10.1007/978-3-319-44878-7_8
33. Waga, M., Hasuo I., Suenaga, K.: Code that Accompanies "Efficient Online Timed Pattern Matching by Automata-Based Skipping". https://github.com/MasWag/timed-pattern-matching
34. Waga, M., Hasuo, I., Suenaga K.: Efficient Online Timed Pattern Matching by Automata-Based Skipping. CoRR, abs/1706.09174 (2017)
35. Watson, B.W., Watson, R.E.: A boyer-moore-style algorithm for regular expression pattern matching. Sci. Comput. Program. 48(2–3), 99–117 (2003)

Reachability Analysis

Let's Be Lazy, We Have Time
Or, Lazy Reachability Analysis for Timed Automata

Loïg Jezequel[1]([⊠]) and Didier Lime[2]

[1] Université de Nantes, LS2N UMR CNRS 6004, Nantes, France
loig.jezequel@ls2n.fr
[2] École Centrale de Nantes, LS2N UMR CNRS 6004, Nantes, France
didier.lime@ec-nantes.fr

Abstract. In a recent work we proposed an algorithm for reachability analysis in distributed systems modeled as networks of automata. The main interest of this algorithm is that it performs its analysis in a lazy way: decision is done by only taking into account the automata potentially involved in a path to the reachability goal. This new work extends the approach to networks of timed automata, lazily considering the automata but also lazily adding the clocks to the analysis, which implies not only to consider clocks tested along the paths to the goal, but also to deal with the special issues due to urgency and shared clocks. We have implemented our approach as a tool and provide some interesting experimental results, in a comparison with the model-checker Uppaal.

1 Introduction

The verification of concurrent timed systems is a crucial and challenging issue. It is subject to both an explosion of the number of discrete states due to the number of concurrent components, and an explosion of the clock space due to the number of clocks.

To model such systems we focus here on networks of timed automata and the verification of reachability properties. Since the seminal article of Alur and Dill establishing the PSPACE completeness of this problem [1], many techniques have been developed to improve the practical efficiency of reachability verification.

Efficient symbolic representations of the clock space have been proposed, implemented using a data structure called Difference Bound Matrix [5,7], as well as efficient algorithms to handle them [16]. Different kind of abstractions have then been devised to further improve them [2,12].

Better exploration orders [13] have also been proposed and quite a few authors have defined partial-order reductions for timed automata (see e.g. [6,10,18] and the references therein). Some decision diagram-based representations of the state-space have also been proposed [15,20]. Several tools are available that implement part of these techniques, this is in particular the case of UPPAAL [17].

In this article, we exploit a technique orthogonal to most of those mentioned above and build on a recently proposed lazy reachability analysis algorithm in

© Springer International Publishing AG 2017
A. Abate and G. Geeraerts (Eds.): FORMATS 2017, LNCS 10419, pp. 247–263, 2017.
DOI: 10.1007/978-3-319-65765-3_14

compound systems modeled as networks of labelled transition systems [14], that we extend to the timed setting. The resulting algorithm can be implemented using the successful DBM data structure. It starts separately from each of the components explicitly mentioned in the reachability property and adds other components, as well as clocks, on demand, based on the analysis of the successive overapproximations obtained by ignoring some components or clocks. Since we start by verifying separately that each component in the property can indeed reach its goal, the algorithm also performs synchronisations to make sure that in reaching its goal, one component does not prevent another one to do so.

The timed setting brings a few difficulties of its own, namely: choosing the clocks to add, handling urgency, and accounting for shared clocks. It can be proven that our algorithm is sound, complete and that it terminates. We provide a rather naive prototype implementation that nonetheless produce some interesting experimental results.

This paper is organized as follows. In Sect. 2 we recall basic definitions about timed automata, give some definitions and notations about compound systems built from timed automata, and we define the reachability problem we consider. In Sect. 3 we briefly recall the lazy reachability algorithm of [14] and we describe the modifications needed to make it cope with timed systems. In Sect. 4 we discuss an implementation of this algorithm as a publicly available tool: LaRA-T and we present an experimental evaluation, comparing its performances to those of UPPAAL on a few classic examples.

2   Definitions

In this section we first recall standard definitions for timed automata and set the notations we use in the paper. Then, we define the reachability problem on compound systems built from timed automata that we aim at solving.

2.1   Timed Automata

Definition 1 (Clocks, clock constraints). *Let X be a set of real-valued variables called* clocks. *A clock constraint over X is a constraint of the form $x \sim k$ with $x \in X$, $k \in \mathbb{N}$, and $\sim \in \{<, \leq, =, \geq, >\}$. The set of all possible such clock constraints over X is denoted by $\mathcal{B}(X)$. The subset of $\mathcal{B}(X)$ where $\sim \in \{<, \leq\}$ is denoted by $\mathcal{B}'(X)$.*

For simplicity, we do not consider clock differences in the above defined constraints. The high level algorithm presented in this paper is however independant of the exact reachability analysis technique used, so our approach is not restricted to these simple constraints.

Definition 2 (Clock valuations). *For a set of clocks X we call* clock valuation *a function $v : X \to \mathbb{R}_{\geq 0}$ associating a non-negative real number to each clock in X. We denote by $V(X)$ the set of all such valuations. Given a subset R of X and a clock valuation v, we denote by $v[R]$ the clock valuation such that*

$\forall x \in R, v[R](x) = 0$ and $\forall x \notin R, v[R](x) = v(x)$. Given $d \in \mathbb{R}_{\geq 0}$, we denote by $(v + d)$ the clock valuation such that $\forall x \in X, (v + d)(x) = v(x) + d$.

Definition 3 (Constraint satisfaction). *A clock valuation v satisfies a constraint $b = x \sim k$, written $v \models b$, if and only if $v(x) \sim k$. A clock valuation v satisfies a set of constraints g, written $v \models g$, if and only if it satisfies each of its elements.*

In this article, we consider timed automata with invariants [11]. Finite automata are extended with clocks that can be tested in guards to allow some transition to be taken, and can also be reset to 0 when some transition is taken. Invariants further specify constraints on clocks that must be satisfied to stay or enter in a given location. They add a notion of *urgency* to the timed automata of [1].

Definition 4 (Timed automata: syntax). *A Timed automaton (TA) is a tuple $\mathcal{A} = (\mathcal{L}, \ell^0, \Sigma, X, E, Inv)$ where $\mathcal{L}$ is a set of locations, $\ell^0 \in \mathcal{L}$ is an initial location, Σ is a set of action labels, X is a set of clocks, $E \subseteq \mathcal{L} \times 2^{\mathcal{B}(X)} \times \Sigma \times 2^X \times \mathcal{L}$ is a set of transitions, and $Inv : \mathcal{L} \to 2^{\mathcal{B}'(X)}$ associates invariants to the locations.*

In the rest of the paper $\mathcal{A}$ will denote the tuple $(\mathcal{L}, \ell^0, \Sigma, X, E, Inv)$. Similarly, $\mathcal{A}'$ will denote the tuple $(\mathcal{L}', \ell^{0'}, \Sigma', X', E', Inv')$. And, for any i, $\mathcal{A}_i$ will denote the tuple $(\mathcal{L}_i, \ell_i^0, \Sigma_i, X_i, E_i, Inv_i)$. For a transition $e = (\ell, g, \sigma, R, \ell') \in E$, we note $\ell(e) = \ell$, $g(e) = g$, $\sigma(e) = \sigma$, $R(e) = R$, and $\ell'(e) = \ell'$. Moreover, $\Sigma(\mathcal{A}) = \{\sigma \in \Sigma : \exists e \in E, \sigma(e) = \sigma\}$ denotes the set of actions actually used by $\mathcal{A}$. Similarly, $X(\mathcal{A}) = \{x \in X : \exists e \in E, g(e) \cap \mathcal{B}(\{x\}) \neq \emptyset \vee x \in R(e)\} \cup \{x \in X : \exists \ell \in \mathcal{L}, Inv(\ell) \cap \mathcal{B}(\{x\}) \neq \emptyset\}$ denotes the set of clocks actually appearing in $\mathcal{A}$. And finally, $\mathsf{Res}(\mathcal{A}) = \{x \in X : \exists (\ell, g, \sigma, R, \ell') \in E, x \in R\}$ denotes the set of clocks reset by $\mathcal{A}$.

A state of a timed automaton consists of a location, and a value for each of its clocks. The state of a timed automaton evolves either by letting time pass, or by taking a transition. This is formalised in the following definition:

Definition 5 (Timed automata: semantics, timed-paths, timed-runs, reachable locations, duration). *A state of a timed automaton $\mathcal{A}$ is a pair $(\ell, v) \in \mathcal{L} \times V(X)$ so that $v \models Inv(\ell)$. A transition relation $\to_{\mathcal{A}}$ is defined over the states of $\mathcal{A}$ as follows: $(\ell, v) \to_{\mathcal{A}} (\ell', v')$ if and only if:*

- *$\ell = \ell'$ and $\exists d \in \mathbb{R}_{\geq 0}$ so that $v' = (v + d)$ (time elapsing of duration d), or*
- *$\exists e \in E$, such that $\ell(e) = \ell$, $\ell'(e) = \ell'$, $v \models g(e)$, and $v' = v[R(e)]$ (discrete transition firing – of duration 0).*

A finite timed-path *(or simply, path) of $\mathcal{A}$ is a sequence $(\ell_0, v_0) \ldots (\ell_n, v_n)$ of states such that $\forall i \in \{0..n-1\}, (\ell_i, v_i) \to_{\mathcal{A}} (\ell_{i+1}, v_{i+1})$. If, moreover, $\ell_0 = \ell^0$ (i.e. ℓ_0 is the initial location of $\mathcal{A}$), we call $(\ell_0, v_0) \ldots (\ell_n, v_n)$ a finite timed-run (or simply, run) of $\mathcal{A}$. When there exists such a run, we say that ℓ_n is reachable in $\mathcal{A}$. The* duration *of a timed-path is the sum of the durations of its transitions.*

In the rest of the paper we denote by $\mathsf{Urg}(\mathcal{A})$ the set of initially urgent locations of $\mathcal{A}$. These locations are the ones appearing on a timed-run so that any location in it has a non-empty invariant. Formally, $\mathsf{Urg}(\mathcal{A})$ is the smallest set such that (a) if $Inv(\ell^0) \neq \emptyset$ then $\ell^0 \in \mathsf{Urg}(\mathcal{A})$, and (b) if $e \in E$ with $\ell(e) \in \mathsf{Urg}(\mathcal{A})$ and $Inv(\ell'(e)) \neq \emptyset$ then $\ell'(e) \in \mathsf{Urg}(\mathcal{A})$.

And we denote by $\mathsf{Req}(\mathcal{A})$ the set of actions that could be requested by $\mathcal{A}$ due to urgency: the actions appearing in transitions originating from locations in $\mathsf{Urg}(\mathcal{A})$. Formally, $\mathsf{Req}(\mathcal{A}) = \{\sigma \in \Sigma \; : \; \exists e \in E, \sigma(e) = \sigma \; \wedge \; \ell(e) \in \mathsf{Urg}(\mathcal{A})\}$.

2.2 Reachability Problem in Compound Systems

We are interested in systems made of several interacting components. To formalise this notion, we define compound systems.

Definition 6 (Compound system). *Let $\mathcal{A}_1, \ldots, \mathcal{A}_n$ be TAs. The compound system $\mathcal{A}_1 \| \ldots \| \mathcal{A}_n$ is the TA $\mathcal{A}$ such that:*

- $\mathcal{L} = \mathcal{L}_1 \times \cdots \times \mathcal{L}_n$, $\ell^0 = (\ell_1^0, \ldots, \ell_n^0)$, $\Sigma = \Sigma_1 \cup \cdots \cup \Sigma_n$, $X = X_1 \cup \cdots \cup X_n$,
- $((\ell_1, \ldots, \ell_n), g_1 \cup \cdots \cup g_n, \sigma, R_1 \cup \cdots \cup R_n, (\ell_1', \ldots, \ell_n')) \in E$ *if and only if* $\forall i \in [1..n]$:
  - $\sigma \in \Sigma_i$ *implies* $(\ell_i, g_i, \sigma, R_i, \ell_i') \in E_i$, *and*
  - $\sigma \notin \Sigma_i$ *implies* $\ell_i = \ell_i'$, $g_i = \emptyset$, *and* $R_i = \emptyset$,
- $\forall \ell = (\ell_1, \ldots, \ell_n) \in \mathcal{L}$, $Inv(\ell) = Inv_1(\ell_1) \cup \cdots \cup Inv_n(\ell_n)$.

Definition 7 (Time-non blocking timed automaton). *A timed automaton $\mathcal{A}$ is* time-non blocking *if, in any state and for any duration d, there exists a finite timed-path from that state with duration d.*

In all this article, we assume that compound systems are time-non blocking TA. Else, an invariant of any TA could block the whole system. This would force to always consider all the TA of a system to perform reachability analysis.

The next definitions allow us to specify reachability objectives related to only a part of the global system.

Definition 8 (Global locations, partial locations, concretisation). *In a compound system $\mathcal{A}_1 \| \ldots \| \mathcal{A}_n$ we call any element from $\mathcal{L}_1 \times \cdots \times \mathcal{L}_n$ a* global location. *We call* partial location *any element from $(\mathcal{L}_1 \cup \{\star\}) \times \cdots \times (\mathcal{L}_n \cup \{\star\}) \setminus \{(\star, \ldots, \star)\}$, where $\star$ is a special symbol not in any $\mathcal{L}_i$. We say that a global location $(\ell_1', \ldots, \ell_n')$* concretises *the partial location $(\ell_1, \ldots, \ell_n)$ if and only if $\forall i \in [1..n]$, $\ell_i \neq \star$ implies $\ell_i' = \ell_i$.*

Definition 9 (Reachability problem). *In a compound system $\mathcal{A}$ we say that a partial location ℓ is* reachable *(in $\mathcal{A}$) if and only if there exists a global location that (1) is reachable in $\mathcal{A}$ and (2) concretises ℓ. Given a set $\mathcal{R}$ of partial locations, we call* reachability problem *the problem of deciding if there exists a reachable element in $\mathcal{R}$. We denote this problem by $RP_{\mathcal{A}}^{\mathcal{R}}$.*

In this paper, we propose a lazy backtracking-based algorithm for solving such reachability problems. We avoid as much as possible to compute the full compound systems considered, only taking into account the subsets of their components and clocks that are needed for reachability analysis. In the remaining of this section we introduce a few more definitions, simplifying the description of our algorithm.

2.3   Partial Compound Systems

The following definitions allow us to reason about only parts of the global system, be they obtained by considering only some of the components, some of the clocks, or even a partial behaviour of some components.

Definition 10 (Isomorphic timed automata). *Let $\mathcal{A}_1$ and $\mathcal{A}_2$ be two TA. We say that they are isomorphic if and only if $\Sigma_1 = \Sigma_2$, $X_1 = X_2$, and there exists a bijection $f : \mathcal{L}_1 \to \mathcal{L}_2$ so that: $f(\ell_1^0) = \ell_2^0$, $(\ell, g, \sigma, R, \ell') \in E_1$ if and only if $(f(\ell), g, \sigma, R, f(\ell')) \in E_2$ and $\forall \ell \in \mathcal{L}_1, Inv_1(\ell) = Inv_2(f(\ell))$.*

Definition 11 (Neutral element). *We denote by $\mathcal{A}_{id}$ the TA such that $\mathcal{L}_{id} = \{id\}$, $\ell_{id}^0 = id$, $\Sigma_{id} = \emptyset$, $X_{id} = \emptyset$, $E_{id} = \emptyset$, and $Inv_{id}(id) = \emptyset$. As, for any TA $\mathcal{A}$, $\mathcal{A} \| \mathcal{A}_{id}$ is isomorphic to $\mathcal{A}$, $\mathcal{A}_{id}$ can be considered as the neutral element for the composition of TAs. For any TA $\mathcal{A}$ we denote by $id(\mathcal{A})$ the TA whose only location is the initial location of $\mathcal{A}$ and which is isomorphic to $\mathcal{A}_{id}$.*

Definition 12 (Clock projection). *For a TA $\mathcal{A}$ and a set of clocks X', we denote by $P_{X'}(\mathcal{A})$ the TA $\mathcal{A}'$ so that: $\mathcal{L}' = \mathcal{L}$, $\ell^{0\prime} = \ell^0$, $\Sigma' = \Sigma$, X' is the set of clocks, $E' = \{(\ell, g \cap \mathcal{B}(X'), \sigma, R \cap X', \ell') : (\ell, g, \sigma, R, \ell') \in E\}$, Inv' is so that $\forall \ell \in \mathcal{L}, Inv'(\ell) = Inv(\ell) \cap \mathcal{B}(X')$.*

Definition 13 (Extensions). *A TA $\mathcal{A}_1$ extends a TA $\mathcal{A}_2'$, noted $\mathcal{A}_1 \sqsupseteq \mathcal{A}_2'$, if and only if $\mathcal{A}_2'$ is isomorphic to some TA $\mathcal{A}_2$ so that: $\mathcal{L}_2 \subseteq \mathcal{L}_1$, $\ell_2^0 = \ell_1^0$, $\Sigma_2 \subseteq \Sigma_1$, $X_2 = X_1$, $E_2 \subseteq E_{1|\mathcal{L}_2,\Sigma_2}$, $Inv_2 = Inv_{1|\mathcal{L}_2}$, with $E_{1|\mathcal{L}_2,\Sigma_2} = \{e \in E_1 : \ell(e), \ell'(e) \in \mathcal{L}_2 \wedge \sigma(e) \in \Sigma_2\}$ and $Inv_{1|\mathcal{L}_2}$ the function defined over $\mathcal{L}_2$ and so that $\forall \ell \in \mathcal{L}_2, Inv_{1|\mathcal{L}_2}(\ell) = Inv_1(\ell)$. If moreover at least one of the above inclusions is strict, we say that $\mathcal{A}_1$ strictly extends $\mathcal{A}_2'$, which we note $\mathcal{A}_1 \sqsupset \mathcal{A}_2'$.*

Definition 14 (Initialisation). *For a TA $\mathcal{A}$ and a set of clocks X' we denote by $ini(\mathcal{A}, X')$ the TA with the same locations, initial location, and transitions as $id(\mathcal{A})$ but with X' as set of clocks, the same set of actions as $\mathcal{A}$, and the same invariants as $\mathcal{A}$ on its initial location. Notice that $P_{X'}(\mathcal{A}) \sqsupseteq ini(\mathcal{A}, X')$.*

Definition 15 (Partial compound system). *A TA $\mathcal{A}'$ is a partial compound system of $\mathcal{A} = \mathcal{A}_1 \| \dots \| \mathcal{A}_n$ if there exist m TAs $\mathcal{A}_{k_1}', \dots, \mathcal{A}_{k_m}'$ with $\{k_1, \dots, k_m\} \subseteq [1..n]$, such that $\mathcal{A}' = \mathcal{A}_{k_1}' \| \dots \| \mathcal{A}_{k_m}'$ and $P_{X_{k_i}'}(\mathcal{A}_{k_i}) \sqsupseteq \mathcal{A}_{k_i}'$ for all i in $[1..m]$.*

In the rest of this paper, for a compound system $\mathcal{A} = \mathcal{A}_1||\ldots||\mathcal{A}_n$, a partial compound system $\mathcal{A}' = \mathcal{A}'_{k_1}||\ldots||\mathcal{A}'_{k_m}$ of $\mathcal{A}$, the set $K = \{k_1, \ldots, k_m\}$, and a set $\mathcal{R}$ of partial locations of $\mathcal{A}$, we adopt the following notations.

By $\mathcal{A}' \to \mathcal{R}_{|K}$ we denote that $\mathcal{R}$ is (partially) reachable in $\mathcal{A}'$. That is, the fact that there exists a location from $\mathcal{R}_{|K} = \{(\ell'_{k_1}, \ldots, \ell'_{k_m}) : \exists (\ell_1, \ldots, \ell_n) \in \mathcal{R}, \forall i \in [1..n], \forall j \in [1..m], i = k_j \Leftrightarrow \ell_i = \ell'_{k_j}\}$ which is reachable in $\mathcal{A}'$.

By $\mathsf{Conf}(\mathcal{A}', K)$ we denote the set of actions in conflict with $\mathcal{A}'$ with respect to K: the actions from $\mathcal{A}_K = \mathcal{A}_{k_1}||\ldots||\mathcal{A}_{k_m}$ originating from locations in $\mathcal{L}'$ but not appearing in transitions from E'. Formally $\mathsf{Conf}(\mathcal{A}', K) = \{\sigma \notin \Sigma(\mathcal{A}') : \exists e_K \in E_K, \sigma(e_K) = \sigma \land \ell(e_K) \in \mathcal{L}'\}$ (assuming not only isomorphism but equality in Definition 13).

3 From Lazy Reachability to Lazy Reachability with Time

In this section we give an as generic as possible description of our lazy reachability algorithm. This description is strongly based on what we proposed recently for non-timed systems [14]. We show that it extends naturally to timed-systems. This however implies non-trivial modifications, in particular to handle invariants and resets of shared clocks. These modifications mostly impact the notion of *completeness*, which is the main notion behind the validity of the approach.

3.1 Introductory Example

The main goal of our algorithm is to be as lazy as possible when solving a reachability problem in a compound system. That is, trying to involve the smallest number of automata and the smallest number of clocks of these automata in the reachability analysis. In order to get an overview of our approach to do so, lets consider the example of Fig. 1.

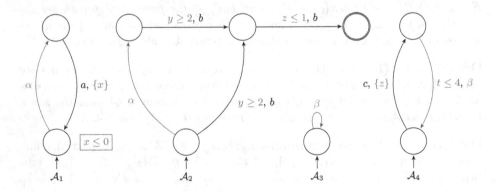

Fig. 1. A compound system involving four timed automata.

This figure shows a compound system made of four TAs: $\mathcal{A}_1$, $\mathcal{A}_2$, $\mathcal{A}_3$, and $\mathcal{A}_4$. Locations are depicted as circles and transitions as arrows with labels indicating guards, actions, and clocks resets (in this order, with empty guards and empty sets of resets omitted). Initial locations are the ones with input arrows coming from no other location. Invariants are depicted in rectangles near the corresponding locations (there is only one invariant, in $\mathcal{A}_1$, in this figure). There are three interactions in this system: $\mathcal{A}_1$ interacts with $\mathcal{A}_2$ because they share the α action, $\mathcal{A}_2$ interacts with $\mathcal{A}_4$ because they share the z clock, and $\mathcal{A}_3$ interacts with $\mathcal{A}_4$ because they share the β action. The objective here is to reach the double circled location in $\mathcal{A}_2$.

One can start from a partial compound system $P_\emptyset(\mathcal{A}_2)$, and look for a path to the objective. A possibility is bb. The clock constraints have to be added, moving to a partial compound system $\mathcal{A}_2$. The constraint $y \geq 2$ for the first b can be satisfied by waiting for (at least) 2 time units. After that, the constraint $z \leq 1$ for the second b cannot be fulfilled. However, z is a clock that can be reset by $\mathcal{A}_4$. One thus adds $P_{\{z\}}(\mathcal{A}_4)$ to the partial compound system. It appears that bcb allows to reach the objective, fulfilling all the timing constraints.

However, in $\mathcal{A}_2$, the first b is in conflict with α. And α is shared with $\mathcal{A}_1$, where it has to be used with no delay, due to the invariant $x \leq 0$. This immediately discards bcb as a possible path to the reachability objective in the global compound system. One thus, looks for another path to the objective in $\mathcal{A}_2 \| P_{\{z\}}(\mathcal{A}_4)$.

A possibility is αbcb. This immediately implies to add $\mathcal{A}_1$ to the partial compound system because of the shared action α. In the partial compound system $\mathcal{A}_1 \| \mathcal{A}_2 \| P_{\{z\}}(\mathcal{A}_4)$, αbb is clearly a timed-run. It can be verified that this run is also a run of the global compound system.

Using this incremental process, one has found a way to satisfy the reachability objective. This has been done without considering the automaton $\mathcal{A}_3$, nor the clock t. This is why we call our algorithm lazy. The remainder of this section formalizes the approach we just exemplified.

3.2 General Scheme of the Algorithm

Algorithm 1 presents the general scheme of our algorithm[1]. This algorithm starts from a partition of the TAs involved in the reachability objective. The idea is to verify this objective separately on each involved component, with the hope to find a solution involving no interaction between these components. The current state of the search is stored in the list Ls which has initially one element per part of the initial partition. Each such element is a list of tuples (A, C, I, J, K, L, M) –

---

[1] Notice that the algorithms presented in this paper make use of the classic abstract list data-structure. The usual operations $hd()$, $tl()$, and $len()$ give respectively the head, tail, and length (number of elements) of a list. The list constructor (prepend) is denoted by: and the list concatenation is denoted by ++. The $rev()$ operator reverses a list. The empty list is denoted by [ ]. Finally, $L[i]$ denotes the ith element of list L.

described in details in the next subsection – that represent more and more concrete partial compound systems: they include more and more automata and take into account more and more clocks. The more concrete partial compound system is at the head of the list.

First note that the initial partition of the TAs has to be well-formed (line 1), by that we mean that it should contain only one element $I_1 = \mathbb{L}_g$ if any TA has an invariant on a reachability objective (that is $\exists i \in \mathbb{L}_g$, $\exists (\ell_1, \ldots, \ell_n) \in \mathcal{R}$, so that $\ell_i \neq \star$ and $Inv_i(\ell_i) \neq \emptyset$).

Algorithm 1. Algorithm solving $RP_{\mathcal{A}}^{\mathcal{R}}$ ($\mathbb{L}_g$: indices of TAs involved in $\mathcal{R}$)

---

1   **choose any** well-formed partition $\{I_1, \ldots, I_p\}$ of $\mathbb{L}_g$
2   **for all** k **in** $[1..p]$ {
3   **let** $I'_k = I_k$
4   **until** stability **let** $I'_k = I'_k \cup \{i \notin I'_k \ : \ \exists j \in I'_k, \mathsf{Res}(\mathcal{A}_i) \cap X(\mathcal{A}_j) \neq \emptyset\}$
5   **let** $ID_k = \|_{i \in I'_k} id(\mathcal{A}_i)$
6   **let** $INI_k = \|_{i \in I'_k} ini(\mathcal{A}_i, \emptyset)$
7   }
8   **let** Ls $= [[(ID_1, INI_1, I_1, \emptyset, I'_1, \emptyset, \emptyset)], \ldots, [(ID_p, INI_p, I_p, \emptyset, I'_p, \emptyset, \emptyset)]]$
9   **let** Complete $=$ false
10   **let** Consistent $=$ false
11   **while not** Complete **or not** Consistent {
12   **let** Complete $=$ IsCOMPLETE(Ls)
13   **if not** Complete {
14   **optional unless** Consistent {
15   **if not** CONCRETISE(Ls) { **return** false }
16   }
17   }
18   **let** Consistent $=$ IsCONSISTENT(Ls)
19   **if not** Consistent {
20   **optional unless** Complete { MERGE(Ls) }
21   }
22   }
23   **return** true

Each element in the initial partition has to be completed with all automata resetting some clocks of the automata in that element (lines 3, 4). Resetting a clock may indeed add some behaviours, which could be overlooked otherwise.

After initialising Ls, we proceed to the main loop, which consists of two operations: concretisation, ensuring completeness, and merging, ensuring consistency. These notions and functions are described in the following subsections.

3.3   Completeness, Concretisation and the CONCRETISE Function

The main loop of Algorithm 1 iterates as long as the current state Ls of the search is not *complete*. We say that Ls is complete (noted IsCOMPLETE(Ls))

if and only if, for any indice k, $Ls[k]$ is complete. Intuitively, this means that the partial compound system represented by $hd(Ls[k])$ contains a path to reach the corresponding local goal. Moreover, this path has to (1) use no action of any automaton not participating in this partial compound system, (2) have no conflict with actions that could be externally forced by an invariant (this was the case of action α in the above example), (3) avoid relying on the satisfaction of a clock constraint involving a clock that is reset by an automaton not from this partial compound system (this was the case of clock z in the above example), and (4) take into account all clock constraints on any transition involved. In other words: a partial compound system is complete if it can reach a local goal alone.

In any tuple (A, C, I, J, K, L, M), in particular in $hd(Ls[k])$, C is the TA representation of the partial compound system considered, and $J \cup K$ contains the indices of the TAs (from the global compound system) involved in this partial compound system. The above notion of completeness can be formalized from only C, J, and K. The other elements of the tuple are instrumental for building our algorithm and are described later. In the following definition of completeness, points (1–4) correspond to intuitions (1–4) above.

Definition 16 (Completeness). *The list $Ls[k]$ so that $hd(Ls[k]) = (A, C, I, J, K, L, M)$ is complete if $\exists C^*$ so that: $C \sqsupseteq C^*$, $C^* \to \mathcal{R}_{|J \cup K}$, and (1) $\forall i \notin J \cup K, \Sigma_i \cap \Sigma(C^*) = \emptyset$, (2) $\forall i \notin J \cup K, \mathsf{Conf}(C^* J \cup K) \cap \mathsf{Req}(\mathcal{A}_i) = \emptyset$ (3) $\forall i \notin J \cup K, \mathsf{Res}(\mathcal{A}_i) \cap X(C^*) = \emptyset$ (4) $\{x \notin X(C^*) : \exists A^*, \|_{i \in J \cup K} \mathcal{A}_i \sqsupseteq A^*, P_{X(C^*)}(A^*) = C^*, x \in X(A^*)\} = \emptyset$.*

In order to achieve completeness, we use the CONCRETISE function defined in Algorithm 2. This is basically a standard backtracking algorithm, specialized for incrementally building more and more concrete partial compound systems: partial compound systems containing (1) more and more states and transitions, for a fixed set of TAs and clocks, and (2) more and more TAs and clocks.

The list $Ls[k]$ contains the search history: backtracking means replacing this list by its tail (else part of the conditional at line 4). Notice that, when backtracking, it could be possible to allow to remember the unsuccessful searches (this can be used for speeding up the future searches). This has been described in [14] for un-timed systems.

Any element of $Ls[k]$, and in particular the one reflecting the current state of the search (the head of $Ls[k]$), is a tuple (A, C, I, J, K, L, M) where: A is the partial compound system computed at the previous call to CONCRETISE, C is the current partial compound system we consider, I gives the initial partition of TAs involved in the objective, J gives the TAs involved in A, K gives the TAs that can be used to build C from A, L gives the clocks involved in A, and M gives the clocks that are used to build C from A.

The main idea of the function consists in first choosing a partial compound system C^* bigger than what we already had, and that can reach the goal. Set $\mathcal{N}_A$ then corresponds to the automata sharing some action with C^*, but not added, and $\mathcal{N}_X$ to the clocks tested, but not present, in C^*. From these sets,

---

Algorithm 2. Auxiliary function CONCRETISE(Ls) for Algorithm 1

---

1   **choose any** k **in** $[0..len(Ls) - 1]$ **such that not** ISCOMPLETE($Ls[k]$)
2   **let** $(A, C, I, J, K, L, M) = hd(Ls[k])$
3   **let** $Back = tl(Ls[k])$
4   **if** $\exists C^*$ **s.t.** $(\|_{i \in K} P_{L \cup M}(\mathcal{A}_i))\|A \sqsupseteq C^* \sqsupset C$ **and** $C^* \to \mathcal{R}_{|J \cup K}$ {
5   **choose any such** C^*
6   **let** $\mathcal{N}_\mathcal{A} = \{i \notin J \cup K \ : \ \Sigma_i \cap \Sigma(C^*) \neq \emptyset\}$
7   **let** A' **be such that** $\|_{i \in J \cup K} \mathcal{A}_i \sqsupseteq A'$ **and** $P_\emptyset(A') = P_\emptyset(C^*)$
8   **let** $\mathcal{N}_X = \{x \notin L \cup M \ : \ x \in X(A')\}$
9   **case** $\mathcal{N}_\mathcal{A} \cup \mathcal{N}_X \neq \emptyset$
10   **choose any** K', M' **such that** $K' \subseteq \mathcal{N}_\mathcal{A}$ **and** $M' \subseteq \mathcal{N}_X$ **and** $K' \cup M' \neq \emptyset$
11   **let** $Back' = (A, C^*, I, J, K, L, M) : Back$
12   **let** $J' = J \cup K$
13   **let** $L' = L \cup M$
14   **let** $K'' = K'$
15   **until** stability **let** $K'' = \{i \notin J' \cup K'' \ : \ \exists j \in K'', \mathsf{Res}(\mathcal{A}_i) \cap X(\mathcal{A}_j) \neq \emptyset\}$
16   **let** A^* **be such that** $\|_{i \in J \cup K} P_{L' \cup M'}(\mathcal{A}_i) \sqsupseteq A^*$ **and** $P_\emptyset(A^*) = P_\emptyset(C^*)$
17   **let** $Ls[k] = (A^*, \|_{i \in J' \cup K''} ini(\mathcal{A}_i, L' \cup M'), I, J', K'', L', M') : Back'$
18   **case** $\mathcal{N} = \emptyset$
19   **let** $Ls[k] = (A, C^*, I, J, K, L, M) : Back$
20   } **else** {
21   **if** $Back = [\ ]$ { **return** false }
22   **else** { **let** $Ls[k] = Back$ }
23   }
24   **return** true

---

we can choose automata or clocks to add to our partial compound system in order to try to make it complete (line 10). The next lines create the new tuple that will be put at the head of Ls as the new current level of concretisation (line 17), to reflect these choices. Line 15 forces the addition of automata that reset some clocks we have chosen to add. This is important because resetting a clock may add some new behaviours. Finally, A^* (line 16) is a version of C^* with the whole set of clocks we have up to now (those we already had and those we have just chosen to add). It will serve as an upper bound (w.r.t. $\sqsupseteq$) for the choice of C^* at the next level of concretisation. Note that at this next level we start with a partial compound system reduced to the initial states of the chosen automata (and with all the chosen clocks). If we have no clocks or automata to add from $\mathcal{N}_X, \mathcal{N}_\mathcal{A}$, then we simply update the current partial compound with C^* (line 19) and back in the main algorithm we will check if this has allowed us to achieve completeness (line 11 of Algorithm 1). If we could not find C^* at all, then it is not possible to reach the goal with the current upper bound an we need to backtrack to extend this upper bound at a lower level of concretisation, i.e., with fewer clocks or automata (line 22).

3.4   Consistency, Merging and the MERGE   Function

Achieving completeness for each element of Ls is not sufficient however to solve our reachability problem. Indeed, it may be the case that some automata appear in several different elements of Ls: we start from a partition but the same automata may be added to elements of Ls during concretisation steps. In this case, it is likely that some paths in different partial compound systems interfere: they use the same actions but not in the same order or they need incompatible valuations of the clocks for satisfying clock constraints. The main loop of Algorithm 1 reflects this by iterating as long as the current state Ls of the search is not complete, as explained above, or not *consistent*.

Definition 17 (Consistency). $Ls = [(A_1, C_1, I_1, J_1, K_1, L_1, M_1) : Back_1, \ldots, (A_n, C_n, I_n, J_n, K_n, L_n, M_n) : Back_n]$ *is consistent if* $\forall i \neq j \in [1..n], (J_i \cup K_i) \cap (J_j \cup K_j) = \emptyset$.

In order to achieve consistency we use a MERGE function to replace two elements of Ls: $Ls[i]$ (with $hd(Ls[i]) = (A_i, C_i, I_i, J_i, K_i, L_i, M_i)$ and $tl(Ls[i]) = Back_i$) and $Ls[j]$ (with $hd(Ls[j]) = (A_j, C_j, I_j, J_j, K_j, L_j, M_j)$ and $tl(Ls[j]) = Back_j$) by a single one $h : Back$ obtained by merging them, thus reducing the length of Ls by one. The simplest such new element would be such that: $Back = [\ ]$ and $h = (ID_i || ID_j, INI_i || INI_j, I_i \cup I_j, \emptyset, I_i' \cup I_j', \emptyset, \emptyset)$. However, it may be of interest to use the current state of the search in both $Ls[i]$ and $Ls[j]$, taking instead: $Back = [(ID_i || ID_j, INI_i || INI_j, I_i \cup I_j, \emptyset, I_i' \cup I_j', \emptyset, \emptyset)]$, and $h = (P_{L_j}(A_i) || P_{L_i}(A_j), P_{L_j \cup M_j}(C_i) || P_{L_i \cup M_i}(C_j), I_i \cup I_j, J_i \cup J_j, K_i \cup K_j)$.

In fact, it is even possible to replace $Ls[i]$ and $Ls[j]$ by any history that could have been produced by a sequence of call to CONCRETISE starting from $(ID_i || ID_j, INI_i || INI_j, I_i \cup I_j, \emptyset, I_i' \cup I_j', \emptyset, \emptyset)$ (of which the two above examples are particular cases). This avoids to un-merge when backtracking, has been formalized as a notion of good MERGE in our previous work [14], and remains essentially the same for timed systems.

3.5   Termination, Soundness, Completeness

Theorem 1 explicits the fact that Algorithm 1 always terminates, and is sound and complete. Due to space limitations, its proof is omitted.

Theorem 1. *Algorithm 1 always terminates. It returns true if and only if the goal is reachable.*

3.6   Example

We get back to the introductory example and see how our algorithm may find the result we intuitively outlined.

First we choose an initial partition of the automata directly involved in the objective. Here there is only A_2 so $Ls = [(id(A_2) || id(A_4), ini(A_2, \emptyset) || ini(A_4, \emptyset), \{2\}, \emptyset, \{2, 4\}, \emptyset, \emptyset)]$. Note in particular that $I_1' = \{2, 4\}$ because clock z is present in $\mathcal{A}_2$ and reset by $\mathcal{A}_4$. Also, since we have only one element in our partition, we will always stay consistent in this example.

Now we can call CONCRETISE and choose $k = 0$ (the only possibility). We choose for instance C^* as the compound system C_{24} made of the path bb in $\mathcal{A}_2$ and the path c in $\mathcal{A}_4$, which permits to reach the goal. Then $\mathcal{N}_A = \emptyset$ and $\mathcal{N}_X = \{y, z\}$. We can now choose $K' = \emptyset$ and $M' = \{y, z\}$ for instance. Then $K'' = \emptyset$. Finally, A^* is $C^* = C_{24}$ augmented by the clocks y and z, slightly abusing notations we denote it by $P_{\{y,z\}}(C_{24})$. The function returns true, and $Ls[0] = [Ls_1, Ls'_0]$ with $Ls'_0 = (id(\mathcal{A}_2)||id(\mathcal{A}_2), C_{24}, \{2\}, \emptyset, \{2, 4\}, \emptyset, \emptyset)]$, and $Ls_1 = (P_{\{y,z\}}(C_{24}), ini(\mathcal{A}_2, \{y, z\})||ini(\mathcal{A}_4, \{y, z\}), \{2\}, \{2, 4\}, \emptyset, \emptyset, \{y, z\})$.

Back in the main algorithm, starting from $ini(\mathcal{A}_2, \{y, z\})||ini(\mathcal{A}_4, \{y, z\})$ we obviously do not have completeness. So we call CONCRETISE again. We choose, for instance C^* as the full $P_{\{y,z\}}(C_{24})$, in which the goal can be reached. Both $\mathcal{N}_A$ and $\mathcal{N}_X$ are empty, so we proceed to line 19 and $Ls[0]$ becomes $[(P_{\{y,z\}}(C_{24}), P_{\{y,z\}}(C_{24}), \{2\}, \{2, 4\}, \emptyset, \emptyset, \{y, z\}), Ls'_0]$. We return true.

Back in the main algorithm, $P_{\{y,z\}}(C_{24})$ is not complete because α is in conflict with the first b in $\mathcal{A}_2$ and α is urgent due to the invariant in $\mathcal{A}_1$ ((2) of Definition 16) so we need to call CONCRETISE again. There, we have to choose something strictly bigger than the C, i.e. $P_{\{y,z\}}(C_{24})$, which is not possible with K being empty. We reach line 22 (backtracking) and $Ls[0]$ becomes $[Ls'_0]$.

In the main algorithm again, Ls is not complete because C_{24} (the C value of Ls'_0) is not complete (for the same conflict with α as above). We choose to add the rest of $\mathcal{A}_2$ and choose therefore C^* as the compound system C'_{24} made of $\mathcal{A}_2$ and the path c of $\mathcal{A}_4$. Then $\mathcal{N}_A = \{1\}$ because α is shared with $\mathcal{A}_1$ and $\mathcal{N}_X = \{y, z\}$. We choose $K' = \{1\}$, $M' = \emptyset$ and since we have no further shared clock, we have $K'' = K'$. Since we have not added clocks, $A^* = C'_{24}$ and finally $Ls[0]$ becomes $[Ls'_1, Ls''_0]$ with $Ls''_0 = (id(\mathcal{A}_2)||id(\mathcal{A}_4), C'_{24}, \{2\}, \emptyset, \{2, 4\}, \emptyset, \emptyset)$, and $Ls'_1 = (C'_{24}, ini(\mathcal{A}_1, \emptyset)||ini(\mathcal{A}_2, \emptyset)||ini(\mathcal{A}_4, \emptyset), \{2\}, \{2, 4\}, \{1\}, \emptyset, \emptyset)$. We return true.

Back in the main algorithm we are not complete since we do not reach the goal in $ini(\mathcal{A}_1, \emptyset)||ini(\mathcal{A}_2, \emptyset)||ini(\mathcal{A}_4, \emptyset)$ so we call CONCRETISE. We choose for instance C^* as the compound system C_{124} made of the path α in $\mathcal{A}_1$, the whole of $\mathcal{A}_2$ and the path c in $\mathcal{A}_4$. Then $\mathcal{N}_A = \emptyset$ but $\mathcal{N}_X = \{x, y, z\}$ because clock x is tested in the invariant of $\mathcal{A}_1$. So we have to choose $K' = \emptyset$ and decide to take $M' = \{x, y, z\}$. We have $K'' = K'$. Hence, A^* is C_{124} augmented by the clocks x, y and z, slightly abusing notations we denote it by $P_{\{x,y,z\}}(C_{124})$. And $Ls[0]$ becomes $[Ls_2, Ls''_1, Ls'_0]$, with $Ls''_1 = (C'_{24}, C_{124}, \{2\}, \{2, 4\}, \{1\}, \emptyset, \emptyset)$ and $Ls_2 = (P_{\{x,y,z\}}(C_{124}), ini(\mathcal{A}_1, \{x, y, z\}) || ini(\mathcal{A}_2, \{x, y, z\}) || ini(\mathcal{A}_4, \{x, y, z\}), \{2\}, \{1, 2, 4\}, \emptyset, \emptyset, \{x, y, z\})$. We return true.

Again in the main algorithm we are not complete because we do not reach the goal in the C value of Ls_2, so we call CONCRETISE. We choose C^* as the compound system C'_{124} made of the path α in $\mathcal{A}_1$ (but with x this time), the whole of $\mathcal{A}_2$ (with y and z this time) and the path c in $\mathcal{A}_4$ (with z this time). Now taking into account the clocks C'_{124} does allow to reach the goal, but only through the path $abcb$. Furthermore, $\mathcal{N}_X = \mathcal{N}_A = \emptyset$ so we proceed to line 19 and $Ls[0]$ is now $[Ls_2', Ls_1'', Ls_0'']$, with $Ls_2' = (P_{\{x,y,z\}}(C_{124}), C_{124}', \{2\}, \{1,2,4\}, \emptyset, \emptyset, \{x,y,z\})$. We return true. Finally, the main algorithm concludes that C_{124}' is complete and terminate, by concluding that the goal is indeed reachable.

4   Experimental Analysis

We implemented an instance of the above algorithm as a tool called LARA-T. The LARA-T tool represents around 2000 lines of code written in the functional language Haskell[2]. It is built over the previous LARA tool for reachability analysis in networks of (untimed) automata [14]. Both tools are available for download[3].

The algorithm we have presented is very general and the current implementation results from some important choices. First, each time we add automata or clocks, we compute the resulting partial compound system completely. This eliminates the need for backtracking, since if we cannot find the goal in this partial compound system then it is for sure not reachable at all. In that respect, this choice also heuristically favors the unreachable case. Second, we only compute the reachable parts of the compound systems, using a classic DBM-based symbolic state exploration [16], with DBM inclusion checking and maximal constant per clock extrapolation. Finally, when we have computed a whole partial compound system, we look at the paths we have followed to reach all goal states. If some automata or clocks are required for completeness with respect to all those paths, then we add them all at the next level. Otherwise, we add one arbitrary required automaton or clock with the following priority: first automata ((1) of Definition 16), then clocks actually used on some path to the goal (4), and finally clocks coming from urgent conflicts due to invariants (2). We have not yet implemented the support for shared clocks (hence (3) of Definition 16 not appearing in the previous priority order).

We compared LARA-T to UPPAAL [4] on several examples from the literature on analysis and verification of timed systems[4]:

CRITREG is a modeling of a critical region protocol from PAT [19] benchmarks. We check the reachability of an error location in one of the automata. This is a true property.

FDDI is a modeling of a communication protocol based on a token ring network presented in [9] and adapted to our setting in [13]. We check the reachability of a couple of mutually exclusive locations. This is a false property.

FISCHER is a modeling of Fischer's mutual exclusion protocol [3]. We check the reachability of a couple of mutually exclusive locations. This is a false property.

---

[2] https://www.haskell.org/.
[3] http://lara.rts-software.org/.
[4] UPPAAL templates and inputs for LARA-T: http://lara.rts-software.org/.

FISCHER2 is a variation of Fischer's mutual exclusion protocol where a time constant has been changed, breaking the mutual exclusion guarantee. In this example, the property is true.

TRAINS1 is the Train model of Uppaal [3]. A controller is responsible for a queue of trains and has to prevent more than one of them to access a bridge together. We check the reachability of a state in which the two first trains are crossing the bridge at the same time. This is a false property.

TRAINS2 is a variation of the TRAINS1 benchmark where the controller manages a set of trains rather than a queue of trains.

TRAINS3 is a model where a railway crosses a road [8]. A controller has to ensure that the gate is closed (cars cannot crosse the railway) as soon as a train crosses the road. We check the reachability of a state in which a train crosses the road while the gate is open. This is a false property.

4.1 Experimental Results

For each example we ran UPPAAL and LARA-T on instances of growing size (the size is, roughly, the number of timed-automata, see Table 2 for precise information), with a time-limit of 20 min at each size. In order to better evaluate the performances of the laziness mechanism (independently of our implementation of the DMB-based computation of the state-space of a TA) we also ran LARA-T with all components and clocks in a single element of the initial partition (LARA-T Full). All the experiments were run on the same machine with four Intel® Xeon® E5-2620 processors (six cores each) with 128 GB of memory. Though this machine has some potential for parallel computing, all the experiments presented here are actually monothreaded.

Table 1 gives the largest instance of each example solved by each tool within the time-limit.

Table 1. Size of last instances solved within 20 min by UPPAAL and LARA-T

	CRITREG	FDDI	FISCHER	FISCHER2	TRAINS1	TRAINS2	TRAINS3
LARA-T	≥1500	≥5000	7	≥500	8	13	7
LARA-T Full	4	15	6	5	8	13	5
UPPAAL	46	13	13	65	10	16	6

For each example, we also evaluated the number of automata and clocks that LARA-T takes into account to decide its result in an instance of size n. In Table 2, we compare it to the total number of automata and clocks in the same instance. Our goal was to evaluate to which extent our algorithm is actually lazy.

Table 2. Number of automata (A) and clocks (C) used by LARA-T for solving instances of size n, and total number of automata and clocks in such instances.

	CRITREG		FDDI		FISCHER		FISCHER2		TRAINS1		TRAINS2		TRAINS3	
	A	C	A	C	A	C	A	C	A	C	A	C	A	C
LARA-T	3	1	4	5	$n+1$	n	3	2	3	3	3	3	$n+2$	3
Total	$2n+1$	n	$n+1$	$3n+1$	$n+1$	n	$n+1$	n	$n+1$	n	$n+1$	n	$n+2$	$n+2$

4.2 Analysis of the Results

We first remark that LARA-T clearly outperforms UPPAAL on three of our seven examples: CRITREG, FDDI, and FISCHER2. This is because the number of automata and clocks considered by LARA-T in these examples does not increase with the size of the instances considered. This is particularly striking in the case of FDDI where the property we consider is false: UPPAAL needs to completely explore a quickly growing state-space.

On three other examples, namely TRAINS1, TRAINS2, and TRAINS3, LARA-T copes with UPPAAL. It is surprising that, while the number of automata and clocks does not increase with the size of the instances considered, LARA-T solves a bit less instances of TRAINS1 and TRAINS2 than UPPAAL. This can be explained by the fact that one of the automata considered by LARA-T represents the centralized data-structure (either a queue or a set) involved in these examples. The size of this automaton increases exponentially with the size of the instances considered. LARA-T does not implement efficient search in large automata (this is orthogonal to our work). On the TRAINS3 example, LARA-T always uses all the automata. However, it needs only a subset (of size independent from the size of the instance considered) of the clocks to conclude. So, the timed reachability analysis is made easier, explaining the fact that LARA-T solves a bit more instances than UPPAAL.

Finally, LARA-T is clearly outperformed by UPPAAL on the FISCHER example. This can be explained by the fact that LARA-T needs to consider all the automata and all the clocks, that is, to perform the full reachability analysis. On such a task it is illusory to be as efficient as UPPAAL.

5 Conclusion

We have proposed a new algorithm for the verification of concurrent timed systems, modelled as products of timed automata. This algorithm extends our previous proposition for untimed systems [14] by considering not only the different automata components, but also clocks, in a lazy manner. By examining closely which actions and clocks are needed to reach some goal locations, and how they interact with urgency, in successive over-approximations of the whole system, we are, in many cases, able to conclude on the reachability property by considering only a subset of the components and clocks. And we can do it regardless of the actual truth value of the property. We have implemented a version of the algorithm in a freely available tool, named LARA-T and we report on its efficiency in comparison to UPPAAL, a state-of-the-art model-checker for timed automata. These experimental results, obtained on classic benchmarks from the timed systems community, are very encouraging, with LARA-T outperforming UPPAAL, sometimes by several magnitude orders, on a few of the benchmarks, and being never too far behind even in the worst cases where all components and clocks have to be considered to decide the property.

The proposed algorithm provides a quite general framework open for many heuristic improvements, and part of future work naturally consists in finding good heuristics for better choosing the components and clocks to add. The computed over-approximations also contain a lot of information on the system and, in practice, we currently only use them to prune actions leading to non-coreachable states. It would be interesting to make a better use of that information, and, for instance in the case of timed systems, to use it to cheaply find good exploration orders minimizing the number of "mistakes" when a bigger DBM is reached after a smaller one for a given location, and all the successors have to be explored again (see [13] for precise account of the problem). Further work also includes extending to properties beyond reachability, and taking discrete variables into account to improve the conciseness of the models.

References

1. Alur, R., Dill, D.L.: A theory of timed automata. Theor. Comput. Sci. **126**(2), 183–235 (1994)
2. Behrmann, G., Bouyer, P., Larsen, K.G., Pelánek, R.: Lower and upper bounds in zone-based abstractions of timed automata. Int. J. Softw. Tools Technol. Transf. **8**(3), 204–215 (2006)
3. Behrmann, G., David, A., Larsen, K.G.: A tutorial on UPPAAL. In: Bernardo, M., Corradini, F. (eds.) SFM-RT 2004. LNCS, vol. 3185, pp. 200–236. Springer, Heidelberg (2004). doi:10.1007/978-3-540-30080-9_7
4. Behrmann, G., David, A., Larsen, K.G., Pettersson, P., Yi, W.: Developing UPPAAL over 15 years. Softw. Pract. Exp. **41**(2), 133–142 (2011)
5. Bellman, R.: Dynamic Programming. Princeton University Press, Princeton (1957)
6. Bengtsson, J., Jonsson, B., Lilius, J., Yi, W.: Partial order reductions for timed systems. In: Sangiorgi, D., Simone, R. (eds.) CONCUR 1998. LNCS, vol. 1466, pp. 485–500. Springer, Heidelberg (1998). doi:10.1007/BFb0055643
7. Berthomieu, B., Menasche, M.: An enumerative approach for analyzing time petri nets. In: IFIP Congress, pp. 41–46 (1983)
8. Berthomieu, B., Vernadat, F.: State class constructions for branching analysis of time petri nets. In: Garavel, H., Hatcliff, J. (eds.) TACAS 2003. LNCS, vol. 2619, pp. 442–457. Springer, Heidelberg (2003). doi:10.1007/3-540-36577-X_33
9. Daws, C., Olivero, A., Tripakis, S., Yovine, S.: The tool KRONOS. In: Alur, R., Henzinger, T.A., Sontag, E.D. (eds.) HS 1995. LNCS, vol. 1066, pp. 208–219. Springer, Heidelberg (1996). doi:10.1007/BFb0020947
10. Hansen, H., Lin, S.-W., Liu, Y., Nguyen, T.K., Sun, J.: Diamonds are a girl's best friend: partial order reduction for timed automata with abstractions. In: Biere, A., Bloem, R. (eds.) CAV 2014. LNCS, vol. 8559, pp. 391–406. Springer, Cham (2014). doi:10.1007/978-3-319-08867-9_26

11. Henzinger, T.A., Nicollin, X., Sifakis, J., Yovine, S.: Symbolic model checking for real-time systems. Inf. Comput. **111**(2), 193–244 (1994)
12. Herbreteau, F., Srivathsan, B., Walukiewicz, I.: Better abstractions for timed automata. Inf. Comput. **251**, 67–90 (2016)
13. Herbreteau, F., Tran, T.-T.: Improving search order for reachability testing in timed automata. In: Sankaranarayanan, S., Vicario, E. (eds.) FORMATS 2015. LNCS, vol. 9268, pp. 124–139. Springer, Cham (2015). doi:10.1007/978-3-319-22975-1_9
14. Jezequel, L., Lime, D.: Lazy reachability analysis in distributed systems. In: Proceedings of the 27th International Conference on Concurrency Theory, pp. 17:1–17:14 (2016)
15. Larsen, K.G., Pearson, J., Weise, C., Yi, W.: Clock difference diagrams. Nord. J. Comput. **6**(3), 271–298 (1999)
16. Larsen, K.G., Pettersson, P., Yi, W.: Model-checking for real-time systems. In: Reichel, H. (ed.) FCT 1995. LNCS, vol. 965, pp. 62–88. Springer, Heidelberg (1995). doi:10.1007/3-540-60249-6_41
17. Larsen, K.G., Pettersson, P., Yi, W.: UPPAAL in a nutshell. J. Softw. Tools Technol. Transf. **1**(1–2), 134–152 (1997)
18. Salah, R.B., Bozga, M., Maler, O.: On interleaving in timed automata. In: Baier, C., Hermanns, H. (eds.) CONCUR 2006. LNCS, vol. 4137, pp. 465–476. Springer, Heidelberg (2006). doi:10.1007/11817949_31
19. Sun, J., Liu, Y., Dong, J.S., Pang, J.: PAT: towards flexible verification under fairness. In: Bouajjani, A., Maler, O. (eds.) CAV 2009. LNCS, vol. 5643, pp. 709–714. Springer, Heidelberg (2009). doi:10.1007/978-3-642-02658-4_59
20. Wang, F.: Symbolic verification of complex real-time systems with clock-restriction diagram. In: Kim, M., Chin, B., Kang, S., Lee, D. (eds.) FORTE 2001. IIFIP, vol. 69, pp. 235–250. Springer, Boston (2002). doi:10.1007/0-306-47003-9_15

Lazy Reachability Checking
for Timed Automata Using Interpolants

Tamás Tóth$^{(\boxtimes)}$ and István Majzik

Department of Measurement and Information Systems,
Budapest University of Technology and Economics, Budapest, Hungary
{totht,majzik}@mit.bme.hu

Abstract. To solve the reachability problem for timed automata, model
checkers usually apply forward search and zone abstraction. To ensure
efficiency and termination, the computed zones are generalized using
maximal constants obtained from guards either by static analysis or lazily
for a given path. In this paper, we propose a lazy method based on
zone abstraction that, instead of the constants in guards, considers the
constraints themselves. The method is a combination of forward search,
backward search and interpolation over zones: if the zone abstraction is
too coarse, we propagate a zone representing bad states backwards using
backward search, and use interpolation to extract a relevant zone to
strengthen the current abstraction. We propose two refinement strategies
in this framework, and evaluate our method on the usual benchmark
models for timed automata. Our experiments show that the proposed
method compares favorably to known methods based on efficient lazy
non-convex abstractions.

Keywords: Timed automata · Model checking · Reachability · Zone
abstraction · Interpolation

1   Introduction

Timed automata [1] is a widely used formalism for the modeling and verification
of real-time systems. The reachability problem deals with the question whether
a given error state is reachable from an initial state along the transitions of the
automaton. The standard solution of this problem involves performing a forward
exploration in the so-called zone-graph induced by the automaton [9].

   To ensure performance and termination, model checkers for timed automata
usually apply some sort of generalization of zones based on maximal lower-
and upper bounds [3] (LU-bounds) appearing in the guards of the automaton.
This can be performed directly by extrapolation [3] parametrized by bounds
obtained by static analysis [2]. Alternatively, bounds can be propagated lazily
for all transitions [12] or along an infeasible path [11], which, combined with

---

   T. Tóth—This work was partially supported by Gedeon Richter's Talentum Foundation (Gyömrői út 19-21, 1103 Budapest, Hungary).

A. Abate and G. Geeraerts (Eds.): FORMATS 2017, LNCS 10419, pp. 264–280, 2017.
DOI: 10.1007/978-3-319-65765-3_15

an efficient method for inclusion checking [13] with respect to a non-convex abstraction induced by the bounds, results in an efficient method for reachability checking of timed automata. This latter approach can be seen as a variant of counterexample-guided abstraction refinement [8] (CEGAR), a technique widely used in model checking.

In this paper, we propose a similar lazy algorithm for reachability checking of timed automata. However, instead of propagating the bounds appearing in guards, the algorithm considers the guards themselves. If the abstraction is too coarse to exclude an infeasible path, a zone representing the guards of a disabled transition is propagated backwards using pre-image computation. Based on the pre-image, we compute a zone strong enough to block the disabled transition in form of an interpolant [14]. In a similar fashion, we use interpolation to effectively prune the search space by enforcing coverage of a newly discovered state with an already visited state when possible. We propose two refinement strategies in this framework. Both methods are a combination of forward search, backward search and zone interpolation, and can be considered as a generalization of zone interpolation to sequences of transitions of a timed automaton.

We compared the proposed interpolation based method and the non-convex LU-abstraction based method [11] on the usual benchmark models for timed automata. Results show that our method performs similarly to the highly sophisticated algorithm of [11], and in cases can even generate a smaller state space. Moreover, it turned out that for some models the proposed refinement strategies are less sensitive to search order, thus are more robust against bad decisions during search.

Comparison to Related Work. Lazy abstraction [10] is an approach widely used for model checking, and in particular for model checking software. It consists of building an abstract reachability graph on-the fly, representing an abstraction of the system, and refining a part of the tree in case a spurious counterexample is found. Lazy abstraction with interpolants [15] (also known as IMPACT) and lazy annotation [16] are both lazy abstraction techniques for software where refinement is performed using interpolant generation.

For timed automata, a lazy abstraction approach based on non-convex LU-abstraction and on-the-fly propagation of bounds has been proposed [11]. A significant difference of this algorithm compared to usual lazy abstraction algorithms is that it builds an abstract reachability graph that preserves exact reachability information (a so-called adaptive simulation graph). As a consequence it is able to apply refinement as soon as the abstraction admits a transition disabled in the concrete system. In our work, we apply the same approach, but for a different abstract domain, with different refinement strategies.

The work closest to ours is difference bound constraint abstraction [18]. The refinement method presented there and our refinement strategy we refer to as the binary (BIN) strategy are highly analogous, and both are very similar to lazy annotation. However, our refinement strategy that we refer to as the sequence (SEQ) strategy is different in concept. Moreover, in [18], abstractions are sets of difference constraints, and refinement rules are defined on a case-by-case basis for guards, resets and delay. In our paper, we represent abstractions as canonical difference bound matrices, and define abstraction refinement in more general terms, as a combination of symbolic forward and backward search and zone interpolation. This formulation enables a simple generalization of our approach to automata with diagonal constraints in guards [6] and to updatable timed automata [5], as well as to the application of backward exploration. Moreover, by representing abstractions as canonical difference bound matrices, known zone-based abstraction methods can be considered orthogonal to our approach.

Organization of the Paper. The rest of the paper is organized as follows. In Sect. 2, we define the notations used throughout the paper, and present the theoretical background of our work. In Sect. 3 we propose a lazy reachability checking algorithm based on zone abstraction for timed automata. We propose two methods for abstraction refinement in Sect. 4. Section 5 describes experiments performed on the proposed algorithm. Finally, conclusions are given in Sect. 6.

2   Background and Notations

Let X be a set of *clock variables* over $\mathbb{R}$. We assume $x_0 \in X$, where x_0 is a distinguished reference clock with constant value 0. A *clock constraint* over X is a conjunction of atoms of the form $x_i - x_j \prec c$ where $x_i, x_j \in X$, $c \in \mathbb{Z}$ and $\prec \in \{<, \leq\}$. We denote the set of clock constraints over X by $\Phi(X)$.

A *clock valuation* over X is a function $\eta : X \to \mathbb{R}$. We denote by $Eval(X)$ the set of clock valuations over X, and by $\mathbf{0} \in Eval(X)$ the clock valuation where $\mathbf{0}(x) = 0$ for all $x \in X$. For a real number $\delta \geq 0$ and for all $x \in X$, let $(\eta + \delta)(x) = \eta(x) + \delta$. Moreover, for $R \subseteq X$ and for all $x \in X$, let $([R]\,\eta)(x) = 0$ if $x \in R$ and $([R]\,\eta)(x) = \eta(x)$ otherwise. For a clock constraint $\varphi \in \Phi(X)$, we denote by $\eta \models \varphi$ iff φ is satisfied under valuation η. Furthermore, let $\llbracket \varphi \rrbracket = \{\eta \mid \eta \models \varphi\}$.

2.1   Timed Automata

Definition 1 (Timed automaton). *Syntactically, a timed automaton is a tuple $\mathcal{A} = (L, X, T, \ell_0)$ where*

- *L is a finite set of locations,*
- *X is a finite set of clock variables,*
- *$T \subseteq L \times \Phi(X) \times \mathcal{P}(X) \times L$ is a finite set of transitions where for a transition $(\ell, g, R, \ell') \in T$, constraint g is a guard and R is a set containing clocks to be reset, and*
- *$\ell_0 \in L$ is the initial location.*

A state of $\mathcal{A}$ is a pair (ℓ, η) where $\ell \in L$ and $\eta \in Eval(X)$.

Definition 2 (Semantics). *The operational semantics of a timed automaton is given by a labeled transition system with initial state $(\ell_0, \mathbf{0})$ and two kinds of transitions:*

- *Delay:* $(\ell, \eta) \xrightarrow{\delta} (\ell, \eta + \delta)$ *for some* $\delta \geq 0$;
- *Action:* $(\ell, \eta) \xrightarrow{t} (\ell', [R]\,\eta)$ *for some transition* $t = (\ell, g, R, \ell')$ *where* $\eta \models g$.

A *run* of a timed automaton is a sequence of states from the initial state along the transition relation $(\ell_0, \eta_0) \xrightarrow{\alpha_1} (\ell_1, \eta_1) \xrightarrow{\alpha_2} \ldots \xrightarrow{\alpha_n} (\ell_n, \eta_n)$ where $\eta_0 = \mathbf{0}$ and $\alpha_i \in T \cup \mathbb{R}_{\geq 0}$ for all $0 \leq i \leq n$. A location $\ell \in L$ is *reachable* iff there exists a run such that $\ell_n = \ell$.

2.2 Symbolic Semantics

As the concrete semantics of a timed automaton is infinite due to real valued clock variables, model checkers are often based on a symbolic semantics defined in terms of zones. A *zone* $Z \in \mathcal{Z}$ is the solution set of a clock constraint $\varphi \in \Phi(X)$, that is $Z = \llbracket \varphi \rrbracket$. For zones Z and Z', we will denote by $Z \sqsubseteq Z'$ iff $Z \subseteq Z'$. Moreover, if Z and Z' are zones and $t \in T$, then

- $\bot = \emptyset$,
- $\top = Eval(X)$,
- $Z \sqcap Z' = Z \cap Z'$,
- $Z_0 = \{\eta \mid \eta = \mathbf{0} + \delta \text{ for some } \delta \geq 0\}$,
- $\mathbf{post}_t(Z) = \left\{ \eta' \mid (\ell, \eta) \xrightarrow{t} s \xrightarrow{\delta} (\ell', \eta') \text{ for some } \eta \in Z \text{ and } \delta \geq 0 \right\}$, and
- $\mathbf{pre}_t(Z') = \left\{ \eta \mid (\ell, \eta) \xrightarrow{t} s \xrightarrow{\delta} (\ell', \eta') \text{ for some } \eta' \in Z' \text{ and } \delta \geq 0 \right\}$

are also zones. Zones are not closed under complementation, but the complement of any zone is the union of finitely many zones. For a zone Z, we are going to denote a finite set of such zones by $\neg Z$.

The functions $\mathbf{post}_t(Z)$ and $\mathbf{pre}_t(Z)$ represent the strongest postcondition and weakest precondition of Z with respect to a transition t of a timed automaton, respectively. We are going to use the following simple lemma.

Lemma 1. *Let A, B be zones and $t \in T$ a transition. Then $A \sqcap \mathbf{pre}_t(B) \sqsubseteq \bot$ iff $\mathbf{post}_t(A) \sqcap B \sqsubseteq \bot$.*

Using **post**, we can define a zone-based symbolic semantics for timed automata.

Definition 3 (Symbolic semantics). *The symbolic semantics of a timed automaton is given by a labeled transition system with states of the form (ℓ, Z), with initial state (ℓ_0, Z_0), and with transitions of the form $(\ell, Z) \overset{t}{\Rightarrow} (\ell', \mathbf{post}_t(Z))$ where $t = (\ell, g, R, \ell')$.*

Definition 4 (Symbolic run). *A symbolic run of a timed automaton is a sequence $(\ell_0, Z_0) \overset{t_1}{\Rightarrow} (\ell_1, Z_1) \overset{t_2}{\Rightarrow} \ldots \overset{t_n}{\Rightarrow} (\ell_n, Z_n)$ where $Z_n \neq \bot$.*

Proposition 1. *For a timed automaton, a location $\ell \in L$ is reachable iff there exists a symbolic run with $\ell_n = \ell$.*

2.3 Difference Bound Matrices

Clock constraints and thus zones can be efficiently represented by difference bound matrices.

A *bound* is either ∞, or a finite bound of the form $(m, \prec)$ where $m \in \mathbb{Z}$ and $\prec \in \{<, \le\}$. Difference bounds can be totally ordered by "strength", that is, $(m, \prec) < \infty$, $(m_1, \prec_1) < (m_2, \prec_2)$ iff $m_1 < m_2$ and $(m, <) < (m, \le)$. Moreover the sum of two bounds is defined as $b + \infty = \infty$, $(m_1, \le) + (m_2, \le) = (m_1 + m_2, \le)$ and $(m_1, <) + (m_2, \prec) = (m_1 + m_2, <)$.

A *difference bound matrix* (DBM) over $X = \{x_0, x_1, \ldots, x_n\}$ is a square matrix D of bounds of order $n + 1$ where an element $D_{ij} = (m, \prec)$ represents the clock constraint $x_i - x_j \prec m$. We denote by $[\![D]\!]$ the zone induced by the conjunction of constraints stored in D. We say that D is *consistent* iff $[\![D]\!] \neq \emptyset$. The following is a simple sufficient and necessary condition for a DBM to be inconsistent.

Proposition 2. *A DBM D is inconsistent iff there exists a negative cycle in D, that is, a set of pairs of indexes $\{(i_1, i_2), \ldots, (i_{k-1}, i_k), (i_k, i_1)\}$ such that $D_{i_1, i_2} + \ldots + D_{i_{k-1}, i_k} + D_{i_k, i_1} < (0, \le)$.*

For a consistent DBM D, we say it is *canonical* iff constraints in it can not be strengthened without losing solutions, formally, iff $D_{ii} = (0, \le)$ for all $0 \le i \le n$ and $D_{ij} \le D_{ik} + D_{kj}$ for all $0 \le i, j, k \le n$. For convenience, we will also consider the inconsistent DBM D with the single finite bound $D_{00} = (0, <)$ canonical. Up to the ordering of clocks, the canonical form is unique. Moreover, the zone operations in Sect. 2.2 can be efficiently implemented over canonical DBMs [4]. Therefore, we will refer to a canonical DBM D (syntax) and the zone $[\![D]\!]$ it represents (semantics) interchangeably throughout the paper.

For two DBMs A and B, we will denote by $\min(A, B)$ the (not necessarily canonical) DBM D where $D_{ij} = \min(A_{ij}, B_{ij})$, which encodes $[\![A]\!] \cap [\![B]\!]$.

3   Algorithm

In this section, we present our algorithm for lazy reachability checking of timed automata.

3.1   Adaptive Simulation Graph

The definitions and propositions presented here are adaptations of concepts introduced in [11] to our convex, zone-based setting.

Definition 5 (Unwinding). *An unwinding of a timed automaton (L, X, T, ℓ_0) is a tuple $U = (V, E, v_0, M_v, M_e, \rhd)$ where*

- *(V, E) is a directed tree rooted at node $v_0 \in V$,*
- *$M_v : V \to L$ is the vertex labeling,*
- *$M_e : E \to T$ is the edge labeling, and*
- *$\rhd \subseteq V \times V$ is the (functional) covering relation.*

For an unwinding we require that the following properties hold:

- $M_v(v_0) = \ell_0$,
- *for each edge* $(v, v') \in E$ *the transition* $M_e(v, v') = (\ell, g, R, \ell')$ *is such that* $M_v(v) = \ell$ *and* $M_v(v') = \ell'$,
- *for all* v *and* v' *such that* $v \triangleright v'$ *it holds that* $M_v(v) = M_v(v')$.

Informally, the purpose of the covering relation $\triangleright$ is to mark if the search space has been pruned at a node due to an other node that admits all runs possible from the covered node. For convenience, we define the following shorthand notations: $\ell_v = M_v(v)$ and $t_{v,v'} = M_e(v, v')$.

Definition 6 (Adaptive simulation graph). *An adaptive simulation graph (ASG) for a timed automaton $\mathcal{A}$ is a tuple $G = (U, \psi_Z, \psi_W)$ where*

- U *is an unwinding of* $\mathcal{A}$, *and*
- $\psi_Z, \psi_W : V \to \mathcal{Z}$ *are labelings of vertices by zones.*

We will use the following shorthand notations: $Z_v = \psi_Z(v)$ and $W_v = \psi_W(v)$. Later, we will ensure that Z_v represents the exact set of reachable valuations for v, and W_v an overapproximation of it.

A node v is *expanded* iff it has a successor for all transitions $t = (\ell, g, R, \ell')$ such that $\ell_v = \ell$. Without loss of generality, we assume that for each location the automaton has at least one outgoing transition, thus if a node is expanded, then it is not a leaf. A node v is *feasible* iff $W_v \neq \bot$. It is *covered* iff $v \triangleright v'$ for some node v'. It is *excluded* iff it is covered, infeasible or it has an excluded parent. A node is *complete* iff it is either expanded or excluded. A node is ℓ-safe iff $\ell_v \neq \ell$.

For an ASG to be useful for reachability checking, we have to introduce restrictions on the labelings ψ_Z and ψ_W.

Definition 7 (Well-labeled node). *A node v of an ASG G for a timed automaton $\mathcal{A}$ is well-labeled iff the following conditions hold:*

- *(initiation) if* $v = v_0$, *then (a)* $Z_v = Z_0$ *and (b)* $Z_0 \sqsubseteq W_v$;
- *(consecution) if* $v \neq v_0$, *then for its parent u and the transition $t = t_{u,v}$ we have (a)* $Z_v = \mathbf{post}_t(Z_u)$ *and (b)* $\mathbf{post}_t(W_u) \sqsubseteq W_v$;
- *(coverage) if* $v \triangleright v'$ *for some node v', then* $W_v \sqsubseteq W_{v'}$, *and v' is not excluded;*
- *(simulation) if* $Z_v = \bot$, *then* $W_v = \bot$.

The above definitions for nodes can be extended to ASGs: an ASG is complete, ℓ-safe or well-labeled iff all its nodes are complete, ℓ-safe or well-labeled, respectively. As the conditions for well-labeledness suggest, the main challenge for the construction of a well labeled ASG is how the labeling ψ_W is computed. In Sect. 4, we propose two strategies for computing a labeling that satisfies well-labeledness. A well labeled ASG preserves reachability information, which is expressed by the following proposition.

Proposition 3. *Let G be a complete, well-labeled ASG for a timed automaton $\mathcal{A}$. Then $\mathcal{A}$ has a symbolic run $(\ell_0, Z_0) \overset{t_1}{\Rightarrow} (\ell_1, Z_1) \overset{t_2}{\Rightarrow} \ldots \overset{t_n}{\Rightarrow} (\ell_n, Z_n)$ iff G has a non-excluded node v such that $\ell_v = \ell_n$.*

Proof. The left-to right direction is a consequence of Lemma 2, and the converse is a consequence of Lemma 3. □

Lemma 2. *Let G be a complete, well-labeled ASG for a timed automaton $\mathcal{A}$. If $\mathcal{A}$ has a symbolic run $(\ell_0, Z_0) \overset{t_1}{\Rightarrow} (\ell_1, Z_1) \overset{t_2}{\Rightarrow} \ldots \overset{t_{n-1}}{\Longrightarrow} (\ell_{n-1}, Z_{n-1}) \overset{t_n}{\Rightarrow} (\ell, Z)$ then G has a non-excluded node v such that $\ell = \ell_v$ and $Z \sqsubseteq W_v$.*

Proof. We prove the statement by induction on the length n of the symbolic run. If $n = 0$, then $\ell = \ell_0$ and $Z = Z_0$, thus v_0 is a suitable witness by condition *initiation(b)*. Suppose the statement holds for runs of length at most $n - 1$. Thus there exists a non-excluded node v_{n-1} such that $\ell_{n-1} = \ell_{v_{n-1}}$ and $Z_{n-1} \sqsubseteq W_{v_{n-1}}$. As v_{n-1} is complete and not excluded, it is expanded, thus by condition *consecution(b)*, there is a successor node v_n for transition t_n such that $\ell_n = \ell_{v_n}$ and $\mathbf{post}_{t_n}(W_{n-1}) \sqsubseteq W_{v_n}$. Clearly, $Z \sqsubseteq W_n$, as $Z = \mathbf{post}_{t_n}(Z_{n-1})$ and $\mathbf{post}_t$ is monotonic for any $t \in T$. Thus if v_n is not covered then it is a suitable witness. Otherwise there exists a node $v \in V$ such that $v_n \triangleright v$. By condition *coverage*, we know that $W_{v_n} \sqsubseteq W_v$ and v is not excluded, thus it is a suitable witness. □

Lemma 3. *Let G be an ASG for a timed automaton $\mathcal{A}$. Let v be a non-excluded, well-labeled node of G such that all its ancestors are well-labeled. Then $\mathcal{A}$ has a symbolic run $(\ell_0, Z_0) \overset{t_1}{\Rightarrow} (\ell_1, Z_1) \overset{t_2}{\Rightarrow} \ldots \overset{t}{\Rightarrow} (\ell_v, Z_v)$.*

Proof. We prove the statement by induction on the depth n of v in the tree. If $n = 0$, then $v = v_0$. Thus $\ell_v = \ell_0$ and $Z_v = Z_0$ by condition *initiation(a)*, and (ℓ_0, Z_0) is a suitable run of $\mathcal{A}$. Assume that the statement holds for nodes in depth at most $n - 1$. Let u be the parent of v. As u is non-excluded, well-labeled, and all its ancestors are well-labeled, there exists a symbolic run to (ℓ_u, Z_u). By condition *consecution(a)*, we have $\mathbf{post}_t(Z_u) = Z_v$ for $t = t_{u,v}$. As v is not excluded, $Z_v \neq \bot$ by condition *simulation*, thus the run to u can be extended to a run to v by appending to it (ℓ_v, Z_v) for t. □

Remark 1. Note that for an automaton $\mathcal{A}$, the labeling ψ_W can be chosen so that the ASG is finite. A way to construct such an ASG is for example by taking $W_v = Extra^+_{LU}(Z_v)$ [3] for some bound functions L and U statically computed for ℓ_v, for all nodes v. Similarly, the termination of any reasonable algorithm for constructing a well-labeled ASG can be ensured by maintaining the additional invariant $W_v = Extra^+_{LU}(W_v)$ for all nodes v. As doing so is straightforward, termination can be considered an issue orthogonal to abstraction computation. In this paper, we focus on the latter.

3.2   Algorithm

The pseudocode of the reachability algorithm is shown in Algorithm 1. The main procedure of the algorithm is EXPLORE, which gets as input a timed automaton $\mathcal{A}$ and an error location $\ell_e \in L$. Upon termination, it either witnesses reachability by a symbolic run of $\mathcal{A}$ to ℓ_e, or proves unreachability of ℓ_e for $\mathcal{A}$ with a well-labeled, complete, ℓ_e-safe ASG.

The main data structures of the algorithm are the ASG G over set of nodes V, and sets *waiting* and *passed*, both of which store nodes from V. Informally, *waiting* stores leaves that are not yet excluded, and *passed* stores nodes that have been expanded. The algorithm consists of three subprocedures, EXPAND, COVER, and REFINE. The procedure COVER attempts to add a covering edge for a node. Procedure EXPAND creates the successors for a node. For a node v and zone W such that $Z_v \sqsubseteq W$, procedure REFINE enforces that also $W_v \sqsubseteq W$ holds. This is performed by calls to a procedure BLOCK, for which two possible algorithms based on interpolation are given in Sect. 4. The contract of BLOCK asserts that whenever zones Z_v and B are inconsistent, then after the call, the inconsistency of W_v and B is also ensured. Note that this condition is sufficient to satisfy the contract of REFINE.

Informally, the algorithm employs the following strategy. The algorithm consists of the single loop in line 10 that consumes nodes from *waiting* one by one. If *waiting* becomes empty, then $\mathcal{A}$ is deemed safe. Otherwise, a node v is removed from *waiting*. If $Z_v \sqsubseteq \bot$, then *simulation* is established by calling to REFINE. Otherwise, if the node represents an error location, then $\mathcal{A}$ is deemed unsafe. Otherwise, in order to avoid unnecessary expansion of the node, the algorithm tries to cover it. This is attempted by a call to COVER to enforce *coverage* by a candidate node v'. As the labeling of v' might be strengthened during the call as a side effect, after the call, the condition for coverage is checked. If it is satisfied, v gets covered. Otherwise, v is put back to *waiting*. If there are no suitable candidates for coverage, then the algorithm expands the node by a call to EXPAND, puts it in *passed*, and puts all its newly created successors in *waiting*.

To show correctness of EXPLORE w. r. t. the annotation specified in line 1, we will refer to the following subsets of V: let *infeasible* $= \{v \mid v$ is infeasible$\}$ and *tentative* $= \{v \mid v$ is covered$\}$.

Proposition 4. *Procedure* EXPLORE *is partially correct: if* EXPLORE$(\mathcal{A}, \ell_e)$ *terminates, then the result is* SAFE *iff* ℓ_e *is unreachable for* $\mathcal{A}$.

Proof (sketch). The main loop in line 10 maintains the following invariants:

1. $V = passed \cup waiting \cup tentative \cup infeasible$,
2. *passed* is a set of non-excluded, expanded, ℓ_e-safe, well-labeled nodes,
3. *waiting* is a set of non-excluded leaves that satisfy all conditions of well-labeledness, except maybe *simulation*,
4. *tentative* is a set of feasible, covered, ℓ_e-safe, well-labeled leaves, and
5. *infeasible* is a set of infeasible, ℓ_e-safe, well-labeled leaves.

Algorithm 1. Lazy reachability algorithm for timed automata

```
1:  ensure ρ = SAFE iff ℓₑ is unreachable for 𝒜
2:  function EXPLORE(𝒜, ℓₑ) returns ρ ∈ {SAFE, UNSAFE}
3:      let v₀ be a node such that ℓᵥ₀ = ℓ₀, Zᵥ₀ = Z₀ and Wᵥ₀ = ⊤
4:      V ← {v₀}
5:      E ← ∅
6:      ▷ ← ∅
7:      let G be an ASG for 𝒜 over V, E and ▷
8:      passed ← ∅
9:      waiting ← {v₀}
10:     while v ∈ waiting for some v do
11:         waiting ← waiting \ {v}
12:         if Zᵥ ⊑ ⊥ then
13:             REFINE(v, ⊥)
14:         else if ℓᵥ = ℓₑ then
15:             return UNSAFE
16:         else if there exists v′ ∈ passed such that ℓᵥ′ = ℓᵥ and Zᵥ ⊑ Wᵥ′ then
17:             COVER(v, v′)
18:         else
19:             EXPAND(v)
20:     return SAFE

21: require Zᵥ ⊑ Wᵥ′
22: procedure COVER(v, v′)
23:     REFINE(v, Wᵥ′)
24:     if Wᵥ ⊑ Wᵥ′ then
25:         ▷ ← ▷ ∪ {(v, v′)}
26:     else
27:         waiting ← waiting ∪ {v}

28: procedure EXPAND(v)
29:     for all t ∈ T such that t = (ℓᵥ, g, R, ℓ′) do
30:         let v′ be a new node such that ℓᵥ′ = ℓ′, Zᵥ′ = postₜ(Zᵥ) and Wᵥ′ = ⊤
31:         let (v, v′) be a new edge such that tᵥ,ᵥ′ = t
32:         V ← V ∪ {v′}
33:         E ← E ∪ {(v, v′)}
34:         waiting ← waiting ∪ {v′}
35:     passed ← passed ∪ {v}

36: require Zᵥ ⊑ W
37: ensure Wᵥ ⊑ W
38: procedure REFINE(v, W)
39:     for all B ∈ ¬W do
40:         BLOCK(v, B)

41: require Zᵥ ⊓ B ⊑ ⊥
42: ensure Wᵥ ⊓ B ⊑ ⊥
43: procedure BLOCK(v, B)
```

It is easy to verify that under the above assumptions, these sets form a partition of V. Partial correctness of the algorithm is then a direct consequence. Since at line 20 the set *waiting* is empty, so G is complete, well-labeled and ℓ_e-safe, and as a consequence of Lemma 2, the location ℓ_e is indeed unreachable for $\mathcal{A}$. Conversely, at line 15, a node is encountered that is non-excluded, well-labeled and not ℓ_e-safe, with all its ancestors well-labeled, thus by Lemma 3, there is a symbolic run of $\mathcal{A}$ to ℓ_e.

Building on the assumption that EXPAND, COVER and REFINE preserve the conditions of well-labeledness, showing that the loop invariant holds is straightforward. For EXPAND and COVER, this assumption can be easily proved. For REFINE, we need to prove that BLOCK preserves the conditions of well-labeledness. As calls to BLOCK might strengthen the labeling, care must be taken that the conditions (and in particular, *initiation(b)* and *consecution(b)*) are maintained In Sect. 4, this assumption is proved to hold.   □

Termination, hence total correctness of the algorithm in this form can not be established, however, with the additional restriction in Remark 1, termination can be guaranteed. This is because refinement progress is ensured by the algorithm. After each call to COVER, either a node v gets covered, or a node $v' \in passed$ gets strengthened. As a node v' does not get strengthened beyond $Z_{v'}$, eventually, either all leaves become covered, an error node gets discovered, or a leaf gets expanded.

4   Abstraction Refinement

To maintain well-labeledness, procedure REFINE relies on a procedure BLOCK that performs abstraction refinement by safely adjusting labels of nodes (see the reachability algorithm in Sect. 3.2). In this section, we propose two methods for abstraction refinement based on interpolation for zones.

4.1   Interpolation for Zones

Let A and B be two canonical DBMs such that $A \sqcap B \sqsubseteq \bot$. An interpolant for the pair (A, B) is a canonical DBM I such that

- $A \sqsubseteq I$,
- $I \sqcap B \sqsubseteq \bot$, and
- clocks constrained in I are constrained in both A and B.

This definition of a DBM interpolant is analogous to the definition of an interpolant in the usual sense [14]. As DBMs encode formulas in $\mathcal{DL}(\mathbb{Q})$, a theory that admits interpolation [7], an interpolant always exists for a pair of inconsistent DBMs. Algorithm 2 is a direct adaptation of the graph-based algorithm of [7] for DBMs. For simplicity, we assume that A and B are defined over the same set of clocks with the same ordering, and are both canonical. Naturally, these restrictions can be lifted. For a more general description, see [17].

Algorithm 2. Interpolation for zones represented as canonical DBMs

---

1: **require** $A \sqcap B \sqsubseteq \bot$
2: **ensure** $A \sqsubseteq I$
3: **ensure** $I \sqcap B \sqsubseteq \bot$
4: **function** INTERPOLATE(A, B) **returns** I
5:     **if** $A \sqsubseteq \bot$ **then**
6:         **return** $\bot$
7:     **else if** $B \sqsubseteq \bot$ **then**
8:         **return** $\top$
9:     **else**
10:         **let** $D = \min(A, B)$
11:         **let** $C = \{(i_1, i_2), \ldots, (i_{k-1}, i_k), (i_k, i_1)\}$ be a negative cycle in D
12:         **let** $C_A = \{(i, j) \in C \mid A_{ij} = D_{ij}\}$

13:         **let** $I_{ij} = \begin{cases} (0, \leq) & \text{if } i = j \\ A_{ij} & \text{if } (i, j) \in C_A \\ \infty & \text{otherwise} \end{cases}$

14:         **let** $I = [I_{ij}]_{ij}$
15:         **return** I

After checking the trivial cases, the algorithm searches for a negative cycle in $\min(A, B)$ to witness its inconsistency. This can be done e.g. by running a variant of the Floyd-Warshall algorithm. As $A \sqcap B$ is inconsistent, such a cycle C exists by Proposition 2. Then the set C_A of edges that come from A is constructed. We can assume that no two such edges are subsequent, as A is canonical. Thus the DBM I induced by the corresponding constraints of A is clearly canonical. Moreover, it is easy to verify that I is indeed an interpolant.

4.2 Interpolation Strategies for Abstraction Refinement

We propose two methods for abstraction refinement based on zone interpolation. Both methods are based on pre- and post-image computation, and can be considered as a generalization of zone interpolation to sequences of transitions of a timed automaton.

Conceptually, both methods for BLOCK work as follows. Given a node v and a zone B for which $Z_v \sqcap B \sqsubseteq \bot$ holds, a zone inconsistent with B is computed in form of an interpolant that is used to strengthen the current labeling. Meanwhile, conditions for well-labeledness are maintained. The condition of *coverage* is maintained by procedure STRENGTHEN that removes covering edges that would violate the condition after strengthening. However, the two methods differ in the strategy to ensure conditions *initiation(b)* and *consecution(b)*.

Algorithm 3 depicts the pseudocode for the two methods. We will refer to procedure BLOCK$_{SEQ}$ as the sequence (SEQ) strategy, and to procedure BLOCK$_{BIN}$ as the binary (BIN) strategy. The main difference is that BIN only applies backward propagation for refinement, whereas SEQ also uses forward propagation.

Algorithm 3. Interpolation strategies for abstraction refinement

1: **require** $Z_v \sqsubseteq I$
2: **ensure** $W_v \sqsubseteq I$
3: **procedure** STRENGTHEN(v, I)
4:     **for all** u such that $u \triangleright v$ and $W_u \not\sqsubseteq I$ **do**
5:         $\triangleright \leftarrow \triangleright \setminus (u, v)$
6:         *waiting* $\leftarrow$ *waiting* $\cup \{u\}$
7:     $W_v \leftarrow W_v \sqcap I$

8: **require** $Z_v \sqcap B \sqsubseteq \bot$
9: **ensure** $W_v \sqsubseteq I$ 25: **require** $Z_v \sqcap B \sqsubseteq \bot$
10: **ensure** $W_v \sqcap B \sqsubseteq \bot$ 26: **ensure** $W_v \sqcap B \sqsubseteq \bot$
11: **function** BLOCK$_{\text{SEQ}}(v, B)$ **returns** I 27: **procedure** BLOCK$_{\text{BIN}}(v, B)$
12:     **if** $W_v \sqcap B \sqsubseteq \bot$ **then**   28:   **if** $W_v \sqcap B \sqsubseteq \bot$ **then**
13:         **return** W_v 29:   **return**
14:     **else**   30:   **else**
15:         **if** $(u, v) \in E$ for some u **then**   31:   **let** $A = Z_v$
16:             **let** $t = t_{u,v}$ 32:   **let** $I = $ INTERPOLATE(A, B)
17:             **let** $B' = \mathbf{pre}_t(B)$ 33:   **if** $(u, v) \in E$ for some u **then**
18:             **let** $A' = $ BLOCK$_{\text{SEQ}}(u, B')$ 34:   **let** $t = t_{u,v}$
19:             **let** $A = \mathbf{post}_t(A')$ 35:   **for all** $B'' \in \neg I$ **do**
20:         **else**   36:   **let** $B' = \mathbf{pre}_t(B'')$
21:             **let** $A = Z_v$ 37:   BLOCK$_{\text{BIN}}(u, B')$
22:         **let** $I = $ INTERPOLATE(A, B) 38:   STRENGTHEN(v, I)
23:         STRENGTHEN(v, I)
24:         **return** I

We show that both procedures are correct w. r. t. the annotations in Algorithm 3 and maintain well-labeledness.

Proposition 5. *Both variants of* BLOCK *are totally correct: if* $Z_v \sqcap B \sqsubseteq \bot$, *then* BLOCK$(v, B)$ *terminates and ensures* $W_v \sqcap B \sqsubseteq \bot$. *Moreover, they maintain well-labeledness.*

Proof. Termination of both methods is trivial, so we focus on partial correctness and the preservation of well-labeledness.

For BLOCK$_{\text{BIN}}$, if $W_v \sqcap B \sqsubseteq \bot$, then no strengthening is needed. If v is a root, it is easy to see that *initiation(b)* is maintained, and the postcondition trivially holds. Otherwise, after the loop, $W_u \sqcap \mathbf{pre}_t(B'') \sqsubseteq \bot$ for all $B'' \in \neg I$ by contract. Thus $\mathbf{post}_t(W_u) \sqcap B'' \sqsubseteq \bot$ for all $B'' \in \neg I$ by Lemma 1. Hence $\mathbf{post}_t(W_u) \sqsubseteq I$, so *consecution(b)* is maintained for v after strengthening. Moreover, $I \sqcap B \sqsubseteq \bot$, thus B is successfully blocked.

For BLOCK$_{\text{SEQ}}$, if $W_v \sqcap B \sqsubseteq \bot$, then no strengthening is needed. If v is a root, it is easy to see that *initiation(b)* is maintained, and the postconditions trivially hold. Otherwise A' is such that $A' \sqcap \mathbf{pre}_t(B) \sqsubseteq \bot$ by contract, thus $A \sqcap B \sqsubseteq \bot$ by Lemma 1. Thus the interpolant I can be computed, and $\mathbf{post}_t(A') \sqsubseteq I$.

Moreover, $W_u \sqsubseteq A'$ by contract, thus $\textbf{post}_t(W_u) \sqsubseteq \textbf{post}_t(A')$ by monotony of $\textbf{post}$. Hence $\textbf{post}_t(W_u) \sqsubseteq I$, so *consecution(b)* is maintained for v after strengthening. Moreover, $I \sqcap B \sqsubseteq \bot$, thus B is successfully blocked.   □

5   Evaluation

We implemented a prototype version of Algorithm 1 in Java as an instantiation of the open source model checking framework THETA[1]. The only optimization we applied in the implementation compared to the presented algorithm is how coverage is handled: in the implementation, REFINE is only called if no covering node is present. Moreover, we implemented the two interpolation-based refinement strategies described in Algorithm 3.

For comparison, we also implemented a version of the lazy refinement algorithm of [11] based on LU-bounds ($\textbf{a}_{\preccurlyeq LU}$, disabled). The main difference in our implementation compared to [11] is that bounds are propagated from all guards on an infeasible path, and not just from ones that contribute to the infeasibility. Because of this, refinement in the resulting algorithm is extremely cheap, but as the comparison of our data with that of [11] suggests, for the examined models, the algorithm is still at least as space- and time-efficient as the original one. In some aspects, this refinement strategy is the opposite of interpolation based refinement: it provides a very cheap, non-convex, specialized refinement algorithm, as opposed to a relatively costly, convex, more general strategy. Apart from the abstraction and refinement strategy used ($\textbf{a}_{\preccurlyeq LU}$, BIN or SEQ), the three implementations of Algorithm 1 are identical.

Table 1 reports the results of our experiments. It contains the execution time (in seconds) and the final sizes of sets V and *passed*. The execution time is the average of 10 runs, obtained from 12 runs by removing the slowest and the fastest one. The input models are based on the PAT benchmarks[2]. For each model, the more efficient of BFS and DFS was applied as search order, which is BFS for all models except FDDI. We performed the measurements on a machine running Windows 10 with a 2.6 GHz dual core CPU and 8 GB of RAM.

For CSMA, FDDI, Fischer and Lynch, the three algorithms generated and expanded the same number of nodes. For FDDI, Fischer and Lynch, all three algorithms are optimal in this sense: the number of expanded nodes equals the number of distinct discrete states (plus one for FDDI), that is, clock variables do not influence the size of the ASG.

With respect to execution time, Fischer and Lynch provide the worst cases for our algorithm. The reason for the higher execution time despite the same number of generated nodes is that for these two models, the more costly refinement was not counterweighed by the smaller number of refinements performed, as opposed to CSMA, where the interpolation-based algorithms performed (as our logs showed) significantly less refinement steps. For FDDI, the three algorithms performed the same small number of refinement steps each, which explains the

---

[1] http://theta.inf.mit.bme.hu.
[2] http://www.comp.nus.edu.sg/~pat/bddlib/timedexp.html.

Table 1. Comparison of lazy reachability algorithms

Model	$\mathbf{a}_{\preccurlyeq LU}$			BIN			SEQ		
	Time	Nodes	Passed	Time	Nodes	Passed	Time	Nodes	Passed
Critical 3	1.8	23428	4923	1.6	14377	3213	1.6	14075	3157
Critical 4	65.0	838213	130779	78.2	536733	83686	75.2	499245	78252
CSMA 9	6.6	99207	30476	7.3	99207	30476	7.9	99207	30476
CSMA 10	21.3	251749	78605	21.0	251749	78605	22.8	251749	78605
CSMA 11	61.4	625215	198670	58.9	625215	198670	63.8	625215	198670
CSMA 12	167.2	1525525	493583	168.7	1525525	493583	179.1	1525525	493583
FDDI 50	1.4	504	402	2.0	504	402	2.0	504	402
FDDI 70	2.9	704	562	3.5	704	562	3.7	704	562
FDDI 90	5.9	904	722	6.8	904	722	7.1	904	722
FDDI 120	12.9	1204	962	15.0	1204	962	15.4	1204	962
Fischer 7	1.9	31060	7737	2.8	31060	7737	2.8	31060	7737
Fischer 8	5.1	111825	25080	7.7	111825	25080	8.7	111825	25080
Fischer 9	21.3	395956	81035	29.0	395956	81035	32.4	395956	81035
Fischer 10	94.4	1382921	260998	133.2	1382921	260998	149.7	1382921	260998
Lynch 7	2.6	51570	9977	3.6	51570	9977	4.0	51570	9977
Lynch 8	7.7	179273	30200	12.2	179273	30200	13.9	179273	30200
Lynch 9	32.8	620236	92555	45.2	620236	92555	54.2	620236	92555

slight relative overhead of the interpolation-based algorithms. However, the three algorithms scale in the same way.

A favorable case for our algorithm with respect to ASG size is provided by the model Critical. For this model, the interpolation-based algorithms were able to generate a 40% smaller ASG as $\mathbf{a}_{\preccurlyeq LU}$, with a 15–20% relative overhead in execution time. Among the two interpolation strategies, SEQ was somewhat more efficient in both aspects.

We also evaluated the three methods under random search order. We used FDDI as an input model, as this model is known to be sensitive to search order: with the right abstraction and search order, it scales linearly in the number of processes (as in Table 1), otherwise, it scales exponentially. The results of our experiment are shown on the boxplot in Fig. 1, which depicts the ASG sizes for 50 random runs of each algorithm. As the boxplot suggests, the interpolation-based refinement methods, and SEQ in particular, are less sensitive to search order with respect to the size of the generated tree, and are better at recovering from bad decisions during search.

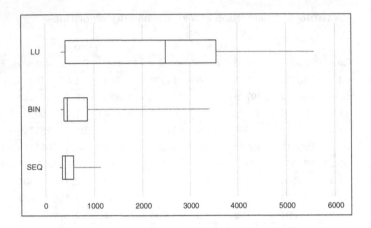

Fig. 1. ASG size for random search of FDDI 10

6   Conclusions

In this paper, we proposed a lazy reachability checking algorithm for timed automata based on interpolation for zones. Moreover, we proposed two refinement strategies, both a combination of forward search, backward search and interpolation. We demonstrated with experiments that - even without the use of extrapolation - the method is competitive with sophisticated non-convex abstractions in both execution time and memory consumption.

Future Work. As the method we proposed computes abstractions in terms of zones, it is straightforward to combine it with existing zone-based abstractions for timed automata. In particular, we believe that a combination with $a_{\preccurlyeq LU}$, disabled would potentially yield a more efficient method with no considerable overhead, as backward propagation of LU-bounds is much cheaper than the propagation of interpolants. In this setting, interpolation can be considered as a further reduction on top of $a_{\preccurlyeq LU}$ abstraction.

An interesting application of our approach would be to apply it to more expressive variants of timed automata, e.g. to automata with diagonal constraints in guards [6], or to updatable timed automata [5] with updates of the form $x_i := c$, $x_i := x_i + c$ (shift), $x_i := x_j$ (copy) or, more generally, even $x_i := x_j + c$. As all these operations yield zones both for forward and backward computation, with a generalization of **pre** and **post**, the approach becomes directly applicable. Naturally, due to general undecidability and the lack of a suitable extrapolation operator, termination can not be guaranteed in some of these cases [5].

We note that by switching the role of **pre** and **post** in the algorithm, a variant can be obtained that performs backward exploration in a lazy manner. Such an algorithm might result in an interesting method for simple timed automata with a restricted use of integer operations.

There are also many possibilities for fine-tuning the proposed algorithm. For example, the algorithm as described applies an aggressive covering strategy, as it tries all possible nodes for coverage before expanding a node. The investigation of more sophisticated covering strategies (e.g. forced covering as in [15]) might yield better scaling with respect to execution time. Moreover, our current implementation is based on DBMs. The adaptation of the method to e.g. minimal constraint systems is straightforward, and is possibly more efficient.

References

1. Alur, R., Dill, D.L.: A theory of timed automata. Theor. Comput. Sci. **126**(2), 183–235 (1994). doi:10.1016/0304-3975(94)90010-8
2. Behrmann, G., Bouyer, P., Fleury, E., Larsen, K.G.: Static guard analysis in timed automata verification. In: Garavel, H., Hatcliff, J. (eds.) TACAS 2003. LNCS, vol. 2619, pp. 254–270. Springer, Heidelberg (2003). doi:10.1007/3-540-36577-X_18
3. Behrmann, G., Bouyer, P., Larsen, K.G., Pelánek, R.: Lower and upper bounds in zone based abstractions of timed automata. In: Jensen, K., Podelski, A. (eds.) TACAS 2004. LNCS, vol. 2988, pp. 312–326. Springer, Heidelberg (2004). doi:10.1007/978-3-540-24730-2_25
4. Bengtsson, J., Yi, W.: Timed automata: semantics, algorithms and tools. In: Desel, J., Reisig, W., Rozenberg, G. (eds.) ACPN 2003. LNCS, vol. 3098, pp. 87–124. Springer, Heidelberg (2004). doi:10.1007/978-3-540-27755-2_3
5. Bouyer, P.: Forward analysis of updatable timed automata. Formal Methods Syst. Des. **24**(3), 281–320 (2004). doi:10.1023/B:FORM.0000026093.21513.31
6. Bouyer, P., Laroussinie, F., Reynier, P.-A.: Diagonal constraints in timed automata: forward analysis of timed systems. In: Pettersson, P., Yi, W. (eds.) FORMATS 2005. LNCS, vol. 3829, pp. 112–126. Springer, Heidelberg (2005). doi:10.1007/11603009_10
7. Cimatti, A., Griggio, A., Sebastiani, R.: Efficient interpolant generation in satisfiability modulo theories. In: Ramakrishnan, C.R., Rehof, J. (eds.) TACAS 2008. LNCS, vol. 4963, pp. 397–412. Springer, Heidelberg (2008). doi:10.1007/978-3-540-78800-3_30
8. Clarke, E., Grumberg, O., Jha, S., Lu, Y., Veith, H.: Counterexample-guided abstraction refinement for symbolic model checking. J. ACM **50**(5), 752–794 (2003). doi:10.1145/876638.876643
9. Daws, C., Tripakis, S.: Model checking of real-time reachability properties using abstractions. In: Steffen, B. (ed.) TACAS 1998. LNCS, vol. 1384, pp. 313–329. Springer, Heidelberg (1998). doi:10.1007/BFb0054180
10. Henzinger, T.A., Jhala, R., Majumdar, R., Sutre, G.: Lazy abstraction. In: POPL 2012, pp. 58–70. ACM (2002). doi:10.1145/503272.503279
11. Herbreteau, F., Srivathsan, B., Walukiewicz, I.: Lazy abstractions for timed automata. In: Sharygina, N., Veith, H. (eds.) CAV 2013. LNCS, vol. 8044, pp. 990–1005. Springer, Heidelberg (2013). doi:10.1007/978-3-042-39799-8_71
12. Herbreteau, F., Kini, D., Srivathsan, B., Walukiewicz, I.: Using non-convex approximations for efficient analysis of timed automata. In: FSTTCS 2011. LIPIcs, vol. 13, pp. 78–89 (2011). doi:10.4230/LIPIcs.FSTTCS.2011.78
13. Herbreteau, F., Srivathsan, B., Walukiewicz, I.: Better abstractions for timed automata. In: LICS 2012, pp. 375–384. IEEE (2012). doi:10.1109/LICS.2012.48

14. McMillan, K.L.: Interpolation and SAT-based model checking. In: Hunt, W.A., Somenzi, F. (eds.) CAV 2003. LNCS, vol. 2725, pp. 1–13. Springer, Heidelberg (2003). doi:10.1007/978-3-540-45069-6_1
15. McMillan, K.L.: Lazy abstraction with interpolants. In: Ball, T., Jones, R.B. (eds.) CAV 2006. LNCS, vol. 4144, pp. 123–136. Springer, Heidelberg (2006). doi:10.1007/11817963_14
16. McMillan, K.L.: Lazy annotation for program testing and verification. In: Touili, T., Cook, B., Jackson, P. (eds.) CAV 2010. LNCS, vol. 6174, pp. 104–118. Springer, Heidelberg (2010). doi:10.1007/978-3-642-14295-6_10
17. Tóth, T., Majzik, I.: Timed automata verification using interpolants. In: Proceedings of the 24th PhD Mini-Symposium, pp. 82–85. BUTE DMIS (2017). doi:10.5281/zenodo.291907
18. Wang, W., Jiao, L.: Difference bound constraint abstraction for timed automata reachability checking. In: Graf, S., Viswanathan, M. (eds.) FORTE 2015. LNCS, vol. 9039, pp. 146–160. Springer, Cham (2015). doi:10.1007/978-3-319-19195-9_10

Safe Over- and Under-Approximation of Reachable Sets for Delay Differential Equations

Bai Xue[1]([⊠]), Peter Nazier Mosaad[1], Martin Fränzle[1], Mingshuai Chen[2,3],
Yangjia Li[2], and Naijun Zhan[2,3]

[1] Department of Computing Science, C. v. Ossietzky Universität Oldenburg,
Oldenburg, Germany
{bai.xue,peter.nazier.mosaad,fraenzle}@informatik.uni-oldenburg.de
[2] State Key Laboratory of Computer Science,
Institute of Software, CAS, Beijing, China
{chenms,yangjia,znj}@ios.ac.cn
[3] University of Chinese Academy of Sciences, Beijing, China

Abstract. Delays in feedback control loop, as induced by networked
distributed control schemes, may have detrimental effects on control
performance. This induces an interest in safety verification of delay differential equations (DDEs) used as a model of embedded control. This
article explores reachable-set computation for a class of DDEs featuring
a local homeomorphism property. This topological property facilitates
construction of over- and under-approximations of their full reachable
sets by performing reachability analysis on the boundaries of their initial sets, thereby permitting an efficient lifting of reach-set computation methods for ODEs to DDEs. Membership in this class of DDEs is
determined by conducting sensitivity analysis of the solution mapping
with respect to the initial states to impose a bound constraint on the
time-lag term. We then generalize boundary-based reachability analysis
to such DDEs. Our reachability algorithm is iterative along the time
axis and the computations in each iteration are performed in two steps.
The first step computes an enclosure of the set of states reachable from
the boundary of the step's initial state set. The second step derives an
over- and under-approximations of the full reachable set by including
(excluding, resp.) the obtained boundary enclosure from certain convex
combinations of points in that boundary enclosure. Experiments on two
illustrative examples demonstrate the efficacy of our algorithm.

1 Introduction

The rapidly increasing deployment of cyber-physical systems into diverse safety-
critical application domains ranging from, among others transportation systems
over chemical processes to health-care renders safety analysis and verification for
these systems societally important. Formally, the safety verification problem can
often be reduced to a problem of deciding whether the system of interest may in

© Springer International Publishing AG 2017
A. Abate and G. Geeraerts (Eds.): FORMATS 2017, LNCS 10419, pp. 281–299, 2017.
DOI: 10.1007/978-3-319-65765-3_16

its evolution touch a specified set of unsafe states [22,24,29]. Reachability analysis, which involves computing appropriate approximations of the reachable state sets, plays a fundamental role in addressing such safety verification challenges. It usually employs either over-approximations (i.e., super-sets of the actual reach set) to determine whether a system starting from legal initial states satisfies some specified safety properties, or under-approximations (i.e., sub-sets [12]) to detect falsification of safety properties by finding counterexamples[1]. The use of such approximations instead of exact reach sets is justified by the fact that the exact sets are generally not computable.

Ordinary differential equations (ODEs) are traditionally used for describing system dynamics within continuous or hybrid-state feedback control loops. Consequently, significant research has been invested in reachability analysis of such dynamical systems. For the problem of computing over-approximations, significant advances have continuously been reported in the literature over the last decades (e.g., [6,9,11,18–21,25]). For computing under-approximation, methods have initially focused on linear systems (e.g., [14,17]), but recently, approaches have been proposed to also tackle nonlinear systems (e.g., [8,12,15,28,30]).

ODEs are, however, an idealized model of the feedback dynamics in control systems. Simply conjoining the ODEs describing the plant dynamics with the ODEs describing control laws may be misleading, as any delay introduced into the feedback loop may induce significantly deviating dynamics. In practice, delays are involved in sensing or actuating by physical devices, in data forwarding to or from the controller, in signal processing in the controller, etc. An appropriate generalization of ODE able to model the delay within the framework of differential equations is delay differential equations (DDEs), as originally suggested by Bellman and Cooke for modeling physical, biological, and chemical processes involving delayed dynamics [4].

DDEs are a class of differential equations where the time derivatives at the current time depend on the solution and possibly its derivatives at previous times as well. The presence of delayed dynamics may invalidate any stability and safety certificate obtained on the related delay-free model, as delays may significantly alter the overall shape of the system dynamics. This situation is illustrated through the following simple example from [16] where arbitrarily small delays have significant effect on state dynamics: the solution of the ODE

$$\dot{x}(t) + 2\dot{x}(t) = -x(t) \qquad (1)$$

is asymptotically stable, converging to the equilibrium point $x = 0$ from any initial state. However, the solution of its corresponding DDE

$$\dot{x}(t) + 2\dot{x}(t - \tau) = -x(t) \qquad (2)$$

is unstable for any positive delay τ. Therefore, taking time-delay terms into account to either verify or falsify properties of systems by performing reachability

---

[1] If the under-approximation intersects a given unsafe set, there is definitely at least one of the trajectories entering the unsafe set, i.e., the system is definitely unsafe.

analysis is not just desirable, but ought to be imperative for systems that are more accurately modelled by DDEs, especially in safety-critical applications.

The problem of computing over- and/or under-approximations for the reachable sets of DDEs obviously is more challenging than for the proper sub-class of ODEs. Recently, a set-boundary based reachability analysis method being capable of generating over- and under-approximations of reach sets of ODEs was proposed in [29,30] making use of the homeomorphism property of the ODE's solution mapping. A homeomorphism is a bijection ψ from a topological space X to a topological space Y with the property that the pre-image $\psi^{-1}(P)$ is an open subset in X if and only if P is an open subset in Y. An important property induced by a homeomorphism from X to Y is that the homeomorphism maps the boundary and interior points of Q onto the boundary and interior points of $\psi(Q)$, respectively. In this vein, the solution mapping to initial value problems (IVP) featuring unique solutions is a homeomorphism between the space of initial values and that of values reached by the solution trajectory at any given time $t \geq 0$. Based on the observation that the DDE will converge to an ODE when the time-lag term tends to zero, this motivates us to explore a class of DDEs with solutions featuring a similar homeomorphism property and to generalize the aforementioned set-boundary based reachability analysis method accordingly.

Membership of a given DDE in the class of DDEs exhibiting the necessary homeomorphism property is determined by conducting a sensitivity analysis on the solution mapping. This sensitivity analysis imposes a bound on the time-lag term as the properties of the solution change when time-lag exceeds certain bounds like the stability border. In an engineering process, this upper bound on time-lag can be considered as an automatically derived design space constraint, asking the development engineers for selection of appropriate components (sensors, processors, actuators, communication networks) guaranteeing sufficiently low latency in the feedback loop.

The main contributions of this paper is the generalization of the set-boundary reachability analysis based method for ODEs to DDEs exposing the necessary homeomorphism property, as detected by the sensitivity analysis. The reachability algorithm is iterative along the time axis and the computations in each iteration are performed in two steps. First step computes an enclosure of the set of states reachable from the boundary of the step's initial state set. Second step derives an over- and under-approximations of the full reachable set by including (excluding, resp.) the obtained boundary enclosure from certain convex combinations of points in this boundary enclosure. We demonstrate the efficacy of our algorithm on two illustrative examples.

Related Work

As mentioned above, the reachability analysis to dynamic systems modeled by delay differential equations (DDEs), especially for computing under-approximations, is in its infancy and thus provides an open area of research.

Zou et al. proposed in [31] a safe enclosure method using interval-based Taylor over-approximation to enclose a set of functions by a parametric Taylor series with parameters in interval form. To avoid dimension explosion incurred by the ever-growing degree of the Taylor-series along the time axis, the method depends on fixing the degree for the Taylor series and moving higher-degree terms into the parametric uncertainty permitted by the interval form of the Taylor coefficients, thereby being able to provide analysis of time-unbounded solutions to DDE. In [23], Prajna et al. extended the barrier certificate methodology for ODEs to the polynomial time-delay differential equations setting, in which the safety verification problem is formulated as a problem of solving sum-of-square programs. The work in [13] presents a technique for simulation-based time-bounded invariant verification of nonlinear networked dynamical systems with delayed interconnections by computing bounds on the sensitivity of trajectories (or solutions) to changes in initial states and inputs of the system. A similar simulation method integrating error analysis of the numeric solving and the sensitivity-related state bloating algorithms was proposed in [7] to obtain safe enclosures of time-bounded reach sets for systems modelled by DDEs. In the aforementioned work, however, the authors focused on over-approximating reachable sets for systems modeled by DDEs with finite or infinite time horizon, not touching on the problem of under-approximation methods of reachable sets for DDEs as needed, e.g., in system falsification.

In this paper, we infer a class of DDEs with solution mappings featuring an appropriate homeomorphism property with respect to initial states, where membership in the class can be determined by sensitivity analysis. For such a DDE, the boundary of the reachable set is maintained under dynamic evolution, thereby enabling us to construct over- and under-approximations of reachable sets by extending the set-boundary based reachability analysis method for ODEs from [29, 30].

Outline. We formulate the reachability problem of interest and give a brief introduction into nonlinear control systems in Sect. 2. In Sect. 3, we expose a class of delay differential equations featuring a desirable homeomorphism property for its solutions and present our boundary-based reachability analysis algorithm for computing over- and under-approximations of reachable sets respectively. Then we illustrate our approach on two examples as well as discuss its impact in Sect. 4. Finally, we conclude our paper in Sect. 5.

2   Preliminaries

In this section, we formally define the dynamical systems of interest and recall the basic notion of reachability used throughout this paper. The following conventions will be used in the remainder of this paper: the space of continuously differentiable functions on $\mathcal{X}$ is denoted by $\mathcal{C}^1(\mathcal{X})$; for a set Δ, the decorations Δ°, Δ^c and $\partial\Delta$ represent its interior, complement, and boundary respectively; vectors in the $\mathbb{R}^n$ as well as of functions are denoted by boldface letters. The set of $n \times n$ matrices over the field $\mathbb{R}$ of real numbers is denoted by $\mathbb{R}^{n \times n}$.

In this paper we consider systems that can be modelled by delay differential equations (DDEs) of the form

$$\dot{x} = \begin{cases} g(x), & \text{if } t \in [0,\tau), x(0) \in \mathcal{I}_0 \\ f(x, x_\tau), \text{if } t \in [\tau, K\tau], \end{cases} \tag{3}$$

where $x(t) = (x_1(t), x_2(t), \ldots, x_n(t))' \in \mathcal{X}$, $x_\tau = (x_1(t-\tau), x_2(t-\tau), \ldots, x_n(t-\tau))' \in \mathcal{X}$, $\mathcal{X} \subseteq \mathbb{R}^n$, $K \geq 2$ is a positive integer, $g : \mathcal{X} \mapsto \mathbb{R}^n$ describes the process which the initial function is determined by the initial value $x(0) \in \mathcal{I}_0$, and $\mathcal{I}_0 \subset \mathbb{R}^n$ is a simply connected compact set and $f : \mathcal{X} \times \mathcal{X} \mapsto \mathbb{R}^n$ is globally Lipschitz continuous over the variables $x(t)$ and $x(t - \tau)$. Also, we require that $g(x) \in \mathcal{C}^1(\mathcal{X})$ and $g : \mathcal{X} \mapsto \mathbb{R}^n$ satisfies the Lipschitz continuity condition w.r.t. the variables $x(t)$, guaranteeing that $\dot{x} = g(x)$ with initial value $x(0) = x_0 \in \mathcal{I}_0$ has a unique solution on $[0, \tau]$. Therefore, Eq. (3) describes a deterministic process on $[0, K\tau]$. Besides, we assume that max norms $\|\frac{\partial f(x,y)}{\partial x}\|_{max}$ and $\|\frac{\partial f(x,y)}{\partial y}\|_{max}$ of the matrices $\|\frac{\partial f(x,y)}{\partial x}\|$ and $\|\frac{\partial f(x,y)}{\partial y}\|$ are uniformly bounded for any combination of $x \in \mathcal{X}$ and $y \in \mathcal{X}$, i.e.,

$$\frac{\partial f(x,y)}{\partial x}\|_{max} \leq M, \|\frac{\partial f(x,y)}{\partial y}\|_{max} \leq N, \tag{4}$$

where M and N are positive real numbers.

Given System (3) with an initial set $\mathcal{I}_0$, and a finite time duration t, where $0 \leq t \leq K\tau$ and $K \geq 2$ is a positive integer, the set of allowable initial functions selected by $g(x)$ is just a set of solutions of the ordinary differential equation (ODE) $\dot{x} = g(x)$ initialised in $\mathcal{I}_0$ w.r.t. the time interval $[0, \tau]$. The trajectory of System (3) is defined to be $\phi(t; x_0) = x(t)$, where $x(t)$ is the solution of System (3) that satisfies the initial condition $x(0) = x_0$ at time instant $t = 0$. In addition, we define the reachable set of a given initial set $\mathcal{I}_0$ for any time $t \geq 0$ and its corresponding over- and under-approximations as follows.

Definition 1. *The reachable set $\Omega(t; \mathcal{I}_0)$ at time $t \geq 0$ is a set of states visited by trajectories originating from $\mathcal{I}_0$ at time $t = 0$ after time duration t, i.e.*

$$\Omega(t; \mathcal{I}_0) = \{x : x = \phi(t; x_0), x_0 \in \mathcal{I}_0\}.$$

Definition 2. *An over-approximation of the reachable set $\Omega(t; \mathcal{I}_0)$ is a set $O(t; \mathcal{I}_0)$, where $\Omega(t; \mathcal{I}_0) \subseteq O(t; \mathcal{I}_0)$. In contrast, an under-approximation $U(t; \mathcal{I}_0)$ of the reachable set is a nonempty subset of the reachable set $\Omega(t; \mathcal{I}_0)$.*

Notice that from Definition 2, the over-approximation $O(t; \mathcal{I}_0)$ is an enclosure s.t. $\forall x_0 \in \mathcal{I}_0 : \phi(t; x_0) \in O(t; \mathcal{I}_0)$ holds, where $0 \leq t \leq K\tau$. On the other hand, the under-approximation $U(t; \mathcal{I}_0)$ is a nonempty set s.t. $\forall x(t) \in U(t; \mathcal{I}_0) : \exists x_0 \in \mathcal{I}_0 : x(t) = \phi(t; x_0)$.

Aiming at computing over- as well as under-approximations, we wish to extend the set-boundary based reachability method for ODEs from [30] to DDEs. This method relies on the fact that the solution mapping is a homeomorphism and thus preserves set boundaries, permitting to retrieve safe over- and under-approximations from enclosures of the dynamic images of the boundaries of the initial set. The solution mappings of DDEs in the form of Eq. (3), however, need not be homeomorphisms. Hence, we devote ourselves to exposing a class of systems of the form (3) with solution mappings having that desirable property. We study, in this paper, the following problems:

Problem 1. Which class of systems characterized by Eq. (3) has solution mappings forming a homeomorphism?

Problem 2. How can we efficiently compute over- and under-approximations of the reachable set for the systems described in **Problem 1** if the initial set $\mathcal{I}_0$ is a simply connected compact set?

2.1 Nonlinear Control Systems

Nonlinear control systems are characterized by the presence of nonlinear elements in the right-hand side of the characterizing differential equation. Such non-linearities may stem from both the system under control (i.e., the plant) and the controller itself. Ordinary differential equations (ODEs) are traditionally used to model the continuous behaviour of such systems. In general, the nonlinear control systems that are modeled by ODEs with a control input are of the following form

$$\dot{x}(t) = h(x(t), u(t)), \tag{5}$$

where $x(0) \in \mathcal{X}_0 \subseteq \mathbb{R}^n$, $u(t) \in U \subseteq \mathbb{R}^m$, and $\mathcal{X}_0$, U are both compact sets. The Eq. (5) is required to be (globally) Lipschitz-continuous and the input trajectory $u(\cdot) : \mathbb{R}^+ \mapsto U$ is required to be piecewise continuous so that a solution is guaranteed to exist globally in the sense for all $t \geq 0$. For convenience, we denote the space of piecewise continuous functions from $\mathbb{R}^+$ to U as $\mathcal{P}$.

Let us denote the solution to System (5) for a given initial state and an input trajectory by $\chi(t; x_0, u(\cdot))$, where $t \geq 0$, $x(0) = x_0 \in \mathcal{X}_0$ and $u(\cdot) \in U$ is the input trajectory within the time interval $[0, t]$. The reachable set at time $t = r$ can be defined for a set of initial states $\mathcal{X}_0$ and a set of input values U as

$$\mathcal{R}(r) = \{\chi(r; x_0, u) \in \mathbb{R}^n | x_0 \in \mathcal{X}_0, u \in \mathcal{P}\}.$$

Althoff's approaches [1,3] are among the many methods for computation of over-approximations of the reachable set $\mathcal{R}(r)$. Such methods can also be applied to over-approximating the reachable set for cases involving DDEs of the form (3) by regarding the delay term x_τ as the time-varying uncertainty u (cf. [13] for such an algorithm).

3   Reachable Sets Computation

This section mainly focuses on solving **Problem 1** and **Problem 2** as presented in Sect. 2. Firstly, we address **Problem 1** by conducting sensitivity analysis on the solution mappings $\phi(t; \cdot)$ w.r.t. the initial states for DDEs of the form of Eq. (3). This facilitates imposition of a bound constraint on the time-lag term such that the homeomorphism property is guaranteed. Then, addressing **Problem 2**, we generalize the set-boundary based method for reachability analysis of [29,30] to the computation of safe approximations of reach sets for systems of the form (3). This way, we can construct over- and under-approximations of their reachable sets.

3.1 Sensitivity Analysis Theory

For a system governed by the ODE

$$\dot{x} = g(x),$$

where $t \in [0, \tau]$, its flow mapping $\phi(t; x_0)$ as a function of x_0 is differentiable w.r.t. the initial state x_0, if $g \in C^1(\mathcal{X})$ and g is Lipschitz continuous. The sensitivity of solutions at time $t \in [0, \tau]$ to initial conditions is defined by

$$s_{x_0}(t) = \frac{\partial \phi(t; x_0)}{\partial x_0}, \tag{6}$$

where $s_{x_0}(t)$ is a square matrix of order n. The $(i, j)_{th}$ element of s_{x_0} basically represents the influence of variations in the i_{th} coordinate $x_{0,i}$ of x_0 on the j_{th} coordinate $x_j(t)$ of $\phi(t; x_0)$. To compute the sensitivity matrix, we first apply the chain rule to get the derivative of s_{x_0} w.r.t. time [10], as follows:

$$\frac{d}{dt} \frac{\partial \phi(t; x_0)}{\partial x_0} = D_g(\phi(t; x_0)) \frac{\partial \phi(t; x_0)}{\partial x_0},$$

which yields the ODE

$$\dot{s}_{x_0} = D_g s_{x_0}$$

describing evolution of sensitivity over time, where D_g is the Jacobian matrix of vector field g along the trajectory $\phi(t; x_0)$. This equation is a linear time-varying ODE and the relevant initial value $s_{x_0}(0)$ is the identity matrix $I \in \mathbb{R}^{n \times n}$.

Remark 1. From the definition of the sensitivity matrix $s_{x_0}(t)$, we observe that $s_{x_0}(t)$ is also the Jacobian matrix of the mapping $\phi(t; \cdot) : \mathcal{I}_0 \mapsto \Omega(t; \mathcal{I}_0)$, where $t \in [0, \tau]$.

Lemma 1. *There exists a $\tau^* > 0$ such that the determinant of sensitivity matrix $s_{x_0}(t)$ in Eq. (6) is different from zero for any $t \in [0, \tau^*]$.*

For the proof of Lemma 1, please refer to the Appendix. Assume that the solution mapping $\phi(t; x_0)$ of System (3) for time ranging over $t \in [(k-1)\tau, k\tau]$ and the state variable $x_0 \in \mathcal{I}_0$, could be equivalently reformulated as a continuously differentiable function of the state variable $x((k-1)\tau)$ in $\Omega((k-1)\tau; \mathcal{I}_0)$ and the time variable $t \in [(k-1)\tau, k\tau]$, i.e.,

$$\phi(t; x_0) = \psi_{k-1}(t; x((k-1)\tau), (k-1)\tau),$$

where $k \in \{1, \ldots, K - 1\}$, and $\boldsymbol{x}((k - 1)\tau) = \boldsymbol{\phi}((k - 1)\tau; \boldsymbol{x}_0)$. Also assume the determinant of the Jacobian matrix of the mapping $\boldsymbol{\psi}_{k-1}(t; \boldsymbol{x}((k-1)\tau), (k-1)\tau)$ w.r.t. any state $\boldsymbol{x}((k-1)\tau) \in \Omega((k-1)\tau; \mathcal{I}_0)$ is not zero for any $t \in [(k-1)\tau, k\tau]$. Then, we deduce what follows. For its proof, please refer to the Appendix.

Lemma 2. *Given the above assumptions, the sensitivity matrix* $s_{\boldsymbol{x}(k\tau)}(t) = \frac{\partial \boldsymbol{x}(t)}{\partial \boldsymbol{x}(k\tau)}$, $t \in [k\tau, (k+1)\tau]$, *for System (3) satisfies the following linear time-varying ODE:*

$$\dot{s}_{\boldsymbol{x}(k\tau)} = \frac{\partial \boldsymbol{f}(\boldsymbol{x}, \boldsymbol{x}_\tau)}{\partial \boldsymbol{x}} s_{\boldsymbol{x}(k\tau)} + \frac{\partial \boldsymbol{f}(\boldsymbol{x}, \boldsymbol{x}_\tau)}{\partial \boldsymbol{x}_\tau} \frac{\partial \boldsymbol{x}_\tau}{\partial \boldsymbol{x}(k\tau)}, \tag{7}$$

where $\dot{s}_{\boldsymbol{x}(k\tau)} = \frac{ds_{\boldsymbol{x}(k\tau)}}{dt}$, *and* $s_{\boldsymbol{x}(k\tau)}(k\tau) = \boldsymbol{I} \in \mathbb{R}^{n \times n}$.

From the definition of the sensitivity matrix $s_{\boldsymbol{x}(k\tau)}(t) = \frac{\partial \boldsymbol{x}(t)}{\partial \boldsymbol{x}(k\tau)}$ together with the fact that its determinant is not equal to zero, the solution mapping $\boldsymbol{\phi}(t; \cdot) : \mathcal{I}_0 \mapsto \Omega(t; \mathcal{I}_0)$ for $t \in [k\tau, (k+1)\tau]$ could be formulated equivalently as a continuously differentiable function of the state variable $\boldsymbol{x}(k\tau) \in \Omega(k\tau; \mathcal{I}_0)$ for any fixed $t \in [k\tau, (k+1)\tau]$, and this mapping from $\Omega(k\tau; \mathcal{I}_0)$ to $\Omega(t; \mathcal{I}_0)$ for $t \in [k\tau, (k+1)\tau]$ is a continuously differentiable homeomorphism between two topological spaces $\Omega(k\tau; \mathcal{I}_0)$ and $\Omega(t; \mathcal{I}_0)$. This assertion is formalized in Corollary 1.

Corollary 1. *If the determinant of the sensitivity matrix* $s_{\boldsymbol{x}(k\tau)}(t)$ *w.r.t. any state* $\boldsymbol{x}(k\tau) \in \Omega(k\tau; \mathcal{I}_0)$ *at time* $k\tau$ *is not zero for any* $t \in [k\tau, (k+1)\tau]$, *then* $\boldsymbol{\phi}(t; \boldsymbol{x}_0)$ *for* $\boldsymbol{x}_0 \in \mathcal{I}_0$ *and* $t \in [k\tau, (k+1)\tau]$ *could be equivalently reformulated as a continuously differentiable function of the state variable* $\boldsymbol{x}(k\tau) \in \Omega(k\tau; \mathcal{I}_0)$ *and the time variable* $t \in [k\tau, (k+1)\tau]$, *and the state* $\boldsymbol{x}(t) = \boldsymbol{\phi}(t; \boldsymbol{x}_0)$ *is uniquely determined by the state* $\boldsymbol{x}(k\tau)$ *for any fixed* $t \in [k\tau, (k+1)\tau]$, *where* $\boldsymbol{x}(k\tau) = \boldsymbol{\phi}(k\tau; \boldsymbol{x}_0)$.

3.2 Generating a Constraint Bounding the Time-Lag Term

According to what we discussed above, here, we will infer a class of DDEs of the form (3), where the determinant of the corresponding sensitivity matrix $s_{\boldsymbol{x}(k\tau)}(t)$ w.r.t. the state variable $\boldsymbol{x}(k\tau) \in \Omega(k\tau; \mathcal{I}_0)$ at time $k\tau$ is not zero for $t \in [k\tau, (k+1)\tau]$, and $k = 0, \ldots, K - 1$. Such a class of equations is derived by appropriately confining the time-lag term of the DDE (3), i.e., τ. In what follows, first, we review the classical result about diagonally dominant matrices from Varah [27].

If a matrix $A \in \mathbb{R}^{n \times n}$ is strictly diagonally dominant, i.e.,

$$\Delta_i(A) = |A_{ii}| - \sum_{j \neq i} |A_{ij}| > 0, \text{ with } 1 \leq i \leq n,$$

where A_{ij} is the entry in the i_{th} row and j_{th} column of the matrix A, then the inverse of the matrix A satisfies the bound

$$\|A^{-1}\|_\infty \leq max_{1 \leq i \leq n} \frac{1}{\Delta_i(A)}.$$

Note that, by convention, $\|\cdot\|_\infty$ is the maximum absolute row sum of a matrix. Based on this classical result, we derive a constraint on the time-lag term τ in System (3) rendering the sensitivity matrix mentioned in Lemma 2 strictly diagonally dominant.

Assume that the sensitivity matrix $s_{\boldsymbol{x}((k-1)\tau)}(t)$ is strictly diagonally dominant s.t.

$$\|s_{\boldsymbol{x}((k-1)\tau)}(t)\|_{max} \leq R, \tag{8}$$

$$max_{1 \leq i \leq n} \frac{1}{\Delta_i(s_{\boldsymbol{x}((k-1)\tau)}(t))} \leq \epsilon, \tag{9}$$

for any $t \in [(k-1)\tau, k\tau]$, where $k \in \{1, \ldots, K-1\}$, $\epsilon > 1$, and $R > 1$. Then, we construct the bound constraint on the time-lag term τ as follows.

Lemma 3. *Based on Eqs. (8) and (9), if the time-lag term is*

$$\tau \leq min \left\{ \frac{\epsilon - 1}{\epsilon(nMR + N\epsilon)}, \frac{ln\frac{R^2+1}{2}}{\sqrt{n}(2\sqrt{n}M + N\epsilon)} \right\},$$

where M and N are presented in Constraint (4), then $s_{\boldsymbol{x}(k\tau)}(t)$ for $t \in [k\tau, (k+1)\tau]$ is strictly diagonally dominant with the property of $\|s_{\boldsymbol{x}(k\tau)}(t)\|_{max} \leq R$ and $max_{1 \leq i \leq n} \frac{1}{\Delta_i(s_{\boldsymbol{x}(k\tau)}(t))} \leq \epsilon$.

Proof. Since the sensitivity matrix $s_{\boldsymbol{x}((k-1)\tau)}(t)$ is strictly diagonally dominant and Eq. (9) holds, the inequality

$$\|s_{\boldsymbol{x}((k-1)\tau)}^{-1}(t)\|_\infty \leq \epsilon,$$

also holds, where $t \in [(k-1)\tau, k\tau]$ and $k \in \{1, \ldots, K-1\}$. Accordingly, this implies that $\|s_{\boldsymbol{x}((k-1)\tau)}^{-1}(t)\|_{max} \leq \epsilon$. This way, according to Lemma 2, the sensitivity matrix $s_{\boldsymbol{x}(k\tau)}(t)$ for $t \subset [k\tau, (k+1)\tau]$ w.r.t. the state $\boldsymbol{x}(k\tau)$ satisfies the sensitivity equation

$$\dot{s}_{\boldsymbol{x}(k\tau)} = \frac{\partial \boldsymbol{f}(\boldsymbol{x}, \boldsymbol{x}_\tau)}{\partial \boldsymbol{x}} s_{\boldsymbol{x}(k\tau)} + \frac{\partial \boldsymbol{f}(\boldsymbol{x}, \boldsymbol{x}_\tau)}{\partial \boldsymbol{x}_\tau} \frac{\partial \boldsymbol{x}_\tau}{\partial \boldsymbol{x}(k\tau)}, \text{ with } s_{\boldsymbol{x}(k\tau)}(k\tau) = \boldsymbol{I}. \tag{10}$$

In the following, we employ the comparison principle for ODEs to derive a bound on the solution to Eq. (10).

Let

$$M_d = max_{(k-1)\tau \leq t \leq k\tau} \sqrt{n}(2\sqrt{n}\|A(t)\|_{max} + \|b(t)\|_{max}),$$

$$N_d = max_{(k-1)\tau \leq t \leq k\tau} \sqrt{n}\|b(t)\|_{max},$$

where $A(t) = \frac{\partial \boldsymbol{f}(\boldsymbol{x}, \boldsymbol{x}_\tau)}{\partial \boldsymbol{x}}$ and $b(t) = \frac{\partial \boldsymbol{f}(\boldsymbol{x}, \boldsymbol{x}_\tau)}{\partial \boldsymbol{x}_\tau} \frac{\partial \boldsymbol{x}_\tau}{\partial \boldsymbol{x}(i\tau)}$. It is obvious that $M_d \leq \sqrt{n}(2\sqrt{n}M + N\epsilon)$ and $N_d \leq \sqrt{n}N\epsilon$.

We take the j_{th} column of the sensitivity matrix $s_{\boldsymbol{x}(k\tau)}(t)$ and the matrix $\boldsymbol{b}(t)$ as a vector $\boldsymbol{y}(t)$ and $\boldsymbol{b}_j(t)$, where $j \in \{1, \ldots, n\}$. Let $u(t) = \|\boldsymbol{y}(t)\|_2^2 = \langle \boldsymbol{y}(t), \boldsymbol{y}(t) \rangle$ with $u(k\tau) = 1$, where $\|\boldsymbol{y}(t)\|_2$ is the 2-norm for $\boldsymbol{y}$ and $\langle \cdot, \cdot \rangle$ is an inner product in $\mathbb{R}^n$.

Based on Cauchy-Schwarz inequality and the fact that $2\|\boldsymbol{y}\|_2 \le \|\boldsymbol{y}\|_2^2 + 1$, we obtain

$$\dot{u} = 2\langle \boldsymbol{y}, \dot{\boldsymbol{y}} \rangle \le 2\|\boldsymbol{y}\|_2 \|\dot{\boldsymbol{y}}\|_2 = 2\|\boldsymbol{y}\|_2 \|A(t)\boldsymbol{y} + \boldsymbol{b}_j(t)\|_2 \le 2\|\boldsymbol{y}\|_2^2 \|A(t)\|_2 + 2\|\boldsymbol{y}\|_2 \|\boldsymbol{b}_j(t)\|_2$$
$$\le 2\|A(t)\|_2 \|\boldsymbol{y}\|_2^2 + \|\boldsymbol{b}_j(t)\|_2 (\|\boldsymbol{y}\|_2^2 + 1) \le M_d \|\boldsymbol{y}\|_2^2 + N_d = M_d u + N_d. \qquad (11)$$

Applying Gronwall's inequality [5] to Eq. (11), we deduce that

$$u(t) \le u_0 e^{M_d(t-k\tau)} + \int_{k\tau}^t N_d e^{M_d(t-s)}\, ds = u_0 e^{M_d(t-k\tau)} + \frac{N_d}{M_d} e^{M_d(t-k\tau)} - \frac{N_d}{M_d} \le R_d,$$

for $k\tau \le t \le (k+1)\tau$, where $u_0 = u(k\tau) = 1$, and

$$R_d = \left(1 + \frac{N_d}{M_d}\right) e^{M_d \tau} - \frac{N_d}{M_d}.$$

Therefore, $\|\boldsymbol{y}(t)\|_2^2 \le R_d$ for $k\tau \le t \le (k+1)\tau$. By solving the inequality $R_d \le R^2$, we conclude that $\|s_{\boldsymbol{x}(k\tau)}(t)\|_{max} \le R$ for $t \in [k\tau, (k+1)\tau]$ holds if

$$\tau \le \frac{ln\frac{R^2+1}{2}}{\sqrt{n}(2\sqrt{n}M + N\epsilon)},$$

where the right side of this inequality could be gained when $M_d = N_d$.

For the sensitivity matrix $s_{\boldsymbol{x}(k\tau)}(t)$ with t ranging in the interval $[k\tau, (k+1)\tau]$, the diagonal element in the i-th row of the matrix $s_{\boldsymbol{x}(k\tau)}(t)$ is equal to

$$1 + \left[\frac{\partial f_i(\boldsymbol{x}, \boldsymbol{x}_\tau)}{\partial \boldsymbol{x}} \frac{\partial \boldsymbol{x}}{\partial x_{k\tau,i}} + \frac{\partial f_i(\boldsymbol{x}, \boldsymbol{x}_\tau)}{\partial \boldsymbol{x}_\tau} \frac{\partial \boldsymbol{x}_\tau}{\partial x_{k\tau,i}} \right]_{t=\xi_i} (t-k\tau),$$

the element in the i_{th} row and j_{th} column is equal to

$$\left[\frac{\partial f_i(\boldsymbol{x}, \boldsymbol{x}_\tau)}{\partial \boldsymbol{x}} \frac{\partial \boldsymbol{x}}{\partial x_{k\tau,j}} + \frac{\partial f_k(\boldsymbol{x}, \boldsymbol{x}_\tau)}{\partial \boldsymbol{x}_\tau} \frac{\partial \boldsymbol{x}_\tau}{\partial x_{k\tau,j}} \right]_{t=\xi_j} (t-k\tau),$$

where $j \in \{1, \ldots, n\} \backslash \{i\}$ and ξ_l, for $l = 1, \ldots, n$, is some value in $(k\tau, (k+1)\tau)$. Thus $\Delta_i(s_{\boldsymbol{x}(k\tau)}(t))$ is larger than

$$1 - \tau \sum_{j=1}^n \left| \frac{\partial f_i(\boldsymbol{x}, \boldsymbol{x}_\tau)}{\partial \boldsymbol{x}} \frac{\partial \boldsymbol{x}}{\partial x_{k\tau,j}} + \frac{\partial f_i(\boldsymbol{x}, \boldsymbol{x}_\tau)}{\partial \boldsymbol{x}_\tau} \frac{\partial \boldsymbol{x}_\tau}{\partial x_{k\tau,j}} \right|_{t=\xi_j},$$

which in turn is larger than $1 - (nMR + N\epsilon)\tau$.

By solving the inequality $\frac{1}{1-(nMR+N\epsilon)\tau} \le \epsilon$, we obtain that $\tau \le \frac{\epsilon-1}{\epsilon(nMR+N\epsilon)}$. Therefore, if

$$\tau \le min\left\{\frac{\epsilon-1}{\epsilon(nMR+N\epsilon)}, \frac{ln\frac{R^2+1}{2}}{\sqrt{n}(2\sqrt{n}M+N\epsilon)}\right\},$$

then $\|s_{\boldsymbol{x}(k\tau)}(t)\|_{max} \le R$ and $max_{1\le i\le n}\frac{1}{\Delta_i(s_{\boldsymbol{x}(k\tau)}(t))} \le \epsilon$ hold, and $s_{\boldsymbol{x}(k\tau)}(t)$ is also diagonally dominant for $t \in [k\tau, (k+1)\tau]$ since $\tau \le \frac{\epsilon-1}{\epsilon(nMR+N\epsilon)}, 1-(nMR+N\epsilon)\tau > 0$ holds. $\qquad\square$

Combining Lemmas 1 and 3, we deduce the following theorem.

Theorem 1. *If the time-lag term of DDE (3) is*

$$\tau \le min\left\{\tau^*, \frac{\epsilon-1}{\epsilon(nMR+N\epsilon)}, \frac{ln\frac{R^2+1}{2}}{\sqrt{n}(2\sqrt{n}M+N\epsilon)}\right\},$$

where τ^* is from Lemma 1, then the solution mapping $\phi(t;\cdot) : \mathcal{I}_0 \mapsto \Omega(t;\mathcal{I}_0)$ to System (3) is a homeomorphism between two topological spaces $\mathcal{I}_0$ and $\Omega(t;\mathcal{I}_0)$ for any $t \in [0, K\tau]$.

When the time-lag τ satisfies the condition presented in Theorem 1, the homeomorphism property in Theorem 1 implies that the solution mapping $\phi(t;\cdot) : \mathcal{I}_0 \mapsto \Omega(t;\mathcal{I}_0)$ to System (3), where $t \in [0, K\tau]$, maps the boundary and interior points of the initial set $\mathcal{I}_0$ onto the boundary and interior points of the set $\Omega(t;\mathcal{I}_0)$ respectively. Therefore, the full reachable set induced by the initial set of System (3) could be retrieved by computing the reachable set just of the initial set's boundary. We illustrate Theorem 1 through the following example involving a delay τ that could be caused by sensor circuitry. Determining a bound on that delay could thus help facilitate the choice of appropriate sensors such that the delay τ incurred satisfies the conditions of Theorem 1.

Example 1. Consider a modified model of an electromechanical oscillation of a synchronous machine,

$$\dot{\boldsymbol{x}} = \begin{cases} \boldsymbol{g}(\boldsymbol{x}), & \text{if } t \in [0, \tau), \boldsymbol{x}(0) \in \mathcal{I}_0 \\ \boldsymbol{f}(\boldsymbol{x}, \boldsymbol{x}_\tau), & \text{if } t \in [\tau, K\tau], \end{cases} \tag{12}$$

with $\boldsymbol{x} = (\delta, w)'$, $\boldsymbol{x}_\tau = (\delta_\tau, w_\tau)$, $\boldsymbol{g}(\boldsymbol{x}) = (g_1(\boldsymbol{x}), g_2(\boldsymbol{x}))' = (0,0)'$, $\boldsymbol{f}(\boldsymbol{x}, \boldsymbol{x}_\tau) = (f_1(\boldsymbol{x}, \boldsymbol{x}_\tau), f_2(\boldsymbol{x}, \boldsymbol{x}_\tau))' = (w, 0.2 - 0.7sin\delta_\tau - 0.05w_\tau)'$, and $\mathcal{I}_0 = [-0.5, 0.5] \times [2.5, 3.5]$, $K = 60$ and $\mathcal{X} = [-100, 100] \times [-100, 100]$. Through simple calculations, we obtain that $M = 1$, $N = 0.7$, $R = 2$ and $\epsilon = 2.5$, thus any $\tau \le 0.104$ satisfies the condition in Theorem 1. In our experiments, we set $\tau = 0.1$.

From the result illustrated in Fig. 1, we conclude that the corresponding solution mapping $\phi(6;\cdot) : \mathcal{I}_0 \mapsto \Omega(6;\mathcal{I}_0)$ maps the boundary and interior points of the initial set $\mathcal{I}_0$ onto the boundary and interior points of the set $\Omega(6;\mathcal{I}_0)$ respectively, as the homeomorphism property suggests.

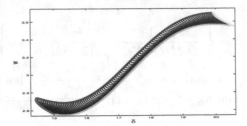

Fig. 1. An illustration of the reachable set for Example 1 at time $t = 6.0$ using simulation methods, (red, green, blue and yellow points – the approximate sampling states reachable from the boundary subsets $[-0.5, -0.5] \times [2.5, 3.5]$, $[0.5, 0.5] \times [2.5, 3.5]$, $[-0.5, 0.5] \times [2.5, 2.5]$ and $[-0.5, 0.5] \times [3.5, 3.5]$ respectively; black points – the approximate sampling states reachable from the entire initial set). (Color figure online)

3.3   Constructing Reachable Sets

We in this section extend the set-boundary based reachability analysis method of [29, 30] for nonlinear control systems to reachability computations of System (3) with a time-lag τ satisfying the conditions of Theorem 1. The reduction is based on regarding the delayed state variable $\boldsymbol{x}_\tau$ in System (3) as a control input $\boldsymbol{u}(t)$, and the confinement to set boundaries adds considerably to precision as it significantly reduces the volume of the tube containing all such input trajectories $\boldsymbol{x}_\tau$. In our algorithm we obviously restrict the initial set $\mathcal{I}_0$ to a specific family of computer-representable sets in the $\mathbb{R}^n$ such as polytopes.

Assume that the initial set's boundary can be represented as an union of m subsets from the respective family, that is, $\partial \mathcal{I}_0 = \cup_{i=1}^m I_{0,i}$. For $t \in [0, \tau]$, the system is governed by ODE $\dot{\boldsymbol{x}} = \boldsymbol{g}(\boldsymbol{x})$. Therefore, we can apply any existing reachability analysis technique for ODEs that is able to deal with reachability computations with initial sets of forms such as polytopes, to the computation of an enclosure $\mathcal{B}_{0,t}$ of the reachable set for the initial set's boundary $\partial \mathcal{I}_0$ at time $t \in [0, \tau]$, where $\mathcal{B}_{0,t} = \cup_{i=1}^m B_{0,i}(t)$ and $B_{0,i}(t)$ is an over-approximation of the reachable set at time $t \in [0, \tau]$ starting from the set $I_{0,i}$, for $i = 1, \ldots, m$. The corresponding over-and under-approximations of the reachable set at time t could be constructed by including (excluding, resp.) the set $\mathcal{B}_{0,t}$ from the set obtained from convex combinations of points in $B_{0,i}(t)$, according to [30].

Based on these computations for the initial trajectory segment up to time τ, for $t \in [k\tau, (k+1)\tau]$, $k = 1, \ldots, K-1$, the following steps are used to compute its corresponding over- and under-approximations of the reachable set respectively.

1. Firstly, we compute an enclosure $B_{k,i}(t)$, for $t \in [k\tau, (k+1)\tau]$, of the reachable set $\Omega(t; I_{0,i})$ for System (3) with the initial set $B_{k-1,i}(k\tau)$ and $\boldsymbol{x}_\tau \in B_{k-1,i}(t - \tau)$. This enclosure can be computed by employing reachability analysis methods for nonlinear control systems of the form (5) with a time-varying input $\boldsymbol{u}(t) = \boldsymbol{x}_\tau \in B_{k-1,i}(t - \tau)$. Therefore, $\mathcal{B}_{k,t} = \cup_{i=1}^m B_{k,i}(t)$ is an enclosure of the reachable set for the initial set's boundary $\partial \mathcal{I}_0$ at time $t \in [k\tau, (k+1)\tau]$.

2. Secondly, we construct a simply connected compact polytope $O_{k,t}$ such that it covers $\mathcal{B}_{k,t}$. The set $O_{k,t}$ is an over-approximation of the reachable set $\Omega(t;\mathcal{I}_0)$ at time $t \in [k\tau, (k+1)\tau]$ according to Lemma 1 in [30].
3. Thirdly, we construct a simply connected polytope $U_{k,t}$ that satisfies two conditions: (1) the enclosure of the reachable set from the boundary of the initial set, i.e., $\mathcal{B}_{k,t}$, is obtained to be a subset of the enclosure of its complement, and (2) it intersects the interior of the reachable set $\Omega(t;\mathcal{I}_0)$. Then, according to Lemma 2 in [30], $U_{k,t}$ is an under-approximation of the reachable set $\Omega(t;\mathcal{I}_0)$ at time $t \in [k\tau, (k+1)\tau]$.

4   Examples and Discussions

In this section, we test our method on two examples of a two-dimensional system and a seven-dimensional system. Our implementation is based on Althoff's *continuous reachability analyzer (CORA)* [2], which is a MATLAB toolbox for prototype design of algorithms for reachability analysis. All computations are carried out on an i5-3337U 1.8 GHz CPU with 4 GB running Ubuntu Linux 13.10.

Example 2. Consider a modified Lotka-Volterra two-variables system with a delay τ, given by

$$\dot{x} = \begin{cases} g(x), & \text{if } t \in [0,\tau), x(0) \in \mathcal{I}_0 \\ f(x,x_\tau), & \text{if } t \in [\tau, K\tau] \end{cases} \tag{13}$$

with $x = (x,y)'$, $x_\tau = (x_\tau, y_\tau)'$, $g(x) = (g_1(x), g_2(x))' = (y, -0.2x + y - 0.2x^2y)'$, $f(x,x_\tau) = (f_1(x,x_\tau), f_2(x,x_\tau))' = (y, -0.2x_\tau + y - 0.2x^2y)'$, $\mathcal{I}_0 = [0.9, 1.1] \times [0.9, 1.1]$ with $\partial \mathcal{I}_0 = \cup_{i=1}^4 I_{0,i}$ and $\mathcal{X} = [0.5, 3.5] \times [0.2, 1.5]$, where $I_{0,1} = [0.9, 0.9] \times [0.9, 1.1]$, $I_{0,2} = [1.1, 1.1] \times [0.9, 1.1]$, $I_{0,3} = [0.9, 1.1] \times [0.9, 0.9]$ and $I_{0,4} = [0.9, 1.1] \times [1.1, 1.1]$.

In this example, the valuations $M = 2.10, N = 0.2, R = 2$ and $\epsilon = 2$ fulfill the condition in Lemma 3. Through simple calculations, $\tau = 0.01$ satisfies the requirement in Theorem 1. Also, K is assigned to 100, i.e. the entire time interval is $[0, 1.0]$. The over- and under-approximation of the reachable set illustrated in Figs. 2 and 3 are represented by polytopes. The computation time for computing over- and under-approximations is 111.56 s.

Example 3. Consider a seven-dimensional system with a delay τ^2,

$$\dot{x} = \begin{cases} g(x), & \text{if } t \in [0,\tau), x(0) \in \mathcal{I}_0 \\ f(x,x_\tau), & \text{if } t \in [\tau, K\tau] \end{cases} \tag{14}$$

---

[2] The delay-free system could be found in the Package CORA.

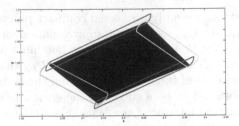

Fig. 2. An illustration of the reachable set of the initial set's boundary for Example 2 at time $t = 1.0$, (red curve – $\partial O(1.0; I_{0,1})$; blue curve – $\partial O(1.0; I_{0,2})$; green curve – $\partial O(1.0; I_{0,3})$; yellow curve– $\partial O(1.0; I_{0,4})$; black points – the approximate sampling states reachable from the initial set $\mathcal{I}_0$ after time duration of 1.0, which are computed using simulation methods). (Color figure online)

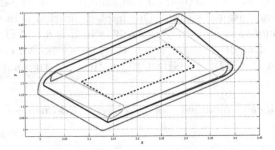

Fig. 3. An illustration of the reachable set of initial set's boundary for Example 2 at time $t = 1.0$, (red curve – $\partial O(1.0; I_{0,1})$; blue curve – $\partial O(1.0; I_{0,2})$; green curve – $\partial O(1.0; I_{0,3})$; yellow curve – $\partial O(1.0; I_{0,4})$; black curve – boundary $\partial O(1.0; \mathcal{I}_0)$ of the over-approximation obtained by our boundary method; black dash curve – boundary $\partial U(1.0; \mathcal{I}_0)$ of the under-approximation obtained by our boundary method; purple curve – boundary $\partial O(1.0; \mathcal{I}_0)$ of less tight over-approximation obtained by extrapolating the entire initial set rather than its boundaries). (Color figure online)

with $\boldsymbol{x} = (x_1, \ldots, x_7)'$, $\boldsymbol{x}_\tau = (x_{1,\tau}, \ldots, x_{7,\tau})'$, $\boldsymbol{g}(\boldsymbol{x}) = \boldsymbol{0}$, $\boldsymbol{f}(\boldsymbol{x}, \boldsymbol{x}_\tau) = (1.4x_3 - 0.9x_{1,\tau}, 2.5x_5 - 1.5x_2, 0.6x_7 - 0.8x_3x_2, 2.0 - 1.3x_4x_3, 0.7x_1 - 1.0x_4x_5, 0.3x_1 - 3.1x_6, 1.8x_6 - 1.5x_7x_2)'$, $\mathcal{I}_0 = [1.1, 1.3] \times [0.95, 1.15] \times [1.4, 1.6] \times [2.3, 2.5] \times [0.9, 1.1] \times [0.0, 0.2] \times [0.35, 0.55]$ and $\mathcal{X} = [0.5, 1.5] \times [0.5, 1.5] \times [1.0, 2.0] \times [2.0, 3.0] \times [0.5, 1.5,] \times [0.0, 0.5] \times [0.0, 1.0]$.

The valuations $M = 3.9, N = 0.9$, $R = 2$ and $\epsilon = 9$ fulfill the condition in Lemma 3. Thus, $\tau \leq 0.01$ satisfies the requirement in Theorem 1. Also, τ and K are assigned to 0.01 and 10 respectively, i.e., the entire time interval is $[0, 0.1]$.

The computed over-approximation at time instant 0.1 is $O(0.1; \mathcal{I}_0) = [1.062, 1.302] \times [1.001, 1.216] \times [1.311, 1.529] \times [2.099, 2.322] \times [0.792, 0.989] \times [0.022, 0.183] \times [0.302, 0.516]$. The computed under-approximation at time instant 0.1 is $U(0.1; \mathcal{I}_0) = [1.113, 1.251] \times [1.052, 1.165] \times [1.362, 1.477] \times [2.150, 2.271] \times [0.843, 0.0.937] \times [0.073, 0.132] \times [0.353, 0.465]$. The computation time for both is 505.03 s. The projections for over-and under-approximations at time instants $t = 0.02, 0.04, 0.06, 0.08, 0.1$ on the $x_1 - x_2$ space are illustrated in Fig. 4.

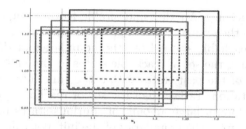

Fig. 4. An illustration of the reachable set on the $x_1 - x_2$ space for Example 3 at times $t = 0.0, 0.02, 0.04, 0.06, 0.08, 0.1$, (yellow solid line – the boundary of the initial set on the $x_1 - x_2$ space at time instant $t = 0.0$; purple, red, green, blue and black solid lines – the boundaries of over-approximations on the $x_1 - x_2$ space at time instants $t = 0.02, 0.04, 0.06, 0.08, 0.1$ respectively; purple, red, green, blue and black dashed lines – the boundaries of under-approximations on the $x_1 - x_2$ space at time instants $t = 0.02, 0.04, 0.06, 0.08, 0.1$ respectively). (Color figure online)

From Fig. 2 that presents the approximation of the reachable set's boundary obtained by applying numerical simulation methods along with the set-boundary based method to Example 2, it is further confirmed that the set-boundary based method is able to produce a valid over-approximation of the reachable set's boundary when the delay-lag term τ satisfies the conditions in Theorem 1. Furthermore, it is concluded from Fig. 3 that the set-boundary based method as in Subsect. 3.3 is able to output validated over- and under-approximations of the reachable sets. Also, the results in Fig. 3 demonstrate convincingly that the set-boundary based method induces a smaller wrapping effect in performing reachability analysis compared with extrapolating the entire initial set, since the boundaries of the initial set definitely have much smaller volume than the entire initial set. For Example 3, the approximations of the interval form as illustrated in Fig. 4 are computed for the sake of reducing computational burden. Note that the bound imposed for maintaining homeomorphism property applies to the time-lag in the DDE only and is not a bound on the temporal horizon coverable by reach-set computation, which can be arbitrarily larger if only the time-lag suits the condition. The relatively small horizons in these examples are due to the wrapping effect in the underlying reachability techniques, not the method itself, as discussed below.

Next, we should point out that the positive aspect induced by this kind of representation, is that they enable the analysis of some properties such as safety and reliability by reasoning in the theory of linear arithmetic. On the other side, they might not be the best representations of the reachable sets for nonlinear systems since the reachable sets of nonlinear systems modeled by ODEs and DDEs may be far from being convex as demonstrated in Fig. 1, thereby generating poor results when employing polytopes to characterize the reachable sets. In order to remedy this shortcoming of conservativeness induced by polytopes, we will struggle to employ representations of more complex shapes such as semi-algebraic sets in the construction of the reachable sets at the expense

of computational efficiency. Another undesirable feature might be in our implementation, is due to the excessive use of previous state information to compute
the set of current reachable states from the boundaries of the initial set. In a
sense, while computing the set of reachable states at time $t \in [k\tau, (k+1)\tau]$, the
entire reachable set of the past states within the time interval $[(k-1)\tau, k\tau]$ is
used for the computations rather than the set of reachable states at just time
instant $t - \tau$. Therefore, a large amount of spurious states not actually reachable at previous time from the boundaries of the initial set might be introduced,
significantly increase the wrapping effect. Due to constructing over- and under-
approximations by including (excluding, resp.) the obtained boundary enclosure
from certain convex combination of points, a pessimistic over-approximation of
the reachable sets from the boundaries of the initial set may reduce the tightness of computed results accordingly. In order to circumvent this issue, we will
extend Taylor-model based reachability analysis for ODEs to the proposed class
of DDEs in the future work. Since Taylor models are functions being explicitly
dependent on time and state variables, this dependence enables the use of an
over-approximation associated with the reachable sets of the boundaries of the
initial set at previous time $t-\tau$ rather than within the time interval $[(k-1)\tau, k\tau]$
to over-approximate the set of states reachable from the boundaries of the initial
set at current time $t \in [k\tau, (k+1)\tau]$, thereby resulting in a significant reduction
in the wrapping effect.

Finally, we should point out that our method, in this paper, is suitable for
systems modeled by DDEs of the form (3) with solutions having homeomorphism
property. But, it is restricted to a class of DDEs with time-lag term τ satisfying
the conditions in Theorem 1. As a future work, we will expand such class of
systems by loosing bound constraints on τ. Also, in order to measure the conservativeness on such bounds, we plan to deduce constraints on τ such that the
solution to the associated system does not equip with homeomorphism property.
Besides, if such homeomorphism property fails, one feasible solution to compute
its over- and under-approximations of reachable sets is first to reformulate the
associated DDE as an ODE via the method of steps in [26] and then apply
the set-boundary based reachability analysis method of [29, 30] to the obtained
ODE. However, the formulated ODE suffers an increase of space dimension over
reachability time of interest. We will investigate more about this in future work.

5   Conclusion

In this paper, we have exposed a class of delay differential equations (DDEs)
exhibiting homeomorphic dependency on initial conditions. Membership in this
class is determined by conducting sensitivity analysis of the solution mapping
with respect to the initial states, therefrom deriving an upper bound on the
time-lag term of the DDE thus ensures homeomorphic dependency. One of the
primary benefits of the existence of a corresponding homeomorphism is that
state extrapolation can be pursued from the boundaries of the initial set only,
rather than the full initial set, as the homeomorphism preserves boundaries and

interiors of sets. As (appropriate enclosures of) the boundaries of the initial set have much smaller volume, such an approach tremendously reduces the wrapping effect incurred when using set-based state extrapolation on ODE with inputs as a means for enclosing solutions to the DDE. Furthermore, it allows us to construct an over- and under-approximations of the full reachable set by including (excluding, resp.) the obtained boundary enclosure from certain convex combinations of points in that boundary enclosure. We have illustrated the efficiency of our method on two examples of dimension 2 and 7.

Acknowledgement. This research from Peter N. Mosaad and Martin Fränzle is funded by Deutsche Forschungsgemeinschaft within the Research Training Group "SCARE - System Correctness under Adverse Conditions" (DFG GRK 1765) and from Mingshuai Chen, Yangjia Li, and Naijun Zhan is supported partly by NSFC under grant No. 61625206, by "973 Program" under grant No. 2014CB340701 and by the CAS/SAFEA International Partnership Program for Creative Research Teams. Besides, Yangjia Li is supported partly by NSFC under grant No. 61502467.

Appendix

The Proof of Lemma 1

Proof. From Eq. (6), we obtain that

$$s_{\boldsymbol{x}_0}^{ij}(t) = \boldsymbol{I}^{ij} + \boldsymbol{J}^{ij}t,$$

where $\boldsymbol{J}^{ij} = \left(D_{\boldsymbol{g}}(\boldsymbol{\phi}(t; \boldsymbol{x}_0)) s_{\boldsymbol{x}_0}(t)\right)^{ij}_{t=\tau_{ij}}$, τ_{ij} lies between 0 and t, $s_{\boldsymbol{x}_0}^{ij}$ is the $(i,j)_{th}$ element of the matrix $s_{\boldsymbol{x}_0}$ and $\boldsymbol{J}^{ij}$ is the $(i,j)_{th}$ element of the matrix $D_{\boldsymbol{g}}(\boldsymbol{\phi}(t; \boldsymbol{x}_0)) s_{\boldsymbol{x}_0}(t)$ with $t = \tau_{ij}$. Also, since $\boldsymbol{g}(\boldsymbol{x}) \in \mathcal{C}^1(\mathcal{X})$, i.e. $\boldsymbol{g}(\cdot) : \mathcal{X} \mapsto \mathbb{R}^n$ is a continuously differentiable function, the element in the matrix $D_{\boldsymbol{g}} = \frac{\partial \boldsymbol{g}}{\partial \boldsymbol{x}}$ is bounded over an arbitrary compact set covering the reachable set $\cup_{t\in[0,\tau_1]}\Omega(t; \mathcal{I}_0)$ in the set $\mathcal{X}$, where τ_1 can be any number in $(0, \tau]$ such that $\cup_{t\in[0,\tau_1]}\Omega(t; \mathcal{I}_0) \subseteq \mathcal{X}$. The bounded property also applies to the matrix $s_{\boldsymbol{x}_0}(t)$. Consequently, a lower bound for all elements of the matrix $\boldsymbol{J}$ exists. Thus, $lim_{t\to 0}s_{\boldsymbol{x}_0}(t) = \boldsymbol{I}$ implies that there exists a $\tau^* \in (0, \tau_1]$ s.t. the sensitivity matrix $s_{\boldsymbol{x}_0}(t)$ for $t \in [0, \tau^*]$ is diagonally dominant. The conclusion follows from this fact.   □

The Proof of Lemma 2

Proof. Since the determinant of the Jacobian matrix of the mapping $\boldsymbol{x}(t) = \boldsymbol{\psi}_{k-1}(t; \boldsymbol{x}((k-1)\tau, (k-1)\tau)$ w.r.t. any state $\boldsymbol{x}((k-1)\tau) \in \Omega((k-1)\tau; \mathcal{I}_0)$ is not zero for $t \subset [(k-1)\tau, k\tau]$, then for any fixed $t \in [(k-1)\tau, k\tau]$, the mapping

$$\boldsymbol{x}(t) = \boldsymbol{\psi}_{k-1}(t; \cdot, (k-1)\tau) : \Omega((k-1)\tau; \mathcal{I}_0) \longmapsto \Omega(t; \mathcal{I}_0)$$

is a bijection and its inverse mapping from $\Omega(t; \mathcal{I}_0)$ to $\Omega((k-1)\tau; \mathcal{I}_0)$ is continuously differentiable. Thus, the sensitivity matrix $s_{\boldsymbol{x}(k\tau)}(t)$ for $t \in [k\tau, (k+1)\tau]$

satisfies the sensitivity equation:

$$\dot{s}_{\boldsymbol{x}(k\tau)} = \frac{\partial f(\boldsymbol{x}, \boldsymbol{x}_\tau)}{\partial \boldsymbol{x}} s_{\boldsymbol{x}(k\tau)} + \frac{\partial f(\boldsymbol{x}, \boldsymbol{x}_\tau)}{\partial \boldsymbol{x}_\tau} \frac{\partial \boldsymbol{x}_\tau}{\partial \boldsymbol{x}(k\tau)},$$

with $s_{\boldsymbol{x}(k\tau)}(k\tau) = \boldsymbol{I} \in \mathbb{R}^{n \times n}$.   □

References

1. Althoff, M.: Reachability analysis of nonlinear systems using conservative polynomialization and non-convex sets. In: Belta, C., Ivancic, F. (eds.) Proceedings of the 16th International Conference on Hybrid Systems: Computation and Control (HSCC 2013), Philadelphia, 8–11 April 2013, pp. 173–182. ACM (2013)
2. Althoff, M.: CORA 2016 Manual (2016). http://www6.in.tum.de/Main/SoftwareCORA
3. Althoff, M., Stursberg, O., Buss, M.: Reachability analysis of nonlinear systems with uncertain parameters using conservative linearization. In: Proceedings of the 47th IEEE Conference on Decision and Control (CDC 2008), Cancún, 9–11 December 2008, pp. 4042–4048. IEEE (2008)
4. Bellman, R., Cooke, K.L.: Differential-difference equations. Technical report R-374-PR, The RAND Corporation, Santa Monica, California, January 1963
5. Bellman, R., et al.: The stability of solutions of linear differential equations. Duke Math. J. **10**(4), 643–647 (1943)
6. Berz, M., Makino, K.: Verified integration of ODEs and flows using differential algebraic methods on high-order Taylor models. Reliab. Comput. **4**(4), 361–369 (1998)
7. Chen, M., Fränzle, M., Li, Y., Mosaad, P.N., Zhan, N.: Validated simulation-based verification of delayed differential dynamics. In: Fitzgerald, J., Heitmeyer, C., Gnesi, S., Philippou, A. (eds.) FM 2016. LNCS, vol. 9995, pp. 137–154. Springer, Cham (2016). doi:10.1007/978-3-319-48989-6_9
8. Chen, X., Sankaranarayanan, S., Ábrahám, E.: Under-approximate flowpipes for non-linear continuous systems. In: Formal Methods in Computer-Aided Design (FMCAD 2014), Lausanne, 21–24 October 2014, pp. 59–66. IEEE (2014)
9. Chutinan, A., Krogh, B.H.: Computing polyhedral approximations to flow pipes for dynamic systems. In: Proceedings of the 37th IEEE Conference on Decision and Control, vol. 2, pp. 2089–2094. IEEE (1998)
10. Donzé, A., Maler, O.: Systematic simulation using sensitivity analysis. In: Bemporad, A., Bicchi, A., Buttazzo, G. (eds.) HSCC 2007. LNCS, vol. 4416, pp. 174–189. Springer, Heidelberg (2007). doi:10.1007/978-3-540-71493-4_16
11. Girard, A.: Reachability of uncertain linear systems using zonotopes. In: Morari, M., Thiele, L. (eds.) HSCC 2005. LNCS, vol. 3414, pp. 291–305. Springer, Heidelberg (2005). doi:10.1007/978-3-540-31954-2_19
12. Goubault, E., Mullier, O., Putot, S., Kieffer, M.: Inner approximated reachability analysis. In: Fränzle, M., Lygeros, J. (eds.) 17th International Conference on Hybrid Systems: Computation and Control (part of CPS Week) (HSCC 2014), Berlin, 15–17 April 2014, pp. 163–172. ACM (2014)
13. Huang, Z., Fan, C., Mitra, S.: Bounded invariant verification for time-delayed nonlinear networked dynamical systems. Nonlinear Anal. Hybrid Syst. **23**, 211–229 (2017)

14. Kaynama, S., Maidens, J.N., Oishi, M., Mitchell, I.M., Dumont, G.A.: Computing the viability kernel using maximal reachable sets. In: Dang, T., Mitchell, I.M. (eds.) Hybrid Systems: Computation and Control (part of CPS Week 2012) (HSCC 2012), Beijing, 17–19 April 2012, pp. 55–64. ACM (2012)
15. Korda, M., Henrion, D., Jones, C.N.: Inner approximations of the region of attraction for polynomial dynamical systems. IFAC Proc. Vol. **46**(23), 534–539 (2013)
16. Kuang, Y.: Delay Differential Equations: With Applications in Population Dynamics, vol. 191. Academic Press, Boston (1993)
17. Kurzhanski, A.B., Varaiya, P.: Ellipsoidal techniques for reachability analysis. In: Lynch, N., Krogh, B.H. (eds.) HSCC 2000. LNCS, vol. 1790, pp. 202–214. Springer, Heidelberg (2000). doi:10.1007/3-540-46430-1_19
18. Kurzhanski, A.B., Varaiya, P.: Ellipsoidal techniques for hybrid dynamics: the reachability problem. In: Dayawansa, W.P., Lindquist, A., Zhou, Y. (eds.) New Directions and Applications in Control Theory, vol. 321, pp. 193–205. Springer, Heidelberg (2005). doi:10.1007/10984413_12
19. Le Guernic, C., Girard, A.: Reachability analysis of linear systems using support functions. Nonlinear Anal. Hybrid Syst. **4**(2), 250–262 (2010)
20. Moore, R.E.: Automatic local coordinate transformations to reduce the growth of error bounds in interval computation of solutions of ordinary differential equations. Error Digit. Comput. **2**, 103–140 (1965)
21. Neher, M., Jackson, K.R., Nedialkov, N.S.: On Taylor model based integration of ODEs. SIAM J. Numer. Anal. **45**(1), 236–262 (2007)
22. Prajna, S., Jadbabaie, A.: Safety verification of hybrid systems using barrier certificates. In: Alur, R., Pappas, G.J. (eds.) HSCC 2004. LNCS, vol. 2993, pp. 477–492. Springer, Heidelberg (2004). doi:10.1007/978-3-540-24743-2_32
23. Prajna, S., Jadbabaie, A.: Methods for safety verification of time-delay systems. In: Proceedings of the 44th IEEE Conference on Decision and Control, pp. 4348–4353. IEEE (2005)
24. Ratschan, S., She, Z.: Safety verification of hybrid systems by constraint propagation based abstraction refinement. In: Morari, M., Thiele, L. (eds.) HSCC 2005. LNCS, vol. 3414, pp. 573–589. Springer, Heidelberg (2005). doi:10.1007/978-3-540-31954-2_37
25. Stauning, O., Madsen, K.: Automatic validation of numerical solutions. Ph.D. thesis, Technical University of DenmarkDanmarks Tekniske Universitet, Department of Informatics and Mathematical ModelingInstitut for Informatik og Matematisk Modellering (1997)
26. Taylor, S.R.: Probabilistic properties of delay differential equations (2004)
27. Varah, J.M.: A lower bound for the smallest singular value of a matrix. Linear Algebra Appl. **11**(1), 3–5 (1975)
28. Wang, T., Lall, S., West, M.: Polynomial level-set method for polynomial system reachable set estimation. IEEE Trans. Autom. Control **58**(10), 2508–2521 (2013)
29. Xue, B., Easwaran, A., Cho, N.-J., Franzle, M.: Reach-avoid verification for nonlinear systems based on boundary analysis. IEEE Trans. Autom. Control **62**(7), 3518–3523 (2017)
30. Xue, B., She, Z., Easwaran, A.: Under-approximating backward reachable sets by polytopes. In: Chaudhuri, S., Farzan, A. (eds.) CAV 2016. LNCS, vol. 9779, pp. 457–476. Springer, Cham (2016). doi:10.1007/978-3-319-41528-4_25
31. Zou, L., Fränzle, M., Zhan, N., Mosaad, P.N.: Automatic verification of stability and safety for delay differential equations. In: Kroening, D., Păsăreanu, C.S. (eds.) CAV 2015. LNCS, vol. 9207, pp. 338–355. Springer, Cham (2015). doi:10.1007/978-3-319-21668-3_20

Testing and Simulation

Simulation Based Computation of Certificates for Safety of Dynamical Systems

Stefan Ratschan[✉] [ID]

Institute of Computer Science, Czech Academy of Sciences, Prague, Czech Republic
stefan.ratschan@cs.cas.cz

Abstract. In this paper, we present an algorithm for synthesizing certificates for safety of continuous time dynamical systems, so-called barrier certificates. Unlike the usual approach of using constraint solvers to compute the certificate from the system dynamics, we synthesize the certificate from system simulations. This makes the algorithm applicable even in cases where the dynamics is either not explicitly available, or too complicated to be analyzed by constraint solvers, for example, due to the presence of transcendental function symbols.

The algorithm itself allows the usage of heuristic techniques in which case it does not formally guarantee correctness of the result. However, in cases that do allow rigorous constraint solving, the computed barrier certificate can be rigorously verified, if desired. Hence, in such cases, our algorithm reduces the problem of finding a barrier certificate to the problem of formally verifying a given barrier certificate.

1 Introduction

A common technique in formal verification is the reduction of a verification problem to a constraint solving problem. A main limitation of such approaches comes from theoretical and practical limitations of the decision procedures used to solve the resulting constraints. In the case of continuous systems, this is usually the theory of the real numbers which is undecidable as soon as periodic function symbols, such as the sine function are allowed. Even in the polynomial case, which is decidable [37], existing decision procedures are by far not efficient enough to be able to solve realistic problems. In contrast to that, simulations of continuous systems, approximating the solutions of the underlying differential equations, are possible for systems far beyond those restrictions.

In this paper, we circumvent the constraint solving bottleneck by using an approach that is data-driven instead of deductive: We use simulation data instead of system dynamics as the main input for computing certificates. From a given set of simulations we compute a candidate for a certificate. If this candidate turns out to not to be a certificate for the system itself, we use a refinement loop to run further simulations. In our concrete case, the certificates are formed by so-called barrier certificates [29].

The algorithm uses optimization as its main workhorse. Here, we allow suboptimal results which enables the use of fast heuristic [22] and numerical [27]

© Springer International Publishing AG 2017
A. Abate and G. Geeraerts (Eds.): FORMATS 2017, LNCS 10419, pp. 303–317, 2017.
DOI: 10.1007/978-3-319-65765-3_17

optimization algorithms. In cases, where the system dynamics can be handled by rigorous decision procedures, the final result can be rigorously verified. This final verification step is then applied to a barrier certificate that is already given. Hence it is a much easier problem than the computation of the barrier certificate itself. In our experiments, the non-verified results always turned out to be mathematically correct. Moreover, the final rigorous verification step always took negligible time. The experiments also show that the approach can compute barriers for ordinary differential equations of a complexity that has been out of reach for computation of barrier certificates up to now.

The structure of the paper is as follows: In Sect. 2 we define the problem that the paper solves. In Sect. 3 we describe the general algorithmic framework. In Sects. 4 and 5 we show how to concretize this framework into a working algorithm, and in Sect. 6 we provide this algorithm. In Sect. 7 we describe our implementation of the algorithm, in Sect. 8 we describe computational experiments on several examples, and in Sect. 9 we discuss related work. Section 10 concludes the paper.

The research published in this paper was supported by GAČR grant GA15-14484S and by the long-term strategic development financing of the Institute of Computer Science (RVO:67985807). We thank Hui Kong for discovering a significant mistake in an earlier version of the paper.

2   Problem Description

Definition 1. *A* safety verification problem *is a tuple* (Ω, f, I, U) *where*

- $\Omega \subseteq \mathbb{R}^n$ *(the* state space *of the safety verification problem),*
- $f : \Omega \to \mathbb{R}^n$, *Lipschitz continuous (the* vector field *or* dynamics*),*
- $I \subseteq \mathbb{R}^n$ *(the set of* initial states*), and*
- $U \subseteq \mathbb{R}^n$ *(the set of* unsafe states*).*

We want to verify that a given safety verification problem does not have a solution of the ordinary differential equation $\dot{x} = f(x)$ that leads from an initial to an unsafe state. The corresponding decision problem is in general undecidable [1], and decidable only for very special cases [14]. Hence we head for an algorithm that successfully solves benchmark problems.

The following object [29,36] certifies successful safety verification:

Definition 2. *A* barrier certificate *of a safety verification problem* (Ω, f, I, U) *is a differentiable function* V *such that*

- $\forall x \in I . V(x) < 0$,
- $\forall x \in U . V(x) > 0$, *and*
- $\forall x \in \Omega . V(x) = 0 \Rightarrow (\nabla V(x))^T f(x) < 0$.

In this paper, we will introduce an algorithm that, for an arbitrary given safety verification problem, tries to compute such a barrier certificate. If successful, this implies safety:

Property 1. If a safety verification problem (Ω, f, I, U) has a barrier certificate, then there is no solution $x : [0, T] \to \Omega$ of the ODE $\dot{x} = f(x)$ such that $x(0) \in I$ and $x(T) \in U$.

Our approach is template based. That is, we introduce parameters into the function V, resulting in a parametric function $V(p, x)$ that we call *template*. This reduces the problem of finding a barrier to the problem of finding parameter values such that the template is a barrier. The template can have an arbitrary form, but we will usually work with polynomial templates, that is, templates of the form $p_0 + \sum p_i x^i$, where the x_i are power products, and $p_0, p_1, \ldots$ are parameters.

So, now we are left with the problem of finding a vector p of parameter values such that $\forall x \in I . V(p, x) < 0$, $\forall x \in U . V(p, x) > 0$, and $\forall x \in \Omega . V(p, x) = 0 \Rightarrow (\nabla V(p, x))^T f(x) < 0$.

We denote the conjunction of these three constraints by C_f. The constraint $\exists p\, C_f$ represents a decision problem in the theory of real numbers with quantifier prefix $\exists \forall$. In the polynomial case, this is decidable [37], function symbols such as sin make the problem undecidable. However, even in the polynomial case, in practice, existing decision procedures can only solve problems with a few variables. Note also, that for a template with k parameters, this constraint has $n + k$ variables.

3   Algorithmic Framework

Even if the dynamics f is complex, it is usually possible to compute simulations of the system behavior. That is, for a given $x_0 \in \Omega$ and a time bound T, one can compute an approximation of the solution of the ordinary differential equation $\dot{x} = f(x)$ of length T, starting in x_0. Simulation is an essential tool in practical systems modeling, and approximation is usually taken into account already during the modeling process. As a consequence such simulations often describe the intended system behavior more accurately than even the precise mathematical solution.

We will represent such simulations by pairs $(s, s') \in \Omega \times \Omega$, where s is the starting point, and s' is the endpoint of the simulation. We will call such pairs *simulation segments*. The straightforward way of computing such a pair (s, s') is to fix s and a time bound T and then to compute s' using simulation. Note however, that it is also possible to do reverse simulation, that is to fix s' and to compute s by solving the ordinary differential equation $\dot{x} = -f(x)$.

We will maintain a set S of such simulation segments. Our goal is to use this set S for computing a solution p of the constraint C_f. For this we relax the universal quantifiers to finite conjunctions. For the first two parts of the constraint C_f we simply replace the set I bounding the universal quantifiers in the first part with the set of all initial points in S, and the set U with the set of all unsafe points in S. However, for the third part of C_f, due to the implication occurring here, it does not suffice to replace the set Ω by a finite subset. This would allow trivial satisfaction of this implication using a parameter vector p such that $V(p, s)$ is non-zero for every element of this finite subset. Instead, we use the observation, that the third part of C_f—which ensures a certain direction of the vector field f on the zero set of the barrier—implies that no solution of $\dot{x} = f(x)$ may connect a point with negative value of V to a point with positive value of V. The resulting constraints are:

- $\bigwedge_{(s,s') \in S, I(s)} V(p, s) < 0,\ \bigwedge_{(s,s') \in S, I(s')} V(p, s') < 0$
- $\bigwedge_{(s,s') \in S, U(s)} V(p, s) > 0,\ \bigwedge_{(s,s') \in S, U(s')} V(p, s') > 0,$
- $\bigwedge_{(s,s') \in S} V(p, s) > 0 \lor V(p, s') < 0$

We will call the conjunction of these constraints *sampled constraint* and will denote it by C_S. Clearly, this approximation of C_f by C_S does not lose barrier certificates:

Property 2. C_f implies C_S.

Unlike the original constraint C_f, the sampled constraint C_S does not contain any quantifier alternation which makes it easier to solve. However, it may have spurious solutions, that is, solutions that do not correspond to a solution of the original constraint and that, hence, do not represent a barrier certificate

In order to handle such a situation, we use the following property:

Property 3. If $S \subseteq S'$ then $C_{S'}$ implies C_S.

So adding more segments to S does not weaken the approximation. To actually strengthen the approximation we use an algorithm based on the principle of counter-example based refinement: The algorithm computes a solution of C_S that we will call *barrier candidate*, checks whether this barrier candidate is spurious, and if yes, generates and adds a counter-example in the form of a new simulation segment that refutes the given barrier candidate. If the barrier candidate is not spurious, we return the vector p which then represents a barrier certificate.

The resulting algorithm looks as follows:

initialize S with some simulation segments
let p be s.t. $p \models C_S$
while $p \not\models C_f$ **do**
  $S \leftarrow S \cup \{(s, s')\}$, where (s, s') is a simulation segment with $p \not\models C_{S \cup \{(s,s')\}}$
  let p be s.t. $p \models C_S$
return p

The algorithm leaves the concrete choice of the barrier candidate and counter-example open. As it is, allowing an arbitrary choice of those objects, it does not work. The main problem is a consequence of the fact that the space of barrier candidates is uncountable. Computing an arbitrary barrier candidate, and then removing this single barrier candidate does, in general, not make enough progress in removing spurious barrier candidates[1]. Moreover, if the system dynamics f

---

[1] Decision procedures for real closed fields, can circumvent this problem [15], due to the fact that semi-algebraic sets possess an algorithmically computable finite cellular decomposition [4].

is non-polynomial, it is, in general, not possible to decide the satisfiability test $p \models C_f$ which is the termination condition of the algorithm.

In the next three sections we will design a variant of the above algorithm that overcomes those problems. We will compute a barrier candidate p s.t. $p \models C_S$ and a counter-example (s, s') with $p \not\models C_{S \cup \{(s,s')\}}$ that ensure as much progress of the algorithm as possible. As a side-effect we will also get a termination condition for the refinement loop that represents a computable and practically reliable replacement for the satisfiability test $p \models C_f$.

4   Computing a Barrier Candidate

The sampled constraint C_S can have many solutions. Which one should we choose? Certainly we should prefer non-spurious solutions that is, solutions that also satisfy the original constraint C_f. Moreover, if a solution turns out to be spurious, removing it should remove as many further spurious solutions as possible. We will work with the assumption, that those objectives will be fulfilled by solutions that are as central as possible in the solution set of the sampled constraint.

For this we replace the inequalities, that can be either satisfied or not, by a finer measure [30]. Observing, that the right-hand side of every inequality is zero, we base this measure on the value of the term on the left-hand side: This value measures how strongly a given point p satisfies a greater-than-zero predicate. In the case of a less-than-zero predicate, we can measure this by multiplying the value of the term on the left-hand side by -1. Moreover, we replace conjunction by the minimum operator and disjunction by the maximum operator in the style of fuzzy logic.

The result is the function

$$\min \left\{ \begin{array}{l} \min_{s \in I, (s,s') \in S} -V(p, s), \min_{s' \in I, (s,s') \in S} -V(p, s'), \\ \min_{s \in U, (s,s') \in S} V(p, s), \min_{s' \in U, (s,s') \in S} V(p, s'), \\ \min_{(s,s') \in S} \max\{V(p, s), -V(p, s')\} \end{array} \right\}$$

which we maximize to find points that satisfy the constraint C_S as strongly as possible.

Now observe that template polynomials $V(p, x)$ of the form $p_0 + \sum p_i x^i$ are linear in their parameters $p_0, p_1, \ldots$. Hence, the result of substituting points s and s' for x in $V(p, x)$ is a linear inequality of the form $a^T p < 0$ with p being the parameter vector $(p_0, p_1, \ldots)$ and a being a vector of real numbers whose first entry, resulting from the monomial p_0, is the constant 1.

For a polynomial template and $\lambda \geq 0$, $V(\lambda p, s) = \lambda V(p, s)$. Hence, also the above function scales in such a way, the corresponding optimization problem is unbounded, and optimization algorithms will usually simply come up with larger and larger values for the vector p. In other words, instead of optimizing for our goal of being as much as possible in the solution set of the sampled constraint this formulation optimizes for large parameter values which, in turn, result in large values of $V(p, s)$. We avoid this by constraining the (max)-norm of the vector p to not to exceed 1.

However, even then, minimizing a linear term $a^T p$ enforces large distance from the boundary of the solution set of C_S, if $||a||$ is small, and vice versa. For avoiding this, we normalize the terms, resulting in $\frac{a^T}{||a||_2} p$. This amounts to computation of the Chebyshev center [2], that is, the center of the largest ball contained in the solution set[2].

So we solve the optimization problem

$$\max_{||p|| \leq 1} F_S(p)$$

where $F_S(p)$ is the minimax function above with all linear terms normalized by dividing them with the 2-norm of their coefficients.

Property 4. $F_S(p) > 0$ iff $p \models C_S$

Hence, a positive result of the optimization problem gives us a solution of the sampled constraint. By optimizing further, we get solutions that are as central as possible in the solution set of C_S, hence also increasing the chances of finding a solution of the original constraint C_f.

5   Computing a Counter-Example

The solution p of the sampled constraint C_S might be spurious, that is, it might not satisfy the original constraint C_f. If the computed solution is spurious, we generate a counter-example, that is, a new simulation segment (s, s') s.t. p does not satisfy the strengthened sampled constraint $C_{S \cup \{(s,s')\}}$. However, this constraint should not only refute the computed barrier candidate p, but as many further spurious solutions as possible. The techniques from the previous section, that is, maximizing F_S instead of computing an arbitrary solution of C_S, alleviates the problem. However, in addition, we also want to add a simulation segment (s, s') that removes as many spurious solutions as possible.

For this we again translate the constraint solving problem of finding a counter-example into an optimization problem. However, searching for a strong violation of $C_{S \cup \{(s,s')\}}$ by searching for a simulation segment (s, s') s.t. $F_{S \cup \{(s,s')\}}$ is minimal, is an ODE-constrained optimization problem. Such problems are notoriously difficult to solve. In order to avoid this, we work with the original constraint C_f, instead.

We have a *fixed* barrier candidate p and look for an x violating one of the individual parts of C_f. By looking for an x violating one of the individual parts of C_f *as much as possible* we hope to construct a counter-example not only for

---

[2] Note that due to the disjunction, we do not have a polyhedron here. Still, this formulation models the Chebyshev center.

the given spurious candidate p, but for as many further spurious candidates as possible.

Applying the constraint-to-function transformation already described in the previous section to the three parts of the constraint C_f, we arrive at the functions

$$\min\{-V(p,x) \mid x \in I\},$$
$$\min\{V(p,x) \mid x \in U\}, \text{and}$$
$$\min\{-(\nabla V(p,x))^T f(x) \mid V(p,x) = 0, x \in \Omega\}.$$

However, the third entry does not fully correspond to the original intention of the corresponding constraint: Its task is to measure, whether all solution of the ODE crossing the zero level set $\{x \mid V(p,x) = 0\}$ do so in the correct direction. This direction should be independent wrt. scaling of $f(x)$ or $\nabla V(x)$. In order to normalize those factors, we replace the objective function $-(\nabla V(p,x))^T f(x)$ with the objective function

$$-\frac{\nabla V(p,x)}{||\nabla V(p,x)||}^T \frac{f(x)}{||f(x)||}.$$

As a result, we have three optimization problems,

- $\min_{x \in I} F_I(p,x)$, where $F_I(p,x) := -V(p,x)$,
- $\min_{x \in U} F_U(p,x)$, where $F_U(x) := V(p,x)$, and
- $\min_{x \in \Omega, V(p,x)=0} F_\nabla(p,x)$ where $F_\nabla(p,x) := -\frac{\nabla V(p,x)}{||\nabla V(p,x)||}^T \frac{f(x)}{||f(x)||}$.

Compared to the problem from the previous section, where the search space is the parameter space, and the state space was discretized, here p is fixed, and we search in the original state space Ω.

Denoting the endpoint of a solution of length T of the ODE $\dot{x} = f(x)$ starting in x_0 by $\phi(x_0, T)$, we have:

Property 5. Let $x \in I$ with $F_I(p,x) < 0$. Then for all $T \geq 0$, $p \not\models C_{S \cup \{(x, \phi(x,T))\}}$.

Property 6. Let $x \in U$ with $F_U(p,x) < 0$. Then for all $T \geq 0$, $p \not\models C_{S \cup \{(\phi(x,-T),x)\}}$.

Property 7. Let x be such that $V(p,x) = 0$ and $F_\nabla(p,x) < 0$. Then there is a $T^* > 0$ s.t. for all $0 < T \leq T^*$, $p \not\models C_{S \cup \{(\phi(x,-T),\phi(x,T))\}}$.

So we add simulation segments approximating $(x, \phi(x,T))$, $(\phi(x,-T),x)$, and $(\phi(x,-T),\phi(x,T))$, respectively. In the case of $(\phi(x,-T),\phi(x,T))$ we have to be careful to not to do too long simulations, due to the upper bound T^* in Property 7.

6 Resulting Algorithm

initialize S with some simulation segments
$(cand, cntrxpl) \leftarrow check(S)$

while $\neg[cand = \bot \vee ctrxpl = \emptyset]$ **do**
    $S \leftarrow S \cup cntrxpl$
    $(cand, cntrxpl) \leftarrow check(S)$
if $cand = \bot$ **then return** "no barrier found"
rigorously verify $cand$ *optional verification step*
return $cand$

subalgorithm check(S): returns barrier candidate and counter-example
let p be s.t. $F_S(p)$ is as large as possible   *compute a barrier candidate*
if $F_S(p) \leq 0$ **then return** $(\bot, \emptyset)$ *no barrier candidate found*
let $x_I \in I$ be s.t. $F_I(p, x_I)$ is as small as possible
let $x_U \in U$ be s.t. $F_U(p, x_U)$ is as small as possible
let $x_\nabla \in \Omega$ be s.t. $V(p, x_\nabla) = 0$ and $F_\nabla(p, x_\nabla)$ is as small as possible
$m \leftarrow \min\{F_I(p, x_I), F_U(p, x_U), F_\nabla(p, x_\nabla)\}$
if $m \geq 0$ **then return** $(p, \emptyset)$ *no counterexample found*
return $(p, \{(s, s')\})$ **where**
$$(s, s') = \begin{cases} \text{a forward simulation from } x_I, \text{if } m = F_I(p, x_I) \\ \text{a backward simulation from } x_U, \text{if } m = F_U(p, x_U) \\ \text{a forward/backward simulation from } x_\nabla, \text{if } m = F_\nabla(p, x_\nabla) \end{cases}$$

Note that here we only need values for which the objective functions are large (small, respectively). We do *not* insist on a lower bound of the minimization problem (upper bound on the maximization problem, respectively), let alone a decision procedure. This allows the use of various heuristic optimization techniques [22] that even can be applied in cases where finding a precise optimum is impossible due to non-decidability issues, for example, due to non-polynomial system dynamics f occurring in F_∇.

Also observe that the optimization of $F_S(p)$ is a search problem of the parameter space dimension k, and the computation of x_I, x_U, and x_∇ is a search problem of the state space dimension n. In contrast to that, directly solving original constraint C_f is a problem in dimension $n + k$.

The final step of rigorously verifying the barrier candidate, that is, verifying $p \models C_f$, is a problem in state space dimension n, as well. Due to the strategy of optimizing for a barrier candidate, the computed candidate will usually satisfy C_f robustly. Hence, even in undecidable cases, this allows the application of procedures that exploit robustness [31].

7 Implementation

In the section, we show how the optimization problems and the final verification step of the algorithm from the previous section can be solved in practice.

As described in Sect. 4, $F_S(p)$ is linear in p. However, it contains a min/max alternation which is beyond the capabilities of usual numerical optimization algorithm. The key to solving this constraint is the observation that the min/max operators occurring within $F_S(p)$ are *finite*. Hence the optimization problem can be rewritten to the following constrained optimization problem: Maximize δ under

$$\bigwedge_{(s,s')\in S, I(s)} -V(p,s) \geq \delta, \bigwedge_{(s,s')\in S, I(s')} -V(p,s') \geq \delta,$$
$$\bigwedge_{(s,s')\in S, U(s)} V(p,s) \geq \delta, \bigwedge_{(s,s')\in S, U(s')} V(p,s') \geq \delta, \text{ and}$$
$$\bigwedge_{(s,s')\in S} V(p,s) \geq \delta \vee -V(p,s') \geq \delta.$$

This is an optimization modulo theory [26,33] problem in the theory LRA (linear real arithmetic).

For minimizing $F_I(p,x)$, $F_U(p,x)$, and $F_\nabla(p,x)$ one can use classical numerical optimization [27]. Since such methods do local search, they may run into local, but non-global optima. To search for global solutions one can start several optimization runs from random starting points which is also known under the term multi-start [23]. Note that this is trivial to parallelize efficiently.

For the final rigorous verification step, one can use a simple branch-and-bound approach, evaluating the terms $V(p,x)$ using interval arithmetic [25], checking the inequalities of Definition 2 on the resulting intervals, and using splitting to tighten the bounds, if necessary.

8   Computational Experiments

We did experiments with a prototype implementation of the method described so far. The prototype requires the state space, set of initial states and the set of unsafe states to have the shape of a hyper-rectangle. We initialize the set S by forward simulations from all vertices of the initial hyper-rectangle and backward simulations from all vertices of the unsafe hyper-rectangle. Due to this initialization, our prototype implementation does not check barrier candidates for violations of the first two conditions of Definition 2, and indeed, even without such a check, the computed barriers do not violate those conditions.

For each example, we set the lengths of all simulations manually to a certain constant σ that we show below. Moreover, we cancel simulations that leave a bloated version of the state space. Here, we simply bloat each interval bound of Ω by a certain percentage from its distance from the interval center: $bloat([\underline{a}, \overline{a}]) = [\frac{\underline{a}+\overline{a}}{2} - b(\frac{\underline{a}+\overline{a}}{2} - \underline{a}), \frac{\underline{a}+\overline{a}}{2} + b(\overline{a} - \frac{\underline{a}+\overline{a}}{2})] = [\frac{(1+b)\underline{a}+(1-b)\overline{a}}{2}, \frac{(1-b)\underline{a}+(1+b)\overline{a}}{2}]$. In our experiments, we use $b = 1.1$.

The examples that we used are:

1. a standard ODE modeling a pendulum with normalized parameters (e.g., Kapinski et al. [18], Example 1), where the variable x models the angle of the pendulum, and y models angular speed.

$$\dot{x} = y$$
$$\dot{y} = -\sin x - y$$

$\Omega = [-10, 10] \times [-10, 10]$, $I = [-10, 10] \times [8, 10]$, $U = [-10, 10] \times [-10, -5]$, $\sigma = 0.5$

2. dynamics from [5, Example 5]

$$\dot{x} = y + (1 - x^2 - y^2)x + \ln(x^2 + 1)$$
$$\dot{y} = -x + (1 - x^2 - y^2)y + \ln(y^2 + 1)$$

$\Omega = [-5, 5] \times [-5, 5]$, $I = [1, 3] \times [-1.5, 3.0]$, $U = [-3, -0.6] \times [1, 3]$, $\sigma = 1$

3. a standard Lorenz system [38], see also [6, Example 7]

$$\dot{x} = 10(y - x)$$
$$\dot{y} = x(28 - z) - y$$
$$\dot{z} = xy - \tfrac{8}{3}z$$

$\Omega = [-20, 20] \times [-20, 0] \times [-20, 20]$, $I = [-14.8, -14.2] \times [-14.8, -14.2] \times [12.2, 12.8]$, $U = [-16.8, -16.2] \times [-14.8, -14.2] \times [2.2, 2.8]$, $\sigma = 0.1$

4. composition of trivial dynamics (variable x_1) and pendulum (variables x_2 and x_3)

$$\dot{x}_1 = 1$$
$$\dot{x}_2 = x_3$$
$$\dot{x}_3 = -10 \sin x_2 - x_3$$

$\Omega = [-10, 10]^3$, $I = [9, 10] \times [-10, 10]^2$, $U = [-10, -9] \times [-10, 10]^2$, $\sigma = 0.1$

5. scalable example, manually constructed

$$\dot{x}_1 = 1 + \tfrac{1}{l}(\textstyle\sum_{i \in \{1,\ldots,l\}} x_{i+1} + x_{i+2}))$$
$$\dot{x}_2 = x_3$$
$$\dot{x}_3 = -10 \sin x_2 - x_2$$
$$\cdots$$
$$\dot{x}_{2l} = x_{2l+1}$$
$$\dot{x}_{2l+1} = -10 \sin x_{2l} - x_2$$

$\Omega = [-10, 10]^{2l+1}$, $I = [9, 10] \times [-10, 10]^{2l}$, $U = [-10, -9] \times [-10, 10]^{2l}$, $\sigma = 0.1$, with $l = 1$

6. same as Example 5, but $l = 2$
7. same as Example 5, but $l = 3$
8. same as Example 5, but $l = 4$

All experiments were executed on a notebook with Intel(R) Core(TM) i7-5600U CPU @ 2.60 GHz and running Ubuntu Linux 16.10. For simulation we used the software package CVODE version 2.5.0 from the SUNDIALS suite of solvers. For optimizing $F_S(p)$ we use the tool OptiMathSAT [34]. For minimizing $F_I(p, x)$, $F_U(p, x)$, and $F_\nabla(p, x)$ we use the function sqp from the software package GNU Octave 4.0.3 which implements the optimization method of sequential quadratic programming. We globalized this method by multi-start with 16 local optimization runs. For the final rigorous verification step, we use our software RSolver (http://rsolver.sourceforge.net) which extends a basic interval branch-and-bound method with interval constraint propagation.

We list the results in Table 1. Here, the column "dim" denotes the problem dimension and "templ" denotes one of the following templates:

Table 1. Results of experiments

	dim	templ	iter	simulation	candidate	counter-example	verif
1	2	Q	10	0.24	1.2	8.21	0
2	2	Q	5	0.11	0.25	5.7	0.41
3	3	T	10	0.3	1.01	17.03	0
4	3	L	1	0.02	0	1.07	0
5	3	L	1	0.01	0.01	1.21	0
6	5	L	1	0.14	0.36	3.51	0
7	7	L	1	1.06	7.38	7.67	0
8	9	L	1	15.81	1340.6	19.76	0.01

Q: $p_0 + p_1x^2 + p_2xy + p_3y^2 + p_4x + p_5y$
T: $p_0 + p_1x^2 + p_2x + p_3y$
L: the linear template $p_0 + p_1x_1 + \cdots + p_nx_n$ with n being the state space dimension

Moreover, the column "iter" denotes the number of iterations of the refinement loop. Further columns denote the time spent in simulation, computation of a barrier candidate, computation of a counter-example, and verification. The time unit are seconds.

As can be seen, in all cases, the computed barrier could be rigorously verified. Moreoever, the time needed to do so is negligible. The whole method scales to higher-dimensional examples, but as the problem dimension increases, the optimization module theory solver used to compute a barrier candidate is increasingly becoming a bottleneck. Note that we used the solver as a black box, with the original parameter settings.

To ensure verifiability of our results, we list the computed barriers:

1. $0.118462553528y^2 - 0.011722981249xy - 0.709542580128y - 0.0550927673883x^2 - 0.0586149062452x - 1$
2. $0.408692986165y^2 - 0.386033509251xy - 0.227005969996y + 0.0866893912879x^2 - 0.925807829028x - 1$
3. $(-z) + 0.0862165171738x^2 + 0.406513973333x - 0.668459116412$
4. $0.12774317671 - x_1$
5. $6.94919072662 \times 10^{-4}x_3 + 7.29701934574 \times 10^{-4}x_2 - x_1 + 0.127740909365$
6. $0.00298446742425x_5 - 0.00705872836204x_4 - 0.00693382587388x_3 + 0.00295825595803x_2 - x_1 + 0.100721787174$
7. $0.00567387721155x_7 + 0.00131139026963x_6 + 0.00409187476431x_5 - 0.00293955884622x_4 - 0.00148234438362x_3 + 0.0102405191466x_2 - x_1 + 0.0693868521466$
8. $0.00474371409319x_9 + 6.04082564889 \times 10^{-4}x_8 + 0.00539357982978x_7 - 3.62914727064 \times 10^{-5}x_6 - 0.00305191611365x_5 + 0.00234411670971x_4 + 0.00308900495946x_3 + 0.00766513576991x_2 - x_1 + 0.0526159036023$

9   Related Work

The original method for computing barrier certificates [29] was based on sums-of-squares programming [28]. Since then, various further methods for computing barrier certificates and inductive invariants of polynomials systems have been designed [10, 12, 19, 32, 39, 40].

To the best of our knowledge, there is only one method capable of computing barrier certificates for non-polynomial systems [6]. The method is not based on simulation but uses interval-based constraint solving techniques, in a similar way as we do in the final verification step, and in a similar way as the algorithm implemented in RSOLVER [31]. This restricts the method to systems where such techniques are available, which corresponds to those systems, where our algorithm can do the final verification step. The method applies branching to *both* the state and parameter space, whereas our algorithm, at a given time, always searches only in one of the two. Instead of our method for computing barrier candidates, the method guesses barrier certificates by simply trying midpoints of intervals which can be very efficient if this guess happens to be lucky, but very inefficient, if not. Especially, if the midpoint of the user-provided parameter space already happens to be a barrier certificate, then the method succeeds without any search. Unfortunately, the paper does not give any information on the computed barriers, which makes comparison difficult.

The approach to generalize or learn system behavior from simulations has been used before for computing Lyapunov functions [17, 18] and for computing the region of attraction [20]. Simulations can also be used to directly verify system behavior [7–9, 11]. For an overview of simulation-based approaches to systems verification see Kapinski et al. [16].

In software verification, the usage of test runs was shown to be useful in the computation of inductive invariants [13, 35]. However, the problem and solution are quite different from what we have here due to the discrete nature of both time and data types occurring in computer programs.

Our algorithm can also be interpreted as an online machine learning [24] process that learns a barrier certificate from simulations, querying for new simulations to improve the barrier certificate. Moreover, the samples reachable from an initial state or leading to an unsafe state can be interpreted as positive and negative examples. However, here we do *not* have a classification problem due to the third property of Definition 2.

10   Conclusion

In this paper, we have presented an approach for synthesizing barrier certificates from system simulations. The resulting method is able to compute barrier certificates for ODEs that have been out of reach for such methods so far.

In the future we will increase the usability of the method by automatizing the choice of the used template and by automatically adapting the length of the computed simulation. We will also combine the method with falsification methods [21] that search for ODE solutions that lead from an initial to an unsafe state. In such a combined method, falsification should exploit the result of failed attempts at computing a barrier certificate and vice versa.

References

1. Bournez, O., Campagnolo, M.L.: A survey on continuous time computations. In: Cooper, S., Löwe, B., Sorbi, A. (eds.) New Computational Paradigms, pp. 383–423 (2008)
2. Boyd, S., Vandenberghe, L.: Convex Optimization. Cambridge University Press, Cambridge (2004)
3. Caviness, B.F., Johnson, J.R. (eds.): Quantifier Elimination and Cylindrical Algebraic Decomposition. Springer, Wien (1998)
4. Collins, G.E.: Quantifier elimination for the elementary theory of real closed fields by cylindrical algebraic decomposition. In: Second GI Conference Automata Theory and Formal Languages. LNCS, vol. 33, pp. 134–183. Springer (1975). Also in [3]
5. Djaballah, A., Chapoutot, A., Kieffer, M., Bouissou, O.: Construction of parametric barrier functions for dynamical systems using interval analysis. arXiv:1506.05885v1 (2015)
6. Djaballah, A., Chapoutot, A., Kieffer, M., Bouissou, O.: Construction of parametric barrier functions for dynamical systems using interval analysis. Automatica **78**, 287–296 (2017)
7. Donzé, A., Maler, O.: Systematic simulation using sensitivity analysis. In: Bemporad, A., Bicchi, A., Buttazzo, G. (eds.) HSCC 2007. LNCS, vol. 4416, pp. 174–189. Springer, Heidelberg (2007). doi:10.1007/978-3-540-71493-4_16
8. Fainekos, G.E., Girard, A., Pappas, G.J.: Temporal logic verification using simulation. In: Asarin, E., Bouyer, P. (eds.) FORMATS 2006. LNCS, vol. 4202, pp. 171–186. Springer, Heidelberg (2006). doi:10.1007/11867340_13
9. Fan, C., Qi, B., Mitra, S., Viswanathan, M., Duggirala, P.S.: Automatic reachability analysis for nonlinear hybrid models with C2E2. In: Chaudhuri, S., Farzan, A. (eds.) CAV 2016. LNCS, vol. 9779, pp. 531–538. Springer, Cham (2016). doi:10.1007/978-3-319-41528-4_29
10. Ghorbal, K., Sogokon, A., Platzer, A.: A hierarchy of proof rules for checking positive invariance of algebraic and semi-algebraic sets. Comput. Lang. Syst. Struct. **47**, 19–43 (2017)
11. Girard, A., Pappas, G.J.: Verification using simulation. In: Hespanha, J.P., Tiwari, A. (eds.) HSCC 2006. LNCS, vol. 3927, pp. 272–286. Springer, Heidelberg (2006). doi:10.1007/11730637_22
12. Gulwani, S., Tiwari, A.: Constraint-based approach for analysis of hybrid systems. In: Gupta, A., Malik, S. (eds.) CAV 2008. LNCS, vol. 5123, pp. 190–203. Springer, Heidelberg (2008). doi:10.1007/978-3-540-70545-1_18
13. Gupta, A., Majumdar, R., Rybalchenko, A.: From tests to proofs. Int. J. Softw. Tools Technol. Transfer **15**(4), 291–303 (2013)
14. Hainry, E.: Reachability in linear dynamical systems. In: Beckmann, A., Dimitracopoulos, C., Löwe, B. (eds.) CiE 2008. LNCS, vol. 5028, pp. 241–250. Springer, Heidelberg (2008). doi:10.1007/978-3-540-69407-6_28
15. Jovanović, D., Moura, L.: Solving non-linear arithmetic. In: Gramlich, B., Miller, D., Sattler, U. (eds.) IJCAR 2012. LNCS, vol. 7364, pp. 339–354. Springer, Heidelberg (2012). doi:10.1007/978-3-642-31365-3_27

16. Kapinski, J., Deshmukh, J.V., Jin, X., Ito, H., Butts, K.: Simulation-based approaches for verification of embedded control systems: an overview of traditional and advanced modeling, testing, and verification techniques. IEEE Control Syst. **36**(6), 45–64 (2016)

17. Kapinski, J., Deshmukh, J.V., Jin, X., Ito, H., Butts, K.R.: Simulation-guided approaches for verification of automotive powertrain control systems. In: American Control Conference, ACC 2015, Chicago, IL, USA, 1–3 July 2015, pp. 4086–4095 (2015)

18. Kapinski, J., Deshmukh, J.V., Sankaranarayanan, S., Arechiga, N.: Simulation-guided Lyapunov analysis for hybrid dynamical systems. In: 17th International Conference on Hybrid Systems: Computation and Control (part of CPS Week), HSCC 2014, Berlin, Germany, April 15–17, 2014, pp. 133–142 (2014)

19. Kong, H., Song, X., Han, D., Gu, M., Sun, J.: A new barrier certificate for safety verification of hybrid systems. Comput. J. **57**, 1033–1045 (2013)

20. Kozarev, A., Quindlen, J., How, J., Topcu, U.: Case studies in data-driven verification of dynamical systems. In: Proceedings of the 19th International Conference on Hybrid Systems: Computation and Control, pp. 81–86. ACM (2016)

21. Kuřátko, J., Ratschan, S.: Combined global and local search for the falsification of hybrid systems. In: Legay, A., Bozga, M. (eds.) FORMATS 2014. LNCS, vol. 8711, pp. 146–160. Springer, Cham (2014). doi:10.1007/978-3-319-10512-3_11

22. Locatelli, M., Schoen, F.: Global Optimization: Theory, Algorithms, and Applications. SIAM, Philadelphia (2013)

23. Martí, R.: Multi-start methods. In: Glover, F., Kochenberger, G.A. (eds.) Handbook of Metaheuristics. International Series in Operations Research & Management Science, vol. 57, pp. 355–368. Springer, US (2003)

24. Mohri, M., Rostamizadeh, A., Talwalkar, A.: Foundations of Machine Learning. The MIT Press, Cambridge (2012)

25. Moore, R.E., Kearfott, R.B., Cloud, M.J.: Introduction to Interval Analysis. SIAM, Philadelphia (2009)

26. Nieuwenhuis, R., Oliveras, A.: On SAT modulo theories and optimization problems. In: Biere, A., Gomes, C.P. (eds.) SAT 2006. LNCS, vol. 4121, pp. 156–169. Springer, Heidelberg (2006). doi:10.1007/11814948_18

27. Nocedal, J., Wright, S.J.: Numerical Optimization, 2nd edn. Springer, New York (2006)

28. Parrilo, P.A.: Semidefinite programming relaxations for semialgebraic problems. Math. Programm. Ser. B **96**(2), 293–320 (2003)

29. Prajna, S., Jadbabaie, A.: Safety verification of hybrid systems using barrier certificates. In: Alur, R., Pappas, G.J. (eds.) HSCC 2004. LNCS, vol. 2993, pp. 477–492. Springer, Heidelberg (2004). doi:10.1007/978-3-540-24743-2_32

30. Ratschan, S.: Quantified constraints under perturbations. J. Symbolic Comput. **33**(4), 493–505 (2002)

31. Ratschan, S.: Efficient solving of quantified inequality constraints over the real numbers. ACM Trans. Comput. Logic **7**(4), 723–748 (2006)

32. Sankaranarayanan, S., Sipma, H.B., Manna, Z.: Constructing invariants for hybrid systems. Formal Methods Syst. Des. **32**(1), 25–55 (2008)

33. Sebastiani, R., Tomasi, S.: Optimization modulo theories with linear rational costs. ACM Trans. Comput. Logic (TOCL) **16**(2), 12 (2015)

34. Sebastiani, R., Trentin, P.: OptiMathSAT: a tool for optimization modulo theories. In: Kroening, D., Păsăreanu, C.S. (eds.) CAV 2015. LNCS, vol. 9206, pp. 447–454. Springer, Cham (2015). doi:10.1007/978-3-319-21690-4_27

35. Sharma, R., Gupta, S., Hariharan, B., Aiken, A., Liang, P., Nori, A.V.: A data driven approach for algebraic loop invariants. In: Felleisen, M., Gardner, P. (eds.) ESOP 2013. LNCS, vol. 7792, pp. 574–592. Springer, Heidelberg (2013). doi:10.1007/978-3-642-37036-6_31

36. Taly, A., Tiwari, A.: Deductive verification of continuous dynamical systems. In: Kannan, R., Kumar, K.N. (eds.) IARCS Annual Conference. on Foundations of Software Technology and Theoretical Computer Science (FSTTCS 2009). Leibniz International Proceedings in Informatics (LIPIcs), vol. 4, pp. 383–394. Dagstuhl, Germany (2009)

37. Tarski, A.: A Decision Method for Elementary Algebra and Geometry. University of California Press, Berkeley (1951). Also in [3]

38. Vaněček, A., Čelikovský, S.: Control Systems: From Linear Analysis to Synthesis of Chaos. Prentice Hall, London (1996)

39. Yang, Z., Huang, C., Chen, X., Lin, W., Liu, Z.: A Linear Programming Relaxation Based Approach for Generating Barrier Certificates of Hybrid Systems. In: Fitzgerald, J., Heitmeyer, C., Gnesi, S., Philippou, A. (eds.) FM 2016. LNCS, vol. 9995, pp. 721–738. Springer, Cham (2016). doi:10.1007/978-3-319-48989-6_44

40. Yang, Z., Lin, W., Wu, M.: Exact safety verification of hybrid systems based on bilinear SOS representation. ACM Trans. Embed. Comput. Syst. 14(1), 16:1–16:19 (2015)

A Symbolic Operational Semantics for TESL
With an Application to Heterogeneous System Testing

Hai Nguyen Van[1]([✉]), Thibaut Balabonski[1], Frédéric Boulanger[2],
Chantal Keller[1], Benoît Valiron[2], and Burkhart Wolff[1]

[1] LRI, Université Paris Sud, CNRS, Université Paris-Saclay, Orsay, France
{hai.nguyen-van,thibaut.balabonski,chantal.keller,burkhart.wolff}@lri.fr
[2] LRI, CentraleSupélec, Université Paris-Sud, Université Paris-Saclay,
Gif-sur-Yvette, France
{frederic.boulanger,benoit.valiron}@lri.fr

Abstract. TESL addresses the specification of the temporal aspects of an architectural composition language that allows the composition of timed subsystems. TESL specifies the synchronization points between events and time scales. Methodologically, subsystems having potentially different models of execution are abstracted to their interfaces expressed in terms of timed events.

In this paper, we present an operational semantics of TESL for constructing symbolic traces that can be used in an online-test scenario: the symbolic trace containing a set of constraints over time-stamps and occurrences of events is matched against concrete runs of the system.

We present the operational rules for building symbolic traces and illustrate them with examples. Finally, we show a prototype implementation that generates symbolic traces, and its use for testing.

Keywords: Heterogeneity · Synchronicity · Timed behaviors

1 Introduction

The design of complex systems involves different formalisms for modeling their different parts or aspects. The global model of a system may therefore consist of a coordination of sub-models that use differential equations, state machines, synchronous data-flow networks, discrete event models and so on. This raises the interest in *architectural composition languages* that allow for "bolting the respective sub-models together", along their various interfaces, and specifying the various ways of collaboration and coordination. Figure 1 shows a conceptual diagram of such a heterogeneous system model.

The Ptolemy project [10] was one of the first to provide support for mixing heterogeneous models. More recently, the GEMOC initiative [9] has been putting the focus on the development of techniques, frameworks and environments to facilitate the creation, integration, and automated processing of heterogeneous modeling languages. While Ptolemy follows a generic approach to architectural

© Springer International Publishing AG 2017
A. Abate and G. Geeraerts (Eds.): FORMATS 2017, LNCS 10419, pp. 318–334, 2017.
DOI: 10.1007/978-3-319-65765-3_18

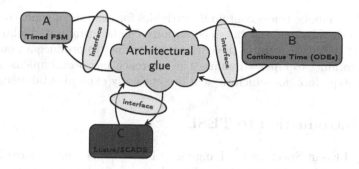

Fig. 1. A heterogeneous timed system

composition, the BCOoL language [20] is more specifically targeted at coordination patterns for Domain Specific Events, which define the interface of a domain specific modeling language.

Our interest in architectural composition has a particular emphasis on sub-systems involving *time* and *timed behavior*. In contrast to BCOoL, which translates its coordination patterns into CCSL (Clock Constraints Specification Language, see [11,15]), we target TESL (Tagged Events Specification Language, see [6]), a language that we designed to allow the specification of durations as differences between tags, and not only as a number of occurrences of an event. This model of time is close to the time in the MARTE [1] profile, or in the Tagged Signal Model [14]. This allows us to coordinate systems with different forms of time that flow at different rates.

The TESL language, which was developed in the ModHel'X [12] heterogeneous simulation platform, was originally targeted only at the timed coordination of sub-models during the simulation of heterogeneous models. It allows sub-systems to live in different "time islands" by supporting the notion of time scale and of relations between the speed at which time elapses for different clocks. TESL is totally synchronous and focuses on *causality* between events and *synchronization* on time scales. Causality is expressed in statements such as: "event X should occur now because event Y occurs now". Synchronization is expressed in statements such as: "event X should occur because time reaches t on the time scale of a clock". This can be used to coordinate the execution of models that have different notions of time (physical time, angular position, distance) that flow at different rates, which are in the most general case only loosely coupled and can even accelerate.

In this paper, we extend our simulation framework to a verification framework: we present a novel *test method* establishing that the time coordination of some sub-models, as it is actually implemented in a given system, conforms to the specification modeled in TESL. Since an enumerative model-checking approach is impossible for real-time systems and infeasible for practical discrete time systems, we develop a novel operational semantics geared to the symbolic execution of TESL specifications. If the latter is run in parallel to a system under test (SUT), symbolic traces containing variables for instants of time, constraints over time scale relations, and causal conditions, can be instantiated following the reactions of the SUT, refining the current constraints to produce a new specification conforming to input stimulus. The approach has been implemented in a novel prototype tool, for which we will present early experimental results.

2   An Introduction to TESL

The Tagged-Event Specification Language (TESL) [6] is a declarative language designed for the specification of the timed behavior of discrete events and their synchronization. Event occurrences (aka *ticks*) are grouped in *clocks*, which give them a time-stamp (aka a *tag*) on their own *time scale*. Tags represent the occurrence of the event at a specific time. The tag domains used for time must be totally ordered; typically, they are reals, rationals, integers, as well as the singleton Unit, which is used for purely logical clocks where time does not progress.

TESL allows for specifying causality and time scales between clocks, basically by three main classes of constraints.

Event-triggered implications. The occurrence of an event on one clock might trigger another one: "Whenever clock a ticks, clock b will tick under conditions". For instance, to model the fact that the minutes hand of a watch moves every minute, we will say that the min clock implies the move clock.

Time-triggered implications. This kind of causality enforces the progression of time. The occurrence of an event triggers another one after a chronometric delay measured on the time scale of a clock. For instance, in order to specify that the min clock ticks every minute, we can require that clock min *implies* itself with a time delay of 1.0 measured on its time scale. It is important to note that this delay is a duration (a difference between two tags) and not a number of ticks.

Tag relations. When all clocks are combined in a specification, each of them lives in its own "time island", with a potentially independent time scale. The purpose of tag relations is to link these different time scales. For instance, time runs 60 times as fast on clock sec as on clock min. This does not mean that the faster clock has more ticks, it only means that in any given instant, the tags of these clocks are in a ratio of 60. In general, TESL allows for fairly general tag relations (permitting even acceleration or slow-down); for the sake of simplicity, we will present only *affine tag relations* throughout this paper; this reduces the complexity of constraint-solving to handling linear equation systems.

Here is a TESL specification for the examples above:

```
1  rational-clock sec
2  rational-clock min sporadic 0.0
3  unit-clock move
4  tag relation sec = 60.0 * min
5  min implies move
6  min time delayed by 1.0 on min implies min
```

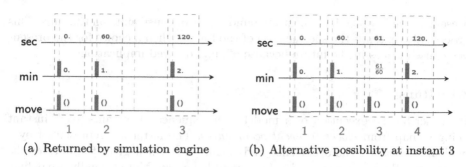

(a) Returned by simulation engine   (b) Alternative possibility at instant 3

Fig. 2. Two partially satisfying runs

Lines 1 to 3 declare clocks sec and min with rational tags, and clock move with the unit tag. The constraint sporadic enforces a tick on min with tag 0. Line 4 specifies that time on sec flows 60 times as fast as on min. Line 5 requires that each time the min clock ticks, the move clock ticks as well. Line 6 forces clock min to be periodic with period 1.0, specifying that it ticks every minute. The grammar of such expressions is detailed in Subsect. 3.2.

TESL is a specification language that defines the *set* of possible execution traces or *runs* of a global system. In Fig. 2 we present two of them; runs are presented by ticks (solid rectangles) timestamped with tags (small numbers) on the time-scales of the clocks sec, min and move; additionally, they are grouped in a sequence of synchronization *instants* (dashed rectangles).

Note that an infinity of other runs satisfy this specification, both from an architectural point of view (runs with additional clocks) and from a behavioral point of view (runs with additional ticks or instants). For instance, Fig. 2(b) shows a run with an additional tick on move, which may correspond to a movement of the minute hand caused by setting the time on the watch.

The original TESL simulator only computes "minimal" runs, as shown in Fig. 2(a), which makes its interpretation deterministic. Since our objective is to turn TESL into a specification language for timed behaviors, we consider not only minimal runs of the system, but *any* run of a given specification.

For more information about TESL and more application-oriented examples involving multiform time and heterogeneous time scales, see the TESL gallery; its engine ignition example[1] may be the most illustrative one.

3   Operational Semantics

In this section, we define an operational semantics of TESL for deriving all possible runs satisfying a given TESL specification. The operational semantics works with a specification of the future of the run, and instantiates it in the

---

[1] http://wdi.supelec.fr/software/TESL/, http://wdi.supelec.fr/software/TESL/GalleryEngine.

present instant, which incrementally builds a set of constraints on the runs. This process also extends the specification of the future when a choice for the present has consequences in the future because of time delayed implications.

3.1 Runs

We describe the execution of a model as a sequence of instants, each instant being a map from *clocks* to *event occurrences*. The latter are represented by a boolean indicating the occurrence and a time tag which gives the date of the occurrence. Such a sequence of instants is called a *run*. More formally, we define:

$\mathbb{K}$	set of clocks $K_1, K_2, \ldots$
$\mathbb{B}$	booleans
$\mathbb{T} = \biguplus_{K \in \mathbb{K}} \mathbb{T}_K$	universe of tags, with $\mathbb{T}_K$ the domain of tags of clock K
$\Sigma = \mathbb{K} \to (\mathbb{B} \times \mathbb{T})$	set of instants
$\Sigma^{\propto} = \mathbb{N}^+ \to \Sigma$	set of runs
ρ_n	n^{th} position (instant) in the run $\rho \in \Sigma^{\propto}$

where $\biguplus$ is the disjoint union operator. Informally, some tag type conditions apply: for a given instant $\sigma \in \Sigma$, a clock K maps to an event occurrence with a fixed tag domain $\mathbb{T}_K$.

Additionally, we define two projections to extract the components of an instant for a given clock:

$\mathsf{ticks}(\sigma(K))$	ticking predicate of clock K at instant $\sigma \in \Sigma$ (first projection)
$\mathsf{tag}(\sigma(K))$	tag value of clock K at instant $\sigma \in \Sigma$ (second projection)

For instance, if we write ρ as the run in Fig. 2(a), we have

$$\mathsf{ticks}(\rho_1(\mathsf{sec})) = \mathsf{false} \qquad \mathsf{ticks}(\rho_1(\mathsf{min})) = \mathsf{true}$$
$$\mathsf{tag}(\rho_1(\mathsf{min})) = 0.0 \qquad \mathsf{tag}(\rho_1(\mathsf{move})) = ()$$

3.2 TESL Specifications

A TESL specification φ is a set of atomic constraints that must all be satisfied by a conforming run. To simplify notations, we write them as conjunctions, and we ignore clock types and some operators of the full TESL. Here is a grammar:

$$\varphi \qquad ::= \quad \langle atom \rangle \wedge \cdots \wedge \langle atom \rangle$$
$$\langle atom \rangle \quad ::= \quad \langle clock \rangle \; \texttt{sporadic} \; \langle tag \rangle$$
$$| \quad \langle clock \rangle \; \texttt{sporadic} \; \langle tag \rangle \; \texttt{on} \; \langle clock \rangle$$
$$| \quad \texttt{tag relation} \; \langle clock \rangle = \langle tag \rangle \times \langle clock \rangle + \langle tag \rangle$$
$$| \quad \langle clock \rangle \; \texttt{implies} \; \langle clock \rangle$$
$$| \quad \langle clock \rangle \; \texttt{time delayed by} \; \langle tag \rangle \; \texttt{on} \; \langle clock \rangle \; \texttt{implies} \; \langle clock \rangle$$
$$\langle clock \rangle \quad \in \quad \mathbb{K}$$
$$\langle tag \rangle \quad \in \quad \mathbb{T}$$

We also define the subset of *sporadic specifications* as follows:

$$\mathsf{Sporadic}(\varphi) \qquad = \qquad \{\varphi_{\mathsf{atom}} \in \varphi \mid \varphi_{\mathsf{atom}} \text{ is a } \texttt{sporadic} \text{ atom}\}$$

The expression c_1 `sporadic` τ `on` c_2 is a generalization of the sporadic statement. It means that clock c_1 has to tick in an instant where time is τ on the time scale of c_2. Therefore c_1 `sporadic` τ is the same as c_1 `sporadic` τ `on` c_1.

3.3 Primitives for Run Contexts

Symbolic runs are defined by *run contexts* constructed from a set of constraint primitives introduced below. Run contexts may contain variables that can be arbitrarily instantiated; instances of symbolic runs with ground terms are called *concrete runs*.

Definition 1 (Run context). *A run context Γ is a set containing constraint primitives of the following kind:*

$K \Uparrow_n$	clock K is ticking at instant index n
$K \not\Uparrow_n$	clock K is not ticking (idle) at instant index n
$K \Downarrow_n x$	clock K has timestamp (tag) x at instant index n
$x_1 = \alpha \times x_2 + \beta$	affine relation between x_1 and x_2 with constants α, β

where symbols x, x_1, x_2 can be variables or tag constants in $\mathbb{T}$.

Note that a symbolic run can be instantiated as an infinite number of concrete runs. We give below the interpretation of symbolic runs as concrete runs:

$$[\![\Gamma]\!] \qquad = \qquad \bigcap_{\gamma \in \Gamma} [\![\gamma]\!]$$
$$[\![K \Uparrow_n]\!] \qquad = \qquad \{\rho \in \Sigma^\infty \mid \mathsf{ticks}(\rho_n(K)) \text{ is true}\}$$
$$[\![K \not\Uparrow_n]\!] \qquad = \qquad \{\rho \in \Sigma^\infty \mid \mathsf{ticks}(\rho_n(K)) \text{ is false}\}$$
$$[\![K \Downarrow_n \tau]\!] \qquad = \qquad \{\rho \in \Sigma^\infty \mid \mathsf{tag}(\rho_n(K)) = \tau\}$$
$$[\![\tau_1 = \alpha \times \tau_2 + \beta]\!] \qquad = \qquad \{\rho \in \Sigma^\infty \mid \tau_1 = \alpha \times \tau_2 + \beta\}$$

It is possible to construct run contexts that contain contradictory primitive constraints. They are interpreted as the empty set reflecting the fact that they do not denote any concrete run. We observe the following:

Lemma 1. *The consistency of a context Γ – i.e. whether $[\![\Gamma]\!] \neq \varnothing$ – is decidable.*

Proof sketch. The affine relations described above belong to the class of linear arithmetic problems which are known to be decidable for integers and rationals, using Fourier-Motzkin elimination. The propositional part is a SAT problem and their combination remain decidable.

3.4   Configurations of the Execution Process

We now define the machinery for constructing symbolic runs. We chose to treat TESL as a logic of resources, where some TESL formulae (such as `sporadic`, which denotes a single event occurrence) are consumed, while others (such as `implies`, which denotes a permanent constraint) are persistent. Processing these formulae produces additional constraint primitives, which refine the shape of satisfying symbolic runs.

The *rules* of our operational semantics relate *configurations* of our symbolic execution process, similarly to triples in a Hoare logic. Configurations consist of:

n	current simulation step index
Γ	run context containing primitives, describing the "past"
ψ	TESL-formula to satisfy in the "present"
φ	TESL-formula to satisfy in the "future" of the process

and are formally introduced in:

Definition 2 (Configuration). *A configuration is a tuple $(\Gamma, n, \psi, \varphi)$ that we write as $\Gamma \models_n \psi \triangleright \varphi$*

The operational semantics can be seen as an abstract machine, in which a configuration corresponds to an abstract state comprising the past (Γ), present (ψ) and future (φ) of the symbolic run under construction. Intuitively, the abstract machine constructs a symbolic run by refining the current configuration via the actions:

1. moving or duplicating parts from the future to the present (introduction)
2. then, consuming the present to produce the past (elimination)

3.5   Execution Rules

The execution rules of our abstract machine are defined by the $\rightarrow$ relation, which we decompose into $\rightarrow_i$ and $\rightarrow_e$ to identify introduction and elimination rules.

Introduction Rule for Instant Initialization. We build a run by adding instants to it. Initializing an instant makes time progress by copying constraints (defined in Subsect. 3.2) from the future to the present. Sporadic constraints are moved (consumed) rather than copied. Initializing an instant consists of:

- checking that the present constraints of the previous instant have been consumed (*i.e.* $\psi = \varnothing$)
- copying permanent constraints from φ to ψ
- moving sporadic constraints from φ to ψ

This is defined by rule instant$_i$, whose goal is to initialize a new instant.

$$\Gamma \models_n \varnothing \triangleright \varphi \quad \rightarrow_i \quad \Gamma \models_{n+1} \varphi \triangleright (\varphi - \mathsf{Sporadic}(\varphi)) \tag{instant$_i$}$$

As an instant has been created, ψ contains instantaneous constraints that are pending to be instantiated into Γ. We now give reduction rules to eliminate formulae from ψ, adding constraints in Γ for the current instant n.

Elimination Rules for sporadic-on. Formula K_1 sporadic τ on K_2 constrains K_1 to tick when the time on K_2 is τ. K sporadic τ is syntactic sugar for K sporadic τ on K. Such a constraint can be satisfied in the current instant, or postponed to a future instant. We therefore have two elimination rules for it:

$$\Gamma \models_n \psi \wedge (K_1 \text{ sporadic } \tau \text{ on } K_2) \triangleright \varphi$$
$$\rightarrow_e \ \Gamma \models_n \psi \triangleright \varphi \wedge (K_1 \text{ sporadic } \tau \text{ on } K_2)$$
$$\text{(sporadic} - \text{on}_{e1})$$

$$\Gamma \models_n \psi \wedge (K_1 \text{ sporadic } \tau \text{ on } K_2) \triangleright \varphi$$
$$\rightarrow_e \ \Gamma \cup \left\{ \begin{array}{l} K_1 \Uparrow_n \\ K_2 \Downarrow_n \tau \end{array} \right\} \models_n \psi \triangleright \varphi \qquad \text{(sporadic} - \text{on}_{e2})$$

Elimination Rule for tag relation. An affine tag relation has to be satisfied at every instant by adding a constraint on the tags of the corresponding clocks:

$$\Gamma \models_n \psi \wedge (\text{tag relation } K_1 = \alpha \times K_2 + \beta) \triangleright \varphi$$
$$\rightarrow_e \ \Gamma \cup \left\{ \begin{array}{l} K_1 \Downarrow_n \mathsf{tag}^n_{K_1} \\ K_2 \Downarrow_n \mathsf{tag}^n_{K_2} \\ \mathsf{tag}^n_{K_1} = \alpha \times \mathsf{tag}^n_{K_2} + \beta \end{array} \right\} \models_n \psi \triangleright \varphi$$
$$\text{(tagrel}_e)$$

where $\mathsf{tag}^n_{K_1}$ and $\mathsf{tag}^n_{K_2}$ are symbolic values, which will be instantiated with ground values in concrete runs.

Elimination Rules for implies. An implication is satisfied at every instant, either by forbidding a tick on the master clock (rule implies$_{e1}$), or by making the slave clock tick also (rule implies$_{e2}$):

$$\Gamma \models_n \psi \wedge (K_1 \text{ implies } K_2) \triangleright \varphi \quad \rightarrow_e \quad \Gamma \cup \{K_1 \not\Uparrow_n\} \models_n \psi \triangleright \varphi \quad \text{(implies}_{e1})$$

$$\Gamma \models_n \psi \wedge (K_1 \text{ implies } K_2) \triangleright \varphi \quad \rightarrow_e \quad \Gamma \cup \left\{ \begin{array}{l} K_1 \Uparrow_n \\ K_2 \Uparrow_n \end{array} \right\} \models_n \psi \triangleright \varphi \quad \text{(implies}_{e2})$$

Elimination Rules for time delayed implication

K_1 time delayed by δt on K_2 implies K_3 means that whenever K_1 ticks, K_3 will tick after a delay of δt measured on the time scale of K_2. It can be satisfied either by forbidding a tick on K_1 (with primitive $K_1 \not\Uparrow_n$), or by making K_1 tick and adding the corresponding sporadic-on constraint to the future formula φ:

$$\Gamma \models_n \psi \wedge (K_1 \text{ time delayed by } \delta t \text{ on } K_2 \text{ implies } K_3) \rhd \varphi$$
$$\to_e \quad \Gamma \cup \{K_1 \not\Uparrow_n\} \models_n \psi \rhd \varphi$$

$$(\text{time} - \text{delayed}_{e1})$$

$$\Gamma \models_n \psi \wedge (K_1 \text{ time delayed by } \delta t \text{ on } K_2 \text{ implies } K_3) \rhd \varphi$$
$$\to_e \quad \Gamma \cup \left\{ \begin{matrix} K_1 \Uparrow_n \\ K_2 \Downarrow_n \text{tag}^n_{K_2} \end{matrix} \right\} \models_n \psi \rhd \varphi \wedge (K_3 \text{ sporadic } (\text{tag}^n_{K_2} + \delta t) \text{ on } K_2)$$

$$(\text{time} - \text{delayed}_{e2})$$

3.6 Termination of a Simulation Step

A *simulation step* consists in building the next instant of the symbolic run by:

1. initializing an instant with reduction $\to_i$ (uniquely defined by rule instant_i);
2. eliminating all ψ-subformulae using $\to_e$ elimination rules until $\psi = \varnothing$.

A simulation step is more formally defined as a reduction rule, with $\cdot$ the composition of relations, and $\to_e^*$ the reflexive transitive closure of $\to_e$:

$$\to_\lightning := \{(\Gamma_1 \models_n \varnothing \rhd \varphi_1) \to_i \cdot \to_e^* (\Gamma_2 \models_n \varnothing \rhd \varphi_2) \mid \Gamma_1 \text{ and } \Gamma_2 \text{ are consistent}\}$$

$$(\text{simulation})$$

Note that we add a consistency constraint on Γ-contexts as we are interested in symbolic runs that have concrete instances. Indeed, reductions given by $\to$ are purely syntactical and do not take into account the constraints in Γ. For instance, $\to_e$ allows adding $K_1 \Uparrow_n$ to a context that already contains $K_1 \not\Uparrow_n$.

The termination of the computation of one simulation step $\to_\lightning$ is ensured by the termination of $\to_e$, because the number of formulae in ψ strictly decreases when a rule is applied. Moreover, whenever ψ is not empty, there is at least one applicable elimination rule, so when $\to_e^*$ terminates, ψ is necessarily empty and we can proceed with the next simulation step.

Following the specification given as an example in Sect. 2 (denoted as φ_0), we illustrate the use of our operational rules in Fig. 3. We start with an empty symbolic run and show the two first simulation steps on the left hand-side. Then we focus on the first step and provide the underlying reduction details on the right-hand side. This step is decomposed into the application of the introduction rule instant_i, then a sequence of elimination reductions (sporadic $-$ on_{e2}, tagrel_e, implies_{e2}, time $-$ delayed_{e1}), until irreducibility.

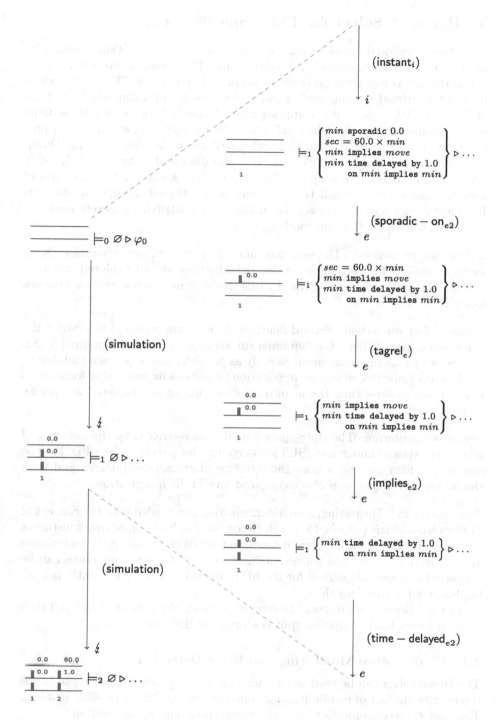

Fig. 3. Detail of the reduction steps of the operational semantics

4   Heron: A Solver for TESL Specifications

Since the operational semantics can be seen as an abstract execution machine, its implementation is conceptually straightforward. The resulting prototype solver, called Heron[2], is more general than the original deterministic TESL solver since it is not restricted to "minimal" runs. It consists of approximately 2500 lines of Standard ML code, and is compiled with MLton [22]. Heron is a standalone command-line interpreter, which takes a TESL specification as input and produces prefixes of satisfying symbolic runs, written in the Value-Change Dump format [3]. The solver is complete in the sense discussed in Subsect. 3.6, *i.e.* it produces all satisfying runs up to a fixed step index. Assuming that the 'future' formula contains no contradiction, this means that the satisfying symbolic runs have instances which are *exactly* the prefixes of *all* satisfying concrete runs.

Heron can be used in four modes:

Exhaustive exploration. The non-deterministic nature of our semantics allows multiple choices for deriving runs. By default, they are all explored when no specific simulation policy is given. In this mode, state-space explosion emerges quickly.

Minimal fast simulation. Several heuristic policies are provided to restrict the state-space, among them, the "minimal run strategy" mimics the original TESL simulator by making events occur as early as possible, and only when mandatory (a clock does not tick unless an implication or a sporadic constraint forces it to tick). These policies turn Heron into an execution engine targeted at specific kinds of runs.

Scenario monitoring. The state-space can also be restricted by the behavior of a concrete system under test (SUT) observed at its interfaces (see Fig. 1). The observed behavior — both from the interface of system components and from the architectural glue — is checked against the TESL specification.

Scenario testing. For testing, scenario monitoring is extended with the concept of distinguished *driving-clocks*, for which Heron can produce tagged event instances that are consistent with the current constraint-set (it essentially picks an instance at each instant among the consistent instances). These event-instances can be converted into suitable stimuli for the SUT (however, we have currently not yet implemented a driver for this).

In the following, we discuss the monitoring scenario in more detail and then refine it into a kind of input-output conformance [19] test scenario.

4.1   Conformance Monitoring and Error Detection

The Heron solver can be used as an online monitoring tool, permitting to tackle the infinite number of possibilities for concrete test-runs at all possible instants. The conformance monitoring scenario makes the following assumptions:

---

[2] Heron is distributed as free software at https://github.com/heron-solver/heron.

1. we assume the monitor has an access to the SUT interfaces (see Fig. 1) via a driver that abstracts observations into tagged events on clocks;
2. we assume that the computing time of the driver and of Heron can be neglected with regard to the execution time of the SUT, and
3. we assume that the system is output deterministic; *i.e* after an initialization of the SUT by the tester, it is possible to track the state of the SUT by only observing its inputs *and* outputs [8].

The idea for the monitoring scenario is to filter out the branches in the set of runs maintained by Heron that are no longer compatible with the behavior of the system, as observed through the interfaces. If the SUT produces a behavior that does not conform to the specification, the solver will fail to produce a satisfying configuration and abort.

A monitoring sequence is illustrated in Fig. 4. The solver first starts by generating all satisfying states (circled ⊨). It then keeps the states that are compatible with the observed behavior of the SUT (plain circles), while dropping the other ones (dashed grey circles). When the SUT produces a bad behavior (circled ⊭), the solver drops all of its states and finds none that match the behavior of the SUT. No further simulation is possible.

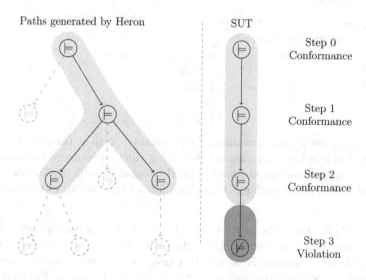

Fig. 4. Executing Heron and the SUT in parallel

Example: based on the specification shown in Listing 2 on page 3, we use the @scenario directive to feed Heron with the observed behavior, and the @step directive to take this behavior into account and update the reachable states:

```
 7  @scenario strict 1 min move
 8  @step
 9  @scenario strict 2 min move
10  @step
11  @scenario strict 3 move
12  @step
13  @scenario strict 4 min move
14  @step
```

For instance in Line 7, we tell Heron that we observed that clocks `min` and `move` tick at instant 1. The `strict` option indicates that only the given clocks tick, all the others remain idle in that instant. Alternatively, we could use:

```
 9  @scenario strict 2 (min-> 1.0) move
```

to indicate that the tag on clock `min` at this instant is `1.0`. This instantiates the symbolic tag variable in the symbolic run with a concrete tag for clock `min`. Thus, the observations on the concrete run of the SUT can be used to prune execution branches that are not relevant for the future of the run.

In the above example, the solver finds 24 symbolic runs, among them the one shown in Fig. 2(b):

```
@print
## Simulation result:
            sec         min         move
    [1]      ⊘         ↑ 0.0        ↑
    [2]      ⊘         ↑ 1.0        ↑
    [3]      ⊘          ⊘           ↑
    [4]      ⊘         ↑ 2.0        ↑
```

The output shows a run containing four instants, with a timeline for each of the specified clocks (`sec`, `min`, `move`). A ticking clock is depicted by the upwards arrow (↑) with the associated time tag on the right. An idle clock is depicted by the circled slash (⊘). If nothing is specified for a clock, it can either tick or not.

Property Violation. As long as the SUT produces behaviors for which the solver does not detect a contradiction, the observed run "potentially conforms" to the TESL specification. However, if a non-conforming behavior occurs, the solver detects a contradiction in its constraint set. For instance, if in step 3, clock `min` ticks but clock `move` does not, we have:

```
 7  @scenario strict 1 min move
 8  @step
 9  @scenario strict 2 min move
10  @step
11  @scenario strict 3 min
12  @step
```

In this case, the solver detects the violation of the `min implies move` formula.

4.2 Input/output Conformance Testing

We consider online testing as an extension of online monitoring with a policy for generating input stimuli on the fly. This policy explores the state space with respect to a particular coverage criterion.

In order to use Heron as an online testing tool, the clocks that are considered as *inputs* must be declared as *driving-clocks*:

```
7  @driving-clock move
```

After this declaration, Heron may be instrumented by:

```
8  @event-solve 2
```

which leads to the invocation of a constraint solver (Lemma 1) for step 2, which by default choses for the driving clocks, an input that satisfies the constraints. More sophisticated generation policies could be implemented.

Conformance: if the future of a configuration (see Subsect. 3.4) becomes empty or *stable*, the observed run "fully conforms" to the TESL specification. A (future) specification is stable, if it represents a Buchi-automaton producing an infinite behaviour such as:

```
min time delayed by 1.0 on min implies min
```

which represents an infinite stream of event occurrences, each separated from the previous one by a 1.0 time delay measured on the time scale of clock `min`. For the moment, we only have an incomplete set of patterns to characterize stable specifications. Moreover, we cannot conclude if we do not reach such a configuration during the test, which corresponds to the classical *inconclusive* situation in conformance testing.

4.3 Performance

We give some benchmarks that were made on a conventional laptop computer with an Intel Core™ i5-2520M CPU @ 2.50GHz and 8 GB of RAM. They are based on examples provided by the official gallery of TESL and fully logged in Table 1. They highlight the state-space explosion for exhaustive paths, while depicting the feasibility of scenario monitoring of a SUT.

Table 1. Time (in sec or min:sec) and memory usage (in kB) with respect to a given policy and a fixed number of simulation steps for several examples of the TESL gallery

Example		Policy and steps											
		Exhaustive				Minimal Run				SUT Monitoring			
		1	2	3	4	1	2	3	4	1	2	3	4
HandWatch	Time	0.02	0.00	0.01	0.07	0.00	0.00	0.00	0.00	0.00	0.00	0.00	0.02
	Memory	2412	3124	6464	10264	2592	2512	3220	3220	2496	3236	3892	5768
LightSwitch	Time	0.00	0.06	3.20	10:02.81	0.00	0.00	0.01	0.02	0.00	0.02	0.04	0.11
	Memory	3132	9872	288120	4029676	3172	5300	7088	7064	3180	7080	8140	12444
ConcurrentComp	Time	0.00	1.77	10:26.32	Timeout	0.02	0.06	0.08	0.06	0.02	0.23	1.19	3.27
	Memory	7064	145208	4029688		7120	7916	7856	7860	7136	15956	68864	121884
LeapYears	Time	0.01	3.24	15:12.41	Timeout	0.05	0.06	0.07	0.08	0.01	0.52	1.12	1.53
	Memory	8320	217688	4029792		8356	8384	8260	8360	8332	39832	39820	39884
Engine	Time	0.00	0.03	0.32	8.34	0.00	0.01	0.01	0.01	0.00	0.02	0.04	0.08
	Memory	3212	7752	20728	342240	3300	4780	6628	7196	3252	7384	8044	8460

5   Conclusion

We have presented the Tagged Event Specification Language (TESL) to specify the timing behavior at the interfaces of components of an heterogeneous system. We have defined its operational semantics by a set of symbolic evaluation rules, permitting the construction of symbolic representations of infinite sets of timed behaviors (runs). We have shown how our semantics leads naturally to an implementation of a solver that can be used to monitor and test the architectural glue of heterogeneous systems with timed behavior.

The introduction of *driving-clocks* (see Subsect. 4.2) paves the way for the distinction between mere observations of the SUT (and their relative check of conformance) and the stimulation by timed inputs consistent with the constraint set that is monitored in a particular symbolic run. This gives TESL the flavor of an input-output automaton or labelled transition system for which a well-known theoretic testing framework exists [19] which also has been extended to timed behavior [13,17]. Due to their proximity to model-checking, these frameworks are usually restricted to discrete time and cannot treat causality. To overcome the former limitation, an entire research community emerged under the label *online testing* [2] which discusses techniques based on symbolic execution in parallel to test execution. Our work can be seen as a form of online testing for heterogeneous timed systems with arbitrary linear relations between time scales.

Related Work. The TESL language is sourced from different ideas. It originally started as a complementary approach to the CCSL specification language, by keeping purely synchronous logical clocks, while adding support for time tags and time scale relations as described in the Tagged Signal Model [14], which allows specifying the occurrence of events after a chronometric delay. The original solving algorithm relies on a constructive semantics in the style of the Esterel synchronous language [5]. Compared to CCSL, the restriction to purely synchronous constraints in TESL comes from the necessity to compute time tags, which is not possible when asynchronous relations give only precedence constraints on event occurrences. The style of executable semantics we give in this article is similar to [23] but we abstract time with symbols while preserving the bounded computability of the run state-space.

The idea of a timed architectural composition language is conceptually similar to orchestration languages for web-services, for example BPEL [4] and more formal treatments thereof such as [21]. BPEL is designed to organize and synchronize a set of communication threads, called conversations. In contrast to TESL, BPEL-like languages allow for dynamic thread creation and therefore a dynamic evolution of channels and interfaces; however, they are not designed to treat time, duration, and causality of possibly periodic events.

Future Work. A strengthening of both foundational as well as practical aspects of the TESL language is desirable. Although the operational semantics has been carefully designed, there is no formal proof of the inherent logical consistency of the rule set: to this end, a denotational version is currently under development (which assures consistency by construction) in Isabelle/HOL [16] which could serve as a reference in a validity proof of these rules (which thus become *derived*). This would allow also pave the way to describe the exchange of *data* between sub-components, either process-oriented [18] or program-oriented [7]. Furthermore, the conformity of a *SUT* to a spec *S* can only be established when the possible futures becomes either trivial or stable. For now, this can only by decided for certain patterns based on an automata-based reasoning. The denotational semantics may help to find a less ad-hoc characterization of "stability" based on co-induction. On the practical side, we wish to explore more refined heuristics to monitor and test heterogeneous systems with Heron.

References

1. UML profile for MARTE^{TM}: Modeling and analysis of real-time embedded systems^{TM}. http://www.omg.org/spec/MARTE/1.1/
2. International online testing symposium (1995–2017). http://tima.imag.fr/conferences/iolts/
3. IEEE standard verilog hardware description language. IEEE Std 1364–2001 (2001). https://doi.org/10.1109/IEEESTD.2001.93352
4. Specification: Business process execution language for web services version 1.1 (2003). http://www-106.ibm.com/developerworks/webservices/library/ws-bpel/
5. Berry, G.: The Constructive Semantics of Pure Esterel (1999), http://citeseerx.ist.psu.edu/viewdoc/summary?doi=10.1.1.46.2076
6. Boulanger, F., Jacquet, C., Hardebolle, C., Prodan, I.: TESL: a language for reconciling heterogeneous execution traces. In: Twelfth ACM/IEEE International Conference on Formal Methods and Models for Codesign (MEMOCODE 2014), pp. 114–123. Lausanne, Switzerland, October 2014. http://ieeexplore.ieee.org/xpl/articleDetails.jsp?arnumber=6961849

7. Brucker, A.D., Wolff, B.: An extensible encoding of object-oriented data models in HOL. J. Autom. Reasoning **41**(3–4), 219–249 (2008). https://doi.org/10.1007/s10817-008-9108-3

8. Brucker, A.D., Wolff, B.: Monadic sequence testing and explicit test-refinements. In: Aichernig, B.K.K., Furia, C.A.A. (eds.) TAP 2016. LNCS, vol. 9762, pp. 17–36. Springer, Cham (2016). doi:10.1007/978-3-319-41135-4_2

9. Cheng, B.H.C., Combemale, B., France, R.B., Jézéquel, J.-M., Rumpe, B. (eds.): Globalizing Domain-Specific Languages. LNCS, vol. 9400. Springer, Cham (2015)

10. Eker, J., Janneck, J.W., Lee, E.A., Liu, J., Liu, X., Ludvig, J., Neuendorffer, S., Sachs, S., Xiong, Y.: Taming heterogeneity - the Ptolemy approach. In: Proceedings of the IEEE, pp. 127–144 (2003)

11. Garcés, K., Deantoni, J., Mallet, F.: A model-based approach for reconciliation of polychronous execution traces. In: SEAA 2011–37th EUROMICRO Conference on Software Engineering and Advanced Applications. IEEE, Oulu, Finland, August 2011. https://hal.inria.fr/inria-00597981

12. Hardebolle, C., Boulanger, F.: Exploring multi-paradigm modeling techniques. Simul. Trans. Soc. Model. Simul. Int. **85**(11/12), 688–708 (2009). http://wdi.supelec.fr/software/downloads/ModHelX/2009MPMSimulation.pdf

13. Krichen, M., Tripakis, S.: Conformance testing for real-time systems. Form. Methods Syst. Des. **34**(3), 238–304 (2009). http://dx.doi.org/10.1007/s10703-009-0065-1

14. Lee, E.A., Sangiovanni-Vincentelli, A.: A framework for comparing models of computation. IEEE Trans. CAD **17**(12), 1217–1229 (1998)

15. Mallet, F., Deantoni, J., André, C., De Simone, R.: The clock constraint specification language for building timed causality models. Innov. Syst. Softw. Eng. **6**(1–2), 99–106 (2010). https://hal.inria.fr/inria-00464894

16. Nipkow, T., Wenzel, M., Paulson, L.C. (eds.): Isabelle/HOL—A Proof Assistant for Higher-Order Logic. LNCS, vol. 2283. Springer, Heidelberg (2002). doi:10.1007/3-540-45949-9

17. Schmaltz, J., Tretmans, J.: On conformance testing for timed systems. In: Cassez, F., Jard, C. (eds.) FORMATS 2008. LNCS, vol. 5215, pp. 250–264. Springer, Heidelberg (2008). doi:10.1007/978-3-540-85778-5_18

18. Tej, H., Wolff, B.: A corrected failure-divergence model for CSP in Isabelle/HOL. In: Fitzgerald, J., Jones, C.B., Lucas, P. (eds.) FME 1997. LNCS, vol. 1313, pp. 318–337. Springer, Heidelberg (1997). doi:10.1007/3-540-63533-5_17

19. Tretmans, J.: Test generation with inputs, outputs and repetitive quiescence. Softw. Concepts Tools **17**(3), 103–120 (1996)

20. Vara Larsen, M.E., Deantoni, J., Combemale, B., Mallet, F.: A Behavioral coordination operator language (BCOoL). In: 18th International Conference on Model Driven Engineering Languages and Systems (MODELS 2015), August 2015. https://hal.inria.fr/hal-01182773

21. Viroli, M.: A core calculus for correlation in orchestration languages. J. Logic Algebraic Program. **70**(1), 74–95 (2007). http://www.sciencedirect.com/science/article/pii/S1567832606000300

22. Weeks, S.: Whole-program Compilation in MLton. In: Proceedings of the 2006 Workshop on ML. ML 2006, p. 1. ACM New York (2006). http://doi.acm.org/10.1145/1159876.1159877

23. Zhang, M., Mallet, F.: An executable semantics of clock constraint specification language and its applications. In: Artho, C., Ölveczky, P.C. (eds.) FTSCS 2015. CCIS, vol. 596, pp. 37–51. Springer, Cham (2016). doi:10.1007/978-3-319-29510-7_2

Semi-formal Cycle-Accurate Temporal Execution Traces Reconstruction

Rehab Massoud[1]([✉]), Jannis Stoppe[1,2], Daniel Große[1,2], and Rolf Drechsler[1,2]

[1] Group of Computer Architecture, University of Bremen, 28359 Bremen, Germany
{massoud,jstoppe,grosse,drechsle}@cs.uni-bremen.de
[2] Cyber-Physical Systems, DFKI GmbH, 28359 Bremen, Germany

Abstract. Today's Real-Time Systems' (RTSs) increasing speed and complexity make debugging of timing related faults one of the most challenging engineering tasks. Debugging starts with capturing the fault symptoms, which requires continuous cycle-accurate execution traces. However, due to limitations of on-chip buffers' area and output ports' throughput, these cannot be obtained easily.

This paper introduces an approach that divides the tracing into two tasks, monitoring on-chip execution to retrieve accurate timing information and high level functional simulation to retrieve signal contents. A semi-formal cycle-accurate reconstruction method uses these two sources to retrieve a complete, cycle-accurate trace of a given signal. An experiment illustrates how this method allows the cycle-accurate reconstruction of on-chip traces of a Real-Time Autonomous-Guided-Vehicle software.

1   Introduction

Locating errors is a crucial part of the Systems-on-Chip (SoC) development process. In order to be able to pinpoint bugs in the design, sophisticated logging and monitoring techniques are used. Usually, designers have to decide between: (1) much information from potentially slow simulations, (2) formal approaches that often limit the model's timing (if considered it at all) to a given upper accuracy and/or duration bounds or (3) limited data from on-chip runs.

Simulation-based techniques may be used to analyze a given system as soon as there is an executable prototype down to the end of the development process. While simulators supposedly provide an exact model of the given design, they inherently only offer (1) an abstraction of the real fabricated final hardware and (2) a fraction of the performance of it (running on general purpose host systems, a full accurate simulation of a single input-output-combination takes much longer than on the final SoC). While this is not much of an issue for a wide variety of

This work was supported by the University of Bremen's graduate school SyDe funded by the German Excellence Initiative, the German Federal Ministry of Education and Research (BMBF) within the project 01IW16001 (SELFIE), the German Research Foundation (DFG) within the Reinhart Koselleck project DR 287/23-1 and the German Academic Exchange Service (DAAD).

© Springer International Publishing AG 2017
A. Abate and G. Geeraerts (Eds.): FORMATS 2017, LNCS 10419, pp. 335–351, 2017.
DOI: 10.1007/978-3-319-65765-3_19

use cases, it is for the location of timing-related errors in today's SoC's. Correct SoC's timing simulations require more details; hence excessive computations causing prohibitive slow-down in the simulation performance. Simulations can count only for those *apriori* known and modeled effects, so they can not cover all possible sporadic executions of the actual system.

Model-based approaches utilize functional hardware models that are e.g. provided to the software developers for functional testing. These models are based on hardware specifications like an instruction set architecture (ISA) [16]. Approaches such as worst case execution time (WCET) analyses [21] and abstract interpretations [19] are using this concept to give some guarantees about the behavior of the software when it operates on hardware. However, the more reliable and formal these methods, the more computation they require to account for every possibility and aspect in reality. The multitude of environment effects and variations of input/output interactions makes these model-based verification techniques very challenging – if not downright impossible. The execution on the fabricated hardware can still differ from its model-specifications due to possible unexpected (and hence non-modeled) process variations or other environmental operating conditions.

On-chip debugging requires stopping the system to get a scan-out of the current chip registers or state. Traditionally, scan-chains, Multi-Input Shift Registers (MISR) and Test Access Points (TAP) are used for post silicon validation [11], whereas specialized trace buffers and debug support units are mainly used in embedded processors [5]. This run/stop approach is inherently unsuitable for temporal behavior debugging, and requires many reruns until the root-cause is identified – which may result in it missing the sporadic behavior. To support continuous logging in embedded processors domain, current solutions are very customized (they use on-chip debugging modules and/or depend on compiler's generated meta data [2,4]), that they cannot be extended to any SoC. Current on-chip techniques are often intrusive, i.e. they alter the temporal behavior itself, potentially affecting the timing that may be causing the error in the first place. Therefore, post-silicon timing aspects are usually addressed by different methods to avoid expensive continuous or time-accurate logging. These, however, focus only on capturing specified timing constraints violations and do not provide further means to detect a violation's root-cause, as in [10,15].

Methods for determining which signals to log or monitor to accurately reflect the system state at a specific instance (enhancing logic visibility) have been investigated [18]. However logging such signals continuously on a temporal accurate base was not considered so far.

Assuming that relevant signals have been identified beforehand to provide the best coverage of possible root-causes, obtaining a temporally accurate access to their evolution over time is still limited by factors such as the trace-buffers' area (if they would be stored on-chip) or the output ports' capabilities (when they are to be logged on-line). For SoCs in general, on-chip area can not accommodate continuous (theoretically) infinite traces; and on-chip signals/transactions speeds are orders of magnitudes greater than current logging ports capabilities [20].

Each of these techniques thus has its specific but severe issues for spotting timing-related errors. To address these shortcomings, this work shifts the focus from full-scale on-chip tracing to only log the temporal behavior accurately, omitting the functional content, which is provided via an off-chip functional simulation. To realize the reduced on-chip logging functionality, the idea of signature-summaries previously used in [8,14] is reformulated and generalized to be applied continuously to any on-chip traced signal. This altered usage of signatures is introduced as the continuous logging of *"footprints"* to denote their light weight and periodic nature. Non-temporal information of the erroneous run is obtained via traces from running a high level functional simulation of the specific scenario. While the logged simulation data lacks precise timing information (due to its potential high-level nature, which may sacrifice timing accuracy to improve the performance), it provides significantly more detail concerning the order and changes in value of the traced signal. This data (logged temporal execution footprints containing timing information and detailed off-chip logs) is combined and used to reconstruct the accurate on-chip behavior.

The contributions of this work are:

1. a novel yet simple consistent methodology for continuous accurate temporal execution tracing and
2. a semi-formal offline Cycle-Accurate Temporal Reconstruction Algorithm (CATRA).

A proof-of-concept implementation for efficiently logging footprints from a running LEON3 processor [3], using functional Transaction Level Model (TLM) simulation traces from the SoCRocket simulator [17], is provided to illustrate how the approach may be applied and used to capture sporadic timing related bugs.

2 Methodology

The core goal of retrieving cycle accurate traces of on-chip temporal behavior drives the ideas and design decisions that are taken for the presented approach. First, an overview of the approach is presented that explains both, the methodology itself and the structures of the implementation. Two major parts of the given approach – the trace logging itself and the merging of on-chip and off-chip (simulation) traces – are discussed afterwards, providing the details of the approach.

2.1 Overview

As sporadic timing-related faults are hard to reproduce, precise information concerning the time *and* the data of erroneous transactions is required to enable the designer to identify the cause of the problem. In order to provide both, the task is split in two parts:

1. Logging precise timing information of the chip's behavior, i.e. storing information concerning *when* something happened and
2. logging the behavioral information itself, i.e. storing information concerning *what* happened.

The first part is needed to properly capture the temporal on-chip behavior, and is required to avoid altering the timing and thus changing what is – by definition – part of the cause of this *timing*-related fault. Thus, this part is explicitly logged from the traced on-chip execution. On the other hand, having an already functioning system removes the burden of logging the exact state *or signal* value itself every clock cycle, so only a data-parity-check is logged.

The second part – the data itself – is calculated off-chip in a functional simulation. Correct abstract functionality is enough to simulate the transitions of states – or signals values changes – irrespective of their timing, which depends on architectural and environmental particularities. In practice, SystemC Transaction Level Modeling (TLM) models are executed to calculate the behavioral data of the design. SystemC itself is a C++ library that allows designing hardware systems using high level language constructs, sacrificing synthesizeability for the sake of being able to quickly develop prototypes, with the TLM additions providing improved simulation performance at the cost of reduced timing accuracy. Notice that while the given example relies on SystemC, any functional simulation framework providing the required data may be used.

These two sources of information are then mapped onto each other, providing designers with a comprehensive continuous capture of the system's behavior. While the hardware is executed, the temporal behavior information (first part) is logged continuously. When a fault becomes visible, the scenario that was run on the hardware and lead to the faulty behavior, is used to start a functional simulation to provide the basic data, of which its temporal behavior was logged from the hardware execution.

2.2 Definitions

A trace τ is defined as a consecutive traced values of a signal over time. Hence, a trace can be represented by an ordered vector $\tau^{u,l} = \{\rho_0, \rho_1, ..., \rho_N\}$ if for the duration l, N different values were traced. Traced values are samples of the signal's continuous value, sampled every clock-cycle. A trace is either timed $\tau^{t,l}$, (it contains a value for every time instance), or un-timed $\tau^{u,l}$ (it only contains the consecutive ordered different values, appearing after each other). An infinite or continuous execution trace is denoted without a period l, i.e. τ^t or τ^u. When a trace is timed, elements of the trace ordered vector $\tau^{t,l}$, namely $\{\rho_{t_0}, \rho_{t_1}, ..., \rho_{t_{l-1}}\}$, represent the value ρ of a signal S at times $t_0, t_1, ..., t_{l-1}$. Due to the time being discrete and the system running on an internal clock, we can state that $t_i = t_{i-1}+1$. Thus, if a value ρ_x remained for two clock-cycles, starting from t_i, then two consecutive values ρ_{t_i} and $\rho_{t_{i+1}}$ would be equal. On the other hand if the trace is un-timed, one value ρ_i which corresponds to both ρ_{t_i} and $\rho_{t_{i+1}}$ is added to the trace ordered vector τ^u.

Traces could be obtained by continuously logging the values of on-chip signal. Such a complete trace is called *Actual Timed Trace* τ_a^t and represents the ideal goal. For cycle accurate tracing, such actual timed trace τ_a^t needs to be either stored on-chip or logged off-chip, the former being not possible due to limited on-chip storage, the latter due to the limited bandwidth of available ports. An alternative is to obtain the information from the simulation, with such a result being called *Simulation Trace* τ_s, or recovered from logged footprints, called *Reconstructed Trace* τ_r. Each of those traces could be either timed or un-timed.

2.3 Footprints Logging

In this work, we choose to generate and then log the temporal footprints periodically. The actual on-chip trace τ_a^t of the signal S is first divided into equal M long *Trace-cycles* $\tau_{r_i}^{t_M}$, where i is the trace-cycle number. M's actual value is a matter of the designer's preferences. It is a trade-off between the time required to decode the information, as shall be seen later, the logging bandwidth being used and the required on-chip storage. The logging is then limited to three distinct types of information:

– The timing information is encoded using periodic signatures. Each clock-cycle within the trace-cycle T_a^t is marked with a unique *time-stamp* TS_n, where $0 \leqslant n < M$ indicates the clock cycle within a trace-cycle. For the given implementation, w_{TS} bits (denoting bit-width of the time-stamps) are used to encode each clock-cycle within the trace-cycle. The traced signal S is sampled/monitored in a clock-cycle accurate basis. The old value of the signal is kept in a register, and is compared to the current value of S, raising a *Temporal Check TC* when it detects a change, as shown in Fig. 1. Time-stamps marking the cycles at which the given signal changes are aggregated (in the suggested implementation using XOR operations) into a single *Tracc – Cycle*'s signature called *Temporal Cyclic Footprint TCF*. In Fig. 1, TC can be seen to invoke the aggregation of time-stamps $TS\,2$, $TS\,6$, $TS\,8$, $TS\,13$, and $TS\,14$ (when the traced signal changes its value) to generate a TCF. Only this generated signature is logged to express change instances. To reduce the amount of data of this TCF to a size that fits through any potential bottlenecks, the time-stamp bit width can be reduced as desired – at the cost of potentially creating ambiguous footprints.
– A similar technique is applied for the considered signal itself: Each change in the observed signal's value at any cycle during the interval, contributes to creating a signature from the signal, called *Functional-Check (FC)*. (In the suggested implementation a simple parity check of the consecutive signal values during the *Trace – Cycle* is used, also in the form of XOR of these values). This functional check is later used to match the un-timed simulation and actual traces.
– Finally, the number of signal changes N is stored and transferred as well.

This data (i.e. the timing and data signatures, and how many signal toggles occurred within the trace-cycle) is encompassed in a structure, that is logged

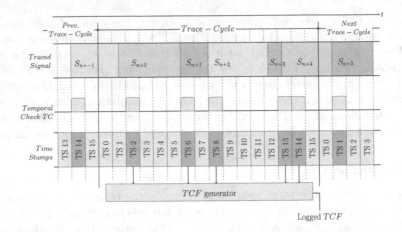

Fig. 1. Time-stamps involved in generating the Temporal Cyclic Footprint TCF

and transferred to the host computer each trace-cycle. This set is called a *footprint* $FP_s = <s.FC, s.TCF, s.N>$ of signal s, describing how the signal s leaves a series of these distinct traits that are unique to the events that happened (or a set of possible events that could have happened) but do not represent the information itself. For a 16-clock-cycles long trace-cycle, a 16 bits-wide footprint gives exactly one solution, which is equivalent to logging one bit every clock cycle. Such footprint of width $w_{TCF} = M$ enables the full recovery of the trace temporal check TC (and thus the times at which the signal was altered), irrespective of the number of changes N. To reduce the required bandwidth, the time-stamps' width w_{TCF} is reduced, and N is used afterwards to narrow the possibilities down. These footprints do not contain any explicit information about the behavior. However, the missing information is generated using a high-level functional simulation.

2.4   Functional Simulation

Techniques such as TLM allow designers to run simulations that sacrifice accurate timing information to gain performance. The assumption is thus that the semantics of the functional simulation are identical to the chip's behavior but the timing may be inaccurate and that the simulation can be executed when the on-chip execution reports an error that needs to be investigated. The data that can be retrieved from the simulation thus complements the footprints, which provide the timing information that the simulation's trace is lacking.

The functional simulation is executed in a controlled environment, so a signal's simulated functional values (constituting an un-timed functional simulation trace τ_f^u) can easily be generated and stored on a host system. Although the simulation is conducted on higher granularity and might differ in some details, it still provides a baseline from which the actual timed trace τ_a^t can be reconstructed. In literature, the different flow possibilities of interrupts and threads of executions

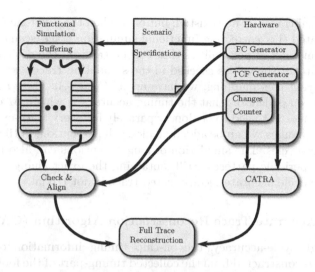

Fig. 2. Methodology for footprints logging and traces reconstruction

of the simulated scenarios can be obtained via methods like [13]. When there is a set of known flow possibilities that could be short-listed for matching, the process becomes easier as shall be seen in the experiments section. In general, the complexity of such dynamic behavior matching was addressed in [9].

The process of retrieving complete traces is illustrated in Fig. 2. For the functional part (left-hand side of the figure), basic scenario specifications (such as e.g. inputs with their schedule, a software image and the set of interrupts to be fed to the system with their periodicity and/or estimated/planned occurrence instances) are needed to execute the functional simulation. From such simulation, the monitored signal values are also stored and then buffered: i.e. repetitions are eliminated to obtain un-timed functional traces (as stated in the definitions section); also the basic trace segments are identified. Segments are those groups of values of the trace known to be consecutive even if other segments came in between. Extracting the trace segments can be done with different granularity levels, in our experiment for example as the SoCRocket simulation already supports interrupts injection, we considered the whole main program as a single segment as obtained from simulation and interrupts service routines each as a segment. These two operations (eliminating repetitions and extracting segments) are called buffering in the figure. Hence, a potential candidate un-timed trace τ_f^u -or group of traces as a result from composition of segments- is obtained.

Then, using N and FC obtained from the hardware (right-hand side of the figure), the un-timed simulation trace τ_s^u can be mapped to trace-cycles $T_{s_i}^u$, of N changes each. Comparing a trace-cycle's logged FC to the simulated N values' generated FC is a parity check of $\tau_{s_i}^u = \tau_{a_i}^u$; i.e. the simulation values matches the actual values, providing a safeguard for the assumption about the simulation's correctness. It can also help amending discrepancies between simulation and actual traces if they existed; but only when the difference's root-cause can be speculated (i.e. correcting functional simulation trace/scenario to match the reality from a set of possibilities that can be tried by the designer until the logged FC matches the values checked in the simulation trace).

After applying this mapping, we have an *M-Cycles-Accurate* reconstructed trace $\tau_r^{t_M}$, where t_M denotes that the timing accuracy is within M clock cycles. This mapping does not need to be done separately for every trace-cycle. Instead, the number of changes N can be added all along the execution, until reaching the suspected trace-cycles. The simulation of long executions can also be projected into repeating periodic patterns. Still, obtaining the exact change clock-cycles, for a complete cycle accurate reconstructed trace is not trivial.

2.5   Cycle Accurate Trace Reconstruction Algorithm (CATRA)

To reach single-cycle-accuracy, the on-chip timing information of particular trace-cycles is reconstructed from the collected timing-part of the footprint TCF. This is done only for trace-cycles that are suspected to be of special interest and require cycle-accurate (i.e. timed) reconstructed trace-cycles $\tau_r^{t,M}$. This allows designers to pick any arbitrary trace cycle to inspect without having to process the whole execution log to get the exact cycle accurate data of a particular part.

In the Trace-Cycle mapping, it is possible that discrepancies in the values could go undetected if the suggested parity-check based functional check FC cannot detect it. For example, if the footprint was generated from the signal S from Fig. 1 and the FC was generated using the suggested XOR-aggregation, as shown in Fig. 3 below, the two identical values S_{n+1} and S_{n+3} would cancel each other out. If $S_{n+1}^c = S_{n+3}^c$ on chip were *both* different from the simulation's $S_{n+1}^s = S_{n+3}^s$, the footprint's FC would not indicate any problem.

Figure 3 shows a set of time-stamps that are aggregated (here using XOR) into the temporal cyclic footprint parts TCF. If a given trace cycle should be analyzed, all possible combinations that could lead to this specific TCF are obtained, with the actual combination that was calculated on-chip being among them. The number of possibilities may be large, though: for the example, when time-stamps of width $w_{TS} = 8$ are used (as indicated in the Fig. 3), there are 256 possible combinations of TSs that could have led to this logged TCF. Of these 256, only one contains 5 changes, which is the number N in our trace-cycle. In this case, an exact cycle accurate reconstruction is obtained. Notice that there may be more than one possible result though, making determining which one exactly is what happened on hardware probabilistic (as the designer can assign probabilities to the obtained solutions).

Reconstruction Using Formal Methods. The footprints contain a set of constraints describing characteristics of on-chip execution. From them, searching for solutions using established formal methods to deduce the actual on-chip trace is a viable approach. The TCF is created by merging all relevant time step signatures into a single footprint; now this process needs to be reversed. In order to quickly retrieve all possible combinations of time steps that result in

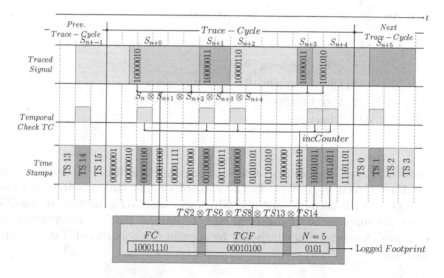

Fig. 3. Example of footprint generation

a given footprint, the relation between footprint and time steps is formulated as a problem for (established) satisfiability solvers. The reconstruction of M cycles from an w-bits-wide signature (footprint) can be formulated as a simple Satisfiability Modulo Theory (SMT) problem as shown in Algorithm 1. The algorithm first initializes the value of the footprint TCF_0 to ρ_0 (which is user defined in reset -for the first trace-cycle- and the previously logged footprint afterwards) in line 1. It then builds a set of M consecutive if-then-else (*ite*) statements to be given to the solver in lines 3 and 4 that instruct the solver how to build the footprint: if the ith bit in the Temporal Check $TC[i]$ indicates a change, the corresponding time-stamp TS is XORed. The solver is then constrained to finding a solution that matches one that has been retrieved from the hardware (*loggedTCF*) in line 6, thus giving a possible solution to when the signal was altered in line 7.

Algorithm 1. TC Reconstruction from Temporal Cyclic Footprints

---

Data: ρ_0, TS, *loggedTCF*

1   $TCF_0 = \rho_0$

2   $bitvector[M]$ TC /* where M is the width of the bit vector variable
    TC */

3   **foreach** i *in* $1 \longrightarrow M$ **do**

4       $TCF_i = ite(TC[i], TCF_{i-1} \oplus TS_i, TCF_{i-1})$
      /* where $TC[i]$ is the ith bit of TC */

5   **end**

6   $AddConstraint(TCF_M = loggedTCF)$

7   $Solve\_SAT \Rightarrow TC$

Table 1. Average run-time in seconds of Algorithm 1 for different M and $w = w_{TCF}$

M	w = M	w = 4	w = 8	w = 16	w = 32
8	Direct mapping	0.02	–	–	–
16	Direct mapping	0.3	1.9	–	–
32	Direct mapping	1.05	1.7	13.9	–
512	Direct mapping	–	–	–	3576

The SMT solver Boolector [7] was used to solve Algorithm 1, reconstructing TC in times shown in Table 1. In the case of smaller time-stamps bit-width w_{TS}, Algorithm 1 is used incrementally. In accordance to the number of possible solutions, the amount of time needed to compute all possible reconstructions of TC grows exponentially, which can be seen in the columns of Table 1, with different w_{TS}.

Improving Results Using Available Information. To improve the scalability, the fact that the number of solutions can be reduced by N (which is the number of changes in the given trace-cycle) can be utilized to exclude all solutions containing number of changes that does not equal N during the solving process itself. N is required to map the functional trace vector's elements to the trace-cycles (and thus is logged anyway), so utilizing it to improve reconstruction performance does not cause any additional overhead. Excluding the solutions obtained by Algorithm 1 that do not match the given amount of changes N reduces the number of possible solutions but not the time required to obtain them. So in Algorithm 2 below, N is used as input to the solver.

Algorithm 2. Bounded to N Changes (No-changes) Trace Reconstruction

---

Data: ρ_0, TS, N

1 $FP_0 = \rho_0$

2 $bitvector[N][\lceil log(M)\rceil]$ $change\_index$

3 $AddConstraint(TCF_N = loggedTCF)$

4 **foreach** j in $1 \longrightarrow 2^{M-w_{TCf}}$ **do**

    /* where M is the trace length after which we log the footprint;
    and w_{TCf} is the footprint's bit-width   */

5   **foreach** i in $1 \longrightarrow N$ **do**

6          $TCF_i = TCF_{i-1} \oplus TS[change\_index[i]]$ /* $change\_index[i]$ is index
        of the clock-cycle in which the ith change happened   */

7   **end**

8      $Solve\_SAT \Rightarrow change\_index_j$

9   **if** $UNSAT$ break

10   AddConstraint($change\_index \neq change\_index_j$)

11 **end**

Algorithm 2 uses N to reduce the amount of possible solutions *and* the time required to obtain them as follows. The algorithm relies on solving for a list of N indices, each indicating the time (inside the trace cycle) where a change occurred instead of a list of bits TC, where each indicates whether a change happened at the given index or not. Table 2 shows the average run times of the modified algorithm. Reductions in computation time are significant if few changes occur within a trace-cycle. It still needs to be applied iteratively to locate all possible (ambiguous) solutions. This algorithm relies on a list of indices, stored in the *change_index* bitvector that is declared in line 2. This set references the timestamps that should be used to calculate the resulting footprint. Table 2 shows the average run times of Algorithm 2 for different N and M. The reduction in computation time by Algorithm 2 is remarkably significant in the two extreme cases: where there are very few and (as explained next) too much changes in a trace-cycle.

For signals that change frequently, the logged footprint may be first XORed with an all-time-stamps-XOR value, hence resulting in a new footprint that carries only the XOR of the remaining instances that were not XORed in the logged footprint; then the algorithm is used to locate those $M - N$ time-stamps that indicate the instances of no change. This reduces the reconstruction complexity for larger N, allowing the algorithm to have an upper worst case for the reconstruction algorithm, which is $N = \frac{M}{2}$. So the algorithm shall be reconstructing either (changing or stagnating) change instances.

Table 2. Algorithm bounded by N, average run-time in m minutes and s seconds, for different trace lengths M and number of changes N. For N = 1, it's just a direct mapping, i.e. the TCF is the single change's time-stamp.

$M \backslash N$	1	2	3	4	5	6
8	0	~0	~0	~0	~0	~0
16	0	~0	0.1 s	0.2 s	0.3 s	0.4 s
32	0	~0	0.5 s	1.6 s	2.1 s	5.4 s
512	0	1 m 16 s	7 m 10 s	43 m 65 s	–	–
1024	0	6 m 42 s	37 m 46 s	–	–	–

This bounded by N-changes algorithm can result in only one solution if the time-stamps are designed to provide unique TCF for each different combination of N aggregated time-stamps. As the time-stamps are set prior to the execution, they may be generated to specifically satisfy this criterion. This is particularly useful, if a given N is assumed to be problematic. For only one change ($N = 1$), the uniqueness of time-stamps is enough for cycle-accurate trace reconstruction; as a logged time-stamp can then be directly mapped to its respective instance.

For $N = 2$ and using XOR gates to merge the time-stamps, the condition is:

$$\forall i, j, k, l, [TS_i \neq TS_j]$$
$$\cap [TS_i \oplus TS_j \neq TS_k \oplus TS_l], \tag{1}$$

where

$$(0 < i, j, k, l \leqslant M) \cap i \neq j \cap k \neq l$$
$$\cap (i = k \Rightarrow j \neq l) \quad \cap \quad (j = l \Rightarrow i \neq k)$$
$$\cap (i = l \Rightarrow j \neq k) \quad \cap \quad (j = k \Rightarrow i \neq l)$$

Similar conditions can be derived for higher N.

In summary, using a combination of on-chip traced footprints, off-chip functional simulation data, and the reconstruction and mapping of this information, a cycle accurate reconstruction of on-chip behavior is possible. The next section illustrates the applicability of the method in practice, showing how the reduction in the amount of logged data allows the approach to be used in continuous logging. This in turn allows the designer to efficiently capture timing related sporadic faults and assists in finding their root-causes.

3 Experiments

As a case study, the presented methodology was used to continuously capture the temporal behavior of a toy software, which contains an integrated safe-zone calculation module for mobile robots from the SAMS project[1]. In the given design, the current angle of the moving robot is updated via an interrupt service routine (ISR), which checks for differences from the previous value $\Delta\theta$ as shown in Fig. 4. If the difference is below an accepted limit θ_1, it continues the previously executed task. Otherwise it restarts the safety zone calculation algorithm with the new values if there is enough time to finish it before the deadline. If restarting the algorithm will result in missing the deadline, the ISR checks whether the difference is less than another value θ_2 where $\theta_2 > \theta_1$. If it is, it adds a margin to the current calculation. The value to be added depends on the time difference between the last two time readings. If the difference $\Delta\theta \geq \theta_2$, it activates a worst case algorithm with the updated values. The maximum interrupt rate is 100 ms. The generated software image was run on a LEON3 processor implemented using Xilinx zync7020 FPGA. The same software image was run on SoCRocket, a LEON3 SystemC TLM simulator to get the functional execution traces.

A trace-cycle with $M = 1023$ clock cycles, given the 83 MHz (12 ns) input clock of the Zynq FPGA, would make 12.276 µs duration of each trace-cycle; during which no interrupt can occur twice (the quickest is the timer interrupt with periodicity 10 ms). Including the watchdog interrupt, the maximum number of interrupts we can have in one trace-cycle is three corresponding to the 3

---

[1] www.sams-project.org, the module is certified for use in safety systems up to SIL-3 according to IEC EN 61508.

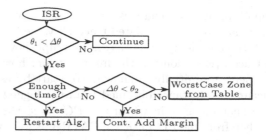

Fig. 4. Interrupt-service-routine

interrupts occurring at the same trace-cycle. The signals chosen for tracing were the program counter (PC, $w_s = 32$ bits) and two interrupts lines ($IRQ\_l_{1,2}$, $w_s = 2$ bits). One of those 2 bits of IRQ_l is our ISR's IRQ line and the other is timer interrupt line. So, here $IRQ\_l.FC$ is not only a check, but it also indicates which interrupts occur. At which clock cycle exactly an interrupt that has occurred starts to be served is not usually known because of the pipeline mechanics and interrupt masking (if used). In our case, there is no masking, no critical sections where interrupts are disabled and the different interrupts are allowed to be nested according to their priorities. So within a trace-cycle at which the interrupt line's footprint indicates an interrupt request, the exact instance of interrupt occurrence is obtained using CATRA and the exact instance where the interrupt starts executing lies within the maximum detailed architectural delay (cache miss, pipeline, interrupt priority ...etc).

A hardware module (implementing the hardware-box in Fig. 2 containing the generators and counter) was implemented on-chip to generate and log FC, TCF and N for both PC and IRQ separately every trace-cycle (for $M = 511$ and $M = 1023$ as in Table. 3 below). Our implementation does not cause any system slow-down, as we used continuous EXORing with previous FC and TCF. So the changes at the borders between trace-cycles do not require any special handling.

Additionally, the values of those two signals (PC and IRQ_l) are logged during the SoCRocket simulation and buffered to eliminate consecutive similar values. SoCRocket enables injecting interrupts via timers and given certain delay from the start time. The exact time when interrupts occurred can be obtained from applying CATRA to the interrupt line footprint. Still during simulation, the actual time in which the interrupt occurs may be not exactly the time the interrupt was fired in the simulation (because the model is not cycle accurate).

The direct way to map changes to their respective trace-cycles is to start from reset where the initial values of both simulation and hardware are similar. Each trace-cycle, the logged $FC.N$ is used to pick N values from the simulation trace and assigning them to a trace-cycle. Then the generated FC for these values is compared to the logged footprint's FC as a check. It is possible to skip this step (when there is high confidence in the functional simulation results) and jump to the suspected trace-cycle ($K^{th}trace - cycle$, where more than one interrupt occur), get the sum of all previous changes ($N_{sum} = \Sigma_{i=0}^{k-1} N_i$) and then get the start of the traced signal from the simulated trace τ_s^u values as the N_{sum}^{th} value.

Within a specific trace-cycle, if there was an interrupt, how many among the N changes in the trace-cycle belong to the interrupt and how many belong to the interrupted segment are initially unknown. We start by assuming that the actual interrupt occurrence instance obtained from the logged IRQ_l footprint via CATRA is the exact instance in which the PC value has switched to the interrupt segment; then from the $PC.TCF$ via CATRA as well, we determine the first change instance appearing at or after actual interrupt occurrence instance. We then assume PC values before this instance belong to the interrupted segment, and from the instance on belong to the interrupt. Then we calculate the FC by EXORing these PC simulation trace values and check if it matches the logged footprint's FC. We increment the PC-switch-to-interrupt instance to the next possibility by considering one more PC value from the interrupted segment and one less from the interrupt. We repeat this to consider the range of possible maximum architectural delay. As a result, candidate traces that match the logged FC for further investigation are collected. If no FC matches were found, then the previous assumption leading to the start value obtained from the simulation is probably wrong, hence earlier trace-cycles are investigated.

Two scenarios in which we used the above mechanism to debug sporadic faults that did not appear consistently are shown in Table 4. In both cases we started our analysis from the last trace-cycles that had more than one interrupt before the fault becomes visible. Then the above described flow was used to get when exactly (after which instruction) the interrupts were executed and arrived to the conclusions in Table 4 about the faults' root-causes.[2]

Table 3. The number of bits logged every trace cycle, and the required bit-rate for logging, in the implementation $w_{FC} = 32 + 2$ and $w_{TCF} = 32$ for both PC and IRQ

Trace-cycle length	Naive logging	Required bit-rate	TC, FC (1 bit per clk)	Required bit-rate	TCF, FC, N(+CATRA)	Required bit-rate
M = 511	17374	2.92 Gbps	1056	171.81 Mbps	109	17.73 Mbps
M = 1023	34782	2.92 Gbps	2080	169.37 Mbps	110	8.95 Mbps

Using naive logging, $M * (w_s(PC) + w_s(IRQ\_l))$ bits are logged per trace-cycle, i.e. 34782 bits for $M = 1023$. Using the proposed logging scheme and CATRA, only: $w_{s.FC}(PC)\ |_{32} +w_{s.FC}(IRQ)\ |_2 +w_{s.TCF}(PC)\ |_{32} +w_{s.TCF}(IRQ)\ |_{32} +w_{s.N}(PC)\ |_{10} +w_{s.N}(IRQ))\ |_2$ bits are logged, i.e. 110 bits for the same setup. Table 3 shows the reduction in the required logging bit-rate. So, instead of logging the signal every clock cycle, a set of footprints are logged periodically. Using the proposed approach cycle-accurate details of the exact on-chip execution trace are captured.

---

[2] Note that using interrupts to alter the execution is not recommended for safety critical software in general. However, it could be unavoidable to fulfill a hard requirement of responding to external changes instantaneously not via pulling.

Table 4. Scenarios that encountered sporadic faults and their symptoms in the second column, root-cause analysis and its computation effort in the 3rd and 4th columns

#	Scenario	Symptoms	Root-cause analysis
1	$\theta_1 < \Delta\theta < \theta_2$ and ISR comes at an instance where there is barely enough time to restart the same task to finish before its deadline.	sams task is restarted, but didn't finish before its deadline.	It was found that ISR interrupted the timer interrupt after it started execution, but before the exact instruction in which it updates the time value. So the ISR used the old time value thinking there is enough time to restart sams so it finishes.
2	$\theta_1 < \Delta\theta < \theta_2$ and ISR runs at its maximum rate, requesting a margin increase each time.	Wrong value of the safe-zone output.	The ISR interrupted the timer twice in row, making the margin calculations inside that interrupt routine being performed using older, non-updated values of the time.

4   Related Work

While formal design based approaches like Backspace [8] and Magellan [6] use the design itself, the presented approach instead relies on a simulated abstract functional execution trace. This hugely reduces the computational requirements and limits the tracing to specific trace-cycles. While other approaches that rely on higher level abstract functional matching may only start from the initial state (as in [6]) or the final state (as in [8]), the presented approach limits the matching process to short time frames (the trace-cycles) within the given traces. Periodic logging is used to check the on-chip computed signatures in [22], where the usage of parity-checks decrease the number of debugging sessions. However, requiring frequent rerunning, scan-chains and run-stop mechanism keeps such methods from detecting inconsistent faults. For circuits implemented on FPGAs, commercial tools like [1] rely on the continuous tracing of values at the operating frequency, which results in log-size issues. For microprocessors, manufacturers provide propriety solutions for temporal accurate logging [2,4]. Their closed nature and reliance on compiler-generated meta-data means that conceptually, these approaches cannot be applied e.g. to ASICs. Recently, NuVA [12] verified high speed on-chip transactions, but in turn caused the overall chip performance to drop slightly. In contrast, the methodology proposed here does not affect the chip's performance, uses very simple logic and is applicable to any signal.

5 Conclusion and Future Work

Temporally accurate logging using today's methods is impractical, although it could be the shortest way for capturing and debugging post-silicon timing related bugs. We proposed a novel non-intrusive logging scheme and a reconstruction approach CATRA to provide accurate information about the on-chip execution. This allows for the first time, to capture and analyze timing-related sporadic errors.

We are currently developing methods for efficient times-tamps auto-generation for less solutions of CATRA under-specific conditions and shorter computation time. Also the computational complexity of using the functional-check part of the footprints in traces alignment is under analysis.

References

1. ChipScopePro (2017). www.xilinx.com/products/design-tools/chipscopepro.html
2. Embedded Trace Macrocell block specification (2017). http://www.arm.com
3. Gaisler Research (2017). http://www.gaisler.com
4. System Navigator Probe (2017). http://www.mips.com
5. Abramovici, M., Bradley, P., Dwarakanath, K., Levin, P., Memmi, G., Miller, D.: A reconfigurable design-for-debug infrastructure for SoCs. In: DAC (2006)
6. Ahlschlager, C., Wilkins, D.: Using magellan to diagnose post-silicon bugs. In: Synopsys Verification Avenue Technical Bulletin, vol. 4, no. 3, p. 15 (2004)
7. Brummayer, R., Biere, A.: Boolector: an efficient SMT solver for bit-vectors and arrays. In: Kowalewski, S., Philippou, A. (eds.) TACAS 2009. LNCS, vol. 5505, pp. 174–177. Springer, Heidelberg (2009). doi:10.1007/978-3-642-00768-2_16
8. De Paula, F.: Backspace: formal analysis for post-silicon debug traces. Ph.d. Thesis, University of British Colombia (2012)
9. Fredrikson, M., Christodorescu, M., Jha, S.: Dynamic behavior matching: a complexity analysis and new approximation algorithms. In: Bjørner, N., Sofronie-Stokkermans, V. (eds.) CADE 2011. LNCS, vol. 6803, pp. 252–267. Springer, Heidelberg (2011). doi:10.1007/978-3-642-22438-6_20
10. Hu, B., Huang, K., Chen, G., Knoll, A.: Evaluation of run-time monitoring methods for real-time events streams. In: ASPDAC (2014)
11. Mitra, S., Seshia, S.A., Nicolici, N.: Post-silicon validation opportunities, challenges and recent advances. In: DAC (2010)
12. Nassar, A., Kurdahi, F.J., Elsharkasy, W.: NUVA: architectural support for run-time verication of parametric specications over multicores. In: CASES (2015)
13. Nguyen, M.D., Wedler, M., Stoffel, D., Kunz, W.: Formal hardware/software co-verification by interval property checking with abstraction. In: DAC, June 2011
14. Park, S., Mitra, S.: IFRA: instruction footprint recording and analysis for post-silicon bug localization in processors. In: DAC (2008)
15. Reinbacher, T., Függer, M., Brauer, J.: Runtime verification of embedded real-time systems. Formal Meth. Syst. Des. 44(3), 203–239 (2014)
16. Schmidt, B., Villarraga, C., Fehmel, T., Bormann, J., Wedler, M., Nguyen, M., Stoffel, D., Kunz, W.: A new formal verification approach for hardware-dependent embedded system software. IPSJ Trans. Syst. LSI Des. Methodol. 6, 135–145 (2013)

17. Schuster, T., Meyer, R., Buchty, R., Fossati, L., Berekovic, M.: SoCRocket-a virtual platform for the European space agency SoC development. In: ReCoSoC (2014). http://www.github.com/socrocket
18. Shojaei, H., Davoodi, A.: Trace signal selection to enhance timing and logic visibility in post-silicon validation. In: ICCAD (2010)
19. Souyris, J., Pavec, E.L., Himbert, G., Borios, G., Jégu, V., Heckmann, R.: Computing the worst case execution time of an avionics program by abstract interpretation. In: 5th International Workshop on Worst-Case Execution Time Analysis (WCET) (2005)
20. Vermeulen, B., Goossens, K.: Debugging Systems-on-Chip: Communication-centric and Abstraction-based Techniques. Embedded Systems. Springer, New York (2014)
21. Wilhelm, R., Engblom, J., Ermedahl, A., Holsti, N., Thesing, S., Whalley, D., Bernat, G., Ferdinand, C., Heckmann, R., Mitra, T., Mueller, F., Puaut, I., Puschner, P., Staschulat, J., Stenström, P.: The worst-case execution-time problem: overview of methods and survey of tools. ACM Trans. Embed. Comput. Syst. **7**(3), 36 (2008)
22. Yang, J., Touba, N.: Enhancing silicon debug via periodic monitoring. In: Proceedings of Symposium on Defect and Fault Tolerance (2008)

Author Index

Printed in the United States
By Bookmasters